W9-ASH-830

FIGURES

2.1 Formal models of hierarchical fiduciary and republican conceptions of accountability *page* 39
2.2 The ideal of a circle of checking and balancing separated powers, each of which is a potentially widening circle 42
2.3 Restorative justice means never giving up on responsibility and accountability 45
2.4 The dominant dimensions of responsibility and accountability for a restorative justice process 48
5.1 Accountability regimes 128
11.1 Actor linkages in a conventional advocacy NGO regulatory environment 298
11.2 Actor linkages in the ISEAL regulatory environment 298

CONTRIBUTORS

John Braithwaite is an ARC Federation Fellow in the Regulatory Institutions Network (RegNet), Australian National University.

Sasha Courville is Executive Director of the International Social and Environmental Accreditation and Labelling (ISEAL) Alliance and a member of the Centre for Governance of Knowledge and Development, in the Regulatory Institutions Network (RegNet), Australian National University.

Michael C. Dorf is Michael I. Sovern Professor of Law at Columbia University.

Michele Ford is Lecturer in the Department of Indonesian Studies at the University of Sydney.

Jody Freeman is a Professor of Law at the Harvard Law School.

John Gardner is a Professor of Jurisprudence at Oxford University and the Georges Lurcy Visiting Professor at Yale Law School.

Christine B. Harrington is an Associate Professor in the Politics Department and the Laws and Society Program at New York University.

Jerry L. Mashaw is Sterling Professor of Law and Management at the Yale Law School.

Bronwen Morgan is Professor of Socio-Legal Studies at the University of Bristol School of Law.

PUBLIC ACCOUNTABILITY

There is an ongoing perception that public accountability in modern-day governance is in "crisis," caused by globalization and the increasing power of private economic interests. This book responds to that idea, providing a comprehensive survey of how different institutions hold persons acting in the public interest to account, and the various problems they face. It shows how key issues – such as public-mindedness, democracy, and responsibility – and structures – such as bureaucracy, markets, and transparency – adopt different and sometimes contradictory interpretations of what constitutes public accountability. It also demonstrates how underlying these differing interpretations are core communities of experiences that bind them into a complex web of mutual interaction and influence. The book includes studies not only of Anglo-American experiences, but also of the experiences of numerous foreign and transnational organizations.

CAMBRIDGE STUDIES IN LAW AND SOCIETY

Cambridge Studies in Law and Society aims to publish the best scholarly work on legal discourse and practice in its social and institutional contexts, combining theoretical insights and empirical research.

The fields that it covers are: studies of law in action; the sociology of law; the anthropology of law; cultural studies of law, including the role of legal discourses in social formations; law and economics; law and politics; and studies of governance. The books consider all forms of legal discourse across societies, rather than being limited to lawyers' discourses alone.

The series editors come from a range of disciplines: academic law; socio-legal studies; sociology; and anthropology. All have been actively involved in teaching and writing about law in context.

Series editors

Books in the Series

The Politics of Truth and Reconciliation in South Africa
Legitimizing the Post-Apartheid State
Richard A. Wilson

Modernism and the Grounds of Law
Peter Fitzpatrick

Unemployment and Government
Genealogies of the Social
William Walters

Autonomy and Ethnicity
Negotiating Competing Claims in Multi-Ethnic States
Yash Ghai

Constituting Democracy
Law, Globalism and South Africa's Political Reconstruction
Heinz Klug

The New World Trade Organization Agreements
Globalizing Law through Services and Intellectual Property
Christopher Arup

The Ritual of Rights in Japan
Law, Society, and Health Policy
Eric A. Feldman

The Invention of the Passport
Surveillance, Citizenship and the State
John Torpey

Governing Morals
A Social History of Moral Regulation
Alan Hunt

The Colonies of Law
Colonialism, Zionism and Law in Early Mandate Palestine
Ronen Shamir

Law and Nature
David Delaney

Social Citizenship and Workfare in the United States and Western Europe
The Paradox of Inclusion
Joel F. Handler

Law, Anthropology and the Constitution of the Social
Making Persons and Things
Edited by Alain Pottage and Martha Mundy

Judicial Review and Bureaucratic Impact
International and Interdisciplinary Perspectives
Edited by Marc Hertogh and Simon Halliday

Immigrants at the Margins
Law, Race, and Exclusion in Southern Europe
Kitty Calavita

Lawyers and Regulation
The Politics of the Administrative Process
Patrick Schmidt

Law and Globalization from Below
Toward a Cosmopolitan Legality
Edited by Boaventura de Sousa Santos and Cesar A. Rodriguez-Garavito

Public Accountability
Designs, Dilemmas and Experiences
Edited by Michael W. Dowdle

PUBLIC ACCOUNTABILITY

Designs, Dilemmas and Experiences

Edited by

Michael W. Dowdle

CAMBRIDGE UNIVERSITY PRESS
Cambridge, New York, Melbourne, Madrid, Cape Town, Singapore, São Paulo

CAMBRIDGE UNIVERSITY PRESS
The Edinburgh Building, Cambridge CB2 2RU, UK

PUBLISHED IN THE UNITED STATES OF AMERICA BY CAMBRIDGE UNIVERSITY PRESS, NEW YORK

www.cambridge.org
Information on this title: www.cambridge.org/9780521617611

First published 2006

Printed in the United Kingdom at the University Press, Cambridge

A catalogue record for this publication is available from the British Library

ISBN-13 978-0-521-85214-2 hardback
ISBN-10 0-521-85214-5 hardback
ISBN-13 978-0-521-61761-1 paperback
ISBN-10 0-521-61761-8 paperback

This book is dedicated to the Columbia Law School and the Regulatory Institutions Network of the Australian National University

7 **Spontaneous accountability** 174
Colin Scott

PART THREE ACCOUNTABILITY AND PARTICIPATION

8 **Accounting for accountability in neoliberal regulatory regimes** 195
Christine B. Harrington and Z. Umut Turem

9 **The mark of responsibility (with a postscript on accountability)** 220
John Gardner

10 **Technocratic v. convivial accountability** 243
Bronwen Morgan

PART FOUR ACCOUNTABILITY AND EXPERIENCE

11 **Understanding NGO-based social and environmental regulatory systems: why we need new models of accountability** 271
Sasha Courville

12 **Problem-solving courts and the judicial accountability deficit** 301
Michael C. Dorf

13 **Public accountability in alien terrain: exploring for constitutional accountability in the People's Republic of China** 329
Michael W. Dowdle

Notes 358
Bibliography 404
Index 446

CONTENTS

List of figures *page* xiii
List of contributors xiv
Acknowledgments xvi

1 **Public accountability: conceptual, historical, and epistemic mappings** 1
Michael W. Dowdle

PART ONE ACCOUNTABILITY AND THE STATE

2 **Accountability and responsibility through restorative justice** 33
John Braithwaite

3 **The myth of non-bureaucratic accountability and the anti-administrative impulse** 52
Edward Rubin

4 **Extending public accountability through privatization: from public law to publicization** 83
Jody Freeman

PART TWO ACCOUNTABILITY AND DESIGN

5 **Accountability and institutional design: some thoughts on the grammar of governance** 115
Jerry L. Mashaw

6 **Emerging labor movements and the accountability dilemma: the case of Indonesia** 157
Michele Ford

Edward L. Rubin is Dean and John Wade-Kent Syverud Professor of Law at the Vanderbilt University Law School.

Colin Scott is Professor of EU Regulation and Governance at the University College Dublin School of Law.

Z. Umut Turem is a PhD candidate at the New York University Institute of Law and Society.

ACKNOWLEDGMENTS

The idea for this book had its germination in a conversation I had with Mark Barenberg at Columbia Law School in the fall of 1999. It was nourished by subsequent conversations with Charles Sabel and Edward Rubin. Jody Freeman, Kanishka Jayasuriya, and Bronwen Morgan then provided critical support and advice that allowed this idea to evolve into a project.

Michael Dorf and Gabriel Soto made the administrative organization of a workshop on this idea a breeze rather than a nightmare. The workshop itself benefited immensely from the contributions of Peter Strauss, Susan Sturm, Gillian Metzger, and Frank Munger.

John Braithwaite, Peter Drahos, and Colin Scott were instrumental in teaching me how to attract the attention of a publisher. Thankfully, that publisher came in the person of Finola O'Sullivan of the Cambridge University Press, whose patience, assistance, and, more importantly, encouragement have been extraordinary and are most gratefully appreciated.

Others who provided vital assistance at times when vital assistance was needed include Frank Upham, Christine Harrington, Randle Edwards, and Randall Peerenboom.

Finally, I would like to acknowledge the vital contribution of two institutions, Columbia Law School and the Regulatory Institutions Network at the Australian National University. I cannot believe that there is any more nourishing intellectual environment on the face of the earth than those found at these two institutions while I was there. This book is really their product.

Chapter 4, "Extending Public Accountability Through Privatization: From Public Law to Publicization," by Jody Freeman, was adapted from "Public Values in an Era of Privatization: Extending Public Law Norms Through Privatization," which appeared in *Harvard Law Review* 116: 1285–1352 (2003).

Chapter 9, "The Mark of Responsibility (With a Postscript on Accountability)," by John Gardner, was adapted from "The Mark of

Responsibility," which appeared in *Oxford Journal of Legal Studies* 23: 157–171 (2003). We are grateful to Oxford University Press for its permission to publish.

Chapter 12, "Problem-Solving Courts and the Judicial Accountability Deficit," by Michael Dorf, was adapted from "Legal Indeterminacy and Institutional Design," which appeared in the *New York University Law Review* 78: 875–981 (2003).

CHAPTER 1

PUBLIC ACCOUNTABILITY: CONCEPTUAL, HISTORICAL, AND EPISTEMIC MAPPINGS

Michael W. Dowdle

INTRODUCTION: ON THE CRISIS IN PUBLIC ACCOUNTABILITY

Many in the Anglo-American world perceive a growing crisis in public accountability. In particular, many fear that privatization and globalization are breaking down the traditional accountability arrangements which give us confidence in our government. Privatization seems to be devolving important political authority and power onto private actors who are able to operate outside of the public accountability mechanisms designed for civil servants. Globalization seems to be shifting governmental powers and responsibilities onto transnational actors, both public and private, that operate outside the jurisdictional reach of domestically formulated accountability systems. All this leads many people to wonder whether the political forces affecting their lives are really acting in the interest of the public.

This perception of "crisis" is further exacebated by the fact that different people seem to have very different and often conflicting ideas as to what constitutes or satisfies a meaningfully "public" accountability. Economic development agencies, for example, often see public accountability primarily in terms of rationalized and transparent systems of bureaucratic control. Human rights activists see it primarily in terms of popular participation in and supervision of political decisionmaking. Legal development agencies see it primarily in terms of judicial enforcement of legal norms. Many regulatory reformers in the United States and Great Britain see it in terms of market-like competition and discipline. Thus, while there is common perception of an accountability problem, there is also deep division about its exact causes and about what our appropriate response to that problem should be.

This book seeks to unpack the nature of this seeming crisis in public accountability. As further explored in the remainder of this chapter, our different visions of public accountability reflect different histories, different experiences and different concerns. Historically, these had been harmonized by the conceptual predominance of what we will call bureaucratic accountability. Recent events, however, have weakened this predominance, and in doing so have catalyzed inconsistencies in the differing logics that underlie these different experiences.

Part I of this chapter will examine the historical roots of present-day Anglo-American understandings of public accountability. As we will see, that understanding is very much the product of historical accretion, embedding within it different ways that generations past perceived and responded to past accountability crises. As we will see in Part II, what stabilized this accretional collection of historical experiences and responses until recently was the relative conceptual dominance of one particular kind of public accountability, that of bureaucratic accountability. Part III will explore how recent evolutions in global and domestic governance have reduced the appeal of bureaucratic accountability, and in the process catalyzed conceptual inconsistencies among the other historical-accretional visions, resulting in a growing fragmentation of our present-day notions of public accountability – the "crisis" referred to at the opening of this chapter.

In Part IV, we will see that underlying this fragmentation is the fact that we experience accountability in a number of different contexts. These include experiencing public accountability as subjects of state power; experiencing public accountability as conceptual designers of state institutions; experiencing public accountability as citizen-participants in the state itself (as popular-sovereigns); and experiencing public accountability as human beings interacting with other human beings. We shall also see that each of these ways of experiencing public accountability has its own distinct logic, its own distinct epistemology. A more robust understanding of the nature of public accountability requires a consilience among these different kinds of experience.

In Part V, we shall explore how this volume contributes to such a consilience. The remaining chapters of this volume provide a good survey of the four experiential perspectives described in Part IV. We will see how each chapter relates to and informs the other chapters in the book. We will see how weaving through these chapters and their diverse perspectives and experiences is a robust web of conceptual linkages. In the Conclusion, we disaggregate one strand of this web, that of bureaucracy, to show how this web is suggestive of a complex network of interdependencies linking these seemingly distinct and divergent visions. I propose that the key to our effectively responding to the accountability crisis may lie in recognizing and exploring these latent interdependencies.

I. AN INTELLECTUAL HISTORY OF PUBLIC ACCOUNTABILITY

In beginning our exploration into the diverse structural and experiential facets of public accountability, we might first ask "what is public accountability?" At its heart, the idea of public accountability seems to express a belief that persons with public responsibilities should be answerable to "the people" for the performance of their duties (see also Mashaw, this volume). But such an idea exists primarily in metaphor, one that borrows very imperfectly from a number of other discourses about "accountability" per se. From private law, it borrows the notion that accountability is a product of a particular kind of relationship existing between two individuals, the principal and her agent, in which the agent is required to demonstrate that her actions conform to the demands, intentions, and interests of the principal. It then borrows from political theory the idea that the "public" itself can be analogized to an individual.

The problem is, of course, that the "public" cannot really be equated with an individual. As an inherently collective phenomenon, the "public" is only vaguely identifiable in space. Its corpus is diffuse and contestable, and its internal dynamics are often so complex as to be opaque. It rarely can be said to have mental-state intentions, as what "intentions" it might meaningfully be said to have are often internally inconsistent.

Perhaps because of this conceptual conundrum, Anglo-American political and legal theory has tended to define public accountability primarily in terms of discrete institutional architectures. Most prominent among these have been elections, rationalized bureaucracies, judicial review, transparency, and "markets." As we shall see, each of these architectures developed as exigent responses to various legitimacy crises that have periodically beset Anglo-American governance.

Elections have been a key component of Anglo-American conceptions of public accountability ever since the founding of the American constitution. In the United States, electoral recall originally represented the principal sanction by which the citizenry were to hold politicians accountable for errant political frolics. James Madison commented upon the centrality of elections to early American notions of public accountability:

> As it is essential to liberty that the government in general, should have a common interest with the people; so it is particularly essential that [the House of Representatives] should have an immediate dependence on [and] an intimate sympathy with the people. Frequent elections are unquestionably the only policy by which this dependence and sympathy can be effectually secured.[1]

But, even in the Anglo-American world, intellectual and political support for electoral democracy has always been decidedly mixed. In the United States at the end of the nineteenth century, the ability of machine-style, patronage-based politics to thrive in electoral competition, at the seeming expense of the public good, caused many to become skeptical of the electorate's capacity to hold politics to true, public account. Reformers sought, instead, to hold political behavior to such account via the construction of rationalized, professionalized bureaucratic frameworks. To these reformers, devices such as meritocratic recruitment, tenure and promotion; professionalization; and scientific administration offered a more satisfying vision of public accountability. It was a vision of public accountability that worked by subjecting political behavior to the oversight of an organizational environment specifically designed to recognize and pursue the public good as opposed to one that relied primarily on corruptible electoral impulses. (See also Dowdle, this volume.)

At the same time as the Americans were turning to bureaucracy as a cure for perceived accountability problems of electoral democracy, constitutional scholars in England began turning to the judiciary as a cure for the perceived accountability problems of both democracy and bureaucracy. Spurred in part by their contact with the Chinese, England had began rationalizing and professionalizing its administrative bureaucracy in the 1850s. They did so, however, not so much for accountability reasons – i.e. to counteract a possibly runaway electorate – but more simply to increase the capacities and effectiveness of executive government. By the 1880s, the influential English constitutional law scholar, Albert Venn Dicey, had become concerned about – some might even say obsessed with – these expanded administrative capacities, arguing that, with these expanded powers, administrative government was increasingly able to operate outside of traditional constitutional constraints. Dicey advanced an idea, what he famously called "rule of law," that such constraints had to be maintained principally by giving the courts oversight over bureaucratic behavior.[2] In the 1930s, American jurists, too, became increasingly concerned about perceived constitutional threats brought about by the emergence of the American administrative state, and they were strongly influenced by Dicey's description of the need for a strong judicial check on the growing administrative state.[3]

Dicey's vision saw judicial review primarily as a substantive constraint on bureaucratic decisionmaking. The American vision, by contrast, adopted a more process-focused approach. This approach became theoretically codified in the 1950s, resulting in what G. Edward White has called the "legal-process school" of American jurisprudence.[4] One of the accomplishments of these process-school jurists was to link the idea of judicial review with that of public accountability by articulating a symbiotic relationship between judicial review, procedural visibility, and public faith in government. Acknowledgment of this linkage can be found in *Amalgamated Meat Cutters* v. *Connally*:

> Concepts of control and accountability define the constitutional requirement. The principle permitting a delegation of legislative power, if there has been sufficient demarcation of the field to permit a judgment whether the agency has kept within the legislative will, establishes a principle of accountability under which compatibility with the legislative design may be ascertained not only by Congress but by the courts and the public.[5]

In the 1960s and 1970s, rising disillusion of American government, generated first by the Vietnam War and later by the Watergate scandal, caused many to become skeptical about the degree to which either professionalized rationalization or judicial review could encourage public officials to actually work in the public interest. This occasioned the appearance of yet another architectural modality for political accountability, that of "transparency" and "open government."[6]

Open government sought to make governmental decisionmaking as visible as possible – not simply to those who directly involve themselves with government, but also to the larger uninvolved portion of the polity. At the heart of this movement at the federal level was a series of laws passed between 1966 and 1978. Principal among these were the Freedom of Information Act,[7] passed in 1966, which generally requires federal agencies to release their records to the public upon request, and the Government in the Sunshine Act of 1976,[8] which requires most federal agencies to hold their meetings regularly in public session. This new vision of open government promised to allow a much wider range of civil society to hold public officials to account even without directly participating in political decisionmaking.

In the 1970s, economic stagnation in the United States and Great Britain caused growing concern about governmental waste, inefficiency, and unresponsiveness. This caused some reformers to look to market-like mechanisms, which they believed more efficient in allocation and usage of resources, as a means of promoting the responsible use of public resources. In some cases, these reformers advocated devolving public responsibilities directly onto private, market-based actors. Beyond this, reformers in the United Kingdom also invented new governance architectures that replicated market-like forces of competition by having different public departments "compete" in the development of effective regulation, while American reformers developed architectures and procedures, like cost–benefit analyses, that sought to replicate market-like pricing and demand mechanisms. (See generally Mashaw, this volume; and Freeman, this volume.)

II. STABILITY AND CONTIGUITY

In sum, the Anglo-American idea of public accountability is not so much the product of extrapolation from core conceptual principles as an accretional layering of responses to periodic legitimacy crises experienced by Anglo-American societies. But why and how did these successive modalities aggregate into a *singular* conceptualization of public accountability, rather than simply producing a sequence of competing conceptual paradigms?

For most of the twentieth century, the stability of this accretional layering has been due largely to the fact that one particular modality of public accountability – that of bureaucracy – has enjoyed a privileged, *primus inter pares* status when it came into conflict with other modalities.[9] (See also Rubin, this volume.) Of course, this predominance was not always the case. We noted above that elections were the principal recognized source of public accountability for the first 100 years of American constitutional government. Indeed, there is some evidence that the drafters of the American constitution were quite distrustful of bureaucratic government. But when American reformers began promoting bureaucratization as an accountability alternative to democracy, they triggered a corresponding reconceptualization of the nature of democracy itself. "Democracy" came to be thought of in the more limited terms of elections and suffrage, as opposed to the more robust notion of "participation" famously described by Tocqueville. Reorienting the idea of democracy in this way avoided conflict with growing norms of bureaucratization and professionalization, both of which sought to remove the more day-to-day, technocratic matters of public administration from the partisan politics that a more participatory vision of democracy seemed to unleash.[10] (See also Dowdle, this volume.)

A similar clearing of space occurred when the expanded capacities of bureaucratized administrative government also brought it into conflict with judicial review. As described above, constitutional scholars in both England and the United States had originally hoped that preexisting processes of judicial review could be used to put a brake on the inherent dangers of bureaucratic administrative governance. This was not to be the case, however. Both English and American courts have adopted a vision of judicial review that is largely deferential to the substance of bureaucratic decisionmaking. During the first two-thirds of the twentieth century, the British courts' deference to the administrative state has been so complete that there was a real question whether judicial review in Britain had any real meaningful impact on the actual operations of administrative governance.[11] On the other side of the Atlantic, the American courts have also decided – wisely in the eyes of many – to defer to bureaucratic judgment, at least when it is properly processed. As recently noted in a germinal article written by Elena Kagan, former Deputy Assistant to the President for Domestic Policy and Deputy Director of the Domestic Policy Council during the Clinton Administration:

> For too long, administrative law scholars focused on judicial review and other aspects of legal doctrine as if they were the principal determinants

> of both administrative process and administrative substance. They are not . . . As this new body of scholarship has shown, much of what is important in administration occurs outside the courthouse doors. It occurs as new views emerge of the appropriate goals and optimal strategies of regulatory programs. Less often stressed, it occurs as bureaucratic institutions, the constituencies with which they deal, and the political environment in which they operate change over time.[12]

Nor did the more recent modalities of public accountability – e.g. open government, deregulation, privatization, contracting out – seriously challenge bureaucratization's dominance as our main paradigm for public control. The "open government" movement of the late 1960s and early 1970s quickly subordinated itself to the perceived needs of bureaucratic government. The Freedom of Information Act is qualified by its famous Exemption 5, which allows an agency to lawfully withhold "inter-agency or intra-agency memorandums or letters which would not be available by law to a party other than an agency in litigation with the agency."[13] The exemption was thought necessary to "protect . . . the decisionmaking processes of government agencies."[14] Similarly, one study suggests that the Government in the Sunshine Act has become so conditioned by exceptions – both legislative and judicial – that it has had little real substantive impact on the character of governmental decisionmaking in the United States.[15]

More recent, market-inspired governmental reforms such as contracting out, devolution, and "streamlined government," despite often being motivated by expressly anti-bureaucratic impulses, have for the most part simply substituted one (often less visible) bureaucracy for another. In the United States, for example, an overall decrease in the size of the federal bureaucracy during the 1990s has been offset by corresponding increases in the size of state government bureaucracies.[16] Decreases in public bureaucratic responsibilities due to "contracting out" have been counterbalanced by increased private bureaucratic responsibilities within contracting firms.[17] Of course, this is not to deny that these reforms have indeed had important effects on regulatory governance in the United States and the United Kingdom (see, e.g., Mashaw, this volume). It is simply to point out that, despite their often expressly anti-bureaucratic intentions, this most recent round of regulatory reforms did not so much challenge bureaucratic accountability as it has shifted it around.

III. FRAGMENTATION

Recent events have disrupted the stability of the Anglo-American, "accretional" vision of public accountability, however. We noted above that this vision has been sustained in part by the pride of place it gives to bureaucratic structuring. One of the reasons why bureaucratization has been able to enjoy this pride of place is because it was most consistent with the evolving organizational trends of what we might call "modernized" Anglo-American society as it emerged in the early twentieth century.[18] Industrialization occasioned a massive rationalization, regularization, and centralization of social life. The rationalization, regularization, and centralization that characterize bureaucratic administration worked in significant part by paralleling this development. (See also Dowdle, this volume.)

Bureaucratized regulation, for its part, depends vitally on a stable regulatory environment for its effectiveness. Bureaucratic rules and procedures designed to address a particular set of circumstances can easily become dysfunctional when those circumstances change. However, recent innovations in information technologies have caused both domestic and international regulatory environments to become increasingly unstable. As a result, regulatory systems are therefore being reoriented to emphasize flexibility and adaptability, at the expense of bureaucratic predictability and control.[19]

Another reason for the disruption of the Anglo-American vision of public accountability has to do with recent developments in the global environment. During the last half of the twentieth century, what we are calling the Anglo-American "model" of public accountability became increasingly internationalized. Following the end of the Second World War, the United States exported its particular vision of bureaucratic regulation to Western Europe – and, to a lesser extent, to Japan – in the process of helping rebuild state and government institutions in the aftermath of the war.[20] American post-war dominance of emerging institutions devoted to international governance and international development also caused the American vision of public accountability to become increasingly embedded in both public international law and the legal and political environments of many developing countries. In this way, the Anglo-American experience of public accountability increasingly came to be regarded as an international standard for governance.[21]

However, the end of the Cold War removed one of the principal transnational incentives for international unity with regard to Anglo-American political models, including that of public accountability. Multilateral tolerance for America's intellectual dominance within international regulatory and intellectual arenas had been sustained in part by the First World's perceived need to present a united front against communism in general and the Soviet Union in particular. With the collapse of the Soviet Union, this united, American-led vision of what constituted good, or even democratic, governance has come under increased scrutiny. At the same time, new technologies have also enabled formerly isolated, localized resistance movements to participate in and gain support from international networks of like-minded resistors and activists (see also Courville, Morgan, Ford, this volume). A growing array of self-consciously "local" interests are now increasingly able to contest, both normatively and practically, their assimilation into centralizing, bureaucratic regulatory frameworks. For both these reasons, the Anglo-American vision of public accountability, which used to be seen as a bulwark for liberal political stability, is now sometimes seen as an instrument of political hegemony.[22]

The result has been a "fragmentation" in public accountability discourse. As the harmonizing dominance of bureaucratic modernization is delegitimated by newer and more localized organizational logics that stress flexibility and decentralization, formerly latent tensions among the diverse architectural modalities that make up the Anglo-American vision of public accountability become more manifest. Different kinds of political interests tend to be attracted to different modalities of accountability. Trade unions, for example, whose impact on political decisionmaking historically has come in large part from their ability to mobilize voters, tend to prefer electoral modalities of accountability. International human rights organizations, whose staff generally includes a high number of persons with legal training, tend to prefer juridical modalities of public accountability. Economically oriented interests tend to be more comfortable with rationalized bureaucracies and open governance, which both mesh with their own institutional practices and make it easier for them to navigate the diversity of transnational and domestic regulatory environments in which they must operate.

Paradoxically, however, the retreat of the logic of modernization has also caused a quickening of public accountability discourse.

Globalization has generated growing demands for more public accountability. The more willing participants in the globalization process – e.g. international business, trading interests, labor activists, and environmental activists – are demanding an ever-more expanding scope of public accountability from domestic government actors, whom they suspect to be illegitimately impeding the implementation of emerging public international norms.[23] At the same time, more reluctant, involuntary, and localized participants in the globalization process are demanding increasing public accountability from transnational regulatory actors, whom they see as illegitimately interfering with what should ultimately be domestic political matters. (See also Morgan, this volume.)

Growth in discourse over public accountability is also catalyzed by the fact that the idea of "public accountability" is common to a wide diversity of domestic and transnational factions and interests. Thus, it provides a common referent around which these factions and interests can try to align, coordinate, or co-opt their diverse agendas. For example, after the World Bank formally recognized "good governance" – which included a strong public accountability component – as a core component of its developmental mandate in the early 1990s,[24] human rights organizations then seized on the accountability aspects of good governance to try to develop institutional dialogue with the World Bank on an array of human rights concerns.[25] And whereas challenges to the reach of human rights were previously expressed primarily in terms of sovereignty, today people increasingly use accountability critiques to try to remove particular interests from the seeming expanding scope of human rights regulation. (See generally Courville, this volume.)

IV. EXPERIENCES AND EPISTEMOLOGIES

Compounding this fragmentation in the ideal of public accountability is the fact that we *as individuals* encounter public accountability in a variety of ways. In other words, one reason why our ideas of public accountability are fragmented is because our own individual consciousness is inherently fragmented.[26] One way we encounter public accountability is as beings subject to the state's coercive forces that dictate what we must, can, and must not do. As subjects, we encounter state power both as beneficiaries of and as subalterns to the state's public accountability demands. On the one hand, public accountability gives us confidence in the reasonableness of state demands. On the other hand, public accountability subjects us to the threat of state sanctions if we ourselves fail to comply with public accountability demands. (For more on how the demands of a distinctly "public" accountability are increasingly being imposed on private citizens, see Freeman, Courville, Ford, and Morgan, this volume.)

Another way we encounter public accountability is as conceptual architects of political institutions. Of course, few of us ever have the opportunity to actually set up a public accountability system. But that does not stop us from thinking about how such a system should be designed or how it should work. Thus, when we think about the viability of electoral term limits, or the problems of judicial activism, political lobbying, or campaign finance, we generally think about these issues from a largely architectural perspective. We are not so much concerned about the subjective implications of these mechanisms – i.e. about how they would affect us personally – rather, we wonder more abstractly and objectively what sort of implications these devices might have on the mechanisms and dynamics of government.[27]

We also encounter public accountability as citizens, or as participants in the state. In many places in the world, public governance itself is an expressly participatory phenomenon. As described above, the general idea of public accountability is often seen as a logical implication of this larger idea of participatory government. "Accountability" is an inherently participatory concept. Accountability is not the same thing as obedience. To give an account is to communicate, not to completely surrender control. Accountability is therefore a discursive condition, something that sets up a dialogue between the public, and the public servants. (See, e.g., Harrington and Turem, and Braithwaite this volume.) As members of the public, we actuate public accountability by participating in this dialogue, for example by thinking for ourselves whether the accounts offered by public officials are proper and in our interest.[28]

Finally, we also encounter public accountability through direct experience. Consider, for example, the experience of being treated with respect and kindness. Such experience implicates a particular form of public accountability. The feeling of being treated with kindness or respectfulness indicates to us that some other person is taking our own concerns into account. (See also Braithwaite, this volume.) Another example would be when we experience ourselves behaving responsibly and accountably. Even as wholly private citizens, we still recognize that in certain aspects we too are and should be held accountable to a larger public. (Cf. Gardner, this volume.) We are and should be accountable for being good parents, for being good colleagues and neighbors, for being good citizens. But our experiences in these regards rarely depend on our contemplated appreciations for the dynamics of political coercion or on how our actions implicate institutional design.[29] They are feelings that operate prior to our rational understandings of larger political contexts, and hence represent an encounter with public accountability that is distinct from the other kinds of encounters described above.

Each of these different ways of encountering public accountability has its own, distinct logic. For example, as "subjects" of public accountability we see public accountability primarily in terms of formal powers, authority, and duties on the one hand, and rights, privileges, and capacities on the other. These are the constructs that "the state" uses to portray and define the scope of its coercive might.[30] We ourselves therefore find these constructs useful in helping us negotiate our way through the state's institutional pathways.

From this perspective, public accountability works to constrain power.[31] This causes this perspective to conceptualize public accountability in terms of discretely bounded terrains: such as public v. private; state v. (civil) society; plan v. market; etc. Because we are subjects of this "power," it is seen as residing in terrains that are outside and beyond our own. Power is thus seen as something alien that imposes itself on us, and for this reason is regarded through a distinctly skeptical lens. (See Gardner, this volume.)[32]

When we look to "design" public accountability, we use another kind of epistemic logic. Here, power is the product of institutional mechanics more than outside forces. The "power-thing" of the subjective vision is replaced by a vision that sees power more in terms of hydraulics, and it sees public accountability as using and channeling (rather than binding and restraining) these hydraulics via effective, *a priori* design of institutional architectures. This *a priori* focus encourages a largely positivist epistemology, one that sees the dynamic of both public power and public accountability in terms of abstracted universals describing the nature of human and institutional behavior. It is therefore a disembodied logic, one that places itself outside the perspective of any particular component of the system it seeks to design.[33]

When we encounter public accountability as citizens, we perceive our environment in more discursive terms. The epistemology of this perspective is dialogic.[34] What the other perspectives see (or explain) in terms of "power," this perspective sees in terms of cooperation and agreement. The knowledge that governs this realm is more intimate, more nuanced, and less conducive to positivist or formal structuring. It is, in significant part, conventionalist – embedded in the stories and symbologies that we are forever sharing with other participants.[35] Its quality sometimes appears "emotive" (see, e.g., Morgan, this volume; cf. Gardner, this volume), and, to outsiders, even fantastical (see especially Dowdle, this volume). In contrast to that of both the design and the state perspectives, the logic of this realm is largely "spontaneous" – designed by the invisible hands of social complexity rather than by the rational minds of human architects.

Finally, the epistemic logic of what we are calling the experience of public accountability is perceptual and phenomenological. It is largely pre-theoretical, founded in the irreducible complexities of tacit or practical knowledge. Like the dialogic epistemology of participation, the epistemology of experience has an emotive quality, often appearing in the form of intuition and gut-feeling. But, unlike that dialogic epistemology the epistemology of this realm can be personal and private. It need not depend on conventionalist confirmation.

The fact that we as individuals encounter public accountability in multiple ways does not distinguish public accountability from any other experienced phenomenon. Human intelligence is inherently multivariate. We as individuals are actually complex bundles of continually interacting identities. Not only do we invariably see ourselves as both subjects and participants, designers and observers, but we generally do so concurrently. In other words, we ourselves are always somewhat cognitively and experientially fragmented. Our on-the-ground interpretations of the phenomenon of public accountability thus invariably involve simultaneously components of each of these categorizations.

The various, accretional "modes" of public accountability discussed at the beginning of this chapter may themselves reflect in some part these different realms of encounter. At least at a superficial level, bureaucratic visions of public accountability seem to emphasize subjective experience; market-based visions would seem to emphasize a more participatory experience. Therefore, our divergent modes of public accountability, and the crisis they have engendered, are not simply the product of different values or material interests. They are likely to be the product of different collections of personal experience and the particular combination of logics one uses to understand those experiences.

But we should not make too much of this superficial correspondence. Our disagreements about the nature of public accountability are not attributable simply to your taking a subjective state-centric perspective and my taking an objective design-oriented perspective. Disagreement and debate occur within these perspectives as well as among them. Bureaucracy, for example, seems to catalyze certain aspects of the subjective experience with public accountability, but, at the same time, it also corrupts other aspects of that experience (compare Rubin, this volume, with Braithwaite, this volume). As we shall see, one can also find support for bureaucratic visions of public accountability from design-based (see, e.g., Mashaw, this volume) and participatory experiences (see, e.g., Harrington and Turem, this volume) – albeit for different reasons.

The reason why it is important to recognize the fragmented nature of our experience with public accountability is not so much because such recognition would resolve our disagreements. Indeed, just the opposite. The fragmented nature of our own experience with public accountability would seem to mean that, at the end of the day, the hunt for a single, grand unified theory of public accountability is likely to be futile. The simple fact that we have distinctly different realms of experience governed by distinctly different logics suggests that, at some fundamental level, these differences are not completely reducible to a single common experiential referent.

And, paradoxically, this suggests that the inherently fragmented, accretional nature of our vision of public accountability is a source of strength, rather than a weakness. While a unified theory of public accountability might be of some degree of psychic comfort, it would not and could not reflect the actual reality of our existence. No matter how structured, a unified theory would invariably delegitimate some experiences that contribute to our thriving. An accretional, fragmented conception, by contrast, allows us to better take all useful experience into account.

Although distinct, our different realms of experience and knowledge are not insular. In fact, they are highly interdependent. New experiences and understandings in one realm can often be translated into new and useful understandings in some other.[36] The fragmented and accretional nature of our vision of public accountability could help catalyze this kind of arbitrage. By simultaneously legitimating a wide diversity of not entirely harmonious experiences, such fragmentation ultimately facilitates an especially inclusive discourse about the experience of public accountability. This diversity of experience represents a unique potential source of knowledge. It represents a unique opportunity to promote what Edward O. Wilson has termed "consilience" – a process of generating new, robust understandings of the human condition that occur when different experiences and epistemologies come in contact with and learn from one another.[37] Our task, in this regard, should not be one of finding ways to dissolve this diversity, but one of finding ways to harness it – of finding ways to use it to catalyze these new, more robust understandings of the human condition.[38]

V. OVERVIEW AND STRUCTURE OF THIS VOLUME

Such is the possibility that underlies this book. In this book, each author and each chapter approaches the issue of public accountability from a different experience, ranging from the more "traditional" governance experiences of the Social Security Administration (Mashaw) and bureaucratic governance more generally (Rubin) to much more "exotic" experiences of transnational grass-roots resistance to international water regulation (Morgan) and labor mobilization in Indonesia during and immediately following the neo-authoritarian presidency of Mohamed Suharto (Ford). This diversity of experiences recapitulates that larger diversity of experiences that we saw above makes present-day understandings of public accountability both so maddeningly fragmented and so extraordinarily promising as a tool of human understanding.

Public accountability and the state

The book is divided into four parts, corresponding to the four epistemic dimensions of public accountability described above. Part I, entitled "Accountability and the state", explores how we perceive this crisis through our encounters as subjects of the state. Our standard modal conceptualizations of public accountability emerge primarily from this realm. It is therefore from this perspective that the present-day "crisis" of public accountability is most commonly articulated.

In Chapter 2, John Braithwaite locates at least part of the crisis in public accountability in the tension between the traditional, bureaucratic structuring of state power and the more intimate needs of human communities. Using criminal justice as an example, he shows how bureaucracy by itself is simply unable to provide the full range of public accountability required by these communities, and how local communities are vitally dependent on a particular kind of accountability, what he calls horizontal accountability, that operates outside the state's bureaucratic reach. Bureaucratic accountability is inherently punitive. It works by isolating misfeasors and punishing them. But communal continuity requires not simply punishment, but restoration from the disruptions both the malfeasance and the subsequent punishment cause. Horizontal accountability is a key feature in promoting this restoration. Using the experiences of restorative justice projects in the United States, Australia and Canada as precedents, he suggests ways by which the state can make use of horizontal accountability to supplement and buffer its more invasive interventions in community life.

In Chapter 3, Edward Rubin also locates the crisis in public accountability in the tension between the state's need for large-scale bureaucratic structurings and the individual's needs for a more intimate governance. But he suggests that, at the end of the day, the state itself is functionally locked into a bureaucratic mode of governance. In today's world, public governance, and hence public accountability, needs to be able to operate on a large scale in order to be effective. He sees the crisis in accountability as due in significant part to this expansion in scale. This expansion generates conflicting imperatives between, on the one hand, the need for ever-larger governmental scope and, on the other, a sentimental desire for a more intimately responsive provision of governmental services. Unfortunately, this more sentimental vision of governance and public accountability simply cannot operate on the scale at which today's government must operate. For this reason, he argues, efforts that seek to resolve the present accountability crisis by relying on alternatives to bureaucratic governance are ultimately going to be futile.

Finally, in Chapter 4, Jody Freeman locates the crisis in public accountability, not so much in the tension between the state's bureaucratic governance and community needs, but in the efficacy limits inherent in bureaucratic government per se. She notes that bureaucratic government often simply does not make particularly good use of the resources available to it, and that some of the crisis in public accountability stems from the public resource waste caused by bureaucratic command-and-control government. Recently, many have begun addressing this problem by partnering bureaucratic governments with markets, which are generally thought to be intrinsically better at making use of available resources. But this creates its own accountability problems because markets operate outside the ambit of our existing public accountability structures. She argues that, while, at one level (what she calls the ideological level), this problem may be intractable (because some visions of public government are opposed to market mechanisms as a matter of principle), we can at least address this problem at a pragmatic level by adapting public accountability mechanisms to market situations, a process she refers to as the "publicization" of such markets.

Public accountability and institutional design

Freeman's chapter could be read as implying that the principal locus of the present crisis in public accountability may lie in the way we think about "state" power, and that one way to resolve this crisis in part is to move beyond the rough-hewn dichotomies of government v. market, public v. private, into more nuanced perspectives that recognize that these seemingly sharp terrains are in fact functionally highly porous. This leads us to the second part of the book, which looks at "Accountability and design." The design aspect of our encounter with the public accountability crisis sees the accountability crisis as due in significant part to the human failure to fully comprehend the diversity of the mechanics that can go into a public accountability system. This aspect thus focuses on identifying, understanding, and manipulating these mechanics so as to create more robust accountability systems.

Part II begins with a chapter by Jerry Mashaw that proposes a systematized grammar for thinking about public accountability regimes from this design perspective. Like Freeman before him, Mashaw starts by showing how the traditional distinction between bureaucracy, market, and community found in what we are calling more state-oriented discourse is highly oversimplified. These different modes of public institutions are in fact intermingled, and much of our confusion and concern about contemporary accountability stems from this intermingling.

Mashaw finds that a more robust approach to the issue of how public accountability manifests itself in any particular situation is to disaggregate the idea of public accountability into six foundational questions.

These are (1) to whom is the accountability owed; (2) by whom is it owed; (3) for what is the person accountable; (4) what is the process by which she is made to demonstrate accountability; (5) what standards does she use to demonstrate accountability; and (6) what happens when she fails to meet these standards. (The different modes of public accountability identified in the state-oriented vision, what he calls "regimes," correspond to particular and distinctive patterns of answers to these questions.) Applying this methodology to analyze ongoing American efforts to contract out social-security disability claims, he shows how careful attention to these design questions can expose in much more detail the complicated webs of accountability flows that can operate in a particular public institution.

Mashaw's chapter looks at the design of public accountability *ex post* – seeing how public accountability flows in institutions after those institutions have already been established. But what about efforts to "design" public accountability *a priori*? In Chapter 6, Michele Ford looks at efforts to promote public accountability in Indonesian labor organizations to suggest that the *a priori* design of public accountability can be much more complicated than an *ex post* perspective might otherwise suggest. These efforts replaced the "alternative" labor organizations that operated under the authoritarian Suharto regime with more democratic labor organizations operating in a more democratic political environment. These alternative labor organizations had been organized largely by intellectuals and had taken the form of NGOs. They therefore seemed to operate outside the direct, electoral and participatory oversight of the workers themselves.

It was thought that replacing these NGOs with traditional trade unions, whose leaders would be subject to the workers' own electoral discipline, would make Indonesia's post-Suharto labor movement more accountable and responsive to Indonesian labor. But Ford finds that, contrary to this expectation, these more traditional, electorally oriented trade unions in fact are not significantly more accountable to Indonesian labor than the paternalistic organizations they succeeded. This is because the accountability dynamics affecting labor organizations in Indonesia are intimately intertwined with and dependent upon larger social and political forces. These interdependencies are so strong as to overpower simple changes in institutional accountability architecture. Ford's study suggests that, contrary to the assumption that often underlies the design perspective, seeing accountability dynamics does not necessarily translate into a power to shape them.

In Chapter 7, Colin Scott expands on Ford's observation, deriving from it a critical gloss on Mashaw's analytic framework. Scott starts by showing how what Mashaw calls accountability regimes – the gross analytic categories associated with what we are calling "state-oriented" perspectives – actually correspond to different kinds of power arrangements that society imposes on different kinds of public institutions. He then shows how the intermingling of accountability regimes explored by Mashaw and Freeman themselves correspond to and appear driven by a growing intermingling of these different kinds of arrangements. This would explain why, consistent with Ford's finding in Chapter 6, changes in accountability architecture do not necessarily produce changes in actual accountability dynamics.

Like Ford, Scott also questions the functional linkage between our ability to map public accountability dynamics *ex post* and our ability to design public accountability *a priori*. If actual accountability dynamics ultimately follow social function, as Scott suggests, then, at the end of the day, these dynamics may often simply be "spontaneous" – in the sense of emerging in ways that ultimately operate outside the scope of human intentionality. And, if this is the case, then our ability to resolve – or even merely to massage – the accountability crisis via resort to design-oriented perspectives may in many instances be chimeric. We will return to this issue in our discussion of Chapter 11 on "Understanding NGO-based social and environmental regulatory systems."

Public accountability and the citizen

Scott's vision of a spontaneous accountability also has some radical implications for the crisis in public accountability. It suggests that our problems with public accountability are not necessarily the product of problems in institutional structure. They may simply be the inevitable product of our larger social environments. Indeed, many have argued that the particular order that characterizes many social and political environments itself may be "spontaneous" in large degree.[39] The spontaneity in public accountability Scott identifies may simply be due to its symbiotic relationship with the spontaneous, evolutionary dynamics of social structure and social participation. This suggests, in turn, that the actual "crisis" in public accountability may lie primarily in the realm of the social, or what we are calling the realm of "participation." This leads us to Part III of our volume, which examines public accountability from the perspective of citizen participation.

In Chapter 8, Christine Harrington and Z. Umut Turem show how strongly the participatory experience can affect perceptions of public accountability. Looking at American efforts to introduce a new form of rulemaking – called negotiated rulemaking – into its federal administrative procedures, they show how efforts to generate or establish new modes of less-bureaucratic governance can be frustrated by a failure of the system to take participation seriously. For this reason, they find, the actual experience of negotiated rulemaking in American federal administrative decisionmaking is often quite different from that intended by the designers of the system.

Even when some newly designed form of public accountability does generally function as intend, it nevertheless disrupts settled anticipations and expectations of the actors, which in turn result in a loss of accountability. In this way, efforts to design novel forms of public accountability in response to particular aspects of the accountability crisis can simply generate novel forms of public accountability crises.

Harrington and Turem's analysis also shows why many civil society participants in administrative rulemaking might actually perceive greater legitimacy in the older, more bureaucratic processes for rulemaking than in the newer, allegedly more participatory "negotiated" rulemaking. This is particularly true of participants that lack more intimate ties with the rulemaking agency, such as public interest organizations. In this way, they give a new force to Rubin's claim in Chapter 3 about the inevitability of bureaucracy in the modern state by exposing an unexplored, symbiotic connection between what we are calling state-oriented explanations of public accountability and participatory experience. More particularly, they suggest that the subsequent efforts to design around Rubin's observation of bureaucratic inevitability may be critically incomplete. Such design solutions invariably see the crisis of public accountability primarily as a functional problem. Harrington and Turem's study, by contrast, suggests that the "crisis" in public accountability may lie in significant part in the unsettling of the conventionalist practices, understandings, and expectations that constitute what we are calling the participatory realm.

In Chapter 9, John Gardner further explores the implications of the participatory reinterpretation initiated by Harrington and Turem, by using it to reexamine the foundational dynamics of public accountability per se. As noted above, the standard understanding of public accountability sees such accountability in terms of making persons with public responsibilities answerable *to the people* for the performance of their duties. As described by Mashaw (this volume), we reify this relational aspect primarily by linking it to threats of possible adverse consequences for malfeasance. Gardner shows how this particular reification of public accountability's relational character actually places public accountability in inherent tension with a critical, foundational aspect of human nature he associates with the idea of "responsibility".

Gardner starts by exploring the nature of responsibility. He finds that inherent in this nature are three implications. First, responsibility is ultimately a justificatory condition; secondly, people have an innate need to be responsible; and, thirdly, responsibility is not a relational phenomenon. What distinguishes public accountability from responsibility is two-fold. The first distinction, as noted above, is its relational character. A second and related distinction is its generally punitive quality – failure to demonstrate accountability to a third party generally subjects one to a sanction of some sort. Together, Gardner shows, these two distinctions cause the idea of public accountability to frustrate our innate drive to be responsible.

Just as Harrington and Turem might be seen as a participation-based "translation" of the observations of Rubin, Gardner might be seen as a participation-based translation of the observations of Braithwaite. As we may recall, Braithwaite ultimately located the crisis in accountability in the innate tension between bureaucratic modes of accountability and society's need for restorative justice. Gardner's analysis suggests that this tension, and therefore this crisis, may actually lie not so much in the linking of public accountability with bureaucracy, but somewhere in the linking of public accountability with punishment.

Gardner's hypothesis finds empirical support in Chapter 10, in which Bronwen Morgan identifies in transnational, grass-roots organizations seeking to resist the internationalization of local water use a particular form of accountability that she terms "convivial accountability". Convivial accountability is a spontaneously arising form of accountability that seems especially resistant to standardization or routinization. This special resistance to routinization could be a product of Gardner's hypothesis. The social-participatory implications of routinization could be analogous to the social-participatory implications of punishment.

Like punishment, routinization ultimately calls into question the actor's intrinsic capacity to act responsibly, since it demands not only that the actor act responsibly, but also that she act responsibly in a way that we demand rather than in a way that allows her to express her own autonomous reasonableness. It would thereby seem to provoke the same, innate "suspicion of wrongdoing" that Gardner associates with punishment and the threat of punishment.[40]

Morgan's analysis also has interesting implications regarding our understanding of bureaucratic rationality. To recall, in Chapter 3, Edward Rubin argued that bureaucratic accountability is an essential response to problems of governmental size. Morgan's analysis seems to challenge that claim somewhat by showing that shared trust and respect can indeed span large organizational environments, and, where that is the case, large-scale alternatives to bureaucratic accountability can arise.

Public accountability and experience

The grass-roots resistance organizations that are the subjects of Morgan's study were all newly emergent at the time of her study. One issue that Morgan expressly leaves open is whether convivial accountability might evolve into or otherwise facilitate more routinized accountability structures somewhere down the line. The question, in other words, is whether and what institutions might "learn" from their convivial or otherwise spontaneous accountability experiences. This brings us to the final part of our volume, that of "Accountability and experience."

In Chapter 11, Sasha Courville studies the experiences of international private and voluntary market-based certification and accreditation systems (such as SAI 8000) to suggest, following on Morgan, that institutions can indeed routinize original, spontaneously emerging accountability regimens as these institutions mature. Key to this developmental capacity are the institution's own willingness to address accountability problems and the degree to which all the institution's members participate in institutional evolution. Under such circumstances, the "legitimacy" of a newly routinized accountability regime comes not from its functionality per se (Courville acknowledges that these regimes can be less effective than more traditional models), but from the participants' experiencing of the institution's continuously recognizing and responding to accountability issues. She refers to this continuous recognizing and responding as "learning."

Courville's learning-based vision suggests some interesting responses to a number of the conundrums raised in previous chapters. One is the role of design. A number of the volume's other chapters have suggested that human capacity to promote institutional accountability via positivist structures of institutional design is fairly limited. If this is so, does this really mean that design-based efforts and approaches like those of Mashaw and Freeman are really "chimeric," as suggested in our discussion of Chapter 7? Courville's analysis suggests that, indeed, it is not. It suggests that the value of design need not lie in the functionality of its product per se. It might lie in the simple act of designing – of searching for and responding to "accountability problems." This is, of course, the whole point of Mashaw's chapter – his "grammar" does not suggest a solution to accountability problems, but a way of thinking about these problems. We wondered above whether the *ex post* analysis that this grammar facilitates can actually be converted into *a priori* design. Courville suggests that this is the wrong question; that "accountability" can actually come simply from analytic effort itself where that effort is "sincere" (i.e. generates sincere response) and broadly participatory.

The other conundrum for which Courville's observation seems particularly relevant is that hypothesized by John Gardner in Chapter 9 and worked out by Bronwen Morgan in Chapter 10. This is the argument that the routinization of accountability works to corrode the very soul of human "responsibility" that accountability itself ultimately seeks to promote. Courville's idea of accountability as learning might suggest that this conundrum can be massaged somewhat by what we might think of as "meta-routinization" of the design features that promote institutional accountability "learning." Of course, this response could be seen as raising a problem of infinite regress. But the ultimately experiential foundations of Courville's study suggests that, despite its philosophical incompleteness, this solution still seems to *work*, at least sometimes, in actual practice.[41]

In Chapter 12, Michael Dorf gives us an example of how we can capture institutional learning in institutional design and then use it to address particular public accountability problems – in this case the democratic accountability deficit that attaches to Anglo-American courts. Building on earlier work that he and Charles Sabel did on structuring institutional learning capacity in public democratic institutions – a design they call "democratic experimentalism"[42] – he shows how one can use experimentalist structurings so as to reduce the courts' accountability deficit, at least in certain kinds of cases.

Somewhat paradoxically, Dorf suggests that we can increase judicial accountability in these cases by making judicial decisions less concrete, less determinative, and thereby more interdependent on the autonomous cooperation of other public actors. Such interdependence, he argues, allows courts to free-ride on the greater accountability advantages of these other public actors, while still taking advantage of the unique institutional contributions that courts are able to bring to public decisionmaking.

Dorf's chapter exposes an important functional correspondence between institutional learning, interdependency, and public accountability. In sum, it suggests that (1) institutional learning is inherently an interdependent phenomenon, and (2) interdependence can be a *sine qua non* of public accountability. The idea of accountability as a form of interdependence also offers a possible resolution to the conundrum raised by John Gardner in Chapter 9 and amplified by Bronwen Morgan in Chapter 10. At the core of this conundrum is the tension between autonomy and control: as evinced in the first two questions of Mashaw's grammar, the common conception of public accountability seeks to control actors whose very responsibilities, as per Gardner, ultimately require autonomy. Dorf implies that we can avoid this conundrum by thinking of public accountability, not in terms of control – i.e. "who is accountable to whom for what" – but in terms of interdependence. Gardner's conundrum could sometimes simply be a product of looking at only one side of what is really an interdependency.[43]

Insofar as the subjects of public accountability are concerned, Dorf's analysis suggests that they may often experience this interdependency, not as an affront to their capacities to behave responsibly, but simply as inevitable but ultimately transcendable limits in human capacity. The crucial word here is "experience" – because the actual experience of learning is ultimately not tied up in any particular formal institutional architecture. This would explain why we often experience our more effective bureaucratic superiors, like we experience our more effective social superiors, as "teachers" rather than bosses. Similarly, markets and democracy are often experienced as teaching institutions, at least when encountered in their more benign guises.

The point here is not that our choice of bureaucracy, community, democracy, or markets does not have real accountability implications. It is simply that, at the end of the day, regardless of the institution, the *experience* of an *effective* accountability is the same regardless of regime. In this sense, the constructs of markets, elections, bureaucracies, and communities may represent not so much different kinds of *solutions* to accountability problems as they do different kinds of accountability problems themselves, problems that arise from the different ways in which humans seek to transcend their inherently limited capacities.

This leads us to another important implication of Dorf's analysis. Dorf himself notes that his proposed response to the courts' accountability crisis is a limited one. In particular, he suggests that this response may not be effective in addressing the courts' accountability deficit insofar as what he calls "hard cases" are concerned – cases whose solution requires choosing among a set of contested value preferences. (See also Freeman, this volume.) But perhaps this is more an observation about the nature of the limits of accountability per se. Gardner's analysis is again instructive in this regard. Ultimately, efforts to make one publicly accountable for one's *existing* value preferences could be inherently self-defeating because *existing* value preferences are the product of an inherently and necessarily autonomous moral judgment, and such autonomy is simply not amenable to the *external* disciplining dynamics that accountability describes.

But of course, as Dorf himself acknowledges, whether or not a particular case is really "hard" as opposed to just "big" in the sense of simply requiring the processing of massive amounts of information, can itself be simply a matter of social construction. If we presume that our values are ultimately compatible, then what we might otherwise think of as hard cases involving contestable choice of competing values become big cases involving discovery of common values. Whether and when such a presumption is actually warranted is another question. And it is very likely to be a question that accountability per se cannot address.[44] Thus, from the perspective of experience, the crisis in public accountability may ultimately spring from a foundational contradiction between our innate desire to trust others[45] and the innate limits in our capacities to trust others.[46]

This brings us to the final chapter of our volume. Our choice as to whether or not to make an initial commitment to the possibility of public accountability in a new situation is not made in a vacuum. Rather, it is based on past observation. We associate certain behaviors with public accountability. And, when we see public officials conforming to these behaviors, it gives us confidence that they probably deserve our trust.

This is fine as far as it goes. The problem is that, in new or alien environments, we cannot really expect to see such familiar signaling behavior. What should we do in such situations? If we allow the alienness of the situation per se to cause us to default to a distrusting rejection of the possibility of public accountability, we effectively prevent ourselves from moving forward, from ever adapting to the inevitable changes that human societies face. We prevent ourselves from ever being able to respond to whatever crises in public accountability we find ourselves facing.

In Chapter 13, Michael Dowdle suggests a way forward. He begins by exploring how the present-day American vision of public accountability as it relates to constitutional institutions (what he calls constitutional accountability) embeds within it certain presumptions about the structure of society that are not always warranted, and how when this vision is applied to other environments in which these presumption do not hold it can produce a very misleading picture of that environment's accountability dynamics. He then argues that, ultimately, the problem with this model lies in its inherently deductive character, and suggests an alternative methodology for evaluating public accountability "inductively."

He demonstrates the utility of this inductive methodology by using it to look at the constitutional environment in the People's Republic of China, a clearly alien constitutional environment insofar as most people are concerned, and one that we generally conclude lacks any meaningful incidence of constitutional accountability. He shows that this inductive methodology exposes important sites of "potential accountability" in that environment that are invisible to traditional constitutional analyses. His point is not that there are no real accountability problems in China's constitutional environment. Rather, his point is that these real problems need not blind us to the simultaneous existence of significant sites of accountability potential.

As noted several times above, there is good reason to suspect that the contemporary "crisis" in public accountability is at some level a reflection of insoluble contradictions embedded in the whole enterprise of public accountability. At the end of the day, this crisis may simply be an inevitable product of human existence and its many, often irreconcilably competing demands. But not all crises are the same, even in their ongoing existence. To say that crisis is necessarily perpetual is not to say that it is necessarily fatal. If this crisis is indeed a moving target (see especially Harrington and Turem, this volume), then we, too, need to keep moving: to keep responding and to keep learning.

CONCLUSION: OF CRISIS AND CONSILIENCE

Collectively, what the chapters in this volume show is how each perspective of public accountability is usefully informed by other perspectives. Take bureaucratic accountability as an example. We saw, initially, that underlying the accountability crisis is a widespread dissatisfaction with modern government's perhaps over-reliance on bureaucratic accountability (see Braithwaite). We also saw, looking at the issue from a state-oriented perspective, that this reliance would seem to be inevitable (see Rubin). A more design-oriented perspective, however, suggests that the dichotomy between bureaucracy and other forms of accountability is not so hard-and-fast as the regime perspective might make it seem (see Mashaw), and that the state-oriented perspective's conundrum of bureaucracy might be dissolved by a more micro-analytic approach to organizational design (see Mashaw, Freeman).[47]

A participant's perspective, on the other hand, suggests that there are critical aspects of bureaucratic accountability that are likely to escape detection by design-based perspectives – aspects that lie in the irreducible complexities of social interaction. What we are calling the state-oriented perspective of bureaucratic accountability is not simply functionalist, it is also a reflection of existing collective expectations and anticipations. Therefore, whatever solutions we find to the problems of bureaucratic accountability must also be learned, and learned collectively. They cannot simply be bestowed from on high (cf. Morgan, Courville).

But in order to be useful, this new learning often has to be folded back into existing understandings and expectations (see Dorf, this volume). Therefore, our collective capacity to learn – or to learn effectively – is itself vitally informed by the broad conceptual mappings that are captured primarily in what we have called the state-oriented perspective.

In other words, no single perspective captures the full dimension of public accountability. Effective understanding of, and responses to, the "crisis" in public accountability must be epistemically collaborative. As noted above, our crisis in accountability is in some sense perpetual. Our disagreements about accountability are therefore also in some sense perpetual. But disagreement is also an excellent catalyst for learning. Perhaps paradoxically, our best hope for the future may well lie precisely in this perpetuity of disagreement.

PART ONE

ACCOUNTABILITY AND THE STATE

CHAPTER 2

ACCOUNTABILITY AND RESPONSIBILITY THROUGH RESTORATIVE JUSTICE

John Braithwaite

I. THE ACCOUNTABILITY CRISIS AS A CRISIS OF DEMOCRACY

Democracy does not work well through the traditional modalities of public accountability outlined by Michael Dowdle in Chapter 1. In contrast to the eighteenth- and nineteenth-century practice of democracy, today we mostly vote for representatives we have never met. They no longer hear our voice in town meetings. Once elected, they go to a legislature on the floor of which few of the major issues that affect our lives are discussed. Most of the really big decisions are made by the circle of policy advisers around the head of state, while a much larger number of middling decisions are taken within public and private bureaucracies without debate in the legislature. So our vote is mostly not the accountability tool it once was. Private law accountability is something only corporations and a tiny number of wealthy individuals can afford, and widespread private prosecution of both what we today call public and private law is no longer something the law allows in the way that was standard up to the nineteenth century.[1] We have more private wealth, even as it becomes more unequally distributed, so we do exercise minute market accountabilities by switching consumer choices more frequently than we did when we were poorer. Perhaps because of the latter, many citizens are satisfied enough, quiescent, not much interested in voting or going before the local magistrate to have their say. Others are cynical and see modern democracy as a sham. They crave voice and political choice on matters that affect them rather than just consumer sovereignty.

Most analysis of democratic accountability is directed at the executive and legislative branches of governance. This essay explores a different path of enriching direct democracy and accountability. This is "restorative justice." Restorative justice as an accountability innovation has developed mostly as an experiment in re-democratizing criminal law. While this essay focuses on the criminal justice system as a core arena of research and development of restorative justice innovation, we must understand that restorative justice is a wider strategy of confronting injustice in any arena where injustice occurs. Injustice in the way states fight wars can be confronted by restorative justice strategies such as truth and reconciliation commissions. Injustice in the way children are treated in schools can be confronted by restorative anti-bullying programs. Injustice in the way large private bureaucracies treat us as employees or consumers can be confronted in restorative justice circles or conferences. Unjust treatment by public bureaucracies, such as tax offices, is equally a site of restorative justice research and development.

There is now a vast literature on the problems and prospects of restorative justice, including more than fifty empirical program evaluations. The contribution of this chapter will be limited to developing a new normative approach to accountability and responsibility in restorative justice, focusing on criminal law. Its importance is in illustrating the possibility of infiltrating a more participatory approach to public accountability into all institutions of private and public governance at any point where injustice is experienced (and thereby creating incentives for organizational investment in injustice prevention). Of course, possibilities are not empirical realities; the intent is to provide a theoretical framework to motivate evaluations of how different innovations in restorative accountability actually work out.

II. THE ARGUMENT SUMMARIZED

Restorative justice is conceived as a horizontal process of democratic deliberation that is integrated into external processes of accountability to courts and the rule of law. This integration of direct democracy and the rule of a representative democracy's laws is an opportunity to enrich thinking about the relationship between responsibility and accountability in a democracy. Responsibility is conceived here as an obligation to do some right thing; accountability as being answerable to give a public account of some thing. The restorative justice ideal of responsibility is active responsibility as a virtue, the virtue of taking responsibility, as opposed to the passive responsibility we are held to. The restorative justice method for engendering active responsibility is to widen circles of accountability. Enculturation of active responsibility drives injustice prevention *before* the event, so the demand for accountability after the event is reduced. This is conceived as part of a civic republican institutional design of a circle of widening circles of deliberative accountability.

When responsibility is taken and accounts accepted as sufficient to acquit that responsibility, justice is done. From a restorative justice perspective, justice is always unfinished business until an account has been accepted by the stakeholders in the injustice. Even when the state intervenes to hold someone passively responsible by imprisonment after they fail to take sufficient active responsibility for their wrongdoing, there should be no giving up on active responsibility. Responsibility may be admitted and acquitted on release from prison. Victims, with the family of the offender and other stakeholders, may accept the offender's account at that time with considerable benefit to all if they choose to be involved. Injustice on all sides may still be hurting at the time of release, so justice can still heal then. Deeper democracy, on this account, is one where the institutional preference is for responsibility that is active rather than passive, bottom-up rather than top-down, but where failure of bottom-up responsibility results in a form of state accountability that never gives up on restoring bottom-up accountability.

III. THE CONCEPT OF RESTORATIVE JUSTICE

Restorative justice is a process to involve, to the extent possible, those who have a stake in an injustice to collectively identify and address harms, needs, and obligations in order to heal and put things as right as possible.[2] Restorative justice shares much in common with other Alternative Dispute Resolution ideologies like mediation. One important difference is that restorative justice facilitators are not morally "neutral" in mediating conflicts. Restorative justice is about righting the wrongs of injustices. A restorative justice conference to confront domestic violence is not morally neutral about violence as merely a conflict between two people. Most mediation is between two parties to a conflict; restorative justice views it as morally important to give an opportunity for all those who see themselves as key stakeholders in an alleged injustice to participate in the deliberation about what to do. So the predominant structural form of restorative justice is deliberation among people seated in a circle, as opposed to two people negotiating across a table. Empirically, the outcomes from a plurality of stakeholders sitting in the restorative justice circle tend to be different from those produced by dyads assisted by professional mediators. Some think they are often better outcomes.[3] Restorative justice is not morally neutral about what are good outcomes. It is value-driven. This is not to suggest that it is settled what those restorative justice values are. One of them is certainly that, because injustice hurts, justice should heal. This has meant that in fields where restorative justice has now been extensively experimented with – criminal law, care and protection of neglected or abused children, societies recovering from armed conflict, and business regulation – restorative justice has meant more serious consideration being given to non-punitive outcomes than other extant dispute resolution practices.

Most nations have a considerable investment in restorative justice programs today, ranging from nations like New Zealand where it is a universally mandated process for juvenile crime, to nations like Norway and Austria where the volume of restorative processing is very high, to nations like the United States where most programs are tiny and at the margins of the criminal justice system.

IV. RESTORATIVE JUSTICE: DEMOCRATICALLY EXPERIMENTAL[4] BUT UNACCOUNTABLE?

Responsibility and accountability are recurrent worries about restorative justice. They are articulated at many levels. Is it right that a restorative justice process like the South African Truth and Reconciliation Commission fails to hold many of the major criminals of Apartheid criminally responsible for their murderous activities? What about accountability to the community when a meeting of victims of a crime and an offender does a deal that gives a lot of compensation to the victims but little guarantee of future protection to the community? Is restorative justice accountable to a rule of law enacted by legislatures elected by the people? The list of particular concerns about responsibility, accountability, and restorative justice is so long that I will not try to address them in all their particulars.[5] Rather I will attempt to do so in an abstract way that cuts a swathe through many of these particular concerns. The next section argues that holding wrongdoers responsible by imposing punishments for past wrongs is only one version of what responsibility can mean. An active version of responsibility is proposed as the stuff of a more meaningful jurisprudence of responsibility.[6]

On accountability, most of the concerns about restorative justice rest on a belief in the virtues of hierarchical accountability. Declan Roche concludes from his survey of accountability in twenty-five restorative justice programs across six nations that, while hierarchical accountability to prosecutors and courts that sit above restorative justice circles does useful work, horizontal deliberative accountability of one actor in the restorative justice circle to others in the circle does more work in practice.[7] For example, accountability of the police for excessive use of force during arrest, or for coercing an innocent person to confess, may be more likely to be forthcoming within the circle from a mother who pleads with the circle that her son has been unfairly treated. In a court case, such a mother will be silenced unless she is called as a witness relevant to the conduct of the offender, as opposed to the conduct of the police. As David Dolinko has pointed out in the case of an innocent offender coerced into a guilty plea:

> [He will find it impossible] to discuss with the victim what he's done and how to repair the harm he's caused when he knows quite well he has in fact done nothing and has caused no harm. And even if his participation in a conference could somehow be secured, the conference will hardly be a success – the putative offender will simply insist "I'm innocent; they're framing me; I didn't do anything to you and there is nothing for me to 'restore' or 'repair'!"[8]

This means that while it is very possible for court cases to proceed against innocents coerced into a guility plea, it is unlikely in practical terms for a restorative conference to be able to proceed against such innocents. The horizontal deliberative accountability in prospect with a restorative conference does the work of dissuading the prosecution of an innocent coerced into a guility plea. More precisely, the impossibility of giving a deliberative account of how we could repair harm to a victim we have not inflicted any harm upon creates too much risk of exposing the coercion of the guility plea.

In criminal cases, Roche argues that there are some simple reasons why empirically it turns out that deliberative accountability in the circle does more of the work of accountability than accounts to higher-level institutions like directorates of public prosecutions and courts.[9] One is timeliness. An obligation to give an account that occurs in the circle in the process of making a decision elicits immediate responses from other stakeholders: "That's no excuse." "Is that all you are proposing to do?" "What about the emotional havoc this has heaped upon your mother?" Such contestation of accounts inside the process of deliberation more often than not attracts an immediate response: "What I want to say to mum is that I recognize that. I am so sorry mum. I will never cause you that pain again." This example of giving an account is not casually chosen. It is meant to illustrate Heather Strang's empirical conclusion that emotional reparation like this turns out to be more important to accountability being accepted in the circle, even to victims of violent crime, than material reparation.[10] Immediate face-to-face accountability therefore not only has the virtue of timeliness, it also has the virtue of authenticity of emotional communication in the giving of accounts.

Emotional authenticity also builds commitment to follow through on accountability. One of the puzzles to those who have not experienced the emotional power that can be generated in a restorative justice conference for serious crime is why compliance is more likely to happen with a victim compensation agreement or community service agreed as a voluntary, non-enforceable outcome of a conference than with the legally enforceable order of a court. One reason is that the emotional dynamic of the offender discussing with a victim the pain she has suffered builds commitment when the offender promises to do something to try to heal that hurt. But, secondly, commitment to follow through is built among other stakeholders in the circle. An offender promises to attend an anger management program. His mother says he was ordered to an anger management program last time he offended. An uncle is moved to say: "This time I'll take responsibility for making sure he goes. I'll pick him up every Tuesday night to get him there." Then the uncle becomes a signatory to a conference agreement that says this particular responsibility belongs to him. Roche found the most elaborated version of this kind of commitment-building to accountability in two American programs that institutionalized a "celebration circle" that reconvened the stakeholders when all the undertakings in the agreement were successfully completed.[11]

As a matter of research evidence, we cannot be sure which of the foregoing mechanisms is most important to the superior accountability restorative justice delivers. What we can now be reasonably sure of is that it does deliver it. In a meta-analysis of thirty-two restorative justice evaluations by the Canadian Department of Justice, the biggest, most statistically robust, effect size was that compliance with restorative justice agreements was higher than compliance with orders/agreements in control groups.[12] A subsequent review by Barton Poulson combined data from several studies to show that both offenders and victims were significantly more likely to perceive offenders to be "held accountable" in restorative justice cases compared to controls that went to court.[13]

V. ACCOUNTABILITY'S INFINITE REGRESS PROBLEM

Now let us return to juxtaposing the immediate deliberative accountability in the circle to the delay of hierarchical accountability. The biggest problem with hierarchical accountability is that it is hierarchical. By this I mean that an infinite regress of accountability is required. If guardians of accountability are arranged in a hierarchy as in the left hand side of Figure 2.1, we have a problem when the top guardian is corrupt. And, unfortunately, criminal justice institutions such as police departments, and indeed whole states, are like fish: they rot from the head down. The only solution to the corruption of *n*th order guardians is to add an *n*+1th order guardian. But if we arrange guardians of accounts in a circle (see Figure 2.1, right side) each guardian can be a check on every other guardian. We can escape

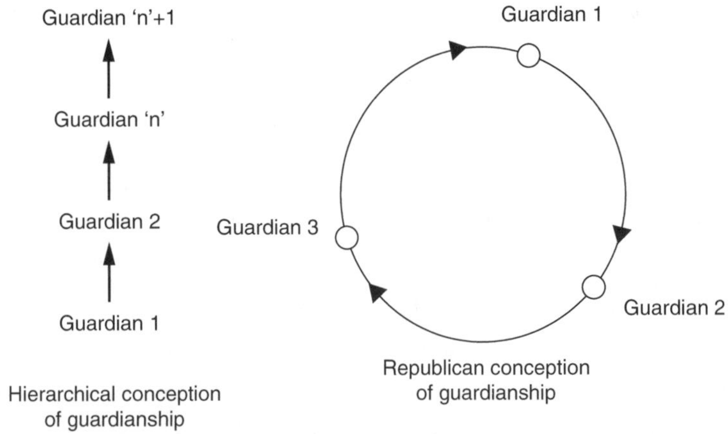

Figure 2.1. Formal models of hierarchical fiduciary and republican conceptions of accountability.

from the infinite regress of hierarchical accountability. The more separated public and private powers there are in a polity, the richer the checking of one guardian by many other guardians can be.[14] So abuse of power by a restorative justice conference might be checked by a prosecutor, while abuse of power by the prosecutor might be checked by a court, the media, human rights NGOs, or indeed by a restorative justice circle reporting a complaint about the prosecutor to a court, an ombudsman, or a human rights commission.

Deliberative accountability among a group of people who meet face to face has its own pathologies – like groupthink.[15] So we actually need a prudent mix of deliberative accountability within the circle and accountability from a separate source of power that is external to the circle. What Figure 2.1 argues is that we can still get that mix of internal deliberative accountability and external accountability by organizing circles of deliberative accountability themselves in a circle.

A good example of this is the republican vision of separation of powers. The republican ideal is for all nodes of governance in a separation of powers to become more deliberative in their decision-making. This means a more deliberative parliament,[16] more deliberative courts,[17] more deliberative regulatory agencies,[18] and so on. So we end up with a checking and balancing circle of deliberative circles.

Christine Parker and I have argued that restorative justice circles should be checked by the rule of law and the rule of law should be permeable to messages bubbling up from the rule of the people as articulated in restorative justice circles.[19] This is Roche's conclusion as well – deliberative accountability and external accountability have different effects: while deliberative accountability is cheaper and more contextually grounded, and can therefore do most of the hard work of practical accountability, external accountability is also needed, particularly because of the superior linkage it can offer to a rule of law enacted by democratically elected governments.[20]

VI. ACTIVE AND PASSIVE RESPONSIBILITY

Restorative responsibility might be conceived as that form of responsibility most likely to promote restoration – of victims, offenders, and communities.[21] Given that framework, a distinction between active and passive responsibility seems informative.[22] This active–passive responsibility distinction usefully maps onto distinctions between active and passive deterrence, active and passive rehabilitation, and active and passive incapacitation. The active versions of deterrence, rehabilitation, and incapacitation are likely to be more effective than their passive versions. While these consequentialist considerations are important in motivating a restorative justice jurisprudence as a jurisprudence of active responsibility, this part of the argument will not concern us here except in one respect.[23]

This respect is that an important part of a mechanism by which active responsibility delivers active deterrence, active rehabilitation, and active incapacitation is that the circle from which accounts are requested is widened. In our development of these ideas with business regulatory agencies in Australia, we would ask for a conference with those causally responsible for an offence within the company. That conference would often break down when these corporate actors refused to accept responsibility, saying in effect, "See you in court." Instead of proceeding to litigation, however, what we would do was widen the circle. The regulator would ask for another conference, inviting the boss of those directly responsible to join the circle. Inviting the boss to give an account would sometimes backfire even more badly because the boss was an even tougher nut than her subordinates. Then our idea was to widen the circle even further. In one case using this approach, an Australian regulator widened the circle right up to the Chairman of the Board.[24] The Chairman was a soft target who could be moved by shame about the corporate offence and by a simple appeal to his sense of moral responsibility. He fired his CEO (not very restorative!) and participated in an agreement where generous compensation was paid to victims and impressive internal compliance measures were put in place to prevent a recurrence of the offence.

The idea is that we can keep widening the circle of accountability; at each step there are extra people with extra capacities to prevent a recurrence of injustice and to right the wrongs of past injustice. With active deterrence, we keep widening the circle beyond hard targets who are not deterrable until we reach a soft target who can be deterred by shame. With active rehabilitation of a homeless young offender, we widen the circle beyond a nuclear family who will not have him back until we find a more distant relative or family friend, perhaps in another city, who will take him into their home.

In Figure 2.1, we ended up with a checking and balancing circle of deliberative circles. Now we have added the further idea that the circles should be iteratively widened to remedy responsibility and

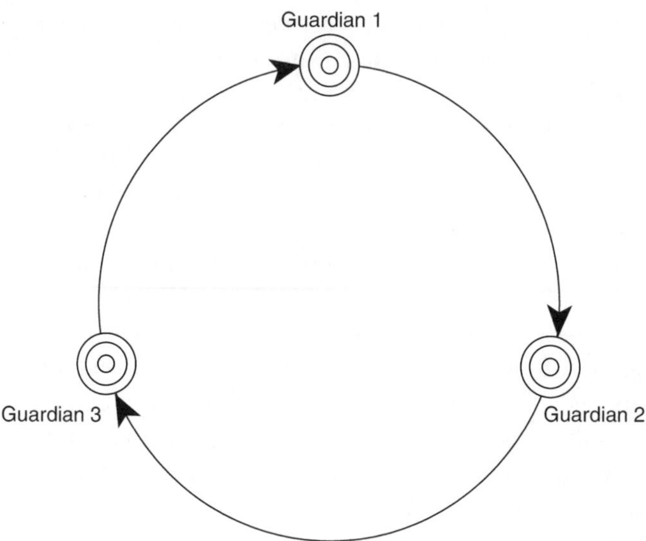

Figure 2.2. The ideal of a circle of checking and balancing separated powers, each of which is potentially a widening circle.

accountability failures. So the ideal is a circle of widening circles of deliberative accountability (see Figure 2.2).

Mark Bovens first distinguished active from passive responsibility.[25] Elaborating Bovens' conception somewhat, passive responsibility is something we hold wrongdoers to; we hold someone responsible for something they did in the past. Active responsibility means taking responsibility for putting something right into the future. One can be actively responsible for righting a wrong in the future without being causally responsible for the wrong in the past. Family members of an offender might offer to work with the offender to help repair the damage a victim of crime has suffered, for example. Restorative justice is partly about community building by encouraging citizens who are not offenders to assist in righting wrongs that offenders have caused. One virtue of the active responsibility of an offender's loved ones is that it nurtures active responsibility on the part of the offender. Restorative justice is about creating a space where offenders are most likely to take responsibility. Conventional Western criminal justice is about creating spaces where offenders will be held responsible in proportion to their culpability.

Building on Brent Fisse's notion that the most important kind of criminal fault is reactive fault, i.e. how praiseworthy or blameworthy is an offender's reaction to the offence,[26] Declan Roche and I argue that, if offenders take active responsibility for apology, repairing the harm, and repairing themselves, then they have acquitted their reactive fault. In conventional criminal law jurisprudence, passive responsibility is acquitted by punishment in proportion to that fault.[27] Under restorative jurisprudence passive responsibility is acquitted by active responsibility as a reaction to the crime. It follows that there remains a role for passive responsibility in restorative justice – both in determining that there is fault that must be acquitted reactively and in determining fault that cannot be let stand if there is a failure to acquit it through active responsibility. In other words, we need passive responsibility to decide that there is an offender who is causally responsible for a criminal offence. And we need the jurisprudence of passive responsibility to guide what is the maximum punishment we should be able to impose when active responsibility is spurned.

But restorative justice is about a major shift in the balance of criminal jurisprudence from passive to active responsibility. This is connected to the restorative justice notion that, because crime hurts, justice should heal. What follows from this is of greater importance for how just we are in the way we heal, as against the more traditional concern of how just we are in the way we hurt others. Justice in the way we hurt others is of course an important concern for restorativists, but the theory articulated here is that it only arises in cases where we have failed to achieve justice in the way we heal.

Another way of summarizing all this is to say that restorative justice has a theory of responsibility that is more demanding than conventional Western justice; it demands active responsibility. But it also demands passive responsibility both as a precondition for restorative justice and as a backstop when active responsibility is not proffered. Moreover, the processes of nurturing active responsibility and allocating passive responsibility are democratically rich compared to conventional justice processes. They depend for their meaning on opportunities for all the stakeholders in an injustice to participate in defining what responsibility for that injustice should mean. Restorative justice conferences are sharply distinguished from criminal trials by the fact that the major stakeholders – the victim and the offender – have an absolute veto over an outcome that they feel allocates responsibility inappropriately.

Not only is democratic participation necessary to give all stakeholders the opportunity to step forward to voice a willingness to take active responsibility, but also recursively taking active responsibility nurtures future democratic participation. Restorative justice is constitutive of actively responsible democratic citizens. We are not born democratic; we learn to be democratic, for example, in the ways that are required to make the kind of participatory accountability discussed in Sasha Courville's chapter work. This is why restorative justice activists place so much emphasis on restorative justice programs in schools[28] and why these are growing faster in the United States than the many hundreds of restorative criminal justice programs that now exist in all states.[29]

VII. RESPONSIBILITY AND ACCOUNTABILITY

Responsibility and accountability are related concepts.[30] (See also Gardner, this volume.) If you are responsible for something, you are liable for giving more than just an account of what you have done in respect to it; you are also liable for acting to fulfill that responsibility. If you acquit the responsibility badly, you are liable for blame; if well, for credit or praise. It is only for some kinds of responsibility that we are publicly accountable. My son is responsible for keeping his bedroom tidy, but there is no requirement for him to be accountable for this in any public way. So responsibility is an obligation to do some right thing. Responsibility is a realm of (private or public) action; accountability is a realm of public justification.

Obversely, we can be required to provide a public account of certain conduct without being responsible for that conduct. This is the role of the auditor of a company's books: to report whether they give a true and fair account of the company's finances. But the auditor is not responsible for the financial performance of the company or even for the state of its financial records; she is responsible only for giving a public account of them. In drawing the distinction this way, I am going with the narrow classical conception of accountability as simply a requirement of giving a public account. This classical conception originates with the ancient Greeks and is elaborated in the Roman and later northern Italian development of the idea of audit.[31]

We can conceive of restorative justice as a process that, by virtue of its dual integration into horizontal processes of community deliberation and external processes of accountability to courts,[32] enriches democratic thinking about institutional relationships between responsibility and

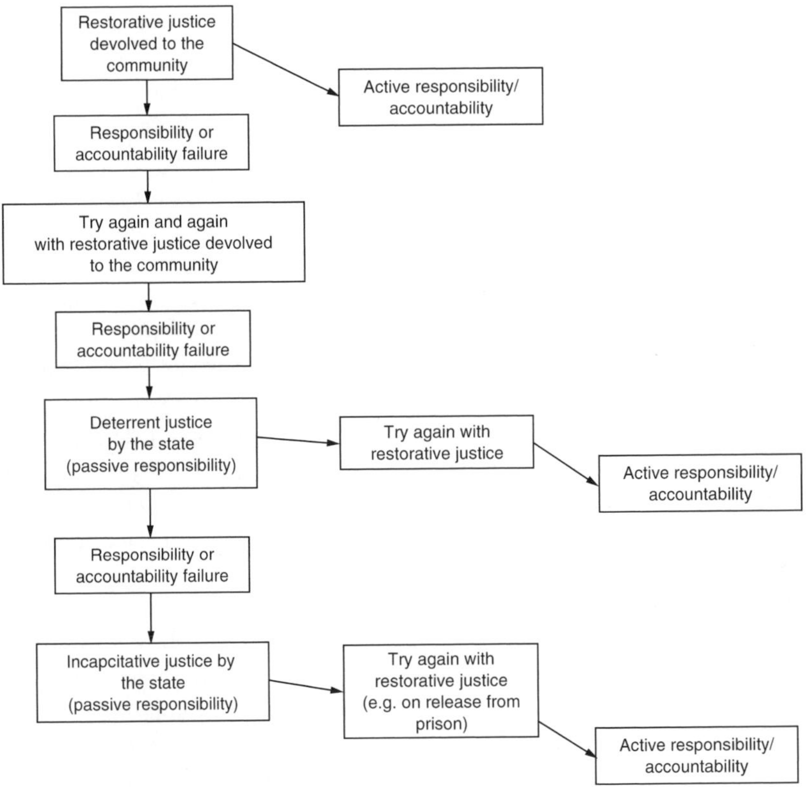

Figure 2.3. Restorative justice means never giving up on responsibility and accountability.

accountability. In the first section of this chapter, we saw that restorative justice is very much a participatory process for fostering responsibility, particularly on the part of offenders but not only on their part. The public accountability dimensions of restorative justice are mostly, though not entirely, about rendering an account of whether the responsibility that has been taken is just. Accountability happens deliberatively when an offender gives an account of what she proposes to do to right a wrong. Accountability is sharpened when the discussion in a restorative justice circle leads to the conclusion that what the offender has proposed is not enough to acquit her responsibility; further deliberation is required and a fresh account must be provided of the responsibility to be taken. Accountability happens externally when a court reads the account of a restorative justice conference and decides that it should overrule the conference outcome.[33]

Figures 2.3 and 2.4 represent what I am conceiving here as the key dimension of accountability for restorative justice, the rendering of an account that acceptable responsibility for an injustice has been taken. Figure 2.3 represents the idea that restorative justice should mean that we never give up on accomplishing active responsibility and assuring accountability for that accomplishment. The figure means that our preference is for restorative justice, devolved to the community, creating a space where: (a) active responsibility is taken; (b) stakeholder citizens in the conference accept the account given of that responsibility (by, for example, signing a conference action plan at the end of a discussion, or later perhaps by holding a "celebration circle" as a ritual recognition that the plan has been completed and responsibility acquitted); and (c) where the state accepts this devolved deliberative accountability (by, for example, a court ratifying a conference agreement and a prosecutor monitoring the agreement and deciding that the conference has accomplished sufficient accountability for there to be no need to take the case to court).

If insufficient responsibility is taken, Figure 2.3 suggests it is best to try again with a restorative justice process devolved to the community. Community stakeholders themselves do best when they have this preference – that is, when their first response to a failure to take sufficient responsibility is to adjourn the restorative justice circle and reconvene when the offender has had more time to think about why his account is not being accepted and perhaps with additional members who can bring fresh perspectives into the circle. But of course it is the free choice of stakeholders to spurn restorative justice and prefer the justice of the courts.

Similarly, the state does best when its presumption is that the best response to an initial failure to accomplish sufficient responsibility is to try again with restorative justice devolved to the community. Moreover, Figure 2.3 suggests that the best response of both community stakeholders and the state when restorative justice fails a second and a third time is likely to continue to be to try again with restorative justice. We tolerate courts failing at the twentieth and thirtieth appearances of repeat offenders; we should tolerate restorative justice failing on a second and third appearance, and beyond.

Ultimately however, the contextual wisdom of the restorative justice circle in a particular case may be that continued restorative justice failure is likely and the case is best handed on to the state to hold the offender passively responsible. But, even when this has happened, there should remain a hope that, once punishment has been imposed, the offender might ultimately come to feel remorse and apologize to the victim, and the victim might ultimately be ready to accept the apology and even to offer forgiveness.

When deterrent punishment fails, when remorse is eschewed, victims are disdained, or reoffending occurs, it may ultimately be necessary to impose an incapacitative punishment – one that actually removes the capacity of the offender to commit this kind of offence again – by locking her up, for example, or by disqualifying her from acting as a company director. But, when that period of disqualification or imprisonment ends, the ideal is that there would be another opportunity for a restorative justice process in which active responsibility is taken, apology rendered, victims assured that they will be safe when the offender is released, and so on.

Such a procedural commitment to never giving up on restorative justice would be expensive. It is an ideal of an exhaustive practice of healing through accountability that can never be perfectly achieved, yet is a yardstick against which we measure different degrees of accountability for the justice of the responsibility that is taken.

Figure 2.4 represents schematically what happens when insufficient responsibility for an injustice is accepted in a restorative justice process. This can arise through a downright refusal of an alleged offender to participate in a restorative justice process or a denial of any responsibility in such a process. Or it can occur because the citizens in the conference do not accept the offender's account of the responsibility she proposes to accept. They think it is not a sufficient response to the degree of wrongdoing. Either way, the state must then step in and signal a willingness to hold people responsible for an injustice. This state actor might be a regulatory authority like the police, a factory inspectorate, a prosecutor, or it might be a court.

When the state takes responsibility for repairing the responsibility failure that has occurred in community justice, under the restorative justice ideal it still hopes that stakeholders will take active responsibility back from the state. When stakeholders, particularly offenders, refuse to do this, the state escalates its response. At each stage of escalation, the state hopes citizens will still not find it too late to take active responsibility for repairing the harm. This escalation can be from a police caution on the street to a more formal caution at the police station (or by taking the offender home to their family), then referral to a prosecutor, then a court hearing, and ultimately

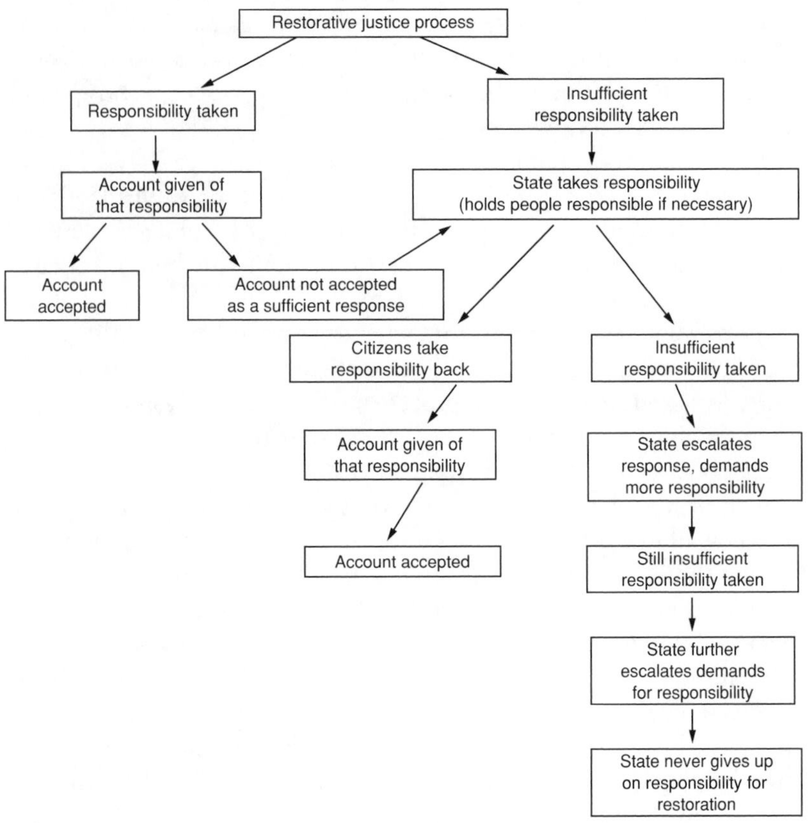

Figure 2.4. The dominant dimensions of responsibility and accountability for a restorative justice process.

incarceration. As in Figure 2.3, the message of Figure 2.4 is that there is no stage when the state gives up on the hope of accountability for active responsibility.

There are other important dimensions of accountability beyond accountability for sufficient responsibility. The state also takes responsibility for holding restorative justice processes accountable for respecting the human rights of victims and offenders, for procedural safeguards, for ensuring all stakeholders are listened to respectfully, for the integrity of the financial accounts of the program and a large variety of accountabilities beyond those for the justice of responsibility attributions. In addition, non-state actors, such as human rights

NGOs, women's shelters, youth advocates, and indigenous community organizations can be more important interveners than states in these responsibility-accountability interventions.[34] Indeed, one of the most effective ways of deepening the furrows of democratic responsibility for justice is to resource and empower organizations in civil society to improve on the state's capabilities to assure accountability for justice failures.

VIII. HOW DOES RESTORATIVE ACCOUNTABILITY DEEPEN DEMOCRACY?

The first respect in which the account of responsibility/accountability sketched here is claimed to deepen democracy is that there is a shift in the balance of how responsibility is exacted from responsibility as a coercive imposition of states upon citizens to responsibility as something autonomous citizens take, after listening to a democratic conversation about harms done and dues owed. Secondly, the principal stakeholders in a directly democratic conversation about an injustice – offenders and victims in the case of a crime – can directly veto any allocation of responsibility they view as unjust. Then, however, these principals must put the determination of responsibility into the hands of the less participatory but more authoritative process for allocating responsibility in the mainstream legal system. That is, principals should retain their right to adjudication of responsibility according to rules of law enacted by a democratic state. Without abandoning this old democratic right, restorative justice can mean a new right to the option of directly participatory democracy over responsibility allocations.

Thirdly, even when the state takes over responsibility for responsibility allocations, there can be further opportunities at each stage of state intervention (police, prosecution, court, prison, parole, etc.) for citizens to take responsibility back into the realm of direct stakeholder democracy. State accountability is reconfigured recursively to enable responsibility to become something autonomous citizens freely choose as opposed to something the state forces upon them. Every time accountability for justice obliges the state to "steal a conflict"[35] from the direct control of stakeholders in that conflict, it can also create a path where the stakeholders can take it back so long as they agree to provide an account to the state of how they use the new opportunity to take responsibility for any serious injustice. This ideal is approximated in the "whole of government" approach to restorative justice in the Australian Capital Territory's Crimes (Restorative Justice) Act 2004.

Hence, on this theory, responsibility for injustice is thrown back into the realm of direct democracy, qualified by accountability to the state to ensure that fundamental principles of the rule of law are not fudged. Yet that state accountability is itself qualified by an exhaustive commitment to keep throwing the game back from external to internal accountability in the circle of stakeholders. Every detour into top-down accountability in Figures 2.3 and 2.4 is itself detoured back to bottom-up accountability. The presumptive path is always direct stakeholder democracy (the justice of the people), but that path is always accountable to the justice of the law. Democracy is enriched when the justice of the people and the justice of the law each become more vulnerable to the other.[36] Democracy can be enriched by the set of preferences for responsibility being active rather than passive, bottom-up rather than top-down, accountable both deliberatively and externally rather than just deliberatively among stakeholders or just externally to a state authority. Together, these preferences might make restorative justice a more deeply democratic practice of justice both in terms of citizen participation and in terms of accountability to a rule of law that is an accomplishment of the people. Not only does it raise the possibility of a practice that takes democratic accountability more seriously than does a rule of law we are held to by grey men in white wigs. It also invokes the possibility of taking responsibility more seriously by never settling for passive responsibility, always struggling to turn passive back into active responsibility owned by wrongdoers and other stakeholders. To settle for passive responsibility, cursed by the criminal as a rope breaks his neck, is to settle for a muted responsibility and a muted democratic conversation about justice.

The final chapter of my book, *Restorative Justice and Responsive Regulation*, argues that it is an institutional possibility to redesign governance to grant citizens universal access to both restorative justice and the justice of the courts when there are reasonable grounds for believing that they have suffered a serious injustice.[37] A key to rendering this seemingly implausible political aspiration plausible is Christine Parker's idea of a regulatory institution that requires all private and public organizations above a certain size to have an access to justice plan and to continuously improve access to justice under that plan.[38] If the kind of consequences Parker proposes for failure to continuously improve access to justice were in place, larger organizations would invest in injustice prevention and in restorative justice not only inside their own organizations but in their interaction with individuals and smaller organizations upstream and downstream. The core idea is that strategic regulation of access to justice would cause the organizational sector of the economy, which it is argued is directly or indirectly implicated in the majority of serious injustices in a complex society, to internalize the costs of injustice prevention and of healing the hurts of their injustices. Universal access of citizens to both restorative justice and to the justice of the courts for any serious injustice would then become fiscally possible. Chapters 3 and 8 of *Restorative Justice and Responsive Regulation* also argue that, because there is overwhelming research evidence that citizens prefer restorative justice to the justice of the courts, faced with universal access to both kinds of justice, people would overwhelmingly choose restorative justice.[39] Since restorative justice is mostly (though not invariably) more immediate and less complex, to the extent that citizens do opt for it in preference to the delay and complexity of litigation, resources are freed up to fund legal aid in the cases where a universal right to access to the courts must be honored.

Readers may conclude that the possibility of a democracy that insists on accountability for universal dual access to deliberative accountability and external accountability to state justice is wild utopianism. It is not the purpose of this chapter to provide the evidence or arguments to dissuade this conclusion. But those who reach it might be persuaded by the arguments herein of the virtues of integrating deliberative accountability and accountability to the rule of law. If so, they might join in demands for incremental reform to deliver both more access to restorative justice for those who want it and more legal aid to improve access to the courts for those who want it. And they might support research on whether restorative justice, especially in schools, actually helps young citizens learn to be democratic.[40] Only by dreaming can we see the steps along the path to a project of larger democratic ambition.

CHAPTER 3

THE MYTH OF NON-BUREAUCRATIC ACCOUNTABILITY AND THE ANTI-ADMINISTRATIVE IMPULSE

Edward Rubin

INTRODUCTION

Accountability has become such a fashionable concept in contemporary legal and political science scholarship that it seems to have expanded beyond any plausible meaning that can be attached to the term. In assessing this concept, the first step is to confine it to specific assertions that can be fitted within a conventional definition. Roughly speaking, accountability can be defined as the ability of one actor to demand an explanation or justification of another actor for its actions, and to reward or punish that second actor on the basis of its performance or its explanation. This chapter focuses on two of the leading uses of this term in contemporary scholarship, two uses that have contributed heavily to the current fashion for accountability. The first is that local and market institutions are more accountable to the people, or that people should be given the opportunity to be accountable for themselves. From this, other observers have concluded that authority should be devolved from the central government to localities and individuals, that policy should be made by officials at the local level or by private parties. The second use of accountability is based on the idea that elected officials – legislators and the chief executive – are accountable to the people, while officials who obtained their position by appointment or examination are not. From this, some observers have concluded that authority should be shifted to elected officials: that policy decisions should be made by legislators, not administrators, that all administrators should be controlled by an elected chief executive, and that the federal government should not intrude on the authority of elected officials in the states.

Some of the proposals that have been associated with these two ideas of accountability have obvious merits, some have subtle merits, and some have obvious or subtle demerits. Very few of them, however, have very much to do with the concept of accountability. Invocation of this concept confers a certain cachet on these proposals – it makes them fashionable – but it neither justifies nor illuminates them. One goal of this chapter is to reveal the conceptual and empirical defects in these two uses of accountability. The ideas of devolving authority to localities and individuals and of shifting it to elected officials will not be critiqued in general, although there is much to be said on this subject. Rather, the argument is that neither of these two ideas is entitled to invoke the notion of accountability.

Because these two notions of accountability are so different from each other, one might expect any discussion of them to be a bifurcated one. After all, the idea that local institutions and individuals are accountable rests on the principle of devolution, where power is shifted to local institutions or private parties so that people make their voice known more effectively or take responsibility for their own actions. The idea that elected officials are accountable, on the other hand, rests on the principle of election, where one chooses another to express, or represent, her views. But these concepts, although divided in their rationale, are unified in their most serious defect. What they share is a pre-analytic hostility to the modern administrative state, an anti-bureaucratic pastoralism that feeds on nostalgia for simpler, more integrated times.[1] The instinct is understandable, but it represents a genuine intellectual sin because it distracts our attention from the government we actually possess. That government can be altered and improved, of course – sometimes in the ways that the proponents of accountability suggest – but there is no foreseeable possibility that it will undergo an essential alteration, and none of those who express hostility toward it have advanced any realistic scenario by which such an alteration could occur. Any proposal that avoids this ineluctable reality of modern government runs a serious risk of doing more harm than good.[2]

One reason that these anti-administrative ideas about elections and participation invoke the term accountability, apart from its cachet, is that they are attempting to expropriate a concept that is essentially administrative in nature, to inoculate themselves against administrative realities by adapting some of those realities for their own anti-administrative purposes. True accountability, in the realm of law and politics, involves many of the features that are central to the administrative state, and that people find so unattractive about it – hierarchy, monitoring, reporting, internal rules, investigations, and job evaluations. Far from being the warm and fuzzy notion that some of its proponents seem to envision, accountability flows along the complex, hierarchical pathways that structure modern government, and reveals the managerial mechanisms of a people who are, in Genet's words, "no longer childish but severe."[3]

Section I of this chapter critiques the idea that accountability can be secured by devolution to localities or private parties. Section II critiques the idea that accountability can be secured by elections. Section III discusses the way in which accountability is an essentially administrative concept, and that the devolution and electoral uses of the concept reflect anti-administrative attitudes.

I. ACCOUNTABILITY AND DEVOLUTION

Arguments regarding the devolution of authority can be divided into two separate sub-categories, the first focusing more on politics, and the second focusing on the enforcement process. The political one, sometimes identified with the idea of federalism, and sometimes with the idea of participatory democracy, argues that local institutions are more accountable to the people than centralized ones, and that devolution of power to such institutions will therefore improve the quality of government. The enforcement sub-category argues that private institutions and individuals can be accountable for their own behavior, and that the government's efforts to enforce the law should allow people to play an active role. These two sets of arguments will be considered in turn.

A. Devolution to localities and the political process

Accountability arguments for the devolution of authority from the central government to localities are based on the idea that a political entity that governs a small group of people can be more readily controlled by those people than one that governs a larger group. In other words, small governmental units are more accountable to their constituents.[4] Implicit in this claim are at least three different thoughts. First, a government is more accountable to those it governs if it is small, because it will need to be more attentive to the concerns of its constituency. Secondly, a government is more accountable to those it governs if the governed group is small, because the members of this group can communicate more readily with each other, and more readily organize political action. Thirdly, a government is more accountable to those it governs if its decisionmakers are physically closer to those whom it governs, because such proximity causes the government to be more attentive and facilitates communication from the constituency.

It is important, in assessing this argument, to distinguish between federalism and decentralization.[5] The idea of decentralization plays an important role in arguments for accountability based on devolution to local authorities, but federalism is a different notion. Federalism grants subsidiary units a final say in certain areas, that is, it grants these governments definitive rights against the center. Decentralization, in contrast, is a managerial strategy by which a centralized regime can achieve the results it desires in a more effective manner.[6] The effectiveness of any decisionmaking unit depends on a variety of factors, including the information available to it, the quality of its personnel, its level of control over its subordinates, and its prestige among those who must follow its commands. These factors sometimes suggest that the most effective decisions will be made by the central government, and sometimes suggest that they will be made by a geographical subdivision. The choice between these two alternative strategies, that is, the particular allocation of responsibility within the overall structure, is determined by the effectiveness of each strategy in achieving the desired result. But it is the central government that identifies this result, and thus defines the criteria for success or failure. And it is the central government that decides how decisionmaking authority will be divided between itself and the geographical subdivisions, and when that allocation will be changed.

The argument that accountability is increased if authority is transferred from national to local authorities is not connected with federalism, and relies only on the more general principle of managerial decentralization. One reason for this is the obvious one that federalism protects the rights of regional political entities – states, in the American system – rather than localities. Regional governments, however, do not display the small-scale features on which the devolution argument depends. A more general reason is that devolution, or decentralization, is a managerial policy that does not depend on the kind of rights that federalism guarantees. Of course, the policy might be more difficult to alter if it were secured by a right, but that is a very different consideration. Many policies that are widely regarded as desirable, such as unemployment compensation, environmental protection, or the regulation of securities markets are not secured by rights because they lack the moral texture that rights seem to possess, and because the considerations that support them might change in the future. Localism seems to belong in this category because arguments for it are almost exclusively functional, not moral, and because these arguments could conceivably change, perhaps as a result of the Internet.

Whatever the virtues of localism, the concept of accountability provides very little support for it. The main difficulty with it involves salience. How many people pay much attention to the political events that occur in their locality? To begin with, many Americans pay relatively little attention to politics at any level: they may have some strongly held beliefs, but their levels of knowledge and their levels of participation are extremely low.[7] One reason for this is that many political issues, in a modern administrative state, are technical and complex, which not only makes them seem daunting, but also dull. Another is that people have so many other sources of stimulation these days, including movies, television, recorded music, spectator sports, participatory sports, the Internet, and convenient travel. Most of these activities, moreover, tend to draw one's attention away from the locality: the entertainment industry is national; the Internet connects people to those with similar interests anywhere in the world; and spectator sports often involve professional or Division I college teams that draw fans from large geographic areas.

Even when people are interested in politics, it is often politics at the state or national level. For many people, large-scale politics are much more interesting, because of the issues involved or the sense of significance that they convey. One simply cannot save the blue whale, or protect Israel, or privatize social security, or eliminate abortion through actions whose effects are focused narrowly on one's local community. While a person can undertake local actions to oppose abortion or protect the environment or alleviate hunger or improve education in a single school, the positions that people formulate on issues such as these are often conceived in comprehensive or national terms.

Social movements that generate relatively high levels of political involvement are generally national in scope.[8] This is readily explained by either of the two dominant explanatory theories for these movements, the American or resource-mobilization approach, and the Continental, or identity-oriented approach.[9] According to the resource-mobilization approach, social movements are generated by leaders using a variety of instrumentally rational strategies, such as fund-raising, dramatic events, and media access.[10] Clearly, these sorts of activities are best organized on the national level, and often depend on their ability to draw support from a large number of widely dispersed people for their effectiveness. According to the identity approach, social movements spring from people's changing self-conceptions, from trends within civil society that generate new opinions and beliefs.[11] Again, such ideological transformations tend to occur on a society-wide level, and most social movements, unless they have overwhelming support, can only flourish by uniting all the widely dispersed people who have developed a novel self-conception.

There is, moreover, a close interconnection between the national character of people's non-political interests and the kinds of political interests they develop. As just noted, entertainment in our society – motion pictures, television, popular music, spectator sports – is often national in scope. As a result, the common inclination to treat politics as a form of entertainment, as a set of contests one watches on television,[12] reinforces the tendency to focus on national, rather than local politics. People's tendency to vote for candidates on the basis of their personalities, rather than on the basis of the issues they espouse, also orients the average citizen toward national politics, since it is national figures who receive media attention and thereby become identifiable. Most Americans know who the President is, and many know their Senators or Representatives, but how many know even the names of their town supervisors or local legislators?

If people fail to attend to local politics, the devolution of political authority to local entities cannot produce decisionmaking that is more accountable to those subject to the decision. Rather, decisions taken at the local level will be opaque to their subjects. They will be low visibility events, because they are not reported in the media that people watch and do not involve the issues that people regularly follow. Instead of being controlled by ordinary citizens, these decisions will be controlled by local elites, that is, those who are already in control and thereby benefit from the devolution of additional authority, or those who are unusually motivated to participate because they have a high economic stake in the outcomes of local decisions. Studies of local government suggest that there may be several different elites competing with each other for control,[13] but these will be elites nonetheless, and not the mass of ordinary citizens that would support an accountability argument for devolution.[14]

Robert Putnam's *Bowling Alone* provides an historical explanation for this present reality.[15] According to Putnam, the American people's sense of social solidarity, their level of participation in all aspects of political and civil society, has been declining precipitously in recent years. We have less contact with our neighbors, we join fewer organizations, we spend less time socializing with our friends, and we often go bowling alone. The culprits are suburbanization, an obsessive dependence on automobiles, and the increasing influence of the mass media, most notably television.[16]

Putnam paints a grim picture of modern society, but it is difficult to imagine how it could be reversed. The causes he identifies are not likely to be abolished, or even abated, in the foreseeable future. Indeed, contemporary demographic trends emphasize their inevitability. Putnam identifies several states that continue to display the sort of communal life he asserts we are losing, such as North Dakota, South Dakota, Montana, and Vermont. He identifies several other states that typify contemporary political disconnection and social dissociation, such as Nevada, Texas, Georgia, and Florida.[17] The fact that people, particularly young people, are fleeing from Putnam's genial, well-integrated states to those he identifies as cauldrons of *anomie* suggests that the trends he observes will continue,[18] as well as raising the question whether the experience of modernity is quite as miserable as Putnam suggests.

The important point is that small-town America is largely gone. The kinds of localities that could exercise increased authority in an accountable manner have been ripped apart by skeins of superhighways, telecommunications networks, and the mass media.[19] Local jurisdictions that can serve as the recipients of devolved authority are no longer self-contained towns, surrounded by ten thousand acres of farmland or forest, but segments of suburban and ex-urban sprawls demarcated by invisible and arbitrary legal lines. In the modern world, these localities are no more salient than the technical issues that confront elected officials. Thus, they are of little use for increasing the accountability of government, and, in fact, devolution of government decisions to this level is more likely to increase their opacity.

The accountability argument for devolution of authority to local governments is conceptually connected to the principle of participatory democracy, as opposed to the principle of federalism. That is, devolution has nothing to do with the rights of states, qua states, and little to do with the rights of any governmental entity, but rather draws its conceptual force from the idea that citizen participation is essential if democracy is to prosper, or perhaps even survive. Participatory democracy is a very popular idea these days, but it presents formidable difficulties when considered from either a descriptive or a prescriptive point of view.

Descriptively, the difficulty is the one just given: that people in modern American society are generally non-participants, particularly in politics. As Putnam has observed, there is an increasing trend toward an atomized social existence, linked to the outside world through passive media such as television. We simply cannot rely on participation at the local level to provide accountability for government. In fact, the devolution of authority to local governments may well produce the opposite effect. If only a minority of Americans in any given locale choose to participate in politics, effective participation may require that this relatively small and generally dispersed group be aggregated at the national level if it is to be effective.

Participatory democracy fares no better as a normative idea. Imposing a moral or legal obligation on people to participate in government could well conflict with our basic commitment to liberty, as Bruce Ackerman points out.[20] Many feel that citizens should be free, if they choose, to be politically inactive, and they should be safe from being reviled as unpatriotic, or from being oppressed for failing to protect their interests, if they make that choice. The devolution of authority to local government in the interest of accountability, by relying on participation to control decisions that were originally made at another level, effectively punishes people for their non-participation. That is, it relies on a control mechanism that real people will not use.

None of this is to suggest that local communities never become mobilized about a given issue, or that local governments are never held accountable. Such events occur, and they may count as some of the more dramatic cases of political participation in our governmental system. But the accountability argument for devolution of authority to local governments cannot rest on intermittent eruptions of political involvement, no matter how dramatic. Rather, the argument depends on the continual involvement and constant vigilance of local populations, and their ability to monitor the quotidian decisions that constitute the bulk of virtually every assignment of government authority. Without such vigilance, the devolution of authority to local government will, on the whole and with a few exceptions, decrease government accountability.

B. Devolution to private parties and the enforcement process

Unlike the accountability arguments for political devolution, the accountability arguments for devolution to private parties do not focus on the structure of government, but rather on the government's relationship to citizens. These arguments begin with the recognition, which other accountability arguments so often ignore, deny, or condemn, that enforcement of public policy directives is a crucial task of modern government. The basic idea is that enforcement will be more effective, that it will better accomplish its ultimate purpose, if private parties, whether organizations or individuals, are accountable for their own actions. Such accountability can be achieved by transferring, or devolving, power from administrative agencies and other governmental institutions to these private parties.[21] Thus, accountability arguments for enforcement devolution recommend that classic command-and-control regulations be replaced with a more cooperative and collaborative approach. The resulting mode of governance is sometimes described as "New Public Management" or the "post-regulatory state."

Arguments for devolving enforcement to private parties draw on some of the most convincing and illuminating insights in modern social science. Human behavior and human institutions, we have learned, are enormously complex. They are grounded on an intersubjective process that creates the interpretive framework, or structure of meaning, that makes individual thought possible, and that generates social institutions. These institutions then become part of the intersubjective process by which new interpretive frameworks and structures of meaning are created.[22] Thus, social scientists are beginning to connect the growth and operation of institutions with the internal experience of individuals, demonstrating the way individual motivation and construction of meaning generate institutions, and that institutions affect individual motivation and meaning. Much of this process occurs in civil society, that is, in the set of interactive relationships among people that is separate from either the economic or political systems.[23] Rejecting the Hobbesian view that society is essentially political, and the Marxian view that society is essentially economic, modern social scientists have revealed the truly *social* character of the process that underlies all human behavior and human institutions.

One of the most important lessons that has been derived from these insights is that neither individual nor institutional behavior can be readily altered by simple government *ukase*. The intersubjective processes of civil society are generally too robust to be effectively controlled in this manner, particularly in an open, non-repressive system like our own. (Indeed, the vigor of the black market in the old Soviet Union suggests that even enormously repressive regimes have difficulty controlling people by direct command.[24]) Sometimes, government commands will provoke resistance because they conflict with personal attitudes, institutional structures, and patterns of meaning in civil society. More often, they will be ignored, or reinterpreted in a manner that undermines their intended purpose. To be sure, the government can impose sanctions on those who violate its commands, but sanctions are too costly, both politically and economically, to be relied on in the face of widespread non-compliance.

On the basis of these insights, social scientists and legal scholars have begun to develop new approaches to the implementation of social policy and administrative programs.[25] This literature is too subtle and complex to be briefly summarized, but it will be enough, for present purposes, to note some of its major themes. First, it argues that effective implementation cannot be based on commands issued by a government agency that emerge from the agency's own needs and modes of thought, without paying any attention to the subjects of the program. Rather, the agency must take cognizance of the organizational structure of the firm, or the meaning structure of the individual. Secondly, the best way to take cognizance of these complex matters is to open a dialogue with the firm or individual, to learn about them through what Weber called *verstehn*, or empathetic understanding.[26] Thirdly, in order to implement the program, to obtain compliance with its essential features, the firm or individual should be allowed to play an active role in the implementation process. This is partially achieved by the dialogue established by the agency, but more effectively pursued by allowing the firm or individual to develop its own strategies for compliance. Fourthly, these strategies will be most effective if the firm or individual internalizes them, that is, absorbs them into its meaning structure so that they become part of its mode of operation or existence. Fifthly, this process can be tied into the layered, or interactive, character of civil society. Instead of interacting directly with the subject, in the manner just described, the agency can interact with an intermediate institution, and that institution, once it has developed and internalized a compliance strategy, can then interact with the subject. In doing so, it can use the same process, often in a more subtle and effective manner than the agency. In summary, new approaches to implementation often devolve the authority to devise implementation techniques to the subject, or to an intermediate institution.

There is widespread enthusiasm for implementation programs of this sort at present. Several have already been enacted into law, while others now serve as a modus operandi for administrative agencies. The US Organizational Sentencing Guidelines, adopted in 1991,[27] recommend greatly reduced penalties for corporate violations if the corporation has developed and implemented its own program for enforcing ethical business conduct. The Guidelines list minimum requirements for an effective program, which include promulgating a written code, communicating the code to employees, establishing monitoring systems to detect violations, encouraging employees to report such violations, responding to any violations that are detected, and taking all reasonable steps to prevent future violations. The Sarbanes–Oxley Act of 2002,[28] passed in response to the Enron scandal, relies heavily on the Guidelines, and requires that all companies subject to the Act file reports describing their internal ethics codes and increases the penalties for firms that fail to meet the criteria specified in the Guidelines.

The term "accountability " is sometimes used to describe the subject's reaction in this New Public Management mode of implementation. The subject, it is said, becomes accountable for its actions by participating in the implementation process. Rather than being told what to do, the firm or individual develops its own approach, through an open dialogue with the agency, and then takes responsibility for implementing or internalizing the approach that it developed. Thus, there has been a devolution of authority from the implementing agency to the subject. Rather than being given a command to end discrimination or control unethical business practices, the firm is invited to develop its own strategy, and is described as becoming accountable for either the strategy itself or the results that it achieves. Similarly, rather than simply being subject to a prescribed punishment, a miscreant individual may be invited to propose a plan for altering his behavior, and then be described as having become accountable for either the plan or the behavior.[29]

To describe implementation programs of this sort in terms of accountability is usually inaccurate, and potentially dangerous as well. The firms and individuals who are subject to these programs are not being made accountable for their own actions, or making their own choices; they are being manipulated by the administrative state. These modern implementation strategies may be more effective, but, if so, they are effective because they get inside the firm's internal structure, or the individual's head, and alter their behavior to achieve a collectively established social purpose. Far from granting the subject autonomy, or making it accountable for its own actions, they undermine its will to resist, making it an accomplice in the governmental effort to control it.[30] The devolution of authority is set within a larger framework of continued supervision. Of course, there may be no supervision, but, in that case, there is no accountability in any real sense. In this case, talking about "accountability" in such situations is potentially dangerous, as it misleads us into thinking that the firm is being supervised or controlled, while in actuality it can violate applicable public norms with impunity.[31]

If the subject firm or individual is truly accountable to the implementing agency in the standard bureaucratic sense that it must answer for disobedience, then it will be punished if it does not behave the way the agency wants. It is true that what the agency wants has become less specific and more rational in the New Public Management Model. Instead of identifying a goal, choosing the implementation strategy it thinks will work, and then requiring the subject to obey that implementation strategy, whether it works or not, the agency now identifies a goal, lets the subject choose part or all of the implementation strategy, and evaluates the success of its efforts by determining whether or not it has achieved its goal. But this does not alter the basic reality that the agency is imposing a particular goal on the firm or individual. It simply means that it is avoiding making unnecessary and possibly counter-productive demands for compliance, demands that it can now avoid because it has the sophistication to get inside the subject and enlist it in achieving the agency's objectives.

Consider the example of combating drug abuse through treatment and rehabilitation programs that ask the individual to propose his own strategy for getting and staying off drugs.[32] Such programs are undoubtedly more humane than incarceration without treatment, and they are almost certainly more effective. They exist, however, in a context where the government is compelling the individual, albeit in a more humane and effective way, to do what the government wants, not what the individual wants. Perhaps the individual really does want to stop using drugs, and welcomes criminal culpability as a means of compensating for a weakness of the will. More often, however, what the individual wants is to be in the same situation regarding his chemical stimulant of choice as alcohol users are regarding theirs, namely to be able to indulge his habit cheaply, safely, and in peace. Society, in its collective wisdom, has decided that he may not do so, however. Given this prohibition of his real desires, the rehabilitation program is probably preferable, in the addict's view, to incarceration, but that does not mean that he has been made accountable or responsible for his actions. Rather, he has been compelled, and given a choice about the method of compulsion.

To be sure, the subject of the implementation program may ultimately accept the government's goal as its own. That is certainly the intention, and it is certainly the most effective implementation strategy, since compliance will then be voluntary, and require many fewer government resources to achieve the same results. But one must be careful about the way one characterizes this process, since it poses real dangers. Our theory of government is based, at least in part, on the idea that people's views are exogenous to their interaction with the government; that the government is supposed to respond to their desires, not create them. Our electoral process provides some guarantee that the new implementation techniques will be used to support collective purposes, and against only those firms and individuals who violate those purposes. Nonetheless, a large enough number of actions taken at the individualized level can have systemic consequences, and one does not need to endorse Genet's view of the criminal as existential hero[33] to perceive a real danger.

The danger can be highlighted by considering Pavlovian thought reform, an early but still important effort to achieve voluntary compliance from a recalcitrant subject. Although Pavlov is associated, in the popular mind, with having trained dogs to salivate at the sound of a bell, he did not discover this technique, but was simply using it to produce saliva for his experiments on digestion. What he did discover was that, when he rescued his dogs from near death in a flood, their conditioned reflex was gone. Further experimentation revealed that the application of stress, if continued long enough, could extirpate a good deal of learned behavior, and leave the subject ready to be taught new behaviors by the experimenter.[34] Use of this technique on human beings in the Soviet Union and China revealed that the stress had to be applied beyond the point when the subject ceased resisting and said what he thought he was supposed to say, and up to the point when the subject ceased thinking for himself, and asked his interlocutor what he was supposed to think.[35]

It is not hard to imagine a variant of this technique being used with a recalcitrant firm. Implementation theorists have suggested that the most effective strategy that an agency can use to obtain compliance from a large group of regulated entities is the "nice" strategy of Tit for Tat, which applies punishment only in response to disobedience, and ceases as soon as the disobedient behavior stops.[36] In a case of genuine recalcitrance, however, the agency might begin imposing sanctions, and then continue imposing them until there was a breakdown in the structure of the firm and a new structure could be put in place. This is essentially what happened in the prison reform cases that the federal courts decided during the 1970s and 1980s, where the federal courts imposed a set of constitutional standards on state prisons. Confronted with recalcitrant state prisons, the judges moved from case-by-case adjudication to continuous monitoring. Retaining jurisdiction of the initial claim, sometimes for as long as a decade, they imposed a continuing stream of orders and sanctions until the old system simply broke down, the wardens retired, and new officials who would voluntarily comply with the constitutional standards were installed in their stead. By that point, these prisons had, through a process of internal reform triggered by the stress of judicial supervision, become different institutions.[37]

There is probably nothing objectionable about what the federal courts did in the prison cases. Prisons are public institutions that do not themselves have rights, and the prisons that were the subject of this intensive supervision were imposing truly barbarous treatment on individuals who, despite their incarcerated status, did have rights. The mere fact that the approach used by the courts can be analogized to Pavlovian thought-reform does not render it invalid. But it cannot truly be said that the prisons became accountable for their actions, or took responsibility for them. Rather, these institutions were transformed by a severe and effective method, a method that reflects sophisticated current thinking about governmental implementation strategies.

It is theoretically possible that administrative agencies or other public institutions would encourage genuine accountability on the part of private actors. To do so, they would need to abandon their fixed commitment to particular goals, as well as to particular techniques, and open themselves to a genuine dialogue about the purposes that regulation was designed to achieve. This would make the private actor an equal partner in the regulatory enterprise, rather than a subject to be manipulated, however subtly. But government agencies are unlikely to adopt this approach, and it would not be normatively desirable for them to do so. Agencies are part of a hierarchically organized government apparatus that transmits goals and expectations from one level to another, a system of superiors and subordinates where subordinates are held accountable in the true, bureaucratic sense of this term. It is not likely that a subordinate official could tell his superior, or his superior tell the President or a congressional committee, that he had changed the purpose of the regulatory program after consultation with the subjects of the regulation. Moreover, these purposes represent the collective decisions of a democratic government. They are not typically selected by the voters, for the reasons described above, but they are selected by elected officials who represent the voters. To allow those purposes to be so readily undermined would raise much more serious normative problems than are raised by the flexible strategies that modern implementation theory recommends.

A separate, and in a way more extreme, version of the idea that the devolution of authority shifts "accountability" to private persons is the argument that deregulation does not release firms from accountability because the market will continue to hold them accountable.[38] The marvelous result, according to this account, is that accountability can be achieved without any governmental supervision whatsoever.[39] But to say this is merely to play with words, and reflects the gaseousness that afflicts contemporary discussions of accountability. While there are certainly issues of bureaucratic accountability within the hierarchical structure of every firm of significant size,[40] market competition does not make the firm answerable to anyone; it is simply a constraint on their actions which sometimes works to the benefit of consumers and sometimes works to their detriment. Their claim is equivalent to saying that Newton's laws of motion make drivers accountable to traffic regulators.[41] The whole point of a free market is that the entrepreneur is able to pursue its self-interest without being accountable to anyone, and that social benefit will result from the operation of the market's invisible hand.

On the other hand, the whole point of economic regulation, at least according to the standard interpretation, is to impose some public accountability on market actors, to make them answerable to some government authority. While the reasons for such regulation are very well known, it may be useful to summarize them at this point to emphasize the extent to which describing markets as a form of accountability misuses the term. First, markets fail in various ways, due to monopolization, externalities, and information asymmetries.[42] When these conditions occur, the market will not achieve efficiency – the monopolist will under-produce its product, the factory will impose costs on its neighbors, the merchant will exploit the consumer. Secondly, there are only certain goals that a market can fulfill. Even perfect markets cannot provide what economists describe as public goods, that is, goods whose benefits cannot be restricted to the delimited group of people who are willing to pay for them.[43] Thirdly, the market distributes its benefits with stunning unevenness. Some people become extremely rich, while others, with less marketable skills, get very little.[44] A significant group of people will get nothing at all.

The correction of market failure, the provision of public goods, and the alleviation of inequality through income distribution or direct services, all require government intervention, at least in the context of the modern world.[45] This intervention is achieved by making private firms accountable to a government authority that can counteract market forces in a variety of ways. The elimination of such intervention may be good public policy, or bad public policy, according to one's views, but it clearly represents the elimination of accountability, and the reversion to the lack of external supervision that is generally regarded as a market's greatest virtue.

II. ACCOUNTABILITY AND ELECTIONS

A second set of contemporary arguments about accountability is that elected officials should make a larger proportion of government decisions because these officials are accountable to their constituents.

There are at least three such arguments: first, that legislators, being elected officials who are accountable to the people, should make basic policy decisions and not delegate extensive authority to administrators;[46] secondly, that the chief executive, being an elected official who is accountable to the people, should control all executive agencies, including those that are currently independent;[47] and, thirdly, that elected state officials, because they are accountable to the people, should not be subject to policy control by the federal administrative agencies.[48] These arguments, including the argument for greater autonomy for elected state officials, are distinct from the arguments about the accountability of local officials that were discussed in the previous section. That section, and the arguments that it discussed, did not turn on whether the local officials were elected or not, but simply on their physical proximity and personal connection to those whom they govern. Here, elections are the crucial factor.

Elections are regarded, in our society, as a Very Good Thing, but their virtues do not correspond to the claims for them on which accountability arguments depend. Perhaps the most important virtue of elections is to solve the problem of succession.[49] Dictatorships are virtually guaranteed to undergo a succession crisis on the death of the dictator, if not before; hereditary monarchies undergo such crises when the monarch fails to produce an heir or when there is a rival claimant. At best, succession crises of this sort disrupt orderly government relations; at worst, they lead to civil war. Moreover, the looming threat of a succession crisis tends to undermine the effectiveness of government. Those who aspire to succeed the ruler must build their own power base, withdrawing their resources from the collectivity, devoting their efforts to self-aggrandizement, and attracting allies to their cause.[50] This activity is often regarded as disloyal by the ruler, and with good reason, since the same actions that position someone to succeed the ruler can position that person to stage a coup while the ruler is alive. Thus, these actions must be conducted clandestinely, and the ruler is induced to devote much effort to discovering and combating this potentially threatening activity.

A functioning electoral democracy provides a remarkably successful solution to this problem. The regular election of political leaders assures an orderly succession, and generally avoids difficulties resulting from the death or incapacity of the existing leaders. It replaces the disruption and inefficiency produced by efforts to succeed the leader with a constructive process. Positioning oneself for succession in an electoral regime, far from being regarded as disloyal, is a highly acceptable activity that confers prestige on any plausible candidate. The best way to do so, moreover, is to offer criticisms that significant parts of the populace regard as helpful, or to demonstrate that one can govern by acting effectively in one's present position. These strategies need not be conducted secretly, and, in fact, are generally most effective when openly pursued. The leader may choose to combat them, but does so most effectively by open debate – more disruptive efforts to thwart opposition are disfavored, and expose the leader to serious political risk. Electoral democracies achieve these beneficial results so effectively and, once they are well established, so effortlessly, that people often forget that the most important virtue of elections is that they solve the problem of succession. This is great, but it has nothing in particular to do with the issue of accountability.

A second crucial function of elections is to produce a government that is responsive to the people's basic desires. They achieve this through the process of representation that is central to our conception of elections,[51] although not necessarily to elections in general.[52] In voting for candidates in a general political election, people tend to choose the person whom they believe best reflects their particular values and interests.[53] This often means a person of their own ethnic background, or a person who can convincingly demonstrate that she has the same attitudes and beliefs as the voters.

This is not accountability, but the opposite of accountability. Voters want to choose a like-minded person because they believe that such a person will take the actions they prefer, even though they are not able to supervise or monitor the person. They know that government policy will involve a succession of quotidian decisions, complex judgments, recondite bargains, and other actions that will be beyond their understanding and attention spans. When someone is choosing a subordinate who is truly accountable – whom the person can monitor on a continuous basis – there is at least a tendency to choose the most talented or capable individual, regardless of his personal views, and rely on instructions to make sure he does what his superior wants. In elections, people generally prefer to choose someone who will act in their interests because she shares their perspective.

Holding the representative accountable is a third function of elections, but it is subsidiary to succession and representation. There is an ongoing debate about whether elected officials are more motivated by ideological considerations[54] or by the desire to be re-elected.[55] Even if one assumes that electoral considerations predominate, however, their effect is likely to be attenuated by a variety of factors. Incumbents are difficult to defeat, which means that the electorate's initial choices tend to become locked in place.[56] In addition, the chief executive is often a lame duck, as are a number of Senators. Most important, however, is that intermittent, highly contested elections are simply a very poor device for holding a person accountable. Most electoral democracies present the voters with only two or three realistic choices, which means that a multitude of issues must map into a small decision set. This is the result of party politics, a feature of democracy that generally develops outside the constitutional structure, but is just as central to its operation as the constitutional provisions. A small decision set means that even perfectly informed voters must make their choice on the basis of the few issues they regard as most important, and then accept their representative's decisions on the other issues, whether they approve of her decision or not. Indeed, some argue that electoral democracy itself is merely symbolic.[57]

Most voters, moreover, are not perfectly informed about the issues, and the evidence suggests that they often suffer from apocalyptic levels of ignorance.[58] Some classic voter studies conclude that people's choices can generally be predicted from their social characteristics, without regard to any particular features of the person they are voting for.[59] More recent studies grant a larger role to attitudes, but identify these attitudes as very general party affiliations or impressions of the candidate's personality.[60] Even if voter attitudes are issue-oriented, they tend to be stable, long-term preferences on leading issues, rather than detailed assessments of particular decisions;[61] in fact, voters often base their decision on the candidates' perception of problems, rather than their actual or proposed solutions.[62] Finally, if an issue becomes truly salient – if it is something that voters become truly exercised about – they are likely to hold those in power responsible for the decision, without making fine distinctions about who actually made the relevant decision. (As noted above, voters often treat elections as a mode of entertainment, rather than as a policy debate about important matters of social policy.)

The highly attenuated nature of electoral accountability means that it will be of limited value for the purposes that proponents of accountability have recommended, that is, arguing against open-ended delegations by the legislature, in favor of a unitary executive, or in favor of federalism. To begin with the delegation issue, compelling legislators to make more policy decisions, rather than delegating such decisions to administrative agencies, will not mean that these decisions are being more closely monitored or controlled by voters.[63] Even at their most extreme, such decisions are simply too fine-grained to become factors in an electoral campaign. In fact, elected representatives often monitor administrative agencies quite closely, and hold them responsible for their actions,[64] but this has very little to do with their accountability to the electorate. Rather, it is the result of their hierarchical position, the fact that they function as agencies' structural superiors in our system. Their monitoring activities are rarely based on any direct accountability to the voters, but rather are carried out, first, because it is their job, because of their representative role, that is, the kind of people that they are, and secondly, to provide favors to important contributors.

Similar problems beset the accountability arguments in support of a unitary executive, that is, an executive who has direct supervisory authority over all administrative agencies. In many cases, proponents of this view argue on either constitutional or policy grounds that the President should be in control of all federal administrative agencies because he is elected, and therefore accountable to the voters.[65] The sort of control that the President would exercise over a presently independent agency, however, will rarely have the political salience that would make a difference in a general election. To be sure, Ronald Reagan ran on a platform that prominently featured deregulation, and it is possible that public approval of this position was a factor in his landslide electoral victory. This was, however, a broadly stated political position, not the sort of quotidian supervision of administrative practices that would be facilitated by eliminating agency independence. In fact, it was the incumbent whom Reagan so resoundingly defeated, Jimmy Carter, who was actually the most effective deregulator, before or since. Carter's deregulatory program was not limited to the quotidian level, but in fact involved rather sweeping policy changes.[66] In addition, most of it was directed toward independent agencies, which tends to contradict the idea that the President must possess the removal power in order to exercise control over these agencies.[67] None of this intensive deregulation, however, seems to have made much of an impression on the electorate. It was Reagan, who accomplished less but spoke about it more, and certainly more effectively, who was apparently able to attract whatever votes this issue was able to produce.

However unconvincing the electoral accountability argument may be when applied to Congress or the President, it is more unconvincing still when applied to state officials. The essence of the argument is that elected state officials, because they are accountable to the people, should not be subject to policy control by the federal government. This serves as the basis of the Supreme Court's anti-commandeering cases, such as *Printz* v. *United States*[68] and *New York* v. *United States*,[69] which assert that state officials, being accountable to their constituents, should retain exclusive jurisdiction over the issues on which their constituents will judge them.[70] For the federal government to commandeer them, to compel them to implement federal statutes, undermines them unfairly because their constituents may hold them accountable for decisions that were forced upon them – as Justice Scalia said in *Printz*, "[t]he Constitution . . . contemplates that a State's government will represent and remain accountable to its own citizens."[71] A secondary concern is for the voters, who will be misled by federal commandeering, and may then fail to hold their officials accountable for matters that these officials decide on their own.

The great difficulty with this argument is that it assumes that voters can distinguish between state and federal areas of jurisdiction as long as the federal government is not allowed to intrude upon the state's prerogatives. This is not an easy thing to do, however, because federal and state responsibilities overlap in so many areas of governance.[72] Consumer sales practices, food quality, securities offerings, worker safety, civil rights, environmental protection, agriculture, mining, and numerous other areas are regulated by the federal government under the Interstate Commerce Clause; banks are chartered under the Money Clause; roads are built under the national defense power. Most of these functions are decentralized within the federal government, which means that there are regional, state, or local offices carrying out the federal functions. But the states also regulate the same areas, charter banks, and build roads as part of their general police power. The result is a complex pattern of overlapping jurisdictions. And again, the regulatory details are generally too technical, too fine-grained to be salient to voters, except under the most extraordinary circumstances.

But the accountability argument for federalism indulges in an even greater level of implausibility than this. Having assumed that the average voter can distinguish between federal and state authority, despite all these overlapping jurisdictions, it then assumes that the voters will be fooled when the federal government gives orders to state officials in one of these areas. In other words, these amazingly sophisticated voters, who understand that some federally insured banks are chartered and supervised by the state, while others are chartered and supervised by the Treasury Department; or that the quality of the food served in a restaurant is monitored by state officials, but the quality of the packaged food sold at the counter is monitored by federal officials, are unable to understand that the federal government is compelling the state to take certain actions. Moreover, the elected officials who are so compelled are absolutely unable to explain this fact to these sophisticated voters. The whole set of assumptions is so implausible as to give rise to the suspicion that accountability is a *post hoc* rationalization invoked by proponents of federalism because of its current cachet.

A second difficulty with the accountability argument for federalism, apart from the existence of overlapping jurisdictions, is that its essential claim tends to be refuted by the interaction between state and local government. The American people are governed by a vast array of local authorities – villages, towns, cities, counties, and special-purpose districts. According to long and essentially unchallenged doctrine, these authorities have no constitutional status of their own; they are creatures of the state.[73] Moreover, within states, the general legal principle that controls state–local relations is Dillon's rule, which is that local governments possess only those powers that have been granted them by state authorities.[74] Some state constitutions provide certain forms of autonomy for local jurisdictions, but others do not, and there is certainly no uniform pattern.[75]

In other words, state governments are authorized, by both the federal Constitution and their own constitutions, to commandeer local officials, that is, to use the employees of the state's subsidiary creations to carry out the state's own programs. The pattern, moreover, is enormously complex. Even those sophisticated voters who can disentangle the strands of federal–state relations may have difficulty knowing precisely where state initiatives end and local ones begin. But the absolute subjugation of some local governments to state authority, and the high level of incomprehension regarding the scope of autonomy possessed by others, does not appear to have prevented people in American cities and towns, or, more specifically, political elites in cities and towns, from developing vigorous political scenes, with intensive competition for electoral office. Elections are still used to determine succession, voters still choose candidates to represent them, and candidates are still held accountable on a few salient issues. The fact that local officials are regularly compelled to implement state programs, to an extent that goes beyond anything in federal–state relations, does not seem to interfere at all with the electoral process for these officials.

Finally, the invocation of accountability on behalf of state officials assumes the very point at issue in the federalism debate, namely the proper balance between state and federal authority. After all, citizens vote for federal officials as well as state officials, and the types of official for whom they vote at the state and federal levels are generally analogous. Which of these sets of elections provides more accountability in a situation where the authority to decide is a matter of debate? Granting authority to the state allows the state voters to control the issue, but it simultaneously denies a voice to voters in the other states. Whether those voters should be given a voice – whether or not the decisionmaker should be accountable to them – is precisely the issue at stake in the federalism debate. The general idea of electoral accountability, which can be invoked on each side, does nothing to resolve the issue, even assuming that it is an operative principle with respect to these relatively recondite and complex matters.

III. ADMINISTRATIVE ACCOUNTABILITY AND THE ANTI-ADMINISTRATIVE IMPULSE

A. The real nature of accountability

If, as argued above, the concept of accountability cannot be used to describe elected officials' relationship to voters, or the devolution of authority to local institutions or to private persons, does this familiar concept have any meaning at all? In fact, it has a well-established meaning, and serves as a useful concept for describing certain relationships in modern government. As used in ordinary language, accountability refers to the ability of one actor to demand an explanation or justification of another actor for its actions, and to reward or punish that second actor on the basis of its performance or its explanation. The concept is useful because it is a basic mechanism of administrative or bureaucratic government, that is, of the mode of government that is dominant at the present time, and shows no sign of being displaced. It is precisely this connection to administrative government that makes the term "accountability" such an appealing device for expressing anti-administrative impulses, such as non-delegation, localism, and the devolution of public authority. And it is precisely this connection that makes these efforts to use the term for anti-administrative purposes so incoherent.

The real role of accountability in a modern state must be sought within the complex structure of the administrative hierarchies that constitute our basic mechanism for governing ourselves. Accountability is one means by which superiors control subordinates, and thus a means by which policies promulgated at the highest levels of government – the President, the legislature, or the heads of agencies – are translated into governmental action. It is not the only means of supervision, however; an understanding of it therefore requires us to determine when it is being used, when it is not being used, and why this choice has been made. Such organizational issues are crucial to the performance of the governmental agencies that we rely on so heavily in the modern administrative state.[76]

Accountability involves two elements: first, a hierarchical relationship; and, secondly, a standard that the hierarchical superior imposes on a subordinate. With respect to the first element of accountability, a recent discussion of the subject by Mark Seidenfeld is particularly helpful.[77] Relying on psychological studies, Seidenfeld suggests that accountability can improve decisionmaking by reducing some of the heuristic biases on which decisionmakers frequently rely.[78] For accountability to produce this effect, these studies suggest, the decisionmaker must be aware that he will be held accountable before he decides, and he must accept the legitimacy of the person imposing the standard. It is the purpose of an administrative hierarchy to resolve these issues in a definitive manner; the hierarchy defines supervisory relationships and declares those relationships to be authoritative.[79] These features are not unique to an administrative hierarchy, of course. They also apply to the legislature's or the judiciary's relationship to the administrative apparatus in its entirety. However, because the command structure in these cases involves the relationship between large institutions, and often occurs only after a considerable period of time has elapsed, a particular administrator's awareness that she will be held accountable by these particular actors is likely to be attenuated. The legislature may not turn its attention to the implementation of the law it has enacted; the judiciary may never consider a case that challenges her decision. But within an administrative hierarchy, these relationships are more definitive. Each decisionmaker is usually aware of the particular person or group of persons who will supervise his decision, and supervision is generally carried out more frequently and more immediately.

In fact, administrative hierarchies typically display a feature that can be described as second-order accountability. Those who supervise subordinates, and hold these subordinates accountable in various ways, are themselves accountable to those superior to them, and, specifically, they are accountable for the way in which they hold their subordinates accountable.[80] That is, one of the crucial tasks that most administrators must perform is the supervision of subordinates, and they are typically judged, or held accountable, for the quality of that supervision. An administrative hierarchy is frequently a chain of accountability, and the idea of accountability serves as an essential feature in the construction and operation of the hierarchy.

The second element involved in holding someone accountable is the standard that is applied. This standard may be either procedural or substantive, that is, it may specify a decisionmaking process or a desired result. A procedural standard instructs a subordinate how to carry out the task in question – how often to inspect factories for unsafe conditions, what reading program to use in elementary schools. A substantive standard instructs a subordinate what results he is expected to achieve – what level of industrial accidents is acceptable, what the children are expected to know when they finish elementary school.[81]

In either case, the subordinate would be responsible for meeting the prescribed standard, and his job performance would be assessed on the basis of his ability to do so. The standard provides the basis on which the subordinate can, and usually must, justify his actions to the superior. Just as the first element of accountability – the hierarchical relationship – creates the structure of administrative governance, the second element – defined standards – establishes the content of this mode of governance. Administrative governance, as Weber pointed out in his seminal discussion of the subject, is instrumental in its basic conception; it is not viewed as divinely inspired, traditionally established, or inherently valuable, but rather as a means by which the people who compose a given society achieve their collective goals.[82] It does not place people in positions of authority because of their birth, their status, or their personal charisma, but because they are qualified to perform specified tasks. The standards that superiors impose on their subordinates are the mechanism by which goals are translated into reality, and the evaluation of subordinates by their superiors is the means by which the administrators' ability to carry out that task is assessed.

B. The anti-administrative impulse

When viewed from this perspective, it seems apparent that voters cannot, through the process of election, hold a public official accountable in any real sense, that local populations cannot hold local officials accountable, and that people cannot really be induced to be accountable for themselves. These relationships are all important ones, and serve useful functions in the governmental process, but they are not mechanisms of accountability. Consideration of the actual mechanisms, as they are implemented in an administrative hierarchy, emphasizes the distance between true accountability and elections, localism, and private responsibility. Elected officials respond to some of the deeply felt, or widely held views of the electorate, local officials exhibit some similarity of outlook with those they govern, and private persons can sometimes be induced to consider the consequences of their actions from a public perspective. But these general and occasional correspondences do not enable one actor to demand an explanation or justification of another actor for its actions, and to reward or punish that second actor on the basis of its performance. Obligations of this sort can only be imposed in a tightly integrated hierarchy, such as those found within the administrative apparatus. One can always slap the word accountability down on the page if one wants to argue for the increased reliance on elected officials, local officials, or private parties, but the underlying concept does not apply.

If this is true, then why have these alternative accountability arguments become so popular? The answer lies in our ambivalence toward administrative government. On the one hand, modern Western societies have irrevocably committed themselves to an administrative system, and can no longer even conceive of parting with the advantages that this system provides. Accountability is one of these advantages; it would simply be impossible to manage the complex tasks of modern government, and implement publicly-debated and articulated policies, without the elaborate administrative mechanisms through which subordinate officials are held accountable for their performance. On the other hand, there is a widespread hostility toward administrative government, a desire for simplicity, community, and freedom of action that the heavy, complex machinery of modern government seems to have obliterated. The discourse of accountability is an effort to argue that we can capture the necessary advantages of the administrative state without subjecting ourselves to its oppressiveness. Let us shift authority from the administrative apparatus back to the President, to Congress, to state officials, to local officials, to private parties, to anyone else. We can still have accountability – in fact we can have more accountability – because elected officials will be accountable to the voters, local officials will be accountable to their communities, and private parties will be accountable to themselves or the "market." We will have then achieved the magical result of supervision without supervisors, of hierarchical control without hierarchy, of effective administration without administrative government.

The idea that devolving authority to local government will increase accountability may not appear to be anti-administrative on its face. After all, the authority might be transferred to local administrative agencies. In fact, there is a close, albeit complex relationship between bureaucratization and scale.[83] Large institutions, at least in the modern world, are almost always organized bureaucratically, while small ones can be organized on different principles, some of which may render them more accountable to those they serve. The devolution of authority to local authorities can thus be viewed as an alternative to bureaucratization. It is also an invitation to nostalgia. During the early Middle Ages, Europe was divided into rather large political entities – e.g. the Holy Roman Empire, France, the Angevin Empire. But the administrative apparatus needed to govern entities of this size was beyond the reach of Europeans at the time (at least those on the continent). Instead, control was decentralized through the device of feudalism, which granted virtual autonomy to subsidiary units in exchange for loyalty to the regime.[84] This complementary relationship between bureaucracy and devolution continues to the present day. Bureaucratization follows almost inevitably from large-scale institutions, and the devolution of authority to smaller units represents the only realistic possibility of avoiding it. Such devolution, for reasons already discussed, will not lead to any real increases in accountability. The claim that it will, however, gains increased appeal from the implicit understanding that devolution is an alternative to the administrative state.

The inclination to describe flexible implementation techniques in terms of accountability also reflects an abiding discomfort or hostility to the realities of the administrative state.[85] If flexible implementation truly made the private parties involved accountable for their actions, then the process could not properly be described as regulation any more. Rather, it would be a truly collaborative enterprise, where individualized interactions replaced hierarchy and a spirit of benign camaraderie replaced the instrumental rationality of the Weberian state. This seems appealing, at first, and all sorts of positive terms such as cooperation, mutual respect, egalitarianism, and open-mindedness come to mind as descriptions of it. The difficulty is that this approach to governance represents a major retrenchment of our ability to achieve collective goals. The majority would no longer be able to deploy the machinery of government to impose its desires on the economic or social system. Instead, each private person or institution would have the opportunity to establish its own goals, with help, guidance, and advice from the un-bureaucratic agents of the collectivity.[86]

To find a government such as this in American history, we must return again to the 1820s, and perhaps earlier. At this pre-regulatory time, government rarely interfered with private enterprise. If one wanted to start a bank, for example, one simply collected some capital and started one. If one had enough capital, one would locate the new bank in a city; if one did not, and was afraid that depositors and payees would make use of their common law right to come in and demand their money over the counter, then one would start a wildcat bank, that is, a bank located somewhere in the woods, where the wildcats lived.[87] Individuals were subject to coercive laws of course, but, as Frederick Jackson Turner noted, if one did not like these laws, one could move to the frontier and live beyond the effective reach of legal rules.[88] The picture is not exact, to be sure, but it seems as close to a non-regulatory state as we have gotten, or are likely to get.

What the bitter experience of the nineteenth century taught us is that a modern economic system of industrial production, when granted such latitude, will lead to grinding oppression, inequality, and social dislocation at a level that the majority of people – those who do not own the means of production – will find unacceptable. Denied the franchise, they will rebel; granted the franchise, they will vote for public officials who will create an administrative state and impose their goals on the owners.[89] One hundred years later, this state, with its health and safety legislation, unemployment compensation, labor regulation, environmental protection, social security, public housing, and innumerable other regulatory programs, is so well established that it is easy to overlook its general significance, and concentrate on its specific and apparent failures. None of its regulatory programs work perfectly, and some do not even work particularly well. But abandoning the entire apparatus is not only infeasible, but inconceivable; it is not on the current political agenda of any industrialized nation.

In fact, administrative agencies make the majority of our rules and carry out the majority of our adjudications.[90] They constitute the basic, operational structure of modern government, and this role necessarily involves a considerable amount of policymaking. The President and his immediate staff, Congress, and the federal courts function mainly to control and direct the bureaucracy, rather than performing basic governmental operations.[91] They make policy in certain areas, and, when they do so, that policy usually prevails, but they could not possibly make all the policy-level decisions that modern government requires.

The anti-administrative character of arguments that authority should be transferred to elected officials, such as the Congress or the President, is even more apparent, since the unelected officials who are now exercising excessive authority in this argument are federal administrators. With respect to Congress, this takes the form of the non-delegation doctrine, the idea that Congress should not enact open-ended statutes that allow administrators to make policy-level decisions. Proponents of this doctrine, fully aware of the irreversibility of administrative government, often insist that their recommendations would not necessarily cause a reduction in the scale of the administrative state, that Congress could make all the basic policy decisions if its members only worked harder, were better informed, and possessed more political resolve.[92] But of course, it would lead to a massive retrenchment of administrative government, beyond anything that any mainstream politician has proposed. For Congress to increase its policymaking activities by such a vast amount would entail vast political costs, and vast monetary costs in staff resources. When costs go up, and the scale of the producer's basic operation does not change, the quantity of production will inevitably decline. For these reasons, enforcing the non-delegation doctrine is politically unrealistic, as the federal courts have long recognized[93] and the Supreme Court has recently reconfirmed.[94] Academic writing urging its enforcement is essentially an expression of hostility toward the administrative state.

Proposals for a unitary presidency are less openly hostile to the administrative state, but ultimately rest on a similar instinct. These proposals, while acknowledging the crucial role that agencies play in modern government, insist that these agencies must be controlled by the President, as an elected, and presumably accountable, official. But there is no particular reason why an elected Congress, as our primary policymaker, cannot deploy the quality of oversight as an elected President.[95] The mere fact that the President cannot remove the top political appointees, which is the hallmark of independence, does not mean that the agency is out of control. A so-called independent agency is generally subject to congressional and judicial control to precisely the same extent as an executive agency. It is equally subject to control by private parties, both through the legally established mechanisms of the Administrative Procedure Act,[96] and through the informal contacts that one court described as the "bread and butter" of the administrative process.[97] It is even subject to control by the President, through his appointment of the Chair and through his influence as the most important person in the government.[98] The idea that an agency is out of control simply because it is not subject to the direct commands of the Chief Executive, betrays an underlying fearfulness of the administrative process.

Federalism arguments often possess an equally anti-administrative tone. It is true that shifting authority from the federal government to the states often means shifting authority from a federal to a state administrative agency.[99] But the growth of administrative government is generally connected to the nationalization process, a connection that is unambiguously true in unitary regimes.[100] In the United States, regulation tends to be associated with federal incursions into state affairs, and arguments for state autonomy are often couched in quasi-deregulatory terms.

There are at least three reasons for the association between regulation and the federal government. First, in federalism-related conflicts between the federal government and the states, the conflict usually manifests itself when the federal government attempts to regulate either the state itself[101] or some entity within the state.[102] To be sure, other federalism cases involve federal legislation establishing court-enforced rights or punishments,[103] but regulatory cases predominate. Secondly, while the federal government does not necessarily take the lead in developing administrative programs, it generally finds itself in the role of imposing regulations on the less progressive states, and often on the majority of states. Given the variations in state adoption of regulatory programs, there will almost always be some states that have not acted by the time the federal legislation passes.[104] The impact of the legislation on these states will be more salient than its lack of impact on the states that have already enacted similar legislation. Thirdly, and closely related to the second, many states are simply too small to develop and operate the kinds of regulatory programs that the federal government imposes. Some thirty American states have fewer than five million people. Program drafting and design costs tend to be somewhat constant, rather than varying with scale, and these states, particularly given the American reluctance to tax, will often find themselves unable to initiate regulation on their own.

Thus, accountability arguments for the devolution of authority to local government or private parties, and for the transfer of federal authority to Congress, the President, or the states, all spring from the same source. It is an abiding hostility toward the administrative state, a desire to deny or dissipate its all-too-evident reality. The idea of accountability serves as an alternative to administration in these arguments; if local governments or private persons are accountable for their actions, then they do not require the sort of regulation or ongoing supervision that has fueled the expansion of modern bureaucracy. Use of the accountability concept in these contexts is alluring, but, because it is essentially political escapism, it will ultimately mislead us, encouraging the adoption of policies that will produce effects quite different from those we are seeking by its invocation.

CHAPTER 4

EXTENDING PUBLIC ACCOUNTABILITY THROUGH PRIVATIZATION: FROM PUBLIC LAW TO PUBLICIZATION

Jody Freeman

INTRODUCTION

Public law concepts and doctrines, based, as they are, on a hierarchical and bureaucratic notion of public action, and prioritizing constraints on government power, tend to ignore the important role private actors play in performing public functions. As a result, they badly underestimate the potential for harnessing private actors in the service of public goals. Private contributions to service provision, and even to regulation, are not necessarily or exclusively dangerous and corrosive of public accountability – which is how they seem to be perceived in mainstream administrative law.[1] Today, many public services and functions are produced by a highly interdependent network of public–private partnerships. These partnerships, which involve for-profit firms, and nonprofit, professional, religious, and public-interest organizations, have the potential to contribute important technical innovation, ingenuity, cost-savings, quality, and diversity to the performance of arguably public functions.[2] Instead of simply constraining the private role in public governance, we should therefore aim, instead, to facilitate, direct, and manage it.[3] Importantly, harnessing this private potential can strengthen, rather than weaken, the state.[4] Yet, for this to be true, scholars and policymakers must rethink the traditional accountability mechanisms that might be imposed upon private actors.[5]

In this chapter, I suggest a counterintuitive way to view American privatization trends. Instead of seeing privatization as a means of weakening the state and reducing public accountability, I imagine it as a mechanism for expanding public accountability's reach into realms traditionally thought private. In other words, privatization can be a means of "publicization,"[6] a process through which private actors increasingly commit themselves to traditionally public goals as the price of access to lucrative opportunities to deliver goods and services, and to perform functions that might otherwise be provided directly by the state. Rather than compromising democratic norms of accountability, due process, equality, and rationality – as some critics of privatization fear it will – privatization might extend these norms to private actors through the judicious use of legislative, executive, judicial, and even social oversight.

This chapter proceeds as follows. In Section I, I explore the present state of the privatization vs. public accountability debate, in which commentators who care about the potential efficiency gains of contracting out are often pitted against those who are more concerned about its potential to result in an accountability deficit. While this debate is frequently conducted along ideological lines, there is also a more pragmatic version that offers prospects for possible convergence between these two viewpoints. In Section II, I explore ways by which we might use legislative, executive, judicial, and social mechanisms to extend public accountability norms to private actors. In Section III, I address possible objections to this proposal. In Section IV, I suggest three considerations that, from the public law perspective, distinguish stronger cases for publicization from weaker ones. Finally, in Section V, I discuss the implications of all this for notions of public accountability.

I. THE STATE OF THE DEBATE

A. Ideological arguments

In the last two decades, privatization – which, in the American context refers to contracting out rather than selling state assets – has been championed by conservative policymakers, academics, and public intellectuals as instrumental to reducing the size of government and broadly restructuring society in line with a conservative agenda.[7] Privatization coincides with other political and economic developments – including globalization, free trade, market integration, and deregulation – that similarly reinforce an ideological preference for private over public ordering and market over noneconomic values.[8]

Ideological support for privatization is matched by a contrary ideological view that holds the public sector in higher esteem. Adherents of this view are more likely to regard government as a force for progressive ideals. They would rule out privatization as a presumptive matter, at least for a subset of functions that go to the heart of what they see as the state's inherent responsibilities in a liberal democratic society. These functions might include criminal and civil adjudication, policing, incarceration, education, transportation, health care, national defense, and foreign policy. Like the pro-privatization position aimed at limiting government, this anti-privatization rejoinder is grounded in political philosophy rather than sound economics. It holds that even if privatization were proven to deliver significant cost savings, it would still be an illegitimate choice for organizing service provision, at least for those functions that are so inherently governmental as to be categorically nondelegable.

The trouble with ideological positions of this sort, on both sides of the privatization debate, is their intransigence in light of arguments about the empirical consequences of privatization. Empirically grounded claims about how privatization works, or might be made to work, are unlikely to move either side from its core beliefs. For this reason, the possibility that public values might extend to private actors through privatization would be less interesting to ideological privatizers than to pragmatic privatizers. Pragmatic privatization arguments, though not free of ideological underpinnings, are potentially more responsive to arguments about the benefits of privatization and the potential for structuring privatization to ensure that it does not erode democratic norms.

B. Pragmatic arguments

A variety of arguments about privatization seem more pragmatic than ideological. As an illustration, I have in mind the paradigmatic public manager – a county official, say – faced with the task of providing high-quality services in a cost-effective way. Pragmatic privatizers of this sort seek more efficient service delivery while adhering to numerous and sometimes conflicting mandates from higher levels of government. Operating under considerable fiscal, institutional, and legal constraints, these local officials try to solve immediate budgetary and service-provision problems rather than seek to transform society's relationship to government.

For example, when a local agency contracts out highway maintenance or garbage collection primarily because of cost considerations, that decision may qualify as an instance of pragmatic privatization: a means of improving productive efficiency by obtaining high-quality services at the lowest possible cost, thereby freeing up resources that might otherwise go to waste and allocating them elsewhere to maximize welfare. Such pragmatic arguments sound largely in the discourse of economics and tend to elevate economic values over other goals.

While such choices have political implications (for example, they might systematically shrink the civil service), they may not be motivated primarily by either political expediency or ideology. Rather, they might represent an attempt to solve a problem in a cost-effective way without compromising either quality or accountability.

Of course, maximizing efficiency in service provision implicates two separate questions. First, who should set the level at which the relevant good is provided and dictate the terms of its provision? Secondly, and independently, who should provide it?

Pragmatic privatizers typically focus on the second question. They take for granted that government has a responsibility to establish service levels, but view government as ill-designed and poorly equipped in most cases to deliver services directly. This view that private entities are better suited to deliver most goods and services reflects a comparison of public and private organizations in which public institutions fare badly. For example, economists point out that civil service protections reduce the government's flexibility to reward and punish employees' performance, making it harder to encourage employees to produce high-quality services and cut costs. Public agencies are generally not client-oriented, economists argue, so agency employees lack incentives to perform well.[9] Agencies are not profit-maximizing entities disciplined by competition and the possibility of bankruptcy, and so will tend to be both less innovative and more wasteful.[10] Because of differences of structure, organization, and institutional culture, private firms are thought to be capable of providing the same or higher-quality services at lower cost than can public agencies.[11] The economics literature is generally optimistic about privatization for reasons such as these, and tends to adopt the view that privatization should be the default assumption for service delivery unless a convincing economic case can be made against it.[12]

Notably, adopting a pragmatic approach to privatization is not the same thing as being pro-privatization. Even if many economists would favor privatization as a default, many others might argue *against* it in particular circumstances by invoking the same kinds of economic considerations identified above – by arguing, for example, that the anticipated benefits of a particular privatization depend on market conditions that frequently fail to materialize; or that particular privatization efforts may fail because of an absence of competition[13] or because of political obstacles that hamper the market regime from the start. What unites pragmatic privatizers is not a commitment to privatization per se, but a commitment to the intellectual terrain on which the debate over privatization takes place, a terrain that is dominated by the normative perspective, vocabulary, and disciplinary techniques of economics.

However, there is another perspective on privatization, one that prioritizes legal and democratic accountability over cost.[14] This view is also pragmatic, in the sense that it is concerned with the consequences of privatization, but it is also ideological in its baseline commitment to democratic norms other than efficiency. Proponents of this perspective might concede that productive efficiency in service provision has value. Indeed, they might be in favor of cost savings in service provision generally. But they would also worry about privatization's implications for what they regard as liberal democratic norms of accountability, due process, equality, rationality, and the like.[15] Adherents of this perspective might be willing to debate the appropriate size, structure, and role of government, but they would argue that, whatever the ultimate public/private mix, privatized service provision must be accountable to the electorate and consistent with liberal democratic norms – even if the precise nature of those norms might be subject to debate.[16]

For convenience, I will call this perspective the "public law" view because I associate it with public law scholars. To my mind, the public law view is represented paradigmatically by administrative law scholars for whom the substantive legality and procedural regularity of government action is the primary preoccupation – though it is certainly not limited to this group. In the United States, adherents of the public law perspective begin with the observation that the Constitution, together with statutes like the federal Administrative Procedure Act (APA),[17] imposes on government a host of obligations designed to render decisionmaking open, accountable, rational, and fair. While they recognize that such impositions generally apply only to government, they bristle at the notion that government would seek to *avoid* these obligations by systematically contracting out functions to private actors who are not similarly constrained.

How might this happen? First, Congress has wide discretion to delegate functions to private actors, so long as it supplies in legislation the requisite "intelligible principle" to guide the exercise of private discretion.[18] And, because it take so little to meet the constitutional standard for providing such guidance, Congress can delegate broad powers that afford private actors considerable discretion without fear of being judicially overturned. In addition, the state-action doctrine insulates most of these private actors from constitutional constraints. Thus private actors avoid the accountability-generating constitutional requirements, including due process, that would apply to the government if it performed the same functions.[19] And, though the Supreme Court occasionally treats private actors as state actors for constitutional purposes, these instances are few.[20]

Private actors can also effectively escape many statutory imperatives designed to promote public accountability. In the US, for example, they need not comply with any of the procedural requirements of the Administrative Procedure Act, nor must they, generally speaking, observe the disclosure provisions of the Freedom of Information Act[21] or the open-meeting obligations of other sunshine laws[22] that apply exclusively to government actors. Private contractors notably escape the civil-service protection rules, as well as the conflict-of-interest and ethics rules that apply to public employers.[23]

To illustrate how privatization can raise public law concerns in both obvious and subtle ways, consider American welfare reform. The elimination of Aid to Families with Dependent Children and its replacement with Temporary Assistance for Needy Families (TANF) via the Personal Responsibility and Work Opportunity Reconciliation Act of 1996 (PRWORA)[24] created a new welfare policy in which the federal government replaced a federal entitlement program with block grants to the states.[25] The Act's emphasis on "welfare to work" and its clear intention to change the "institutional culture" of welfare administration encouraged states to use these block grants to contract with private, sometimes for-profit, providers to furnish welfare-related services.[26] Under the new TANF program, many administrative functions once reserved to public agencies were increasingly performed by private, often for-profit, actors.[27] These include functions such as case management, child care, transportation, education, job training, and placement services for TANF recipients. At least one state had sought to put its entire program, including eligibility determinations, out for bidding to private firms before the Clinton administration prohibited the outsourcing of some eligibility determinations.[28]

This has resulted in an apparent erosion of public law protections. For example, contracts with private providers are typically awarded without notice and comment, preventing TANF recipients and their advocates from influencing the contractual terms or, at a minimum, having their views heard in the process of constructing the contracts. The new array of contracts has produced a more fragmented network of local agencies and private providers which makes it more difficult to obtain information, lodge complaints, and monitor quality.[29] And fewer welfare-related decisions – many now made by private contractors – are considered "determinations" or "denials of benefits" which, if made by an employee of a public agency under the old regime, would be subject to due process hearings and judicial review.[30]

As suggested above, a pragmatist might respond that this kind of contracting out is inconsequential because government typically sets the level of service provision itself and delegates only implementation to private providers. This arrangement seems to preserve traditional accountability, since it is the level of service, not the nature of the deliverer, that ought to concern us. As long as government retains its role in setting the standard and in monitoring its contractors, the system is accountable. But this claim is too formalistic to provide much comfort to those who share the public law perspective. Providers (whether public or private) enjoy considerable discretion when implementing the policy choices of elected officials. This discretion affords them an opportunity to redefine policy choices or to specify them at a level of detail unanticipated by policymakers.[31] Decisions at the ground level of policy implementation can be as consequential as decisions, such as eligibility standards or general program directives, set directly by a centralized public authority.[32] Even the power simply to provide the most carefully specified services creates a principal–agent problem in which a contractor may, without violating any technical contractual terms, enjoy substantial room to maneuver.[33]

Those who subscribe to what I have called the public law perspective worry more, then, about the nature of the provider than do those who advocate privatization on the ground of costs savings. This is not only because they are concerned about the quality of service, but because they elevate the importance of accountability over other values. Empowered with so much discretion, and facing incentives to further their self-interest at the expense of the "public interest," private providers seem risky from a public law perspective.

II. PRIVATIZATION'S POTENTIAL TO EXTEND PUBLIC LAW NORMS TO PRIVATE ACTORS

A. An impasse?

To an outside observer, the choice between these two positions – one generally pro-privatization and one generally wary on accountability grounds – can appear to be all or nothing: either privatize and hope for the best, or refuse to privatize for fear of the worst. Part of this may be due to the compartmentalized and self-referential nature of the privatization literature: most analyses seem oriented to a single community that tends to agree with itself – either the generally pro-privatization economists or the frequently more trepidatious administrative lawyers. Rarely does one encounter an argument aimed at those who do not share common disciplinary tools and normative frameworks. But there remains the potential for translation across this divide.

To this end, one might try to express the value of public accountability mechanisms that economists might otherwise find to be costly and cumbersome, in terms that economically minded pragmatic privatizers would appreciate. For example, one might argue that notice-and-comment rulemaking feeds important information into the administrative decisionmaking process, which might assist agencies as they translate legislative generalities into the operational specificity of rules. In this way, legal procedures provide a mechanism for preference elicitation and preference aggregation, which economists might consider valuable.[34] In the same vein, broad consultation with interested parties who have a concrete stake in an issue can also force the agency to consider a wide range of scientific and economic data it might otherwise ignore or treat less seriously, which can help minimize costly policy errors.[35]

Too, just as proponents of the economic perspective might come to acknowledge the value of legal procedures, public law scholars might come to see that pragmatic supporters of privatization have a point about the potential value of enlisting private providers in public service delivery, or in the performance of what are generally regarded as public functions. Many publicly provided services deservedly attract criticism for being costly and inadequate.[36] One need not be a conservative ideologue to criticize the quality of education in public schools, the dangerous conditions in overcrowded prisons, and the dilapidated state of much urban infrastructure. If private provision might improve these services and do so for less, surely, one might argue, it is worth a try. Feelings like these explain why parents of all political persuasions might support school vouchers, for example, even at the risk of having their children attend private schools where they would be exposed to religious instruction the parents would rather avoid. Whatever its downside, these parents might think, privatization has to be better than the status quo.

Good translation across the disciplinary, conceptual, and linguistic divides between the two views only goes so far, however. Even if the prospect of cost savings and improved quality seems promising, many adherents of the public law view would decline to take the risks that, in their estimation, widespread contracting out entails. Such objections could be overcome, however, if one could show that privatization could in fact *extend* public law norms to private actors under some circumstances – a process I call "publicization." This would allow one to obtain some of the benefits of privatization without systematically eroding democratic norms. In this vision, public and private power might grow simultaneously: services might improve and diversify, and the worst fears of the public law perspective need never materialize. Below, I describe a host of measures that might help to accomplish this goal. Though I decline to advocate any particular combination, and though some are less likely to materialize than others in the current political climate, they nevertheless exist, and under the right circumstances might well come to shape the terms of public–private contracting in important ways.

B. Legislative mechanisms

There are a variety of legislative mechanisms to accomplish publicization and they are by no means new. Since the late nineteenth century, federal and state governments have imposed requirements on both private for-profit corporations and nonprofit organizations through direct regulation, conditioned grants, and the conferral of tax subsidies, among other instruments.[37] Common law courts have long imposed legal restrictions on private actors through evolving tort, contract, and public nuisance standards.[38] Extending compliance with public law norms to private actors engaged in service delivery would, therefore, be an expansion of a traditional practice.

To illustrate, Congress could extend by statute some or all of the public law requirements discussed in Section II to private actors – requiring them to disclose information in a public record, hold public hearings and take public comment, and justify their programmatic decisions with reasons that would be subject to judicial review.[39] Congress could conceivably amend the Administrative Procedure Act to eliminate the public participation and reporting exemption for contracts and grants. This would allow members of the public to participate in agency decisions related to these instruments, which would help to produce a record for judicial review. Congress could also extend other statutes, such as the Freedom of Information Act, to private entities.

Congress might also accomplish much of this indirectly, through the federal grant system pursuant to its spending power. As a condition of federal grants, Congress could tailor privatization experiments to extend federal goals not only to the state and local government grantees that directly receive the funds, but also to private contractors with which these governments contract for service delivery. Congress might minimize the discretion of private contractors by specifying performance criteria or dictating substantive contractual terms, including requirements for regular and detailed reporting that may currently be lacking. Congress could also demand closer or more extensive monitoring of private contractors by federal agencies, not only for cost control and fraud prevention (the purpose of most traditional agency oversight), but also for quality control, a task that contracting agencies have not to date performed very effectively.[40] To accomplish this, of course, Congress would need to fund and empower these agencies to monitor in a serious way, and hold them to account through oversight.[41] In addition, Congress might provide for supplementary contract enforcement by granting private rights of action in legislation, or by requiring contracts to provide for suits by third-party beneficiaries.

Even if this kind of congressional action is not forthcoming, federal agencies charged with awarding grants could themselves impose – in many cases without any additional delegated authority – a wide variety of substantive regulations on recipients of those grants or on contractors with whom the granting agencies do business. This is possible because, despite some legislative constraints and notwithstanding the coordinating directives of the Office of Management and Budget,[42] agencies nevertheless generally have considerable discretion over grant implementation. Imposing regulations designed to generate accountability would not be especially difficult.[43] And, finally, even without congressional or federal agency action, state governments could adopt similar measures independently, either through direct regulation of private contractors or by inserting terms into the contracts themselves.

C. Judicial mechanisms

Courts could also extend their scrutiny of both legislative and bureaucratic efforts to contract out government functions, and might invalidate them for constitutional or statutory violations. As an initial matter, the Supreme Court may find some functions non-delegable. The Court has already suggested that in addition to conducting elections and running towns, some other government functions may be non-delegable, such as tax collection, fire and police protection, and education.[44] And, though the Court has been reluctant to act on its suggestion, or to expand this list, perhaps it will do so as experience with privatization develops.

Indeed, courts could conceivably invalidate private delegations while leaving delegations to public agencies in place. Private delegations create a set of problems that public delegations do not, and have historically been more suspect.[45] Jack Beermann has also suggested that the Supreme Court's concern with political accountability, evinced in its Tenth Amendment jurisprudence, could provide the basis for invalidating some delegations to private actors on the ground that such delegations may confuse the public about whom to blame when things go wrong.[46] In addition, many state constitutions contain "accountability clauses" that may limit privatization.[47]

Short of invalidating delegations to private providers, however, courts have other options at their disposal. For example, they may choose to scrutinize contracts with private providers more carefully to ensure they provide for adequate supervision by the legislature.[48] Alternatively, courts might soften their approach to state action, perhaps relaxing the conditions under which they are willing to find that private contractors are performing functions traditionally and exclusively performed by the states. This move would limit the impact of broad delegations and provide a mechanism for extending public norms to private actors without invoking the blunt instrument of the non-delegation doctrine, which the US Supreme Court so resoundingly and unanimously declared defunct in the recent *American Trucking* case.[49]

The Supreme Court has spoken on at least two occasions about privately run prisons and detention centers, with the result that these are now equally and, some might argue, more accountable as a constitutional matter than public prisons.[50] While private prisons may still present dangers that public prisons do not, the Court has shown some willingness to ensure that privatization does not compromise constitutional norms, at least with regard to a sensitive function such as incarceration. In addition, the Appointments Clause might serve as a constitutional constraint on privatization. When Congress delegates authority to private actors and equips them with significant federal law enforcement responsibilities, it must arguably appoint them in a manner consistent with the Appointments Clause because they are Officers of the United States.[51] These are just two examples, but they offer some reason to believe that courts might fill the gap should legislatures and agencies fail to extend public norms to private actors exercising their contractual duties.

And while courts have been reluctant to construe statutes to afford plaintiffs private rights of action absent express congressional intent, courts could still construe contracts to afford third-party beneficiaries the right to sue to enforce contractual terms, whether or not Congress or state legislatures expressly build such causes of action into contractual schemes.[52]

With regard to agency decisions to issue grants and award contracts, courts might simply determine that the relevant governing statutes do not preclude judicial review and then impose on agencies a duty to oversee their contracts more vigorously under pain of being found to be acting arbitrarily or capriciously. In other words, courts might jettison the traditional deference they afford such informal policymaking if it becomes the primary tool of contracting out traditional government functions and if courts detect a serious erosion of public law norms. Critics of regulatory reform have called for a similar reconsideration of judicial deference to an agency's exercise of enforcement discretion, when that discretion has arguably been used to undermine otherwise mandatory statutory or regulatory requirements.[53] Courts are free to scrutinize agency contracts and grants for arbitrariness, even when those contracts are not subject to the

Administrative Procedure Act's notice-and-comment requirements for rulemaking (unless Congress provides otherwise).[54]

Short of such steps, courts might simply elaborate common law contract principles that require fair procedure and rational decision-making to force private actors to comply with rudimentary due process. Such obligations have historically applied to health care providers excluded or expelled from private associations on which they depended for their livelihood,[55] and state courts have begun applying these obligations more broadly. In 1998, a Californian court imposed procedural obligations on a private employer seeking to dismiss an employee for sexual harassment.[56] It is conceivable, then, that courts might find such obligations applicable to private contractors in control of an important service when they are in contractual relationships with consumers (for example, nursing home residents and utility customers). The California Supreme Court has held, for example, that private utilities are bound to comply with antidiscrimination norms because of state-conferred monopoly status and pervasive state regulation.[57] In addition, private actors are generally more vulnerable to tort liability than public entities. The US government has waived its sovereign immunity for some tort claims, but its liability is still subject to substantial exceptions, such as for intentional torts, defamation, and harm resulting from discretionary decisions.[58] It is conceivable that courts could increasingly rely on tort law as a mechanism for disciplining private decisionmaking.

In addition to constitutional, administrative, contract, and tort law doctrines, corporate law may be a driver of publicization, primarily through information disclosure. Beermann argues that corporate law functions, much like administrative law, to force accountability in private decisionmaking.[59] For example, corporations must disclose information and submit to public scrutiny, much as public agencies do. The securities laws and the general demands of capital markets "place a great deal of information about private corporations in the public domain. With regard to publicly traded corporations, it is not hyperbole to state that nearly as much information about them is easily accessible to the public as is available about the workings of many administrative agencies."[60] Moreover, Beermann notes, publicly traded corporations must also submit many decisions for shareholder approval, a process that, while rarely resulting in shareholder dissent, does guarantee information disclosure.[61] Both the investment and the insurance industries are subject to disclosure demands as well, either as a result of legal requirements or because consumers demand information.[62]

Though Beermann may be somewhat optimistic about the extent to which corporate law doctrines currently discipline private firms, the host of requirements imposed on governing corporations reminds us that regulating private entities is nothing new. Granted, information disclosure alone may do little to make private firms accountable in the absence of an oversight body equipped to discipline them for infractions. (The spate of accounting fraud at Enron, Tyco, and other corporations comes to mind.) And the analogy between corporate disclosure and agency accountability may be overdrawn because agencies are accountable to many different overseers, including all three branches of government. Still, Beermann's argument suggests that regulating private actors as a condition of awarding them contracts would be perfectly consistent with existing requirements. Private firms and nonprofit organizations – including charities – are already forced to adhere to public law norms to some extent, as a consequence of either direct regulation or licensing, or as a condition of receiving government grants or tax-exempt status.[63] The federal government already uses its spending power to condition federal funding on state and private compliance with antidiscrimination norms.[64] And, already, some federal government programs extend nondiscrimination requirements beyond state and local government grantees to private subcontractors.[65]

D. Supplemental measures

The measures above are familiar and depend mostly on government or judicial oversight. Yet there are supplementary accountability mechanisms available as well, which rely on a more diverse set of participants. The project of extending public norms to private actors need not fall exclusively to the three branches of government. Examples of such alternatives include relying on private accreditation to certify compliance with standards, building in third-party participation in the form of an ombudsperson or an intermediary organization that could advocate for consumer interests in the design of service contracts, or requiring private firms to provide opportunities for public participation. In addition, information disclosure requirements could be improved, with a priority placed on producing information in a usable form, meaning that it must be accessible and able to be used by interested parties in subsequent proceedings or actions. To this end, independent auditors might be enlisted to ensure that the information generated is reliable, comprehensible, and widely available. In addition, contracts could require performance audits by independent third parties. Some supplementary accountability measures might also come from private providers themselves in the form of self-regulation (voluntary adoption of standards and benchmarking) or through management systems that require firms to adopt structural reforms that govern decisionmaking. Lenders, insurers, and investors might be relied upon to place additional demands on firms. These are just a few ideas for alternative accountability mechanisms that could respond to public law concerns. While they may not satisfy the public's demand for accountability when used instead of government oversight, they may be helpful when used to supplement that oversight. In this way, privatization might end up generating accountability rather than undermining it. As this Section has made clear, there is no shortage of tools for this purpose. The challenge is to deploy them in appropriate combinations, commensurate with the threat that any particular contracting scheme poses to public law norms.

III. SKEPTICISM

The notion that privatization can be a means of extending public norms to private actors will likely invite skepticism. The three principal criticisms I envision are these: the institutions capable of extending these norms to private actors are not motivated to do so; even if they were, publicization will not achieve its aims; and, even if it did, the result would be effectively to turn private institutions into public institutions, thus undermining the benefits of privatization.

A. Lack of motivation

It is easy to explain why the executive and legislative branches might pursue privatization, but harder to predict why they would structure it in the ways I suggest. Although the tools of publicization are available, it is not obvious that the government would be motivated to use them.[66] Indeed, relatively unfettered privatization might be in the interest of both the executive and legislative branches, but for different reasons. For example, a large private contract workforce and a smaller civil service might enhance executive power. In theory, a president stands to gain by contracting out agency functions because he can appeal to voters as doing more with less and simultaneously diffuse discretionary executive power through a wide range of loosely tracked instruments, barely visible to Congressional oversight, but within the control of political appointees.[67] While fragmenting authority through these mechanisms could make executive oversight somewhat difficult, the president's political appointees, with daily control over small-scale decisions relevant to contract management and performance assessment, may be in a better position than Congress to oversee a vast network of contracts, grants, and mandates. This could help the president fend off congressional encroachment on executive power, which most scholars acknowledge has been increasing steadily since the Watergate era.[68]

For their part, members of Congress might favor privatization because it provides opportunities to enhance their prospects of reelection. Contracting can be a means of bestowing favors on supporters.[69] Privatization could enable legislators to take credit for program successes in the form of lower costs and improved services – which they can opportunistically draw to the public's attention – while blaming private contractors, executive agencies, and lower levels of government for program failures, if and when these come to light. In this way, members of Congress can use the contracting process to further their self-interest which, from a public choice perspective, explains much of congressional behavior. This can be done without attracting public scrutiny because members can award benefits to supporters through a web of contracts, subcontracts, grants, and mandates buried deep within the recesses of an agency program.[70] Congress might also delegate broad powers to private actors as a way of insulating discretionary authority from executive control.[71] In their most sweeping formulations, such delegations could raise separation of powers concerns.[72]

But a Congress or an executive that expects to use privatization simply to escape public responsibilities is likely to be disappointed. When privatization runs smoothly, the public appears complacent; when it goes badly, as it did during the brief Californian energy crisis, the public expects government to step back in.[73] As privatization begins to affect politically contentious services (for example, prisons and schools) in a more enduring way, the public may demand greater accountability from, and increased governmental supervision of, private contractors. Recent experience with contracting for private military and interrogation functions in Iraq suggests that the more sensitive the task, the more likely will be the public demand for accountability from private contractors.

If scholarly and judicial attention are any measure of an issue's political salience, then this prospect seems likely. Private prisons comprise only a small percentage of all prisons and detention centers nationwide, but they have prompted a firestorm of academic commentary and two Supreme Court decisions in a relatively short time.[74] The reaction to vouchers and privately managed schools has been similarly intense, producing a spate of empirical studies, a significant amount of commentary in the popular press, and a recent Supreme Court decision (this one upholding a voucher program).[75] Perhaps the best example of public demand for publicization is the outcry over health management organizations (HMOs). In response to concerns that HMOs deny care in order to cut costs, most states have passed "patients' bills of rights," and similar federal legislation has been introduced in Congress.[76] The state laws generally require HMOs to provide some measure of due process before making determinations regarding care or to submit contested decisions to independent review boards.

Moreover, some legislators will be moved to oppose privatization out of principle or ideology.[77] Indeed, the most simplified public choice account, which neatly attributes all legislative behavior to an obsession with self-interest and, therefore, reelection, is widely considered flawed because it does not account for cases in which members of Congress have legislated to benefit the interests of the diffuse public, even at some personal risk.[78] And even if the simplified account were an accurate depiction of member motivation generally, there are still instances in which an issue's political salience is so high, and the public so vocal, that a member normally oriented to the concerns of concentrated interest groups will cater instead to the more diffuse interests of her constituents. In some cases, moreover, members are freed of the need to cater to reelection considerations because they occupy relatively safe seats.

Indeed, Congress has already demonstrated a willingness to regulate at least some kinds of government contracting stringently: the procurement process, by which the government contracts for goods and services for its own consumption, is subject to detailed restrictions, including provisions for bid protests and other challenges, which are adjudicated by the federal Court of Claims.[79] And, as argued earlier, Congress already conditions federal grants on compliance with a host of regulatory requirements.

Courts, too, could be motivated to extend public accountability to privatized government. Again, skeptics will claim that this possibility seems unlikely. The Supreme Court shows no sign of, for example, broadly reconsidering state-action doctrine or recognizing implied private rights of action to allow private parties to enforce federal funding conditions.[80] However, the Court did find a private doctor under contract with a state prison to be a state actor for purposes of the constitutional duty to provide adequate medical treatment. Writing for the majority in *West* v. *Atkins*,[81] Justice Blackmun noted that the state bore an affirmative obligation to provide adequate medical care to West, which it had delegated to Atkins, and which Atkins had "voluntarily assumed . . . by contract."[82]

In addition, there has been some movement in this direction in the lower federal courts. In *J. K. ex rel. R. K.* v. *Dillenberg*,[83] a federal district court held that a private regional health facility was a state actor because it was created exclusively to deliver mental health services to children entitled to care pursuant to a federal statute. The provider was not merely "doing business" with the state, but executing an entirely delegated responsibility for state health care duties. Echoing *West*, the Court held that it would be "patently unreasonable to presume that Congress would permit a state to disclaim federal responsibilities by contracting away its obligations to a private entity."[84] Several other federal district and appellate courts have held that constitutional due process applies to private firms when they assume a state's mandated duties and are the exclusive service providers.[85] Admittedly, these are only a few cases, and it would overstate matters to suggest there is a judicial trend toward cabining privatization. The point is simply that judicial intervention is possible and that already there are signs of it intensifying.

While some species of private decisionmaking may not easily submit to judicial review, as long as there are contracts, regulations, and grant conditions to enforce, courts will be a possible venue for those seeking to protect public law norms. And, despite the doctrinal hurdles and obstacles to judicial access that remain, courts are arguably the most likely of the three branches to extend public norms to private actors. The legislature's constitutionally assigned role is to tax and spend – to occupy itself with policymaking and budgeting. The executive must use appropriated funds to implement those policy decisions effectively. Both of these branches face incentives to focus on productive efficiency, that is, accomplishing social policy goals at the lowest possible cost. The executive branch in particular must determine the best way to provide the social services that Congress funds. And, because of electoral discipline, both the legislative and especially the executive branch (which makes the front-line decisions regarding implementation) face incentives to cut costs. Courts, however, do not.

The judiciary's formally assigned role of legal interpretation could not be further from the world of productive efficiency. And insulation from electoral politics lets courts impose public law values on the other branches. The courts may be particularly sympathetic to public law concerns. The judiciary, trained in the rigors of procedural regularity, arguably has greater institutional sensitivity to these norms than do the other branches. After all, due process, rationality, equality, public participation, and openness are *legal* norms that courts routinely enforce through constitutional adjudication and statutory interpretation. Without delving into the long history and rich literature on the "counter-majoritarian difficulty" posed by an unelected judiciary, the claim here is simply that, partly because of their constitutionally assigned roles, courts may be more likely than the legislature or executive to extend public law norms to private actors.

B. Publicization will not work

There is not much to say in response to this objection except to counter that it might. Undoubtedly, there will be instances in which the paper assurances of cost and quality diverge considerably from actual performance. But while this ought keep us from blind enthusiasm and complacency, such problems arise with both public and private service provision. The possibility that agents will shirk their responsibilities and not live up to their commitments is endemic to principal–agent relationships wherever they arise: in corporations, administrative agencies, and legislatures. For privatization to deliver on its promise, we will need a greater political commitment to oversight of both cost and quality than we have today. But while this is a reason for vigilance, it should not, by itself, be a reason for preferring government provision to private provision in all cases.

Much of the skepticism about publicization is really skepticism about the potential of for-profit firms to serve the public interest. One might argue that the profit motive is simply incompatible with certain policy goals. Under no circumstances, one might claim, will private for-profit prisons actually protect public law norms. How could they, when the profit motive creates incentives to enlarge the prison population, whereas a rational criminal justice policy ought to seek to reduce it? Publicization efforts may be insufficient to overcome such misaligned incentives. And even where the incentives are not so askew, the inevitable difficulties of specifying performance objectives in a contract will always leave slack for providers to exploit, which will always lead to the erosion of public law norms.

In the end, one's optimism or pessimism on this score depends largely on one's predispositions to market and government. If one believes that private power is a great threat to individual rights, and if one skeptically views public–private partnerships in light of a long process of corporate resistance to state regulation dating back to the nineteenth century, then one might dismiss any project aimed at enlisting the for-profit private sector in public service delivery more broadly as both naïve and dangerous.

However legitimate the historical account that provides the basis for this skeptical view, there is another historical account that is equally powerful: the long tradition of successful *combination* of public and private entities, together providing a variety of publicly desired goods and services that neither could effectively provide alone. As noted earlier, many of the services we now take for granted as state obligations (for example, education, welfare, and even the police) were once privately provided, and a variety of "intermediary" institutions such as nonprofits and religious and charitable organizations emerged early on to provide those services with public-goods dimensions. The story of the expansion of government services in the twentieth century is in part a story of standardizing, secularizing, and democratizing service provision through expanded regulation of these private-sector players, while at the same time multiplying and diversifying those services that the government felt obligated to see provided. This required the development of complex, multilayered relationships between governments at all levels and private contractors (both for-profit and nonprofit), resulting in an interdependent network of actors connected to each other by, among other things, funding, contract, practice, and mission.

Against this background of deep public–private interpenetration, it seems both premature and drastic to suggest that the current trend toward privatization will, as a general and absolute matter, irretrievably compromise public law norms regardless of the context in which it is being tried, the availability of accountability mechanisms, and the intentions of government. And it seems unrealistic to think that direct government provision of services is a panacea or even, at this point, a viable alternative. If nothing else, we ought not to romanticize the capacity of public agencies, without very significant reform, to directly produce the services and perform the functions that are now provided by this network.

C. Publicization will turn private firms into public agencies and undermine gains from privatization

This final objection is both serious and hard to answer. Adherence to public law norms might be costly for private providers, and those costs might undermine the potential for efficiency gains to some extent. Beermann has a point when he argues that for privatization to achieve its promise of dramatic cost reductions, it would have to be accompanied by deregulation.[86] But it is far less obvious that selectively adding due process, public participation, or oversight will undermine *all* of the economic gains and technical innovations that might come from reliance on private service providers. Surely it depends on the instruments we use. While publicization will lead to different outcomes than if private providers were entirely unfettered, it remains to be seen just how costly publicization will be. The task now is to describe the circumstances in which some measure of publicization makes sense, and to weigh the tradeoffs that will inevitably arise when choosing among the available publicization tools.

Some of the accountability mechanisms discussed above, such as information disclosure, might be less costly to implement than others. Some measures may effectively pay for themselves. For example, greater attention to contract design through a consultative process, though perhaps costly on the front end, might produce better ideas about how to provide services effectively and at lower cost. A more careful and inclusive drafting process could conceivably save costs down the line by reducing to some extent future conflict over the meaning of contractual terms. While some contractual incompleteness is unavoidable, many badly drafted service contracts would benefit from greater clarity and specificity. Similarly, enlisting third-party auditors for oversight creates monitoring costs, but might be less costly than relying directly on government monitoring. And, to the extent that monitoring ferrets out fraud and noncompliance with contractual terms, it can prevent even greater losses over time. This is not to suggest that publicization will be costless, just that it need not entirely compromise the purported benefits of privatization.

Nor will it turn private firms into public agencies. While the extension of public law norms might change how private firms operate, this is nothing new and it is consistent with the profit motive. Private-sector firms are already heavily regulated for a variety of other purposes, such as workplace safety, environmental impact, and employment discrimination. Compliance with such regulations alters firm practices and can be costly, but surely does not transform firms into public agencies. Concededly, extreme publicization could produce such an effect – if, for instance, a private firm were required by statute or as a condition of a grant to adopt all the civil-service protections, procedural rules, and sunshine laws governing public agencies, and if courts treated the firm as a state actor. To become like public agencies, in other words, firms would have to be dramatically and systematically reorganized and reoriented, which seems highly unlikely. Surely both nonprofit and for-profit firms would balk at competing for service contracts under such conditions. I suspect, however, that we can fall well short of this dramatic result and still provide some protection of public law norms.

IV. THE STRONGEST CASES FOR PUBLICIZATION

Capitalizing on privatization while reassuring adherents of the public law perspective depends on our ability not only to think inventively about prospective tools of publicization, but also to use them judiciously. In what instances should we seek to extend public norms to private actors?

Three considerations affect the desirability of publicization from the public law perspective: (1) the relative precision with which a service can be specified and, relatedly, the extent of the provider's discretion; (2) the potential impact on the consumer; and (3) the government's motivation for privatization. The strongest cases for extending public norms to private actors, from the public law perspective, involve highly contentious and value-laden services that are hard to specify and over which providers have significant policymaking discretion; that affect vulnerable populations with few exit options and little political clout; and for which the motivation for privatization is discernibly ideological rather than pragmatic.

Each of these considerations has a rough economic analogue: the first overlaps considerably with "contractual incompleteness"; the second might be lumped into what economists count as "quality"; and the third might be expressed as a concern over "patronage and corruption." While these are not perfect analogues, and the two sides diverge in important ways, there is nonetheless considerable convergence between the economic and public law perspectives on the conditions under which privatization is risky.

In other words, the considerations that matter most from the public law perspective are linked to similar considerations that come from the economic view. Conceivably, then, there might be substantial agreement among both public law proponents and privatization advocates over cases in which we should never privatize; cases in which we should do so with little hesitation; and hard cases in which some publicization might be preferred to abandoning privatization altogether. Below I examine each consideration in turn.

A. Ease of specification and degree of discretion

Some tasks are relatively easy to specify in a contract, whereas others defy the most scrupulous attempts at clear definition. For example, specifying what constitutes a quality education is more difficult than defining satisfactory road repair or quality waste collection. This difficulty is unavoidable when a task is highly complex and when reasonable people can easily differ over what constitutes quality, especially with functions or services that implicate deeply held beliefs and involve contestable value judgments. Additionally, specifying a task can be difficult when it involves competing goals that are hard to accomplish simultaneously. For example, we might expect prisons to punish prisoners, not only to register society's disapproval, but also to reduce recidivism. We might expect welfare benefits both to provide a social safety net and to encourage recipients to move from welfare to work.

The inability to specify a task because it is value-laden, politically contentious, and complex militates in favor of very strenuous publicization efforts. Vague contracts leave contractors with considerable flexibility to make judgment calls, trade-offs, and policy decisions to fill in the contractual gaps. In the public law view, filling these gaps should be entrusted to government, which is bound to make policy decisions in an open and accountable way, and in adherence with public law norms. Public law scholars fear that private contractors are more likely to exploit these gaps in favor of cost-cutting measures by, for example, eliminating expensive programs in schools, reducing quality of care in hospitals, or hiring unqualified guards in private prisons. They are also concerned about the political legitimacy of conferring policymaking discretion on otherwise unaccountable nongovernmental actors.

Economists would call the difficulty of specifying quality "non-contractab[ility]"[87] and express similar concerns in different terms. For example, Hart, Shleifer, and Vishny refer to gap-filling as the allocation of "residual control rights."[88] When quality is hard to specify, it becomes harder to prove that the provider has fallen short of contract specifications. Moreover, non-contractibility can create incentives for providers to cut costs at the expense of quality because the quality loss may not technically violate the terms of the contract.[89] This is known as the "quality-shading hypothesis."[90] Where quality is non-contractable, government will likely measure performance in terms of inputs, such as time and materials invested in a task, rather than outputs such as product quality. This means payment will be "based in large part on activity rather than on results."[91]

The economic perspective is not as concerned as the public law view with the legitimacy of conferring policymaking authority on nongovernmental actors. Indeed, non-contractability is portrayed as problematic primarily because it could compromise service quality and create costly monitoring problems, not because of a concern about democratic accountability. Nonetheless, both perspectives agree that privatization is riskier when quality is harder to specify.

B. The potential impact of the service on the consumer

Some services involve policy decisions and raise normative questions about which people care deeply, whereas other services are more routine in the sense that they tend not to raise questions of individual rights or of fundamental fairness; nor do they substantially affect the more important conditions of life. This standard is of course imprecise: one person's routine service might be crucially important to another. Nevertheless, it seems plausible that services that directly and substantially affect health, liberty, safety, and personal autonomy should qualify as important and nonroutine. By comparison, highway maintenance, solid waste collection, and mail delivery seem routine. While these might be difficult tasks that involve important judgments and affect human health and commerce, they are not especially value-laden activities and do not generally implicate our most cherished freedoms and aspirations.

From a public law perspective, these comparatively routine services are not strong candidates for our most strenuous publicization efforts.

This is not only because they do not tend to implicate fundamental rights or affect the most important conditions of life, but also because they can be relatively easily specified and monitored so they pose fewer non-contractability problems.

Nonetheless, even for routine services, the public law concerns about fairness and nonarbitrariness suggest the need for some minimal extension of public law norms to private contractors. For services like waste collection and mail delivery, as with utilities like water, gas, and electricity, we might demand that contractors provide universal access, comply with antidiscrimination norms, and put procedures in place to prevent arbitrariness in termination decisions. This is especially important when the provider has a monopoly, a point with which economists, for whom the absence of competition augurs ill for the success of privatization, would likely concur.[92]

The public law concern about adverse impacts on the consumer is especially great where the populations most directly affected by privatization are vulnerable. This vulnerability might arise because these populations lack resources and political clout, enjoy few viable exit options, or are relatively invisible to the population at large[93] – such as prisoners, detainees, persons involuntarily committed to institutions, and welfare and disability-aid recipients, Medicaid patients, and school-age children.

Vulnerability can be exacerbated when the consumers of the service are not the same as the payers, such as when taxpayers finance prisons occupied by convicts, welfare received by eligible low-income applicants, and schools attended by other people's children. In such instances, privatization may present a choice between taxpayers' and consumers' interests. For example, taxpayers might be willing to compromise prisoner safety and medical care to conserve resources.[94] Prisoners will likely think differently.

The potential for such conflicts is greatest with despised and dependent populations, whom taxpayers may regard with little sympathy. So again, the vulnerability consideration has an augmenting effect here. Where such conflicts between constituencies arise, the case for publicization, from the public law perspective, will tend to be stronger – in large part because payers may wield more power than the consumers who bear the risk of grave injury or loss should the service be inadequate.

From the economic perspective, the concern about privatization's impact on the consumer – specifically the concern about vulnerable populations that might suffer great harm – might count as part of the "quality" of the service. Economic accounts of privatization rarely define quality specifically to include public law concerns. But conceivably, adherents of the economic perspective might be willing to accord weight to such considerations. Undoubtedly, they would be sympathetic to the monitoring costs that arise when the interests of consumers and payers conflict. And they would agree, as argued above, that the absence of competition can be problematic, although not primarily because it might lead to abuse of power by private actors with monopoly power, but rather because it undermines the potential for cost savings.[95]

C. Motive

From a public law perspective, the motivation behind the government's decision to privatize would likely influence judgments about the extent of publicization required. Because they are attuned to the implications of privatization for democratic norms, adherents of the public law view would be especially suspicious if government privatizes primarily to *avoid* constitutional and legal accountability. Discovering that this, and not just the pragmatic desire to cut costs and improve quality, is the impetus behind privatization would militate in favor of publicization.

It may be impossible to detect government's true motivation for privatization, and in many cases that motivation may be mixed.[96] However, if a commitment to avoiding the accountability usually required of public institutions does emerge as the primary motivation for privatization, the public view counsels caution.[97] Implemented on a broad enough scale, privatization fueled by this commitment alone would lead to anemic government rather than the proliferation of public accountability explored in this chapter.

The economic perspective may share the concern that privatization be economically justified, but would likely frame this concern as a worry about corruption and patronage rather than a commitment to avoid legal and political accountability. As Hart, Shleifer, and Vishny explain, the presence of corruption in government would create incentives to privatize, whereas the presence of patronage would cause government to prefer public provision of services.[98] The case for privatization is weaker, therefore, when government is corrupt. Moreover, the economic perspective demands adequate enforcement of contractual terms, so ideological considerations that result in less monitoring of contractors' performance, or grants of monopoly power, may also weaken the case for privatization.

Thus, both economic and public law perspectives are sensitive to the need for privatization to be justified by *pragmatic* concerns about both cost and quality. It seems plausible that adherents of both views would support publicization when these pragmatic motivations for privatization are weak or absent.

D. Conflicting factors

The most difficult cases will arise when the considerations discussed above pull in different directions. On the one hand, water and electricity provision are services on which both highly vulnerable and less vulnerable people are heavily dependent. On the other hand, the delivery of water and electricity does not involve as much discretion as other services. What publicization efforts should attend these services? From the public law perspective, are utilities more like education and incarceration than like waste collection? And, if forced to choose, which of the considerations discussed above is most important: the absence of exit options, the involuntariness of the consumer's situation, or the degree of the provider's discretion? To answer difficult questions such as these requires agreeing on the relative weights that each of these considerations should have, and developing a framework for making tradeoffs among them. The further task of elaborating that commonality is an endeavor from which both the economic pro-privatization perspective and the skeptical public law perspective might profit. As described earlier, these two perspectives each has its own menu of concerns, accessible in a different language and stemming from different cultural and normative frameworks. Some of these concerns are incommensurable, and there will be resistance to giving them up. Nonetheless, there might be substantial agreement about those instances in which publicization is warranted, and perhaps even some overlap in consensus about which tools to use when.

CONCLUSION: RETHINKING PUBLIC ACCOUNTABILITY

Recognizing the ideal of publicization ultimately requires breaking with traditional notions of accountability.[99] Rethinking what accountability requires is necessary because public law tends to define accountability as formal and hierarchical, whereas public–private arrangements function as horizontal networks. In the traditional approach, political accountability is envisioned in terms of nested principal–agent relationships: the general public is the principal for elected representatives; elected representatives are principals for a public agency; the agency is the principal for private contractors; and so on. While the public law perspective traditionally has been satisfied with formal accountability of this sort – which relies on the theoretical possibility of tracing responsibility back to a public decisionmaker who can be punished for poor performance – this hierarchical model of accountability becomes more symbolic and less functional with each step away from the electorate.[100]

The other primary source of public accountability in the traditional view is legal accountability to courts, which as many of the other chapters in this book clearly demonstrate, suffers – at least under their more traditional guise – from some of the same problems of formality, remoteness, and inaccessibility. (See, for example, the chapters by Braithwaite, Mashaw, and Dorf.)

It might be more productive, then, to think of public accountability design as a deeply contextual process, and to imagine it more broadly in terms of measures that spring not exclusively from top-down oversight by legislatures, executive branch agencies, and courts, but from a variety of participants – public and private – who are actively engaged on the ground in the contractual regime. (See also Mashaw's chapter in this regard.) This helps to explain why I define publicization in terms of *extending* public law norms to private actors. I use this word to suggest that private-sector entities could be enlisted in the project of protecting democratic norms, and not just in ways they will resent and resist.

To my mind, this new vocabulary of accountability evokes a broadly consultative process. It seems more inclusive and multilateral than the language of bureaucratic and electoral constraint, and more compatible with the possibility of devising creative approaches to accountability, including new accountability instruments that private providers might themselves suggest or generate. Private organizations are familiar with a variety of accountability techniques, even if these techniques have not proven entirely effective: auditing, information disclosure, "total quality management" systems, benchmarking, and the like.[101] Moreover, many industries have long set privately generated standards (even if motivated largely by a concern about government regulation) and have established elaborate standard-setting processes to do so;[102] some even include government-style deliberation.[103]

The contract negotiation process is thus promising in this regard. As with informal rulemaking, a consultative approach to contract design may inform the agency about a variety of considerations – desired features of the service, possibilities for quality improvements, and opportunities for cost cutting – that it might otherwise have overlooked or designed badly. Such consultation confers additional legitimacy on the resulting contract, too. And, although we cannot be certain, compliance with contractual terms might increase if the contracting parties view the process that produced the terms as legitimate.[104] The likelihood of compliance might also increase as a result of greater consultation with contractors themselves,[105] especially if the consultative process is ongoing and explicitly aimed at facilitating performance *ex ante* rather than simply punishing nonperformance *ex post*.[106]

PART TWO

ACCOUNTABILITY AND DESIGN

CHAPTER 5

ACCOUNTABILITY AND INSTITUTIONAL DESIGN: SOME THOUGHTS ON THE GRAMMAR OF GOVERNANCE

Jerry L. Mashaw

INTRODUCTION

Accountability is a protean concept, a placeholder for multiple contemporary anxieties.[1] Worried about the arrogance and inefficiency of government bureaucrats? The problem, as often stated, is that unelected bureaucrats are not politically or economically accountable. Concerned that corporations are fleecing their shareholders, endangering consumers, and despoiling the environment? The task, as we are almost daily exhorted to understand it, is to make them more accountable for their actions. Nervous about the emerging powers of supranational organizations like the World Trade Organization, the European Union, the International Monetary Fund, or the World Bank? The cause of this unease is probably the perception that such bodies are outside domestic processes of political accountability, yet weakly policed by a still patchy international political and legal order. Shocked that private contractors are running prisons, dispensing welfare benefits, and planning defense strategies? That alarm is almost certainly traceable to the suspicion that placing these activities in private hands allows them to escape the political and legal accountability processes that normally surround exercises of domestic public power.

I do not doubt that accountability is a problem. But exactly what sort of problem? And why so much concern about it now? Are well-understood structures for accountability failing to keep pace with real changes in how our world is organized? Or have we suddenly become sensitive to problems that were there all along? Perhaps our demands or "tastes" for accountability have shifted? And, assuming, as is likely, that our current anxieties about accountability have multiple and intersecting causes, what accountability structures would suffice to assure the public that the behavior of powerful actors is subject to effective oversight and control?

My purpose in this chapter is not to exhaust all these subjects, but to try to bring a bit of order to an important and nested set of inquiries. The first objective, therefore, is to argue for a way of thinking about accountability that provides some analytic purchase when sorting through myriad claims of accountability deficits and when attempting to design acceptable accountability regimes. I begin in the next section by "unpacking accountability" to demonstrate that accountability talk is at base talk about the answer to six linked questions – answers that will form the basic building blocks of what I will refer to as "accountability regimes." These questions take on multiple meanings in diverse contexts, but my claim is that they are a set of questions that must be addressed to make sense of any claim about the efficacy of accountability.

I then present a partial taxonomy of accountability regimes. The approach here is to seek to group the potentially enormous variety of accountability arrangements by type to see how they differ in their responses to accountability questions. This taxonomic exercise provides a basic map of the choices available to institutional designers (or institutional critics) when addressing accountability questions. It also begins to illustrate why institutional design issues are at base a set of choices among competing and overlapping accountability regimes. This section also explores the down-side of three major forms of accountability regimes. Accountability approaches are not just competing and overlapping, they are also imperfect. Institutional design is therefore an activity directed at weighing the comparative competence or incompetence of alternative accountability arrangements.

In Section II, I illustrate the way this conceptual framework of accountability, a sort of grammar of governance for addressing accountability issues, can be deployed in a contemporary arena of increasing importance and widespread dispute: contracted-out governance. This section looks at the accountability concerns that contracting out generates and sets those anxieties within a framework of long-standing debates about the relative roles of government, the market, and civil society in pursuing collective projects. This sets the stage for an exercise in "auditing the accountability books" – a demonstration of how accountability issues might be analyzed systematically within the specific context of contracted-out governmental functions. The "account books" on the universe of contracted-out activities are, of course, too numerous to pursue. I have chosen to highlight a particular example of contracting out, adjudication of social security disability claims. That example illustrates both the complexity of accountability issues that arise in a highly contracted-out system and some of the difficulties and unanticipated accountability consequences of particular design choices.

Finally, in my conclusion, "Norms, accountability, and institutional design," I address an issue that lurks beneath the surface of the whole discussion: how should we assess the acceptability of particular accountability arrangements? The point here is not to suggest that if we get the normative stance right we can always solve our accountability problems through clever institutional design. That discussion illustrates instead that, once we get the analytics or grammar of accountability reasonably straight, and understand the basic purposes of different forms of accountability, we can then see more clearly what many accountability disputes really entail. For, at base, much of the dispute about accountability is a dispute about what particular institutions are meant to do, not how accountable they are in the doing of it.

I. UNPACKING ACCOUNTABILITY

The millions of words spilled on the subject of accountability are often confusing for a quite simple reason: authors are talking about different methods and questions of accountability without specifying with any precision either the particular accountability problem that engages their attention or the choices that they are making implicitly among differing accountability regimes. The challenge is to devise a general approach to analyzing instances of accountability that will allow us to see and discuss common problems across multiple domains.

Start with a dictionary definition: "liable to be called to account; answerable."[2] So far so good, but this definition is pretty vague. Accountability seems to be a relational concept, but the parties to the relationship remain unspecified. Some sort of account is to be given by someone to someone else, but what is the subject matter of this accounting? And, how is an account to be given? How are its facts and reasons developed, conveyed, and tested? What are the criteria or standards by which the acceptability of conduct is to be judged? Finally, someone is supposed to be "liable" or answerable for consequences, but liable for what and to what extent? Unless we know the answers to these questions we do not know much about what accountability means in any particular domain or instance.

On the other hand, by simply unpacking this vagueness we can begin to make some progress. For what our questions tell us is something like this: in any accountability relationship, we should be able to specify at least six important things: *who* is liable or accountable *to whom; what* they are liable to be called to account for; *through what processes* accountability is to be assured; *by what standards* the putatively accountable behavior is to be judged; and, what the potential *effects* are of finding that those standards have been breached. These basic features, *who*, *to whom*, *about what*, *through what processes*, *by what standards*, and *with what effect*, describe what I will call an "accountability regime."[3] These six inquiries allow us to give an account of accountability. With the answers to these questions in hand we can not only evaluate the potential capacity of any particular regime to satisfy our demands or aspirations, we can compare it to other regimes, evaluate their differential capacities, and perhaps articulate hybrid regimes that approximate optimal institutional designs.

A. Accountability regimes: a partial taxonomy

We all feel ourselves accountable in one way or another to scores of other people and institutions. Our families, our friends, our colleagues, our employers, our bankers, our sports clubs, our churches, our neighbors, the Internal Revenue Service, and the Motor Vehicle Department, all make demands upon us that we view as, in one way or another, legitimate. For certain aspects of our actions in certain ways and with certain effects, all of these people, groups, and institutions, call us to account. The ubiquity of accountability regimes, and our entanglement in scores if not hundreds of them simultaneously, complicates the task of sorting regimes by family, genus, and species. It also explains much of the apparent incoherence of claims about accountability gaps, deficits, or lapses. The same action can implicate numerous accountability relationships. It may be perfectly acceptable from the perspective of some of them, while deficient from the perspectives of others. We need some way to group accountability regimes in order to better see their similarities, differences, and interconnections.

To simplify matters, I will borrow an old idea (traceable at least to Hegel)[4] that Claus Offe has deployed recently[5] as a means of better understanding the idea of corruption. Corruption, of course, is one of the many problems that societies seek to solve by increasing the effectiveness of accountability. But, as Offe points out, in a pre-modern society, where the three realms of community, economy, and governance are not distinct arenas of human action, corruption is a meaningless concept. Rewarding your family or friends is not corrupt if governance, productive activity, and social relations are all fused within the communal group. It is only when we moderns recognize ourselves as acting in distinctive domains – the public forum, the market, and the community – that the idea of corruption emerges. For corruption can almost always be understood as the (inappropriate) use of rules of behavior that apply in one realm of human action in another.

The same can be said for accountability regimes.[6] When we punish a politician for accepting a bribe, our complaint is at base that the rules applicable to the market have been improperly applied in the public forum. When a corporate buyer is fired for making sweetheart deals with his brother-in-law, he is being held accountable for confusing family with workplace responsibilities. At a high level of generality, therefore, accountability regimes should be roughly of three types: those associated with public governance; those that police the marketplace; and those that inhabit the non-governmental, non-market, social realm.

As a preliminary matter, we should also note that in liberal democracies these three domains have strikingly different legal characteristics. When we act as public officials we act in a constitutional culture devoted to limited governance and elaborate ideas of official accountability. For public officials it is not hyperbolic to suggest that the basic legal principle is that everything not authorized is prohibited.

As we move to the market, the law becomes much more facilitative and structural. We are responsible for playing within the rules of the game as enunciated by both public and private law. But the legal rules that structure markets are designed to promote individual initiative and to reward productive performance. Conduct is disciplined largely by the market itself – that is, by the needs of economic actors to maintain the loyalty of their transactional partners in the face of competition from others.

In the social realm, legal constraints are weaker still. Here the law facilitates and protects, but also carves out "law-free" zones of privacy and association. In the current vernacular, this is an arena of norms rather than law.

As we will later develop, these generic differences in public law, private commercial law, and the law of private social relations are much in evidence within contemporary debates surrounding the wisdom of moving from publicly administered to contracted-out government and from hard-law sanctions to more soft-law incentive systems. For now, however, we need to say something more about the various genera and species of accountability regimes that inhabit our family-level categories.

1. Public governance

As a rough cut, think of public governance accountability regimes as using three principal devices: There are political regimes that operate through electoral processes and other forms of legitimating institutions; administrative (or "bureaucratic") regimes that operate through hierarchical control of subordinates; and legal regimes that operate through the authoritative application of law to facts, often by formal adjudication. In each of these regimes, the issues of who, to whom, about what, through what processes, by what standards, and with what effects are answered rather differently.

For example, in a *legal* public accountability regime, *public officials* are responsible *to individuals and firms, about* their respect or lack of respect for legal requirements or legal rights *through* processes of administrative and judicial review, *judged* in accordance with law, *resulting in* either validation or nullification of official acts (and sometimes compensation for private parties affected by official illegality). This legal regime is structured by a host of doctrines, rules, and norms that define who has "standing" to complain (to whom), who is a public authority subject to public law norms (who), what sorts of claims qualify as "legal" claims and are thus "justiciable" (about what), through what procedures administrative or judicial consideration can be obtained (what process), and the limits on the reviewing body's competence. These competence rules include limits on remedies that define the effects, or possible effects, of being held legally accountable.

Consider, by contrast, a public administrative regime. There, lower-ranking officials are responsible to superiors for their compliance with official instructions. Once again, there are a host of rules and doctrines that structure these public accountability relationships and provide the standards against which performance is measured. But the administrative regime is dramatically different from the legal regime. It is hierarchical rather than coordinate – officials (*to whom*) call other officials (*who*) to account within the same organization. The operation (*process*) of accountability is managerial rather than legal, continuous rather than episodic. And superiors have the power not merely to sanction wayward actions, but to remake them, remove errant officials, and redesign decision structures (*effects*).

Political accountability regimes, the third genus of accountability regimes for public governance, are of two general types. Perhaps the most visible form of political accountability is the election. In electoral regimes, elected officials are responsible to the electorate for their choices of public policies. That responsibility is effectuated through voting, combined with other political and party processes of candidate selection, that lead to either reelection or dismissal of elected officials – and, in the latter case, to the substitution of different ones, including different governing coalitions.

But many non-electoral accountability regimes are also essentially political in terms of the subject matter (*about what*) of accountability, that is, their focus on approval or disapproval of public policy choice, and in terms of the standards (*by what criteria*) for judgment, that is, political acceptability. Top-level bureaucrats, for example, are responsible or accountable to an elected official – a president, a governor, or a minister in parliamentary systems – for carrying out their discretionary functions in accordance with their political superiors' policies or ideological commitments. But the process of calling to account is not an election, responsibility is only mediately or indirectly to the electorate, and sanctions range from removal to simple displeasure, or perhaps ostracism from the inner councils of the ruling elite. Similarly, parliamentarians are responsible to party leaderships, administrative officials to Congressional or parliamentary review and appropriations committees, and so on. In short, political accountability includes standard electoral processes and a host of other political processes in which elected officials hold their fellows, or non-elected officials, accountable for their actions based on essentially political criteria.

These public governance regimes, legal, administrative, and political, have been described in highly stylized ways. Within each regime, our six critical variables – who, to whom, about what, through what process, by what standards, and with what effects – have their own complexities, and their articulation within any particular regime varies from issue to issue. If "public governance" is the family, and "political," "legal," and "administrative" the genera, there are countless species.[7]

2. Accountability in the market

Nongovernmental or private activities are subject to similar structures of accountability. One is market accountability, as organized through product markets, capital markets, and labor markets (the other, social, accountability will be examined in the next subsection). And, once again, this tripartite division suggests that the "who, to whom, about what, how, by what criteria, and with what effects" questions are answered differently in these different market arrangements.

In product (including service) markets, for example, producers are responsible to consumers (or other producers who use their components) for their products' quality and price. The process or mechanism of accountability is market competition – within the constraints of various public and private law frameworks that structure the rules of the competitive game. The standards are customers' individual preferences. The effects of accountability to the market are, immediately, the willingness of consumers to buy the product at the offered price, and, ultimately, the product's capacity to maintain itself in the market.

As was hinted at earlier, market accountability is considerably more fluid than public law accountability. In product markets, company charters no longer specify what firms will produce or what services they will render, as would be true of any public bureau. Consumers self-select which products or services they will monitor, unlike electors who can only vote for certain representatives within certain localities or precincts. And, the process of market competition, while constrained by boundary requirements designed to eliminate force and fraud, and to limit negative externalities, permits – indeed encourages – innovation in techniques for facilitating consumer choice. This is not the constrained world of judicial process, administrative decisionmaking, or even legislative bargaining. And, the market provides its rewards or sanctions incrementally and over time. Products or services are selected for success or failure not by discrete acts of collective judgment, but by the aggregation of individual consumer choices.

In somewhat similar ways, financial markets make firms or managers accountable to those who provide debt or equity capital, and labor markets make firms and workers reciprocally accountable to each other for the quality of the human capital available in the market and for the pay, benefits, and working conditions that are provided. The level and style of legal intervention to structure and regulate markets of all types is, of course, remarkably heterogeneous across space (polities) and time (regulatory reform is always on the agenda). And market actors always operate in a world structured by public accountability regimes. Indeed, what we normally mean by "regulation" is some system of behavioral controls that makes private parties accountable to the state, which serves as a placeholder for the general public, in ways that are difficult or impossible to accomplish through regimes of market accountability.

Yet, regimes of market accountability are sharply distinguishable from public law accountability systems. While they operate within constraints supplied by both public and private law, many of those constraints are designed largely to make the competitive process work more effectively. To that degree, they do not change the persons to whom market actors are accountable, what they are accountable for, or the effects of failing to live up to the market's expectations. Moreover, regulation leaves market accountability restructured, but intact as a decentralized mechanism for policing the satisfactoriness of private behavior.

Indeed, public governance and market accountability are sufficiently distinct that some, like Ed Rubin in Chapter 3, may object to the use of the concept of "accountability" to describe the disciplining effects of markets. In one particularly well-thought-out example of this argument, Richard Mulgan advises that "[a]rguably, it is a misuse of the concept of accountability to apply it to the responsiveness of providers to consumers generated by competitive markets. Accountability is essentially connected with authority relations and concerns the rights of owners or principals to instruct their agents and to call them to account."[8] To him, markets are about efficiency, not accountability, and in designing institutions, we should think carefully about trading off accountability for efficiency. Calling markets a form of accountability seems to obscure this tradeoff.

I do not want to argue that there are not crucial differences between systems of bureaucratic authority and systems of market behavior. But categorical classification of these systems obscures the degree to which these systems actually blend into each other and provide alternative paths to a similar overall goal, that of promoting publicly responsible behavior.

For example, Mulgan's vision of accountability as an authority system contrasts mechanistic images of commands backed by sanctions with weaker and more amorphous forms of discipline that may or may not provide effective incentives for proper behavior. But bureaucratic authority systems are considerably less "authoritative" and more amorphous than they might seem from Mulgan's account. Superiors seldom "command" their subordinates in any straightforward way. Instead, they exert influence and negotiate for authority. Hierarchies turn out to be, not pyramids, but dense networks.[9] The tradeoffs that Mulgan refers to are more complex than is captured by a system-level contrast between market-based efficiency vs. authority-based accountability.

The analysis of institutional arrangements involves, therefore, not just recognizing that there are accountability differences between markets (and societies) and hierarchies, but also in understanding exactly what those differences might be. Ultimately, markets, too, are created to serve social purposes[10] – such as cost control, innovation, productivity growth, full employment, and the like. Proponents of contracted-out or voucherized public education are not advocating trading accountability for efficiency. They are indeed seeking enhanced accountability.[11] Their arguments are ultimately over questions of who should be responsible to whom, about what, through what processes, and with what effects.

3. *Social accountability*

Social accountability is such a fluid concept that there is some difficulty in wrapping one's mind around it.[12] That these ideas are dynamic and complex does not, of course, mean that they do not describe real phenomena. Indeed, our accountability to others within our various social networks are often more meaningful for us than anything that we do in the public forum or the marketplace.

I am accountable to my wife for being a good husband, but to whom else? My children, her parents, my parents, her brothers and sisters, her friends, our acquaintances, my pastor, my boss? All of these people, and perhaps others, have stakes in our relationship. Should they be able to call me to account? For what? What is the meaning of "good husband"? The possibilities are almost endless and utterly contextual, shifting perhaps almost by the minute. On what occasions and through what techniques am I to be called to account? What are the fair processes of enforcing spousal responsibilities within the pair? In relation to others? With what effects over what domains of our relationship and over what time periods?

These are the questions that marriages negotiate over years and decades. The contexts for the answers are so various that we can hardly imagine giving a cogent explanation of "spousal accountability," save perhaps by giving an ironic "cf." citation to a fair slice of the world's literature. Nevertheless, it is obvious that "accountability" is indeed demanded in such situations. And it is plain that that "spousal" accountability traverses the six issues that structure all accountability regimes.

Social accountability regimes are a world of what we might call "community and culture" – infinitely negotiable, continuously revisable, often unspoken; oscillating between deep respect for individual choices and relentless social pressure to conform to group norms. To be sure, there are hard legal constraints on the structure of social accountability. But the constraints are large and loose, and importantly so because, in a liberal democracy, rights of private association are fundamental to human dignity and civic identity. The law's character here is thus distinctive. It serves primarily to recognize and give legal legitimacy to certain standard relationships. It polices the outer boundaries of power. It structures both the creation and the dissolution of certain forms of association. It protects domains of privacy and association against encroachment from both governmental and commercial interests. By contrast with the hard law structuring of market accountability regimes, legal regulation of family and other networks in civil society operates under strong constraints of respect for privacy, freedom of association, and freedom of speech and assembly that are often given constitutional status.

On the other hand, many social networks are more structured or formalized. They have nonprofit, corporate charters and bylaws; they make rules and adjudicate cases. And as social networks expand and take on formal structure they tend to become more narrowly purposeful as well. Moreover, the more these private associations take on regulatory functions that operate in lieu of or coordinated with state governance,[13] the more the law is likely to intrude upon them. And because many private organizations, trade and professional associations chief among them, are organized around common economic interests, many familiar groups in "civil society" have a contestable, hybrid legal character.[14]

Still, the accountability regimes generated by social networks have a distinctive character. They apply only to members (who). They usually involve reciprocal obligations among members (to whom). Issues regarding "about what," "through what process," and "according to what standards" tend to be internally generated rather than externally imposed by legal rules or market structures. And rewards and sanctions are uniquely, but not exclusively, related to the group or network itself, involving such things as acceptance into or expulsion from membership or a change of status within the group.

Because social networks are implicitly normative and rely importantly on voice as a mechanism for calling members to account, social accountability may not generate the same sorts of "category-mistake" objections that were noted concerning market accountability. Yet, from an institutional design perspective, network accountability may seem even more problematic. Social networks are the home of cultures and subcultures. They often arise spontaneously as contested sites of "meaning-making," and they define for their participants the boundaries between the thinkable and the unthinkable, the appropriate and the inappropriate. Culture is not necessarily malleable from the outside. Does it make any sense to talk about institutional design as involving a choice of social accountability regime, or about their comparative utility in relation to governance or market mechanisms?

It does make sense, but the simultaneous power and fragility of social accountability systems makes institutional engineering both a delicate and a chunky enterprise. Consider the American Bar Association (ABA), for example. Federal and state governments sometimes seek to use the ABA to appropriate the professional standards of state bar associations as a means for regulating both admission to the bar and professional conduct. But in so doing they buy into a cultural package that may have unwanted as well as desired normative characteristics. This chunkiness is difficult to address because attempting to shift culture by external sanctions almost always has unpredictable consequences. Government can also make the bar more accountable to the market by prohibiting mandatory fee schedules or a ban on advertising, but it cannot easily predict whether this legal demand for market accountability is a small adjustment or will work massive changes in the internal culture of the profession. In the limit, the "professionalism" that argued for self-regulation might become so attenuated by market forces that other, second-best, techniques will have to be employed.

B. Fixing ideas

Figure 5.1 pulls together in tabular form much of the preceding discussion. Putting the characteristics of these accountability-regime types into boxes or grids surely overstates the degree to which they are distinctive. In the real world, these "regimes" flow and blend into each other in just about every imaginable way. Nevertheless, broad differences in kind are clearly distinguishable.

For example, consider the differences between accountability regimes associated with public governance and those that inhabit private markets and social networks. In the public governance realm there is significant role differentiation. And accountability obligations tend to flow in only one direction. Elected officials owe an obligation of political accountability to citizens, for example, but not vice versa. By contrast, in markets, both buyers and sellers are subject to the same market discipline, and in networks, because obligations are based on agreement or mutual alignment, they are reciprocal. In both contexts, mutual adjustment is to be expected and the accountability regime is to that degree more flexible or responsive than a state governance regime.

Similarly, in the realm of public governance, the processes of holding to account tend to be formalized, structured, and collective. Competitive contracting in private markets, by contrast, is decentralized, informal, and individualized. The aggregation of individual actions by markets produces outcomes or effects, but not because mechanisms of collective choice are actuated to hold firms, employees, or products accountable for their market performance. And, while families, professions, or teams may act collectively, the social relations among their members are also defined by continuous interactions that display approval or disapproval of any member's behavior.

The proposed "grammar" permits us to notice at least some of the crucial differences among the accountability regimes that we have discussed. It allows us to see, for example, that, insofar as the administrative and legal subcategories of public governance accountability are concerned, the "for what" question generally is rigidly defined and jurisdictionally cabined. The first response of any legal defendant or uncooperative regulatory agency to a complaint or request is usually that the request revolves around a right that is not recognized in formal law. By contrast, in social network situations, the things about which one might be held accountable often remain more fluid and contestable.

	Who	To whom	Standards of appraisal	About what	How	Rewards and Sanctions
State governance						
• Political	elected officials, administrators	citizens, elected officials	ideology or political preference aggregation	policy choice	voting oversight	approval or removal, funding, authority
• Administrative	public officials	superiors	instrumental rationality	implementation	monitoring	approval, substitute action, etc.
• Legal	officials, individuals, firms	affected persons, states	legal rules	legality	judicial review, enforcement	affirmation, remand, injunction, penalties, compensation
Private markets						
• Product	firms and customers	product markets	preference aggregation	payment, price, and quality	competitive contracting	profit or loss, refusal to deal
• Labor	employers and human capital suppliers	labor markets	preference aggregation	remuneration and performance	competitive contracting	maintenance, severance, or alteration of contracts
• Financial	management and capital suppliers	capital markets	preference aggregation	acceptable terms and returns	competitive contracting	acceptance, refusal, provision, or withdrawal of capital
Social networks*						
• Family	members	each other	group norms	appropriate behavior	individual and collective appraisal	praise and blame, affection, support, etc.
• Profession	members	each other	group norms	satisfaction of professional norms	individual and collective appraisal	esteem, status, exclusion, penalties, etc.
• Team	members	each other	group norms	contribution to joint effort	individual and collective appraisal	comradeship, status, exclusion, etc.

*The networks here are illustrative, not exhaustive.

Figure 5.1 Accountability regimes.

Similarly, insofar as public governance is concerned, the content of the relationship between the "who" and the "to whom" tends to be both hierarchical and asymmetrical. Obligations may flow up or down the hierarchy, but their content will differ depending on direction. Market and social accountability regimes tend to have a more coordinate structure, in which many obligations are mutual, and the persons to whom or from whom obligations are owed shift with context and role, not with formal office.

The "how" of public governance accountability regimes tends to revolve around formal processes – votes, adjudications, executive orders, and notices of termination. Administrative acts operate through transparent and regularized procedures which even outsiders can know and appeal to in seeking to trigger accountability processes. Sanctions in official accountability regimes proceed from some formally designated authority and are themselves constrained by very public norms. At the other end of the spectrum are informal acts of social sanctioning – raised eyebrows, frowns, and turning a deaf ear. To know the "rules" by which these acts can be judged appropriate or inappropriate, one has to be within the particular culture or subculture.

Finally, insofar as standards of appraisal are concerned, public governance accountability regimes tend to present themselves as epistemically complete. Criteria for judgment are established and exposed to public view and actions are judged in accordance with those preexisting norms.[15] At the other end of the accountability spectrum lie normatively open social systems – systems that are, in Robert Cover's famous denomination, "jurisgenerative" rather than "jurispathetic."[16]

Given these differences, it is hardly surprising that shifts in accountability structures generate anxieties. Whether or not to deliver services to welfare beneficiaries via public officials, the Maximus Corporation, or a group of local charities is not just a question of technical capacities. These organizations operate within different accountability systems or regimes. But we should not mistake what is at issue. These sorts of choices do not make actors accountable or unaccountable. Instead, they institute regime changes. Whether we have gained or lost by shifting from one accountability regime to another depends upon who we want to be accountable, to whom, about what, through what processes, judged by what criteria, and with what effects.

C. The uses of taxonomy

1. Critique, dysfunction, and conflict

Let me reemphasize that the distinctiveness of governance, market, and social accountability regimes can be oversold. These systems are, to put it mildly, fuzzy at the margins. Electoral voting looks a lot like a market test for political viability; and, like social institutions, administration and adjudication are norm creating, not just norm applying. Most actors operate within overlapping regimes. Firms are market actors, but managerial action within firms substitutes administrative for market accountability; and products and firms compete for customer or investor loyalty based on a host of shared social norms ranging from environmental trusteeship, to promotion of public health, to support for the arts. Meanwhile, civic associations attract members with market-like offerings from calendars and coffee mugs to health and casualty insurance. We operate within fluid accountability regimes that sometimes reinforce and sometimes are in tension with each other.

These regimes are not only potentially reinforcing or competitive, they also have different strengths and weaknesses. From an institutional design perspective, a perceived weakness in one regime leading to irresponsible behavior is not necessarily a signal that that form of accountability should be *strengthened*. It may be more effective to attempt to weaken the accountability constraints of a competitive regime or to amplify the effects of a potentially reinforcing one. Consider, for example, K-12 educational reform. Stringent bureaucratic accountability of public school teachers and principals is often viewed as the problem, to be solved by instituting market-like accountability (vouchers) or perhaps the peer accountability of like-minded professionals (contracted-out charter schools). In these reforms, therefore, ineffective, but powerful, bureaucratic accountability is not reinforced; it is jettisoned for different accountability regimes that answer every accountability question other than *what* (educational quality) very differently. And those choices will themselves inevitably raise further questions about the capacity of the new regime to satisfy accountability demands – e.g., can parents really act effectively to monitor quality? can for-profit charter school managers really be constrained by contract to serve public interests? and so on. Our choices are always from among imperfect alternatives – a topic to which we now turn.

Up to now, our discussion of governance, market, and social accountability regimes has presented these regimes as functional systems structured in different ways. But, we have said nothing about the possible dysfunctional aspects of these regimes and the degree to which they conflict. The topic is crucial. For contemporary anxieties about accountability are not only the result of changes in the organization of governments, markets, and society. They also proceed from concerns about the efficacy of any one of these accountability regimes to do what it claims, and from disputes about which regime should have prominence in rendering particular behaviors appropriately accountable.

2. *The perplexities of institutional design*

Every action we take, we take within a set of overlapping accountability regimes. From this perspective, it may be that there are no gaps in accountability. If markets or social networks do not hold us accountable, state governance regimes will. And vice versa. In many, perhaps most, instances our conduct is subject to all three.

But this trivializes the problem of effective institutional design. For, all systems of accountability have failures. And they are directed at different things. Every exercise in devising appropriate accountability systems is thus an exercise in comparative incompetence.[17]

Take, for example, recent critiques of the hard-law nature of public governance. Public law as we have described it, that is, administrative and constitutional law, mostly regulates regulators. It establishes the institutions and processes of governance and mediates between the claims of the state as a public collective and the claims of those individuals and private collectivities subject to state power. In liberal states, that is, those in which individuals are seen as the basic unit of social and political value, the exercise of state power is conditional on respect for individual autonomy or moral agency and must, therefore, be made accountable to those it governs.

But how effective are the standard political, bureaucratic, and legal accountability regimes at making public governance accountable? The unhappy fact of the matter is that few believe that these approaches do more than put loose boundary conditions on the exercise of official discretion.

Critiques of liberal legality's claims to legitimacy, premised on the ineffectiveness of voting, hierarchical control, and reason-giving to ensure real accountability, are ubiquitous. Depending upon the critic's disciplinary and political perspective, liberal legal processes are described as a mystification that provides symbolic comfort to the uninformed; a cover for interest group diversion of public resources to private ends; or an instrument of class, racial, or gender oppression. On these accounts, accountability as control has failed and with it the liberal project of moral autonomy within a framework of collective action.

These critiques may be overdrawn, but they rightly give rise to anxiety about the feasibility of the accountability project upon which so much of liberal legality depends. Control of government through "hard" law – "rights" to the franchise, institutional checks and balances, procedural regularity, and compulsory judicial jurisdiction – is surely incomplete. Moreover, it may miss much of the action.[18] The accountability demanded by hard law techniques is often an accountability for prior actions to external controllers. But *ex post* sanctioning is likely to be evidence of a poorly functioning accountability mechanism, not a successful one – just as widespread bankruptcy might suggest a poorly functioning market system. The crucial purpose of accountability is really forward-looking or prophylactic.

Moreover, these approaches may stifle more effective and responsive accountability processes that can only flourish if shielded from the threat of hard-law incursions.[19] Authoritative resolution through hard-law processes can stamp out interactive problem-solving, stifle experimentation, and stymie recursiveness. Being called to account by judges wielding legal rules[20] or by political controllers with urgent political demands (expressed through the inevitably clumsy vocabulary of legislative command or removal from office), can both delegitimate and demoralize efforts to develop more responsive stewardship.

Notice that one way of thinking about these critiques is as recommending a shift from government accountability through public law to either market or social accountability regimes. A multi-decade-long critique of command-and-control regulation in the United States, for example, has focused on the inefficiency of regulatory requirements. In some cases, the call has been for deregulation and a return to the market. In others, it has featured the insinuation of market-like devices into regulatory systems.[21] Critics of rule-bound public law regimes also suggest movement toward "soft law" regimes that emphasize negotiation, trust, and the development of common normative understandings.[22] Whether in the development of environmental regulations or the treatment of drug offenders, reformers suggest that better, more effective, and more acceptable results can be effected by developing communities of interest that rely on techniques of social accountability to promote appropriate conduct.

These alternative approaches employing market and social accountability regimes need not be *strongly* competitive with standard public law accountability ideas. They could merely be a means of reform and reinforcement. Indeed, to the extent that the "soft law" techniques described above already inhabit the interstices of hard law, recognition of their role and its contribution to accountability – exemplified by the reemerging-norms literature[23] – could form an important part of the accountability project implicit in public law liberal legality.

But this optimistic "soft law" view of careful institutional design to integrate divergent accountability regimes may describe a world that is not wholly available to us. Demands for hard-law forms of public governance accountability are difficult to suppress.[24] Scandal often rears its ugly head, as it has recently in the US concerning accounting standards. The political demand for hard-law reforms may be irresistible – whether or not the scandalous behavior was an anomaly in an otherwise well-functioning regime, or was probative of widespread ineffectiveness in the prior system of professional self-regulation.

Moreover, an idealized vision of efficient markets and social systems generating and implementing shared normative visions is also an obviously incomplete account of the functioning of market and social accountability regimes. Indeed, the critiques of these regimes are as well known as those of "government failure" and we need not belabor them here. Information asymmetries, externalities, and collusion in markets are standard grounds for declaring "market failures." And, even well-functioning markets pursue only one goal – efficiency. Evidence of social network failures is also abundant. The American Catholic church's soft-law approach to pedophile priests is perhaps the current poster child of a failed social accountability regime. Indeed, much of the governmental action that gives rise to the need for structures of state governance accountability is directed precisely at rectifying the perceived defects in the outputs generated by regimes of market and social accountability.

But defects in particular accountability regimes, while ubiquitous, need not counsel despair. Indeed, by recognizing that accountability's basic structure is an answer to six common questions, and by recognizing that we have choices across differing types of accountability regimes, we can make some progress on the design of institutions that satisfy our accountability demands. To illustrate how these ideas work, or can work, I will explore a contemporary issue in the structure of governance – the increasingly common phenomenon of contracting out government functions.

II. AUDITING ACCOUNTABILITY: THE ANXIETIES AND COMPLEXITIES OF CONTRACTED-OUT GOVERNANCE

A. Contracting out and the structure of accountability

Sometime in the 1970s, the tide began to run against "big government" in the Anglo-American world. Informed by intellectual commentary and concrete experience, both governing elites and ordinary citizens began to feel that modern "welfare" and "regulatory" states had over-promised and underperformed. "Privatization," "contracting out," "deregulation," and "devolution" became the watchwords of governmental reform, and a "new public management" was created to try to align the theory of what had been "public administration" with the realities of governments who sought, in the now-fashionable image, "to steer rather than row."[25]

In many cases in the US, contracting out was also an undertheorized response to necessity. Most government departments and agencies at the national level in the US have operated under some version of a hiring freeze, punctuated by substantial workforce reductions, for the past thirty years. There are one-third fewer federal civilian employees in relation to the total US workforce in 2004 than in 1954.[26] Yet over that period the responsibilities of the federal government have grown spectacularly. The only way to do more with less has been to borrow someone else's employees. Analysts estimate that, for every federal civilian employee, there are eight private, nonprofit, state or local employees carrying out federal policies under varying forms of contractual, quasi-contractual, or "mandate" arrangements.[27]

B. Accountability concerns associated with contracting out

The "contracted-out" state, sometimes called the "hollow" state, has produced new anxieties of accountability.[28] To some degree those anxieties are a sort of equal and opposite ideological response to the phenomenon itself. The apparent displacement of public law accountability regimes by markets disappoints those who trust government action more than market outcomes.[29] And, because contracting out is also sometimes contracting for a particular regime of social accountability – for example, the culture of a profession, nonprofit organization, or a religious group – concerns about whether that contractor's particular social norms are appropriate rise quickly to the forefront of debates. Government contracting with religious groups has been a recent sore spot in the United States,[30] but the problem is much more widespread. Many also have questions about whether the culture of the Martin-Marietta Corporation, shaped by the constraints of the firm's accountability to financial markets, is appropriate to the provision of back-to-work services for welfare recipients. And disputes about whether professionals like doctors or lawyers can effectively police themselves through networks of peer review have raged over hundreds of years.

Contracting out, therefore, is not just ideologically upsetting, it is conceptually destabilizing. It mixes accountability regimes in ways that we find difficult to understand, and may have multiple, dynamic effects across differing regimes. To see how this occurs, consider a few of the problems that critics assert to be necessary or potential features of contracted-out governance.

1. *Blurring*

One possibility is that contracting out blurs the line between public and private in ways that make accountability more difficult. In a standard case of a mixed-economy hybrid, market actors subject to environmental regulation, for example, are accountable to both markets and public regulators. Markets police the price and quality of goods and services as private firms operate within the constraints established by private law and regulatory rules. Public regulators, for their part, are accountable via public law and political processes for the appropriateness of the regulatory norms adopted and the efficacy and fairness of their monitoring and enforcement efforts. The regime is hybrid, but it is clear who is accountable to whom for what outputs and through what processes.

Some forms of contracting out, on the other hand, seem to confuse the provision of goods and services with the establishment of systems of social control in ways that appear different from the standard case of mixed-economy hybrids. In these, the government contracts with private parties to provide a particular set of goods and services. But those goods and services constitute a regime of social control that entails norm creation, monitoring, and sanctioning. The special accountability concerns here are that the activities normally subject to public law accountability regimes may no longer be subject to those forms of discipline because the critical actors are private rather than public entities. That social control is being privately exercised is, of course, not a problem in itself. We expect such arrangements in civil society. The problem as many see it is that state power has been added without customary accountability arrangements for the use of that power. Similarly, the "private" market may demand productive efficiencies in the "service" of social control that impose inappropriate accountability constraints on private actors carrying out public functions.

In the contracting out of social welfare, for example,[31] public assistance payments are routinely combined with, and conditioned on, acceptance of social services designed to assure family well-being and to develop capacities for self-support. Providing these services includes determining a client's eligibility and need for the service; monitoring client "compliance" with the requirements of "parenting," job training, or other service regimes; and sanctioning noncompliant behavior. When these activities are in the hands of public administrators, background norms of equal treatment, fair processes for dispute resolution, and transparency of rules and routines are a part of the public law package. Private providers are not necessarily subject to any of these public law requirements. And, as in the case of "faith-based" providers, they may be subject to social norms that could make their approach to service provision inappropriate for publicly funded activities.

Public law accountability might, of course, be imposed by statute, regulation, or contract. But, if the contract requires that private actors behave just like public officials, little may be gained by contracting out. And, if contracting out is designed to get the benefits of market discipline or social commitment, then some of the incentives associated with market and social accountability regimes – that is, to cut costs by underserving difficult and therefore costly "customers," or to promote behavior modification through religious indoctrination – may be difficult to eliminate.

2. *Opacity*

Private actors are presumptively entitled to privacy; public officials are not. Private actors generate "proprietary" information; the information produced by public agencies is "owned" by the public.[32] Public actors must often give public reasons for their actions; private preference motivates markets. Hence, to the extent that public accountability depends upon transparency, contracting out to private parties would seem a retreat from accountability.

Of course, we could compensate for this possible loss of transparency by including public transparency conditions in the contract. But this could be self-defeating. If firms gain no competitive advantage from creating information that yields efficiencies (for example, internal rules, routines, monitoring techniques, and incentive schemes), they will have little incentive to innovate, and contracting out may yield limited efficiency gains for government.

There may also be cases in which there is an effective loss of transparency because contracting out redefines the issue in a way that minimizes public attention, or otherwise avoids certain forms of political or legal accountability. Hiring private security forces to protect the Afghani President has a different political valence than sending troops abroad – particularly if some of them come back in body bags. And, as in Kosovo, "contractors" can be sent to do jobs that would be a violation of international law if engaged in by state armed forces.[33] On the domestic scene, contracting out for the construction and management of prisons or schools may be driven by a desire to avoid capital budget restrictions or required referenda on bond issuance – that is, precisely to evade political accountability regimes.

3. *Entropy*

This latter concern is related to the fear that "marketization" via contracting out shifts the grounds of public discourse not only in ways that impoverish the public sphere and render public accountability impossible or inept, but also in ways that are difficult to undo. This anxiety has two dimensions.

One has to do with a loss of public space because the "meaning" of certain issues changes from a question of collective action to one of private choice or preference. The result may be a loss of connective tissue or social capital that has important implications for how we view society and governance.[34] Schooling and the "privatization" of old-age pensions illustrate this sort of concern. For example, buying education, either by contracts to run schools or providing vouchers with which parents can shop, raises questions for public discussion, but not necessarily the same ones that surround government-run public schools. Contracted-out schooling most directly presents us with the question: "Are we (individually or collectively) getting good value for our money?" Public schools pose that question too. But they tend to highlight a different issue as well: "What is public schooling for?" Concern that privatization causes this issue to slip off the public table, with the result that no one is accountable for providing an answer, fuels at least part of the opposition to school privatization schemes, whether or not these concerns are well founded.

The other dimension of the entropy story concerns public sector capacities. Contracting out public services to obtain superior performance may be a self-fulfilling, but unwelcome, prophecy. Much, perhaps most, human productive capacity is acquired in a learning-by-doing mode. If public bureaucracies do not do, they will not learn; and this trained incapacity will have consequences for their ability to enforce accountability through contracting. When information asymmetries are acute, one side dictates the contract terms. And recapturing lost capacities may turn out to be very difficult in a world in which existing public sector capacities are weak.[35]

Political capacities may also be at stake. School voucher systems, for example, are criticized for their potential for splintering the electorate. The fear is that the most concerned and active parents will use vouchers to abandon troubled schools. This would enfeeble the political and social accountability systems that surround those schools, render them even less accountable than they are today, and create even larger gaps between the haves and the have-nots in primary and secondary education.[36]

C. Putting concerns in context

While contracting out may pose unique institutional design issues, the anxieties of accountability that surround contracted-out governance are not unique to that organization of state activities. Capture theorists and scholars of various critical stripes often argue that the public/private distinction cannot be maintained in standard public law regimes (blurring) and that the public interest is constantly in danger of being hijacked by private interests. Lack of transparency is a familiar complaint and has been a standard feature of public law reform activities across the Anglo-American legal world for decades. And concerns about the hijacking of the public sphere by the hegemonic ambitions of economic rationality (entropy) might be said to be commonplace in the political discourse of the late twentieth and early twenty-first centuries.

Conceptually nothing new is at stake. What contracting out adds is a context within which these relatively familiar anxieties have not been domesticated or ameliorated by a set of equally familiar techniques for redress. There is no standard set of institutional designs that we recognize as responsive to these various accountability concerns.

But fears of accountability dysfunctions based on contextual novelty are not necessarily persuasive grounds for limiting this form of privatization. As was mentioned earlier, many instances of contracting out are driven as much by ideology or institutional necessity as by careful analysis of the comparative advantages of public or private provision. Designers of contracted-out systems will simply have to work with the cards that they are dealt.

That means that, within the context of particular programs and particular contracted-out functions, systems will need to be devised that exploit the comparative competences of different modalities of accountability. That social or market accountability regimes must be used does not necessarily specify which species within those generic categories; what specific contractual structures, incentives, or constraints will help to reinforce strengths and ameliorate weaknesses; or how those accountability regimes can be articulated with preexisting public law accountability techniques.

D. The example of social security disability insurance

The concerns just raised about the effects of contracting out should not be dismissed just because they are not truly novel issues. They point to potential dangers and pitfalls that are often ignored by enthusiastic privatizers. Nevertheless, there is in the critical literature on contracting out a tendency to assume that potential dangers are always real and that good institutional design is incapable of ameliorating even real problems. There is also sometimes more than a glimpse of the "Nirvana fallacy," the implicit comparison of potentially faulty privatized activities with an idealized, and therefore perfectly functioning, public bureaucracy.

A more nuanced idea of the accountability challenges posed by contracting out can only be obtained by examining particular instances. For purposes of illustration I will here look at the adjudication of social security disability claims. The adjudication of public pension entitlements seems quintessentially a public function. Yet, this is a highly contracted-out system that has never before been analyzed from the perspective of the ways in which contracting affects accountability. The idea in pursuing this example is to provide a feel for how an audit of the accountability characteristics of particular contracted-out activities might proceed under the conceptual structure that has been developed earlier in this chapter.

Disability benefits policy pursuant to Title II of the US Social Security Act is a policy domain of constant ferment and constant complaint, about both its effectiveness and its accountability.[37] Disability income policy is also subject to a host of differing accountability regimes. I will first attempt to "audit" the system to discover how contracting out affects accountability, and then look briefly at a recent reform that substantially alters the accountability universe by emphasizing market accountability devices rather than political, legal, or bureaucratic controls.

1. The disability determination system in a nutshell

The Disability Insurance Program under the federal Social Security Act pays disability retirement benefits to covered workers who, given their impairment, age, education, and work experience, are unable to do any job available in substantial numbers in the national economy. Disability must result from a clinically determinable condition and be expected to last at least twelve months or result in death.

Initial determinations of disability are made by state disability determination services (DDS) under contract with the federal Social Security Administration (SSA). Disappointed applicants may appeal denials, first to the reconsideration branch of the DDS, then to independent federal Administrative Law Judges (ALJs) who provide de novo hearings, then to the SSA Appeals Council, and finally to the federal courts.[38]

Disability insurance pensions are legal entitlements and are claimed by about 1.5 million applicants each year. DDS examiners reject about one million of these claims. Over one-quarter of rejected applicants pursue ALJ hearings and about 6,000 cases are submitted every year to federal courts for review. This is a legalistic and contentious system where non-trivial expenditures (approaching US$100 billion annually) and large numbers of claimants and beneficiaries make it a politically salient program as well.[39]

Disability determination is notoriously difficult. There is no external referent against which to measure work disability. Individual responses to disease or injury are highly varied and the capacity to work with an impairment depends, under the statutory definition, upon the interaction of medical conditions, personal vocational characteristics (age, education, and work experience), and the characteristics of the job market for the whole economy. Other even less observable factors clearly also affect work behavior, ranging from individual motivation to the structure of an individual's family, community, and workplace supports. Satisfying disappointed claimants and the public at large that disability determinations are "correct" and that the system operates fairly is a major accountability challenge.

Many activities within this system are contracted out. Initial and reconsideration decisions are made under contract by DDS personnel, and for the vast majority of claimants these decisions are effectively final. Whether claimants will receive vocational rehabilitation services in addition to or instead of a disability pension is determined by state-level vocational rehabilitation agencies, again under contract to the SSA. DDS officers contract with physicians in private practice to provide a crucial link in the disability determination process, the characterization of claimants' "residual functional capacity" (RFC) given their medical conditions to engage in various classifications of work. RFC ratings range from none, through the capacity to do "sedentary," "light," "medium," or "heavy" work. These categories are defined by regulation in terms of strength and exertional capacities, which in turn map onto job descriptions contained in the Labor Department's "Dictionary of Occupational Titles," a compendium of the demands of all jobs that exist in substantial numbers in the national economy.

Contracts with the medical profession extend further into the adjudicatory process. To get a clearer picture of their medical situation many claimants are sent to board-certified specialists for a consultative examination (CE), which is purchased by the SSA and reported to the claimant and to the DDS or ALJ ordering the examination. ALJs are also authorized to hire medical advisors in particular cases to assist them in understanding the medical evidence and the probable impact of clinical findings on claimants' work capacities. ALJs often also hire vocational experts to testify in hearings concerning the work prospects of claimants given hypothetical findings of fact concerning their impairments and vocational characteristics.

Finally, the SSA lets scores, if not hundreds, of contracts each year to consultants for advice or research on every aspect of the agency's disability insurance mission. Many of these contracts make available specialized knowledge that would not normally reside in the agency, or relate to one-of-a-kind projects for which the agency would not want to maintain sufficient full-time staffing levels. Many consultants provide services, however, that are indistinguishable from research and statistical work that would once have been done in-house, but that has been shed because of an approximate 20 per cent reduction in SSA staff during the past two decades.

2. Auditing the disability insurance accountability books

The standard governance accountability regime for the disability insurance program is very complex. I will provide only a thumbnail sketch before looking at the impacts of contracting out on these accountability relationships.

In a well-known book, Martha Derthick[40] argues that the whole of the US social security system has been constructed and operated by political and bureaucratic specialists free from sustained political accountability to the electorate. That may be true, but weak citizen control would not distinguish the disability insurance system from much of public policy. Electoral accountability is at best a very loose-jointed enterprise. "Social security" is an issue in most federal elections, as is "Medicare," but the disability insurance program is much less electorally visible.

Nevertheless, Congress (through its General Accounting Office) and the Executive Office of the President (through the Office of Management and Budget) pay close attention to disability insurance program trends and expenditures. A continuous stream of reports about disability insurance flows from both these sources and from the independent Social Security Advisory Council, established by Congress to provide continuous expert oversight concerning all social security programs. Congressional oversight by the Sub-Committee on Social Security of the House Ways and Means Committee is episodic in hearings, but continuous at the staff level. Moreover, individual congressional offices file more than 100,000 requests each year for information regarding disability insurance claims involving constituents.

Notwithstanding the recent reorganization that made the SSA an "independent agency," accountability to political controllers remains substantial. "Independence" tends to make agencies somewhat more accountable to Congress and less to the executive branch, but these shifts may be barely perceptible to administrators who find themselves in constant contact with political principals from both branches, or their staffs. Legislatively mandated reports by the Social

Security Advisory Board and the annual Social Security Trustees, Report are widely reported in the press and often generate sustained congressional committee attention.

Legal accountability to claimants is obviously extensive. The availability of evidentiary hearings before ALJs followed by judicial review is but one mode of legal accountability. Class action suits to remedy systemic maladministration and challenges to agency rules are less frequent, but important means of making the agency legally accountable for its policies and practices. Indeed, these more policy-oriented lawsuits may have considerably greater impacts on agency functioning. A number of the most important administrative law cases in the US that define adjudicatory due process,[41] explicate the power of agencies to narrow adjudicatory issues by rules,[42] and demand transparent promulgation of policy,[43] arise out of the disasbility insurance context. By contrast, the thousands of cases that simply review ALJ judgments for "substantial evidence" have little discernible impact on administration.

Bureaucratic oversight of disability determinations within the SSA hierarchy is clearly affected by the contracted-out adjudicatory structure.[44] This distinguishes the disability insurance system from typical adjudicatory hierarchies in the US. Most high-volume adjudicatory decisions begin with line personnel and proceed by appeal to ALJs and the courts. The question is whether there are real differences in "bureaucratic" and "contract" accountability.

At one level, the answer is "no." The contracts with the DDSs are highly detailed. Moreover, they require the state agencies to act in accordance with the Disability Insurance State Manual, promulgated by the SSA, and updated continuously. That manual specifies routines, procedures, evidentiary requirements, and decision rules in as much detail as might be expected were DDS personnel SSA staff. DDSs must make dozens of mandated reports on their activities to SSA regional offices, including monthly results from an elaborate statistical quality assurance system designed to identify patterns of either procedural or substantive error. Bureaucratic oversight through instructions and audits works here as if state personnel were federalized.

On the other hand, many forms of standard bureaucratic control are missing. Hiring, promotion, compensation, and removal of personnel are state agency functions. So are training, evaluation, and day-to-day counseling by superiors. The state DDS shapes agency culture, and differences in award rates and "error" rates across states can be dramatic. This interstate variance is not well understood, but surely results in part from differences in agency political culture and the level of "professionalization" of staff. A state that organizes these functions in a department of education may employ only adjudicators with master's degrees in vocational education. Its neighbor that uses welfare department personnel may not even require university training for its "eligibility technicians."

Differences in the organization of state government also determine the degree to which the DDS is seen as a quasi-independent adjudicatory bureau or is more closely monitored and controlled by state elected representatives. The result is a DDS culture that ranges from the highly professional to the highly political. Because of intergovernmental politics, the SSA has been unable to control many of these aspects of state organization and personnel practice by either contract or regulation.

This loss of "internalized" bureaucratic control and accountability at the state level cannot be recaptured by managing second-level, federal adjudicators. SSA line officials do not review individual awards or denials. Denials only may be appealed to independent ALJs, who are qualified by and hired off lists provided by the Office of Personnel Management, which also sets their compensation. By statute, ALJs may not be subject to any "efficiency" standards set by an agency and may be removed only for cause. They are organized in a separate unit (the Office of Hearings and Appeals), which does not report to policy divisions of the SSA. ALJs sit in offices around the country separate from SSA facilities, and have their own professional organization with close connections to the American Bar Association. Through judicial review, ALJs are "legally" but not bureaucratically, or indeed politically, accountable.

Conflicts among political, bureaucratic, and legal accountability systems are, of course, common. Because these regimes presumably answer the questions, "who, to whom, about what, through what process, using what criteria, and with what effects" differently, making adjudicators (or any official) accountable in one fashion may entail curtailing accountability in another. ALJs cannot be accountable to claimants to act according to law unless they have a significant degree of independence from bureaucratic and political controllers.

3. *Observations: contracting out in a systemic perspective*

So what does contracting out do to or for "accountability" in the disability insurance system? First, the DDS contracts. Contracting with states to determine eligibility for disability benefits initially had at least two purposes. First, every state had a vocational rehabilitation service that provided rehabilitation and job services to state citizens. These officials presumably had the expertise relevant to making disability decisions. Contracting with these bureaus seemed more efficient than hiring and training a new cadre of federal officials and deploying them all over the country. Secondly, rehabilitation professionals had an orientation – get people back to work and pay them benefits only if that is impossible – that the federal government wanted.

Problems of buying into professional [treatment] culture. Contracting out was not just an attempt at "efficiency," it was an attempt to buy into a professional culture. The federal government was going to be politically accountable for the fiscal integrity of the disability insurance program. A stringent definition of disability and relatively low replacement rates were designed to constrain demand, but that might well not be enough. Disability insurance has famously difficult moral hazard problems. By buying into a treatment culture in vocational rehabilitation that emphasized work and return to work, the federal government was contracting for a particular professional social network – a network whose members were accountable both to each other and to their state political controllers for successfully returning people to employment. That accountability system or regime was meant to reinforce whatever legal or political accountability regimes could be constructed to reinforce fiscal responsibility at the national level.[45]

Unfortunately, the federal government failed to understand how professional and bureaucratic accountability at the state level would affect the disability determination process over time. Because the definition of disability in the disability insurance program is so stringent, the people who showed up as claimants were mostly very poor prospects for return to work. Because vocational rehabilitation professionals tend to be judged, and to judge themselves, by their success rates, they did not want to handle these clients. And, because the vocational rehabilitation statutes allowed them to classify persons referred to them as unable to benefit from rehabilitation services, most disability insurance claimants received that classification. In short, the tie-in between rehabilitation and income maintenance did not work very well. Most states eventually shifted the disability insurance determination question to other employees who did not have the training or pay scales of people who provided vocational rehabilitation services.

Contracts with the medical profession also make the SSA's disability insurance adjudications and policies accountable to "private" professional norms. Doctors participating in the adjudicatory process as witnesses, consulting examiners, advisors, or RFC evaluators bring to bear a clinical judgment that responds to an extra-bureaucratic, treatment culture. Unlike state vocational rehabilitation professionals, doctors participating in the disability insurance process are part-timers whose mentality is shaped by medical training, personal experience, and peer group understandings, not bureaucratic culture or imperatives.

The heavy involvement of the medical profession in disability determination is also based, in part, on fiscal concerns. Congress was fearful that disability insurance would become a form of residual unemployment insurance. Hence, pensions were to be paid only to people who were out of the workforce because of a "medically determinable" physical or mental impairment. Doctors were to be the gatekeepers who separated the "work disabled" from unemployed people with health complaints.

Medical professionals in academic centers also strongly influence SSA policies through research contracts and contract service on advisory panels that review adjudicatory criteria. If SSA evaluative standards diverge too much from current medical thinking, the medical literature will take note. Pressure will mount to reevaluate the SSA's guidelines and regulations and ultimately an advisory committee of high-status physicians will be empanelled to make revisions. Again, medical professional influence – the accountability of the SSA to the professional norms of the treatment and research medical culture through contracted-out (and other) relationships – lessens bureaucratic and political control. But it simultaneously strengthens accountability to the claimants who are the medical profession's patients.

This informal accountability to norms of treatment-oriented professionals is reinforced by political and legal accountability regimes. The Congress in some sense borrowed the legitimacy of the medical profession in the making of disability judgments by defining "disability" as "a medically determinable impairment." And reviewing courts, when looking for "substantial evidence" to support ALJ findings, rely almost exclusively on the reports and testimony of physicians.

A similar story might be told about "vocational experts" who testify for a fee in ALJ hearings, and about the implicit contracting out of the definition of "vocational factors" (the educational, strength, and exertional requirements of jobs) to the Department of Labor. Here again, an outside specialist culture is borrowed, which then exerts "horizontal" accountability pressures on the SSA to accede to its professional norms. And, once again, this contracting out is reinforced by the reviewing courts' search for "substantial evidence" – indeed, the vocational expert program at the SSA was constructed in response to judicial requirements.[46] In both these cases, "contracted-out" professional accountability, and standard political and legal forms, are symbiotic, not competitive.

Nevertheless, borrowing the physicians' treatment culture has had legitimacy costs as well as benefits. Treating physicians put the health of their patients above other considerations when giving medical advice. The SSA thus sees millions of claimants who have been advised by their physicians that they should not work. And the agency has struggled since the program's inception to justify denials in the face of a treating physician's conclusions that a particular claimant is "disabled." To satisfy reviewing courts, this has generally meant the purchase of additional medical evidence from more highly-qualified medical consultants. But, whether paper credentials or experience with the applicant provide a better basis for credible testimony in disability cases remains contentious, both at the administrative hearing level and in reviewing courts.[47]

With the disappearance of vocational rehabilitation professionals from state DDSs, the first-level adjudicators in the disability insurance program became simply a new state bureaucracy that was specialized to disability benefits adjudication. And, having failed to gain accountability through the purchase of a professional social network, the SSA clearly lost a considerable degree of ordinary bureaucratic accountability through contracting out. It is harder for the SSA to make the patterns of decisionmaking in individual state DDSs fit overall national policy than it would have been if these first-level adjudicators were federal employees. Variances in grant and denial rates are geographically patterned and not explicable by differences in the ecology of disability in differing locales. For example, in one study, the General Accounting Office gave 221 disability claims to ten states and asked them to adjudicate them. The states agreed on only forty-eight of the claims.[48]

Although the federal government has considerable power to direct state agency activities by contract, it does not have the authority to train state adjudicators, oversee and manage their careers, provide selective rewards and sanctions, or create an "agency culture" or "adjudicatory climate" that would tend to unify practice. These continuous and intense forms of managerial accountability may simply be impossible to construct by contract. The federal government cannot move state employees from place to place to give them broader or different experiences. It cannot even require that they come to nationally sponsored training seminars, given that about half of the states about half of the time have prohibitions on interstate business travel by state employees. This is one of state governments' favorite responses to fiscal difficulties.

Gaining political accountability. On the other hand, loss of bureaucratic hierarchical control at the national level may mean that disability determinations are responsive to state political cultures because of the DDS's accountability within state political processes. Indeed, this hypothesis is demonstrable on some occasions when shifts in federal policy are resisted by the states. In a high-visibility incident in the 1980s, for example, twenty-nine states refused to honor their contracts in protest against a Reagan administration policy shift that purged nearly 400,000 beneficiaries from the disability insurance benefit rolls.[49] State (and federal court) resistance fueled congressional intervention to overturn the new policies by statute. If first-level adjudicators had been federal employees, a similar political uprising by states, who are powerful actors in the national political process, would have been unthinkable.

Hence, contracting out to the states can, and sometimes does, increase political accountability to claimants and beneficiaries in the disability insurance system precisely because it decreases decisionmakers' bureaucratic accountability to the SSA. To put the matter slightly differently, the states' "conflict of interest" in controlling state employees who hand out *federally* financed pensions, may help stabilize a system that otherwise has relatively weak political constraints on excessive stringency in the adjudication of claims.

The public nature of the contractor may not be crucially determinative here. The other candidate for such contracts, private disability insurance companies, would have a similar (probably excessive) conflict built in. Virtually all private disability insurance is structured to reduce the private insurer's payment amounts by whatever amount is received from a federal disability insurance pension. Indeed, most private policies require long-term recipients to apply for disability insurance benefits, and insurers often assist policyholders in the federal application and appeals process.

Opacity and entropy. Perhaps the most complicated and subtle contract accountability story revolves around contracted-out research and evaluation activities. The SSA's massive information needs concerning population health, demographic trends, medical knowledge, labor market demands, not to mention the effects and effectiveness of its own programs, are met by an army of outside consultants and contractors. What are the accountability effects of contracting out for critical programmatic information?

The primary effect may be to increase the transparency of the agency's operations. The SSA must open itself up to contractors, often providing them with huge amounts of program data, in order for their research to be useful. These researchers, in turn, have academic publication agendas that make it difficult to keep their findings "in-house." And, because these contracts are known to congressional committees, who also want to be informed, contracting for confidentiality (other than protection of claimant and beneficiary privacy) is not a politically viable option.

Contract research hence reinforces both bureaucratic accountability (the agency is better informed about its own system and possibilities for reform) and political accountability (via congressional oversight and press reporting). It also serves as an outside check on political controllers who, under fiscal pressures, might want to trim expenditures at the expense of politically unorganized populations. Administrative policies adopted under political prodding, but that go against the weight of credible scientific evidence, fare badly on judicial review. The SSA's contracting out thus makes it both more and less accountable to elected officials.

The degree of contracting out clearly matters to bureaucratic capacities. An increased information base contributes to effective management and accountability within the agency, and to legal accountability in the face of political stresses. But massive contracting out can deplete the human capital necessary to contract out effectively or to use the information gained in productive ways. Too much externalization of information generation and analysis can trade staff for interest group capture, and distort policy. The decimation of the Office of Research and Statistics at the SSA in the

1980s and 1990s arguably had precisely this result, and the office is currently being rebuilt.[50]

Shifting to market accountability. A recent reform in the disability insurance program illustrates shifting forms within contracting-out regimes – shifts designed to increase both effectiveness and accountability by generating market forms of accountability. As was described earlier, the original vision of DI was one to be run by vocational rehabilitation professionals. When that failed, the program still required that all claimants be referred to vocational rehabilitation for assessment and service, where appropriate. Provision of those services was contracted out to vocational rehabilitation units at the state level. This contracting system has never worked well. State vocational rehabilitation agencies have many other clients, most of them with greater work potential than the people who show up as disability insurance beneficiaries. As a consequence, providing services for these beneficiaries has been a low priority for vocational rehabilitation agencies, and their placement record is abysmal. Only a fraction of 1 percent of all beneficiaries ever leaves the rolls and returns to work. And it is unclear whether these agencies have much to do with those success stories.

A study panel at the National Academy of Social Insurance recommended in 1996[51] that Congress take competition seriously in the provision of return-to-work services for persons on disability insurance pensions. Congress responded with the awkwardly named Ticket to Work and Work Incentive Improvement Act (TTWIIA).[52] In simplified terms, this statute provides that disability insurance recipients may seek vocational rehabilitation and return-to-work services from any provider – public or private. Payments to the providers are largely on a commission-for-performance basis. If a recipient returns to work and leaves the disability benefits rolls, the provider is entitled to a portion of the disability benefits that would have been paid to the recipient for every year the recipient continues not to receive disability insurance payments. This is a high-risk, high-return form of contract that may have a small pay-off in terms of the total number of recipients who return to work. But, it tends to get the incentives right. Providers are accountable to recipients because the latter hold the vouchers and the providers must compete in the market for their business. The government gets what it pays for because it pays (mostly) for performance.

But the TTWIIA program was a hard sell in both Congress and the vocational rehabilitation communities. People had to be convinced to accept an entirely new accountability regime, to prefer the accountability of the market to the accountability of public governance. They had to be convinced to give up on the very strong protections for recipients that are built into a process that requires that everyone at least be evaluated, and that publicly accountable agencies provide or contract for vocational rehabilitation services. They had to be convinced in short that market accountability would monitor and enforce contracts in a way that produced the desired services and supports for disability insurance beneficiaries that would actually allow them to return to work.

The relevant parties are not yet totally convinced. Concerns about leaving behind public sector accountability devices, even in a program that demonstrably produced poor results, yielded a compromise "demonstration project" that may demonstrate little because its scale is so small. And, of course, the lesson may be that market accountability fails to produce much improvement here either – or that losses of other forms of accountability yield unhappy results of other sorts.

E. Lessons learned?

What does this audit of the disability insurance accountability books tell us about some of the accountability anxieties that are generated by contracting out government service? In the disability insurance case, contracting out was partly about the purchase of organizational or professional cultures, not just an attempt to substitute market competition for collective action. And "culture" turned out to be a lumpy and unruly good. Using social networks is tricky.

Opacity did not result from contracting out in this system: contractual relationships were structured to preserve and enhance transparency; and contracting out research and monitoring responsibilities to academics actually increased transparency. There was some clear loss of bureaucratic accountability, understood as managerial control over lower-level actors. But this loss produced some forms of enhanced political accountability. The direction of entropy, at least as concerns research and evaluation capacities, seems reversible: loss of capacity within the SSA has been noticed and addressed. But other forms of entropy may be less easily remedied. While contracting out for medical expertise has produced a highly "medicalized" model of disability evaluation, which has been exploited for its legitimating effects by the political, bureaucratic, and legal systems, many observers of the DI system believe that the reinforcement of this medicalized model – with its emphasis on impairments rather than capabilities – has had baleful effects for claimants and for the country as a whole.

The form of contracting may also be crucial. Contracting with state vocational rehabilitation services looks superficially like the addition of a market to bureaucratic accountability. But, because these contracts are not competitive, no market discipline attaches. Giving beneficiaries return-to-work tickets makes providers accountable to beneficiaries and harnesses competition in ways that may improve accountability for results – a desired outcome that bureaucratic contracting failed to achieve.

Much more could be made of this example, but enough has been said to allow us to grasp its central lesson: the potential gains and losses along different dimensions of accountability regimes or across them are so complex that knowing that a function is "contracted out" tells us virtually nothing about whether "accountability" has been strengthened or weakened. It all depends on how the contracts and the accountability relationships are structured. Every case must be examined carefully and on its own terms. Contracting out for the implementation of public welfare, national defense, the management of prisons, and the provision of elementary and secondary education will all turn out to have substantially different characteristics than those just discussed for disability insurance.

CONCLUSION: NORMS, ACCOUNTABILITY, AND INSTITUTIONAL DESIGN

This chapter has argued that any accountability regime will offer an answer to at least six basic questions: who is accountable to whom; about what; through what processes; in accordance with what criteria; and with what effects? When critiquing any particular regime or designing new ones, we must be careful to specify what sort of accountability is wanted, why it is thought to be appropriate to the particular activity under examination, and what the accountability tradeoffs are of organizing activities in one form or another.

These are the necessary, but hardly sufficient, conditions for having a meaningful conversation about the structure of accountability. The missing ingredient is a normative stance toward accountability regimes. It would be nice if we could view institutional design as a straightforward, instrumentally rational, quasi-engineering process. In such a world, we would specify our normative commitments and the goals those normative commitments implied, and choose accountability regimes appropriately designed to mold behavior in the direction of our commitments. And, to some degree, this straightforward approach to institutional design of accountability structures is available.

In broad terms, accountability regimes directed toward public governance are meant to reinforce the normative commitments of the political system. In a liberal democratic polity, for example, we expect governance accountability to reinforce mechanisms of consent and to ensure that collective judgments (legal standards and public policies) are impersonally applied. Put in conventional terms, governance accountability is meant to reinforce democracy and the rule of law.

Market accountability, by contrast, is meant to ensure that resources are devoted to their highest valued uses. Efficiency is the goal, and we want our product, financial and labor markets organized, at a minimum, to ensure efficient allocation of resources.

The normative underpinnings of social networks are somewhat more mysterious, but in one way or another social networks support particular ideals of human flourishing. As social animals we need solidarity with others in the project of developing and maintaining a culture that we recognize as our own. These cultural practices give meaning to our lives and are reinforced by our sense of reciprocal obligation to the members of the groups that we recognize as having claims on us.

This understanding of the normative underpinnings of public governance, market, and social network accountability systems might lead to a straightforward set of rules of thumb for institutional design. Worried about the protection of democratic values and the rule of law? Emphasize public governance accountability regimes. Interested in efficiency? Try to construct markets that are truly responsive to the demands of producers and consumers, lenders and borrowers, and employers and employees. Seeking to promote human flourishing through the authentic creation or recognition of social norms? Design institutions to leave space for the development of group norms and rely on the reciprocal obligations of group members to maintain fidelity to the particular network's normative commitments.

But the normative issues surrounding any accountability system are hardly exhausted by attention to the "fit" between the normative commitments that various accountability regimes might arguably support and the normative commitments of particular programs. No institution really serves only one purpose or goal, and, therefore, no institution should be expected to be responsive to only one form of accountability regime. In a different, but related, context, Gunther Teubner has argued[53] that regulatory institutions face what he styled a "regulatory trilemma." We demand that regulatory institutions be simultaneously coherent (the rule of law or regularity norm), effective (a variant of the efficiency norm), and responsive (open to the influence of social demands and cultural understandings). The trilemma for Teubner is that virtually any attempt to reinforce one of these demands works to limit the capacity of the regulatory institution to satisfy another.

Because accountability regimes are essentially regulators of institutional performance, Teubner's point applies here as well. To return to the disability adjudication example, early discussions about administering that program considered using a local "social network" approach modeled on local draftboards. The argument was that, not only was information local, the judgments involved were essentially based on cultural norms – who should be expected to work and who not given the complex interaction of medical conditions, personal circumstances, and local economic environments.

Fears of bias, particularly racial bias, made this approach less attractive than the one chosen, that is, delegating responsibility to professionals who were imbued with labor market values. Vocational rehabilitation specialists would produce efficient allocation of claimants to pensions or back-to-work programs based on their understanding of the technical characteristic of job demands.

As we have seen, that approach morphed into a medico-legal model featuring one type of expert evidence and expansive opportunity for a legal contest to ensure regularity in the application of standards. The conversation has now come full circle with widespread demands for rethinking the definition of disability so that the social and economic environment of claimants can be taken more fully into account. Disability advocates often lament the "medicalization" of disability and the failure of disability policies to pursue a broader goal of integration of persons with disabilities into the community. These critics often seem to have in mind some form of community-based and multidisciplinary approach that would deploy financial assistance, medical care, rehabilitation, and transportation services, among other things, to promote the overall well-being and highest possible functioning of disability beneficiaries.

The design details of such a system cannot be explored here. But this much is clear: this vision reimagines the goals of disability adjudication in ways that would demand highly discretionary judgments. Like restorative justice conferences and other similar models discussed in this volume, these decisions would be difficult to subject to standard public governance accountability regimes. Beliefs about how decisions should best be made, and how they should be made accountable, are thus parasitic on beliefs about the true purposes of the program. And, because that is true, many disputes about programmatic purpose are articulated as disputes about the efficacy of accountability regimes.

At least some clarity can be brought to these disputes by sorting questions of public purpose and questions of accountability into separate bins. It matters to know whether disputes are about what a public program should be doing or about whether it is appropriately accountable. And if we can achieve consensus on the question of purpose, we can surely have a more sensible discussion about which accountability mechanisms are likely to support those purposes.

But the normative issues surrounding any accountability system are hardly exhausted by attention to the "fit" between the normative commitments that various accountability regimes might arguably support and the normative commitments of a particular program. When pursuing any of the six questions that I have argued any accountability regime must answer, normative controversy reemerges. Exactly why should this power wielder be expected to be accountable to these parties about these activities or outcomes? By what normative criteria are these actions to be judged? Why are those sanctions for failing to behave properly appropriate? And how are we to judge whether these particular accountability processes satisfy our normative demands for either fairness or efficacy? When answering these questions, it will not be possible to cabin discussion by relentless consequentialist attention to programmatic goals. For no particular public function defines our vision of good public policy or a good life. We have commitments to cross-cutting purposes, often vaguely articulated as concerns with fairness, efficiency, human dignity, or social solidarity. And the way that accountability regimes are structured affects these values, both practically and symbolically.

It may be clear, for example, that in providing effective social supports, income security, and economic opportunity for disabled workers, market incentives operationalized through return-to-work service vouchers, or through support and rehabilitation plans negotiated through some sort of disability amelioration conferences, provide a better fit between program goals and implementing instruments. But how can we ensure that all workers will be treated with equal concern and dignity? That like cases will be treated alike? That public funds will not be wasted on ineffective nostrums?

And, if accountability regimes that provide the best fit with programmatic purposes cannot provide adequate answers to these questions, we may well decide to jettison those purposes in favor of a more restricted set of ends (income security, as in the current program) that can be made more accountable for these cross-cutting values. In so doing, we in some significant, but surely justifiable, sense turn the design enterprise on its head. We design programs that can be made accountable, not accountability regimes that support programs.

CHAPTER 6

EMERGING LABOR MOVEMENTS AND THE ACCOUNTABILITY DILEMMA: THE CASE OF INDONESIA

Michele Ford

INTRODUCTION

A dominant concern in discussions of the accountability crisis is the potential impact of blurring boundaries between public and private accountability regimes. Opponents of privatization (and pseudo-privatization) argue that the modes of accountability characteristically adopted by private institutions are inappropriate for their public counterparts. Organized labor movements in developing countries such as Indonesia provide useful examples with which to explore these claims. Normatively speaking, labor unions are inherently "public" bodies: they have uniquely public responsibilities – namely the procurement of social citizenship for working-class citizens – and they are subject to a distinctly public mechanism of accountability, namely electoral democracy. In contrast, the nongovernmental organizations (NGOs) who have challenged, even undermined, unions' monopoly on worker representation in emerging economy contexts in recent decades are inherently private organizations that are not directly bound to the workers they serve. NGOs' growing engagement with labor issues is thus portrayed as bringing with it a shift away from the electoral mode of accountability considered synonymous with unions towards the inferior modes of accountability adopted by NGOs.

Analyses of labor NGOs' growing involvement in labor issues highlight widely recognized concerns about labor NGOs' accountability to the workers who comprise their "target groups." However, they fail to acknowledge that many unions in emerging economies are only marginally, if at all, more accountable to workers. In Indonesia, both labor unions and labor NGOs are enmeshed in complex webs of accountability, in which their relationship with workers represents just one of many strands. These webs of accountability equally define – and limit – labor unions' and labor NGOs' abilities to "answer" to workers, suggesting that public accountability is perhaps sometimes more a product of the political and economic environments in which labor movement organizations operate than of the structures of those organizations themselves.

This chapter begins by examining the arguments most often made about the differences between labor unions and labor NGOs and the effects those differences have on the nature and extent of their accountability to workers. It then explains the context in which NGOs came to dominate the Indonesian labor movement in the early 1990s and the web of accountability in which Indonesian labor NGOs and unions find themselves today. The chapter concludes by outlining the implications of the "accountability dilemma" faced by unions and labor NGOs. It argues that – despite their formally democratic accountability structures – Indonesian unions are not necessarily always more accountable to workers than their undemocratic labor NGO counterparts. This suggests that a multidimensional model of accountability is required that recognizes the impact that pressures associated with a particular environment have on labor movement organizations' ability to be accountable to workers.

I. QUESTIONS OF ACCOUNTABILITY IN THE LABOR SPHERE

As unions are the primary organizational vehicle for workers' collective action, most discussions of accountability within the labor movement are located in the literature on labor union democracy where accountability is a major, if not always explicit, theme. Discussions of labor union accountability, like most discussions of public accountability, are generally framed in terms of a relationship between two entities: the institution whose level or type of public accountability is to be examined, and "the people" (or representatives of "the people") to whom (or to which) they are accountable. The idea of accountability is implicit in the analyses of tensions between unions' institutional interests and the interests of union members that characterize much of this literature.[1] Scholars concerned with labor union democracy also raise the possibility that different unions may emphasize different measures of accountability.[2] For example, Morris and Fosh identify four major models of labor union democracy, namely liberal pluralism (which stresses electoral accountability); consumer unionism (where accountability is measured through outcomes rather than internal processes); grassroots activism (which stresses accountability through direct collective decisionmaking); and individual accountability (which stresses the role of the state as an external arbiter of labor union democracy which guards against leaders' radicalism).[3] Yet, although these modes of labor union democracy represent quite different approaches to labor unions' public accountability, a common premise underpins all four: that the public to which a union is accountable is comprised only of its due-paying members.

NGOs' contribution to campaigns around labor issues may be increasingly acknowledged, but labor NGOs are seldom considered to be labor movement organizations in their own right because they are not organizations "by, for and of" workers. As a result, in contrast to the literature on labor union democracy, which focuses more or less entirely on unions' accountability to their worker-members, the much smaller literature on labor NGOs emphasizes NGOs' relative lack of accountability.[4] Critiques of labor NGOs' accountability echo the three major concerns regarding NGO accountability more generally that Sasha Courville identifies in Chapter 11: that NGOs are insufficiently accountable to either their members or the groups they serve; that they are even less accountable to society as a whole; and that NGOs' multiple roles inherently diminish their ability to be accountable to workers because of the potential conflicts of interest inherent in seeking to meet the requirements of a whole range of different "publics".[5]

Scholars like Gallin and Compa rightly argue that a labor NGO's public is much less clearly defined than that of a union because labor NGOs are closed-membership organizations whose members are generally middle-class activists who engage with labor issues on behalf of workers, in contrast to unions, which are open-membership, mass organizations comprised of workers themselves.[6] In the case of labor NGOs engaged in grassroots organizing, it is often unclear whether those NGOs are accountable to the workers' groups they sponsor (if indeed they sponsor workers' groups); to all workers employed in a particular occupation, industry, or sector; or to any workers at all. Furthermore, relatively few NGOs are involved in grassroots labor activism: in situations where local NGOs engage in advocacy on labor issues alongside other social issues such as human rights abuses and democracy, their "public" may be better defined as the entire local community than a much narrower constituency of workers.

Even when workers are recognized as a part – big or small – of a labor NGO's public, the NGO's ability to be accountable to those workers is constrained by a whole range of factors. First, labor NGOs, like other NGOs, are principally dependent on external funding, sometimes supplemented by income generated by the NGO itself. It is often argued that labor NGOs' dependence on foreign donors means that they are primarily accountable "upwards" beyond national boundaries to the community of donors who support their work, rather than "downwards" to their target groups or even to society as a whole.[7] A related issue is the extent to which local labor NGOs' links with, and dependence on, international organizations and transnational networks place them outside state systems of accountability and encourage them to pursue external agendas not necessarily compatible with the needs of workers in their particular host society. Another concern is that labor NGOs' own internal accountability structures are weak because NGOs are often "directed" by a founder or group of founding members who cannot be voted out or sacked, and are not subject to the same internal transparency requirements as other social organizations.[8]

Perhaps the strongest theme in critiques of labor NGOs concerns the third point raised by Courville: that NGOs have multiple roles which inevitably create conflicts of interest, thus diminishing their ability to be accountable. As I have argued elsewhere,[9] although labor NGOs should be considered part of the labor movement, it must be recognized that their organizational identities and operational imperatives are not necessarily wholly focused on their role within that movement. All local labor NGOs have multiple roles in the sense that they are engaged with worker communities and/or labor issues within a particular national setting on the one hand, and with their community of donors, which is most often international, on the other. Many local labor NGOs also adopt multiple "horizontal" roles, engaging directly with workers, becoming involved in national-level and transnational advocacy networks, and simultaneously taking on a range of projects (each potentially funded by a different donor) that focus on matters that may or may not be related to labor. Each of these roles comes with a specific set of expectations which NGOs must meet and measures through which NGOs' accountability must be demonstrated. It is not surprising that conflicts of interest arise, which may lead to accusations that the labor NGOs concerned are pursuing their own interests rather than the interests of the workers they claim to support.[10]

On the surface, then, it appears that very different models are required to analyze the public accountability of unions and labor NGOs. However, evidence from developing-country contexts such as Indonesia suggests that differences between the types of accountability demanded from labor NGOs and unions may be less concrete than they first appear. Although labor unions operating in these contexts generally have fewer competing roles than labor NGOs, they are seldom accountable only to their members. Like local labor NGOs, they are required to be accountable to a whole range of other parties (such as to their often charismatic founders and to their own set of overseas donors.) whose demands influence their ability to be accountable to their worker public. And also like local labor NGOs, unions in developing-country contexts often lack organizational transparency or are not particularly internally democratic. This might be because of the dominant role of a central union executive or because of government-imposed restrictions on shop-floor organizing. Yet, whereas scholars are extremely cognizant of the risks competing claims on labor NGOs pose for their ability (and desire) to be accountable to workers, they assume that the definition of a union's public is unproblematic. In other words, unlike the literature on labor NGOs, scholarly accounts of labor union democracy focus on what unions' obligations to workers are and to what extent unions deliver on those obligations, but almost always fail to really ask to whom those unions are really accountable.

The narrow focus in the labor union democracy literature is based on the assumption that unions are essentially, primarily, and uniquely accountable to their members because electoral procedures are used to select union leaders. But, while most unions' publics are indeed defined by membership (and within national boundaries), international unionism and transborder solidarity activities weaken the direct correspondence between a union's membership and its public. One example of this that is immediately obvious to students of emerging labor movements is the campaigns run by national unions' international solidarity organizations – such as the American Federation of Labor-Congress of Industrial Organizations' (AFL-CIO) solidarity wing, the American Center for International Labor Solidarity (ACILS). There is a clear distinction between the public served by unions' international solidarity organizations (generally located in emerging-economy contexts) and the members to whom the parent unions are electorally accountable in their country of origin.[11] This means that, while the unionists and non-union workers targeted by a union's international programs in countries such as Indonesia are part of that union's public, they are not members of the group of workers to which that union is electorally accountable.

The assumption that a union is only accountable to its membership has other implications for the relevance of the labor union democracy literature in the study of emerging labor movements. Most importantly, perhaps, it largely ignores the influence of other forms of accountability on a union's ability to be truly accountable to its worker public. In emerging-economy contexts, at least two very tangible pressures impinge on a union's ability to be accountable to its worker public: state demands that unions be accountable to all citizens (where the means of "being accountable" is defined by the state); and donors' demands that unions be accountable for funds provided for union activities (where the nature and targets of those activities are often significantly influenced by the donor organizations concerned).

The state's potential to determine unions' opportunities to organize and to limit their ability to be accountable solely to their members in all national contexts is widely recognized by labor scholars. However, the extent to which that potential is realized (and therefore the seriousness with which that potential is examined) varies enormously. In liberal democracies, the state's influence over unions changes over time, depending on variables such as the union movement's strength relative to other social interest groups or the extent to which the union movement is captured by state interests. The mainstream labor union democracy literature reflects this reality, with even theorists promoting the fourth model identified by Morris and Fosh – the model which identifies the state as a self-appointed gatekeeper of union accountability – assuming that a union's only public (and ultimate focus of union accountability) is its membership.[12] However, as suggested by the emphasis on state–union relations in the literature on labor unions in emerging economies, particularly labor regimes underpinned by developmentalist models of corporatism,[13] unions are often as, or even more, accountable to the state (theoretically representing "the people" as a whole) than to their own members. In what Alfred Stepan refers to as "exclusionary" state corporatist systems, "unions" are workers' organizations in nothing more than name. However, in many developing-country contexts, under what Stepan calls "inclusionary" state corporatism, unions simultaneously attempt to meet both the developmentalist demands of the state and the demands of workers.[14] This implies that unions in inclusionary state corporatist systems are accountable not only to their members, but also to a broader national public, courtesy of state demands that unions encourage their members to contribute to economic development rather than to fight for their "narrow" sectional interests at the expense of the national interest.

Unions' lack of internally generated resources in emerging-economy contexts also impinges on their ability to be accountable to their members. In theory, unions' primary funding base is drawn from members' contributions, but the low wages of workers in emerging economies mean that financial assistance from abroad is often more important than members' dues in maintaining union facilities and activities.[15] Members' dues alone seldom provide enough finance to obtain technologies now considered basic requirements even in emerging-economy contexts, such as computers and telephones, or to resource everyday union activities. External funding (from international or transnational union bodies, or from other sources including international NGOs) provides a union with the wherewithal to acquire the technology required to achieve their organizational aims and to fund grassroots organizing activities.

However, that funding is accompanied by many pressures. International funding bodies seldom provide resources to all unions in a particular national context – they pick "winners" that match their expectations of what a union is and does. Nor is international funding bodies' provision of resources unconditional: whether funding is provided for particular projects or for general running expenses, international funding bodies generally specify what types of expenses are acceptable and what outcomes they expect. To whom, then, in these conditions, is a union accountable? To its members, who may or may not pay the dues that represent such a small part of a union's operating budget, or to the donors who fund the bulk of it?

As this discussion has suggested, it is not necessarily helpful to focus simply on unions and workers – or even on unions, workers, and labor NGOs – when discussing the accountability of emerging labor movement organizations for two reasons. First, it is often not the case that the public to which labor movement organizations are accountable consists entirely of worker-members. Unions and local labor NGOs working at the local level in emerging-economy contexts are subject to multiple layers of accountability, which impact on their ability to be publicly accountable at all. Secondly, as both labor unions and local labor NGOs operate in particular national contexts, their ability to be accountable to workers is influenced by the political and economic specificities of those contexts. This means that, even if we define all labor movement organizations' public narrowly as consisting of workers (in the case of NGOs) or worker-members (in the case of unions), we cannot ignore either the context in which they operate or the other sorts of accountability to which these organizations are subject, because they impact on unions' and labor NGOs' ability to be accountable to that worker public.

II. UNION AND LABOR NGO ACCOUNTABILITY IN INDONESIA

The Indonesian case provides a particularly fertile context in which to explore the nuances of labor union and labor NGO accountability, not least because labor NGOs played a pivotal role in the reconstruction of the labor movement between 1985 and 2005 – a labor movement decimated by Suharto's authoritarian New Order regime (1967–1998) in the preceding two decades.[16] Labor NGOs' intense and relatively long involvement at both the grassroots and the policy advocacy levels of the Indonesian labor movement, in conjunction with the reemergence of independent unions after the fall of Suharto in 1998, provides a wealth of examples through which the extent and nature of labor movement organizations' accountability to a worker-public can be examined.

Indonesia has a long history of organized labor.[17] Unions played an important role in the nationalist movement in the late colonial period (to 1945) and under Indonesia's first President, Sukarno (1945–1967). However, organized labor entered a new phase when Suharto's New Order seized power in 1966–1967 after an attempted coup and the ensuing massacre of Indonesians associated with the Indonesian Communist Party (PKI, *Partai Komunis Indonesia*) and other leftist groups. Building on the concepts of functional groups formulated during the Guided Democracy period (1959–1965), the New Order encouraged unionists who had survived the purges of left-wing union activists carried out in 1965 to establish the All-Indonesia Labor Federation (FBSI, *Federasi Buruh Seluruh Indonesia*), a single peak body comprised of twenty-one industrial sector unions.[18] State control of organized labor reached new heights in 1985, when the FBSI was replaced by a single union called the All-Indonesia Workers' Union (SPSI, *Serikat Pekerja Seluruh Indonesia*).[19]

Suharto's New Order imposed a series of structural and ideological controls on the forms of representation available to workers.[20] Structurally, workers were integrated into the New Order's broader system of organic state corporatism, in which designated social interest groups (including labor, but also groups such as women and youth) were each "represented" by a single, state-sanctioned mass movement organization.[21] Ideologically, labor unions, along with the other "functional group" organizations in the system, were expected to promote the interests of the "community" as a whole rather than the interests of their members. This had very real consequences for the nature of unionism, and the state-sanctioned union's relationship with its worker-members. There was little pretence of electoral labor union democracy in New Order Indonesia, as the state both provided the bulk of the union's financial resources and appointed union officials – many of whom were bureaucrats or even entrepreneurs.[22] Although the SPSI was officially restructured as a federation in 1993 (FSPSI, *Federasi Serikat Pekerja Seluruh Indonesia*) and unaffiliated enterprise unions were permitted from 1994, little real change was achieved before the fall of the Suharto presidency in 1998.[23] In practice, the New Order government effectively maintained a one-union policy by preventing alternative unions organizing above plant level.[24]

It was in this context that NGOs became involved in labor organizing in Indonesia in the 1980s and 1990s.[25] The first labor NGOs were established by disenchanted unionists and human rights activists between 1978 and 1985. By 1991, labor NGOs had become the major proponent of the right to form independent workers' organizations, and, by 1998, more than a dozen labor NGOs had emerged in the regions of Greater Jakarta and West Java alone, whilst others were established in the industrial cities of Surabaya and Medan, and later in less industrialized cities and provincial towns.[26]

Unlike the Philippines or Malaysia, where labor NGOs have mostly been active on the fringes of traditional labor union activity,[27] Indonesia's labor NGOs engaged very broadly in the labor movement. In addition to the advocacy, educative, and campaign functions commonly associated with labor NGOs worldwide, Indonesia's labor NGOs became involved in grassroots industrial organizing, generally considered the heartland of union activity in other countries. Individual NGOs concerned with industrial labor tended to adopt one of these two primary strategies, although some combined both.[28] Some worked mostly at the grassroots level in an attempt to compensate for the failures in the operation of the official union, using a combination of legal advocacy, workers' education, and associated activities, which usually involved either sponsoring or cooperating with workers' groups. Others focused primarily on policy advocacy or research, engaging in local and international campaigns about labor rights violations, publishing independent assessments of labor conditions, and attempting to engage the government in a public dialogue about military involvement in industrial relations and problems in the implementation of existing labor law.

Local NGOs became involved in labor issues precisely because both the state-sponsored union, and the state itself, were seen to be insufficiently accountable to either workers or the general public on labor issues. Consequently, their demands focused on the legal and policy reforms required to provide greater protection for individual workers and ensure workers' access to their collective right to form independent unions. Labor NGO activists' attempts to achieve better conditions for workers were not always successful. The limited organizational reach of these NGOs meant that they had direct contact with only a small percentage of Indonesian workers employed in the manufacturing sector. Their attempts to encourage the formation of independent workers' organizations (while quite fruitful in many instances) were also inhibited by a whole range of structural factors such as high worker turnover.[29] However, labor NGOs' high-profile campaigns on issues ranging from the minimum wage to military involvement in labor disputes attracted international attention and forced the Suharto regime to significantly modify some aspects of its labor policy. In short, while NGOs' involvement in labor issues theoretically threatened the public accountability of the labor movement by shifting the locus of labor movement activism at least partially away from labor unions, in practice labor NGO activism demonstrably increased the state's accountability to the public on labor issues through their advocacy campaigns and grassroots activities.

Labor NGOs – like other groups opposed to the New Order – were subjected to bureaucratic, legal, and even physical sanctions, including military raids and even imprisonment.[30] However, their links with international NGOs (in conjunction with their connections with key reformist figures within the political elite) accorded the mainly middle-class labor NGO activists a measure of protection not enjoyed by worker-activists. Courville notes that NGOs more generally are often criticized for their lack of accountability to the community as a whole,[31] but it was precisely because of labor NGOs' lack of integration within the New Order's corporatist system that they were organizationally more able to defy the New Order state than domestic mass organizations, including unions. This lack of integration enabled labor NGOs to circumvent anti-union regulations and criticize the New Order's labor relations policy and practices with relative impunity, because they did not directly challenge the one-union system.

In contrast, despite the NGO connections of two of the three "alternative" unions of the late Suharto period, these "alternative" unions fared less well, primarily because their stated desire to formally register as unions posed a direct threat to the New Order's one-union policy. The first, the Solidarity Free Trade Union (SBM-SK, *Serikat Buruh Merdeka-Setiakawan*), was never officially banned, but disintegrated less than two years after it was established in September 1990 as a result of disagreements about whether it should take an industrial or political role.[32] Two years later, Muchtar Pakpahan's union, the Indonesian Prosperous Labor Union (SBSI, *Serikat Buruh Sejahtera Indonesia*), was set up. Pakpahan, a lawyer and former labor NGO activist, was imprisoned by Suharto for his union activities in 1994 after the SBSI was accused of inciting race riots in the Sumatran city of Medan. Dita Sari's Indonesian Center for Labor Struggle (PPBI, *Pusat Perjuangan Buruh Indonesia*) was established in 1994, but was effectively destroyed in mid-1996 when Dita Sari and other PPBI activists were jailed for subversion. Although the SBSI survived and the PPBI regrouped after the fall of Suharto as the National Front for Indonesian Workers' Struggle (FNPBI, *Front Nasional Perjuangan Buruh Indonesia*), all three of those "alternative unions" faced far more serious persecution by the military and the bureaucracy than their labor NGO counterparts in late New Order Indonesia.

Tensions created by contradictions between labor NGOs' responsibilities not only to workers, but also to donors, the international and local NGO communities, and to NGO activists themselves, were evident throughout the 1990s.[33] Interviews with activists conducted in 1999, 2000, and 2001 found that criticisms made of labor NGOs by workers, unionists, and even labor NGO activists themselves, centered on a number of interrelated concerns. The first of these was individual and organizational competition, driven at least in part by the strong convictions of the middle-class activists that control most labor NGOs and in part by pressures to appear more successful than other labor NGOs in order to compete for donor funding. Activists interviewed referred to both "individual egotism" (for example, personally claiming credit for organizing a campaign actually organized by a number of NGO activists) and "institutional egotism" (for example, claiming credit for a demonstration actually organized by either workers or another labor NGO). The second major concern identified by interviewees was donors' priorities, which respondents saw as a major force driving labor NGOs' agendas, particularly where funding was project-based. Donors' priorities (and accompanying funding opportunities) can divert NGO activists' attention from existing projects, and determine what new projects are established. Respondents argued that changing donor priorities demonstrably created a series of "fads" where labor NGOs almost all suddenly turned their attention to a particular issue (such as gender) for which funding was available. A related concern identified in these interviews was that labor NGOs' need to ensure their organizational viability often resulted in conflict between their interests and the interests of workers, for example, cases where labor NGOs had insisted that the worker groups they sponsored deal with a donor through the NGO rather than by approaching the donor directly, or where labor NGOs stopped supporting particular worker-activists because they had established contact with a rival labor NGO.

As labor NGOs have no formal mechanisms through which they are held accountable to workers involved in their programs, it can be argued that workers have little means to hold NGOs accountable beyond choosing whether or not to participate in activities sponsored by a particular NGO. However, this logic does not explain why similar criticisms were made about the alternative unions of the period. Although all three alternative unions were headed by non-worker labor activists, relied on financial and political support from overseas, and had no formal access to the machinery of industrial relations, structurally they were very different from the labor NGOs. In contrast to the labor NGOs' closed membership structure, they were open-membership organizations that had worker-members to whom they were formally accountable. Nevertheless they too were criticized for using workers for their own ends, and were accused of being captured by personal or institutional egotism.[34]

Worker criticisms of both labor NGOs and independent unions were voiced much more openly after the fall of Suharto.[35] Initially, it seemed as if labor NGOs had outlived their usefulness after the lifting of policy restrictions on independent unionism by Suharto's successor, President Habibie. But many of the tens of thousands of unions that sprang up after the fall of Suharto were in fact yellow unions, sponsored by companies in an attempt to prevent independent unions from entering a workplace, or vehicles for individuals' or non-union organizations' political aspirations. Even unions genuinely concerned with their worker-members faced many of the same challenges experienced by labor NGOs. Despite independent labor unions' newfound ability to organize openly, access the shop floor, and engage in collective bargaining, they continued to suffer from the same general kinds of accountability problems as those which plagued labor NGOs.

Like labor NGOs, Indonesia's new unions tend to be driven by individual personalities. Although these unions are theoretically electorally accountable to their members, in fact, as Gerard Greenfield notes, many union leaders "are not directly elected by the rank-and-file, but are appointed by a central executive committee which itself is not elected but is decided through closed discussion among an elite core of activists."[36] This has been a problem not only in small unions or in the local branches of large unions, but also in major independent unions, most notably the SBSI (which was restructured after the fall of Suharto as a Confederation known as the KSBSI). Muchtar Pakpahan continued to serve as the union's chair despite criticisms from his former NGO colleagues and some worker-activists who felt that the union should be headed by a worker rather than a non-worker intellectual, and in 2002–2003, the KSBSI experienced a major split as a result of accusations that Pakpahan was politicizing the union and using union resources to promote his political party.[37]

Accountability problems are also evident in unions' funding arrangements. All three major union confederations claim large numbers of members and all have intricate funding formulae, but the majority of their members are not due-paying.[38] The issue of due collection is a complex one because the low earning base of most Indonesian workers restricts the levels at which dues can be set. In addition, the availability of relatively large amounts of external funding has made the difficult work of due collection unattractive, especially for large unions, whilst at the same time leaving unions vulnerable to pressure from donors. For example, the KSBSI's triennial report shows that member income accounted for just 2.3 percent of its total income in the period between May 2000 and February 2003. Some 84 percent of the KSBSI's income in that same period came from overseas donations, whilst a further 3.5 percent was obtained in the form of overseas loans.[39]

Most importantly, perhaps, foreign interest groups have also been very active in directly reshaping the Indonesian labor movement. In August 1998, the American solidarity organization, the ACILS, supported a split in the FSPSI, the official union of the New Order period, which resulted in the formation of FSPSI-*Reformasi*. In 1999, the ACILS sponsored again the creation of new peak union bodies, neither of which survived.[40] Finally, in 2002, the Indonesian Trade Union Congress (KSPI, *Kongres Serikat Pekerja Indonesia*) was established, this time with the tacit support of the ICXTU. The KSBSI continued to receive significant training and financial support from the ACILS, as did even the FNPBI, despite its focus on political action rather than factory-based organizing.[41]

III. WEBS OF ACCOUNTABILITY

The similarities described here between the limits on labor unions' and labor NGOs' levels of accountability to workers can be at least partially explained by the context in which they operate. Although the Indonesian labor movement had a relatively strong organizational culture before Suharto came to power in 1967, the long years of the New Order destroyed much of that culture, leaving workers suspicious of unionism (because of its perceived associations with communism) and unused to demanding accountability from union leaders.[42] Indeed, a strong focus in labor NGOs' educational programs both before and after the fall of Suharto has been to train workers to expect – and implement – democratic procedures in their organizations. However, structurally, Indonesian unions face a much bigger challenge than their poor internal procedures: like labor NGOs, they are embedded in a web of non-worker accountability that diminishes their ability to be accountable to workers.

The webs of accountability that ensnare Indonesia's labor unions and labor NGOs have both international and domestic dimensions. Labor NGOs and unions are heavily influenced by organizations based outside Indonesia, primarily international unions, transnational union solidarity organizations (some of which are structured as NGOs), and international NGOs. Indonesian unions and labor NGOs rely heavily on the same set of international donors for funding, which is either project- or time-based. For example, the Netherlands Organization for International Development Cooperation (NOVIB, *Nederlandse Organisatie voor Internationale Bijstand*) provided recurring base funding for some NGO-sponsored workers' groups which succeeded in registering as unions after 1998, while the German labor NGO, the Friedrich Ebert Foundation (FES, *Friedrich Ebert Stiftung*), has been a long-time contributor to union training programs and NGO initiatives. For example, the FES funded an NGO labor clipping service, *Problema*, for approximately a decade beginning in the early 1990s.[43] Some solidarity organizations worked primarily with the official union during the Suharto period (for example the Australian Council of Trade Unions' solidarity NGO, APHEDA). Others, including the ACILS, provided a combination of project-based aid and recurring funding for both labor NGOs and alternative unions. Although union solidarity organizations such as the ACILS have focused almost exclusively on the major union confederations since 1998, they continue to work at some level with some of the labor NGOs they formerly funded on a regular basis.[44] Meanwhile, international NGOs such as the Ford Foundation continue to fund a range of local NGOs' labor-related activities, for example the publication of research and worker magazines.[45]

External funding brings with it formal responsibilities not only for financial accountability, but for program design which meets the terms of reference (TORs) donors set out for particular projects. Although donor TORs do not necessarily set unions' or labor NGOs' agendas, they certainly influence them.[46] In addition, donor-funded programs can suddenly stop because a project comes to an end, or donor priorities change. While these programs are clearly aimed at helping Indonesian workers, workers have no formal control over their content or implementation – control they theoretically would if those programs were funded from union dues or on a user-pays basis.

Labor unions and local labor NGOs are also drawn into domestic webs of accountability deriving from personal and institutional alliances.[47] These internal webs are less formal than the external webs (particularly those that bind unions and labor NGOs to donors), but they are no less influential. As is the case at the international level, there is not always a clear divide between union and labor NGO networks. At one end of the spectrum, many local-level unions registered after 1998 grew out of NGO-sponsored workers' groups, and retained close (albeit often fraught) relationships with those NGOs.[48] At the other end of the spectrum, some key personnel in at least two of the major union confederations have links with NGOs, either as former NGO activists, or as worker-activists who were strongly influenced by NGO training. The strength of these union–NGO networks is demonstrated by initiatives such as the union–labor NGO forum initiated by activists in East Java in 2002. Furthermore, although conditions for labor organizing have improved markedly in Indonesia since the fall of Suharto, the organized labor movement is still far from institutionally stable.[49] Individual labor movement organizations rely heavily on the goodwill of others – goodwill which is often undermined by institutional jockeying for status with particular groups of workers or with donors. Unions and labor NGOs are thus also informally accountable to their peers – a form of accountability which, again, excludes workers.

CONCLUSION: THE ACCOUNTABILITY DILEMMA

There is growing recognition in the scholarly and activist communities that unions are not the only kind of organizations that can promote labor interests. Contemporary labor activism in emerging-economy contexts occurs through at least two very different organizational forms. On the one hand are the labor unions, structured according to long-cherished traditions around struggles to promote the common interests of their worker-members, who are generally drawn from a particular occupation, industrial sector, or region. On the other hand, there are local labor NGOs: closed-membership "other-centered" organizations of generally middle-class activists which work on behalf of "target groups" of workers.

Analyses of the form and focus of labor union and labor NGO accountability are largely predicated on these differences in membership structure and class background. The literature on trade union democracy recognizes that unions may be held accountable in different ways, but assumes that all unions are always – and only – accountable to their worker-members because those worker-members have a *right* to hold their unions accountable through electoral processes. In contrast, scholars emphasize the impermanence and incompleteness of labor NGOs' commitment to workers, based on suspicions about their motives and assumptions about their priorities. Evidence from the Indonesian context in no way negates the organizational differences between labor unions and labor NGOs. However, it does indicate that models of labor union accountability premised on a single, particular relationship between labor movement organizations and workers are fundamentally flawed. This chapter has demonstrated that the accountability webs in which Indonesia's new "real" unions find themselves are little different from those that surround the labor NGOs they are supposed to make redundant, which in turn suggests that public accountability is not as much a product of one's choice of institutional regime as it is of the micro-dynamics that shape the institution's needs and capacities.

CHAPTER 7

SPONTANEOUS ACCOUNTABILITY

Colin Scott

INTRODUCTION

Contemporary ideas about governance are dominated by a loss of faith in both hierarchical modes of control and state-centric conceptions of governing. This tendency has caused both scholars and public-policymakers to search for evidence that other modes and loci of control are or might be effective in supplementing or replacing hierarchy and the state.[1] These other modes include governance through networks and communities, governance through competition and markets, and governance through architecture. Contemporary analysis of governance invites us to reconceptualize governing and challenge the centrality of the hierarchical instruments of state law and institutions. Such a reconceptualization requires us to examine the full range of organizations and modes of control at play in any particular domain, for the purposes of understanding both how the regime operates and how it might be enhanced in terms of securing appropriate outcomes. It entails identifying the ways in which diversity in the modes of control matches diversity in the way that social and economic activities generally are carried out. This chapter extends the discussion beyond the modalities of control by focusing on the question of how narratives can be developed which might give some process-based legitimacy to those regimes which displace state and hierarchy at the centre of accounts of contemporary governance. In particular, it examines how regimes of accountability emerge more or less spontaneously and attach themselves to different regimes of control. My use of the term "spontaneous" here implies the emergence of accountability regimes in a manner which is neither intended (or wholly intended) nor directed toward particular ends. This is not to suggest that the actors involved in at least some accountability structures lack intention or views on ends, but rather that accountability regimes, overall, are complex and not liable to be the product of intended actions (and therefore not directed toward particular ends).

Accountability is traditionally defined as the obligation to give an account of one's actions to someone else, often balanced by a responsibility of that other to seek an account.[2] As applied in the public sector, accountability commonly refers to the hierarchical relationships entailed in the duty of public sector organizations to account for their activities to elected politicians, to the courts, and to public sector audit institutions (political, legal, and financial accountability, respectively).[3] The presence of this template of hierarchical accountability for public sector actors is a central aspect of the procedural dimension of legitimacy claims for the public sector, and is closely linked to ideas of control.[4] Only at the margins do accountability regimes have to be planned for any particular governance regime.

A common response to the accountability problems raised by the recognition of the heterarchical nature of contemporary governance is to identify deficiencies in accountability regimes which might be remedied by applying hierarchical and *ex post* accountability mechanisms to the diffuse nodes of power. Contrary to that approach, this chapter argues that different governance mechanisms bring with them distinctive accountability templates – the modality of control shapes accountability as much as the other way around.

We examine the potential for the phenomenon of spontaneous accountability to offer a superior narrative for understanding the legitimacy of governance as being rooted within the distinctive accountability templates which attach to the particular modalities of control. Thus markets, networks, and communities each have distinctive accountability features that are integral to their capacity to operate as modes of control. In each case, these accountability templates are in part spontaneous features and in part supplied by state underpinning.

This analysis generates a puzzle surrounding the existence of a less-well-explored fourth modality of control, said by some to be randomness and by others to be architecture, but which I will call more generally "design." However it is conceived, the problem with this fourth modality is that it does not appear to offer an accountability template. The limits to spontaneous accountability with regards to this fourth modality of control present an important challenge which is resolved in this chapter by suggesting that design, by itself, is less than a full modality of control, precisely because it does not create responsibility on the part of the regulator or human agency on the part of the object of regulation. At best, design is an adjunct to, or a technique available within, the other modalities.

More generally, robust accountability templates are likely to be generated where control is premised on a combination of two or more modalities of control such that hybrid accountability regimes are generated. Thus spontaneity in accountability tends to be oriented around hybrid rather than archetypical accountability templates. I argue in this chapter that such hybrid accountability templates are a product of evolution in particular domains. A central consequence of this understanding of the phenomenon of accountability is that its character is more pragmatic than planned. Such spontaneous evolution of the accountability templates observable within particular domains creates a problem for any attempt to conceive of accountability structures as being amenable to processes of institutional design and planning. While we do not question the possibility of making interventions to change the character of accountability templates, such interventions are, necessarily, mediated through changes in the regime itself which may not be predictable.

I. MODES OF CONTROL AND ACCOUNTABILITY TEMPLATES

The bias toward hierarchical modes of control evident in much thinking about governance historically has derived from the idea that governance is something that is done by governments through law. It may be more helpful to displace the focus on government and its various institutional forms (for example, departments, agencies, and boards) with a regimes approach of the type developed in international relations scholarship and applied to regulatory governance.[5] A regimes approach invites us to look beyond governmental actors to the role of firms and non-governmental or civil society organizations as powerful participants in governance regimes, in both policymaking and implementation, but also as originators and developers of governance beyond the state.[6] Firms have a key role in organizing their own management and compliance, but also in governing others through their decisionmaking.[7] Alongside this shift in organizational focus we need to consider alternatives and supplements to the hierarchical modality of control.

Social science analysis of mechanisms of governance has long recognized the existence of three basic modalities organized around hierarchy, competition or market, and community.[8] Recognition of the distinctive structures and properties of these three sets of institutions is said to be a defining feature of the modern state.[9] The search for the appropriate balance between these three modes of governance is one of the basic questions of contemporary political theory[10] and an issue preoccupying both practitioners and analysts of public management.[11]

The analysis of variety in modalities of control enables us to see the narrowness of conceiving of governance as consisting exclusively of what state organizations do using hierarchical instruments, whilst opening up the possibility of seeing control through market and community-based control as alternatives or supplements to hierarchy.[12] Whilst the existence of three modalities of control associated with the state, the market, and the community is well established in the literature, some argue that there is a fourth distinctive modality premised upon, variously, the possibilities of contriving randomness into the control of human behavior,[13] and the use of architecture as a physical inhibitor on human behavior.[14]

The analysis of these three or perhaps four modalities of control emergent within contemporary governance arrangements has been deployed chiefly with a focus on understanding the available variety of bases for governing, controlling, or regulating social and economic activity. Within the study of public management the analysis makes clear the possible alternatives to hierarchy and law as means for making difficult resource-allocation decisions, for evaluating the effectiveness of public services, or for steering such service provision in new directions.

My interest in this chapter is on the accountability implications of recognizing and deploying these different modalities of control. Each modality has associated with it an "accountability template" – distinctive features of the control dimension which map onto and generate distinctive dimensions of accountability. In the remainder of this section, we discuss each modality of control and examine the characteristics of its associated accountability template.

A. Governance through public law

Within a state-centric conception of regulatory governance, control is often premised upon the use of law to make rules or standards, the capacity of departments and agencies to monitor for compliance, and the power to apply or to seek the application of formal sanctions to those whose behavior deviates from the required norms. In practice, of course, much regulatory activity is rather less mechanical than the model suggests and involves the assertion of mandates over activities for which there is no legal basis, and responsive approaches to enforcement which do not routinely invoke the power to apply formal sanctions.

The hierarchical model of and accountability based on legal regulation of the activities of departments and governmental agencies is attractive because it has a good fit with theories of constitutional governance and delegation of power. It is a necessary incident of the use of public law as the basis for control.[15] For example, New Public Management (NPM) reforms have been advanced as significant alternatives to hierarchy in public governance.[16] But research in the UK found that NPM reforms, which involved a significant downsizing of the public sector, were accompanied by massive growth in ultimately bureaucratic mechanisms of oversight over public sector activity.[17] The observation that these oversight structures remain as strong as ever is a central basis for claims that the UK continues to embrace the regulatory-state model of governance despite these NPM reforms.[18] Within the OECD generally, the picture is more mixed, with evidence of effective enhancements to bureaucratic accountability template in some domains in some jurisdictions, but not in others.[19] In all this variation, it is possible to identify a distinctive hierarchical accountability template that attaches more or less spontaneously to the use of public law as the basis for organizational and normative control.

B. Governance through markets and competition

Control through markets and competition is premised upon the idea that the behavior of dispersed buyers and sellers, when aggregated, creates a discipline on all actors in the market determining not only price but also the acceptable ratio between quality and price. The central mechanism of this modality is competition. Thus a form of standard is set through the interaction of buyers and sellers, which also forms the basis for monitoring and rewarding compliant behavior through loyalty and for punishing deviant behavior through exit.[20] Markets are not restricted to product markets, but also include markets for capital and labor in which similar disciplines apply.[21] In processes of public management reform, one attraction of markets as determinants of how resources are allocated and used is precisely the tendency to remove from governments the responsibilities for these matters.[22]

Many market actors exercise power over others in a way that they are not simply takers of market signals as to the price and quality of products, but actually regulators of other actors. Thus insurance companies are key regulators of public and private actors in respect of their risk-related behavior.[23] Credit rating agencies similarly set standards and monitor for compliance in respect of the financial behavior of both firms and governments. The products offered in both these sectors are market-driven, but the market is for effective private regulation of other market sectors.

With markets we may want to analyze the strength of the pull of market mechanisms over decisionmaking and ask whether it can perform functions similar to more traditional accountability structures. Control through competition centrally involves the discipline that is involved in participating in a market. Accountability here emphasizes results.[24] The mechanism of "the invisible hand," as Adam Smith famously described it, is premised upon individuals acting in pursuit of their self-interest,[25] and it is those actions in aggregate which discipline others. The selfish pursuit of self-interest, as a motivation, is liable to be condemned within many hierarchical and community settings, but applauded within the market. A key feature of market accountability is its "intensive" nature and straightforward metrics of success and failure.[26] It is this aspect which has generated renewed faith in markets to exert accountability on public service providers under conditions where both more hierarchical structures of accountability and more diffuse structures of accountability (see below) are perceived to have failed.[27]

The introduction of competition also brings with it, more or less spontaneously, new forms of accountability. This is particularly evident in those environments which use competition as a regulatory device in the absence of markets or real markets. A key virtue claimed for publication of data about the performance of educational institutions is that it enables users of services to use the information to make choices. Provided users have real choices to make, then those choices create competitive pressures which simultaneously offer control over service providers and a measure of accountability for the allocation, quality, and, sometimes, price of those services. In the absence of such competitive pressures, the management by public (and private) sector actors of contracts for the provision of services can prove to be very difficult – it involves the substitution of contracts for the assertion of hierarchical accountability rather than the application of the market accountability template.[28] A key example of conditions under which competition operates to create an accountability template for governments occurs where regulatory regimes are in competition with each other to attract inward investment. The desire to attract investment may exert a downward pull on the stringency of regulatory rules to balance the upward pull which may result from constitutional politics.[29]

C. Governance through networks and communities

Activities of networks and communities are able to exert control both on members of and outsiders to the community in processes of "mutual monitoring among a band of well-intentioned co-equals."[30] The mechanisms of standard-setting, feedback, and realignment of behavior here are rooted in the capacities of communities to develop social norms and to police them through noncoercive mechanisms such as disapproval and, at the highest level, ostracization. Thus the central mechanisms of this modality of control are rooted in capacities for cooperation (and noncooperation). I use the terms "networks" and "communities" to capture the idea that this modality of governance may emerge in communities that exist and gradually develop a capacity for control over members, and in networks that are formed amongst diverse actors for the very purpose of building up a form of control built upon mutuality.[31]

Mechanisms of community governance are often institutionalized within discrete organizational structures. It has long been recognized that associations of firms either formally or informally are liable to "self-regulate" the behavior of their members. Such self-regulatory regimes often take on some of the characteristics of hierarchical control, with the promulgation of hard rules, systematic monitoring of compliance, and the application of formal sanctions for breach of the rules. This kind of activity may affect firms outside the association if they feel they need to develop or meet similar standards, and even if they decide to operate by different standards. Nongovernmental organizations not only lobby governments on regulatory behavior and performance, but also carry out their own standard-setting and substantive monitoring in fields as diverse as prison conditions and environmental performance. These activities are not restricted to the domestic level of governance, and have considerable importance at the supranational level, for example in efforts to plug the gaps in hierarchical control in European Community energy policy,[32] and for compensating for recognition of the limited capacities of national governments operating alone.[33]

Participation in communities and networks brings with it an accountability template which is a product of this particular modality of control. As with markets there is not necessarily a governance organization required to account for its conduct. Rather behavior which has governance effects falls to be evaluated and responses generated by reference to the communities' norms and processes of showing approval and disapproval – the "intangible hand."[34] The focus of accountability is oriented toward intentions, in contrast with hierarchy (actions) and competition (results).[35]

D. Governance through design

The existence of a fourth modality of control was suggested more or less simultaneously by Christopher Hood and Lawrence Lessig, though their analyses are suggestive of markedly different conceptions of the phenomenon. For Hood, the idea of randomness as a modality of control is grounded in the observation that uncertainties as to consequences and payoffs lead us to behave in certain ways.[36] Hood's examples are drawn from attempts to regulate the public service. He suggests that contrived randomness may be explicitly deployed in public management through the use of lotteries for making decisions on the allocation of scarce resources and the random assignment of unannounced inspections.[37] In both these cases contrived randomness is used as a form of control in conjunction with hierarchy and it must be questionable whether contrived randomness, by itself, is a free-standing modality of control.

Architecture has received rather more attention as a candidate for the fourth modality of control. It was the experience of attempts to control activities on the Internet which caused Lawrence Lessig to place particular emphasis on the capacity of software code to act as an instrument of control over the behavior of users in cyberspace. For Lessig, the fourth modality of control (alongside his other three categories labeled "law," "norms," and "markets") is architecture.[38] Thus, Lessig has revived arguments about the possibility of using physical controls over behavior as the basis for regulation.[39] Whilst information technology firms have made extensive use of this possibility, Lessig's argument is that software code can be deployed, like law, for public purposes.

Hood and Lessig's versions of the fourth modality have in common a link to fatalism,[40] in the sense that, when contrived randomness and architecture are operating properly, there is nothing the object of regulation can do to change the way these modalities are applied.[41] By the time the auditor has been randomly assigned to audit your tax file, it is too late to do anything about it. Control through architecture nevertheless involves choices about the built environment which simultaneously assert a standard or norm that is self-enforcing through the physical properties of buildings, roads, software, and so on. Thus a concrete parking bollard asserts a standard that insists on no parking in a particular location through physically preventing a vehicle from entering the space. The simple presence of a physical barrier determines one's choice – free will has nothing to do with it.

Control through design presents us with a significant problem in terms of identifying an accountability template. In trenchant criticisms of the architectural modality of control, Roger Brownsword has highlighted the extent to which this form of control removes human agency from the object of regulation. The aim of control through design is "to secure [a] pattern of behaviour by designing out any options of non-conforming behaviour."[42] We have no choice about whether to park illegally when faced with a concrete parking bollard in the ideal space. Similarly, we lose the choice as to whether or not to engage in Internet gaming of questionable but nevertheless possible legality when our financial intermediaries' payment software automatically blocks the transaction.[43]

This denial of human agency for the objects of regulation is mirrored by a lack of responsibility for the originator of the architectural control. Parking bollards cannot be complained to, and effective software-based controls cannot be worked around. (The possibility of arguing with randomized audits of inspections results from the appearance of an official with some hierarchical authority, and it is not the randomness of the relationship of scrutiny that can be then argued with). The absence of human intermediation means that the feedback loop between the monitoring and behavior modification function found with the other three modalities is absent.[44] In many instances, it may not even be apparent that design-based control is in play at all, or, where it is apparent, who has initiated it and for what ends. Lessig himself recognized that the deployment of code as a modality of control is liable to be less transparent than the use of law.[45] A key consequence is that the minimal accountability associated with explaining one's regulatory position is lost.[46] Brownsword suggests that, even if this problem of transparency were overcome through processes of deliberative decisionmaking linked to the introduction of measures of control through design, we still risk losing the form of accountability which emerges from the day-to-day interactions of those involved with other modalities such as law enforcement officials, market actors and community members. Without such human intermediation "designed solutions might become so embedded in everyday life that it is only outsiders and historians who can trace the invisible hand of regulation."[47]

This lack of accountability for authors of control, coupled with the denial of agency for its objects, causes us to question whether design is a distinctive modality of control at all. We have observed that each of the other three modalities bring with it a distinctive accountability template. With design, the features of responsibility, accountability, and agency can only be supplied through one of the three other modalities. In this sense, at best, design is not a freestanding modality. Put more forcefully, it is merely an adjunct or technique of the other three modalities.

II. SPONTANEOUS ACCOUNTABILITY

The argument about problems of accountability invariably starts with an observation about the virtues and problems of hierarchical (typically public) governance. Resort to markets and competition as modalities of control appears to remove bureaucratic obstacles to efficiency and innovation,[48] whilst governance through communities and networks appears to be valued as a solution precisely because it offers an alternative to constitutional governance and the capacity to get things done which could not be done by the state using hierarchical modality.[49]

The analysis offered thus far suggests that the problems of accountability that present themselves when governance departs from the hierarchical modality may be more apparent than real. It suggests that each modality of control (with the exception of the fourth) brings with it an accountability template as a more or less spontaneous incidence of the control modality. In many instances, the selection of particular modalities of control is made, with some deliberation, in order to invoke also the particular accountability template. Control and accountability are opposite sides of the same coin.

Thus, in some domains it may be appropriate to think about extending hierarchical mechanisms of accountability to embrace them. Thus self-regulatory associations may have their decisionmaking subjected to judicial review, decisions of human rights watchers, and even the scrutiny of legislative committees.[50] However, to apply such hierarchical models of oversight to market actors such as insurance companies and credit rating agencies seems less appropriate. There appear to be risks that asserting the mechanisms of accountability centrally associated with hierarchy over nonhierarchical modalities of control might rob these alternative governance mechanisms of some of their key properties, undermining the particular forms of responsibility associated with the modality.[51] For example, the creation of conditions under which civil society organizations compete with firms for the provision of contracted-out services neglects the distinctive benefits of community-based governance (and the potential for civil society organizations to do things the market cannot do) "undermining their distinctive accountability regime and eliminating the distinctive contribution they could have made to the overall accountability mix across society as a whole."[52] Tendering for government contracts introduces not only pressures of competition, but also locks contractors into the choices and accountability structures set hierarchically through government.

A central consequence of thinking about governance regimes, rather than organizations, is that we must then consider the aggregate accountability of the regime, rather than retain a focus on the accountability of some discrete governance organization.[53] As we will see, much of modern government involves a heterarchical mixing of these modalities of control. Conceptual problems of accountability arise because this mixing results in aggregate governance structures for which no single accountability template seems suitable. The notion of spontaneous accountability argues that we do not need to fear a mixing of accountability templates. The mixing of control will itself generate the proper mix of accountability structures.[54]

III. SPONTANEOUS ACCOUNTABILITY IN HYBRID ACCOUNTABILITY REGIMES

Oscar Wilde said of truth that it is "seldom pure and never simple." The same might be said of patterns of control and the accountability templates which are incidental to them. Thus far we have suggested that each of the three principal modalities of control (with the exception of control through design) carries with it a template of accountability which attaches spontaneously where the particular modality is chosen. The nature and operation of the accountability template is likely to vary in different settings. The study of any particular regime may reveal weaknesses in the operation of these distinctive accountability processes. It is common to find that the archetypical accountability template has been supplemented by other accountability mechanisms, sometimes drawn from other templates. Furthermore, regimes in which controls occur through a hybrid of modalities are likely to involve hybrid accountability regimes.[55] Thus public management reforms which have invoked the capacity of communities and markets as alternative forms for the delivery of public services, bringing hybrid modalities of control, are also likely to involve the generation of hybrid accountability regimes, which combine the features of two or more accountability templates. For these various reasons, hybridity, rather than purity, in accountability regimes is likely to be the norm.

We have noted that design-based control brings with it no accountability template. Accountability for design-based control measures is therefore dependent upon one or more of the other three modalities being linked to it, offering accountability rooted in community, competition, or hierarchy. More generally, accountability structures in any particular domain are likely to be more robust where two or more modalities of control are deployed because such circumstances offer multiple accountability templates and the prospect of redundancy such that the failure of one aspect of accountability may be compensated by the presence of another.[56] Hybrid accountability may not, of course, always be efficient. Redundancy may be valuable up to a point, but may also be costly in imposing excessive accountability requirements. More critically, the cross-over of accountability templates with other modalities of control may cause interference. Thus accountability templates which emerge in markets may be disrupted by the imposition of the hierarchical accountability template. Community-based accountability may be disturbed where the requirements of competition or hierarchy accountability templates intrude.

The hybridity of control regimes testify to the spontaneity of public accountability. The hybrid regimes discussed below invariably arose spontaneously. They nevertheless seem to work in acceptably accountable fashion. This combination of unplanned hybridity and undesigned accountability suggests that public accountability may be the product of techniques of control, rather than the other way around.

A. Hybrids in public government

Government departments and agencies do not operate only through hierarchical governance instruments. Observation of the "Japanese paradox" is suggestive of a system of governance in which "in terms of authority to act and intervene, the jurisdictional mandate as it were, government or the state seems pervasive yet its capacity to coerce and compel is remarkably weak."[57] Whilst Japan may be an outlying case, it is clear that governments in other OECD countries also exploit their membership in networks and communities to exert control which is not capable of being exercised hierarchically, but in which the state's position at the centre of information networks is a key dimension of its capacity.[58] A more recent trend has been the explicit harnessing of competition as an instrument to secure governmental objectives, not only through privatization and liberalization of utilities services and other state-owned enterprises, but also with services which continue to be owned and operated by the state, and for which there is no proper market, as with healthcare.

Similarly, a key aspect of NPM reforms over the past twenty-five years or so has been to supplement the accountability template for hierarchical control with other accountability forms premised upon participation in communities and networks. But accountability through networks and communities for bureaucracies is hardly new. Thus, for example, an ethnographic study of the UK Treasury undertaken in the early 1970s found that control over senior civil servants was largely based upon mutuality of esteem and respect which they sought for their activities.[59] Thus, to the extent that such actors were also subject to the hierarchical accountability mechanisms, they were operating in a hybrid accountability template. Many areas of public service have been deliberately disrupted through the introduction of control through markets and competition. Policies of privatization and liberalization of utilities sectors in many countries have involved subjecting service providers to the twin market disciplines of performance in capital markets for the securing of funds for investment and retail markets for competition for customers.

B. Hybrids in markets

Similarly, the accountability template for markets is not restricted to pressures of competition. Foundational underpinnings of market activity, such as the recognition of property rights and the capacity to enforce contracts, generate forms of accountability to courts which are hierarchical in character. In many jurisdictions, sellers acting in the course of business are subject to rules on honesty in describing products and general quality standards which do not apply to non-business sellers. Most forms of business association are subject to a myriad of rules on such matters as accounting and audits, and increasingly also guidance and codes on how they conduct their business.

Participation in stock markets entails subjection to a variety of forms of hierarchical accountability for conduct in the market to self-regulatory and/or governmental agencies. In many other markets, the incidents of participation include subjection to accountability to regulators concerned with such matters as protection of consumers and environment, occupational health and safety, and so on.[60] Recognition of the fragility of competition in markets causes hierarchy to be invoked, in the form of competition or antitrust law for example, to address various forms of market failure. All forms of business association carry with them hierarchical mechanisms of accountability, which are perhaps most pronounced for listed companies. In this last case, the concern is to impose accountability on firms and their senior employees to their shareholders.[61] Additionally, the market-driven behavior of firms can lead some to gain formal power over others.[62]

Thus, with the modality of control based in competition and markets, the accountability template may be centered on market mechanisms, but appears typically to invoke also, at a minimum, elements of hierarchy. We see this also in how the process of changing the accountability structures for former state-owned enterprises (often apparently regulated through community-type controls) has frequently involved introducing new layers of hierarchical regulation and thus also accountability to address risks of market failure associated with limited competition.[63]

Markets also frequently evince more communal modes of control and accountability. Empirical research has revealed that business people routinely ignore the terms of the contracts which underpin their exchange, finding appropriate solutions to disputes without recourse to the law.[64] Where such contractual behavior is premised upon trust in continuing relationships, the mode of governance is more akin to community than competition. Whilst some might take these phenomena as evidence that markets operate less than perfectly, for the purposes of this chapter the significance lies in indicating the hybridity of control (and thus, in my argument, also accountability) within market settings.[65]

Another key example of community-based control and accountability in markets is provided by the ratings systems developed by Internet selling sites, such as eBay, in which deficiencies of information that would otherwise create problems of control over actors frequently engaged in discrete transactions are overcome through the building of transparent records of buyer and seller conduct in sending out goods in accordance with description, making payment, and so on. A somewhat different example is provided by attempts to reorient firms away from operation by reference purely to market considerations through the corporate social responsibility movement, which invites firms to open themselves to some of the values and structures associated with community-based mode of accountability. The credibility of such corporate social responsibility practices is built not only on community-based accountability, but also on the techniques of audit which are associated with hierarchy.[66]

C. Hybrids in communities

Community organizations are also frequently hybrid in character. Community organizations which adopt charitable status are, variously, subjected to hierarchical accountability obligations to charities, regulators, and tax authorities so as to ensure compliance with charitable purposes. The use of formal organizational structures brings with it not only the accountability structures incidental to it, but also a sharper focus on participation in networks, both as a mode of governance and of accountability. Though such networks are a feature of governance and accountability for state and market actors, they are a distinctive feature of community-based control.[67] The power wielded by NGOs, professional associations, and other civil society organizations is often both substantial and more concentrated than is the case of public agencies.[68] It is vital for the legitimacy of such activities that there is a plausible narrative for their accountability rooted in the community-based modality of control and their embeddedness within networks, and/or derived from other modalities. Inevitably, participation by civil society organizations in markets (for example, for the provision of public services) draws in other mechanisms of accountability drawn from both competition-based and hierarchical modes of governance.

Similarly, self-regulatory regimes based on trade or professional associations may evolve in such a way as to substitute for the exercise of state hierarchical power and, linked to this, become targets of hierarchical accountability. A well-established doctrine in English public law has seen self-regulatory organizations such as the City Panel on Takeovers and Mergers and the Advertising Standards Authority subjected to the discipline of judicial review over their self-regulatory decisions for this reason.[69]

Indeed, governments may deliberately invoke such self-regulatory capacity as a mechanism for delivering public objectives, steering organizations toward the introduction or development of regimes of rules and enforcement over their members so as to stave off the state version of hierarchical control.[70] Self-regulatory organizations may choose to invoke the hierarchical capacity of the state as a means to increase the credibility of their community-based activities, creating accountability not only of their members but of the association itself to the state's hierarchical enforcement capacity or the "gorilla in the closet."[71]

Community-based regimes may similarly invoke the capacity of markets for supporting the control and accountability functions which cannot be wholly effective where the community in question lacks the necessary embeddedness with the firms whose decisions are critical to its success. Thus with the Forest Stewardship Council an accreditation scheme was created through the partnership of environmental NGOs and producers in which a central driver of take-up is market positioning of major retailers.[72] As higher education institutions have scrambled to recruit students (and sometimes faculty also) from overseas, national, and international rankings published in newspapers and magazines have taken on a significance that is based on more than just prestige.[73] The UK government has developed performance league tables for schools and hospitals and linked this to the right to choose service providers as a way of harnessing competition as a mechanism for exerting control over the quality of public service offerings, often alongside other modalities of control.[74]

D. Design hybrids

As noted above, accountability structures involving design are liable to be based in other modalities of control to which techniques of design have been applied. Thus the use of unannounced inspections for purposes of schools and prisons regulation is an adjunct to the hierarchical capacity of state inspectors to demand the right of access to such organizations. The use of software filters to block access to certain types of website is an architectural technique used both by market actors (accountable through sales figures) and community groups (mutually accountable to each other for their intentions) to offer particular opportunities for reducing the alleged harmful effects of the Internet.

CONCLUSION

In this chapter, I have argued first that contemporary recognition of the diffuse nature and fora of contemporary governance appears to create something of a problem for public accountability. Public actors are liable to perform their tasks through harnessing the variety of modalities of control, with an apparent risk that traditional public sector accountability mechanisms will be evaded. Furthermore we recognize the extent to which non-state actors play distinctive roles in contemporary governance, not simply through participation in processes of constitutional governance, but through the development of their own distinctive governance forms, rooted in the institutions of communities and markets. Conventional accountability narratives, emphasizing *ex post* and hierarchical forms of accountability, with only very limited reach beyond state actors, are unable to support the burden of providing a narrative of accountability that can legitimate governance structures involving diffuse actors and methods.

The solution to the problem offered in this chapter is to reconceptualize hierarchical accountability as but one of the available accountability templates and to recognize that diffuse modalities of control bring with them, to a greater or lesser degree spontaneously, variety in the ways of holding actors to account. I suggest that each modality of control has a distinctive accountability template associated with it that operates as a mirror image. But the spontaneity of accountability extends beyond these archetypal or pure accountability templates, and finds its most interesting and pervasive expression in hybrid accountability regimes which are a product of hybridity in the modalities of control that are typical of contemporary governance across state, market, and third sectors. Hybrid accountability regimes evolve in a way that might be expected to counter-balance weaknesses that are found in pure forms of accountability rooted in hierarchy, competition, and community.

Hybrid accountability regimes are difficult to locate and characterize with clarity. They are liable to change through indirect response to the changing structures of control within any particular domain. This observation makes problematic the argument implicit in Mashaw's chapter[75] and made more explicitly by others to the effect that delivering credible and legitimate structures of accountability is a matter of institutional design. Such an approach appears to risk laying a veneer of legitimacy through accountability over the accountability template which operates dynamically in any particular domain, with the effect of obscuring or stifling it. A more fruitful approach may be found in the empirical observation of accountability regimes and the development of strategic and indirect interventions to address identified weaknesses. Such interventions will necessarily affect not only accountability, but also the modality of control. The effects of such interventions cannot be calculated with precision, but may rather be directed at shifting the accountability template away from undesirable effects and toward something more ideal. Furthermore, such interventions, and intentions to steer accountability templates toward changed objectives, need not be a monopoly of state actors, but might equally well emerge from the institutions of markets and communities.

PART THREE

ACCOUNTABILITY AND PARTICIPATION

CHAPTER 8

ACCOUNTING FOR ACCOUNTABILITY IN NEOLIBERAL REGULATORY REGIMES

Christine B. Harrington and Z. Umut Turem

INTRODUCTION

As the US federal regulatory state formed in the early twentieth century, concerns about democratic accountability also emerged. How could non-elected, administrative officials be held accountable to public law values such as fairness, openness, and transparency (see also Chapter 4)? Criticism of the broad delegation model focused on the accountability costs of building administrative capacity. Yet, once the New Deal "truce" was reached,[1] liberal-welfare state policies endured through to the mid-1970s with judicial blessing, and more institutionalized methods of monitoring "bureaucratic drift" were put in place.[2] In the recent shift toward neoliberalism, however, it is claimed the traditional mechanisms of accountability, through which the "demos" holds public officials accountable for their actions, cannot account for administrative accountability. This chapter examines contemporary neoliberal US administrative procedure in order to better understand the logic and practice of neoliberal administrative accountability. Specifically, what are the sociopolitical and juridical features of the new market-based accountability? To what extent is this particular logic of administrative accountability transforming welfare-state mechanisms of accountability by infusing, if not preempting, the rulemaking process with institutionalized "consent agreements" negotiated by "stakeholders"? How capable is neoliberal accountability of redeeming its own mythic origins, which are located in a story about the "crisis" in liberal-welfare state accountability?

Beginning in the early 1980s, informal negotiation processes, along with other reforms such as cost–benefit analysis, were hailed by reformers as workable solutions. The most notable practice of informal negotiation in administrative procedure was the creation of "negotiated rulemaking" – allegedly a consensus process to craft an administrative rule *before* the traditional "notice and comment" procedures as outlined in section 553 of the Administrative Procedure Act.[3] Legal services entrepreneurs, such as the Harvard Program on Negotiation, and corporate spinoffs, like NDispute, claimed that by bringing together parties affected by, or interested in, particular regulations, informal negotiations between them would practically eliminate the "distance" between the regulators, the regulated, and the public. Alleging that "consensus" among "stakeholders" would alleviate an "accountability deficit" they perceived with traditional "notice and comment" procedure, advocates of negotiated rulemaking (led by the Administrative Conference of the United States, ACUS) urged administrative agencies to experiment with negotiated rulemaking during the 1980s.[4] The institutionalization of this procedure then followed in 1990 with an amendment to the Administrative Procedure Act titled "The Negotiated Rulemaking Act of 1990" (NRA).[5]

In this chapter, we analyze negotiated rulemaking as part of a larger structural and ideological transformation of the American nation-state, rather than seeing it simply as a solution to the problems of the administrative state – including lack of accountability. Other studies detail how negotiated rulemaking works, examine the extent to which it responds to the alleged "crisis" in regulatory litigation, and analyze it as part of the legal profession's "professional project" in the late twentieth century.[6] Our focus here is on its emergence within the current accountability struggle, and hence its relationship to and role in constituting neoliberal regulatory regimes. Conceptually, we treat the jurisprudence of negotiated rulemaking as a *form* of describing, containing, and legitimating controversies over administrative accountability. Our approach thus seeks to interpret the sociolegal meanings of the accountability practice as it is mobilized and justified by both administrative agencies and federal courts.

This chapter, therefore, is more fundamentally concerned with explaining how US regulatory processes are mobilized and transformed to effect state formation and development through law. We argue that, in the period of neoliberal development (1975 to the present), the state, its authority, discretion, and executive powers are consolidated.

Internal and external checks are becoming less visible and more difficult to mobilize against. At a less general level, we argue that accountability practices favoring "participation" and "transparency" among "stakeholders," such as negotiated rulemaking, are themselves a form of knowledge production. As such, they may have the capability of undermining the neoliberal search for accountability which they were established to secure.

In one sense, therefore, we view the institutional and jurisprudential logic of negotiated rulemaking in reverse form. Instead of seeing proposals for increased participation by stakeholders as a solution to an "unresponsive welfare state," we look at the production of this negotiated-participatory mechanism in terms of the kind of state authority and discretion it solidifies. This in turn may trigger a new crisis of accountability, this time for neoliberal regulatory regimes.

I. THE 'PROBLEM OF ACCOUNTABILITY' AND THE PRODUCTION OF NEW ACCOUNTABILITY DISCOURSES

We start by unpacking the observation that negotiated rulemaking is a solution to the problems associated with traditional practices and understandings of accountability. It is commonly argued that expansion of the administrative apparatus has created a crisis of *political* accountability, which is the result of transferring democratic authority to unelected and unrepresentative administrators.[7] A major strand of this analysis sees an accountability problem in the bureaucracy, where a great majority of decisions related to the lives of the citizens are made.[8] The main problem of bureaucracy and of delegation in this context is that the "chain of command" and the hierarchical structure guaranteeing bureaucratic accountability (via political oversight) are almost always broken. In addition, there are too many actors (elected politicians or high-level bureaucrats) between "the principal" (the public) and "the acting agent" (administrative officials) who make and implement public decisions, such that the accountability *relationship*, or *distance* between the principal and agent, is too remote to be meaningful.

Similarly, there is a general consensus in this literature on accountability that structural changes brought about by major transformations, such as deregulation and globalization in the post-1980s, produce a vacuum wherein traditional practices of accountability are deemed "inefficient." For example, the increased public/private blurring, whereby certain state functions are delegated to private actors, requires the creation and adoption of more "efficient" accountability mechanisms. Traditional forms of accountability are seen as too rigid to deal with the new, blurred boundaries. This is particularly so, it is argued, because "power" is no longer (if it ever was) centralized or hierarchically organized. New mechanisms of accountability are needed to more accurately portray and allocate responsibility.[9]

Related to this point is the view that the restructuring and rescaling of the state and the multiplication of the levels at which state actors and bureaucrats function (i.e. global, national, local, regional, etc.) brought about a need for novel mechanisms of oversight.[10] "In the new world of enterprising government," Considine suggests, "the public official is expected to both honor his or her official mandate and to move freely outside the hierarchical constraints of government in search of collaborative and quasi market relationships with contractors, competitors and co-producers."[11] These concerns about new ways of organizing public bureaucratic work overlap with the "widespread adoption of strategies of privatization, decentralization, and contracting-out."[12] And these developments, it is argued, require new mechanisms of control that go beyond traditional methods of command and control, or checks and balances.[13]

Adding to these factors is a more abstract and conceptually driven, yet equally significant, critique of accountability. This body of work begins by outlining the assumptions of traditional understandings of accountability. Accountability is meaningful only in relation to something else. In this sense, it is not *possessed.* There is always the "accountable to" dimension of any relation of accountability. Furthermore, it can only be actualized or realized in the existence of a relationship between the parties. The nature of this relationship is not a given, to be sure. It may be different in different contexts.[14] The "principal–agent" relationship, mentioned above, is perhaps the most frequently theorized nexus for constituting accountability. Fearon describes agency relationships as follows: "one party is understood to be an 'agent' who makes some choices on behalf of a 'principal' who has powers to sanction or reward the agent."[15]

Political accountability in democratic systems also depends heavily on this type of framework in Whig liberal theory. The "principal" is the public at large who "consents" to be governed in exchange for the protection of individual rights (life, liberty, and property). The principal ("we the people") delegates power to its agents (political parties,

MPs, legislature, the executive, judiciary, and administrative apparatus) and holds them accountable through various means, such as elections or legal mechanisms. Thus, accountability "focuses on the obligation owed by all public officials to the public, the ultimate sovereign in a democracy, for explanation and justification of their use of public democracy, for explanation and justification of their use of public office and the delegated powers conferred on the government through constitutional processes."[16] This "vertical" accountability coexists and may even interact with "horizontal" accountability between governmental agents or institutions.[17] Different organs of the government are accountable to one another, theoretically enabling a competitive system of "checks and balances" that limits the abuse of power, and is also held responsible to the public and its representatives.[18]

The concept of horizontal accountability applies more often to the system of checks on "bureaucratic" or "administrative" discretion. Indeed, the problem with bureaucratic accountability is that it has a weak relation to the public at large, since bureaucrats are not directly elected by the people. In this regard, there is no direct accountability link between the "agent" (the bureaucracy) that should respond to the demands of the "principal" (the public). Nevertheless, theoretically there are mechanisms to hold the administrative state accountable to the public. First, bureaucrats are accountable to elected officials. This creates a link through which the public can exert its influence on the non-elected segments of the government. As a "hierarchical" structure, which also creates low-level bureaucrats as subjects accountable to those in the higher chain of command, the mechanism is meant to create a system of checks that ultimately puts elected officials in charge of the non-elected bureaucrats. Secondly, the bureaucratic layer of the government is subject to the rule of law and accountable to the judiciary.

For a considerable number of scholars who are more interested in an analytical approach, traditional theorizations have become problematic. According to both Fearon and Ferejohn, for instance, elections, the primary medium by which the power of the principal is delegated to the agents, do not really work to ensure accountability. They are not, in other words, punishment or reward mechanisms through which the electorate plays its "principal" role.[19] Relations of accountability that link principals and agents in general are extremely complex and delicate in a modern democracy, so that it is nearly impossible to sort out a meaningful relationship between the principal and the agent, except at the theoretical level. These difficulties point essentially to the fact that the mechanics of accountability relations should not be taken for granted. Elections, representation mechanisms, and the relationships between politicians and the people, in other words, cannot and should not be theorized as problem-free, according to these accounts.[20]

On the one hand, scholars argue that accountability mechanisms we took for granted have never been sufficiently meaningful. On the other hand, it is argued that with the recent social, economic, and political changes, traditional mechanisms of accountability which locate the "power" in the ranks and hierarchies of government became problematic. This resulted in diversification of alternative mechanisms of accountability. There is a sharp contrast, in this regard, in US academic writings on accountability between the post-war period and today. In the late 1940s, accountability centered on questions of *accountable to whom* and *for what*.[21] In contrast, recent writings draw attention to systems or styles of accountability, such as "output accountability," "public/private blurring," or "network governance,"[22] rather than concern for who is answerable and on what issues. While only two decades ago "congressional oversight," "executive control," "judicial review," and "tort liability" were among the dominant mechanisms for holding administrators accountable,[23] now we are inundated with talking about "peer reviews," "benchmarking," "Neo-Madisonian competition" between different agencies, or "pools of experience" as parts of democratic experiments, or experimentalist governments.[24]

An analysis that accounts for changing accountability regimes as primarily the structural-functional consequence of changing circumstances tends to disregard the "political" dimension of transformation processes. While it is possible to detect some etymological or semantic "essentials" in meaning, accountability is fundamentally "constructed" and "reconstructed" in different social, political, and historical contexts. It is useful, therefore, to analyze the concept in *relational* terms, within the interpretative web of sociopolitical dynamics, rather than viewing it as merely an effect of changing social and political environments. In particular, historical transformations in the conceptual tone and repertoire of scholarly works on accountability, as outlined above, serve as a good indicator of the contextually nuanced nature of the concept of democratic accountability.

Pointing to differences in accountability discourses does not mean, however, that there is necessarily a lack of conceptual continuity over time. Indeed, certain continuities are obvious. Most importantly, questions of bureaucratic or administrative accountability are situated in, and related to, the larger issues of democratic accountability most of the time. There is a constant concern here with the lack of public control and the need for democratic oversight of administrative actions. Reforms are constantly being generated to overcome this problem.[25] However, the parameters of "who is the relevant public," "what is the scope of control," and which "techniques of monitoring agency discretion perform best," are three key features of democratic accountability that have changed over time. There has been a shift from emphasizing hierarchy, or "chain of command," to theories of "democratic experimentalism."[26] Core features of accountability are in flux.

As we note, it might be possible to explain these differences simply as reflections of changing political and social life. Alternatively, we can analyze accountability to see *how it is understood, shaped and ultimately mobilized as a powerful political symbol to legitimate a certain type of regulatory regime*. The strengths of this approach are that it locates "accountability" in concrete sites and contexts, and allows us to see the relationship between distinct accountability discourses and broader social, political, economic, and legal relations they are part of. By contrasting traditional mechanisms of accountability with emerging (current) conceptualizations in the discourses of accountability, we can determine and document the dynamics of "transformation" in the meaning and practice of accountability.

Our approach, therefore, shifts attention away from the qualitative and quantitative comparisons between old and new mechanisms of accountability (more or less; better or worse), to an inquiry aimed at understanding how the overall framework of making sense of these questions (more or less, better or worse), as well as the accountability practices themselves, are transformed during the formation of a new regulatory regime. In this regard, we do not ask the question whether cost–benefit analysis or market mechanisms provide better schemes for ensuring accountability. Our concern is with analyzing the sociopolitical web of relations through which the cost–benefit analysis or democratic experiments become the dominant methods for ensuring accountability.

The shift we refer to here is one that does not involve a total break with previously dominant accountability logics. Indeed, traditional methods and practices are still operative, yet emphasis is placed more on novel forms of controling and checking. Insertion of cost–benefit analysis into existing processes of administrative rulemaking[27] or experimental governing mechanisms[28] is an example. So, too, is infusing stakeholder participation into the rulemaking process, which constructs a totally different picture of the traditional relation of accountability between the principal and agents. The state, with its legislature, judiciary, and administrative agencies, also contributes to the production of this new discourse of accountability by emphasizing the need to blur public/private boundaries and elevating market values as the main criteria for judging "governance." These new discourses and mechanisms all build upon existing discourses and practices on accountability, but they are stressed and applied more often than their traditional counterparts.

For example, the emerging accountability regime still emphasizes "public interest" at the abstract level, and it is still possible to talk about a principal–agent relationship, even when, through the "networks" and informal mechanisms, the distance between the principal and the agent is eliminated. The conceptualization of public interest, however, is essentially reshaped to include a cost–benefit analysis through which market logic is taken as the standard for governing the public. Additionally, although at the abstract level it is possible to claim that network-driven accountability makes a strengthening of the principal–agent nexus possible, this dimension appears to get silenced, and networks and network governance are treated as goals in themselves, rather than the means to a substantive end.[29]

II. ADMINISTRATIVE MECHANISMS OF THE NEOLIBERAL STATE

The new generation of market forms of regulation *reconfigures* rather than *replaces* state authority. In the abstract, one might assume that state discretionary authority would "shrink" with the transfer of some government roles to private actors. But there are at least two counter-dynamics. First, exercising the power to design models of accountability and shaping the mix between "public" and "private" are within the discretion of state actors. Secondly, the decision by state actors to make some aspects of administrative decisionmaking immune from judicial oversight, as in the case of negotiated rulemaking, enables the consolidation of state administrative discretion early on in the rulemaking process "by excluding concerns of social justice in many arenas of public decisionmaking at the expense of 'rationality' and 'efficiency'."[30]

This exercise of discretionary state power in turn produces ways of governing that reconfigure the meaning of "accountability" as a public law value. We suggest that these are not "new ways in which states carry out their responsibilities,"[31] but rather they are what could be called "embedded options" pursued periodically under the exercise of agency discretion. To date, we have no systematic historical or empirical study of negotiated processes in US federal administrative agency practice. However, there is some evidence to suggest that negotiated processes are an important element in the dynamics of the administrative state. Cary Coglianese notes the "trade practice submittals" that were used in the formative years of federal agencies.[32] It is generally accepted that during the New Deal, both existing agencies and those that were created at that time employed hybrid public–private approaches to decisionmaking that relied on negotiation. In other studies, it is also argued that New Deal administrative processes embraced features of "corporatism," incorporating private actors through informal administrative processes for decisionmaking.[33]

We also know, in a general historical sense, that *how* agencies regulate is linked to *what* they regulate. For example, the rise of modern twentieth-century legal consciousness, which embraced stronger notions of public rights in administrative jurisprudence, followed the collapse of a stricter private law model associated with the late-nineteenth-century laissez-faire market economy.[34] If the collapse of legal formalism and the rise of modern legal consciousness are symptomatic of a more general historical relationship between economic philosophy and administrative jurisprudence (the political economy of administrative law), then today's juridical embrace of the "private law model" on the domestic and global fronts highlights a need to look at the relationship between neoliberal regulatory practices and administrative jurisprudence.[35]

Important jurisprudential and political elements of the current neoliberal regulatory regime formed in relation to new interpretations of administrative due process protections by the US Supreme Court. From the mid-1970s onward, the Court's majority preference erred on the side of supporting the "reduction of administrative burdens" in state institutions (prisons, social welfare agencies, schools) at the expense of limiting the scope of constitutional due process protections for individuals.[36] This was an early procedural indicator of what was to later come to be the procedural dismantling of some portions of the welfare state. These procedural due process cutbacks went hand in hand with substantive deregulation reform policies. In 1978, President Carter announced the first US act of deregulation, the Civil Aeronautics Board Deregulation Act. More than two-and-a-half decades later, privatization policies from both Republican and Democratic administrations have been able to organize neoliberal reforms in administrative procedure.

Judicial deference to agencies after the groundbreaking decision in *Chevron* constitutes one other milestone in the jurisprudential leg of the neoliberal regulatory regime.[37] Viewed from a broader perspective, *Chevron* indicated that the internal checks within the state that had constituted an important mechanism for holding agencies accountable would wither somewhat. This decision marked the beginning of the end of active engagement by the courts to define and formalize the boundaries of rulemaking in the 1960s and 1970s.[38]

The key sociopolitical forces at work in this recent period of regulatory change are three-fold. First, there has been increased pressure since the mid-1970s on state agencies to accommodate the policy and fiscal demands of private actors – also known variously as "deregulation," "delegalization," and "privatization." Secondly, new entrepreneurs have emerged in the nongovernmental sector of negotiation services (i.e. arbitrators, mediators, facilitators, neutrals).[39] And, thirdly, there has also been a broader cultural critique of "state-centered" decisionmaking, or bureaucratic decisionmaking, which market-based regulatory reformers use to produce a "regulatory crisis" (a crisis of legitimacy as well as efficiency) that can be cured if "stakeholders" participate more directly in regulatory regimes. These sociopolitical forces produce procedural and political change as they combine and overlap.[40] And, in combination with state restructuring, these forces are elements of the more general transformation toward neoliberalism.

Neoliberalism, itself, can be understood in a number of ways. In broad terms, the concept implies the (re)emergence of the market and economic rationale as the dominant organizing logic in the society. Referring to Karl Polanyi,[41] the phenomenon can be understood as the disembedding of the economy from the social and political. It emphasizes the rise to dominance of economic ways of thinking. In political economy terms, neoliberalism refers to the ideological and material complex surrounding the shifting regime of capital accumulation starting from the early 1970s onwards. At a more descriptive level, dismantling of the welfare state, erosion of social provisions, turn to monetarism in fiscal and financial management, tax cuts for business, and increasing disciplining of the state via markets and market mechanisms, can all be cited to describe neoliberalism.[42]

At a more concrete historical level, policies associated with Thatcherism and Reaganism, including the attack on the welfare state, increasing emphasis on individualism and individual ethics, and decreasing utilization of Keynesian economics can be counted among the pillars of neoliberalism.[43] These also point toward the idealization and iconization of the rational market actor, and thus toward the spread of economic understanding to the social realm.

This disembedding and rise of the market does not, however, mean a total "deregulation" or "delegalization" of state functions, as was generally accepted to be the case with the initial years of the Reagan and Thatcher administrations. Neoliberalism is as much about construction as it is about destruction.[44] Similarly, it has its own distinct phases, where destruction of the old structures is followed by the institutionalization of the new regime protocols.[45] In this regard, rather than a "weakening" of the state, neoliberal reforms reconfigure *how* the state operates.

State transformation and regulatory change, viewed from a broad perspective, are, in other words, parts of the neoliberal transformation that is taking place. This does not suggest, however, that the changes in the regulatory field are the direct results of such sociopolitical changes or that neoliberalism is a historically inevitable phase which is manifested in the institutional changes we view. On the contrary, neoliberalism itself is a construction, and the state, the judiciary, and the regulatory agencies for that matter, have their autonomous spheres through which they contribute to the transformation. In this sense, the process of negotiated rulemaking is not just a reflection of a grand transformation or a mechanism to reproduce fully the "logic" of the transformation, but it also contributes to the transformation at large. Once the political, social, and institutional forces "combine and overlap" and create fixations of structure and meaning, at least to a certain extent, those fixations, which we can call the transformation (as a process) or new structure (as a more or less finished outcome) can also have their transforming or reproducing power on different elements and dimensions of the transformation itself. In this regard, there is a structuration[46] between what we call the neoliberal transformation and negotiated rulemaking. The transformed state and the new regulatory regimes we are analyzing are thus neoliberal in that they are significant sites where the system is produced and reproduced.[47]

First introduced in the early 1980s under the rubric of "regulatory negotiations" or "reg neg," negotiated rulemaking is an administrative rulemaking process based on parties negotiating a "consensus agreement" that becomes the announced rule of the regulatory agency. The 1986 recommendations issued by the Administrative Conference of the United States (ACUS) encouraged agencies to "review the areas that they regulate to determine the potential for the establishment and use of dispute resolution mechanisms by private organizations as an alternative to direct agency action."[48] Negotiated rulemaking may be initiated by either an agency or one of its constituencies, who are the "interested parties," or, in the lingua franca of neoliberalism, "stakeholders." Under the authority of the Federal Advisory Committee Act of 1976,[49] an agency empanels the interested parties to serve as an advisory committee. The agency designates a "neutral convener" – a mediator or facilitator whose job is to identify the interested parties and the relevant issues. The convener undertakes a "feasibility analysis" to establish whether or not the parties, including agency actors, will agree to negotiate a rule. Facilitators or mediators are selected from outside the agency to help the parties reach an agreement on a rule. If negotiations produce agreement among the parties, a rule will be announced in the *Federal Register* and then a period for public notice and comment is set.[50] If a consensus agreement is not reached, the agency is left to determine whether it will or will not propose a rule based on some aspects of the negotiated rulemaking.[51]

As with other proposals for alternative dispute resolution (ADR), advocates are very enthusiastic about the advantages of rulemaking through negotiation. Specifically, they see the following advantages: first, negotiated rulemaking offers the parties direct participation in the process; secondly, the mediator is more active in "outreach" to the parties affected by regulation than in the "customary rulemaking route";[52] thirdly, the parties are engaged in direct substantive decisions rather than appearing as expert witnesses providing testimony before the agency; fourthly, the costs of participation are reduced because the parties need not prepare "defensive research";[53] fifthly, the quality of participation is richer because the parties are in a setting that provides incentives to rank their concerns; and sixthly, according to reform activists, regulatory negotiations cannot fail because "[a]t the very least, conflicts can be clarified, data shared, and differences aired in a constructive way[, and thus e]ven if consensus is not achieved the negotiation process will still have narrowed the issues in disputes."[54] Negotiated regulation is most successful, according to its proponents, when the agency participates, because then interested parties are more likely to participate to avoid the uncertainty of agency review.[55]

Leaving aside an assessment of the positive and negative aspects of negotiated rulemaking, we focus on the question of agency accountability in this process. We suggest that the practice of accountability appears to be significantly different in a negotiated rulemaking setting when compared to traditional methods. Negotiated rulemaking produces a seemingly more open and transparent regime, where private actors have greater opportunities to negotiate their views, which suggests that this is a move toward a market-based approach to accountability. We contrast this with the so-called "rigid" command-based political accountability structure and discourse of the previous era, which emphasized the principal–agency nexus.

This comparison suggests that agency accountability is reconfigured to expand "transparency" and "participation" for nongovernmental actors, while mechanisms to ensure public accountability, such as judicial review, are minimized. Thus neoliberal regulatory regimes are creating new, and more "flexible" discretionary fields for state agencies. Based on our analysis of how reviewing courts have interpreted agency discretion to use negotiated rulemaking, and our analysis of negotiated rulemaking in practice, we suggest that this reform represents a deeper structural and ideological transformation within the state.

One need not argue, however, that current market approaches are no more than a return of the "laissez-faire"[56] in order to justify the need to reemphasize public law values. A serious analysis would seek to include those values that are discarded, as well as those that are embraced, so as to comprehensively specify the constitutive elements of the procedural change. If we understand these elements as tensions within liberalism – a conflict within a consensus – we may then ask different questions, and consider different answers as well, about "accountability" as it is being configured today. The importance of this theoretical point is that we are concerned with knowing what happens during periods of political change – periods when state actors in administrative agencies alter how they make rules in order to incorporate nongovernmental actors in regulatory policymaking. How are public law values, such as "transparency, participation, and fairness," reconceptualized and reconfigured through negotiated rulemaking?

If the regulatory state has embraced negotiated regulation as one way to manage the policy and fiscal demands of private actors, so too has the construction of a new regime of accountability ended up managing two different kinds of "legitimation crises."[57] On the one hand, there is the "legitimation crisis" that proponents of negotiated rulemaking perceive is being produced by "state-centered" "traditional administrative decisionmaking," that they allege is evidenced by a rise in regulatory litigation.[58] ADR proponents argue that this can be cured with increased transparency and participation for nongovernmental stakeholders in negotiation processes, such as negotiated rulemaking. On the other hand, there is a second kind of "legitimation crisis" arising for the state if it is not able to ensure that market approaches serve no more than private interests – capture theory all over again.[59]

Herein lies a fundamental paradox of neoliberal regulatory regimes: because "participation" is an important symbolic political and cultural resource in this particular regulatory reform,[60] and because participation is also an essential public law value, what happens when transparency and participation are "maximized" for nongovernmental actors but "minimized" for the public at large?[61] What are the downsides for democratic accountability when the administrative state adapts public law values by incorporating market approaches? In other words, while market-oriented regulatory reformers see a cure for the "legitimation crisis" of traditional administrative decisionmaking, will the administrative state nonetheless be left to manage a different sort of "crisis of legitimacy" produced by this market approach itself?[62]

"Stakeholder" participation in the rulemaking process, as in negotiated rulemaking, transforms accountability in an important respect. The agency representative joins the rulemaking process as the "convener", but a convener who appears to be on an equal footing with those parties whose interests are being regulated. This structure blurs the distance, perhaps even erases the difference, between the principal and the agent. Since the decisions are taken and the rules are made by the participation of the private actors, it is difficult to talk about separate principals and agents. This, as a result, destroys to a great extent the architecture on which the traditional accountability regime is built, the principal–agent nexus. In other words, "participation" replaces the principal–agent nexus in the neoliberal regime.

Similarly, the notion of transparency is frequently stressed in the negotiated rulemaking process in particular, and in neoliberal regulatory regimes in general, as a "public value" assumed to increase public input as well as oversight of the administrative process. In the neoliberal regulatory regime, transparency becomes synonymous with "accountability," such that the "answerability" and "enforcement" dimensions of accountability, highlighted in the traditional understanding of the concept, get lost. In addition to redrawing the conceptual boundaries of accountability (the public–private relationship), the criteria used to hold agencies accountable is also transformed. An emphasis on cost–benefit analysis, as well as new ways this analysis is carried out through statistical aggregation of "risks and benefits," all point toward the transformation of accountability in the administrative law field.

To a certain extent, these shifts may be viewed by some as a cure for the "democratic deficit" in the bureaucracy as well as a solution for "inefficiency." There is more to these shifts in accountability, however. The public–private blurring, delegation of state responsibilities to the market, or democratic deliberation and participation do not fully capture the transformations that are taking place in the field of accountability. What we have found in our fieldwork on regulatory negotiation, as well as in our LEXIS search on the subject, is telling in this regard. These findings, which we are going to elaborate on in the next sections, show basically that the agencies who carry out negotiated rulemaking are almost immune from judicial review with regard to their practice of negotiated rulemaking.

Administrative immunity in this instance is a result of the statutory design of the Negotiated Rulemaking Act and the uniform deference courts affirm to the independence and discretion of the agencies who are engaged in negotiated rulemaking. Market forms of accountability are sufficient to "legitimate" agency action simply by being embedded in agency decisionmaking. The essential mechanism for holding agencies accountable, judicial review, then become inoperative.

A neoliberal regime of accountability has emerged through state institutions, such as Congress and the courts. "Participation" and "transparency," the neoliberal criteria for judging accountability, shifts from the political and public interest realms to a more market-based paradigm of private interests. This generates, on the one hand, solutions to the legitimacy crisis concerning the democratic deficit of bureaucracy. On the other hand, however, and paradoxically, such democratic deficit is not being fixed at all. Instead, as we will demonstrate in the next section, this reconfiguration of accountability opens up more discretionary space for state actors and agencies. So, although mechanisms of accountability begin to include market-based structures and incentives, as well as public participation, the regime of accountability does not result in a "contract among stakeholders."

III. NEGOTIATED RULEMAKING JURISPRUDENCE

The context for negotiated rulemaking jurisprudence is the increasing willingness on the part of the US Supreme Court and Congress to enable discretionary decisionmaking by agencies. The Court was a leader in shaping administrative procedural reform in this direction – reform that eventually cut across many public institutions.[63] It might be argued that negotiated processes have *always* been available to agencies as one method for making administrative decisions. In this sense, negotiated rulemaking is not an exception to the broader norms of administrative practice, but rather it is an "embedded option." Indeed, as we mentioned above, it is an embedded option, but what makes neoliberal negotiated processes distinctive is that this option is now formally recognized and recommended,[64] authorized under an amendment to the APA,[65] and even required by some legislation (see below).

Judicial review of agency decisions is one way agencies are theoretically held accountable for their actions. The NRA, however, precludes judicial review of "any agency action relating to establishing, assisting, or terminating a negotiated rulemaking committee under this subchapter."[66] Our LEXIS search of federal court decisions from 1980 to 2004 found that, while this preclusion has not been challenged per se, several other challenges to it have been raised by nongovernmental actors.[67] These disputes and judicial interpretations are an aspect of current negotiated rulemaking jurisprudence. Four themes emerged from our research, which taken together form a jurisprudence that not only broadly defers to agency discretion to convene a negotiated rulemaking process, but supports greater "administrative flexibility" as a central goal of this procedural option.

A. Are agencies mandated to convene negotiated rulemaking under the NRA?

In *Texas Office of Public Utility Counsel* v. *FCC*,[68] the Fifth Circuit rejected the argument put forward by the Texas Public Utility that the

FCC's private contact with interested parties must trigger procedural mandates of the Negotiated Rulemaking Act of 1990. Judge Emilio M. Garza ruled that the "plain language of the statute undermines the notion that the NRA's procedures are mandatory," and that the "substantive provisions of the statute further reinforce the permissive nature of the NRA."[69]

According to the court, there is no specific action that could "trigger" negotiated rulemaking other than the explicit decision of the agency. If an agency has "private contact" with "interested parties," the court maintained, that does not impose a procedural mandate on the agency to establish a negotiated rulemaking process under the NRA. The court interprets the statute as creating a procedural option not a procedural mandate.

B. If a statute mandates negotiated rulemaking, is there a right to participate?

In *Center for Law and Education, et al.* v. *Department of Education*,[70] District Court Judge John D. Bates (who also accepted the agency's argument that the court lacks jurisdiction over the dispute because the No Children Left Behind Act (NCLBA)[71] incorporated, by reference, the NRA and its preclusion of judicial review[72] agreed with the agency that there is no right to participate in a negotiated rulemaking committee. Plaintiff, a public interest law firm, was excluded by the Department of Education from a negotiated rulemaking process. The plaintiffs sought a preliminary injunction (1) to enjoin the negotiated rulemaking process until a new committee, with a more "equitable balance" representing educators and education officials, could be appointed; and (2) to prohibit the Department of Education from using any proposed rules approved by the existing committee on the ground that the plaintiffs would be "harmed by the ongoing injury to their right of participation, and that parents and students will be harmed by the risk of a final regulation that fails to account for their interests."[73] Judge Bates denied the preliminary injunction.

Judge Bates maintained that the House Conference Report – which the plaintiffs had argued intended that representatives of program beneficiaries (i.e. parents and students) constitute a majority of the committee – intended only that the Secretary select individuals to participate in the Title I negotiated rulemaking in numbers that will provide an equitable balance between representatives of parents and students and representatives of educators and education officials. The report's drafters did not, in the court's view, intend this language to require strict numerical equality or comparability among these representatives.[74] Here, the court held that the drafters intended the Secretary to have "flexibility in selecting the conferees," while ensuring that the views of both program beneficiaries and program providers are fairly heard and considered. Administrative flexibility in selecting participants is affirmed by the court as Congress' will over an assertion by nongovernmental actors (public interest law organizations) that they have a right to participate in a mandatory negotiated rulemaking under the NCLBA.

It is interesting to note that, while the courts find some "inconsistency" between the "required" negotiated rulemaking provision in the NCLBA on the one hand, and the "voluntariness" of this option in the NRA on the other, this inconsistency does not entitle the court, says Judge Bates, to read into either Act an artificial distinction between "process" and "non-process" provisions. The better reading of section 1901(b)(4)(B), says the court, is that all the provisions of the NRA are to be incorporated except those that are inconsistent with the NCLBA, and those which are expressly exempted.

What may appear here as a seemingly technical point, is in fact a very significant turn in the ADR reform movement that is then embraced by negotiated rulemaking jurisprudence. Other ADR reforms that were also introduced as "voluntary" have also subsequently been legislated as mandatory. In the late 1970s, for example, ADR reformers argued that, because participation in ADR processes, such as the Neighborhood Justice Center, was "voluntary" (i.e. consent to participate), it would be a more legitimate dispute process than adjudication. We witnessed the withering away of "voluntary processes" in the 1980s and a shift toward mandatory ADR, where proponents now focus on the ends (i.e. "consent agreements") rather than the means. This too appears to be the direction of statutorily mandated negotiated rulemaking.[75]

Further, the shift from voluntary to mandatory negotiated rulemaking contains the seeds for a new legitimation crisis. Although proposed and represented as a mechanism to legitimize administrative rulemaking by adding a democratic participatory agenda to it, the mandatory move here risks deepening what ADR reformers saw as the legitimation crisis ADR was created to fix. Mandatory regulatory negotiation runs counter to the initial voluntary notion of a "democratic" procedure. Mandatory applications are also problematic if they are understood as in fact restricting access to a required administrative process.

C. What's at stake for stakeholders who agree to a consent agreement?

In *Association of American Railroads* v. *Department of Transportation*,[76] three years earlier than the two previous cases, the DC Circuit rejected a challenge by the Association of American Railroads (AAR) to a Department of Transportation (DOT) "technical bulletin" issued subsequent to a negotiated rulemaking process, that required railroads not simply to demarcate areas undergoing trackwork with red flags, but also to inform engineers of approaching trains in advance of the exact trackwork location within the demarcated area. That bulletin clarified a textual ambiguity in the Roadway Worker Protection Rule.[77] The Roadway Worker Protection Rule had been produced through a process of negotiated rulemaking. The AAR sought to invalidate this bulletin, arguing, in part, that their consent to the Roadway Worker Protection Rule during the regulatory negotiation had been dependent on an understanding that they would be able to use red flags alone to demarcate working limits.[78] They claimed that changes to this negotiated consent could only be made via notice and comment rulemaking.

The DC Circuit disagreed, saying that, even if crucial to the agreement, a presumed understanding about the proper interpretation of ambiguous text did not constitute a "definitive interpretation" of that text that could only be changed by notice and comment rulemaking.[79] Moreover, the court argued:

> If, as the AAR urges, the record in this case reflects a definitive interpretation of paragraph (c)(5), it would mean that an agency's initial, often chaotic process of considering an unresolved issue could prematurely freeze its thinking into a position that it would then be unable to change without formal rulemaking. Not only would this blur the distinction between definitive agency action and informal, uncoordinated communications, it would seriously hamstring agency efforts to interpret and apply their own policies.[80]

Although the court does not directly say "caveat emptor" to the AAR, the court in *Association of American Railroads*, like the courts in the previous cases we discussed, ultimately failed to acknowledge the "negotiated" component of negotiated rulemaking.

D. Are consent agreements legally enforceable?

In *USA Group Loan Service, Inc.*, v. *Riley, Secretary of US Department of Education*,[81] a group of corporations servicing federally insured student loans ("servicers") challenged a rule adopted by the Secretary of Education as violating the conditions of negotiated rulemaking. A 1992 amendment to the Higher Education Act, under which the regulation was promulgated, *required* that the Secretary submit all draft regulations to a process of negotiated rulemaking.[82] The servicers argued that the Department negotiated in "bad faith" with them. In particular, they argued that:

> [t]he draft regulations that the Department submitted to the negotiating process capped the servicers' liability at the amount of the fees they received from their customers, yet when it came time to propose a regulation as the basis for the notice and comment rulemaking the Department abandoned the cap. The breach of the promise to abide by consensus in the absence of compelling reasons not here suggested, and the unexplained withdrawal of the Department's proposal to cap the servicers' liability, form the basis for the claim that the Department negotiated in bad faith.[83]

But, ultimately, Judge Posner, writing for the court, maintains that "we have no doubt that the Negotiated Rulemaking Act did not make the promise enforceable."[84] He goes on to argue the practical effect of enforcing what was agreed to in this negotiated rulemaking "would be to make the Act extinguish notice and comment rulemaking in all cases in which it was preceded by negotiated rulemaking; the comments would be irrelevant if the agency were already bound by promises that it had made to the industry."[85]

Judge Posner's analysis of negotiated rulemaking equates it to the process of a settlement conference. He argues that neither can be expected or required to "produce a comprehensive administrative record, such as notice and comment rulemaking."[86] He further concludes that the servicers' conception of "bad faith" is based on a misconception of the negotiation process itself. For Judge Posner, the NRA's purpose was to "reduce judicial challenges to regulations by encouraging the parties to narrow their differences in advance of the formal rulemaking proceeding." This purpose, he concludes, "would be poorly served if the negotiations became a source and focus of litigation."[87] Here Judge Posner embraces the reform agenda of the ADR movement, namely to reduce judicial challenges to administrative rules. That agenda is not served if traditional forms of agency accountability, such as establishing a record (to enable transparency) of the process, are judicially mandated.

Our analysis of the emerging jurisprudence on negotiated rulemaking suggests that the federal courts interpret the NRA, as well as substantive legislation mandating negotiated rulemaking, as a resource for agencies rather than a right for interested parties. This constitutes an interesting dynamic in which private parties and actors are incorporated into the rulemaking processes, yet without having formal rights. The scope and limits of their rights, in other words, depend on the discretion of the agency, which gives the agency, and thus the state, an unprecedented power and flexibility to advance its agenda. Further empirical research is required to determine whether the exercise of this kind of discretion favors certain groups in society as opposed to others. What we can suggest, relying on our data and findings about regulated negotiation disputes in the courts, is that administrative discretion is consolidated – state power is amassed, if you will – while rights of non-state actors are formally weakened.

Empirical data on negotiated rulemaking also supports the thesis that a neoliberal regulatory regime does not displace the state, or even necessarily weaken its role in administrative decisionmaking. It may in fact formalize new agency actions that in a general sense will become "committed to agency discretion" as it were. Christine Harrington's two-year-long study of the negotiated rulemaking, convened by the Nuclear Regulatory Commission to establish a licensing procedure for the Yucca Mountain Nuclear Waste Repository, found that in practice the facilitator, Howard Bellman, viewed negotiated rulemaking as requiring more of the state by way of participation and commitment to making a "good" rule than conventional agency rulemaking.[88] Bellman viewed the state neither as a "neutral" nor as a "mission-oriented" actor. Instead, he operated from a "pragmatic" standpoint, wherein the best he can do is to try to allow the parties to have some "autonomy." For Bellman, negotiated rulemaking was "an opening" for interested parties to make their demands clear and get the state to do its work in a setting which he believed more fully exposed the state.

This aspect of Bellman's practice could be characterized as an unorthodox orthodoxy. That is, he rejected much of the "theory" about negotiated rulemaking, and hence thought of himself as unorthodox. At the same time, however, he embraced a traditional welfare-state perspective on regulation. On both accounts, he placed considerable responsibility with the sponsoring agency. Bellman described this as a "problem" for him in the contemporary ADR community. He thinks that most practitioners do not go along with his view of negotiation because he relies heavily on the capabilities of the parties and the sponsoring agency in particular. Given how Bellman staged the deliberations – his strong effort to place the "laboring oar" in the hands of the state – it may appear that the parties are doing all the work.

The process of getting the parties to realize "their investment" in a consent agreement combined two strategies in Bellman's practice. First, he continually reminded the parties that, if they did not agree to one part of the negotiated rulemaking, they would destroy the whole rule – this was an "all-or-nothing" procedure. Yet we have seen above that federal judges do not take this position toward the agency after a consent agreement is reached. The second strategy encouraged the parties to stay at the table by paradoxically telling them "you can leave anytime." Bellman led the parties to believe that, if they wanted to reach an agreement, it must be an agreement on the whole rule, yet they could "opt out at anytime." It seemed for many of the participants that they had little to lose by participating, but, as the negotiations drew to a close, many of the parties felt they had invested too much to withdraw. This did not mean, however, that all of the parties felt equally invested in the deliberations. In the end, industry did indeed "pull out" of the agreement, but only after it had secured substantial changes in the adjudicatory process for licensing the nuclear waste dump. The NRC, however, walked away with the central outlines of a licensing procedure which it would then publish for notice and comment in the *Federal Register*.

CONCLUSION

Several political and legal ironies of neoliberal accountability are revealed in this analysis. Although nongovernmental actors are incorporated more directly in negotiation processes, the absence of a meaningful judicial check leaves these actors in a precarious situation and status. They are ultimately subject to agency discretion even after reaching a consent agreement, one in which they may or may not have had a considerable hand in producing. In the final analysis, if there can be one at this stage in the development of this practice, the administrative agency is the key actor, the primary institution to hold accountable, but through what mechanisms? If the discretionary field created by negotiated rulemaking has no external mechanism of accountability then it is similar perhaps to an "autopoietic system."[89]

This does not, of course, mean that there is no blurring between the public and the private or that public functions have not been delegated to private entities. It is not so difficult to find examples of such blurring – regulated negotiations would be one of the examples – or detect instances of private actors taking on public functions, such as private prisons. The important point to recognize is that the authority to alter or play with public/private boundaries is located in the state, in the field of administrative discretion.

Forms of accountability that stress market norms may to a certain extent manage the crisis of legitimacy ADR reformers believe is the product of remote and opaque traditional administrative decisionmaking. Similarly, replacement of accountability by transparency or participation may prove to be beneficial in certain contexts. However, judged by other features of traditional accountability, the neoliberal form of accountability is unable to guarantee accountability in the current regime because agencies are immune from the legal gaze and the traditional methods of accountability are silenced by the formal deployment (statutory and judicial) of this embedded option.

A reconfiguration of the public law values such as accountability, transparency, or participation is taking place which may eventually be a cure for the crisis of legitimacy. Meanings of these three symbolically powerful concepts become intermingled – and interchangeable – during this process of reconfiguration. Although there is no more accountability in regulated negotiations in the traditional sense, participation and transparency in the process replaces accountability as a mechanism for managing the potential crisis of legitimacy.

However, neoliberal forms of governance and rulemaking still have the potential to generate novel crises of legitimacy. This is because in periods of political change traditional practices have not yet been fully replaced. Their co-existence provides a standpoint from which it is possible to critique an emerging new "doxa." This is not to say that, once settled and stabilized, new practices of accountability cannot be criticized; indeed, they can be contested on various grounds. However, after the meanings and institutional practices are solidified or once "closure" is produced, it is much more difficult to destabilize the taken-for-granted assumptions for the structures and meanings in the social matrix of institutions. It is therefore important to see both frameworks simultaneously in the period of transition to see what historical path is taken and why.

In this regard, all democratic participatory processes can be problematized. Democratic participation and a stakeholder model of accountability may work for those who are at the table or those who participate in the rulemaking process. For those at the table, rulemaking (not the rulemakers) is perfectly transparent and accountable and includes benefits such as "more learning," "better quality rules," and "more legitimate outcomes."[90] For those who are not at the table, however, there is a severe problem of accountability.[91] Since accountability is equated with participation and bargaining in the negotiation process, those who are excluded from the conversation are only able to hold agencies accountable through traditional practices. Given the impossibility of questioning the selection by the agency of who gets to the table even in the courts, novel discretionary powers are created for the state. Given this increased judicial deference to agency discretion,[92] one might argue that exclusions are even more problematic in the neoliberal regimes. Ackerman, for instance, claims that the entire system of negotiated rulemaking is inadequate if there is a commitment to democratic legitimacy for administrative rulemaking.[93] Public interest law organizations, such as the Center for Law and Education, are likely to mobilize against negotiated rulemaking (with the help of the transparency of the negotiated rulemakings) and challenge the practice of accountability as an exclusive benefit only for those at the table.

Similarly, the question of who participates in negotiated rulemaking with the agency and whether these groups or individuals have any representative capacity, and thus accountability, may trigger an important crisis of legitimacy. At a broader level, this can generate criticisms in terms of the principal and agent framework. The traditional understanding of accountability formally recognizes a public, which holds the right to keep elected politicians accountable. And elected politicians are supposed to oversee the appointed bureaucrats. In the neoliberal regulatory regimes, however, there is no unified or coherent understanding of representation. Industry representatives, NGOs, and public interest organizations certainly have always been active in terms of shaping regulatory policy. On the other hand, courts, both as part of the checks and balances system within the state and as part of "the state" in more general terms, acted in ways to complete the circuit of accountability, by acting as a forum where any citizen or group may go in the case of an allegedly unfair exclusion from the rulemaking system. Now that this forum appears to be no longer available, the checks and balances system within the state may be destabilized. Together with the opening up of new spaces of discretion, this destabilization is likely to produce a legitimacy crisis.

Other responses and challenges to neoliberal practices of "governance" that may accumulate over time include challenges to substantive policies, not just procedural concerns about accountability. Over time, the inner dynamics of negotiated rulemaking may reveal a bias in favor of "repeat players" whose material resources, legal experience, and technical guidance give them an unjustified advantage over "one shot players."[94]

Even for those who regularly participate in the decisionmaking process, transparency and participation alone may not mean much. In the absence of formal procedures, internal checks on discretion and a general understanding of answerability and enforcement mechanisms, an otherwise "transparent" decisionmaking process may not fulfill its promise of bringing about regular oversight, and "participation" cannot fulfill its promise of democracy.

Shifting the criteria for rulemaking from an earlier definition of public interest, to cost–benefit analysis, conceptualized in the last three decades, and consolidating this shift with regulatory models emphasizing private/public blurring, or stakeholder rights, ends up dismantling the previous regulatory system simultaneously with the dismantling of the welfare state structure of the postwar period. This may end up creating new crises of legitimacy, even as these new regulatory practices, such as negotiated rulemaking, seek to solve crises of regulation.

CHAPTER 9

THE MARK OF RESPONSIBILITY (WITH A POSTSCRIPT ON ACCOUNTABILITY)

John Gardner

I

We all want our wrongs and mistakes to have been justified. Failing that, we want them to have been excused. No sooner have we noticed that we did something wrong or mistaken than we start rolling out our justifications and excuses. Why is this? You may say the answer is obvious. By justifying or at least excusing our wrongs and mistakes we may be able to avoid shouldering some or all of the nasty moral or legal consequences of committing them. We may be able to avoid a liability to be punished or admonished, or a duty of reparation or apology, or the loss of a right to be rescued or compensated, or various other unwelcome changes in our moral or legal positions. In short, we may be able to avoid being held *responsible* for what has gone amiss. Ronald Dworkin usefully calls responsibility in this sense "consequential responsibility."[1] I am consequentially responsible if some or all of the unwelcome moral or legal consequences of some wrong or mistake (whether mine or someone else's) are mine to bear. Responsibility in this consequential sense is by its very nature an unwelcome thing to have descend upon one, and hence something that, all else being equal, any rational being would rather avoid. So, all else being equal, a rational being will resort to any argument she can lay her hands on that might possibly help her to avoid it. Which arguments will succeed in eliminating her responsibility will vary depending on what wrong or mistake has been committed and what unwelcome moral or legal consequence is stored up for her. But valid excuses will help to get her off the hook at least in some cases, and valid justifications more often. That is why it is as well for her to have her justifications, and failing that her excuses, at the ready.

This is hunky-dory as far as it goes. But I do not think it goes very deep. There is another deeper story that also helps us to see why, as rational beings, we might want our wrongs and mistakes to be justified, or failing that excused. It is what we could call the Aristotelian story. As rational beings we cannot but aim at excellence in rationality. The only way we have to question that aim – by asking "What reason do I have to excel at rationality?" – already concedes the aim by demanding a reason, by demanding that the case for rationality be made rationally. And of course at that point rationality makes its own case: what else could we have reason to do, or think, or feel, but whatever reason would have us do, or think, or feel? So as rational beings – beings who are able to follow reasons – we cannot but *want* to follow reasons – to excel in rationality.[2] One implication of this, among many, is that as rational beings we cannot but want our lives to have made rational sense, to add up to a story not only of whats but of *whys*. We cannot but want there to have been adequate reasons why we did (or thought or felt) what we did (or thought or felt).

You will not be surprised to hear that, at least where our actions are concerned, these rational explanations come in two different flavors, namely the justificatory flavor and the excusatory flavor.[3] The case of justification is the case of direct rational explanation. Under the heading of justification we claim to have done what we did for adequate reasons. More exactly we claim that the reasons in favor of what we did were not all of them defeated by conflicting reasons, and that our action was performed on the strength of some or all of the undefeated reasons in its favor. The case of excuse, meanwhile, is the more complex case of indirect rational explanation. We concede that we did not act as we did for adequate reasons, but we did act on the strength of beliefs or emotions or desires that were themselves adequately supported by reasons. Suppose that we injured someone in what we thought was an act of self-defense, because we strayed accidentally onto the set of an action movie and found ourselves caught up in the action. Maybe we did act excessively in the thrall of fear or confusion, but the fear or confusion itself was not excessive. We were not being hysterical or gullible in reacting as we did. Here the justification of the fear or confusion does not transmit itself onwards to justify the action that was taken *in* fear or confusion. Nevertheless it does excuse that action. Such an indirect rational explanation is obviously second best. It includes an admission of rational defeat: one was not justified in what one did. But it is better than nothing. It explains why one did what one did in terms of reasons, albeit not exactly reasons for doing it. And explanation in terms of reasons is what a rational being aspires to. That is why, as rational beings, we cannot but want our wrongs and mistakes to have been justified, or failing that at least to have been excused. This makes it part of our *nature* (in Aristotle's sense of *ergon*, purpose, destiny) to hunt for justifications and excuses as soon as we spot that we have done something wrong or mistaken – *never mind what unpleasant moral or legal consequences we can or can't avoid thereby*.

In my experience even the most thoughtful of lawyers tends to find this second story academic, in the pejorative sense, especially when I end the story with those words "never mind what unpleasant moral or legal consequences we can or can't avoid thereby." Even as morally sensitive lawyers we are prone to embrace and promote a largely Hobbesian view of human nature, according to which the only natural aim of rational beings is to stop nasty consequences, including nasty moral and legal consequences, from descending upon their own heads. The job of lawyers, on this same view, is mainly to make sure that the nasty consequences do not descend on the heads of their clients, or in the case of more crusading lawyers, on the heads of a certain supposedly deserving class of potential clients. Either way, everything comes down to who wins and who loses, who gets off the hook and who stays on it. To be fair, lawyers do often have to deal with people whose predicaments are towards the Hobbesian end of the spectrum: desperate people faced with the threat of prison or deportation or bankruptcy, destructively bitter people who have been betrayed and deserted by their spouses and partners, and of course corporations (to whom the Aristotelian considerations arguably do not apply). I am not encouraging lawyers to treat such clients to disquisitions on the deeper implications of their rational natures. But nor, on the other hand, should lawyers regard themselves as being professionally unaffected by these implications.

My favorite illustration of the importance of the Aristotelian story is an illustration from the criminal law. During the early 1990s there was in England a string of legally problematic and politically controversial cases concerning the scope of the provocation defense as it was available to women victims of domestic abuse who killed their abusers.[4] Various judge-made restrictions on the provocation defense (some of them hard to fathom) made it foreseeably difficult for these defendants to plead it successfully. At least some of them, however, could alternatively or additionally[5] have mounted a successful defense of diminished responsibility, based on psychiatric evidence that their long exposure to domestic abuse had reduced them to a condition of "learned helplessness" or had inflicted a similar personality disorder. The effect of a successful diminished responsibility plea, like that of a successful provocation plea, would have been to substitute a manslaughter verdict for a murder verdict. Purely from the point of view of consequential responsibility – getting off the murder hook – the diminished responsibility defense seemed to be just what some of these defendants needed. The sophisticated campaign on their behalf proceeded, however, on the footing that a diminished responsibility verdict, however easily secured, was not at all what these defendants needed. What they needed, even if it was bound to be trickier to argue, was a provocation defense.

Now why would that be? You may say that a finding of provocation sounds better, does more to rescue the defendant's reputation and perhaps the reputation of abused women in general, than one of diminished responsibility. But that just returns us to the question. Why would *that* be? The answer, it seems to me, lies in the moral and legal structure of the provocation defense. To successfully argue provocation, one need not argue that one had valid, let alone adequate, reasons to kill. One need not present one's actions as even partly justified. One certainly does need, however, to make an excusatory case. One needs to argue that, even if one had inadequate reasons to kill, one had adequate reasons to get angry to the point at which one killed. In the term favored by law, one needs to argue that getting angry to a murderous extent was *reasonable*. No such reasonableness test applies in the defense of diminished responsibility. This is the main reason why diminished responsibility is less complicated to plead. But at the same time the absence of any reasonableness test is also the main reason why any rational being would resist making use of the diminished responsibility defense if the provocation defense were available to her instead, all else being equal. By making use of the diminished responsibility defense she demeans herself as a rational being. She opts for a non-rational explanation of what she did, one that makes do with attributing the fact that she killed to her disturbed emotional condition. By making use of the provocation defense, by contrast, she defends herself against the same charge with her head held high as a rational being. She relies not simply on her disturbed emotional condition, but on the *rational defensibility* of her disturbed emotional condition. There were *reasons* for her to get angry or aggrieved to a murderous extent, and she got angry or aggrieved *for* those reasons, and as a rational being she wants the law to recognize this rational explanation. She does not want to be dismissed as someone who can't explain herself rationally, someone whose responsibility, and hence whose participation in the human good, was diminished. She wants to give an account of herself as a fully responsible adult, sane, human being.[6]

I may have used this illustration too often but for present purposes it does have a special claim to be mentioned. By introducing us to the legal defense of diminished responsibility, the tale of the provoked victims of domestic abuse introduces us to a second notion of responsibility, distinct from the notion of consequential responsibility with which we started. I will call it responsibility in the basic sense, or "basic responsibility" for short. Like any rational being, the defendants in the cases just mentioned wanted to avoid responsibility in the consequential sense; they wanted to avoid facing the unwelcome moral or legal consequences of their wrongs. But they did not want to do so by denying, or casting doubt on, their responsibility in the basic sense, at least not if they could avoid it. On the contrary, they wanted to *assert* their responsibility in this basic sense. They wanted to assert that, in spite of all they had been through, they were fully responsible adults. And they asserted this precisely by arguing that, although unjustified, their actions were excused. You may ask: "How can offering an excuse serve as an assertion, rather than a denial, of responsibility?" The answer is breathtakingly simple. Only those who are responsible in the basic sense *can* offer excuses. That is because responsibility in the basic sense is none other than an ability to offer justifications and excuses. In the idioms we more often use, it is the ability to explain oneself, to give an intelligible account of oneself, to answer for oneself, as a rational being. In short it is exactly what it sounds like: response-ability, an ability to respond.

II

I just said that only those who are responsible in the basic sense can *offer* excuses. You may think "offer" was a strange choice of word.

Rather than focusing our attention on the time when the wrong or mistake was committed, this fast-forwards us to a later time when the person who committed it is in the dock, literally or figuratively. At the earlier time we might say that the wrongdoer *has* an excuse; only at the later time can she *offer* it. Which time do I have in mind as the time when her responsibility is settled?

We are used to thinking that responsibility is settled at the earlier time, at the time of the wrong or mistake. Nothing that happens later can make a difference. When we come to the trial – or the nasty scene or the difficult telephone call – everything is in principle retrospective, including the question of responsibility. But I think this is a mistake. I think it is one of the many symptoms of a common tendency to confuse excuses with denials of responsibility in the basic sense. To assess people's excuses, as well as their justifications, we have to stop the tape at the moment at which the wrong or mistake was completed. That's because excuses and justifications are putative rational explanations of the wrong or mistake, and rational explanation is explanation in terms of the reasons that the agent had, and acted on, at that time.

But a denial of responsibility, not being a putative rational explanation of what one did, is not subject to the same freeze-frame restriction. On the contrary, one's responsibility, in the basic sense, has a diachronic (cross-temporal) aspect. I do not mean that the determinants of basic responsibility are status conditions, such that they necessarily eliminate one's responsibility for everything one does over a certain period. Some factors bearing on basic responsibility – such as infancy – do set status conditions in this sense. But others do not. One may be responsible for one thing one is doing and not for another thing one is doing at exactly the same time. For instance, if I am suffering from a delusional mental illness, my responsibility is only absent in respect of the actions which are explained by the delusions.[7] And maybe even the delusions are occasional. So I do not mean to suggest that one's basic responsibility, or lack of it, is necessarily an ongoing condition.

What I mean when I say that basic responsibility has a diachronic aspect is that in respect of any one action relative to which one's responsibility is in question, the question of whether one is responsible straddles the gap between the time at which the action was performed, and the time at which the question itself arises. It straddles the gap between the time of the crime and the time of the trial. The simplest instance of such straddling in the law is the argument of rational incomprehension that applies at the time of the crime under the name of insanity, and then again at the time of the trial under the name of unfitness to plead. One of these we tend to think of as a doctrine of substantive law affecting criminal guilt. The other we think of as a doctrine of procedure affecting the right to proceed with the trial. But in respect of rationale both are part of the same diachronic standard, which is a legal standard of basic responsibility.

So when I said that responsibility in the basic sense is an ability to *offer* justifications and excuses – or alternatively the ability to explain oneself, to offer an account of oneself, to answer for oneself – I meant what I said. I meant to refer to an ability that the responsible person has at the time of the confrontation with her accusers, at the trial or the public inquiry or the family inquisition or the exchange of angry letters, a time when her wrong or mistake is already in the past.

But I also meant, of course, to build into my expression a reference to the time of the wrong or mistake itself. An ability to offer justifications and excuses, in the sense I had in mind, implies an ability to *have* a justification or excuse. If you prefer to spell this out, you could say that basic responsibility is an ability to give a rational explanation for one's actions without giving one's actions any rational explanation that they did not actually have, i.e. without inventing reasons for what one did. Naturally we should expect some people to fib or self-deceive or misremember, to *rationalize* their actions *ex post facto*. You may say, indeed, that everyone has a tendency to rationalize. They present their reasons as better than they were, or they present themselves as having reasons when they had none. But I reply: no wonder they do. After all, as the Aristotelian story showed, any rational being wants to be responsible. The fact that people sometimes try to make themselves seem to be responsible for their actions by rationalizing what they did *ex post facto* is a sign of how badly they want to be responsible. They make themselves seem to be responsible agents by making themselves seem to have had a rational explanation, which they now present as if it were real, maybe even convincing themselves. Perhaps we should sometimes, for practical purposes, give these people the responsibility they want. Perhaps we should treat them as if they were the responsible agents that they claim to be. Perhaps they should still bear some of the consequential responsibility that they might bear if they were indeed responsible in the basic sense. But that is another question.

The key point for present purposes is that the ability that constitutes one as responsible, in the basic sense, is a *composite* ability. It is an ability which straddles the temporal gap between the wrong or mistake and the trial or recrimination, and which also straddles the conceptual gap between the ability to respond to reasons in what one originally does or thinks or feels etc., and the ability to use those same reasons in explaining what one did or thought or felt.

Aristotle had a single word to straddle the conceptual gap. He spoke of *logos*, and the word captured for him, and presumably for his contemporary readers, a single concept. But translators find it hard to capture in English. In the *Ethics* they generally render it as "reason,"[8] but in the *Rhetoric* and *Politics* as "speech."[9] Maybe the closest equivalent we have in English is the word "argument." An argument is an inference from premises to a conclusion, and all rational thought is in that sense argumentative even when it is only the inference from "man-eating tiger" to "run." But an argument is also something that we have with each other, a kind of dialogue in which inferences are used to make progress. Unfortunately the word "argument" has distracting overtones on both sides, making one think, on the one hand, of a rather intellectualized kind of thought, and, on the other, of a rather aggressive kind of dialogue. *Logos* had neither overtone, so far as one can tell from the contexts in which it is used in the classics.

The problem for us seems to be that a millennium of empiricist overindulgence has dulled the Anglophone conceptual palate. We have come to think, when we think about it at all, of the human abilities of reason and communication as two distinct abilities only contingently related. But that is a mistake. To have the distinctively human form of each is not, as Hobbes imagined, just to be able to do a better job than other creatures of anticipating and avoiding nasty consequences descending upon us, or even a better job of warning each other about those consequences by making a wider range of noises. It is not just to have a more developed form of reason and a more developed form of communication than other creatures. It is to have the reason of a communicator, and the communication of a reasoner. The distinctively human form of reason is one which grasps the meaning of things as well as their instrumentality, and hence which depends on the ability to conceptualize and interpret that is part of being a human communicator.[10] Meanwhile the distinctively human form of communication is one which offers reasons or challenges them or purports to create them and hence which requires on both sides (speaker and hearer) a developed ability to use reasons.[11]

In short, to grasp our natures as human beings, we need to think of ourselves in terms of a composite speech-and-reason ability of the kind that Aristotle called *logos*. If I am right, one central component of this ability is our basic responsibility: which is a compound – *not a mixture but a compound* – of our ability to use reasons in acting, thinking, choosing, wanting, etc. and our ability to use those reasons *again* in giving an account of whatever it was we did, thought, chose, wanted, etc., and in that sense, as rational beings, giving an account of ourselves.

III

In these remarks some may see the beginnings of a philosophical basis for the currently fashionable idea that responsibility must be understood *relationally*. Roughly the idea – we find it made explicit by Rorty, and regularly gestured towards by Rawls – is that responsibility, in the basic sense, is always responsibility *to* someone.[12] If asserting one's responsibility means not only having a rational account of oneself but also giving such an account, as I have claimed, then surely there must be someone to whom this rational account is owed, someone with whom one is supposed to enter into the Aristotelian dialogue. We need to begin by finding out who. We need to begin there because who is to receive the explanation, in turn, affects what suffices as a rational explanation. One must justify oneself or excuse oneself *to* that person. So justifications and excuses are also relational things. When people speak of justification or excuse tout court, they are suppressing a crucial variable. They always need to ask: "To whom am I justifying or excusing myself?"

I agree that this last question has its moments. There is often a strong case for framing or editing one's justifications and excuses to suit particular audiences, or more generally to make them engage with the interests of particular people. Those charged with serious offences are heading for big trouble, for example, if they did not take professional advice on how to explain in court the reasons for which they acted. Should they conceptualize the attack that they fought back against as having been a reason for self-defense, or a reason for anger under the heading of provocation, or a reason for emergency steps to be taken under the heading of necessity? It can make all the difference to their chances of conviction or acquittal. Meanwhile, those who are threatened with a duty of reparation rather than a liability to punishment had better take account of the fact that not all the justifications and excuses that may help them to avoid the latter are equally relevant to the former: morally as well as legally, a duty of reparation arises in respect of many wrongs that are justified or excused, where the justification or excuse in question is not related to the interests of the very person to whom the reparation would be paid. These are two different types of cases in which we might like to speak of someone justifying or excusing herself *to* someone.

But these types of cases provide no comfort to believers in the relational view. Remember the contrast I drew at the outset between the two explanations of why we all hunt around for justifications and excuses whenever we perpetrate wrongs and mistakes. One – the shallower, Hobbesian explanation – was that as rational beings we all want to avoid consequential responsibility. The other – the deeper, Aristotelian explanation – was that as rational beings we all want to assert basic responsibility. In cases of the types just mentioned one certainly needs to tailor one's justifications and excuses to make them serve the Hobbesian objective better. But this assumes that one already has non-tailored justifications and excuses that one can tailor to suit the occasion. In other words, it assumes that if one were pursuing one's Aristotelian objective free from the pressures of one's Hobbesian objective, one would be able to offer a different justification or excuse, less narrowly conceptualized or less focused on the interests of a particular person. What believers in the relational view need to explain is why *that* justification or excuse – the one that would be made in pursuit of the Aristotelian objective and free from the Hobbesian objective – would necessarily also be relational.

I suspect that some supporters of the relational view fail to keep the two concepts of responsibility as sharply distinct as they should, and the appeal of their views rests to some extent on that lack of sharpness. At any rate, as soon as one brackets the Hobbesian factors – if I could call them that for short – it becomes much harder to see where the relational view gets its appeal. That asserting ourselves as responsible beings requires some interlocutor, someone to talk to, is not in doubt. But why does it need a *particular* interlocutor? In respect of the same wrong or mistake, could I not assert my basic responsibility by offering the same account of myself to everyone I come across, from judges in the Old Bailey to friends in the pub to strangers on the bus? Remember that, by hypothesis, I am no longer interested in whether my account of myself makes my interlocutors sympathetic, rebuilds my friendship with them, persuades them to let me off punishment, or anything like that. Those are just more of the same Hobbesian factors: more unwelcome consequences that I might want to avoid and that we have, for the sake of argument, bracketed out.

What I care about, under the Aristotelian heading, is giving, so far as I am able, a *good* account of myself. If it really is a good account and other people can not see how good it is then, relative to the Aristotelian story of basic responsibility, that is *their* problem. Naturally not every account I give of myself that is rationally intelligible will be a good one. Naturally not every justification or excuse I offer as a responsible agent will be a successful one. But that is not the point. The point is that the *test* of its success, within the Aristotelian story, is whether it succeeds in providing good reasons why the wrong or mistake was perpetrated, or at least why the agent was driven or drawn to perpetrate it. Whether it succeeds in persuading its audience of the quality of those reasons is another matter altogether.

Probably some extreme supporters of the relational view do not regard this as another matter altogether. They regard the quality of reasons as simply reducible to their ability to persuade some actual person or constituency of people. But, if they think that, then rather than regarding them as champions of the classical idea of *logos* – reason as a dialogical activity – we should regard them as solipsists who have lost touch with the commonality of purpose that unites us all as rational beings and brings us into dialogical engagement with each other. As if to reaffirm his belief in commonality of purpose, Rorty says he prizes "solidarity" over "objectivity."[13] But in the only senses of "solidarity" and "objectivity" that matter one cannot have one without the other.[14] It is central to the classical idea of *logos*, and central to our nature as rational beings, even in these dark post-Hobbesian days, that all involved in the dialogue are aiming at successful understanding of the world around them, and not at mere mutual persuasion. Persuading someone to accept inadequate rational explanations is, for rational beings, the epitome of a pyrrhic victory, even if it means – no, *especially* if it means – that we get away with murder by doing so.

IV

I gave particular attention to the relational view because I think it holds special temptations for lawyers, especially common-law lawyers, and perhaps my last remarks on the subject helped to show why. Did my claim that we are "aiming at successful understanding of the world around [us], and not at mere mutual persuasion" ring any bells? I think it might well be interpreted by some common-law lawyers as a coded warning of an imminent attack. It may seem to herald yet another in a long line of criticisms of the common law's adversarial process. But I am not heading towards any such criticisms now. On the contrary, I am heading for a guarded commendation. For all its vulnerability to abuse by crafty and sometimes unscrupulous lawyers excessively pre-occupied with getting people on or off the hook, I think we should mostly try and take a prouder attitude towards the legal process. We should not think of it as mainly an instrumental appendage to substantive law. In fact we should think of its value as first and foremost intrinsic rather than instrumental.

The intrinsic value I have in mind is, of course, the value of basic responsibility itself. It is the value of being able to offer an account of oneself as a rational being. Naturally not all those who are accused of legal wrongs or mistakes offer personal accounts of themselves in court. Yet all who get as far as trial have the opportunity to do so. Those who choose not to nevertheless typically offer their self-explanations via their legal representatives. In the common law, these explanations tend to take the form of long stilted conversations, involving statements of claim and defenses, counterclaims and counterdefenses, and then (in the courtroom) opening speeches and replies, examinations-in-chief and cross-examinations, and summings-up on both sides. In comparing these stilted conversational devices with rival mechanisms – for instance with civilian inquisitorial processes or with less formal dispute resolution models such as mediation – we all tend to assume in our usual Hobbesian way that they are to be compared first and foremost in terms of their effects on getting people on or off the hook – where that includes reaching agreed solutions about who pays for the window and who says sorry and who has to feel remorse etc. (which are also allocations of consequential responsibility). Even those who like to evaluate rival legal procedures in terms of their fairness – and they often like to say that this is a *non*-instrumental way of evaluating it – tend to default to thinking of fairness, in this procedural context, in terms of the relative ability of the two sides to get on or off the hook. Does someone hold disproportionate sway over the way the case turns out? But it seems to me that if we are thinking in this way then we are missing the most fundamental point of all this legal rigmarole, all these pleas and committals and verdicts and even the physical layout of the courtroom with the dock and the stand and the bench. The fundamental point is to have structured explanatory dialogues in public, in which the object of explanation is ourselves. This point is not a point relative to which the procedure is instrumental; rather the point is *in* the procedure.

I just threw in, as if it were somehow integral to the value I am identifying, the fact that the explanatory dialogues of the law are held in public. What is the sudden significance of this? Well of course like everything under discussion here it has more than one significance. But the pertinent significance right now seems to me to be this. The public character of self-explanation in court constitutes the law's most forthright rejection of the relational view. The law admits that some people – the plaintiff in a civil suit, and the prosecution in a criminal case – have the right to bring people to account. It insists on its own right to do the same. But the account they bring people to is not, at the deepest level, an account addressed specifically to them. It is addressed to the world at large, to be assessed on its merits as a rational explanation.

If it is to be assessed on its merits, you may say, the law has a strange way of showing it. It forces the explanation into conceptual strait-jackets and ties us all in procedural knots. But that is an easy caricature. Certainly the law is a highly technical pursuit. But the self-explanations that people give of themselves when they take the stand are rarely highly technical in the same way. True, if their lawyers present the case then things may be different. But even then the *facts* must first be explained by non-lawyers and merely squeezed into the legal categories by the lawyers. Moreover the legal categories themselves are typically left more elastic in respect of justifications and excuses than in respect of the definitions of the wrongs themselves, precisely to allow for accommodation of (at least some) meritorious but unanticipated self-explanations.[15] And, in a criminal case, before a jury or lay magistrate, even the lawyer's technical handling of these already more elastic categories is controlled by the need to convey the gist of the defense case to lay people. I am inclined to think that this fact provides the beginnings of a case for jury trial. But more importantly, for present purposes, it helps us to defuse the myth that legal fora make people's self-explanations arcane.

I should stress that these remarks are not, at least I hope not, the signs of an early onset of common-law chauvinism. I tend to think that, thanks to the pervasive collision of incommensurable values, there is no one best way to run a legal system. My remarks were only intended to draw attention to one of the several incommensurable values that is often neglected in legal debate and commentary, as well as in some legal and moral philosophy, namely the value of basic responsibility which is instantiated in, rather than instrumentally served by, the legal process. My point was the (I thought) rather intriguing one that, although this value is neglected in Anglophone legal debate and commentary, and is completely at odds with the still studiously Hobbesian thinking of most common-law lawyers, it is not neglected in the common law itself. Possibly the opposite: possibly it is overindulged and/or captured in an exaggerated way by the common law. Possibly some or all of the common law systems have come to embrace the pursuit of "argument" complete with its extra overtones of intellectualization on the one hand and aggression on the other. Possibly some other legal systems in rival traditions have all this in healthier perspective. All of that is beyond my ken.

So, in short, the point I am making is not really about the common law, or its adversarial processes, in particular. It is simply that these processes bring out my broader point in a vivid way. And my point is that we should think of the courtroom struggle as a site of intrinsic as well as instrumental value. So, even if for some reason we abolished the whole apparatus of criminal sentences and civil remedies, we should still think twice about abolishing the trials themselves. In fact, one important (although not sufficient) reason for *having* the apparatus of criminal sentences and civil remedies is to *motivate* the trials themselves. It is to put people under extra instrumental pressure to give decent public accounts of themselves, in the knowledge that doing this will normally help them to eliminate or reduce the burden of consequential responsibility that they might otherwise bear. To that extent, the importance of basic responsibility is not derivative of the importance of consequential responsibility. The reverse is true. The importance of consequential responsibility derives from that of basic responsibility. To this extent, consequential responsibility is justified as the *mark* of basic responsibility.

V

This is just one of several ways in which the importance of consequential responsibility derives from that of basic responsibility. As I have admitted all along, there are also ways in which, conversely, the importance of basic responsibility derives from that of consequential responsibility. It is a two-way street. The only reason I have for thinking that basic responsibility is the more basic of the two is this. To the extent that the importance of basic responsibility derives from that of consequential responsibility, the derivation is entirely instrumental. It all rests on the fact that basic responsibility has consequential responsibility among its consequences. But to the extent that the importance of consequential responsibility derives from that of basic responsibility, the derivation is not only instrumental. I just mentioned the important argument that having a regime of consequential responsibility dependent on basic responsibility encourages people to give proper accounts of themselves, and hence serves the value of basic responsibility instrumentally. But beyond that, being held consequentially responsible can also, in at least some of its forms, be important as a way of *expressing* one's basic responsibility. Since the reverse is not true, basic responsibility is more basic than consequential responsibility. In the mutual exchange of value between the two, basic responsibility is the only one that pays its way in intrinsic value.

The exact way in which being held consequentially responsible can express one's basic responsibility requires careful handling. There are many modes of consequential responsibility (a liability to be punished, a duty to atone, the loss of a right to be compensated, etc.) and there is probably no single thing that subjection to each of them expresses in common with all the others. In particular, the expressive relationship to basic responsibility probably varies from mode to mode.

But the core idea that consequential responsibility can express basic responsibility is clear enough. It underlies the much maligned proposal (usually associated with Hegel) that all wrongdoers have a right to be punished.[16] I think the way this proposal is usually formulated is unfortunate, and the widespread maligning of it is consequently mistaken. It would be better to say less melodramatically that, if they are basically responsible, all wrongdoers have an *interest* in being punished. Since all rational beings want to assert their basic responsibility, all else being equal they cannot but welcome whatever contributes to that assertion. Punishment contributes to that assertion if it expresses their basic responsibility – if that is the public meaning of a punitive action. So all else being equal rational beings do have an interest in being punished whenever they are basically responsible for their actions.

The problem is that as soon as we look at that proposition we realize that all else is *not* equal. Punishment is always at the same time, in its Hobbesian way, an *un*welcome consequence, which every rational being would wish to avoid. There is a necessary conflict here between the demands of the assertion of one's basic responsibility and the avoidance of one's own suffering.

Cases like this led Kant down the road to his radical split of morality from prudence, via the distinction between the noumenal and the phenomenal. He was inclined to say that noumenally we welcome our own punishment, whereas phenomenally we do what we can to escape it.[17] That way of putting the point has its merits. It reminds us of the distinction with which I started, the distinction between the two stories, the Aristotelian story and the one that I later dubbed the Hobbesian story. Kant saw the force of the Aristotelian story very clearly. He saw that there are some abilities that are such that any being that has them necessarily aims to excel in them. And he agreed with Aristotle that our rational ability is such an ability.[18]

But whereas Aristotle meant to *include* our Hobbesian ability to avoid nasty consequences descending upon us under the heading of our rational ability,[19] Kant thought that this aspect of our rationality, belonging to the part that we share with less developed rational creatures, could not be embraced within our rational ability in the sense that mattered for the Aristotelian story. It had to be relegated to a distinct domain of lesser "prudential" reason.

This was a fallacious move. Alas, Kant then compounded the fallacy. In building up the rival "moral" domain he mistakenly focused not on our sophisticated communicative powers as human beings, but on the power of our *wills* to defy our reason, and hence optionally to follow it. He built this up as the special ingredient *x* that distinguished our rational ability from that of other, less rational creatures. By this route he arrived at an account of our basic responsibility in which the acid test was freedom of the will. Corroborating some earlier Christian myths, this account disastrously set the tone of our secular folk theory of responsibility, and indeed our secular folk theory of morality, for the intervening two hundred years – even though throughout this time our lives were still lived exactly as if the folk theories were as false as they really are.

In saying this I am not allying myself with those post-Kantians who doubt whether we have this famous power to confront reasons as options. I agree that we have it. In the face of incommensurable values we cannot but exercise it. And those of us who are lucky enough to live our lives above the desperate Hobbesian threshold of a struggle for survival, and who inhabit certain propitious cultural conditions, are able to live our lives largely as we choose. Our freedom is not, as some post-Kantians argue, a fiction or a myth. On the other hand, contrary to what many post-Kantians assume, our freedom is totally irrelevant to our responsibility.

What our responsibility depends on is our ability to explain ourselves rationally, and that is totally unaffected by whether we confronted or engaged with our actions and thoughts and feelings as optional, as things that we could opt to have or not to have by sheer force of will. You can work back from this bold assertion to certain of my detailed views about the conditions under which we are responsible. You can work out, for example, that I for one do not think coercion generally eliminates or even diminishes our responsibility for our actions. I think it furnishes us with a justification, or failing that an excuse. It can do this only if our responsibility survives it intact, for only those who are responsible can have, and make, justifications and excuses.

You may be surprised that I have managed to get this far without saying more about this kind of problem – more about exactly which circumstances eliminate or diminish our basic responsibility, and which circumstances on the other hand serve to justify or excuse us. I have even managed to avoid explaining even in outline how to distinguish a rational explanation from a non-rational one. And obviously I am not about to do it now. You may have thought that a paper about the "mark of responsibility" would be about these problems. But first things first. The most elementary problem of what we inherited from Kant has been that it has distracted us altogether from the reason–communication interface at which our responsibility resides, and focused our attention on the red herring of the reason–will interface instead. In the process we lost sight, or should I say lost folk-theoretical sight, of the important corollary of the Aristotelian story, that our basic responsibility depends not only on the conditions that obtain when we commit our wrongs and mistakes, but also on the conditions that obtain later when we are confronted with those wrongs or mistakes. It depends not only on our ability to *have* a certain kind of explanation for what we do or think or feel, but also our ability to *offer* that explanation. And it depends not on our ability to offer that explanation to a particular audience, but on our ability to offer it tout court – at the bar, if you like, of reason itself.

POSTSCRIPT

In many contexts the words "responsibility" and "accountability" are interchangeable.[20] But contemporary political discourse has also carved out a special niche for the word "accountability." One is accountable, to contemporary ears, only if there is someone to whom one is responsible. Accountability therefore has a relational aspect that responsibility lacks. It is not enough to make one accountable that one is apt to (and hence reasonably expected to) justify or excuse one's actions. There must also be a person or body of people to whom one owes the justification or excuse. This is the person or body that *holds one to account*.

One currently fashionable mode of accountability is public accountability, meaning accountability to the electorate, or to the taxpayers, or to the citizenry, either directly or through their representatives. Some seem to think that this is the default mode of accountability – that the electorate, or some similar popular body, is the natural body to hold one to account. You may say that I already gave succour to this idea in section IV above. I pointed to the public character of proceedings in court – an accounting that is offered to the whole world – as a way of expressing a defendant's basic responsibility, the raw nonrelational condition on which all relational modes of responsibility are based. Is not accountability to the electorate, through Parliament or the media, just the same kind of thing?

No. An electorate, or a taxpayer population, or a citizenry, is not the world at large. It is a special constituency with its own sectional interests, apt to extract correspondingly distorted justifications and excuses from those who are accountable to it. Besides, accountability *in* public is not the same as accountability *to* the public. Defendants in court are (luckily) not accountable to the public. They are accountable to the court. The court merely puts their account in the public domain – gives it a public audience – to convey that the defendant is before the court *qua* person, and not qua occupant of some specialized social role with some specialized line of accountability. Public accountability, accountability to the electorate or the taxpayers or the citizenry, is by contrast a specialized line of accountability, a relational mode of responsibility that is an incident of only some specialized social roles. It belongs first and foremost, although perhaps not only, to certain public officials who wield executive authority.

The case of the courts highlights some interesting questions about what accountability is *for*. It is currently fashionable to deride judges as "unaccountable," usually as shorthand for "publicly unaccountable." Yet judges are bound to, and normally do, give much more detailed accounts of themselves than do many other public officials. They give reasoned judgments in open court to justify most of the actions they take. And their reasons are apt to be scrutinized closely on appeal, more closely than the reasons of most other public officials, who are subject only to the lighter touch of judicial review. Judges are, in short, the public servants who are already bound to give, and already give, the fullest account of themselves in public. So what is the supposed problem to which greater public accountability would be a solution? Of course we all know the depressing answer. The real gripe of those who deride judges as "unaccountable" is that judges can not be ejected from office by the electorate, or by their elected representatives, when their very full justifications for acting as they do are disliked. There are no electoral sanctions or remedies for bad self-explanations.

Since judges exist mainly to provide a check on the inevitable populist excesses of the elected branches of government, thoughtful people must regard this lack of electoral accountability on the part of judges as at least partly a blessing. But that is not the theme I want to explore here. The theme I want to explore here is connected with a point I made at the end of section IV above. As I said there, one important (although not sufficient) reason for having a regime of sanctions and remedies is to motivate those subject to those sanctions and remedies to give a decent account of themselves. The puzzle is this. When people are inclined to give such an account anyway, as judges generally are, one important reason for subjecting them to a regime of sanctions and remedies is missing. What is the residual case for having a regime of sanctions and remedies in such circumstances? Is there a suspicion that the justifications and excuses would tend to be better – such that the actions being justified or excused would also be better – if there were sanctions and remedies to concentrate the minds of those who offer them? Or is it that the justifications and excuses being given are somehow not the real ones, so that one needs to have some way of applying pressure for a more frank self-explanation?

It seems to me that, whatever case may be made for the availability of sanctions and remedies in such cases, it cannot but rely on the suspicion of wrongdoing. To challenge someone to justify or excuse herself, with a threat of punishment in the event that her justification or excuse is unsatisfactory, is to accuse her of committing a wrong. This accusation is part of the public meaning of such an action of challenging-and-threatening even if the person doing the challenging-and-threatening tries to repudiate it. He cannot escape it by saying: "I'm not accusing you of wrongdoing, but you'd better have a good explanation of why you did that, or else." This is crude doublespeak.

It is true that wrongs are not the only things that call for justification or excuse. A justification or excuse – an answer to the question "Why did you do that?" – is called for whenever anyone does anything that she has any reason not to do, and this condition is met by virtually everything we do. But only some of the things that we do that we have a reason not to do are things that we have an *obligation* not to do, such that doing them is wrongful. And only when we do something wrongful, and lack justification or excuse for doing it, are we aptly punished for doing it. Punishment is an apt response only to unjustified and unexcused wrongdoing.

Accordingly, threatening punishment for an action already done is accusing the agent of having committed an unjustified and unexcused wrong. When coupled with an opportunity to offer a satisfactory justification or excuse and thereby to avoid the punishment, threatening the punishment is accusing the agent of wrongdoing, albeit maybe not unjustified and unexcused. There is no morally acceptable case for making such an accusation unless one makes it sincerely, i.e. unless one reasonably suspects that the accusation is true. So anyone who threateningly asks "Why did you do that?" is claiming to have a reasonable suspicion that the person she is addressing is a wrongdoer.

You may object that not every sanction or remedy, not every adverse consequence that might ensue in the event of an unsatisfactory justification or excuse, is a punitive one. People may lose their jobs simply because they are no good at them, and this need not be a punishment for anything. This is true, but irrelevant to the argument just set out. By *threatening* any adverse consequence in the event of inadequate justification or excuse, one turns the threatened adverse consequence into a threatened punishment. How so? One reacts punitively to what someone did whenever one reacts with the intention that she should suffer for having done it. By threatening adverse consequences in the event of an inadequate justification or excuse, one evinces this intention in advance.[21] That is because one cannot use the threat as the incentive one intends it to be unless, were it carried out, the person to whom it is addressed would suffer. This makes the suffering part of one's intention. It follows that whatever adverse consequences one threatens are rendered punitive by one's act of threatening them, wherever the threat is also designed to be an incentive.

Thus, for example, reparative damages in tort law are not in their nature punitive. They can and should be exacted without the intention that the defendant should suffer. That is why it is consistent with the principles of tort law that the defendant be fully indemnified by an insurance company. But anyone who threatens to exact reparative damages in the event that the person threatened does not settle the case or give in to some other demand turns the threatened exacting of damages into a threatened punishment for non-cooperation. Likewise, dismissing an employee in the event of underperformance need not be punitive. But using the threat of dismissal to secure better performance from the employee turns the threatened dismissal into a threatened punishment. If exacted, it would now be a punishment for underperformance – which entails an accusation of wrongdoing – not only a way of replacing an underperforming employee. For the suffering involved in being dismissed would no longer be a side-effect but rather an intended effect of the dismissal. That is why securing self-explanation by threats is necessarily accusatory, however it is dressed up.

I am not saying that one cannot have a culture of accountability that is not a culture of suspicion and accusation. A culture in which people routinely explain themselves without fear or favor is such a culture. But the culture of accountability that we now seem to have – in which requests for self-explanation are routinely coupled with threats of loss of office, loss of promotion, loss of funding, loss of contracts, and so on – is unavoidably a culture of suspicion and accusation. Most of the time, it seems to me, such suspicion and accusation is unwarranted.

There is usually no reason to suspect a breach of any obligation by anybody. For example, it is part of the job of most public officials to spend public money. Some of them may spend it badly, and among those who do there may be a further subgroup who spend it wrongfully (e.g. feather-bedding their friends, failing to keep an eye on where it is going). To demand that every spender of public money be "held to account for every penny spent" – where this carries with it an implicit threat of adverse consequences in the event that it was not spent wisely – is to accuse every spender of public money, even those who spend public money impeccably, of spending it wrongfully. In this regime everyone is always a suspect. If politicians wonder why trust in politicians has declined when the trustworthiness of politicians (let us concede) has not, they need look no further for an explanation. The system of accountability on which politicians themselves have come to insist as part and parcel of "New Public Management" is an ideology of total suspicion (or, to put the same idea in other words, total mistrust).[22] It should come as no surprise that the more this system comes to be taken for granted as the way to run the country (and indeed the way to run everything else), the more suspicious everyone is of those whose upstandingness the system is meant to secure.[23] These people must be up to something, observers conclude, because the system constantly accuses them of being up to something.

No doubt this line of thought can be developed further. There are reasons to think (although empirical work would be needed to establish) that there is an element of self-fulfilling prophesy in the ideology of total suspicion. Probably, as people are routinely accused of wrongdoing, they become dispirited and less inclined to cooperate in the activity in respect of which they are accused. Possibly they also become more inclined to conceal and dissemble and react defensively for fear of what will become of them if they reveal their ordinary human limitations.

If these hunches are true, then the threat-based mode of accountability to which people are now routinely subject in their working lives is doubly counterproductive. In the first place – a trite point – inasmuch as organizations depend for the quality of their work on the spirit of those who work in them, this mode of accountability is apt to reduce organizational performance. In the public sector in particular, the "New Public Management" may make public services cheaper but also worse value (by eroding the surplus of unpaid cooperation that was once called the "public service ethos"). In the second place, the same threat-based mode of accountability may be counterproductive even from the point of view of accountability itself. That is to say, people may be disinclined to explain themselves honestly and openly for fear that every little slip they make will be punished.

Of course the fear of exposing oneself to terrible consequences by telling the truth can equally be a distorting force in the criminal justice system. But at least in the criminal justice system the accusation of wrongdoing must be based on a reasonable suspicion and those who are accused are therefore, within limits, reasonably put in peril of exposing themselves. There is no similar excuse for today's systems of bureaucratic accountability to have driven ordinary innocent people into the fearful Hobbesian defensiveness and evasiveness that now often seems to dog their working lives. Yet – and here is the element of self-fulfilling prophesy – to the extent that ordinary innocent people are indeed driven into Hobbesian defensiveness and evasiveness, the culture of suspicion has, perversely, helped to create the very conditions that are supposed to necessitate it. The ideology of total suspicion makes people more worthy of suspicion by constantly suspecting them. It helps to dig the hole from which it is supposed to extract us, and thereby prolongs its own miserable life. That, at any rate, is my hypothesis.

CHAPTER 10

TECHNOCRATIC V. CONVIVIAL ACCOUNTABILITY

Bronwen Morgan

INTRODUCTION

Public accountability, in its most Spartan form, is the "liability to reveal, to explain, and to justify what one does."[1] This communicative understanding of accountability is neutral as to institutional design, as well as between different conceptions of value and purpose. It can be mobilized within intimate communities or between far-flung groups of strangers. Substantively thicker accountability paradigms tend to have embedded in them assumptions about institutional design, empirical context, and the values and purposes served by the paradigm in question. Traditional classifications of these competing modes of public accountability (legal, democratic, bureaucratic, market) are grounded on spheres of law, politics, and economics undisturbed by globalizing and privatizing trends. Recent scholarship has been more successful in describing the blurring and melding of these various structural paradigms in terms of their *effectiveness* as governance mechanisms than it has in terms of the implications for accountability.

It is helpful to think of two dimensions of "fit" between the "new regulatory models of collaborative governance" and the changes induced by privatization and globalization. One level of fit is with the descriptive level of emerging institutional arrangements: the use of specific regulatory techniques, the relationships between actors in the overlapping regulatory spaces. Very valuable work has been done here in articulating, however diffuse, models of "network governance," "collibrated governance," and "collaborative governance" to name but a few.[2]

However, precisely because network governance blurs previously distinct institutional and empirical contexts, approaches that assume the distinctiveness of accountability paradigms with competing values and purposes no longer "fit" our understanding of how these new modes of governance are held publicly accountable. That understanding is especially destabilized by the increasing porousness of national territorial boundaries. Popular oversight over political actors, for example, may underpin the integrity of and endorse the shared values of a bounded territorial community, but its darker side – the capacity to foster factionalism and "special interest" rent-seeking behavior – is likely to have even more space in a globalizing context than in a stable national setting.

The classical liberal values underpinning the benefits of market accountability are also less obvious in a global context where, as privatization trends increasingly blur public and private spheres, the integrity of market accountability as a distinct structural paradigm is less and less persuasive. Indeed, the domain of market accountability has actually expanded to regional and global levels in large measure by virtue of a legally imposed mandate. Under the auspices of institutions such as the European Court of Justice and the World Trade Organization, legal accountability is at least in part a handmaiden to market accountability rather than a foil. And this increasingly instrumental role accorded to legal mechanisms of accountability itself undercuts the values and purposes of neutral arm's-length oversight where judicial actors, "independent" as they might be, are not embedded in a bounded national community. Such boundedness provides a context and a constraint for the inevitably contested dimensions of that neutrality. This can be inferred from the greater perceived legitimacy of the European Court of Justice in comparison to the World Trade Organization. The institutional context of multi-level governance for the former incorporates national-level democratic accountability mechanisms at a much more thickly embedded level than the latter.

One could respond to this by constructing a fresh normative framework of values or purposes, almost tantamount to a theory of justice, as suggested but not attempted by Jody Freeman.[3] Or one could reject altogether the salience of normativity for public accountability, as Edward Rubin assumes in the theoretical framework he proposes as necessary for accommodating the deeply changed empirical and institutional landscape.[4] Or – and this is the goal of this chapter – one can retain the notion that normative frameworks remain salient in animating public accountability, but take as a modest starting point the notion that they grow organically and incrementally out of institutional and material changes, while not being determined by them. In this context, a necessary first step towards being able to articulate a language of public accountability that will better "fit" our changed landscape, is to avoid any overt discussion of values and purposes, yet still seek to identify what might be missing from approaches to accountability that give primacy to institutional design.

My argument has three parts. In Section I, I argue that a particular institutional architecture is increasingly *common* to the various modes – whether judicial, bureaucratic, or democratic – of accountability that compete at the centre of the accountability crisis. This institutional architecture, a generalized version of the triadic logic at the heart of legal accountability, is essentially technocratic. The examples I give will demonstrate its pervasiveness across spheres often thought to bolster different types of values and purposes: regulatory policymaking, human rights enforcement and democratic monitoring.

In Section II, I will discuss how the *critique* of technocracy is the crucial axis in debates over accountability. Technocratic accountability misses a crucial aspect of social systems – a particular lucidity of discussion, a particular tenor or texture of discourse, a particular set of implicit or tacit shared assumptions, all of which link to a sense of implicit community. Historically, this particular tenor of discourse has been associated with geographic and cultural commonality, revolving around shared identity and custom. We might call the kind of accountability that operates in these communities "convivial accountability," and its absence or dilution, I argue, underlies many discomforts with structural paradigms of accountability.

The axis between technocratic and convivial accountability cuts across classifications of competing modes of accountability in a way that better "fits" the emerging patterns of network or collibrated governance generated by privatization, globalization, and decentralization. Globalization has increasingly displaced geographical communities with functional, non-geographically defined communities whose common language is often one of technocratic accountability. But, while globalization exacerbates the tendency of technocratic accountability to crowd out convivial accountability, it need not. In Section III, I will conclude by using the example of transnational struggles around the provision of urban water services to show how geographically dispersed communities *can* foster convivial modes of accountability, although the possibilities are sporadic and face significant constraints.

I. TECHNOCRATIC ACCOUNTABILITY

A. Triadic logic: judicial accountability and beyond

Public accountability is, as Michael Dowdle's opening chapter demonstrates, at its heart about making the exercise of political power answerable to some conception of "the people." In the modern context, a self-consciously held appreciation of the pluralities of "peoples," together with pervasive problems of scale, results in accountability debates being typically situated in contexts where dispersed groups of strangers hold multiple and competing understandings of the values and purposes served by the exercise of political power. In such contexts, justifying the exercise of political power is increasingly similar to processes of conflict resolution, and this is what we see developing in modern governance contexts.

I would suggest, as an alternative, that public accountability is a particular institutional architecture that is *common* to the various modes – whether judicial, bureaucratic, or democratic – of accountability that compete at the center of the accountability crisis. This institutional architecture is a generalized version of the triadic logic at the heart of legal accountability. The triadic logic is grounded on disinterested decisionmakers using objective, rationalist, and universalized forms of knowledge to justify decisions that are communicated in an expert language. While its *locus classicus* may be judicial accountability, its extension to other, apparently competing, modes of accountability is possible at least in part precisely because what some characterize as the "legalization" of politics is just one form of bureaucratic or Weberian rationalization. All these forms are what I shall call technocratic modes of accountability. As we shall see – not least by the fact that technocratic forms of accountability can extend even as far as the democratic paradigm – the root of the accountability crisis is more a product of the limitations inherent in the triadic logic, rather than a conflict between bureaucracy, judicialization, and/or democracy.

The core of the triadic logic that underpins modern technocratic forms of public accountability is its delegation of the communicative processes of revelation, explanation, and justification involved in accountability to an arm's-length, neutral, and independent institution. Since modern governance operates under conditions of value pluralism and at a scale where justification takes place largely between and for actors that are strangers to each other, accountability processes must find a language that bridges social, normative, and geographical space. Bridging the normative space between groups of actors that have competing value systems demands disinterestedness and neutrality, and bridging social and geographical space is facilitated by technical abstract languages that apply, or at least purport to apply, in a relatively context-free manner. The essence of this comes close to the logic that underpins the role of courts in society, which Martin Shapiro long ago characterized as triadic in nature. As he summarizes it in a recent joint publication with Alec Stone Sweet:

> If a conflict arises between two persons and they cannot resolve it themselves, then in all cultures and societies it is logical for those two persons to call upon a third to assist in its resolution . . . The triad contains a basic tension. To the extent that the triadic figure appears to intervene in favor of one of the two disputants and against the other, the perception of the situation will shift from the fairest to the most unfair of configurations: two against one. Therefore the principal characteristics of all triadic conflict resolvers will be determined by the need to avoid the perception of two against one, for only then can they rely on their basic social logic.[5]

Where triadic institutions are relatively highly formalized, two devices are especially important in preventing perceptions of "two against one": office and rules.[6] That is, the personal neutrality of the judge, and the resolution of the dispute by reference to preexisting rules expressed in general terms, together ensure that the triadic logic is maintained.

This pared-back perspective on the social logic underlying judicial institutions is an approach that challenges too bright a distinction between courts and other governmental organs. In a technocratic governance environment, the actions of an "objective" official holding other actors to account are epistemically much closer to those of a judge than is usually acknowledged. The distinctiveness of what judges do can be expressed in more general and abstract terms that widen the lens of triadic logic to encompass other institutions and personnel within the modern state. Through this lens, the inspectorate of an education department when performing "quality assessments" of schoolteachers is not so distinct from a court deciding on the legality of resource allocation under public powers.

The similarity between juridical and technocratic decisionmaking is so striking that a group of international relations scholars recently proposed the concept of "legalization" as an analytic device that has the capacity to capture a broad variety of ways in which "law and politics are intertwined across a wide range of institutional forms":[7]

> Legal [and other technocratic] processes involve a discourse framed in terms of reason, interpretation, technical knowledge, and argument, often followed by deliberation and judgment by impartial parties. Different actors have access to the process, and they are constrained to make arguments different from those they would make in a nonlegal [or non-technocratic] context. Legal [and other technocratic] decisions, too, must be based on reasons applicable to all similarly situated litigants, not merely the parties to the immediate disputes.[8]

For a legal audience, the most ready referent of the above description is of course courts. Slightly looser but still recognizably "legalized" in the terms quoted above, is the process of challenging or justifying economic policies that impact on cross-border trade before a panel of the World Trade Organization. But what of a requirement to justify regulatory policy before an economists' commission appointed with relative independence of tenure, as Australia has done by creating a National Competition Council? Or a dialogue between specialized units in the executive branch and bipartisan parliamentary committees as to whether regulatory reform proposals retain the "necessary protection" against harm required by the public interest, an innovation the UK recently implemented in its Regulatory Reform Act 2001? I want to suggest that these developments are, together with the more obviously "legalized" modes, all instances of technocratic accountability. That is to say, they impose a "liability to reveal, to explain, and to justify what one does" in ways that mirror the triadic logic underlying legality, even if they do not share the function of resolving specific disputes that is core to the purpose of judicial adjudication.

B. Technocratic accountability: from regulation to human rights

The pervasiveness of a triadic logic of technocratic accountability in modern governance can be demonstrated by reference to examples from spheres usually thought to encompass very different ranges of values and purposes: from the economic policymaking functions at the core of regulatory politics to the enforcement of fundamental rights, and even to certain forms of democratic monitoring.

1. Economic and regulatory policymaking

To take economic policymaking first: a marked shift can be noted away from the historical preference of many industrialized countries for shaping economic policymaking via a dialogue between government and bureaucracy. Bureaucratic consensualism, as for example in corporatist negotiations between peak trade and labor associations and a government, is a non-triadic logic by virtue of the absence of a neutral mediator who frames the issues at stake in a purportedly disinterested, objective language. But its historical prevalence in economic policymaking has more recently given way to a greater role for courts. As linkages between economic policymaking, regulatory reform, and legal processes have intensified, courts are coming more and more to play a role as *architects* of economic policy.

Sometimes these linkages instance an intensification of the relative involvement of courts and judges in the implementation of economic policies, particularly when they are delivered via regulatory agencies. For example, utilities sectors particularly, in the UK but also in other countries, have become increasingly juridified as policymaking in those sectors is shaped and delivered by independent regulatory agencies.[9] An independent regulatory agency is already in itself an instance of triadic logic: institutionally protected from direct political command by legislatively guaranteed terms of office and a ring-fenced budget, they are often staffed by personnel who are versed in the technical and "objective" aspects of the policy issues they decide, such as electricity and gas pricing policy. The processes of regulatory agency decisionmaking are often carefully defined by explicit statutes and soft law, and, as such, become subject to supervision by courts who also assess their legality in technical and objective language – albeit a language often very different from those of the regulatory officials.

But going beyond regulatory implementation, legalization constraints also increasingly apply at a *policymaking* stage. For example, trade regimes such as that supervised by the World Trade Organization or the internal market project of the European Union are regularly analyzed in terms of the growing "judicialization" of their trajectories.[10] That is to say, the judicial and quasi-judicial institutions in these regimes do not simply resolve disputes that arise from time to time, but also have a powerful and continuing influence on the scope of major policy choices – an influence that is expressed in neutral, disinterested, and objective terms by actors who function at arm's-length from those making the major policy decision. Thus the World

Trade Organization panel recently rejected the United States's claim that a ban on cross-border Internet gambling is legitimate because the activity violates public morals: a decision that cuts off the policy trajectory previously chosen by the United States of banning this activity.[11]

The important point here is not the "juridical" nature of trade panels, but rather the fact that the institutional design of trade review is based on a triadic logic, whether judicial or non-judicial. Indeed, regulatory scholarship of recent years has emphasized the importance of *non-judicial* institutions in this respect. For example, in relation to the carrying out of governmental functions generally, across a wide range of policy areas, Christopher Hood and his colleagues' exploration of bureaucratic regulation within government finds pervasive "oversight of bureaucracies by other public agencies operating at arm's length from the direct line of command, the overseers being endowed with some sort of official authority over their charges."[12] In regulatory arenas that affect economic policymaking, prescriptions for the delegation of dispute resolution and even policymaking to politically insulated independent agencies are pervasive.[13]

One form of monitoring grounded on triadic logic that illustrates particularly well the technocratic nature of this mode of accountability are processes that embed regulatory review mechanisms relying on economic rationality into the everyday routines of governmental policymaking.[14] Australia, for example, has via an intergovernmental compact among its constituent states – the Competition Principles Agreement, or CPA – imposed pro-competitive disciplines on public rulemaking and policymaking processes. The CPA requires policymakers to satisfy a public benefit test to justify the maintenance of any public policy that prima facie restricts competition. Policies for which a public benefit cannot be demonstrated must be repealed or modified so that they do not reduce competition. This commitment is overseen by a newly created national independent agency – the National Competition Council – which evaluates policymakers' outputs on an annual basis to ensure "effective implementation" of the pro-competitive discipline, and awards substantial "competition payments" (in the order of Aus$16 billion over five years) for good performers. The National Competition Councillors are, all but one, five private sector appointees from business backgrounds, and its 20–23 staff members are mostly economists, with a few lawyers. The Council is appointed for a three-year term and makes annual assessments of the rate of progress of each jurisdiction in legislation review, in which it evaluates the justifications advanced by each state for retaining their regulatory programs.

Empirical investigation of this particular example shows that, over time, the regulatory reform regime in Australia not only "came to shape how individuals interact with each other" in economic policymaking fora, but also "develop[ed] authority over the normative structure in place," at least within a community of central agency officials who shared a certain blend of ideological commitment and bureaucratic mission that gave them a "professional and bureaucratic interest in providing disinterested . . . interpretation."[15] The regime placed well-defined, mandatory boundaries upon the exercise of regulatory policymaking power, and required those policies to be justified in the technical discourse of economic analysis. Like legal processes, the *locus classicus* of triadic logic, the Australian regime "involve[d] a discourse framed in terms of reason, interpretation, technical knowledge, and argument . . . [and was] followed by deliberation and judgment by impartial parties . . . based on reasons applicable to all similarly situated [policymakers]."[16] Even though delegation to a detached third party in triadic mode may not usually be as intense as it is in the case of the WTO or Australia's National Competition Council, these are simply more detailed examples of a host of accountability techniques in regulatory spheres that mimic the dynamics of triadic logic in more or less weaker forms, including efficiency auditing, competition benchmarking, cost–benefit analysis, and the like.

2. *Fundamental rights*

The triadic logic underpinning technocratic accountability can also be observed in relation to human rights. The spread of judicial review of "fundamental rights" is perhaps the most obvious facet of this:

> Judicial review was introduced in Europe after the Nazi-Fascist era shook the faith of Europeans in the legislature, making them reconsider the possibility of giving the judiciary the power to check the legislature's respect for the fundamental rights of the people.[17]

Since then, there has been a steadily increasing trajectory of scholarship on the spread of judicial review in relation to human rights.[18] There is also a growing critique of this trend which is, arguably, substantially grounded on opposition to the technocratic nature of judicialization as a strategy of accountability for the human rights dimensions of political affairs, viewing this development as a dilution of vigorous democratic virtues.[19]

Yet non-judicial accountability mechanisms institutionalized in triadic form (and therefore just as technocratic) are also increasingly pervasive within the realm of human rights policymaking. For example, gender impact statements, social auditing, and human rights benchmarking are, like the regulatory sphere techniques alluded to above, fundamentally technocratic, managerial paradigms of accountability. They are focused on *systemic* justification – revealing, explaining, and justifying policymaking choices at one remove from the substantive issues of the policies themselves, focusing instead on the procedures that produce the policies. More "hybrid" forms of review of fundamental rights, such as those institutionalized in New Zealand and the UK, are wary of giving the "last word" (or even a particularly decisive word) to actors that stand at a remove from the values and purposes of the social activity for which accountability is demanded. But they still mandate inter-institutional dialogues between arm's-length institutions (such as courts and judges) and more purely political actors.[20]

Notwithstanding the apparent gulf between economic regulatory issues and issues of fundamental rights, modern forms of governance in both these disparate areas evince commonalities in the underlying social logic and institutional architecture of accountability mechanisms. Both are infused with an ostensible form of neutral and objective knowledge, capable of being wielded only by those versed in its intricacies and, in particular, capable of speaking its expert language. Thus where, in regulatory or human rights matters, the actors who justify, reveal, or explain their actions do so, when they are embedded in modes of technocratic accountability, with reference to explicitly articulated criteria, whether from science, economics, or "principled" theories of human rights, these criteria and the language in which they are expressed gradually develop an increasingly powerful hold on matters that may previously have been issues of "pure politics". However different economic theories may seem from universal human rights principles, common to both those visions is an idea of neutrality or disinterestedness. In such situations, actors possess incentives that push them in the direction of offering interpretations that are not substantially less disinterested than the interpretations offered by judges. What matters here is a "professional and bureaucratic interest in providing disinterested . . . interpretation."[21] Such an incentive may be secured by a blend of ideological commitment and bureaucratic mission vested in actors possessing some institutionally secured independence. Judges may be one such set of actors, but judicialization is in fact a *subset* of broader forms of technocratic accountability. All mechanisms of accountability that build institutionally upon a triadic logic and the concomitant need to infuse the process of "explaining, justifying, and revealing" with discourses of neutrality will result in the penetration of normative structures by ostensibly objective, relatively opaque, expert knowledge, and it is this that makes this form of accountability distinctively technocratic.

C. Democratic accountability: different by species or genre?

Thus far, I have insisted the conception of technocratic accountability is capacious enough to include both judicial and more traditionally "bureaucratic" modes of accountability. But now I take an even more expansive step, with a claim that even democratic modes of accountability, at least when expressed in routinized form, replicate the triadic logic of technocratic accountability. This may seem initially jarring for at least two reasons. First, democratic accountability is grounded in conceptions of self-rule ('by the people, for the people') that abnegate the kind of specialized, delegated decisionmaking that is crucial to the triadic logic. Secondly, its core logic of aggregating subjective choice would seem to run directly counter to the invocation of objective or neutral knowledge by disinterested actors who communicate in expert languages, also a key facet of triadic logic.

But, if we look more closely at the institutionalization of democratic accountability in the context of modern governance, we can see that both the aggregation of subjective choice and the aspirations of self-rule are increasingly muted. Representative democracy implemented by periodic elections, after all, quite consciously delegates the exercise of political power to a range of representatives, who then govern between elections as much with the assistance of bureaucratic expertise as under pressure from subjective preferences of the governed.

Indeed, to the extent that concentrated subjective preferences of powerful groups within the governed do shape the exercise of political power, democracy is understood to be subverted, and it is consequently increasingly common for modes of technocratic accountability, such as the Australian regulatory reform regime described in Section I, to claim *democratic* credentials as well as credentials accrued through technical expertise. The argument here is that the constraints of processes like the Australian reform regime are put in place as a battle on behalf of diffuse, unorganized groups such as taxpayers or consumers who, because of collective action problems, are effectively suffering "taxation without representation" when regulatory policies are implemented by governments.[22] From this perspective, technocratic accountability regimes such as the Australian one "represent" a set of otherwise silenced interests.

Relatedly, the stress placed by some strands of democratization scholarship on elite models of representative democracy has acquired a Schumpeterian texture of bracketing out in the name of democracy the more intensely participatory forms of democratic accountability. This stress has become more pervasive as globalization shrinks the discretionary policy that national governments, particularly of poorer countries, are capable of exercising. As Benjamin Barber recently observed, in a comment glossed by myself to link it to the current argument: "vertical integration and vertical communication, which is the strength of representative democracy [and is intensified by globalization], disallows to a large extent the forms of horizontal and lateral communication that are essential to participatory or strong democracy."[23]

But, even if we consider some of the more participatory, locally embedded modes of democratic accountability, such as John Braithwaite's responsive regulation,[24] or the democratic experimentalism endorsed by Michael Dorf and Charles Sabel,[25] we can see that these, too, maintain some distinctly technocratic turns. While not quite in "pure" triadic mode, certainly by contrast with a judicial mode of accountability, there is, nonetheless, much less of the flavor of spontaneous choice and collective self-rule than one might expect. In Charles Sabel's extended discussion of the organizational theory underlying democratic experimentalism, for example, both the routinized nature of the relevant techniques and the expert language mastery they require are evident:

> [W]hat the new institutions [of benchmarking, simultaneous engineering and error-detection methods] do as a matter of course [is to] routinely question the suitability of current routines for defining and solving problems.[26]

Thus even organizational techniques that constantly feed new information into systems of provision from those that work in or benefit from those systems, acquire a triadic logic once they are institutionalized in the routines that Sabel alludes to. Note, for example, how Sabel describes the benchmarking process industry undertakes to assess the potential of new products.[27] The process begins with asking technical experts to produce engineering simulations of possible outcomes, which an industry team then assesses by reference to leading examples and a comparison of possibilities. The task is then "chunked" and a number of specialist teams from inside or outside the parent company produce work to the initial specifications, constantly comparing the production processes central to their eventual products to ensure that the methods employed will meet or surpass the efficiency of their most capable competitors. Thus there is a continuous separation of tasks, delegation of expertise, and evaluation of the results according to pre-agreed expert languages.

Similarly, while responsive regulation does emphasize in part the fostering of a culture of compliance by creating an interpretive community of shared values and purposes between regulator and regulated, its elaboration depends crucially on *arm's-length* monitoring by "public interest groups" who possess incentives and professional commitments of disinterestedness (see also Chapter 2). These features echo both horizontal accountability design features and the turn to discourses of ostensible neutrality that are commonly found in the triadic logics identified in bureaucratic and judicial modes of accountability.

Moreover, in the transnational context of diluted state power fostered by the currents of globalization and privatization that underpin the accountability crisis, there is if anything an *increased* tendency for the triadic logic to prevail. We see this, for example, in interactions between non-state actors (often invoked as institutions that give voice to the otherwise unrepresented in the international arena) and multinational corporations in the area of social auditing to ensure compliance with international labor standards where arm's-length independence, and a discourse of facts, statistics, and technical standards, are both arguably more prominent than in any analogous labor dispute at national level.[28] In the global arena, where repertoires of justification or indeed even relationships are not as well established as they might be between repeatedly interacting players in a national arena, there is a need to find a neutral language that will serve instead to bind the various players into a shared sense of what makes accountability meaningful. Technocratic discourses of social auditing do just this – and relatedly, it is arguably no accident that international labor law is increasingly deeply linked to international human rights law, drawing upon the latter's claim to objective principles that transcend contextually specific politics. While it may well be true that the increasingly strident critique of NGO participation in transnational politics is grounded at least in part on charges of a "democratic deficit," this in a sense posits an ideal of democracy as an ever-receding utopia. Democratic accountability mechanisms once actually implemented have more in common, in our fragmented polities, with the triadic logic of technocratic accountability than our institutionally elusive ideals of democracy, and particularly in the contexts most under strain from trends of privatization and globalization.

II. CONVIVIAL ACCOUNTABILITY

A. Reframing, participation, and implicit communities

The implication of the extensive reach of technocratic accountability is that the accountability "crisis" is more a product of the limitations inherent in the triadic logic, rather than a conflict between bureaucracy, judicialization, or democracy. By mining the vein of these limitations, we can excavate a conception of what I will call "convivial accountability." Convivial accountability cuts across the apparent differences between competing modes of accountability. Its visibility may point us toward a route away from the seemingly vicious collapse of the existing alternatives into bureaucratized versions of each, or into "networked" amalgams that muddy the distinctive contributions of each. In essence, while technocratic accountability is founded on a triadic logic and a focus on disinterestedness, convivial accountability is grounded in social identities and tacit knowledge.

Let me illustrate how a process of technocratic accountability can eliminate or mute these convivial dimensions from a decisionmaking process. I draw here on the Australian regime of regulatory reform discussed in Section I, summarizing its effects when scrutinizing the regulation of migration advice. This policy issue was initially framed as one of protecting vulnerable clients from being given poor advice. Once under the analytical lens of national competition policy however, it was reframed as correcting the market failure of information asymmetries between advisor and client. The welfare state's protective obligation of integrity toward vulnerable citizens were translated, under the regime of technocratic accountability, into one of correcting market failures in respect to information asymmetries that denied consumers the precondition of fully informed and autonomous choice necessary to participate in the market for migration advice. The effects of this translation included a notable insensitivity to issues of redistributive inequity, particularly in relation to the free community advice provided by nonprofit agencies for especially vulnerable individuals, such as asylum and refugee applicants. From the perspective of "redress of market failure," this free advice became a "cross-subsidy which distorts the migration advice market." Under the framework design for protecting the vulnerable, the elimination of free services now is counted as a benefit.[29]

The above example shows, I would argue, that technocratic accountability has important limits to its capacity to legitimate substantive political stakes. To see this, we must actually bracket out the substantive aspect here, i.e. that a particular policy choice (in favor of competitive markets) has been imposed by the logic of technocratic accountability. This policy choice may in and of itself lack legitimacy, at least with certain groups, but equally it may *enhance* legitimacy with other groups. Indeed, the notion that a result lacks legitimacy with those "special interest" groups whose livelihoods or fates depend on the status quo (as the migration agent's livelihoods did here) is precisely what gives it enhanced legitimacy with other groups. This, in a sense, is an inevitable facet of political conflict in a world of scarce resources. But, leaving this substantive dimension aside, there are two facets of the *mode* of technocratic accountability employed here that are important to understanding the "missing piece" and thus the idea of conviviality in accountability contexts. Both flow from the communicative demands of disinterestedness, which require the use of expert language, the explicit and technical rationalization of the reasons for a decision in universalizable terms. This has two effects.

First, the interpretive process of justifying policy decisions to disinterested actors who use expert language mutes the discretionary, value-laden dimensions of those decisions. Muting raw politics in this way, especially over redistributive issues, never quite succeeds: there is arguably a certain disingenuousness about the evasion of the value-laden issues, illustrated by the migration example, that undermines effective accountability. If we ask why imbalances in information counted as market failures, but imbalances in material resources not, the perception of disinterested triangulation of conflict is undermined.

A second, and perhaps deeper effect, is that the communication of tacit identities is barred and distorted, further hollowing out the discourse that animates effective accountability. For those working in the field of migration advice work, the separation of vulnerable asylum and refugee applicants from other groups of citizens needing migration advice seems to undermine a sense of professional ethic; for citizens at large the division seems to undercut a sense of collective solidarity and inclusion. Even if the application of an alternative triadic logic founded on a different set of policy goals reintegrated this division, its articulation in *explicit* terms will still have undermined the *taken-for-granted* shared understandings underpinning collective identities or professional ethics. Convivial accountability is, then, at its core about transference of tacit knowledge, of local knowledge about one's own identity.

To explore the nature of convivial accountability from a broader angle, consider a topic frequently raised by those who *contrast* technocratic accountability with democratic accountability – participation. There has been extensive scholarly criticism directed at technocratic modes of participation in collective decisionmaking, excoriating the replacement of the citizen by the consumer as the prototypical "figure" of political discourse.[30] Much of this criticism has a neo-republican inflection, assuming that technocratic modes of accountability have the effect of marginalizing the active creation of community. Active political citizens are, it is feared, replaced by apolitical, passive consumers, or by depoliticizing legal strategists.

Those who mourn the effects of technocratic accountability have long called for deeper, more participatory modes of democratic accountability,[31] yet often these calls understate the possibilities for participation in technocratic modes of accountability. They are arguably not as limited as the "participatory" critique implies, even given the constraining effects of the need to employ expert language. For institutionally, the separation between monitoring and delivery implied by the triadic logic can foster transparent justification of regulatory policy choice and practical avenues for citizens to voice their concerns. In this way, settings characterized by multiple overlapping triadic logics can arguably create more opportunity for constructive engagement and dialogue over policy than hierarchically-controlled political avenues dominated by symbolic politics. Genuine deliberation is facilitated rather than narrowed, even though it takes place in technocratic terms, because the overlapping veto points and hurdles required to reverse change raise the stakes of securing policy gains.

But while opportunities for deliberation and participation may be expanded and even deepened under conditions of technocratic accountability, there is still "something missing" that only convivial accountability captures. This "missing piece" is elusive precisely because it is connected to a sense of "implicit community." Convivial accountability mechanisms are more adept than technocratic ones at creating a space for frank debate about values, especially in justifying decisions that aggregate or make tradeoffs between competing interests, which are the glue that binds together such competing interests into community. Technocratic accountability does not easily accommodate debate focused on tradeoffs between competing values, because of the important role of disinterestedness in triadic logic. By contrast, where convivial modes of accountability flourish, the tacit nature of the expertise that underpins shared experiences, values, symbols, identities, and understandings allows multiple implicit communities to co-exist peacefully, and to adjust to conflict incrementally and pragmatically. The "missing piece," then, is a particular *tenor or texture* of debate, a texture that transmits and generates implicit senses of community because of its capacity to defy routinization and the explicit codes of expert knowledge.

B. Territorial and functional communities in the shadow of globalization

The link between convivial accountability and implicit community can be illustrated by showing how globalization creates especially acute pressures for the flourishing of convivial accountability. Implicit communities are constructed much more easily in small-scale settings where repeated interactions can generate and sustain shared identities. Where scale constrains or dilutes face-to-face interactions, there are two primary modes of grounding attempts to "explain, reveal, and justify" actions taken in a particular policy arena. Those two modes are representation and expert knowledge communicated in expert language. In institutionalizing representation, *territorially defined communities* typically construct meaning around identity and custom, while the deployment of expert knowledge typically occurs in *functional communities* (groups of actors who come together for instrumental purposes in relation to clearly defined policy areas). Functional communities are generally more reliant on science or other forms of rational-technocratic knowledge for shaping meaning, and thus often have in common languages of technocratic accountability. And the social salience of these languages intensifies in proportion to the dislodging of the nation-state as the geographical unit that provides a baseline for both technocratic and convivial accountability.

The nation-state, as a prototypical territorial community grounded mainly on identity and custom, has until recently integrated convivial and technocratic accountability mechanisms relatively effectively. As the state increasingly harnessed the scientific knowledge generated by modernity, functional communities have generated institutionally distinct "expert networks." Within a nation-state, expert networks began as subsidiary governance mechanisms feeding into democratic decisionmaking procedures in order to enhance their knowledge base. Over time, the increasing influence of such functional communities within the representational process has begun to infuse even democratic accountability with a triadic logic, as discussed in Section 1 – for example, via lobbying activities within technocratic policy networks that shape the content of policy agendas, or via third party monitoring of social regulation by civil society groups. Thus, as complexity and specialization have grown in the political arena, the impact of expert networks cuts across democratic decisionmaking procedures, and – in the context of the greater influence of supranational actors and processes – even displaces them.[32] In this way, globalization increasingly displaces territorial communities with functional, non-geographically defined communities.

Now many scholars have suggested that transnational networks enhance effective governance. The network of powerful committees in the European political space, the collective processes of which are referred to as "comitology," is one particularly developed example of this.[33] But fewer are optimistic about their contribution to *accountability*: despite some notable exceptions,[34] the wider scholarly community views expert networks in a transnational context as a threat to accountability.[35] This unease is based, I would suggest, at least in part on the unconvivial nature of such mechanisms of accountability – their lack of capacity to reveal, explain, and justify the actions of distant actors in ways that are meaningful for those affected by their actions. When the knowledge deployed and communicated by expert networks is integrated into electorally or democratically grounded processes, then the territorial community thereby created acquires some basis for developing customs and identities and thereby a deeper sense of implicit community. As the conversation becomes increasingly between multiple expert languages, it is unleavened by such implicit communities. Even where multiple overlapping fora hold actors to account via *cumulative* triadic logics for disparate sets of values and purposes (and as Section I demonstrated, there are now numerous fora institutionalizing triadic logics, encompassing values as diverse as fundamental rights and wealth maximization), this seems as often as not to *undercut* broader and deeper social cohesion. For articulating disparate sets of shared assumptions in expert languages makes *explicit* their precise scope and renders them more transparently in conflict with each other. The question therefore arises whether functional communities in a widely dispersed geographical context can develop non-technocratic identities and customs: if this is possible, then globalization does not necessarily have to crowd out the possibility of convivial accountability.

III. WATER STRUGGLES AS CHALLENGE TO TECHNOCRATIC ACCOUNTABILITY

In this final section, I will apply the issues discussed in previous sections to a concrete example of transnational struggles over access to water, to illustrate more concretely the implications for understanding accountability. The "problem of water" is increasingly framed as a global policy issue.[36] Water – in particular the provision of rural and urban water services including dams, irrigation, and household use – is at the center of a complex policy field populated by multiple competing social understandings of water. Each of these typically generates its own discrete zone of technocratic accountability organized around a triadic social logic where expert decisionmakers deploy precise technical knowledge in accordance with a limited and variously binding set of mandates. Each understanding presupposes a different set of relevant actors as well as a different epistemic base, but, as the field of water policy globalizes, the ability to make tradeoffs across the overlapping modes of technocratic accountability at the national level decreases. As a result the plurality of communities underpinning this technocratic network becomes less and less integrated – in part because the salience of territorial communities declines.

We can see this if we document some of the competing understandings of water in circulation at present. Historically, connections between state-building and the control of water resources privileged a political understanding of water as a means of patronage or oppression, such that the implicit community that underpins this control has often been coterminous with nation-state borders. However, functional communities implicit in competing understandings of the meaning of water have an increasing influence on the global water policy field.

For example, environmental and public health values are two scientifically grounded discourses that demarcate the appropriate boundaries of water's community either by reference to the physical dimensions of a watershed, or by reference to demographically identified populations, whose distribution in terms of the health effects of clean water will usually track watershed boundaries. While territorial in nature, these communities do not map onto the boundaries of a nation-state. Economic understandings of water also presuppose, from a different angle, communities the boundaries of which are radically disjunct from those of political nation-states. Increasingly central to global water politics and enshrined as the fourth of the four so-called "Dublin Principles," the notion of water as an economic good focuses on classes of "users" disaggregated primarily by considerations such as cost-reflective pricing. Even an understanding of water as a fundamental human right is an approach which privileges abstract universal principles over locally-specific communities, and while day-to-day struggles to implement such human rights are far more grounded, a rights-based approach to water policy can be just as technocratic as economic ones, as illustrated in Section I above. When *each* of these understandings is institutionalized in a field of decisionmaking and decision-justification grounded on triadic logic, a situation of multiple overlapping modes of technocratic accountability results.

While a detailed discussion of the global politics of water cannot be undertaken here, I want to sketch selected events that illustrate different modes of accountability in relation to water. These do not illustrate any sort of connected coherent narrative about the trajectory of water policy: they are intended instead to illustrate the potential inherent in different textures of "accounting for" or "holding others to account" – sometimes with the potential to evolve into conviviality, and sometimes to collapse back into technocracy. I stressed at the end of Section I that convivial accountability sits uneasily with routinization, and we will see in the following scenarios varying resistances to, and effects of, routinization.

A. Resisting routinization and unruly accountability

The first scenario concerns Cochabamba, Bolivia, between late 1999 and early 2000. The city's water system had come under the control of foreign operators, in accordance with a complex concession contract between the Bolivian government and International Waters, Ltd of London, themselves controlled by the Californian infrastructure company Bechtel. The private company raised the rates for local water users by an average of 35 percent, in some cases as much as 200 percent. In a city where the minimum wage is less than US$100 per month, many families were hit with increases of US$20 per month and more. Public anger over the rate increases escalated over the next few months, with repeated series of marches, demands, negotiations, and ongoing protests that became increasingly tense and eventually violent, leaving five protesters and one policeman dead. Martial law was then imposed, but at the same time the Bolivian government announced it would cancel the contract with International Waters, Ltd.

The fluid social protest at the heart of this scenario illustrates what could be called *unruly accountability*. This is not simply about hostile, extra-legal or violent action. It expresses the constructive dimensions of what Roberto Unger calls "destabilizing" rights,[37] enacting a mode of accountability that resists an understanding of water in technocratic terms of instrumental rationality, and highlights the spiritual, and collective symbolic meanings attached to water in local community contexts. The protestors urged preservation of the "ancient usages and customs" relating to water, which they called the "lifeblood of our ancestors." They meant by this more than simply the allocative and distributive norms for water irrigation that were informally embedded in local community practice, though this was certainly an important part of what they aimed to preserve. But the cumulative quantities of time, volume, price, and distribution of water amounted for the protestors to more than the sum of their instrumental value: they were expressive of and constitutive of, in a taken-for-granted and implicit fashion, the territorial community that used this water. They embodied the tacit knowledge that was crucial to the ongoing existence of that implicit community.

B. Creating implicit communities across distended territory

During the course of the rising tension in Cochabamba, a document called the Cochabamba Declaration was drafted. This document is an illustration of an attempt to shape a community of shared custom and identity across distended geographical spaces, where repeated face-to-face interactions are impossible. The Cochabamba Declaration of December 8, 2000 declared that "We, citizens of Bolivia, Canada, United States, India, Brazil: Farmers, workers, indigenous people, students, professionals, environmentalists, educators, non-governmental organizations, retired people, gather together today in solidarity to combine forces in the defense of the vital right to water." The document then declared a range of disparate principles that should shape the governance of water, constructing water as, variously, a fundamental human right, a public trust, a sacred aspect of the natural world, and a local community resource. The persistent *simultaneous* heterogeneity of the modes of justification is an indication that convivial accountability is a gesture toward something deeper than the substitution of an alternative expert discourse such as environmental science. And the ground of this conviviality is a conception of implicit community, arguably one that shows that functional communities in a widely dispersed geographical context *can* develop non-technocratic identities and customs.

The Declaration mirrors a heterogeneity and plurality of social actors that cannot be comfortably fitted into a representational model where formal arenas for functional decisionmaking feed into territorially defined political structures. Less unruly than fluid social protest, this nonetheless still unsettles the premises of technocratic delegation at the heart of the triadic logic of technocratic accountability by disrupting settled understandings about both representation and expertise. At the territorial level, the Declaration constitutes a people thus: "We, citizens of Bolivia, Canada, United States, India, Brazil . . .". This implies a cosmopolitan flux reaching out beyond any conventional groupings, possibly toward the future – this particular group of nations is not typically massed together in any particular institutional setting. At the functional level, the yoking continues to be mildly eccentric: "farmers, workers, indigenous people, students, professionals, environmentalists, educators, nongovernmental organizations, retired people gather[ing] together . . . in solidarity." This is provocative too, because it collapses a false dichotomy between "new" and "old" social movements: the former based on identity and new forms of politics (such as human rights, gay rights, environment rights, etc.) while the latter movements struggle for resources to cope with the contradictions of the capitalist economy (such as urban squatters', peasant and fishworkers' movements, and farmers' movements).

Ethnographically observed accounts of the Cochabamba water wars confirm the significant extent to which the grassroots mobilization bridged traditional political differences, including rural–urban, mestizo-indigenous, and middle and working class interests.[38] In this way the praxis of the Cochabamba water wars creates a selectively multinational, self-consciously non-state "we." It is also a "we" that resists cohesion through shared epistemologies or value commitments: some less (workers, retired people, students) oppose the distributional impact of markets while still accepting capitalism as a basic framework; others wish to substitute for economic rationality some other basically technocratic instrumental knowledge base (professionals, educators, mainstream environmentalists and NGOs); still others invoke deeply different cultural traditions that resist instrumental rationality altogether (indigenous people, farmers, radical environmentalists, some students, some NGOs).

The "we" therefore has no physical ground and speaks in many different voices. This is the subject of convivial accountability, one that de-territorializes the practice of citizenship in such a way as to gesture toward what Friedmann has called "insurgent citizenship." Insurgent citizenship characterizes active participation in social movements as the creation of "communities of political discourse and practice, that aim at either, or both, the defense of existing democratic principles and rights and the claiming of new rights that, if enacted, would lead to an expansion of the spaces of democracy, regardless of where these struggles take place."[39] The struggles around access to water that radiate outwards from Cochambamba are arguably just such a species of citizenship, congealing around a specific issue in a manner that belies instrumental functionality even while it is delinked from a territorially bounded notion of community. It expresses a community whose practices and norms are sufficiently locally-embedded to generate daily practices that are meaningful for the actors affected, but that takes its cues for the articulation of its shared identity from connections to other actors scattered across the globe who share the values and purposes of the affected local actors. This insurgent, de-territorialized citizenship is a perhaps paradoxically willed expression of implicit community, one that gestures toward conviviality.

C. The incipient routinization of convivial accountability

But the Declaration is a single moment, a moment of drama and a sense of a new beginning. Could such an expression ever become sufficiently routinized to constitute and constrain "everyday" power? Otherwise put, how can the demands of social movements translate into accountability mechanisms that are responsive to the everyday bureaucratic demands of policy implementation? Arguably it could be relevant and responsive if the implicit community presupposed by the strategies of unruly accountability, and the alliances that such strategies build, were to persist into more "everyday" management contexts. In this respect, routinization is crucial and also constructive: it brings in its train a set of administrative practices that rearrange power relations in systematic ways.

One example of embedding the kind of implicit community expressed by the Cochabamba Declaration in more routine practical strategies of governance is the World Commission on Dams (WCD). Established in 1998 as a novel two-year experiment in a new form of global governance, the WCD was a mixture of a research commission, an inquiry, and a legislature, with the aim of providing some constructive ways forward in the context of planning and building large dams, an issue attracting increasing social and political tensions in countries all over the world. The twelve Commissioners of the WCD came from ministries, regulatory agencies, private industry, NGOs (both environmental and development), and academia. They spanned seven countries: including three from the US, two from Western Europe, two from India, and two from Australia. Latin America and the Middle East appeared to lose out, but the balance between "North" and "South" was in fact reasonably even. They served not as representatives of constituencies but rather in their individual capacities. Their role expressed a novel blend of charisma, technical knowledge, activist experience, and de facto yet unacknowledged representation, not so much of constituencies as of a wide range of viewpoints and backgrounds.

The WCD could be viewed as formalizing the "odd bedfellows" facet of the Cochabamba water wars, institutionalizing it with the aim of generating systematic principles that might guide, in this case, the building of major dams. While those who signed the Cochabamba Declaration were in a sense the contingent product of an ad hoc situation, the WCD representational formula was a little more systematic, aiming to capture not the representation of geographic territories or particular political constituencies, but rather the full range (including, at the extremes, those such as activists committed to civil disobedience) of "positions in the dam debate." As such, it aimed to formalize, at a level that transcended national territorial control, the kind of functional array of perspectives that has traditionally remained subsidiary to territorial mechanisms of governance.

After the Commission had completed its work, it attempted to state in more general terms the principles upon which participation in such a governance endeavor might rest. Here too we see an increasing formalization of the patterns of unsettled flux and social protest that characterize a more grassroots activism in Cochabamba style. Participation should be based, the WCD argued, on a "rights and risks" framework, including all those who have a "legitimate claim and entitlement under law, constitution or custom" that might be affected by a dam project. In other words, "stakeholders" in dam decisions include *all* those who take on risk, not only the private sector infrastructure investors (labeled as the key risk-takers in conventional technocratic processes), but also the non-voluntary risks imposed on all project-affected peoples. In additional statements of principle, the WCD prohibited utilitarian tradeoffs and balancing in the resolution of conflicts between all these right-holders and risk-bearers, and mandated instead either good faith negotiations or the decisions of independent courts as accountability mechanisms. We can see here the reemergence of familiar competing modes of accountability – legal, democratic, bureaucratic – in the governance principles generated by even such an innovatively designed institution as the WCD. The question, however, is whether the working through of such familiar institutionalized modes would destroy the implicit community constructed through the original institutional innovation of the WCD?

CONCLUSION

This question will not be answered here, but its persistence poses the main challenge to the viability of a non-bureaucratic alternative to the accountability crisis, one that can operate in large-scale, geographically distended environments and not become inevitably colonized by bureaucracy. The weight of the argument in this Chapter has been directed toward two ends: first, establishing a set of common features that cut across traditionally distinct modes of accountability and renders them all, in varying degrees, technocratic; and secondly, identifying the "missing element" that constitutes a more fundamental basis of current crises of accountability, i.e., a "convivial accountability" generated by tacit shared knowledge and identities and grounded in implicit community.

This convivial form of accountability may indeed be vulnerable to the effects of definition and routinization, which could range from reduction to technocratic manifestations or boiling up into unruly protest. But this chapter has aimed mainly to convince readers that it exists, and that there are indeed possibilities for convivial accountability in technocratically governed, functionally oriented, geographically dispersed policy settings. It points to the possibility that a sense of integrated identity and shared understandings can develop around routine collaborations, such that beyond the willed and self-conscious creation of community evinced by practices like the Cochabamba Declaration lie future and less abstracted possibilities, eloquently captured in Dan Jacobson's evocation of certain forms of social exchange:

> shared, unspoken assumptions; oblique allusions and quasi-familial understandings; mutually recognized expectations and discreet, insistent curiosities; obligations informally accepted and returned; rights to both intimacy and aloofness acknowledged; practices and forms of speech cunningly coded to include some and exclude others.[40]

It is these kinds of practices that lend a sense of collective identity to the process of justifying the exercise of political power that lie at the heart of public accountability. This dimension of assumed identity underpins and stabilizes the dispersed and disaggregated activities characteristic of triadic accountability processes. If it is inaccessible, its absence creates a residual undertow, a falling away of taken-for-granted stability. Yet it must be accessible in ways that make it politically and pragmatically relevant, without diluting the aesthetic or cultural dimensions that make it meaningful.

This fragile balance, if achievable, would create a "convivial society . . . where technologies are servants to politically interrelated individuals not managers."[41] Charles Sabel's work claims to "expand our capacities for problem-solving while inviting us to exercise our capacities for self-rule" through organizational approaches that "develop corrigible institutions through peer review and local experimentation informed by lay knowledge."[42] Whether lay knowledge and peer review can be durably employed across borders and between strangers without relying on expert language and delegation to "objective" professionals is a challenge that accountability debates must integrate. This, I have argued here, is a challenge that is evaded by thinking of it in terms of the appropriate balance between legal, bureaucratic, and democratic modes of accountability. The deeper and more crucial question is whether technocratic accountability necessarily crowds out convivial accountability.

PART FOUR

ACCOUNTABILITY AND EXPERIENCE

CHAPTER 11

UNDERSTANDING NGO-BASED SOCIAL AND ENVIRONMENTAL REGULATORY SYSTEMS: WHY WE NEED NEW MODELS OF ACCOUNTABILITY

Sasha Courville

INTRODUCTION

With the recent rise of NGO power in global civil society, the question "to whom are NGOs accountable?" has been a key topic for discussion. Two fatal flaws have characterized most of the ensuing analysis. The first is that all nongovernmental organizations (NGOs) are generally lumped into one generic category, regardless of significant differences in function, scope, structure, constituency, and boundary. The second is that traditional state-based democratic and corporate-economic notions of accountability have been simply lifted from these contexts and applied to the NGO world.

The NGOs and accountability debate is examined in the first and second sections of this chapter. In the third section, a specific sub-set of international NGOs is introduced in order to narrow the discussion and allow for more detailed analysis later. That subset consists of the members of the International Social and Environmental Accreditation and Labelling (ISEAL) Alliance. In the fourth section, a few examples taken from the ISEAL Alliance and its members are used to put forward the argument that accountability regimes can evolve over time through pragmatic responses to pressures and demands as they arise, rather than solely as the outcome of pre-envisaged institutional design. The fifth section develops this further, outlining how institutional "learning" can play an important role in the evolution of accountability regimes. Based on insights gained from examining the accountability mechanisms of the ISEAL Alliance members, the sixth section offers a conceptualization of accountability relationships based on the concept of differentiated accountability boundaries. The seventh and final section then outlines some thoughts on the limits to NGO accountability.

I. NGOS AND ACCOUNTABILITY

The rise of NGOs has accompanied and influenced the processes of globalization of the late twentieth and early twenty-first centuries. While public welfare issues (social justice and environmental protection, among others) have historically been seen as primarily, and indeed exclusively, the business of national governments, this conceptualization of responsibility has been eroded in recent years.[1] One contributing factor is that neoliberal government policies of the late 1980s and early 1990s, such as trade liberalization and privatization, have been instrumental in shifting economic power from the national level to the international level, from states to other actors, including corporations. This has led to a fracturing of governance, including the creation of new institutional structures and the reshaping of old ones.[2] At the "new frontier zone" where national and global economies interface,[3] the ability and willingness of states to effectively regulate economic policies, and the social and environmental impacts of these economic policies, has been called into question.[4]

Concerned by the lack of effective governmental action across a range of social justice and environmental issues – from poverty alleviation in developing countries to the unrelenting destruction of critical habitat for endangered species, and from clear inequalities of international trade rules to the lack of enforcement of national labor and environmental laws leading to corporate abuses of human rights and environmental destruction – individuals, networks, and organizations outside the realm of the nation-state have begun to take a more active role in processes of social change. These individuals, networks, and organizations comprise global civil society, where people interact across borders outside their identification with a specific state.[5]

I situate NGOs as being embedded within global civil society. Their constituent bases and networks are located within global civil society though global civil society is a much wider concept than NGOs alone. But what are NGOs that makes them different from other types of actors? According to Anna Vakil, NGOs are "self-governing, private, not-for-profit organizations that are geared toward improving the quality of life of disadvantaged people."[6] This definition is useful in providing certain basic structural characteristics with an underlying normative disposition, though I would add a further objective in that a large number of NGOs focus specifically on environmental protection, though some do address both social and environmental goals.

The growth in the number of NGOs in the past two decades is dramatic. NGOs registered in the Organization of Economic Cooperation and Development (OECD) increased from 1,600 in 1980 to 2,970 in 1993.[7] In 2000, the *Economist* put the number of NGOs operating in the USA alone at two million, with most being less than thirty years old.[8] In other countries the numbers are significant as well, with 18,000 registered NGOs in the Philippines, 3,000 in Brazil, and 65,000 in Russia.[9]

With increasing numbers, it has been argued that NGOs are wielding significant power, holding states and intergovernmental organizations accountable "by serving as independent sources of criticism."[10] NGOs, through transnational advocacy, can act to redress a democracy deficit caused by the dispersed nature of decisionmaking across international borders.[11] In their role as "champions of the public good," NGOs appear to be trusted by the public, at least in Europe, much more than governments, companies, or the media.[12]

However, in recent years, NGOs have come under increasing scrutiny. A recurring theme in recent attacks on NGOs is their lack of accountability. Such critiques range from questions about whether NGOs are really the legitimate voice of the poor and disadvantaged to extreme statements that "international NGOs [are not] merely undemocratic, but . . . profoundly antidemocratic."[13] A core question is to whom are NGOs accountable. The answer to this question pivots on the very legitimacy of NGOs as actors in national and global polities.

The issues raised in critiques against NGO accountability center around three main concerns. The first is that NGOs are not accountable to their members or beneficiaries. In this perspective, it is usually stated that NGOs lack customary mechanisms for reporting on their activities, unlike other agents such as firms or elected officials in democratic state systems.[14] Concern is raised that most NGO leaders are not elected and that members are generally passive (since their material commitment generally does not exceed nominal membership fees). The fact that NGOs often have advisory committees incorporated into their structures is not seen as a real check to management, as these committee members share the same ideological perspective as the management representatives.[15] In a recent study of eighteen global entities, NGOs were found lacking in transparency to their members about their operations compared to IGOs and transnational corporations, particularly with respect to how they spend their money or how well they achieve their goals.[16]

The second concern raised refers to the external accountability of NGOs to the wider society. There is a feeling that NGOs need to earn their role in society.[17] Given that NGOs seek to convert their reputations into power, skeptics are concerned about the scientific validity of NGO claims; the high-risk stunts that NGOs may participate in; the way NGOs spend their money; and whether NGOs actually achieve their goals.[18] Concerns have been raised that even when NGO leaders are elected, they are elected from NGO members, not from society in general. In sum, the issue is how, as political actors in national and global polities, NGOs can be held accountable for the information they provide and the actions they undertake when these affect others beyond their membership bases.

This is especially important in the area of international development and international solidarity work, where NGOs are extremely active. The difficulty of applying the concept of external accountability to NGOs at the international level is that these organizations are not recognized by the international system as actors. Given this, there are no mechanisms for ensuring accountability to the system.[19] While international NGOs often work as agents on behalf of disadvantaged people in developing countries, how can we be sure that the outcomes are to the liking and benefit of the intended beneficiaries?[20]

A third concern is the danger of conflicts of interest when NGOs attempt to balance multiple roles.[21] NGOs carry out a range of activities, from advocacy work and research and campaigning roles to service delivery in international development, among others. One example of a potential conflict of interest situation is as follows. An NGO has developed a strong reputation with its advocacy work on the need to improve compliance with and monitoring of labor rights in a specific industry sector, such as the apparel industry. After a period of time, a company that was one of the targets of the NGO's campaign makes a public commitment to address the concerns, and asks the NGO for advice on how best to implement such changes. Concerns are raised about NGO accountability in such a situation, where their role as an advisor seems to jeopardize their status as an independent watchdog.[22]

II. ALTERNATIVES FOR NGO ACCOUNTABILITY

Before addressing each of the concerns about the accountability of NGOs point by point, two overriding flaws of analysis need to be highlighted. First, the majority of critiques about NGO accountability use the word "NGO" as a generic category, lumping all NGOs together with all destined to suffer the same criticisms and concerns, regardless of whether they are appropriate to the specific context or not. In reality, NGOs themselves are a highly diverse group, ranging from extreme environmental organizations, such as Earth First, that use confrontational tactics in their political protests, to international human rights organizations, such as Amnesty International, with strict internal governance procedures.[23] The term NGO also includes emergency and long-term development aid NGOs such as CARE, World Vision, and the Red Cross, as well as private social and environmental certification systems like those affiliated to the International Federation of Organic Agriculture Movements (IFOAM). Many of IFOAM's 700 members are also NGOs, active at the local level in agricultural extension work or consumer-awareness-raising activities.

In sum, NGOs differ dramatically in their core functions, organizational structures (including mechanisms for accountability), scope of activities, constituencies, and intended beneficiaries among other parameters. Given these phenomenal differences, it is simply impossible to address concerns about NGO accountability without focusing on a specific sub-group of NGOs that share a number of similarities. Given this, the next section of this paper will move to a concrete discussion of one of the most sophisticated groups of NGOs in terms of accountability mechanisms, the members of ISEAL, the International Social and Environmental Accreditation and Labelling Alliance.

A second fundamental flaw characterizing most analysis regarding the lack of NGO accountability is the cut-and-paste method of transferring traditional conceptions of democratic and economic accountability to the NGO world. For example, concerns are raised that NGOs are not accountable to their members and/or beneficiaries because these members and/or beneficiaries often do not participate in the election or selection of the NGOs' leaderships. But, of course, where NGO constituencies and beneficiaries are difficult to identify and/or maintain because of rapid growth of the initiative, or large geographic distances and uncertainty, the electoral model may not be the most appropriate. Similarly, as NGOs are operating within a larger societal context that may be hostile to their objectives of social change, there may be a need for gatekeeping of membership and leadership.

In these cases, the NGOs will need other mechanisms of accountability to their members, affiliates, and beneficiaries. One of the most effective internal accountability mechanisms for NGOs is Hirschman's concepts of voice and exit.[24] If NGOs are not providing an effective vehicle for addressing their members' and other internal stakeholders' concerns (voice), then these stakeholders have a powerful tool at their disposal – they can easily exit.[25] Increased membership means higher levels of credibility that can translate into stronger influence for social change. Membership fees are also a fundamental operational baseline for NGO funding. If NGOs do not maintain their membership base, then their very survival is at risk. It should be noted that, while exit may be a low-cost option for NGO members, other beneficiaries of certain NGOs, including international development NGOs, may not have this possibility.[26]

Donors are another group of internal actors that also have the option to exit if they find that NGOs are not accountable to them. Structurally, donors have contracts with clearly defined project objectives and timelines for achieving outcomes that increase NGO accountability; while logistically, donor funding is usually critical to the ability of most NGOs to carry out projects and campaigns. While exit is not an easy option in traditional democratic notions of accountability, it certainly is applicable in the context of NGOs, given the wider context in which they operate. This provides a powerful accountability loop to ensure that NGOs are responsive to their members and donors.

In terms of external accountability, how can NGOs be held accountable to the wider society in which they operate and seek to influence? A key problem is that NGOs are not officially recognized by the international system that they seek to influence. However, conceptualizations of external accountability of all actors operating in the international system, including states and corporations, are weak and somewhat nebulous. While there are no formal mechanisms of accountability operating at the international level, there are a number of softer mechanisms that contribute to the accountability of NGOs. These include engaging in public debate, reputation, peer accountability through networks, and relationships with intergovernmental organizations ("IGOs"). There is also a limited degree of legal accountability acting on NGOs.

First, by actively engaging in public debate, NGOs are presenting their perspectives and views on particular issues and are participating in societal processes of discussion and decisionmaking. By openly and transparently presenting their positions, NGOs leave themselves open to criticism but also open a window for dialogue with other actors. Successful NGOs gauge their members' and civil society's views on specific issues and are responsive to new ideas and pressures.[27] A key role for many NGOs is creating space for their members and other actors in civil society to come together to discuss serious problems facing society and to attempt to outline possible solutions. In this way, NGOs play the role of facilitator between different positions, with a view to moving toward consensus on ways forward.

Secondly, the currency by which an NGO trades is its reputation. According to Ed Mayo, former executive director of the New Economics Foundation, "Legitimacy is at the heart of effective NGO operations: erode it or remove it and the NGO is left stranded, like a business facing overnight market collapse."[28] The skeptics' concern that NGOs will send out false or misleading information to sway public opinion is minimized by the risk of endangering their reputations through such actions. While the system may not recognize them, most NGOs are indeed "repeat players" due to the complex nature of the problems they seek to address and the slow processes of social change that are required to address them.[29]

An NGO's reputation is also critical in establishing and maintaining relationships with other NGOs. The effectiveness of NGO advocacy activities depends on the ability of NGOs, through networking, to ensure widespread support in global civil society.[30] Networking enlarges the circle of decisionmaking, requiring coordination, cooperation, and, at times, compromises. To the extent that NGOs are also interested in influencing IGOs and nation-states through participation and cooperation, they also need to be sensitive to the political and economic interests and constraints of these actors.[31] Through meeting criteria for participation in certain international organizations and fora such as the Food and Agriculture Organization or specific treaty negotiations, a formal, though weak, mechanism for accountability is provided.

A final formal mechanism for external accountability of NGOs to the wider society in which they operate is a legal mechanism binding

NGOs to meet national laws. Even international NGOs need to be registered in one country and the laws of that country must be complied with.

In terms of concerns about conflict of interests between different but overlapping functions of NGOs, these can be addressed through structural solutions. Where potential conflicts of interests arise, NGOs can take steps to ensure that these are minimized, either through organizational structure, as will be seen in the discussion of ISEAL organizations, or through NGO networks. Using networks, NGOs can divide responsibility for certain functions where conflicts of interest exist between different organizations, minimizing the risks.

III. NARROWING THE DISCUSSION: ISEAL ORGANIZATIONS

The NGO and accountability context provides fertile ground for raising a number of fundamental questions about current conceptualizations of accountability, and for pointing to how new forms of accountability could take shape. This section provides a brief overview of the International Social and Environmental Accreditation and Labelling Alliance and a couple of its members to illustrate how NGO labeling initiatives in particular construct their accountability regimes and respond to the criticisms raised against NGOs outlined in the previous section.

A. Introducing the ISEAL Alliance and member initiatives, IFOAM and FLO

The ISEAL Alliance was established, at least in part, to grapple with the concept of international NGO accountability vis-à-vis an international system that is, as mentioned earlier, largely unable to recognize such organizations. ISEAL members, such as the Forest Stewardship Council, Social Accountability International, and the International Federation of Organic Agriculture Movements (IFOAM), include some of the more sophisticated private regulatory structures for social justice and environmental protection.

ISEAL was founded in 1999 by eight social and environmental accreditation and certification systems, in the belief that by working together they could improve their verification systems – ISEAL was also seen to be a vehicle through which these verification systems could become more recognized by governments through developing coordinated tools that would increase the legitimacy of member voluntary systems. ISEAL organizations also seek to ensure that production and process method certification is recognized as valid and that social and environmental concerns are safeguarded within international trade. By coming together, ISEAL members felt that they could deliver a clear message to consumers, ensuring widespread confidence in the quality of members' systems, thereby supporting growing market success. In a world where new corporate social responsibility and environmental schemes seem to pop up every minute with varying degrees of credibility, ISEAL members felt that together they could deliver a clear message to consumers about how to differentiate credible verification initiatives from green wash.[32]

ISEAL's full members include the International Federation of Organic Agriculture Movements (IFOAM), the Forest Stewardship Council (FSC), the Fairtrade Labelling Organizations International (FLO), Social Accountability International (SAI), the Sustainable Agriculture Network (SAN) of the Rainforest Alliance, the Marine Stewardship Council (MSC), and the Marine Aquarium Council (MAC). These members share a common vision of a world where ecological sustainability and social justice are the normal conditions of business.[33]

Membership in ISEAL is conditioned on the following five requirements. To be a member, one must: (1) be an international body establishing accreditation or standard-setting programs at the international level; (2) generate or accredit to private sector product and/or performance-based standards that focus on social and/or environmental issues, incorporating both performance and management-based elements, being voluntary in nature, and taking into account the ecological, cultural, and economic realities of the parts of the world in which they operate; (3) be a registered legal entity; (4) demonstrate a documented management structure that safeguards impartiality and enables participation of all parties significantly concerned, or provide evidence of moving toward this; and (5) agree in writing to abide by ISEAL visions and objectives.[34]

The International Federation of Organic Agriculture Movements (IFOAM) is the oldest member of the ISEAL Alliance, having been founded in 1972 to bring together the various actors in the organic movement worldwide. IFOAM is still "uniting the organic world" over thirty years later with more than 700 organizations as members in over 100 countries – half of which are developing and Central European countries. IFOAM's mission is to lead, unite, and assist the organic movement in its full diversity, and its goal is the worldwide adoption of ecologically, socially, and economically sound systems that are based on the principles of organic agriculture.[35]

IFOAM's members include producer organizations, nongovernmental organizations, traders, retailers, consumers, and researchers, among others. Any organization with a primary interest in organic agriculture can become a member with full voting rights; those with some degree of interest and activities can become associates. IFOAM's main decisionmaking body is its General Assembly, held every three years at different locations around the world. At the General Assembly, members vote for the IFOAM World Board, the body that implements the strategic directions approved at the General Assembly. As its name suggests, the World Board is constituted of members from different regions of the world. Current membership includes representatives from Sweden, Argentina, Germany, Australia, Italy, Senegal, the US, India, and Japan. Apart from the World Board, IFOAM members have significant flexibility to organize themselves through committees, working groups, and task forces according to geographic regions or sector interests. For example, there is an IFOAM Asia working group (which had its fifth scientific conference in China in 2001), an IFOAM Development Forum, and an IFOAM Trade Forum, in addition to a Standards Committee and Norms Management Committee, among others.

In terms of IFOAM's scope, the following are the goals and activities as defined by the IFOAM World Board:

- To provide authoritative information about organic agriculture and to promote its worldwide application;
- To exchange knowledge;
- To represent the organic movement at international policymaking forums;
- To make an agreed international guarantee of organic quality a reality;
- To establish, maintain, and regularly revise the international "IFOAM Basic Standards" as well as the "IFOAM Accreditation Criteria for Certifying Programmes"; and
- To build a common agenda for all stakeholders in the organic sector, including producers, farm workers, consumers, the food industry, trade organizations, and society at large.[36]

Another ISEAL member is the Fairtrade Labelling Organizations International (FLO). FLO was founded in 1997 to bring together the various fair trade labeling initiatives in consumers' countries, the first of which was Max Havelaar in the Netherlands in 1988. Currently there are nineteen such initiatives operating in twenty countries, the newest of which are in Mexico and Australia/New Zealand. FLO is internally focused with respect to stakeholder relations, with key constituents including the national initiatives, the 422 producer groups certified in the system from forty-nine developing countries and trading companies.[37] FLO's highest decisionmaking body is the FLO Board, made up of national consumer-country initiatives, and producer and trader representatives, though the national initiatives hold the balance of power. These national initiatives meet twice a year at the so-called "meeting of members." The national initiatives are the legal owners of FLO, contribute financially every year to its functioning, and hence approve FLO's budget. A separate certification body, FLO Cert, was recently established to manage the certification and trade audit functions of the Fairtrade system.

FLO's mission is to improve the position of the poor and disadvantaged producers in the developing world, by setting the Fairtrade standards and by creating a framework that enables trade to take place with respect to these standards. Standards are set by the Standards and Policy Committee, comprising representatives across the range of stakeholders plus external experts and approved by the FLO Board.

B. Accountability and the ISEAL Alliance

The ISEAL Alliance and its member organizations have a pronounced and distinctive accountability framework, which extends accountability to their members and to wider society. They also have complex organizational structures that address potential conflicts of interest. Critiques of NGO accountability are addressed in this section using examples from the ISEAL Alliance itself, as well as from IFOAM and FLO.

With respect to the claims that NGOs are not accountable to their members or beneficiaries, both informal and formal accountability mechanisms can be seen within the ISEAL Alliance.

Formally, ISEAL's membership criteria are important as they outline several key differences between ISEAL members and other social and environmental initiatives. ISEAL members are stakeholder-based; their standards are performance-based; they are grounded in independent third party verification; and they are ideologically driven. These provide key benchmarks ensuring mutual accountability of the ISEAL member organizations and help to differentiate ISEAL members from other initiatives, such as ISO's 14001, that because they are solely based on management system standards, make it very difficult for consumers to know the actual environmental performance of a given company or product. Another example for comparison is the Euro-Retailer Produce Working Group's EurepGAP standard on food safety with minimal social criteria that is becoming a de facto requisite for placement into European supermarkets. While EurepGAP claims to be stakeholder-based, significant concerns have been raised by the lack of participation by the very people who would be most affected by this standard: producers. Apart from mutual accountability among members, the ISEAL Alliance Executive Director directly reports to the Executive Board, made up of elected representatives from its membership.

ISEAL members address the issue of internal accountability in a number of ways. As was mentioned above, IFOAM is a member-driven organization with the highest decisionmaking body being the General Assembly, now held every three years. Members elect the World Board, which serves as the vehicle for implementing the strategic directions agreed at the General Assembly. There are geographic requirements for Board membership, ensuring that all regions of the world are represented. Members also vote on any revisions to the IFOAM Basic Standards. As one example of responsiveness to member needs, IFOAM is extremely sensitive to ensuring that members from developing countries are able to actively participate in IFOAM activities. The single largest pool of funds that IFOAM has access to is dedicated to supporting organic agriculture in developing countries, and this can only be spent on initiatives and activities by and for developing-country participants.

FLO defines its internal stakeholders as all those actors that can actively participate in the FLO system, including producers, traders, processors, and national initiatives in consumer countries. While this can be criticized as not being entirely open to any interested party, it has the benefit of limiting the scope of stakeholders to those who do actively participate in the system, making such participation more manageable. Many of the national initiatives have direct or indirect links to wider membership structures that allow for broad-based participation. For example, in Australia and New Zealand, the labeling initiative is supported by a broader umbrella association that has open membership, welcoming any individual or organization interested in promoting fair trade.

In order to ensure accountability, all key stakeholder groups participate in the highest decisionmaking body, the FLO Board, through elected representatives. Producers and traders are elected at the FLO Fair-Trade Forum (the largest meeting of FLO, with all producer groups invited), while national initiative members are elected from the Meeting of Members. FLO is also involved in providing producer and fair trade marketing support. This makes FLO fundamentally different from most other certification systems, in that it has an explicit development function within its organizational structure since its target client base is disadvantaged in the marketplace and generally requires such support to access markets and develop trading relationships.

The ISEAL Alliance and its members are all dependent on financial contributions provided by members, affiliates, users, and donors. The accountability relationships with such actors are very important, especially as they all have strong possibilities for using both voice and exit options. Members have many opportunities for varying degrees of participation through the structures, committees, and boards of the organizations.

When entering into the realm of external accountability, ISEAL and its member organizations are plagued by the same problems facing other NGOs: there is no easily identifiable actor or set of actors to whom they can be held accountable at the international level, beyond their own constituencies. It may be possible to recognize certain members of ISEAL initiatives operating at the national level, but the international level poses a problem. Even international institutions such as the International Accreditation Forum (IAF) have been unable to recognize ISEAL members, due to the fact that these members represent new structures in international space and the rules of the game have not yet expanded to include them. Members of ISEAL have applied to the IAF for membership but were told that they were ineligible because they were international accreditation systems and the IAF membership was based on the concept of national accreditation systems.[38]

A further gray area is with respect to the status of private voluntary certification and labeling initiatives in international trade law, and their ability to discriminate between products based on production and process methods. If states were involved in such initiatives, then they would technically conflict with international trade law – namely with Articles I and II of the General Agreement on Tariffs and Trade,[39] but, as these initiatives are voluntary private systems, the exact implications are unclear. The Technical Barriers to Trade Agreement (TBT)[40] could pose a further threat to ISEAL member initiatives. If deemed to fall under the scope of the TBT, then ISEAL member organizations could be in conflict with international trade law due to the fact that they incorporate production and process methods into their standards. The TBT Agreement applies to "technical regulations" and "standards" with trade effects. ISEAL member initiatives would be covered by the TBT Agreement under the standards provisions, if they were considered to be "recognized bodies."[41] If they are not deemed to be recognized bodies, then their standards and initiatives fall outside the scope of the TBT Agreement.

A clear interpretation of the definition of a "recognized body" is lacking. That IFOAM's Basic Standards and Accreditation Standards were accepted by the ISO into the 1999 edition of the ISO Directory of International Standardizing Bodies, and that this directory is used by WTO members and others to identify international standardizing bodies in trade policy matters and dispute resolution, might possibly result in the interpretation that IFOAM could be considered to be a recognized body.[42] This example highlights the lack of clarity on the role of, let alone accountability mechanisms needed for, ISEAL organizations operating in global political and economic spaces.

To whom are ISEAL members accountable in international space? They desperately want to be accepted as credible, as legitimate by IGOs and by nation states, but there seems to be no clear vehicle for direct accountability. While this is lacking, there are other forms of accountability operating on ISEAL organizations. First, ISEAL organizations all use market-based mechanisms of accreditation and certification. While imperfect, market forces do act on these initiatives to the extent that, if they were not seen to be providing a useful service, they would cease to exist. Secondly, aspects of legal accountability do impact on ISEAL member initiatives. There is no such thing as a physical international space; ISEAL and its member organizations must comply with the laws of the countries in which they are registered. Thirdly, as actors operating in a contested, evolving global polity, acting in part to govern the global economy, they are participating in a process that will redefine the structures, processes, and membership criteria of this space. In fact, this is one of the core objectives of the ISEAL Alliance.

Through various projects and activities, the ISEAL Alliance is seeking to demonstrate to the global polity that its members are indeed credible, accountable, and legitimate international actors. ISEAL's membership criteria outlined above provides transparent information about the structures and objectives of ISEAL members. ISEAL's various activities on developing objective performance benchmarks for standard-setting and accreditation activities provide tools that the international community can use to evaluate ISEAL members and other initiatives.

In terms of official recognition of ISEAL members in the international system, IFOAM is recognized by a number of IGOs – including the Food and Agriculture Organization (FAO), which has a small office dedicated to evaluating and promoting organic agriculture in developing countries. It has worked with the United Nations Conference on Trade and Development (UNCTAD) and the FAO to establish a Task Force on Harmonization of Organic Regulation. FLO has worked with other main fair trade organizations internationally to set up an umbrella fair trade advocacy network, called FINE, with the principal objective of lobbying governmental entities such as the EU for official recognition and support of fair trade. The ISEAL Alliance itself will shortly begin to focus on international policy monitoring and advocacy activities with key government bodies and IGOs.

Apart from seeking recognition from the international system, and apart from engaging in peer accountability activities through networks, the ISEAL Alliance and its members are accountable to the general public through ensuring transparency of their activities and operations. The standards of all ISEAL members can be found on their websites, often in various languages to increase accessibility. Through the ISEAL Code of Good Practice for Setting Social and Environmental Standards, ISEAL members are also required to have accessible standards development and revision policies that include at least two rounds of comment submissions by interested parties.[43] Many ISEAL members have electronic newsletters that provide regular information updates to anyone who signs up.

In the arena of standard-setting and accreditation, conflicts of interest need to be handled very carefully. All the ISEAL members have developed different structural mechanisms to address conflicts of interest. In the case of IFOAM, while the federation was always involved in standard-setting, when it became necessary to extend its focus to conformity assessment activities, the membership decided to establish a separate legal entity to manage the accreditation program, that being the International Organic Accreditation Service (IOAS). There are also clear accreditation criteria and procedures for evaluating whether a certification body is eligible for accreditation, as well as an appeals mechanism in case of disputes. With IFOAM handling standard-setting activities and the IOAS managing the accreditation program, conflicts of interest are significantly reduced.

FLO has addressed the issue of conflicts of interest in a slightly different way. FLO undertakes standard-setting, producer support, and certification functions. While most members of the ISEAL Alliance have moved to separate out accreditation from certification functions, FLO felt that, given the unique developmental focus of Fairtrade, it would be difficult to identify other certification bodies to carry out such tasks. In addition, given that producer support activities are based in part on the information obtained in inspection reports, there was a need for close communication between those functions. However, there was also a need to separate standard-setting from certification activities. And for this reason, a separate legal entity was established to carry out certification functions: FLO Cert.

IV. EVOLUTION V. ARCHITECTURAL DESIGN

As new and complex systems operating in a highly uncertain external environment, the ISEAL Alliance and its members are continually revising their accountability structures to meet the changing needs of their members and to respond to external pressures. While architectural design is always important in the initial development of accountability mechanisms for any system, given the ever-changing and highly uncertain context in which these organizations operate, they evolved through pragmatic responses to particular challenges as they arose. A few examples drawn from the ISEAL Alliance and its members will help to demonstrate how accountability is not solely the product of design, but can also be the product of institutional evolution.

A key component of the ISEAL Alliance's mission statement is "to support members' standard and verification systems to attain a high level of quality and to gain public credibility, political recognition and market success."[44] One example of an accountability project that has evolved over the past number of years to work toward achieving ISEAL's mission is the development and launch of the ISEAL Code of Good Practice for Setting Social and Environmental Standards, mentioned above. After identifying the need for internationally recognized criteria for standard-setting relevant to voluntary social and environmental process and production method standards, and following a comprehensive review of existing guidelines for how international standards are set, the ISEAL Alliance developed its own code of good practice, launched in April 2004.

The drafting of the code was largely based on relevant concepts in existing standards guidance documents and on the personal experiences of ISEAL members in standards development and revision, as amplified by an extensive public consultation process. An implementation manual was also developed to accompany the code, incorporating a number of case studies of how particular standard-setting organizations implement various principles of the code. This has also been followed by opportunities for members to exchange ideas on how to implement the code, including a series of training workshops. In time, it will become mandatory for all ISEAL members to comply with the code. In this example, through sharing experiences and codifying best practice, the ISEAL Alliance has facilitated improvements to its members standard-setting processes. While the code was specifically designed to achieve such an objective, it has supported the revision and evolution of its members' accountability systems and has developed a tool that can itself be revised to support continued revisions over time.

A second example comes from IFOAM, focusing on its initial development and the evolution of its standard-setting and conformity assessment functions. The origins of organic agriculture can be traced back to the 1920s, with the first informal regulatory tools developed around loose codes of conduct and informal inspections in the 1950s and 1960s.[45] During the 1960s and 1970s, pioneering farmers' organizations began to feel the need for more precise definitions of organic farming, in order to give guidance to new groups interested in organic agriculture.[46] In order to facilitate communication among various groups interested in organic agriculture across an increasing geographical spread, IFOAM was formed in 1972. Processes to develop the first IFOAM Basic Standards ensued, leading to the first international organic standard published in 1980, based on the standards of member organizations. These standards have since undergone many revisions, with the last version approved at the IFOAM General Assembly in Canada in 2002. New standards sections are periodically added; for example, a chapter on social justice was developed and approved in 1996, and chapters on aquaculture and forestry have been added through the current revision process.[47]

Parallel to the evolution of organic standards, the regulatory mechanisms by which the organic movement verifies that organic farmers comply with such standards have also evolved over time and in response to particular needs. As organic markets grew beyond direct local relationships between producers and consumers, consumers began to ask for independent guarantees that products really were organic. In response, organic farmers' associations were the first to develop private certification bodies to meet this market need.[48] By the mid-1980s, members began to ask IFOAM to evaluate the performance of an increasingly large number of certification bodies, as a way to enhance mutual trust leading to cooperation and facilitation of organic trade.[49] With that in mind, the IFOAM General Assembly approved the development of the IFOAM accreditation program in 1992. By 1997, the International Organic Accreditation Service (IOAS) was finally established to operate the accreditation program after years of discussion over the need to separate standard-setting from accreditation functions.[50] By December 2004, there were thirty-two IFOAM accredited certification bodies, operating in over seventy countries.[51]

With the success of organic agriculture and increased international trade in organic products, governments began to take an interest in organic regulation. Sixty countries were involved in developing organic regulations by 2003, including thirty-seven with fully implemented regulations.[52] This had led to a regulatory nightmare, with duplications between the private system run by IFOAM and governmental programs. And with no multilateral arrangement among governments, this resulted in increased costs, wasted human resources, and trade barriers, particularly for developing-country exports. The IFOAM membership is currently revising its role within this duplicative regulatory context, evaluating what activities and functions would best promote the further development of organic agriculture. It was also active in the establishment of an international Task Force on Harmonization with UNCTAD and the FAO which seeks to find harmonizing solutions to simplify organic regulation which, if successful will require power-sharing and the development of new forms of hybrid regulatory relationships between IFOAM and governmental entities.

A third example is the evolution of FLO's organizational and accountability structures. When FLO was originally established in 1997 as an umbrella organization for global fair trade labeling, its highest decisionmaking body was the Meeting of Members, a forum of seventeen national member initiatives based in consumer countries. This attracted criticism by external actors, as well as from the internal actors who are supposed to be at the very core of FLO's activities – the producers, as they felt that they were not sufficiently represented in FLO's decisionmaking processes. FLO standards were fragmented and lacked standardization as they had come from a number of different national initiatives. Its certification system was also inconsistent due to a lack of strong internal guidelines and consistent training and reporting requirements. This was due to the fact that FLO was initially organized to focus on issues of fair economic development rather than issues of effective monitoring and certification of labeling standards.

While the process of harmonization and restructuring was difficult, especially as FLO needed to keep operating during the changes, it responded to such criticisms in its new structure and operational processes. As mentioned above, the highest decisionmaking structure now includes producers and traders, its standards have been reworked and revised, and its certification functions are now undertaken by a separate legal entity, FLO Cert. A further aspect of the restructuring was to move away from a system of sending Bonn-based auditors to conduct monitoring visits of producer groups, to contracting local consultants in areas where FLO is active. This has dramatically increased the confidence of producer groups as language and cultural differences are much less likely to cause misunderstanding and create tensions. While these structural revisions have brought about improvements, a new round of organizational restructuring is currently underway that will likely see the national initiatives giving up sole ownership of FLO, enabling further power-sharing between producers and the national initiatives.

The three examples above illustrate the critical role of evolution in the development and improvement of the ISEAL Alliance and its member organizations. The ISEAL Code of Good Practice was developed as a response to calls for increased accountability and credibility of its members' standard-setting processes. The process of developing it was in itself a learning process, stimulating sharing and exchange between members and leading to innovation and concrete change. The history of IFOAM's development is a powerful example of evolution with the federation growing and taking on new functions as required to support the organic movement over the past three decades: from initial harmonization of standard-setting activities, to facilitating coordination at the conformity assessment level, and finally to a review of its role given that governments have taken over many functions that it previously accomplished by itself. Likewise, the continual development of FLO's organizational structures demonstrates that there are no perfect models of NGO accountability that fit with its unique mission, objectives, and stakeholder constituency, and that constructing such structures and accountability regimes requires an ongoing process of development, evaluation, review, and restructuring.

V. ACCOUNTABILITY AS LEARNING

The previous section introduced the idea that the accountability regimes of the ISEAL Alliance and its member organizations evolved over time in response to particular needs as they arose. This section explores this idea further, arguing that learning is a critical element in accountability regimes, adding a dynamic understanding of accountability as a continual process of development, as opposed to a static notion of design. This section begins with a discussion of the relationship between quality and learning, followed by reflections on the importance of learning in accountability regimes and an examination of the design implications of learning for accountability regimes.

A. Quality and learning

A core component of most definitions of accountability is that there is an evaluation as to whether stated objectives have been met, or, in a more nuanced context, how well such objectives have been met.[53] As an example, Mashaw's six questions on "who is accountable to whom, about what, through what processes, in accordance with what criteria, and with what effects" (see Chapter 5) are tools that can be used to evaluate accountability regimes. Responding to Mashaw's last two questions that seek to address how well institutional systems or organizations achieve their objectives ("about what"), a potentially useful framework for evaluation focuses on the concept of quality.[54]

Quality of performance in meeting stated objectives is what would need to be evaluated to fulfill the above conceptualization of accountability in the world of NGOs. In that world, the objectives and visions are for societal change, the timeframe is long-term, and the activity to be monitored is a complex set of processes. This has serious implications for evaluating the meeting of objectives. The term "continual improvement" has recently gained favor in management literature, as it allows for changes over time and encompasses the concept of learning. It has also become increasingly popular in the field of humanitarian assistance through the initiative of the Active Learning Network for Accountability and Performance in Humanitarian Action (ALNAP). ALNAP links the concept of quality with a culture of active learning in order to improve accountability in the humanitarian sector.[55]

ALNAP carries out an annual review of humanitarian NGO assistance performance through self-assessment questionnaires, interviews, documentary sources, and workshops, with the goal of providing the humanitarian system with a means to reflect annually on performance, to increase awareness of the principal findings of evaluations, as well as to monitor and encourage improvements in the quality of evaluation work undertaken.[56] According to ALNAP, learning is an internally driven approach to evaluation, while accountability approaches are seen as externally driven, independent evaluations; given this, the latter is not conducive to genuine learning at both the individual and group levels.[57] It is clear that learning approaches and external accountability checks can sometimes conflict. For example, corporate management systems that focus on individual accountability, linking incentives and forms of punishment to individual performance can inhibit the building of an atmosphere of collective responsibility and shared learning.[58] However, in a new conceptualization of accountability, could a culture of accountability *and* learning not be integrated in some way?

If the concept and practice of individual and organizational learning could be fostered and integrated into conceptualizations of accountability, organizations could be more responsive to different actors' needs within the wider societal context. In our "stakeholder society," this could be a critical measurement of external accountability. However, this requires the ability to discuss problems, both internally within a given organization and externally. This requires changes in both internal culture and in the wider culture of society – a change wherein the admission of mistakes is encouraged and the allocation of blame is minimized, with the proviso that new knowledge is gained, changes are made to address problems, and the same mistakes are not repeated. In an increasingly complex world of multiple regulatory agents and levels of activity, surely we need more nuanced conceptualizations of accountability, quality, and improvement.

B. The role of learning in accountability regimes

In Chapter 5 of this volume, Jerry Mashaw notes that accountability regimes change, reform, shift, and morph over time. He also acknowledges that institutional designers can learn from other cases and examples. For example in his discussion of contracted-out governance for prisons, Mashaw notes that the institutional designers have "surely learned by experience" given the careful way that public control was maintained over management issues.[59] Furthermore, he calls for a systems approach to the evaluation of accountability issues, presumably so that one can learn from such an evaluation toward the improvement of the institutional structures.[60] While there seems to be an implicit role for learning lurking in the background of Mashaw's argument, what is lacking is an explicit acknowledgment of the central role that learning plays in good institutional design, review, and adaptation.

As Mashaw observes, most accountability systems have failed to live up to the expectations of their designers.[61] One must ask the question why is this so? Perhaps it is because, in complex systems, no designer is ever going to get it just right. Perhaps accountability regimes will always be imperfect, as they are designed to meet particular requirements at particular points in time while the institution itself and the external environment are constantly changing. Perhaps the "fit" between the public purpose of a given program and questions of accountability will always require constant or at least periodic revisiting and renegotiation.

The case studies of the ISEAL Alliance and its members such as FLO and IFOAM have much to contribute to our understanding of how accountability structures can evolve and improve given that they have significantly revised their organizational structures in a relatively short period of time in order to improve their accountability regimes. Such changes are partly a response to new pressures and are partly due to learning gained from evaluations of the effectiveness of past accountability systems.

As has been outlined earlier, the world in which the ISEAL Alliance and its members operate is highly uncertain, with no clear determination whether such systems are compliant or in conflict with international trade law given that they discriminate between products based on production and process methods. Furthermore, as NGO-based initiatives operating across international trade, there is no clear vehicle for the recognition of such systems by the weak and fragmented political and legal orders that currently exist at the international level. With the rise of civil society activity taking many forms and the emergence of a sea of corporate social responsibility initiatives, the landscape in which the ISEAL Alliance members operate is constantly shifting, with new players, threats, and opportunities arising all the time. This is the context in which ISEAL members have developed. As such, they have had to build into their organizational designs, features that would allow for flexibility and for continual improvement. These are discussed below.

C. Implications for organizational structures

Linking the concepts of improving quality through learning with accountability has certain implications for institutional design. In order to take advantage of learning processes to improve accountability, institutions and organizations need to be structured in ways that allow for some degree of permanence while at the same time ensuring flexibility for change in a timely manner. While ISEAL organizations are not able to change as quickly as some of their adversaries and supporters wish, they do recognize the need for changes both in terms of improvement and in order to keep up with the changes taking place in the contexts in which they operate. This may be one area where nongovernmental forms of governance have an advantage over state governance structures, given their smaller sizes and their focus on a narrower range of issues.

The linkage also allows for a clarification of the concept of accountability. Quality, like accountability, is not an absolute concept where humans are able to identify what 100 percent or complete coverage would require.[62] Instead, we have a general understanding of what the concepts mean and how it can be applied to different contexts. This is enough to be able to conceptualize a scale or continuum of accountability. Learning provides a vehicle to move along the continuum of improvement.[63] Given that our world is complex and is in a state of flux with respect to governance structures and the actors involved, perhaps this is as good as can be expected.

The ISEAL Alliance and its members are characterized by flexible structures and programs that allow for revision and changes over time. For example, the activities of the ISEAL Alliance on standard-setting can be characterized by a process of learning, involving a number of steps beginning with an examination of existing guidance documents on standard-setting, a review of member procedures, and the drafting of the code. Training workshops and opportunities for exchange of experiences were then held, leading to the eventual implementation of the code by the members and verification of compliance. This process-driven approach provides for a number of opportunities for reflection and review before making the next big decision.

A further example of embedding learning into institutional design is with respect to standards-revision processes. As was mentioned earlier, all ISEAL members must have periodic standards-revision processes. These generally take place every few years, much more frequently than most governmental regulation review processes. While these require significant human and financial resources, they also provide important vehicles for member and stakeholder participation and engagement, strengthening feelings of ownership and loyalty. They also allow the member initiatives to play leadership roles in the area of social and environmental standard-setting through the ability to incorporate best practices and new issue-areas into harmonized rules for widespread use in a timely manner. For example, IFOAM set an important precedent for governmental regulators by adding a social justice chapter into its Basic Standards, signaling that the social dimension of organic agriculture is indeed important.

A further reason why the ISEAL members have been able to incorporate learning into their accountability regimes is due to the fact that they are all multi-stakeholder initiatives, structured to allow for debate and discourse among members, users, and affiliates. Given this stakeholder forum feature, there are regular opportunities for feedback about performance and for discussions about how to improve the functioning of the initiatives. IFOAM's General Assembly and FLO's Fairtrade forum are examples of such spaces.

As outlined above FLO has been involved in a number of restructuring processes during its short life to date, due largely to frustrations and concerns raised by its key constituents. During the last restructuring process, the national initiatives agreed to producer and trader representation on the FLO Board, but were not prepared to move to a situation where they would cede sole ownership over the initiative. Since then, producer groups have been able to effectively organize through regional forums, and have begun raising well-articulated issues for FLO to address, including demands for more balanced representation. With a view to improving governance structures, this current round of restructuring will see further changes to improve accountability to key stakeholders, based on lessons learned over the past few years.

As was described above, IFOAM's structures and core functions have evolved over the past thirty-three years in order to meet the needs of its membership in responding to new challenges as the organic movement grew and expanded internationally. At the 2002 General Assembly held in Victoria, Canada, the IFOAM membership decided to separate out discussions of standards-revision processes from the General Assembly, in order to leave more time for strategic discussions about the future direction of the organic movement, and to ensure that members who were not able to travel to the Assembly would be able to contribute to the standards-revision process via mail and electronic means. This example illustrates the degree of sophistication of the discussion among members to commit to changes that will improve the movement's effectiveness and accountability.

Through participation in the ISEAL Alliance, member initiatives are encouraged by their peers to think about new ways to structure their own accountability regimes. Given the existence of spaces where members and affiliates come together periodically to discuss the future of their initiatives, significant learning can take place, supported by the political will for incorporating such learning into institutional review and redesign.

It should be noted that, while quality discourses focus on *continual* improvement, in practice, even though learning is amassed continuously, implementing revisions based on such learning can only take place periodically. Otherwise, building accountability into design processes would be the only activity that the initiatives would ever achieve.

Based on the experiences of the ISEAL Alliance and its members, in order to integrate learning into institutional design, what is needed is a culture that supports continual improvement and periodic revision; a space where key stakeholders can discuss the performance of the regime to date and outline possibilities for improvement; and an ability to incorporate and maintain flexibility in its programs and procedures. Instead of thinking in terms of static conceptions of institutional design, perhaps a more dynamic notion of a design cycle would be useful.

VI. INTERNAL AND EXTERNAL ACCOUNTABILITY: BOUNDARIES AND DEMOCRACY

A final contribution of the ISEAL Alliance case study to understanding accountability regimes is the suggestion that a graduated and multi-layered concept of accountability may be useful in complex systems, in which there are multiple accountability relationships. As Mashaw notes, "accountability seems to be a relational concept, but the parties to the relationship remain unspecified." Mashaw's question of "who is accountable to whom" urges us to examine the accountability relationship in detail, naming the particular actors for a given context. However, this may not be able to capture the full relational component in situations where there is no well-established hierarchical chain of command or a simple duality in the accountability relationship. This section outlines a sketch of accountability that provides for a more meaningful evaluation of complex accountability relationships using the concept of boundary. There may also be certain implications for our understanding of democracy, particularly at the international level.

The first section of this Chapter made significant use of the concepts of internal and external accountability, both within an organization and between an organization and a wider societal boundary, be that a polity, an economy, or a society. Embedded in these concepts is a conceptualization of boundary: the boundary that separates what is internal within an organization or an institution from what is external. However, this particular boundary is increasingly affected by changes in other boundaries, namely the interface between national- and the international-level polities and economies.

For most advocacy-oriented member-driven NGOs operating at the national level, it is still possible to identify what spaces and actors lie internally, and what spaces and actors are external to the organization. Figure 11.1 illustrates one extreme simplification of the linkages between different actors in such a context.

In Figure 11.1, the size of the actors represents their influence in a particular society. The widest boundary drawn is that of a particular society or nation-state. A range of actors, including NGOs, corporations, and perhaps even the media, are involved in lobbying governments and public opinion to further their interests. Society provides a space for different viewpoints and actors to clash as well as cooperate that is filtered using democratic political and regulatory processes. In this scenario, it is clear that NGOs should be accountable to their members, but they are also being asked to be accountable to the society in which they are operating. One could ask how accountable are governments to their citizens? In most countries, financial interests tend to have much greater influence in shaping government policy than other stakeholders.[64] How accountable are corporations to the wider society in which they operate, including their consumers? Legally, a corporation's main responsibility is to its shareholders through fiduciary obligations on the part of a board of directors. Accountability to other stakeholders is minimal. There are different degrees or intensities of accountability toward different actors or stakeholders. How these degrees or intensities of accountability are identified and applied is a political construct.

Figure 11.2 provides a conceptualization of the spaces in which ISEAL organizations might operate, using IFOAM as a specific example. In this example, the widest boundary is the international political and economic system. IFOAM is represented in the diagram as a network of its members, each of which is located within a specific national space. The boundary that envelops IFOAM and its members is particularly strong, as are the forms of democratic accountability and other accountability mechanisms in operation within this space. IFOAM then can be conceptualized as a type of transnational democracy, located within a poorly defined international space that also crosses national boundaries. However, it can also be conceptualized as a commons, whereby any actor can self-select to participate in that system and agree to follow the rules. If one is not interested in producing, trading, processing, researching, or eating organic food, one does not have to. One is alway free to enter, or to stay on or move to the other side of the boundary.

IFOAM was set up for a specific purpose, addressing a limited range of issues, with members participating because they share certain core values and beliefs. Because of its highly specific nature and strong alignment of values across its entire membership, IFOAM members are in a better position to monitor leadership and to guide strategic decisions than citizens of a nation-state.[65]

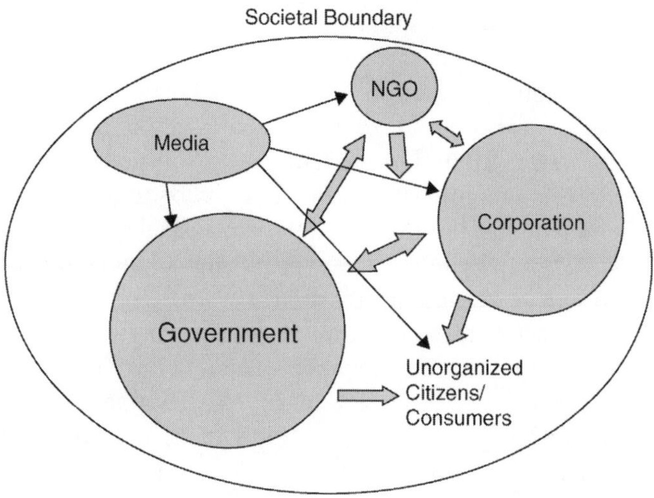

Figure 11.1. Actor linkages in a conventional advocacy NGO regulatory environment.

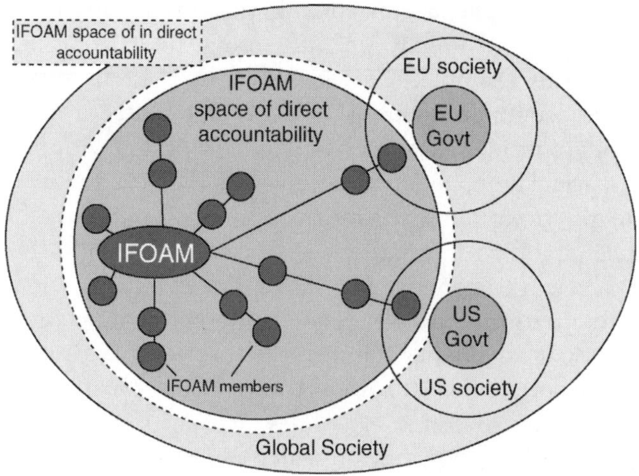

Figure 11.2. Actor linkages in the ISEAL regulatory environment.

If the accountability mechanisms are so strong between IFOAM and its members, then to what extent should it be accountable to external actors, and to which actors? In the case of IFOAM, consumers could be one set of actors to whom it needs to be accountable.

While there are a number of consumer groups that are members of IFOAM, the vast majority of organic consumers do not directly participate in IFOAM, though they are indeed affected by its activities. A second set of actors who influence, and are, in turn, influenced by, IFOAM are the agricultural departments of most national and regional governments who seek to monitor and regulate organic production and imports within their own jurisdictions. However, recognizing obligations to other actors, such as national governments, could put IFOAM in conflict with its responsibilities to its membership. Given this potential tension, perhaps it is useful to think in terms of a graduated set of boundaries, where each movement away from the center means reduced responsibilities and requirements for accountability.

VII. CONCLUSIONS: LIMITS OF ACOUNTABILITY

While accountability is a critical element in any governance system, it should be noted that it is not a "pure good."[66] ISEAL organizations expend a great deal of energy to ensure that they are accountable to their members and affiliates. This includes information exchange, and management activities such as maintaining websites and email newsletters, responding to questions and concerns, and organizing training sessions, workshops, and conferences. This may also require translation into a number of languages, adding significantly to human and financial resource costs. It also includes organizing spaces for member and affiliate discussion and decisionmaking on key strategic issues, such as annual general assemblies and standards revision processes. In addition, ISEAL organizations need to be responsive to non-members, including governments and, at various levels, other initiatives in similar fields, potential certification bodies, and companies interested in certification.

All these activities have their own costs, both in financial and in human resource terms. ISEAL member organizations are chronically understaffed and under-resourced; they survive because of high levels of dedication and commitment on the part of their staff and their members. In many cases, member organizations of ISEAL take an active role in their "parent" initiative, by providing pro bono services and by representing the organization at key events and meetings, among other ways. Given their limited human and financial resources, ISEAL organizations need to prioritize the degree of effort and activity they undertake for different accountability relationships. For example, in recent years IFOAM has had to deal with an increasing number of national governments developing their own organic standards. While it is critical for IFOAM members that IFOAM participates in these processes to ensure that government standards are as close as possible to IFOAM standards, this drains significant resources away from other services that IFOAM needs to provide to its members.

A further area that highlights the limits of accountability is in the operationalization of the concept of participation. While stakeholder participation is critical in all of the ISEAL organizations, there are practical difficulties in even identifying who the relevant stakeholders are when these organizations operate across a number of countries and continents. Providing information and invitations to these stakeholders is a further task, especially as some of these stakeholders may be smallholder farmers in rural communities in remote regions of the world. Further, to organize spaces in which these stakeholders can participate effectively requires even more time and financial resources, as does synthesizing the input from a such a wide range of stakeholders. With higher numbers of participants, the process for achieving a majority opinion or even a consensus takes longer and becomes increasingly difficult, even among a group of stakeholders who basically share the same set of core values and beliefs.

Costs need to be included in any new conceptualizations of accountability. While accountability is critical to ISEAL members, this needs to be balanced with the ability of the organizations to achieve their objectives.

CHAPTER 12

PROBLEM-SOLVING COURTS AND THE JUDICIAL ACCOUNTABILITY DEFICIT

Michael C. Dorf

INTRODUCTION

Courts sit uneasily in the American system of public accountability. Especially since the middle of the twentieth century, they are the government institution most clearly identified with holding other government institutions accountable to fundamental norms. Yet courts themselves have been understood as exhibiting an accountability deficit. The constitutional and other legal norms they invoke to discipline other government actors rarely speak in terms so specific as to allow no room for interpretation, thus raising the question of why judges, who (typically) are unelected and (typically) are insulated from the bureaucratic control of those who are elected, should be permitted to impose their own views about liberty, equality, and the like, upon the public as a whole. Alexander Bickel famously termed this problem the "counter-majoritarian difficulty,"[1] and legal theorists have been struggling with it for generations.[2]

Most accounts of constitutional democracy treat the counter-majoritarian difficulty as requiring a tradeoff. On the one hand, in the wake of legal realism, the notion that judges mechanically apply a disembodied entity called "The Law" has become untenable. Yet, on the other hand, in the wake of Nazism, fascism, and communist totalitarianism, Americans and others in democratic countries have been understandably reluctant to let go of the idea of using judicially enforceable rules of law not only to regulate private actors but also to circumscribe government power itself. Thus, we confront the question, as it is usually posed, of how much self-rule we are willing to sacrifice in order to keep the Leviathan within tolerable limits. Although some legal theorists have argued that the tradeoff sacrifices only that quantum of positive liberty that majorities have no right to exercise in the first place,[3] even on these accounts, the choice is seen in zero-sum terms: either a decision is taken by national, state, or local majoritarian processes or it is taken by the unelected judiciary.

This chapter argues that the zero-sum picture of courts versus other government actors is inaccurate. Given the appropriate decisionmaking structures and doctrines, it is possible to shrink courts' democratic accountability deficit without a fully equal corresponding sacrifice of the judicial checking function. When faced with gaps in the law, judges need not simply choose between the Scylla of deference to elected actors and the Charybdis of usurpation of the latter's functions. Trial courts can address broad social problems without directly taking over responsibility for running institutions like prisons, schools, and police forces, while appellate courts need not themselves fill the gaps in constitutional and other open-ended legal norms; they can instead, or at least in addition, instigate reform by other actors.

Elsewhere, Charles Sabel and I have described an emerging ensemble of new public problem-solving institutions that together comprise what we call "democratic experimentalism."[4] In democratic experimentalism, local units of government are broadly free to set goals and to choose the means to attain them. Within these units, individuals – acting alone, through stakeholder organizations, and through local elected officials – engage in a form of practical deliberation that permits the discovery of novel solutions to their shared problems, thereby at least partially relaxing the grip of familiar political animosities, though in the process opening the way to new conflicts and in any case not tending to pacification or complete harmonization of interests. Concurrently, legislative bodies or regulatory agencies use the pooled experience of relatively local actors to set and ensure compliance with framework objectives. These framework objectives shape and in turn are shaped by means of performance standards based on information about current best practices that regulated entities provide in return for the freedom to experiment with solutions they prefer. Although it is nowhere fully realized, Sabel, myself, and others have argued that the ideal of democratic experimentalism bears a sufficient similarity to emerging institutions to warrant studying them as a group.[5]

Democratic experimentalism – as the name suggests – is principally a model of participatory administration. Indeed, it might be best understood as an alternative to bureaucracy. Conventional wisdom holds that, as the tasks of government become more complex, bureaucracy – in the sense of a top-down, rule-driven, hierarchical organization – is the best or perhaps the only means of holding government accountable.[6] Democratic experimentalism challenges this conventional wisdom, suggesting that the virtues of local responsiveness associated with local decisionmaking need not come with the vice of discretion. Although I won't belabor the point here, the clearest illustrations come from the private sector, where not all that long ago it was also thought that large firms had to be organized top-down, but where organizational changes over the last generation have replaced the assembly line designed by headquarters with local team-based flexible production.[7]

Broadly understood, then, my thesis is that the conventional wisdom is wrong: accountability on a large scale need not take the form of bureaucracy. I do not, however, make the argument in that general a form here. Instead, I focus in this chapter on the role of courts in the emerging architecture of democratic experimentalism. Whereas my prior work aimed to show that experimentalism provides a superior form of accountability to bureaucracy in administrative settings, my ambition here is both narrower and larger – narrower because I restrict my attention to courts but larger because with respect to courts I make two claims rather than just one. First, I claim that the experimentalist methods that are succeeding in the private sector and beginning to succeed in public administration can be readily adapted to the work of courts. Second, I argue that adapting experimentalist methods to the context of judicial decisionmaking can reduce the sting of the courts' own accountability problem, namely the counter-majoritarian difficulty.

These theoretical claims are rooted in practical experience. I begin by looking at experimentalist trial courts, sometimes called "problem-solving courts," which are structured along the same lines as their administrative counterparts. For example, drug courts, to date the most widespread exemplars of problem-solving courts, serve primarily to monitor the performance of defendants and treatment providers. They thus act on social problems like drug addiction and crime, but in doing so they may escape one critique of activist courts of the 1960s and 1970s: by acting at the retail level of individual criminal and other cases, rather than by issuing injunctions to institutions that are nominally responsible to the democratic process, problem-solving courts do not directly usurp the role of political actors.

However, as I explain below in Sections I to III, the affinity of experimentalist courts with (experimentalist) administrative agencies raises a question of indirect usurpation: granting that problem-solving courts do not displace existing administrative agencies, why should courts, rather than new administrative agencies, perform the roles described herein? Below I provide a partial defense of a judicial role, even while conceding that the important question is not whether the institution carrying out reform is formally denominated a court or an agency, but how it is structured.

Section IV below explains how experimentalist judging can respond to the courts' accountability deficit in the area in which courts are most frequently under attack – the resolution of questions, such as abortion, affirmative action, and other "cultural" issues, as to which policy disagreement seems to be rooted in the plurality of values held by a diverse citizenry. First, I draw a distinction between "big" cases – those that appear to require panoptic knowledge on the part of the judge – and "hard" cases – those that seemingly call for choosing one set of values rather than another. I then explain that experimentalism is primarily a strategy for attacking big cases, but that some hard cases will, based upon practical experience, prove to be big cases, and thus amenable to experimentalist solutions. By sharing decisionmaking authority with other actors, I argue, courts can simultaneously improve the quality of their decisions and make themselves more accountable to these other actors.

My proposed solution to the courts' accountability deficit is necessarily a partial one. Inevitably, even framework rules revised in light of pooled experience will conflict with some citizens' views, values, or policy preferences. Yet one should not underestimate the power of direct deliberation among citizens of diverse backgrounds and views to produce workable accommodations – and even to prompt a rethinking of seemingly unshakeable first-order beliefs. Forced together to solve problems to which ideology provides no obvious solution, or to which ideological solutions have manifestly failed, citizens may find that their commitment to solving problems is, by itself, sufficient to bridge their other differences.

I. EXPERIMENTALIST COURTS OF FIRST IMPRESSION

Suppose you are a trial judge whose docket mostly consists of misdemeanor and non-violent felony charges. What is your job? The traditional answer is straightforward: you mete out justice. Sometimes you adjudicate guilt or innocence; more frequently, you conduct a colloquy to ensure that the defendant's guilty plea is voluntary; and, by whichever route a defendant's guilt is determined, you impose a sentence – time served in jail pending trial, probation, community service, restitution, or perhaps some additional weeks or months in jail. Over time, however, you notice that many of the defendants appearing in your courtroom have been there before. You might want to impose ever-stiffer sanctions, but the prisons are already crowded with inmates who have committed violent offenses, and in any event a lengthy prison sentence strikes you as disproportionate to the offense in most instances. Thus, you continue to rely on your familiar repertoire of unsuccessful responses to the revolving door of arrest, arraignment, guilty plea, sentence, release, and rearrest.

In the late 1980s and 1990s, the frustrating circumstances just described led increasing numbers of judges, prosecutors, and policymakers to explore the long-discarded notion that at least some criminals can be rehabilitated.[8] Because the majority of lawbreakers are also illegal drug users, efforts initially focused on drug addiction as a substantial factor contributing to crime. With support from studies showing that drug treatment is more cost-effective than imprisonment,[9] what are now called "drug courts" emerged as an alternative to cycling non-violent offenders through the conventional criminal justice system. The Department of Justice under the Clinton Administration provided seed money for states and localities to establish such courts, a policy that has continued under President Bush, so that, as of May 2004, there were 1,160 operating drug courts, with another 517 in the planning stage.[10]

What is a drug court? Glossing over important local variations, it is a court that closely monitors treatment for drug-addicted defendants brought before it. After the defendant pleads guilty (or in some jurisdictions is found guilty at a trial on the merits), the court sentences him to a treatment program chosen by the court's clinical staff based on an assessment of the defendant's needs. The judge and court personnel then closely monitor the defendant's progress in treatment, using a system of graduated rewards for successes and punishments – including, ultimately, the threat of imprisonment – for failures. Defendants who complete their course of treatment "graduate" in a ceremony that typically expunges the predicate conviction.

Now suppose that you are a drug court judge. What is your job? "Meting out justice" is at best a small part of what you do. You are fundamentally a problem-solver. Collaborating with your court's own clinical staff, service providers, prosecutors, defense attorneys, the police, and others, you attempt to reduce the personal and social cost of crime committed by drug addicts. But, if you are a problem-solver, you will not be content with evidence that your approach to non-violent crime fares better than the revolving-door system in the courtroom down the hall. "Better than a broken system" is a low bar indeed.

Accordingly, you will want to know how you can ensure more effective treatment. You will want to keep close tabs on the treatment providers to which you refer defendants. You need to know that the services promised are being provided, but that alone is insufficient. You got into the drug court business because you thought that conventional courts did not address the underlying social problems – in this instance, addiction – that lead to criminal conduct. Which forms of treatment, provided by whom, under what circumstances, to what client population, do best at retaining clients? At keeping them drug-free? At reducing crime? To answer such questions requires that you have access to rich information about clients and providers.

Thus, drug courts use sophisticated databases to track client performance. In a prior article on drug courts, Professor Sabel and I observed that drug court clinical staff also used information about clients to monitor treatment providers, but not systematically:[11] judges and case workers would notice over time that clients assigned to a particular provider frequently missed their court dates despite reports that the client was attending sessions, and, in response, an inquiry would be initiated or referrals would be diverted. But at least one important player in the drug court movement, the Center for Court Innovation – the research and development arm of the New York State Unified Court system – which also runs a number of demonstration projects, is taking steps to systematize the monitoring of service providers. That project aims to develop a provisional monitoring protocol for drug courts and other problem-solving courts nationwide.[12]

Now imagine that a full-fledged monitoring regime exists. The court superintends drug treatment for its clients while simultaneously acting to improve the quality of services through a networked form of learning. Successful innovations in one treatment provider set new benchmarks by which other providers are measured. Because drug courts are themselves part of a national network, successful innovations both in service provision and in the monitoring of service provision rapidly diffuse around the country by virtue of the continual ratcheting-up of performance benchmarks: a treatment standard that may have been acceptable in the early days of drug courts is superseded by a more demanding one, as documented experience reveals which practices succeed and which, by the ever-more-stringent relative standards, fail.

In one obvious but important sense, problem-solving courts shrink the judiciary's accountability deficit: almost no decision made by a problem-solving court requires the application of unguided judgment. Court sessions serve mostly as an opportunity for the judge to verify that the exhaustive information on the progress of each defendant (or on other "clients" subject to the problem-solving court's jurisdiction) comports with his or her own perception and to ritualize the imposition of graduated rewards or punishments. There is very little "judging" in the sense of making a decision by interpreting a complex set of substantive legal norms.

But the foregoing is a weak justification at best, because even conventional trial courts do very little in the way of this kind of "judging." Mostly they approve plea bargains or settlements, sometimes they adjudicate factual questions, and when they resolve questions of law, their rulings typically set no precedent binding on anyone other than the immediate parties to the case (who can seek reversal on appeal, in any event).

A better account of how problem-solving courts respond to the accountability deficit would first have to grapple with the suspicion that because they participate in the actual administration of drug treatment, such courts bear a troubling resemblance to judges supervising structural injunctions.[13] The structural injunction has been widely regarded as problematic because running schools, prisons, and other complex institutions taxed both the resources and legitimacy of the courts.[14] The best that can be said for conventional structural reform litigation is that, where the need for reform is urgent and politically accountable institutions do not act (as in the case of prisons), courts may legitimately step in. Yet, even if we count prison reform, some school desegregation, and a few other instances of judicially led structural reform as modest successes, that fact hardly justifies converting courts into nothing but managers of complex social change. Even the most enthusiastic defenders of structural reform litigation recognize that courts are at best sub-optimal decision-makers in these contexts.[15]

A defense of problem-solving courts must therefore begin by differentiating them from courts enforcing structural injunctions. The most important distinction is that problem-solving courts act on individuals rather than institutions. The brief against conventional structural reform litigation begins with the fact that institutions like prisons, schools, and police forces have their own mechanisms of accountability to the public – typically via elected officials – that courts displace without legitimacy or expertise. That brief simply does not apply to contemporary problem-solving courts, however. Focusing on drug treatment, drug courts do not issue orders to state or local bodies charged with addressing drug addiction. Moreover, problem-solving courts are considerably more modest than courts engaged in structural reform. A problem-solving court faces fewer competency obstacles than a court overseeing structural reform because the former does not itself run any institutions, nor does it place itself atop a hierarchical organization of personnel resentful of its authority. A problem-solving court is the hub through which the providers it monitors – the spokes – learn to improve their respective performance.

If these distinctions suggest that problem-solving courts act legitimately and can succeed where courts engaged in more direct forms of structural reform sometimes ran into obstacles, there is a similarity that raises an urgent question. Just as courts that attempted to run complex social institutions such as schools and prisons prompted the question of why such tasks should be undertaken by the judiciary rather than legislative, executive, or administrative bodies, so too does having courts administering drug treatment programs. In other words, why courts? If the problem-solving apparatus I am calling a problem-solving court need not be located in the judicial branch, why not spin it off into an administrative agency – albeit one that operates through what might be called "coordinated decentralization" rather than hierarchy? Accountability to the various stakeholders whose cooperation is essential to the success of a problem-solving court may indeed provide greater accountability than we traditionally associate with courts, but is it a form of accountability that is consistent with the function we expect courts to play in a democratic society?

II. ARE PROBLEM-SOLVING COURTS REALLY COURTS?

The "why courts" question poses no mere theoretical worry, as a 2002 appellate ruling in Oklahoma illustrates. In *Alexander* v. *State*,[16] the defendant pled guilty to drug possession and illegal firearm possession charges and agreed to complete a drug court program. After repeatedly testing positive for cocaine and being given additional opportunities to comply with program rules, he was terminated from the program. On appeal to the Court of Criminal Appeals, the defendant argued, inter alia, that the drug court judge was biased because he served as "part of the treatment team."[17] Although the appeals court denied relief because the defendant had waived the objection by not presenting it at the trial level, the appeals court agreed with the general thrust of the defendant's claim, prescribing that, in future cases, a drug court participant facing ejection from his program (and therefore a prison term) should be able to have the termination proceeding adjudicated by a judge who is not a member of his treatment team.[18] A concurring judge went so far as to say that drug courts violated the Oklahoma Constitution's separation-of-powers requirement by mixing legislative, executive, and judicial functions.[19]

The *Alexander* case therefore raises two related questions: First, is it appropriate for drug courts to undertake the activities that they do when these activities could, perhaps more appropriately, be located in the executive branch of government? And, second, assuming that the answer to the first question is the one given by the majority in *Alexander* – namely a qualified yes – is the participation of the judiciary in collaborative problem-solving inconsistent with the ideal of neutrality associated with adjudication?

These questions take on greater urgency when we realize that, if we deem the drug court experiment a provisional success, there is no reason not to apply the model to other domains. Successful treatment for drug-addicted misdemeanants and non-violent felons has already led to calls for drug courts or their equivalent for violent offenders. Moreover, drug treatment may also ameliorate the problems that give rise to cases in family court, housing court, and juvenile court, to name just three problem-plagued specialty jurisdictions. Likewise, addiction is not the only social problem that leads to criminal or otherwise harmful behavior. Any number of other problems could provide the opening for the government to deliver more effective medical, employment, housing, and general counseling services. Although courts addressing these issues may lack the ability to threaten parties with imprisonment, they do have at their disposal other sticks, not to mention carrots, with which to induce compliance with their orders.

Therefore, it does not take a great leap of the imagination to envision a not-so-distant future in which much of what front-line courts do is monitor the delivery of services – serving, in other words, as the mechanism by which society holds service providers accountable. To be sure, there will remain categories of disputes that call for conventional judicial decisionmaking: A claims B breached a contract; C claims D committed an intentional or negligent tort; the state charges E with murder. Conventional courts would still be needed to resolve contested questions of law and fact in the relatively small percentage of such cases that are not resolved by settlement or plea. But, even in contract, as one moves from relatively simple, one-time, bilateral disputes, to questions involving multiple parties over time, it is not difficult to imagine that some of the most important work of the courts will be remedial or problem-solving.[20] Structuring long-term relationships between contracting parties, providing compensation to victims of mass torts, and addressing the aggregate costs of crime are not the sorts of problems that courts have traditionally addressed, or at least they are not the sorts of problems that they have traditionally addressed well. This, too, is the domain of experimentalist courts or agencies.

Yet this observation raises an immediate question: what makes problem-solving courts, "courts," as opposed to administrative agencies? Of course, the problem-solving courts envisioned here would not look like conventional top-down bureaucracies;[21] they would instead be federated agencies that address issues through coordinated decentralization. But, even granting their newfangled structure, why use courts rather than newfangled agencies?

The answer is that despite their similarities with administrative bodies, problem-solving courts still have important institutional advantages that administrative bodies lack. First, as courts, they have what champions of problem-solving courts describe as the convening power,[22] i.e. the ability to bring together the various actors needed to craft effective solutions to multi-dimensional problems. This is a polite way of saying that judicial decrees are backed by the threat of force, a point that is perhaps ultimately true of administrative action as well, but not nearly so directly (since administrative bodies must typically depend on the courts for enforcement). The convening power is parasitic on courts' coercive power.[23]

Second, unlike other actors in the legal system, courts are perceived as neutral parties that lack a direct stake in the outcome of litigation or substitutes for litigation.[24] Neutrality or its perception permits courts to function as honest brokers when problem-solving becomes a matter of negotiation. In addition, the courts' perceived neutrality, when combined with such quasi-mystical symbols of judicial power as the robe and gavel, lends prestige to the courts, thereby enabling courts to command respect where other actors might not.

Third, courts have what might be called a *disentrenching* capacity.[25] The ability to declare some course of conduct unlawful, even where a court does not have a solution ready at hand, enables courts to force other actors to address their problems immediately.[26] En route to becoming a full-fledged problem-solving court that is the hub of some wheel of services and actors, a disentrenching court can impose a "penalty default," a state of affairs so unpalatable to all parties that they have no choice but to hammer out some solution that is, from the perspective of the default, a pareto optimal improvement.[27] The disentrenching power is especially important in circumstances – unlike those of drug courts and other problem-solving *front-line* courts – in which there is no administrative apparatus associated with the judiciary itself. In such circumstances, the court's disentrenching decision can call into existence an experimentalist process in other institutions. In recent years, court-initiated reform of public schools, mental health services, prisons, policing, and public housing have all provided examples of a new model of public law litigation in which courts do not attempt to solve the problems they identify, instead simply acknowledging the violation of a right, disentrenching the status quo, and convening the interested parties to work together to formulate a plan for improvement.[28]

One might worry that courts can maintain their advantages relative to agencies – the convening power, perceived neutrality, and disentrenching power – only so long as they act primarily *as courts* – i.e., as traditional resolvers of disputes. This is the worry of the concurring judge in *Alexander*, writ large. Once courts become active problem-solvers enmeshed in the messy business of ordering real-world institutions, they will no longer be perceived as neutral, and, once the perception of neutrality goes, that will also signal the end of the courts' convening and disentrenching powers, both of which depend upon the willingness of other actors to accept the courts' coercive authority.[29]

If stated as an analytic claim, this last objection misses the mark. One could take simple measures such as the one adopted by the *Alexander* majority – where termination from the program is a possibility, giving each client a right to go before a judge who has not previously worked on his case – that would effectively address claims of improper bias. A legal order that employed such safeguards whenever the coercive power of the state was needed to enforce the edicts of problem-solving courts could, in principle, persist indefinitely. One could even imagine that the public would continue to accept the legitimacy of problem-solving courts' coercive power even long after the actual exercise of such power in problem-solving courts and traditional courts had become truly exceptional.

Yet the traditionalist's objection is not so easily dismissed, for it ultimately poses a question about actual, not just perceived, legitimacy. In other words, even if the people could be "fooled" into thinking that courts were doing nothing extraordinary in solving social problems, if that role is nonetheless inconsistent with the basic premises of self-government, then there remains a deficit of democratic accountability. Organizing and coordinating problem-solving actors is the activity in which problem-solving courts engage, but it is also the activity in which other actors – in particular, administrative agencies superintending systems of coordinated decentralization of the sort I described above – engage.[30] To give a very concrete example, there is no reason to think that judges rather than prosecutors must be the people responsible for diverting defendants to drug treatment, and indeed, in some jurisdictions, diversion to drug treatment has been organized by prosecutors.[31] More generally, administrative agencies exercising their prosecutorial discretion can play much the same role as problem-solving courts. So, the traditionalist is really asking, what makes a problem-solving court a court rather than an (admittedly newfangled) administrative agency superintended by a person wearing a robe? If there is no functional distinction, why not place problem-solving courts in charge of the problem-solving work of administrative agencies? If we were to do that, the traditionalist concludes, then surely the advantages that accrue to courts would dissolve, as "court" would simply be a different word for "agency."

Although the traditionalist is right to think that actual legitimacy matters, he is wrong to think that perception is irrelevant to actual legitimacy. In a legal system in which the people who actually consented to our Constitution are long dead, most of the actual legitimacy the system has arises out of a form of tacit consent, and people will tacitly consent only to those institutions that they deem fair and appropriate.

The fact of our inability to draw a sharp distinction between the activities of problem-solving courts and administrative agencies operating by similar principles in addressing the same or similar problems does not, in the public mind, warrant abandoning the idea that some social problems might usefully be tackled by courts, even if those courts are structured in much the same way as agencies. Even if, in their actual operation, problem-solving courts are largely indistinguishable from administrative agencies, the path by which people enter into the monitoring regime that is constituted by a problem-solving court places boundaries on the sort of institution it can be.

Consider two schematic examples. First, suppose that Smith, a drug addict, decides to seek treatment for his addiction. Smith goes to a well-functioning administrative agency that coordinates drug treatment in the jurisdiction in which he resides. Smith accepts an intrusive monitoring regime replete with carrots and sticks because that is the price of eligibility for public funding. The agency in charge of this monitoring regime will look much like a drug court (without the possibility of using jail as a stick), but few will think that it needs to be a court.

Now suppose that Jones is arrested for shoplifting and is brought before a court. Jones's lawyer learns that Jones is a drug addict who steals to support his habit. She asks Jones if he would be willing to plead guilty to the charged offense, enter a drug treatment plan, and accept an intrusive monitoring regimen, in exchange for avoiding imprisonment. At the moment that Jones makes his choice, the state is exercising the full force of its coercive power, and that fact distinguishes Jones from Smith. Whereas Smith's decision to enter treatment was voluntary, the background threat of criminal sanctions that triggers Jones's decision means that we need special safeguards to ensure that Jones's decision is likewise voluntary. One could imagine an administrative law judge doing the job, but, in our legal culture, courts are the institution that connotes neutrality. The perception in large part makes the reality.[32]

We can also answer the traditionalist critic in a way that does not simply rely on perceptions by observing that courts qua courts have a procedurally fair culture that administrative agencies cannot readily copy. Part of what it means to act as a judge is to maintain a degree of neutrality, in the sense of not having a stake in the outcome. Especially in an era when the power of administrative agencies is rationalized as flowing from the political accountability of the executive officials who supervise administration,[33] it will be much easier to create the perception and reality of neutrality by making judges rather than bureaucrats responsible for protecting the rights of citizens subject to the coercive power of the state – even if the judges, having exercised that gatekeeping function, run their institutions in much the same manner as parallel administrative agencies are run.

The *Alexander* case holds that a judge cannot simply change hats when he shifts from the superintending role back to the gatekeeping role, and that is probably a sensible precaution to avoid the appearance of bias. Similar precautions can be, and generally are, taken by problem-solving courts to ensure compliance with due process norms at other stages of the proceedings.[34] Thus, the preliminary evidence suggests that courts can become problem-solving institutions without necessarily sacrificing the qualities that make them valuable as courts. They can use experimentalist means to hold themselves and other actors accountable to performance standards, without unduly sacrificing their distinctively judicial character.

III. APPELLATE JUDGING IN A WORLD OF EXPERIMENTALIST INSTITUTIONS

Should problem-solving courts continue to play an increasingly large role in the American judiciary, they will narrow the courts' accountability deficit. By deciding less, courts will have fewer opportunities to make controversial choices. More importantly, by addressing large-scale social problems through means other than direct decree aimed at institutions that are nominally accountable in other ways, they will escape the critique of the structural injunction. What about the residual role of courts in resolving contested questions of fact and law?

Because it fits the traditional understanding of the role of courts relative to the political branches, judicial resolution of contested questions of fact raises fewer legitimacy questions than judicial resolution of contested questions of law. Although courts exercise enormous power in resolving contests over facts, that power has rarely engendered much controversy – probably because courts appear to be among the best institutions we have for ascertaining certain kinds of facts. When called upon to make judgments about discrete past events, the courts' neutrality relative to political actors gives them a marked institutional advantage. Broadly speaking, our legal culture accepts that facts, unlike values, are simply "out there" to be found. Furthermore, in those jurisdictions in which juries play the leading fact-finding role, the directly deliberative participation of ordinary lay citizens gives to this judicial function the stamp of democratic legitimacy.[35]

The courts' role in resolving contested legal questions, however, raises the problem of accountability, and the experimentalist judging of problem-solving courts does not appear to provide any direct leverage on that problem. Questions about the meaning of ambiguous legal provisions do not present themselves as problems in the delivery of social services. Accordingly, a model of appellate experimentalist judging must look rather different from experimentalist judging as it works in problem-solving courts of first instance. Along these lines, this section describes experimentalist appellate judging as a review of decisions by experimentalist institutions such as problem-solving courts. The next section then explains how experimentalism might address the judicial accountability deficit with respect to questions of value.

Let us begin with the question of appellate review of decisions made by problem-solving courts. As cases like *Alexander* illustrate, appeals courts can examine whether a problem-solving court has complied with norms of due process. However, as was true in *Alexander* itself, appellate review is typically limited by the fact that the parties who appear before problem-solving courts – and especially drug courts – generally waive the right of appeal. The standard plea colloquy in which a criminal defendant accepts responsibility for his conduct includes this waiver along with that of other procedural rights.[36] A client who is unhappy with his court-mandated treatment can negotiate, through his defense attorney, for some other course of treatment – for example, outpatient rather than inpatient in the case of clients who need to maintain their jobs or tend to family obligations – but the final say remains with the trial court judge. There is usually no appeal to a higher authority.

Although most drug courts and other problem-solving courts do not currently provide for appeals of treatment decisions, there is no reason in principle why they could not. The current dearth of appellate procedures probably results from two features of drug courts. First, as I just noted, drug court clients accept their treatment program as a contract, in just the same way that other plea agreements are enforceable as contracts. Accordingly, lawyers and others accustomed to conventional plea agreements may believe that there is no appeal, because conventional plea agreements typically waive the right to an appeal. If a client does not like his course of treatment, this reasoning goes, he has only himself to blame for having accepted it in the first place. Second, and perhaps more fundamentally, architects of and participants in problem-solving courts may take the view that appeals to higher authority are a form of adversarial behavior, best left in the zero-sum world of litigated cases rather than in the collaborative new world. In my own interactions with personnel in the problem-solving courts, I have found that this attitude is widespread (though hardly universal).

Neither causal explanation for the absence of appellate review amounts to a justification. It may well be true that drug court clients have no right to drug treatment, but that does not mean that they could not be provided with a right, by law, or as part of the standard contract they sign upon entering treatment, to effective treatment and judicial review.

The second, cultural explanation, I believe, accurately describes the attitude of many of the actors involved in collaborative problem-solving processes that have grown up where command and control formerly reigned. Onetime antagonists – environmentalists and industry, labor and management, prosecutorial drug warriors and defense attorneys – who see negotiation, mediation, or deliberative collaboration as superior to deadlocked adversarial processes, can lose sight of the fact that power and interests do not simply vanish in non-adversarial settings. Given the opportunity, the strong can still oppress the weak, capturing decentralized collaborative processes in much the same way that they can capture top-down administrative processes.

Champions of collaborative problem-solving such as myself have three linked answers to the risk that the non-adversarial processes will simply reproduce external power hierarchies. First, we can complain about the yardstick. It is true that power disparities load the dice against the weak, but that fact is hardly uniquely true of collaborative processes. The poor and weak do not hire powerful lobbyists to do their bidding in the halls of Congress or the Administration, nor do they have the resources to fund expensive litigation. Traditional forms of litigation and politics afford the weak only formal equality. Therefore, unless one thinks that no social problems can be addressed before a redistributionist revolution, the relevant question about collaborative processes is not whether they afford opportunities for the powerful to oppress the weak, but whether they provide more such opportunities than conventional adversarial processes. They do not appear to do so.

That takes me to the second response: collaborative decisionmaking typically emerges precisely where adversarial processes fail because none of the parties can clearly identify their interests or go it alone. Because neither the strong nor the weak are monolithic entities, commonalities of interest cross these categories. As Sabel and I put the point:

> [T]he pursuit of new alliances can reveal novel solutions to complex problems, just as the exploration of novel solutions can give rise to new constellations of harmonious interests [and] these possibilities are likely to be especially salient in periods of disorientation marked by the kind of volatility and diversity that recommend experimentalism. Alliances and confusion do not nullify the bargaining disadvantage of inequality, but they can transform what might appear to be an insurmountable obstacle to any but radically redistributive reforms into one of the many considerations that would need to be addressed by experimentalist means in making participation in experimentalist deliberation as fair and comprehensive as it can be.[37]

The third answer to the problem of power imbalances is, frankly, to attempt to remedy them through procedural rules. For example, to prevent collaborative ecosystem governance from becoming a mechanism by which corporate and landowning interests simply weaken environmental rules to suit themselves, it may be necessary for environmentalists to retain a right to sue. This de facto exit right enhances the environmentalists' voice in the collaborative process.[38] More generally, one might characterize collaborative processes or "soft law" as parasitic upon adversarial "hard law," at least in the sense that the latter provides for a penalty default.[39]

If a right to participate backed by a right to sue is sometimes necessary to ensure the evenhandedness of collaborative processes, it will rarely be sufficient. As Archon Fung and Eric Olin Wright argue, groups such as environmentalists and labor organizations must figure out how to exercise their "countervailing power" within collaborative processes.[40] Merely threatening to walk or to sue is not a strategy for solving problems, even if it can effectively guarantee a seat at the table.

In the context of problem-solving courts, those who exercise countervailing power – criminal defense attorneys – appear to have solved the problem of how to cooperate with their traditional adversaries. They continue to press for their clients' interests, with the difference that they tend to accept a broader definition of client interest. The compromise is with client autonomy. Whereas a defense attorney acting within the traditional zealous advocate model pursues any lawful aim of the client, a defense attorney operating within a drug court accepts that it will sometimes be in the client's best interest to receive court-mandated treatment, even if zealous advocacy might result in a technical diminution in the degree of control the court exercises over the client. In the end, the decision remains with the client, but by conceptualizing her role as part of a problem-solving team that includes the client, the prosecutor, the judge, and the clinical staff, the defense attorney inevitably takes a less adversarial position.

Even if defense attorneys have mastered the art of collaboration, they and their clients remain vulnerable to abuse, absent some form of procedural guarantee. A drug court client who consistently violates the rules of the court of his treatment provider is subject to discipline, including, ultimately, expulsion from the program and imprisonment. What happens if the client upholds his end of the bargain but the treatment provider does not reciprocate? A well-functioning problem-solving court monitors treatment providers to detect and prevent poor practices. But what if the court is not well functioning? Surely it is not a sufficient answer to say that the defendant can "exit" by subjecting himself to prison. Such an exit right punishes the client without imposing any substantial cost on the court. In contrast to an environmental organization's threat to sue or a union's threat to strike, the defendant's exercise of his traditional countervailing power – insisting on utilizing the conventional adversary system – is no threat at all. Effective countervailing power for a drug court client must take a different form: perhaps a non-waivable right of appeal.

What question would an appeals court reviewing treatment decisions by drug courts address, given that the trial court itself does not resolve contested questions of law or fact? In short, whether the drug court is doing its job. Does the trial court monitor service providers to detect and prevent abuses? Does it continually update and upgrade treatment quality by demanding that less effective providers adopt the methods employed by or otherwise meet standards set by their more effective counterparts? Does the problem-solving court itself perform at roughly the same level as the better problem-solving courts in jurisdictions with comparable populations?

Thus, the appellate court would apply to the trial-level problem-solving court the same monitoring techniques as the problem-solving court applies to the service providers it monitors. In that way, just as an experimentalist trial court's monitoring of individual clients' performance is, ipso facto, a form of monitoring of treatment providers, so too would the appellate court's adjudication of individual claims of inadequately monitored treatment be, ipso facto, a form of monitoring of the trial court.

The foregoing sketch of appellate review of problem-solving courts also describes appellate review of problem-solving or experimentalist institutions more generally – for recall that, in their practical operation, problem-solving courts act similarly to experimentalist administrative agencies. Accordingly, whether reviewing the activities of problem-solving courts or other problem-solving institutions, experimentalist appellate courts would mirror the activities of those institutions at one remove, i.e. at a meta-level. Where a front-line problem-solving institution monitors the provision of services, reviewing courts monitor the monitoring of the provision of services. Therefore, and for the same reasons, just as front-line problem-solving courts rarely resolve contested questions in the sense of choosing one from a number of possible outcomes, so appellate courts would rarely resolve contested questions of law in the sense of choosing one rather than another meaning of authoritative text.

Describing problem-solving appellate courts as, in effect, meta-problem-solving courts thus casts them as a mechanism for narrowing the accountability deficit. If lawmakers increasingly address social problems by creating open-ended problem-solving institutions, rather than by directing solutions through authoritative but ultimately indeterminate instructions, the accountability deficit will correspondingly shrink in two respects. First, courts will have fewer occasions to attribute their own normative views to ambiguous authoritative text nominally traceable to the popular will. Second, courts, as experimentalist bodies, will be better able to hold primary actors accountable to the mandates that society truly has imposed.

IV. FROM HARD CASES TO BIG CASES

In my judgment, public institutions will become increasingly experimentalist. However, I could be mistaken, and, even if I am right about the long term, the law will continue to contain numerous authoritative yet ambiguous instructions. No complete legal system can be thoroughly experimentalist. Some classes of problems demand categorical, i.e. command-and-control, approaches. For example, it would be dangerous to phrase prohibitions on murder, rape, slavery, and other intentional offenses against the person, as well as some minimum regulatory standards, in experimentalist terms. Categorical rules clearly have their place,[41] and the accountability deficit will loom largest when courts confront the boundaries of such rules. Accordingly, we may properly ask whether experimentalism can narrow the judicial accountability deficit where courts are called upon to make value judgments in the substantial residual category of cases that involve categorical (but often ambiguous) rules. Is affirmative action consistent with "the equal protection of the laws"? Do abortion restrictions deprive women of "liberty . . . without due process of law"? Do publicly funded vouchers redeemable at parochial schools constitute "an establishment of religion"? How can different structures for decisionmaking provide broadly acceptable answers to such fundamentally contested legal questions, given the fact that, in a pluralistic society, reasonable persons will hold diverse views?[42]

The short answer is that experimentalism cannot eliminate the fact of moral diversity. But the slightly longer answer is that, surprisingly, it has some purchase on the problem. To see how experimentalism sometimes addresses moral diversity, consider two accounts of normative reasoning. The first account is modeled on a debating society. Each of the participants in the debate begins by figuring out what she thinks about the controversy at issue. Participants may consult religious authority, or they may turn to the writings of moral philosophers and attempt, after consulting their own moral intuitions, to arrive at a reflective equilibrium. The debaters then come together and butt heads. If the process is functioning at its best, an aggregated consensus may be found, but if not, the position that attracts the most votes prevails.

This first conception of moral reasoning fairly characterizes the conventional view of judicial resolution of moral questions. Ronald Dworkin's account is revealing. His ideal judge, whom he calls

"Hercules," attempts to resolve legal ambiguity by finding the result that best fits with prior law as organized by the best understanding of moral and political principles, while seated in, as it were, a metaphorical armchair (perhaps perched on Mount Olympus).[43] Rather than go out into the world or even discuss cases and principles with his colleagues, Hercules can learn all he needs to know by reading prior decisions as well as works of moral philosophy, and by thinking hard about what he has read. Collective deliberation plays almost no role.[44]

Under this account, if we imagine conventional appellate courts engaged in moral deliberation, the image that comes to mind is simply a sort of interactive search for an aggregate consensus. The process, which I have called "Socratic deliberation," closely tracks discussion in a law school classroom, except without the feeling that there is a single puppeteer leading the marionettes down an unseen path.[45] Whatever its virtues for training students how to trace the implications of their moral intuitions, Socratic dialogue typically cannot, in the end, resolve first-order value disagreement, which perhaps explains why the legal academic literature on the subject constructs multi-member courts as places in which judges individually decide outcomes and then aggregate what are taken to be preferences.[46]

Now contrast a second, quite different, conception of normative reasoning. In this conception, people come together or are thrust together, to solve their common problems. Instead of asking "vouchers: pro or con," they ask what can be done to improve education. Rather than reasoning from first principles to a list of what is and what is not impermissible sexual harassment, they work toward the common goal of a workplace in which all employees can concentrate on doing their jobs effectively.[47]

Practical deliberation does not depend on homogeneity of values or persons. Indeed, it is striking that responses to workplace sexual harassment provide a leading example of practical problem-solving, given the diversity of the American workplace, and the fact that the question of what constitutes sexual harassment can be highly contentious. Yet, as Cynthia Estlund observes, "[i]n the workplace, and often only there, citizens must find ways of cooperating on an ongoing basis, over weeks or years, outside of and often counter to traditional racial, ethnic, or sexual hierarchies."[48] To cooperate, of course, is not necessarily to agree, and it is precisely for that reason that experimentalism – by imagining law as a pathway to cooperative problem-solving rather than as a tool for adjudicating conflicting claims – promises a path around the problems arising from moral diversity.

In contrasting, on the one hand, individual normative reasoning via processes of rational introspection and Socratic dialogue with, on the other hand, collective practical problem-solving around rationally fragmented, value-laden issues, I do not mean to suggest that the latter can wholly supplant the former as a method of adjudication within the courts. The idea, instead, is that, where legal ambiguity appears to raise divisive issues, the courts need not necessarily take it upon themselves to choose one rather than another side in the contest. They can instead fashion doctrines that give front-line actors primary responsibility for working out the practical meaning of contested terms, thereby (partly) reducing the judicial accountability deficit.

The courts' accountability deficit manifests itself in two kinds of cases – what I call "hard cases" and "big cases." A hard case is hard because fleshing out ambiguous legal text calls for a controversial moral judgment. Abortion, affirmative action, euthanasia, gay rights, school prayer, and other issues caught up in the culture wars present hard cases. Big cases, by contrast, tax the administrative capacities of courts. Electoral redistricting, prison reform, school desegregation, and other tasks that do not seem readily amenable to supervision by less-than-panoptic courts present big cases. One might think that because judicial experimentalism – as a mechanism for courts to overcome their bounded rationality by monitoring without superseding the efforts of local actors – has to date been employed primarily in answer to the charge that courts cannot handle big cases, this seemingly technocratic solution does not apply to hard cases.

In order to address this concern, we might first recognize that there is not necessarily any sharp division between hard cases and big cases. Consider school desegregation. For roughly the decade after *Brown v. Board of Education*,[49] that decision was understood as a hard case, with academic efforts focusing on justifying the Supreme Court's adoption of the moral principle that racial apartheid contravenes the constitutional guarantee of equal protection of the laws.[50] When that point became clear to nearly everyone, *Brown* morphed into a big case. Then the question became: given massive resistance to desegregation in the South during the first decade after *Brown*, and persistent de facto racial segregation since then, can the courts really alter large-scale social institutions?[51]

Yet, as perhaps should have been obvious all along, *Brown* was always both a hard case and a big case, and the features that made it hard were tied up with the features that made it big. *Brown* was a big case because dismantling de jure segregation meant taking apart and replacing school assignment systems affecting tens of millions of schoolchildren. That daunting challenge led the Supreme Court in the first instance to provide public school officials with some breathing space through the formula of "all deliberate speed."[52] The fact of segregation's entrenchment was both what made the case big – it would be difficult to disentrench – and a reflection of the fact that the case was, by the lights of the population circa 1954, hard – for de jure racial segregation could not have been so firmly entrenched throughout the South were there a national consensus that the practice was an affront to the moral principle of equality.[53]

In pointing out that *Brown* was both a hard case and a big case, I do not mean to imply that an experimentalist approach in 1954 would have caused Southern resistance to the decision to evaporate. On the contrary, sometimes – as in *Brown* – the moral import of a legal command will be so clear to the judge that, notwithstanding vociferous disagreement by many in the population at large, fidelity to law requires choosing what will be received as a controversial path. Experimentalism, in short, does not eliminate that portion of the accountability deficit that arises out of moral diversity. Nevertheless, I want to suggest that even in such cases, moral diversity may be less of an issue than it appears. If effective, participatory, remedial structures are adopted, then the process of hammering out practical solutions can have an impact on how people understand the underlying value. If ordered by a court to work together on a solution to a problem that is both complex and morally divisive, parties who perceive themselves as holding antagonistic interests – elected officials, teachers, and parents of white and black schoolchildren in a formerly segregated district, say – may find that in fact they share a common interest – in my example, that of providing the best possible education for their respective children and the children of the community as a whole.[54] Practical deliberation, in other words, can work around value differences, and, in the long run, even change them.

The desegregation example is hardly unique. Even when engaging in the conventional task of resolving legal ambiguity, experimentalist courts differ in a crucial respect from constitutional and other courts as conventionally understood within the academic debate: when experimentalist courts must resolve the most contentious questions the legal system poses, they give deliberately incomplete answers. Instead of directing solutions themselves, experimentalist courts direct interested parties to solve problems collectively, as in my schematic desegregation example. They include ambiguity in their own pronouncements by establishing frameworks for resolution, rather than anything like comprehensive blueprints. They declare, for example, that employers are vicariously liable for sexual harassment by their employees absent an adequate program of prevention and remediation, but they leave to employers in the first instance the task of formulating such programs.[55] Or they announce that criminal suspects are entitled to safeguards to prevent undue coercion in interrogation but leave to local determination the decision of what safeguards to employ.[56] As these examples drawn from Supreme Court precedents illustrate, experimentalist principles sometimes inform current practice, so that the transformation envisioned here does not require wholesale reinvention.

We might think of experimentalist judging as operating principally in what would traditionally be understood as the remedial domain. Because the typical problem for courts in selecting remedies is one of institutional competence, the remedial character of experimentalism would again suggest that it is a strategy for dealing with complexity rather than moral diversity. Yet the relationship between rights and remedies is frequently symbiotic. As Daryl Levinson nicely puts the point: "Rights are dependent on remedies not just for their application to the real world, but for their scope, shape, and very existence."[57] If experimentalism is a strategy for enabling courts to overcome the complexity that bedevils the selection of a remedy, it can also be a strategy for announcing – or perhaps for facilitating the unfolding of – rights, notwithstanding the fact of moral diversity.

But not always. My strategy for showing that experimentalism could have utility in hard as well as in big cases has been to show how the distinction between the two categories is not always so clear. However, I must admit that there are some cases that are simply hard without being big, and that therefore may not be amenable to experimentalist solutions.

For example, the question whether the First Amendment protects a right to burn an American flag as a means of expressing disapproval of government policy – to which the Supreme Court answered yes by a five-to-four margin in 1989[58] – was a hard but not a big question. By saying the case was hard I do not mean that it presented especially difficult issues of doctrine. Prior precedent had established that laws targeting expressive conduct because of hostility to the speaker's message are subject to exacting judicial scrutiny,[59] and flag desecration did not fit into any of the Court's previously announced categorical exceptions to freedom of speech.[60] Nonetheless, the closeness of the vote in the Court, and the strong negative political reaction to the decision,[61] demonstrated that the case was hard in the sense that matters from the perspective of the courts' accountability deficit: Most Americans did not think that the First Amendment's protection for "freedom of speech" encompassed the right to burn an American flag, and the constitutional text was not a sufficient basis for showing them to be wrong.

The flag-burning case was not big, however. The Court's invalidation of the Texas statute and its subsequent invalidation of a similar federal statute[62] did not require the judiciary to root out a deeply entrenched social practice, nor to set up or oversee some large administrative apparatus. These decisions simply excised crimes from the statute books, and for that reason there was no occasion for the Court to establish any remedial scheme at all.

Much the same might be said about a case like *Griswold* v. *Connecticut*,[63] which invalidated a ban on contraceptive use. *Griswold* actually was hard in the doctrinal sense: given the constitutional text's failure to mention contraception or a general right of autonomy, the challenge for the Court was to justify a penumbral right of privacy without seeming to license, as the dissent accused the majority of licensing, the sort of open-ended judicial power that had fallen into disrepute by the end of the 1930s.[64] And *Griswold* was also hard in the sense that there was moral opposition to contraceptive use. However, by 1965, when the case was decided, the number of people who strongly believed the government ought, on moral grounds, to forbid contraceptive use, was sufficiently small that the Court's decision engendered nothing like the resistance to *Brown* or to *Griswold*'s most famous successor in the privacy line of cases, *Roe* v. *Wade*.[65]

I shall return to *Roe* momentarily, but first I want to pause over a point that may seem too obvious even to warrant mention, namely the question of whether a case is hard in the sense of bringing into play the problem of moral diversity is always a contingent social fact. Slavery was a hard question in 1856 but is easy today – and not simply because the Constitution now contains the Thirteenth Amendment. Arguments that the antebellum Constitution prohibited slavery were a staple of (one branch of) abolitionist discourse.[66] In a counterfactual world in which slavery died out without a Civil War and without the Reconstruction Amendments, eventually the near-global consensus against slavery surely would have found expression in American constitutional law. To be sure, in such a world, a few curmudgeons would argue that slavery remained compatible with the Constitution, but without a substantial moral or material investment in slavery as an institution, legal elites and society at large would soon dismiss such arguments. The shift in popular opinion over time would have transformed slavery from a hard to an easy question, in much the same way that, in our actual world, shifting public opinion over time has transformed the constitutionality of de jure segregation from a hard to an easy question.[67]

Slavery on the eve of the Civil War, of course, was not merely a hard question. It was also a big question. Suppose that, instead of declaring the Missouri Compromise invalid in the *Dred Scott* case,[68] the Supreme Court had invalidated slavery. The Court would have stood no realistic chance of implementing its decision, no matter what means it might have chosen. That is not to say that the antebellum Court acted correctly in making its peace – and then some – with slavery. When faced with an undeniable evil that a substantial fraction of one's fellow citizens do not recognize as evil, one may have a moral duty to act in contravention of the norms of one's profession.[69] But that problem is not peculiar to the law or judging. In a society not on the verge of civil war and in which the spirit of tolerance prevails, even on most issues as to which there is substantial moral disagreement, one will not find the sort of moral certainty that might be thought to justify civil disobedience by judges and others.

Perhaps abortion and a handful of other profoundly divisive moral issues are to our age what slavery was in the nineteenth century; they create such polarization and depth of feeling that no judicial resolution – not even a decision not to decide – will be viewed as legitimate by those who would have preferred a different outcome. If so, however, that is a contingent historical fact about these moral issues at this moment in time. The current intractability of some moral questions is certainly not an indictment of experimentalism.

Experimentalist appellate judging offers two advantages over conventional appellate judging. First, in those cases that are primarily big, i.e. those cases where the judiciary's competence but not its moral authority seems doubtful, experimentalism offers courts a mechanism for coordinating local learning without having to superintend a top-down bureaucracy. Second, in those hard cases in which the Court's resolution of the central issue does not simply put an end to some practice, an experimentalist approach – by devolving deliberative authority for fully specifying norms to local actors – can soften the sting for those on the losing end of the initial decision. By bringing them together with those who hold different values to solve common problems, experimentalism can also reveal previously unseen commonalities of interest and even constitute common values.

CONCLUSION

If and when it works, democratic experimentalism facilitates discovery of novel solutions to shared social problems. Whereas bureaucracy generates accountability in large-scale institutions by reiterative articulation of ever higher levels of command and control, democratic experimentalism generates accountability in large-scale government by reiterative articulation of ever higher levels of learning. We might say that just as bureaucracy addresses the problem of size and scale by watching the watcher, democratic experimentalism can also address the problem of size and scale by teaching the teacher.

As I have argued here, adapting experimentalist methods to judicial settings has the added benefit of providing for the courts a somewhat different kind of accountability; experimentalism provides at least a partial response to the counter-majoritarian difficulty. I would add in closing that, in doing so, experimentalism offers a superior institutional response to the courts' accountability deficit than the standard alternative – judicial deference to legislative determination. Various critics of judicial supremacy have taken the Supreme Court to task for its arrogation to itself of the sole power of constitutional interpretation.[70] The milder form of this criticism (which I myself have made) urges the Court to give greater deference in its own decisionmaking processes to legislative judgments.[71] Harsher forms would either strip the courts of the power of judicial review or, as in Canada, make their decisions subject to a legislative override.[72] Yet, to the extent that the problems bedeviling judicial resolution of ambiguity are rooted in complexity, the refractory nature of our social problems is likely to pose difficulties for any centralized decisionmaker, whether it is a court, the legislature itself, or a traditionally hierarchical administrative agency to which a legislature delegates power. The crucial question for addressing issues of size and scale, in other words, is not whether the task goes to a court, a legislature, or an agency, but whether whichever institution is charged with the relevant task adopts problem-solving methods equal to the challenge. And, given the connections between complexity and moral diversity, that observation is likely to be true of many divisive moral controversies as well as seemingly more technical questions. In the end, then, the way to make our courts and other institutions more accountable is to make them more effective, and vice versa.

CHAPTER 13

PUBLIC ACCOUNTABILITY IN ALIEN TERRAIN: EXPLORING FOR CONSTITUTIONAL ACCOUNTABILITY IN THE PEOPLE'S REPUBLIC OF CHINA

Michael W. Dowdle

INTRODUCTION

Public accountability looks different from the outside than it does from the inside. The insider is privy to a wealth of information and understandings that eludes the outsider.[1] As long as the outsider remains unaffected by what goes on inside, this discrepancy generally does not merit her concern. But as both transnational and domestic governance reconfigure the parameters of what is public and what is private, what is national and what is transnational, it upsets existing distinctions between insiders and outsiders. Much of the ongoing crisis in public accountability might be attributed to this kind of disruption.[2]

One particular kind of outsider who is vitally interested in the public accountability workings of systems from which she is removed is the comparative constitutional scholar. Just as public accountability is core to the constitutionalist project, understanding its dynamics and reification is core to the comparativist project. But the inherently outsider status of the comparativist always threatens to render her blind to core accountability dynamics. When and where this is the case, it can fatally corrupt comparative understanding.[3]

This problem is not unique to comparativists. As noted above, new evolutions in governance, economics, and communications have caused previously distinct and insular regulatory environments to become interpenetrated. Interest in public accountability thus increasingly transcends traditional institutional boundaries. In a sense, our increasingly "post-regulatory," "post-Fordist," "post-modern," or perhaps just "globalized" world ultimately requires us all to become comparativists. A key issue we face both in comparativist constitutional law and in our practical need to understand our rapidly evolving political, social, and regulatory environments is the need to develop analytic methodologies that are sensitive to as yet unfamiliar aspects of public accountability – aspects that are effective but do not correspond to the structural, institutional, or cultural configurations we use to identify public accountability in our own environments.

Comparative constitutional law can thus provide a useful foil for exploring today's apparent accountability crisis, and perhaps even for addressing some aspects of that crisis. This chapter uses the experience of constitutional development in the People's Republic of China to explore what such a methodology might look like. Anglo-American scholars are clearly "outsiders" insofar as China's constitutional system is concerned. On the one hand, that system lacks the defining attributes we associate with constitutional accountability, namely the use of direct public election to fill principal constitutional offices and a bureaucratic, "rule of law" architecture that binds lower-level civil servants to more politically responsive principals.[4] On the other hand, China's constitutional system has experienced a significant quickening over the past fifteen years, showing increasing and recognizably-constitutional effectiveness.[5] There clearly seems to be something going on there that escapes our cognition. An analytic methodology that is able to give usable comparative meaning and insight into China's constitutional system would seem to be of use, not only to our understandings of comparative constitutional law, but also to our more domestic efforts to identify the public accountability possibilities that might exist in the new and unfamiliar arenas and institutions that are coming to characterize governance in the post-regulatory era.

We begin, in Section I, by exploring the cognitive limits in our traditional model of constitutional accountability. That model sees constitutional accountability as a two-level dynamic. At the elite level, the model says that political actors are to be subject to periodic election. The processes of being elected via direct, free, fair, and universal vote is believed to provide the popular sovereign an essential opportunity to respond to and, if need be, discipline public servants for errant political frolics. More subordinate-level political actors who are not directly elected are made constitutionally accountable indirectly by subjecting them to the bureaucratic command and control of persons who are subject to direct election. We will refer to this as the "regulatory" model of constitutional accountability, in order to reflect the idea that embedded in this conception is a presumption that the constitutional environment – the social space that is structured by the constitutional order – is "regularized" in such a way as to be directly comprehensible to a centralized administrative apparatus.

As we shall see, this regulatory model is really a projection of late nineteenth-century industrialization. Embedded within this model are particular presumptions about the functional structure of socio-political organization. These structures are neither universal, nor historically or functionally inevitable: many recognizably 'constitutional' structures have been founded in their absence. When applied to such "non-regularized" structures, the regulatory model can give a very misleading picture of the constitutional potentialities of the system.

In Section II, we see how the real problem with the regulatory model lies in its deductive character. Exploring for constitutionalism in more alien, "non-regularized" constitutional environments ultimately requires a more inductive conceptualization of what constitutional accountability would look like "from the outside." Section II concludes by outlining the basic features of this inductive methodology.

Section III tests this new, inductive methodology by using it to explore what I have elsewhere termed "the curious case" of meaningful constitutional development in China. We shall see how this inductive approach reveals important structural features that are invisible to more traditional analyses. These features offer an explanation why constitutionalism might be developing in China even in the absence of meaningful elections or rigorous bureaucratic oversight. They are also consistent with evolving scholarship on institutional dynamics, and thus would seem to represent significant constitutional discoveries, rather than simply figments of some inductively-induced constitutionalist fantasy.

I. THE "REGULATORY" MODEL OF CONSTITUTIONAL ACCOUNTABILITY AND ITS LIMITATIONS

The argument for a different, more inductive methodology for exploring comparatively for constitutional accountability implies a claim that the present, deductive, regulatory model does not always work. In this section, we will explore the limits of this regulatory model. As we shall see, the regulatory model presumes a modernized, visibilized constitutional-regulatory environment of the kind that rapidly emerged in the United States in the wake of the late nineteenth-century corporate industrialization. Many constitutional environments are not necessarily so structured, however. Where this is the case, analyses that derive from this particular model can provide a very misleading picture of the true shape of constitutional dynamics.

A. History and development of the regulatory model of constitutional accountability

Today, constitutional accountability is conceptualized primarily as a two-level construct.[6] At the top level, what we will call the "electoral component" of constitutional accountability makes elite political actors accountable to the public via the process of subjecting them to popular election. At the subordinate level, what we will call the legal-bureaucratic component makes subordinate political actors accountable by subjecting them to the bureaucratic command and control of higher level, elected officials. For convenience, we will call this conceptualization the "regulatory" model of constitutional accountability, because, as we shall see, it assumes a particular "regularization" of society.

For the first 100 years of American constitutionalism, however, the dominant model for constitutional accountability was not the regulatory model. Rather, it was a more *res publica* – or "republican" – model, in which constitutional accountability was thought to stem primarily from the constitution's capacity to populate elite levels of government with enlightened, public-minded intelligentsia, while at the same time leaving most political decisionmaking in the hands of largely autonomous, generally intimate, local communities.[7]

Indeed, many early American political thinkers would likely have been quite skeptical of both the electoral and the legalist-bureaucratic components of the regulatory model of constitutional accountability. The founders' belief that electoral politics corrupted rather than engendered accountability to the public good is well rehearsed.[8] Their suspicion of legalist-bureaucratic modes of command and control is less explored, but still fairly evident: the institutional devices that collectively define our particular constitutional structure are overwhelmingly anti-bureaucratic, in that their principal purpose is to disperse and derationalize power, whereas bureaucratic command and control demands a unified and rationalized power structure.[9] Nor was legalism a defining element of the original constitutional structure. Indeed, Tocqueville praised the American constitutional structure precisely because its unique federal system reduced the need for legislation and legalism.[10]

The first articulations of what we are calling the "regulatory" model of constitutional accountability appear in the early twentieth century.[11] Prior to the Civil War, "governance" in the United States was primarily a local phenomenon.[12] But, in the forty years following the Civil War, the localized character that had defined antebellum American political society was effectively erased in an explosion of mass-production, managerial capitalism, and industrialization.[13] Economic firms were transformed from localized entities into nation-sized creatures of private corporate capitalism. This catalyzed two corresponding transformations in American political society. First, the formation of powerful, nation-sized, private entities and organized interests required the parallel creation of powerful, nation-sized, administrative entities to regulate them. As we shall see, this led to the legal-bureaucratic component of the regulatory model of constitutional accountability. Secondly, the formation of powerful, nation-sized, private economic actors pushed the locus of governmental decisionmaking upward. This gave rise to a need for new, less intimate, conceptions of democracy that could claim to legitimate government at more remote distances. As we shall see, this gave rise to the electoral component of the regulatory model of constitutional accountability.

The key to mass production industrialization's ability to catalyze economies of scale was standardization.[14] Standardized work responsibilities decreased the costs of monitoring large numbers of employees. Standardized financial accounting decreased the costs of monitoring geographically dispersed economic activity and performance. Standardized firm structure allowed centralized firm administration to readily evaluate and assign responsibilities to employees in dispersed, remote locales. When tied into a Weberian bureaucracy, such standardization allowed firms to increase their size – and hence their income – without corresponding and proportionate increases in operating costs.

As economic firms expanded in size and scope, they outgrew the governance capacities of the local governments, on which America's original constitutional order was founded. Nation-sized economic actors could only be governed by nation-sized administrative entities.

And just as firm growth depended critically on standardization, so too did the development of this new nation-sized style of government. Whether out of necessity[15] or simply through a lack of ingenuity,[16] this new nation-sized style of government took the form of modern bureaucratic organizations.

Herein lies the conceptual core of what we are calling the regulatory model of constitutional accountability. At the heart of both the economic and governance aspects of this late-nineteenth-century transformation was the exponential expansion of a particular organizational technique that would later be termed "modernism." As explored by James Scott, "modernism" describes a process by which remote, centralized administrators standardize (or regularize) local social activity so as to make it comprehensible – "visible" in his terms – to persons, like themselves, who lack intimate knowledge of the local dynamics of that locality.[17] This linkage between regularization and (remote) visibilization is integral to the regulatory model, in both its electoral and the rule-of-law aspects. The electoral component reflects in significant part a presumption that standardized processes of election can make public concerns visible to the increasingly remote political apparatus that would oversee our new nation-sized governance.[18] Legalist-bureaucracy, for its part, reflects an underlying presumption that a particular positive command will have a standardized and standardizing effect (an effect often captured by the ideal of "predictability") throughout the larger constitutional environment.[19]

Mass-production industrialization did not simply standardize firm-based economic organization, it also standardized larger society. Exploiting economies of scale meant that firm profits corresponded in part to the size of the firm's market: the larger the market, the more profit could be generated by exploiting economies of scale. Firms therefore sought to *create* larger markets in part by standardizing market and labor activity – particularly terms of exchange, employment, and risk allocation – across dispersed locales.[20] Indeed, large firms often welcomed nation-sized government regulation because, by standardizing governance in diverse locales, such regulation often promoted large-scale social standardization that in turn promoted the development of larger markets.[21] We will refer to this larger, societal manifestation of industrially driven standardization as "regularization."

In other words, the fruits of late-nineteenth-century American industrialization were not simply the product of more bureaucratized forms of business activity. They were the product of more bureaucratized forms of business activity interacting with a more regularized society. The benefits of organizational regularization are thus symbiotic on a larger regularization of society as a whole.

Of course, economically based firms could be proactive in regularizing society, because the cost of this regularizing could be funded by the profit gains from market expansion that regularization allowed.[22] But governments are not profit-making institutions. They cannot so easily generate the funds needed to regularize their operating environments (so as to facilitate regulatory governance) simply by borrowing against the future efficiencies associated with that governance. Therefore, in developing and implementing large-scale governance, government often had to rely on the social and economic regularizations generated by private firms.

A good example of this new, regulatory government's reliance on a prior industrialized regularization of society is found in the vital role that preexisting accounting practices played in the success of America's early experiments with regulation. The single most important regulatory tool possessed by early regulatory agencies was the uniform system of accounts, developed by Milo Maltbie in the late 1890s.[23] The uniform system of accounts required all firms within the regulated environment to keep uniformly detailed and integrated records of revenues, expenses, and earnings for each part of their operations. The principal responsibility of early regulatory agencies was to prevent private firms operating in markets for public goods – like railroads and public utilities – from using the inherently monopolistic tendencies of these markets to impose unreasonable charges on their customers. The uniform system of accounts was crucial to effectuating this responsibility, because it allowed regulators to visibilize and generate evaluations and comparisons of pricing and profits across and within firms in the regulated industry, in a way that could be defended against political attack.[24]

The uniform system of accounts was really just a tweaking of the already established industrial practice of cost accounting. Cost accounting – an accounting system in which firms itemize individual sources of cost, expenditure, and revenue – had become a popular practice among the larger, industrialized firms that emerged following the Civil War. By making the corporate activities of local actors more visible to remote, centralized supervisors, cost accounting facilitated centralized control in these larger but more dispersed industrial organizations. At the same time, the visibility benefits of cost accounting accrued not only to firm managers, they also accrued to suppliers of firm capital. Capital markets and bank lenders both began demanding access to these accounts as a condition for investing in the firm.[25]

All this resulted in an explosion in the private demand for persons trained in integrated cost accounting systems. Such demand was met through a corresponding post-Civil War explosion in the number of proprietary business colleges and public and private universities in the United States offering training in accounting. This, in turn, created a market for accounting textbooks. As an increasing proportion of accountants received their education from these colleges or otherwise from these textbooks, accounting practices became more uniform.[26] By the late 1870s, accountancy practices had become standardized and rationalized enough to support the emergence of accounting theory.[27] One of these theorists was Henry Carter Adams, a professor of economics at the University of Michigan and one of the co-founders of the American Economic Association, who devised a cost accounting system specifically for railroads and public utilities.[28] It was from this system that Maltbie adapted his uniform system of accounts.[29]

A similar story can be told about the earliest successful workplace-safety regulatory regimes – workers' compensation, railroad safety, and the regulation of boilers. All of these piggybacked on existing industrial practices.[30] Workers' compensation piggybacked on the widespread establishment of private accident relief funds championed by US Steel. Railroad safety regulation piggybacked on the railroad's own efforts to reduce the costs associated with workplace accidents. Boiler safety regulation piggybacked on the efforts of the insurance industry to reduce payouts. By contrast, legislative efforts to promote workplace safety that did not take into account existing industrial practice had little significant effect on actual workplace safety.[31]

Early regulation's dependence on the prior existence of industrial standards and practices is further evinced in the "case-by-case" strategy that the Interstate Commerce Commission and other early regulators used to develop regulatory standards. A critical component of that strategy was a continuous dialogue between the regulator and the regulated community, manifested primarily in public and private hearings. Crucial to this dialogue was the pre-existence of private regulatory institutions – trade associations, labor unions, professional organizations – that were originally spawned by the growing coordination problems associated with industrialization's ever-more extended market networks. These institutions "gave voice" to their particular component of the regulatory environment, serving as the principal organizational interfaces through which the regulator and regulated spoke to one another.[32]

The other component of the regulatory model of constitutional accountability, electoral democracy, is also a product of the social regularization brought about by industrialized corporatization. Prior to the onset of industrialization, American government remained primarily localized, and democratic legitimacy was founded on the local politician's responsiveness and effectiveness in securing public resources for his community.[33] As industrialization and regulation pushed the locus of American government upward, however, they rendered the older, localized mechanisms of political accountability increasingly unworkable. Governance became remote from its constituencies. The kind of personal, face-to-face interaction with government that in an earlier era was seen to define American democracy – as exemplified by Toqueville's celebration of the town meetings of antebellum New England – came to be seen as elitist, corrupting, and antidemocratic. Political attention began to focus more on elections and their rationalization, because rationalized (or "modernized") elections seemed more adept at transmitting public concerns to remote political decisionmakers.[34] Eventually, rationalized, supra-local elections replaced town meetings as the defining symbol of American democracy.

Just as the effectiveness of early legalist-bureaucratic regulation was dependent upon prior industrial regularization of diverse socioeconomic localities, so too was the effectiveness of supra-local elections. This is clearly seen in William Jennings Bryan's 1896 campaign for the US presidency. Prior to Bryan's campaign, presidential candidates functioned more as remote and symbolic figureheads for their respective parties. They enjoyed little autonomous policymaking authority, and were in general organizationally and politically subservient to party and congressional leadership.[35]

By contrast, Bryan and his supporters initiated a campaign – first within the Democratic Party, and later (albeit less successfully) against the Republican Party – which appealed directly to a broad electorate by evoking a variety of nation-wide policy interests, primarily those concerned with labor rights, monetary policy, and national-level governmental reform.[36] Of course, Bryan's new campaigning style was not successful in winning the Presidency. But it was successful in securing for him the Democratic nomination in the face of broad-based opposition from the party elite. Eight years later, the Republican president Theodore Roosevelt would use this same general strategy – direct, issue-based appeal to the voting electorate, what he famously referred to as the presidential "bully pulpit" – to wrest his presidency away from the control of a hostile Republican Party leadership.[37] With Roosevelt, the modern, what some have termed "imperial," presidency – i.e. a presidency whose considerable power flowed more from his capacity to mobilize the electorate rather than from the favor of party elite – became a ubiquitous feature of the modern American political landscape.[38]

Crucial to Bryan's supra-local mobilization of electoral democracy was the preexistence of social organizations and institutions that had formed in response to industrialization.[39] As mentioned above, Bryan mobilized the electorate primarily by appealing to three large, nation-spanning interests – agrarian interests, industrial labor interests, and silver interests. Each of these nation-spanning interests had distinctly industrial predicates that had already caused them to create nation-sized organizational structures. Agrarian interests had earlier formed the People's (or Populist) Party in order to address nation-spanning social disruptions caused by the early industrialization of American agriculture (particularly the introduction of large-scale cash-crop farming). Industrial labor interests had earlier formed the Knights of Labor in order to address nation-spanning social disruptions caused by the explosive growth of wage-labor sparked by industrialization. Silver interests were driven by an already organized silver-producing industry taking over and uniting the remnants of regional Greenback parties that had formed in reaction to the increasing monetarization of the economy, again caused by industrialization. Bryan used the superior mobilizing capacities of these national-level organizations to overwhelm the political energies that the more established leadership of the Democratic Party could mobilize through the Party's traditional, local-based, patronage-based structures.[40]

At the same time, the Republican Party's success in overcoming Bryan's new 1896 campaign strategy was due to its exploitation of another aspect of social regularizations brought about by late-nineteenth-century industrialization, an exploitation that ultimately produced another core feature of modern electoral democracy – modern campaign finance.

Modern campaign finance is part of a larger bundle of public finance inventions that were both necessary to the success of large-scale electoral democracy and facilitated by industrialization. Throughout the nineteenth century, one of the biggest obstacles to electoral accountability was the spoils system – the system popularized by Andrew Jackson in which jobs in public service were the principal currency by which party leadership bought institutional loyalty and coherence. The spoils system was thought to impede democratic accountability, both by making civil service more accountable to the private corporate interests of political parties than to the public interests of the people as a whole, and by making the parties themselves more accountable to the interests of potential spoils-holders than to the interests of voters.

The spoils system was a creature of necessity, however. With the development of national political parties, national political success became a large-scale endeavor, and, as famously demonstrated by Mancur Olson, effective large-scale organizational discipline has to be bought.[41] Placement in public office was often the principal resource available to political parties with which they could reward and promote large-scale party discipline.[42] This is why even strong, ideological opponents of the spoils system, like Woodrow Wilson, often found themselves dependent upon that system for political effectiveness after they achieved office.[43]

At the national level, the real death-knell to the spoils system came from the invention of modern campaign finance and from the implementation of a centralized, direct-tax system. The advent of a centralized, direct-tax system greatly increased the revenue the federal government could use to fund civil servants. Campaign finance provided political parties with an alternative way of purchasing party discipline. The overall effect of this was to cause civil servants to become more responsive to elected government and less responsive to party interests.[44]

Both these developments were made possible by industrialization. Industrialization's concentration of wealth and income into a smaller number of large financial organizations greatly reduced the monitoring and collection costs associated with a direct-tax system. The standardized and comprehensive accounting and auditing practices that it engendered facilitated the central government's ability to observe, monitor, and tax corporate income flows. Industrialization's tendency to replace production-based sources of wealth with wage-based sources of wealth also facilitated the taxation of individual incomes, which in turn greatly expanded the potential tax base.[45]

Modern campaign finance, for its part, used the centralizing economic tendencies of industrialization to catalyze large-scale political mobilization. As industrialization concentrated wealth in corporate hands, it made it much easier for political parties to identify and target productive sources for campaign contributions.[46] This greatly reduced party dependence on the spoils system, which in turn made party politics more responsive to political issues and less responsive to personal loyalties.[47]

The symbiosis between electoral accountability and industrialization is further demonstrated by looking at environments in which electoral regulation and reform failed to have significant effect on political dynamics. One of the principal intended targets of local urban electoral reform was the patronage-driven, machine-style democracy that operated in many large cities. Ironically, however, electoralization often had only a marginal effect on these urban machines. This is because early-twentieth-century industrial regularizing effects generally did not extend to poor, immigrant, urban communities that supported and maintained these machines. Well into the twentieth century, these communities continued to be characterized by reliance on direct associational ties, which in turn made them more comfortable with the localized, relationship-oriented dynamics of machine-style politics than the more remote and professionalized dynamics of a more regularized electoral democracy.[48]

Similarly, electoral reforms also failed to have significant impact on national and state-level agricultural policies, despite being heavily promoted by widespread, populist, agrarian interests who felt strongly aggrieved by these policies. Agrarian populists believed that electoralizing rural politics by itself would allow local, agrarian majorities in agrarian states to wrest control of politics away from organized industrial interests. By the opening of the twentieth century, most rural jurisdictions had implemented the core modernizing electoral reforms advocated by populist agrarians. But with the collapse of the Populist Party in the wake of Bryan's defeat in 1896, the particular agrarian interests who pushed the populist agenda reverted to a pre-industralized political existence. For this reason, even after winning these electoral reforms, the populist agrarian interests who had promoted these reforms had no significant effect on rural politics and policy formation. It was only after establishment in 1919 of the American Farm Bureau Federation – a nationwide, industrial-interest organization devoted to promoting agricultural interests – that these interests began to have significant impact on American politics.[49]

B. Limitations of the regulatory model

Present-day evidence suggests that the effectiveness of the regulatory model of constitutional accountability continues to be highly dependent upon a prior regularization of society of the kind often initiated by industrialization. The positive correlation between industrialization and the sustainability of electorally-based constitutional systems is well documented.[50] Ronald Inglehart has shown how industrialization correlates with the emergence of political values associated with liberal, electoral democracy.[51] Przeworski *et al.* have shown how the survival of large-scale electoral democratic systems corresponds to higher per capita levels of private wealth.[52] Higher levels of wealth, in turn, tend to correlate with industrialization. For example, larger, relatively wealthy nations ("wealthy" by the standards Przeworski *et al.* found to be sufficient to sustain democracy) that have not modernized or industrialized, primarily those found in the Middle East, have not been particularly effective at sustaining democracy.[53]

A similar story, albeit one that is less examined, can be told about what I am calling legalist bureaucracy, but which is more commonly referred to under the rubric of "rule of law." One of the few comparative studies of the relationship between rule of law and economic development, Katharina Pistor and Philip Wellons' *The Role of Law and Legal Institutions in Asian Economic Development 1960–1995*, suggests that "market/rule-based law might have a measurable effect on future economic development only after economies have reached a certain threshold of development."[54] Again, the strong correlation between economic development and modernization suggests that it could well be industrialization rather than economic development per se, which is driving the correlation observed by Pistor and Wellons.

I am not at all suggesting that democracy, rule of law, or public accountability is impossible in non-industrialized societies. What I am suggesting is that in those non-modernized societies in which recognizable constitutionalism and democracy can be found, the public accountability dynamics that underlie that constitutionalism and democracy are likely to be quite different from those predicted by the regulatory model. A good example of this might be Japan. Japan is often characterized as a post-industrial society – i.e. a society in which economic activity is characterized more by concerns for flexibility and adaptiveness than by concerns for standardization and regularization.[55] Japan also clearly enjoys what most would agree is a vibrant constitutional democracy, and its public officials appear to act in the public interest.[56] But, because of its post-industrial status, its constitutional dynamics do not necessarily conform to the predictions that underlie the regulatory model of constitutional accountability. Administrative governance in Japan does not seem particularly constrained by bureaucratic legalism.[57] And elections seem to have only marginal effect on policy formation.[58] Thus, whatever it is that is making public behavior responsive to the public interest, it does not appear to be something captured by the regulatory model of constitutional accountability.

The symbiosis between regulatory accountability and industrial modernization is also evinced in recent international efforts to help Thailand provide social welfare protection to rural populations in the wake of the East Asian Economic Crisis.[59] When that crisis hit in June of 1997, many in the international development community attributed it at least in part to a failure on the part of East Asian countries to adopt effective "rule of law" – what we are calling legal-bureaucratic – institutions. Lack of effective rule of law, it was argued, allowed corruption and cronyism to corrode the efficiency of these countries' economic and political markets. The crisis was simply a return to equilibrium that resulted when these inefficiencies finally became visible to these markets.

Initial efforts to assist Thailand in building a social safety net to aid persons left vulnerable by this crisis, undertaken primarily by the Asian Development Bank (ADB) and the World Bank, bought into the "corruption and cronyism" argument issued by Western analyses and many Thai NGOs. As a result, they framed their assistance projects in rigorous bureaucratic protections – namely detailed, rationalized standards for eligibility, project structure, and fiscal monitoring – that were intended to prevent the cronyism and state corruption that was supposedly endemic to this region from diluting the effectiveness of these projects.

The result was a failure. In August 1998, the World Bank instituted a "Social Investment Fund" (SIF) designed to promote local community welfare, conservation, and skill-development projects. By the end of 1998, the fund had approved only 12 out of 836 applications. By June 1999, the SIF had disbursed only 5 percent of its available capital. In July of that year, the World Bank itself admitted that, as then structured, the SIF had been ineffective, and that the Bank would have to rethink its project.

The failure of the SIF program was due in significant part to the fact that rural Thailand – the part of Thai society most in need of social-welfare assistance – does not sport an industrialized, modernized economy. Thailand's economy is dominated by small enterprises and agriculture, rather than large enterprises and manufacturing.[60] This non-industrialized condition would make it difficult to centrally identify and target at-risk rural populations. We noted above how the success of early regulation in the United States vitally depended on its cooption of widespread, uniform accounting and managerial practices spawned by industrialization. The SIF's stringent, rationalized application and monitoring requirements presumed the preexistence of such practices. But the vast majority of social-welfare providers operating in Thailand's largely non-industrialized rural sector had not adopted such practices. Consequently, few of the local welfare organizations that were best placed to identify and assist these at-risk populations possessed the experiences necessary to allow them to comply with the World Bank's stringent application and monitoring requirements.[61]

On the other hand, abandoning bureaucratic, "rule of law" monitoring protections actually proved much more effective at reaching Thailand's rural populations. In late 1998, Japan inaugurated its "Miyazawa Scheme" for promoting recovery in East Asia. In stark contrast to the SIF, in Thailand the Miyazawa Scheme "abandoned all pretence of careful targeting [and] elaborate bureaucratic procedures," and "disbursed funds through local government bodies."[62] And the Miyazawa Scheme was significantly more successful in providing social welfare security to vulnerable populations than was the SIF program. Both the SIF program and the Miyazawa fund had budgets of around 10 billion baht. Both sought primarily to provide immediate and substantial assistance to rural welfare development. But, whereas the SIF was only able to disburse some 5 percent of its funds in nine months of operation, the Miyazawa fund successfully disbursed most of its funds within the same timeframe.[63] Moreover, there were no widespread reports of corruption or misuse of funds. Follow-up studies found these rurally located Miyazawa-funded projects to have been relatively well managed.[64]

None of this is to suggest that the regulatory model of constitutional accountability is simply a myth used to perpetuate certain power hierarchies brought about by industrialization.[65] In fact, quite the opposite: as described above, key aspects of both the bureaucratic component and the democratic component of constitutional accountability arose out of efforts to combat and counteract the power hierarchies of industrialization. The universal popularity of the regulatory model in the United States suggests that the model has been at least somewhat successful. Still, whatever success the regulatory model enjoys in effectively fashioning public accountability it is often vitally dependent on the prior presence of a regulatorized society. Not all constitutional environments are so structured.

II. VISIBILIZING PUBLIC ACCOUNTABILITY IN A NON-REGULATORY SPACE: INDUCTIVE ACCOUNTABILITY

A. The pervasiveness of non-regulatory environments

The long-standing dominance of the regulatory state in American political society has caused us to forget just how fortuitous was its development and perhaps even how delicate is its survival. The success of the regulatory state seems likely to depend on what, following Bob Jessop, we might think of as the "improbably stability" of modernism.[66] It is a stability that does not exist in many political, social, and regulatory environments. It is a stability that is not completely pervasive even in modern constitutional democracies.

Even within advanced, stabilized, modernized countries like the United States, there still exist crucial regulatory environments that are effectively "non-modernized." One obvious example of this would be the Anglo-American court system. Anglo-American courts are quintessentially pre-modern constitutional institutions.[67] They are distinctly anti-bureaucratic[68] – lower level judges are not supervised or disciplined by bureaucratic superiors. At the highest level, they are intentionally insulated from electoral processes.

Many question the public accountability of the judiciary precisely on these modernist grounds. As described in Chapter 12 of this volume by Michael Dorf, this is the heart of the "counter-majoritiarian difficulty" that has plagued the courts for the past 100 years.[69] But the counter-majoritarian difficulty is a modern discovery. For the first 100 years of the American Constitution, the courts lay at the very heart of American governance – "a state of courts and parties," as Stephen Skowronek has famously referred to it.[70] During that pre-modern time, few questioned their accountability to the public. It was the process of regulatory modernization that pushed the courts to the periphery, replacing them with the modern administrative state. And, not incidentally, it was during this transformative period when regulatory modernization was being born that the courts' accountability "deficit" started becoming an ongoing national issue.[71]

This is not to suggest that the courts' anti-modernist character is necessarily ill-advised. Again as Michael Dorf demonstrated in Chapter 12 the courts' anti-modernist character can be exploited so as to allow judges to make important, unique contributions to American constitutional governance. The problem here lies not in the anti-modernist character of the courts, but in a vision of constitutional accountability that preemptively excludes non-modernized regulatory environments from its analytic purview. This is precisely what the "regulatory" model of constitutional accountability does. By tacitly presuming the presence of regularized social structures associated with modernism, that vision leaves itself with nothing meaningful to say about the many important political-regulatory environments that have not been colonized by such structures or may otherwise be moving outside their ambit.

B. Towards an inductive methodology for exploring for constitutional accountability

Ultimately, there is more in constitutional accountability than is dreamt of by our regulatory philosophy, even insofar as mature constitutional systems are concerned. How might we escape the cognitive limitations of the regulatory model?

One way is simply to use alternative models, such as the market-based models described by Jody Freeman in Chapter 4, or community-based models described by John Braithwaite in Chapter 2. But, while there is much power to these alternative analyses, they too are limited in scope. Insofar as market-based models are concerned, the "markets" these models seek to recapitulate are invariably modeled after those found in advanced industrialized societies. These models are therefore as likely to be ill-suited to non-regularized regulatory environments as is the regulatory model.[72] Community-based models, for their part, work by trying to ensure that all responsible persons are "insiders" – to return to the terminology I used to open this chapter. But, as noted at the outset of this chapter, that is not always possible: there will always be situations in which an outsider needs to understand the accountability dynamics of a particular system without becoming an insider.

Ultimately, the real problem lies with the use of models per se. Models invoke an intrinsically deductive form of analysis. In a deductive form of analysis, "knowledge" is embodied in the rules or heuristics that make up the model. Since these rules and heuristics operate prior to the application of the analysis, they are largely immune from critical evaluation. The deductive process does not facilitate the development of new or more refined knowledge.

However, new knowledge is precisely what is needed when looking at an unfamiliar system, i.e. when we are looking at a system from the perspective of an outsider. Such situations require us to develop new theoretical understandings instead of simply applying existing theoretical understandings. This, in turn, suggests a mode of analysis that relies on inductive rather than deductive reasoning. Inductive reasoning extrapolates generalities from particulars, rather than the other way around. It works by examining individuated instances of effect, with an eye toward identifying larger patterns – heuristics – that conceptually link these instances. These *new* patterns represent new knowledge.[73]

How would an inductive approach to constitutional accountability work? If we are trying to find out what possibly unforeseen forces might generate constitutional accountability in an unfamiliar system, we first need to be able to identify incidences of possibly accountable constitutional behavior. Such instances could include any behavior that seems to support public norms because at this point we cannot preemptively dismiss possible instances of constitutional accountability merely because they did not conform to our existing understandings of how accountability is generated. Enriching these understandings is precisely the point of our enterprise. Therefore, "sample" instances would include, for example, an instance where a congressional delegate argues on behalf of her supposed constituency, even where the delegate is neither elected by nor meaningfully overseen by that constituency. It would include an administrative actor changing her behavior in such a way as to bring it into greater conformity with constitutional law, even where she was under no threat of electoral or legal sanction or compulsion. It could even include a public official simply appealing to constitutional norms in seeking to justify a particular course of action. Having identified a series of such instances, one would then examine for structural commonalities that would seem to link these instances. Discovery of such commonalities would represent potential new knowledge about the accountability dynamics of the system.

A good precedent for this kind of analytic process can be found in the evolution of English jurisprudential attitudes toward French administrative law. English jurisprudence's first encounter with French administrative law occurred in the latter part of the nineteenth century, when Albert Venn Dicey, in the process of demonstrating the superiority of England's "unwritten" constitutional system, denounced the French administrative law system for its failure to conform to the basic principles of natural justice.[74] Dicey's conclusion resulted largely from a deductive line of reasoning. English principles of natural justice equated parties sitting in judgment of their own case with judicial bias. Under the French system, members of the administrative branch sit in judgment of the actions of that branch. Therefore, according to Dicey, French administrative tribunals must be biased and ineffective.

Dicey's critique quickly became canon to English constitutional jurisprudence.[75] However, as dissatisfaction grew with the increasing inability or unwillingness of English common law courts to discipline administrative actors, English jurists in the 1970s and 1980s began to reexamine the French administrative law system.[76] In reexamining that system, they focused – not deductively, on procedural conformity with established English understandings of natural justice, as did Dicey – but rather inductively, on the actual decisional product of that system.[77] What they found was a system that was not ineffective and biased, but rather was more aggressive in protecting French citizens from administrative overreach than the British courts. Advocates of administrative law reform in England, such as Lord Diplock in the House of Lords, began importing and adapting French administrative law doctrines, such as the doctrine of proportionality, as a means of revitalizing English administrative common law.[78] In sum, this 'inductive' approach to examining French administrative law not only gave these jurists new knowledge about the French system, but also gave them new understandings useful to the development of their own administrative law.

III. A DEMONSTRATION: FINDING CONSTITUTIONAL ACCOUNTABILITY IN THE PEOPLE'S REPUBLIC OF CHINA

A. Indications of constitutional development in China: the political emergence of the national parliament

The utility of inductive accountability can be further explored by using it to analyze the phenomenon of constitutional and parliamentary development in the People's Republic of China ("China"). China would be a particularly useful test case for an inductive approach because none of the existing models for constitutional or public accountability – regulatory, market-based, or societal – seems particularly applicable to China's situation. China's constitutional framework appears to operate outside the disciplining effects of elections or bureaucratic legalism. Market dynamics are also quite stilted, as the state continues to intervene pervasively in market activity. China also lacks a truly independent "civil society" of the type presumed by societal models.[79]

Nevertheless, recent developments in China bear the unmistakable mark of growing constitutionalism. This mark centers primarily around the political emergence of China's national parliament, the "National People's Congress" (NPC). Through the mid-1980s, the NPC was politically irrelevant. All meaningful political decisions were formulated in either the State Council (China's executive branch) or the Chinese Communist Party (CCP) and then forwarded to the NPC for pro forma approval. The NPC had no staff or significant internal resources. It operated as a "rubber stamp" for legitimating executive and party initiatives.

Beginning in the late 1980s, however, the NPC began exerting increasing influence in Chinese political decisionmaking. The NPC started taking over legislative drafting responsibilities from the State Council. It began to refuse to consider bills submitted by the State Council, as well as – on one occasion – a bill submitted by the CCP itself. Delegates began to challenge Party-backed platforms, such as China's joining the WTO. They began to challenge and affect policymaking in other constitutional branches. Between 1980 and 1997, the support services of the NPC grew from a staff of 100 to a staff of over 1,000. When the central government experienced broad staffing cuts in the latter half of the 1990s, the NPC staff was not affected. In 1997, fierce political competition broke out over who would head the NPC over the next five years, a competition that was eventually won by Li Peng, the second-most-powerful man in the CCP. The fact that the second-most-powerful man in China would fight for a position in the NPC leadership suggests that the NPC has indeed become relevant in China's political system.[80]

How do we explain this emergence? Unlike administrative or judicial actors, the NPC cannot found its authority on some superior technocratic skill. The NPC cannot claim to know more about securities markets than the China Securities Regulatory Commission, and it cannot claim to know more about crime control than the Ministry of Public Security. Its only real comparative advantage within China's political structure would seem to derive from its position as China's paramount "democratic" and constitutional body.

Chinese advocates of the NPC's political expansion constantly played up its unique constitutional and "democratic" posture in both public and internal party discussions.[81] And we cannot dismiss this as mere propaganda. At the same time as the NPC was advertising its constitutional-democratic status to the rest of China's political elite, it was also reforming its internal procedures to bring its internal operation more into line with its constitutional-democratic responsibilities. The NPC has increasingly opened itself up to public input; delegates are increasingly representing constituent interests even where their interests conflict with leadership goals.[82]

Nevertheless, many China scholars have dismissed the constitutional import of these developments. They claim that meaningful constitutionalism cannot possibly operate in a political environment in which there is no democratic, bureaucratic, or legal accountability. But as we discussed above, that is a claim that needs to be explored, not presumed. And that is precisely the kind of claim for which the inductive approach was developed. Can a more inductive approach shed any light on this curious development?

B. A case study: Alford and Liebman's account of the development of clean air legislation in China

We can test our inductive approach by applying it to a recent case study by William Alford and Benjamin Liebman of the legal and political dynamics underlying China's recent amendments to its Air Pollution Prevention and Control Law[83] (hereinafter "Alford and Liebman"). Two things make Alford and Liebman an excellent vehicle in this regard. First, they themselves clearly interpret their observations through a "regulatory" lens, and this leads them to conclude, like many others, that the parliamentary developments they find are of no real constitutional import. At the same time, however, their description of the political dynamics surrounding this legislation is admirably thorough. This thoroughness allows us to see if by simply adapting a more inductive analysis, we can take the same factual record and find within it dynamics of significant constitutional accountability.

1. Alford and Liebman's findings

China's first clean air law, the Air Pollution Prevention and Control Law (APPCL) was passed by the NPC in 1987. But the regulatory regime set up by that law assumed a highly controlled economy and society. By the early 1990s, it was clear that that assumption no longer held, and there was widespread recognition among China's political elites about the need for a more effective law. This awareness arose at the same time that the NPC began wresting control of China's statutory development from the State Council, and so, in 1993, it was the NPC's own, newly formed Environment and Natural Resources Protection Committee (ENRPC), rather than the State Council's more established National Environmental Protection Agency (NEPA), that assumed principal responsibility for drafting amendments to the APPCL.[84]

In drafting these amendments, ENRPC received strong cooperation from NEPA. Both NEPA and ENRPC were very much in favor of stringent statutory protections for clean air, and their draft reflected this. However, opposition to their position began to coalesce once the draft was passed on to the NPC's Committee for Legislative Affairs (CLA), a body that functions somewhat like a central clearinghouse for bills presented to the NPC.[85] In particular, the CLA complained that ENRPC/NEPA had not given opposition concerns adequate opportunity to participate in the development of their draft, a complaint that Alford and Liebman themselves find to be valid. ENRPC, with the support of NEPA, refused to compromise on the contents of its tendered draft. The CLA therefore consulted with these other interests on its own, and, despite lacking expertise in environmental issues, significantly amended the ENRPC draft to reflect some of these interests. This resulted in a watered-down version of the amendments, and it was this version that the NPC ultimately passed in 1995.[86]

Many administrative and local entities resisted complying with even the CLA's watered-down provisions. NEPA and some local urban jurisdictions, for their part, sought to strengthen the effect of the 1995 amendments by drafting administrative regulations that contained some of the provisions removed by the CLA. Such attempts were often thwarted, however, when other constitutional actors (including on at least one occasion the State Council itself) expressed concern that allowing executive and local agencies to enact as national and local regulations provisions that had been expressly considered and rejected by the NPC itself would be contrary to the spirit of "rule of law."[87]

At the same time, China's air quality continued to worsen at an alarming rate, thus attracting the attention of more and more political elite. During the course of the formulation of the 1995 amendments, the central apparatus of the CCP and its political elite generally did not concern themselves with the content of these amendments, leaving the development of this content to the constitutional system. After the passage of the 1995 amendments, however, prominent party leaders, including Party Secretary Jiang Zemin, began to show much more interest in the issue, to the point of expressly endorsing in public speeches some of the major provisions that had been removed in the CLA's version of the 1995 draft. ENRPC also instituted a national awareness campaign, intended to promote popular awareness of environmental problems and popular support for environmental protection, which further spurred CCP interest in this matter. By 1997, there was widespread agreement among Chinese constitutional and party-based policymakers that the 1995 amendments were inadequate, and the NPC began organizing the drafting of a succeeding set of amendments.

ENRPC was again given principal responsibility for the development of these amendments. This time, however, ENRPC officials had clearly learned their lessons. ENRPC and NEPA (now renamed the State Environmental Protection Agency, or SEPA) started the drafting process by developing strong support among a wide range of governmental, academic, and GONGO (government-organized non-governmental organization) institutions. They conducted a much more open drafting process that solicited and seriously considered the opinions of entities that opposed stringent clean air legislation. Their draft, which included many of the core provisions that had been removed from the 1995 draft amendments, encountered little opposition from the CLA. In 2000, it was enacted as law in virtually the same shape as it was when it left the ENRPC.[88]

2. *Alford and Liebman's interpretation and its regulatory predicates*

Despite the relatively happy ending from the perspective of environmental protection, Alford and Liebman appear fairly pessimistic about the the implications of this study for political-legal reforms in China. Ultimately, they find that their study "provides scant consolation to those who hope to bring law to bear in addressing the PRC's many and serious environmental issues"[89] – a conclusion that they see in turn as impugning the NPC's capacity to resolve the larger constitutional-regulatory problems of which these environment problems are but a part.[90]

Alford and Liebman derive this pessimistic conclusion from a number of observations of China's constitutional structure. One of these is the NPC's general incapacity "to secure agency [and sub-national] compliance" with their laws.[91] This lack of capacity they attribute in part to a lack of judicial independence and in part to the NPC's "attenuated public mandate" caused by the fact that NPC delegates "are not elected by the public."[92] They also point to the institutional ambiguities that permeate discrete constitutional institutions, such as the CLA's dual role as drafter and supervisor of draft legislation, which they argue contributes to an "opacity of governmental processes that remains a deterrent to the creation of 'pluralistic political dynamics' involving more than political elites."[93] Similarly they point to ambiguities in the legal status of the Constitution itself, noting in particular that China's supreme constitutional authority, the NPC, seems only able to effectuate significant change in China's constitutional-regulatory environment, not through its own legal-constitutional authority per se, but rather by politicizing these issues in order to mobilize extra-constitutional CCP-based political forces.[94]

These observations all have merit. But they also embody a distinctly "regulatory" vision of constitutional order. Their critique of role ambiguity, for example, parallels the regulatory model's demand for institutional regularization and the particular visibility it provides.[95] Their critique of the constitutional efficacy of NPC legislation centers on the twin observations that executive agencies and sub-national actors are able to "re-write or veto [the positive] laws duly passed by the NPC,"[96] and that the NPC only enjoys an "attenuated public mandate" because its delegates are not elected.[97] This parallels the regulatory model's analytic focus on centralized, rule-based governance and mass-based electoral processes. Finally, their complaint about the NPC's continued reliance on the support of extra-constitutional actors, namely the Party, parallels the regulatory model's fundamental delegitimation of influences that affect the "constitutional" system by other than standardized bureaucratic or electoral means.

3. *An alternative "inductive" exploration of Alford and Liebman's account*

As discussed above, an inductive approach begins by looking for what we call "possible incidents" of constitutional accountability – incidents in which political actors do appear to have modified their behavior so as to be more consistent with the stated demands of constitutionalism. Many such instances are found in Alford and Liebman's account. Examples include ENRPC and NEPA adjusting their own drafting processes in response to critiques from the CLA that were founded on appeals to the NPC's constitutional authority. They would include how after ENRPC and NEPA/SEPA adopted more open and participatory (i.e. constitutional) drafting procedures in response to CLA critiques, the CLA itself accepted numerous ENRPC/SEPA regulatory positions that it had earlier opposed. They also would include how administrative actors and local governments, who historically tended to ignore the NPC's constitutional authority when it interfered with their own regulatory strategies and concerns, nevertheless used the APPCL as an "impetus . . . to revise their own environmental standards."[98]

We also see a number of such instances involving the CCP itself. Consider, for example, the CCP's interest the use of total loading plans to measure and control air pollution. Both ENRPC and NEPA had included such plans in their draft of the 1995 APPCL amendments. But these provisions had been removed by the CLA, and thus were not included in the final version of that legislation. Nevertheless, NEPA continued to support total loading, and its position appeared to receive a big boost in 1996 when China's paramount political figure, Jiang Zemin, endorsed the use of total loading plans in a public speech. After this endorsement, NEPA tried to end-run the 1995 legislation and simply enact total loading provisions in its agency regulations. But the State Council refused to approve these regulations. Despite the fact that total loading represented the clearly stated policy preferences of the elite leadership of the CCP, the State Council held that implementing such plans in administrative regulations after they had been expressly considered and rejected in the NPC's drafting process would be contrary to the spirit of the law.[99]

Another incident of this sort involves the CCP's involvement in the 2000 amendments. According to Alford and Liebman, that involvement appears to have been determinative in the effectiveness of that legislative project. But they also suggest that it was an involvement that was itself significantly shaped and triggered by social and political forces running through the NPC. In particular, they describe how the NPC catalyzed CCP interest by encouraging emergent civil society organizations to speak up about environmental problems. In their own words, "The impetus for [the party's embrace of stronger clean air regulation] owes something to rising public opinion that the ENRPC has helped articulate."[100] Also notable is how the CCP cooperated with such social demands, despite its traditional distrust of civil society.

4. Inducing implications

One striking thing about these instances is how they all run through the NPC. Alford and Liebman cite no instance in which the CCP injected policy preferences *directly* into the State Council, or vice versa. This is particularly noteworthy given the virtual omnipotence they ascribe to the Party. Social forces, too, seemed to run through the NPC. Alford and Liebman frame their study as a politically inclusive one, one that implicates, not only the NPC, but also "relations . . . between Beijing and sub-national units of government, and between state and society, all transpiring . . . against the backdrop of the Communist Party."[101] This suggests that the centrality of the NPC in this collection of incidents is not simply an artifice of their particular analytic scope. It would appear to be structural.

In other words, this collection of instances suggests that the NPC might be serving as a "structural bridge" that links up other parts of the constitutional-political apparatus. As we saw above, when the CCP wanted to coordinate with the rest of the constitutional apparatus on the development of clean air policy, it ultimately did so through the NPC. When the State Council sought to coordinate with local actors on regularizing enforcement norms, it did so using NPC norms as the basic referents, rather than those of NEPA. When local policymakers developed their own local regulations, they did so through the NPC via consultations with ENRPC. When China's nascent "civil society" wanted to communicate its environmental concerns to the constitutional apparatus and to the CCP, it too did so through the NPC.

This particular pattern of incidences evokes what Ronald Burt has famously termed a "structural hole." A structural hole is a gap in the communications network of an institution that prevents two or more significant segments of institutional actors from communicating effectively with each another.[102] Burt and others have shown that institutional actors that bridge structural holes – i.e. actors like the NPC who are able to provide conduits that allow relatively direct communication between otherwise separated entities – enjoy a competitive advantage in shaping the opinions and norms of the larger institutional environment.[103] This, too, corresponds with Alford and Liebman's analysis, which shows how agreements and consensuses reached through NPC-sponsored legislative bargaining served as foundational points for the next round of policy exploration, as well as how constitutional arguments issuing from the CLA and the NPC induced significant changes in the way other constitutional and political actors – including the CCP, the State Council, NEPA, local actors, and the NPC's own ENRPC – made policy decisions.[104]

Recall also our earlier discussion about how, within China's political environment, the NPC's principal "comparative advantage" comes from its constitutional status. In other words, not only is the NPC uniquely positioned for disseminating new normative values within China's larger constitutional-political environment, it also has a strong institutional incentive to do so. And in Alford and Liebman's account, we frequently find the NPC aggressively and successfully appealing to constitutional norms in its interactions with other constitutional-political actors. They were a part of the NPC's successful efforts to induce NEPA to change its drafting procedures. They were a part of the NPC's successful efforts to induce greater cooperation from State Council and local policymakers and implementers. They were also part of effective *internal* advocacy within the NPC, such as where they were used to get the NPC's own ENRPC to changes its legislative drafting processes, and where they convinced the CLA to accept ENRPC's now properly drafted draft of the 2000 amendments.

In sum, an inductive analysis of Alford and Liebman's study suggests that the NPC seems to have both a unique capacity and incentive to promote constitutional values within China's larger political environments.[105] This picture of the NPC as a constitutional catalyst is a very different picture from the one painted by Alford and Liebman's more "regulatory" analysis, which led them to conclude that the NPC was "[just] another elite bureaucratic entity whose role remains incompletely defined in a world in which political power, at least in central government and party circles, continues to be tightly held."[106] Of course, viewed from a regulatory perspective, this is indeed the case: the NPC does not have any special regulatory means to forcibly impose its constitutional visions on recalcitrant politicos in other political institutions.

But, as we saw above, the regulatory model does not exhaust the possibilities for exercising effective constitutional authority. In his germinal analysis of Japanese regulation, John Haley identified a particular phenomenon he termed "authority without power."[107] "Authority without power" allowed seemingly innocuous regulatory institutions in Japan to guide regulatory development in the absence of visible means of institutional support. Our inductive analysis of Alford and Liebman's study reveals that the NPC could also be exerting such force in China's constitutional arena.

5. *Contrasts and comparisons*

The point of all this is not to suggest that Alford and Liebman are wrong in their analysis. The regulatory model of constitutionalism has its uses. At the very least, it is the principal template by which many try to make sense of comparative constitutional systems. It may also be a necessary step on the road to developmental maturity.[108] Alford and Liebman's description thus helps us understand how and where China's constitutional system fits into our larger, conventionalist conceptions of constitutionalism.

The inductive analysis neither disputes nor contradicts any of this. From a regulatory perspective, the NPC does indeed appear to be just like any other elite bureaucratic organ in China. But viewed inductively, we see that it could actually be a unique disseminator of constitutional norms. Alford and Liebman are absolutely right to question skeptically claims about how far China actually has moved along the path to comparative constitutional maturity, and their reliance on the regulatory model is well suited to this purpose. But such a snapshot of China's present constitutional nature actually tells us very little about the system's dynamic capacities for further constitutional consolidation and evolution. By exposing developmental forces invisibilized by the regulatory model, an inductive analysis shows that there does indeed appear to be something in China's constitutional environment that might "[console] those who hope to bring law to bear in addressing the PRC's many and serious [regulatory] problems."[109]

CONCLUSION: LEARNING FROM CHINA

The observations revealed by our inductive analysis also have significant implications that go beyond China. The constitutional *behavior* of the NPC in Alford and Liebman's story (as distinct from what we might think of as its constitutional "*legitimacy*") resembles that of parliaments everywhere. Underneath it all, Alford and Liebman show a picture of a parliament, despite its significant electoral and democratic infirmities, doing what parliaments everywhere do: working with a diversity of public and private constitutional actors to craft legal-regulatory responses to social problems. And, therefore, it is possible that there is nothing unique about its particular role in promoting constitutional development.

Traditional Anglo-American analyses of constitutional development focus overwhelmingly – some suggest obsessively – on courts. But, as many have noted, courts may actually be ill-suited institutionally for propagating social *norms*.[110] Our inductive analysis of China suggests that, outside the limited territory of Anglo-American culture, investigations into the dynamics of constitutional development – at least during its preliminary stages – may be wise to center their attention on parliaments rather than the courts.[111]

Herein lies the true promise of this inductive methodology. It allows one not only to understand alien accountability experiences, but also to learn from them new ideas about what we might call, following John Gardner, the "mark of public accountability."[112]

NOTES

1 Public accountability: conceptual, historical, and epistemic mappings

1. James Madison, "The Federalist No. 52," in Jacob E. Cooke, ed., *The Federalist* (Middletown, CT, 1961), p. 355. James Madison, "The Federalist No. 57," in Jacob E. Cooke, ed., *The Federalist* (Middletown, CT, 1961).
2. See Albert Venn Dicey, "The Development of Administrative Law in England," in *Introduction to the Study of the Law of the Constitution* (London, 1959), pp. 496, 498–499; see also Albert Venn Dicey, *Introduction to the Study of the Law of the Constitution* (London, 1959), pp. 389–390, 394–396; Morton Horowitz, *The Transformation of American Law, 1870–1960: The Crisis of Legal Orthodoxy* (New York, 1992), pp. 225–226.
3. See Morton Horowitz, *The Transformation of American Law, 1870–1960*, pp. 225–228.
4. G. Edward White, *Patterns of American Legal Thought* (Indianapolis, 1978), pp. 136–163.
5. *Amalgamated Meat Cutters and Butcher Workmen of North America, AFL-CIO* v. *Connally*, 337 F Supp 737, 746 (DDC 1971).
6. See Frank Anechiarico and James B. Jacobs, *The Pursuit of Absolute Integrity: How Corruption Control Makes Government Ineffective* (Chicago, 1996), pp. 8, 23–26. See also Carolyn Bingham Kello, "Drawing the Curtain on Open Government? In Defense of the Federal Advisory Committee Act" (2003) 69 *Brooklyn Law Review* 345, pp. 348–349.
7. Pub. L. No. 93-502, 1–3, 88 Stat. 1561, 1563–1564 (1974), codified as amended at 5 USC § 552 (2002).
8. Pub. L. No. 94-409, 90 Stat. 124 (1976), codified as amended at 5 USC § 552b (2002).
9. See, e.g., Charles F. Sabel, "Learning by Monitoring: The Institutions of Economic Development," in Neil J. Smelser and Richard Swedberg, eds., *Handbook of Economic Sociology* (Princeton, 1994).
10. See Alexamder Keyssar, *The Right to Vote: The Contested History of Democracy in the United States* (New York, 2000), pp. 117–171.
11. See, e.g., JUSTICE-All Souls Review Committee, *Administrative Justice: Some Necessary Reforms* (Oxford, 1988).
12. Elena Kagan, "Presidential Administration" (2001) 114 *Harvard Law Review* 2245, p. 2383.
13. 5 USC § 552(b)(5).

14. *NLRB* v. *Sears, Roebuck & Co.*, 421 US 132, 150 (1975).
15. See especially Jennifer A. Bensch, "Government in the Sunshine Act: Seventeen Years Later: Has Government Let the Sun Shine In?" (1993) 61 *George Washington Law Review* 1475, pp. 1508–1513.
16. John Dilulio, Jr and Donald Kettl, *Fine Print: The Contract with America, Devolution and the Administrative Realities of American Federalism* (Brookings Institution's Center for Public Management, CPM 95-1, March 1, 1995).
17. See Paul Light, *The True Size of Government* (Washington, DC, 1999).
18. See Michael J. Piore and Charles F. Sabel, *The Second Industrial Divide: Possibilities for Prosperity* (New York, 1984), pp. 49–104.
19. See *ibid.*, pp. 205–220.
20. See Mark Mazower, *Dark Continent: Europe's Twentieth Century* (New York, 1999), pp. 294–296.
21. See also James Thuo Gathii, "Retelling Good Governance Narratives on Africa's Economic and Political Predicaments: Continuities and Discontinuities in Legal Outcomes Between Markets and States" (2000) 42 *Villanova Law Review* 971, pp. 985–1016; Jacques deLisle, "Lex Americana? United States Legal Assistance, American Legal Models, and Legal Change in the Post-Communist World and Beyond" (1999) 20 *University of Pennsylvania Journal of International Economic Law* 179. Cf. Joseph E. Stiglitz, *Globalization and its Discontents* (New York, 2002).
22. See, e.g., Paul Krugman, "The Ugly American Bank," *New York Times*, March 18, 2005; Kanishka Jayasuriya, "Governance, Post Washington Consensus and the New Anti-Politics," in Tim Lindsey and Howard Dick, eds., *Corruption in Asia: Rethinking the Governance Paradigm* (Annandale, NSW, 2001).
23. See, e.g., Dani Rodrik, *The New Global Economy and Developing Countries: Making Openness Work* (Washington, DC, 1999), p. 151; Human Rights Watch Press Release, "No Kosovo Settlement Without Accountability for War Crimes," February 6, 1999; AFL-CIO, *AFL-CIO Twenty-Fourth Biennial Convention 2001: Executive Council Report* (Washington, DC, 2001), pp. 47, 60.
24. See Joel M. Ngugi, "Searching for the Market Criterion: Market-Oriented Reforms in Legal and Economic Development Discourses," Harvard Law School, Unpublished SJD Dissertation (Cambridge, MA, 2002), chapters 1 and 2.
25. See, e.g., Human Rights Watch Press Release, "World Bank Should Monitor Abuses in India," April 21, 1998; Amnesty International, "Statement by Amnesty International on the Occasion of the World Bank/IMF Annual Meetings Hong Kong," September 23, 1997.
26. Cf. Steven Pinker, *The Blank Slate: The Modern Denial of Human Nature* (New York, 2002), pp. 220–221.
27. Cf. Thomas Nagel, *A View from Nowhere* (New York, 1986).
28. Cf. H. Richard Niebuhr, *The Responsible Self: An Essay in Christian Moral Philosophy* (New York, 1963), p. 64.

29. See also Bernard Williams, *Moral Luck* (Cambridge, 1981), p. 18.
30. Cf. Wesley Newcomb Hohfeld, *Fundamental Legal Conceptions as Applied in Judicial Reasoning* (Aldershot, 2001).
31. See also Steven Winter, "The 'Power' Thing" (1996) 82 *Virginia Law Review* 721.
32. See also Michael W. Dowdle, "Of Parliaments, Pragmatism, and the Dynamics of Constitutional Development: The Curious Case of China" (2002) 35 *New York University Journal of International Law and Politics* 1, pp. 44–50.
33. Cf. Michael Foley, *Laws, Men and Machines: Modern American Government and the Appeal of Newtonian Mechanics* (London, 1990).
34. Cf. M. M. Bakhtin, *Speech Genres and Other Late Essays* (Austin, 1986); also Erik Dop, "A Dialogic Epistemology: Bakhtin on Truth and Meaning" (2000) 4 *Dialogism: An International Journal of Bakhtin Studies* 7; see, e.g., David Zaret, *Origins of Democratic Culture: Printing, Petitions, and the Public Sphere in Early-Modern England* (Princeton, 2000), pp. 176–183.
35. See generally Julian E. Orr, "Sharing Knowledge, Celebrating Identity: Community Memory in a Service Culture," in David Middleton and Derek Edwards, eds., *Collective Remembering* (London, 1990), pp. 169–189; Peter L. Berger and Thomas Luckman. *The Social Construction of Reality: A Treatise in the Sociology of Knowledge* (Garden City, NY, 1966), pp. 92–103.
36. See Dan Hunter, "Reason Is Too Large: Analogy and Precedent in Law" (2001) 50 *Emory Law Journal* 1197, pp. 1204–1229. See also George Lakoff and Mark Johnson, *Metaphors We Live* (Chicago, 1980).
37. See generally Edward O. Wilson, *Consilience: The Unity of Knowledge* (New York, 1998).
38. Cf. Robert Looney, "DARPA's Policy Analysis Market for Intelligence: Outside the Box or Off the Wall?" (September 2003) 2(9) *Strategic Insights* (http://www.ccc.nps.navy.mil/si/sept03/terrorism.asp).
39. See, e.g., Robert C. Ellickson, *Order Without Law: How Neighbors Settle Disputes* (Cambridge, MA, 1991).
40. Gardner, this volume.
41. Cf. Stanley Fish, "Almost Pragmatism: The Jurisprudence of Richard Posner, Richard Rorty, and Ronald Dworkin," in Michael Brint and William Weaver, eds., *Pragmatism in Law and Society* (Boulder, CO, 1991), p. 57; Lynn M. LoPucki, "Legal Culture, Legal Strategy, and the Law in Lawyers' Heads" (1996) 90 *Northwestern University Law Review* 1498, pp. 1499–1500.
42. See generally Michael C. Dorf and Charles F. Sabel, "A Constitution of Democratic Experimentalism" (1998) 98 *Columbia Law Review* 267; Michael C. Dorf and Charles Sabel, "Drug Treatment Courts and Emergent Experimentalist Government" (2000) 53 *Vanderbilt Law Review* 831.
43. See, e.g., J. Mark Ramseyer and Francis McCall Rosenbluth, *Japan's Political Marketplace* (Cambridge, MA, 1993), pp. 1–2.
44. See Russell Hardin, *Trust and Trustworthiness* (New York, 2002), pp. 69–73.

45. See Pinker, *The Blank Slate*, pp. 242–244.
46. See Hardin, *Trust and Trustworthiness*, pp. 93–94.
47. Edward L. Rubin, "The New Legal Process, the Synthesis of Discourse, and the Microanalysis of Institutions" (1996) 109 *Harvard Law Review* 1393.

2 Accountability and responsibility through restorative justice

1. See generally Peter King, *Crime, Justice, and Discretion in England, 1740–1820* (Oxford, 2000) and John H. Langbein, *The Origins of the Adversary Criminal Trial* (Oxford, 2003).
2. This is adapted from Howard Zehr, *The Little Book of Restorative Justice* (Intercourse, PA, 2002), p. 40.
3. John Braithwaite, *Restorative Justice and Responsive Regulation* (Oxford, 2002).
4. Michael C. Dorf and Charles F. Sabel, "A Constitution of Democratic Experimentalism" (1998) 98 *Columbia Law Review* 267. See also Braithwaite, *Restorative Justice*, and Heather Strang and Lawrence Sherman, "Effects of Face-to-Face Restorative Justice on Repeat Offending and Victim Satisfaction" (May 16, 2003) (unpublished).
5. See, for example, Jennifer Gerada Brown, "The Use of Mediation to Resolve Criminal Cases: A Procedural Critique" (1994) 43 *Emory Law Journal* 1247, and Kate Warner, "The Rights of the Offender in Family Conferences," in C. Alder and J. Wundersitz, eds., *Family Conferencing and Juvenile Justice: The Way Forward or Misplaced Optimism?* (Canberra, 1994). See also Chapter 5 of Braithwaite, *Restorative Justice*.
6. See generally Brent Fisse, "Reconstructing Corporate Criminal Law: Deterrence, Retribution, Fault, and Sanctions" (1983) 56 *Southern California Law Review* 1141; Mark Bovens, *The Quest for Responsibility* (Cambridge, 1998); John Braithwaite and Declan Roche, "Responsibility and Restorative Justice," in M. Schiff and G. Bazemore, eds., *Restorative Community Justice* (Cincinnati, 2000).
7. Declan Roche, *Accountability in Restorative Justice* (Oxford, 2003). Cf. Colin Scott, "Accountability in the Regulatory State" (2000) 27 *Journal of Law and Society* 38, p. 43.
8. David Dolinko, "Restorative Justice and the Justification of Punishment" (2003) *Utah Law Review* 319.
9. See generally Roche, *Accountability in Restorative Justice*.
10. Heather Strang, *Repair or Revenge: Victims and Restorative Justice* (Oxford, 2002).
11. Roche, *Accountability in Restorative Justice*, p. 159.
12. Jeff Latimer, Craig Dowden and Danielle Muise, *The Effectiveness of Restorative Justice Practices: A Meta-Analysis* (Ottawa, 2001).
13. Barton Poulson, "A Third Voice: A Review of Empirical Research on the Psychological Outcomes of Restorative Justice" (2003) *Utah Law Review* 167, pp. 187–189.
14. John Braithwaite, "On Speaking Softly and Carrying Sticks: Neglected Dimensions of Republican Separation of Powers" (1997) 47 *University of Toronto Law Journal* 1.

15. Irving Janis, "Groupthink Among Policy Makers," in N. Sanford and C. Comstock, eds., *Sanctions for Evil* (San Francisco, 1971).
16. John Uhr, *Deliberative Democracy in Australia: The Changing Face of Parliament* (Melbourne, 1998).
17. Cass Sunstein, "Beyond the Republican Revival" (1988) 97 *Yale Law Journal* 1539.
18. Braithwaite, *Restorative Justice and Responsive Regulation*.
19. John Braithwaite and Christine Parker, "Restorative Justice is Republican Justice," in Lode Walgrave and Gordon Bazemore, eds., *Restoring Juvenile Justice: An Exploration of the Restorative Justice Paradigm for Reforming Juvenile Justice* (Monsey, NY, 1999).
20. For example, Roche finds that horizontal accountability more often leads to interventions to "prevent overly harsh outcomes," while vertical accountability more often leads to interventions to prevent outcomes that are "too lenient." Roche, *Accountability in Restorative Justice*, p. 216. Put another way, horizontal accountability works best for checking upper limits on punishment, vertical accountability for checking lower limits on punishment.
21. Braithwaite and Roche, "Responsibility and Restorative Justice."
22. Bovens, *The Quest for Responsibility*.
23. Braithwaite and Roche, "Responsibility and Restorative Justice."
24. Braithwaite, *Restorative Justice and Responsive Regulation*, p. 110.
25. Bovens, *The Quest for Responsibility*, p. 27.
26. See Fisse, "Reconstructing Corporate Criminal Law."
27. See Braithwaite and Roche, "Responsibility and Restorative Justice."
28. Brenda Morrison, *Restoring Safe School Communities: A Whole School Response to Bullying, Violence and Alienation* (Sydney, 2006).
29. Gordon Bazemore and Mara Schiff, *Juvenile Justice Reform and Restorative Justice* (Portland, OR, 2005).
30. See Peter Cane, *Responsibility in Law and Morality* (Oxford, 2002), pp. 32–34.
31. See Patricia Day and Rudolf Klein, *Accountabilities: Five Public Services* (London, 1987); Richard Mulgan, "The Processes of Public Accountability" (1997) 56 *Australian Journal of Public Administration* 25; Richard Mulgan, "'Accountability': An Ever-Expanding Concept?" (2000) 78 *Public Administration* 555; Roche, *Accountability in Restorative Justice*.
32. Declan Roche, *Accountability in Restorative Justice* (Oxford, 2003).
33. Or, as in the Australian insurance regulation cases of the early 1990s, the legislature can react to what they learn about defects in the law from the outcomes of the restorative justice processes and enact new laws in response. See Braithwaite, *Restorative Justice and Responsive Regulation*, pp. 22–24.
34. See Braithwaite, *Restorative Justice and Responsive Regulation*.
35. Nils Christie, "Conflicts as Property" (1977) 17 *British Journal of Criminology* 1.
36. John Braithwaite and Christine Parker, "Restorative Justice Is Republican Justice," in Lode Walgrave and Gordon Bazemore, eds., *Restoring*

Juvenile Justice: Repairing the Harm of Youth Crime (Monsey, NY, 1999), pp. 103–126.
37. Braithwaite, *Restorative Justice and Responsive Regulation.*
38. Christine Parker, *Just Lawyers* (Oxford, 1999).
39. Braithwaite, *Restorative Justice and Responsive Regulation.*
40. Morrison, *Restoring Safe School Communities.*

3 The myth of non-bureaucratic accountability and the anti-administrative impulse

1. Regarding the pastoral impulse, see Raymond Williams, *The Country and the City* (New York, 1973), pp. 13–45.
2. See Max Weber, *Economy and Society* (Guenther Roth and Claus Wittich, eds., Berkeley, 1968), vol. 2, pp. 987–989; see also Max Weber, "Parliament and Government in a Reconstructed Germany," in Weber, *Economy and Society* (Berkeley, 1968), pp. 1401–1402.
3. Jean Genet, *The Thief's Journal* (Bernard Frechtman, trans., New York, 1965), p. 62
4. See Henry Butler and Jonathan Macey, *Using Federalism to Improve Environmental Policy* (Washington, DC, 1996); Henry Butler and Jonathan R. Macey, "Externalities and the Matching Principle: The Case for Reallocating Environmental Regulatory Authority" (1996) 14 *Yale Law and Policy Review* 23.
5. See Malcolm Feeley and Edward Rubin, *Judicial Policy Making and the Modern State: How the Courts Reformed America's Prisons* (Cambridge, 1998), pp. 180–188; Akhil Amar, "Some New World Lessons for the Old World" (1991) 58 *University of Chicago Law Review* 483; Richard Briffault, "'What About the "Ism"'? Normative and Formal Concerns in Contemporary Federalism" (1994) 47 *Vanderbilt Law Review* 1303; Edward Rubin and Malcolm Feeley, "Federalism: Some Notes on a National Neurosis" (1994) 41 *UCLA Law Review* 903.
6. See Kenneth Arrow and Leonid Hurweiz, "Decentralization and Computation in Resource Allocation," in Ralph Pfourts, ed., *Essays in Economics and Econometrics: A Volume in Honor of Harold Hotelling* (Chapel Hill, 1960), p. 34; Peter Blau and Richard Scott, *Formal Organizations: A Comparative Approach* (San Francisco, 1962).
7. See Ruy Teixeira, *The Disappearing American Voter* (Washington, DC, 1992); G. Bingham Powell, "American Voter Turnout in Comparative Perspective," in Richard Niemi and Herbert Weisberg, eds., *Controversies in Voting Behavior* (3rd ed., Washington, DC, 1993) p. 56.
8. See Donatella della Porta and Mario Diani, *Social Movements: An Introduction* (Oxford, 1999); Barbara Epstein, *Political Protest and Cultural Revolution: Nonviolent Direct Action in the 1970s and 1980s* (Berkeley, 1991).
9. See Jean Cohen, "Strategy or Identity: New Theoretical Paradigms and Contemporary Social Movements" (1985) 52 *Social Research* 663; Bert Klandermans, "New Social Movements and Resource Mobilization: The European and American Approach Revisited," in Dieter Rucht, ed.,

Research on Social Movements: The State of the Art in Western Europe and the USA (Boulder, 1991), p. 17.

10. See, e.g., William Gamson, *The Strategy of Social Protest* (2nd ed., Belmont, CA, 1990).
11. See, e.g., Alberto Melucci, *Nomads of the Present: Social Movements and Individual Needs in Contemporary Society* (John Keane & Paul Mier, eds., Philadelphia, 1989); Claus Offe, "New Social Movements: Challenging the Boundaries of Institutional Politics" (1985) 52 *Social Research* 117.
12. See Ronald Collins and David Skover, *The Death of Discourse* (Boulder, 1996); Douglas Kellner, *Television and the Crisis of Democracy* (Boulder, 1990).
13. See Robert Dahl, *Who Governs? Democracy and Power in an American City* (New Haven, 1989); Nelson Polsby, *Community Power and Political Theory* (New Haven, 1963).
14. See Richard Foglesong, *Married to the Mouse: Walt Disney World and Orlando* (New Haven, 2001); Paul Peterson, *City Limits* (Chicago, 1981); William W. Buzbee, "Urban Sprawl, Federalism, and the Problem of Institutional Complexity" (1999). 68 *Fordham Law Review* 57, pp. 63–76.
15. Robert Putnam, *Bowling Alone: The Collapse and Revival of American Community* (New York, 1996).
16. *Ibid.* See also Collins and Skover, *The Death of Discourse*, pp. 9, 13.
17. Putnam, *Bowling Alone*, pp. 287–363.
18. US Census Bureau, *Current Population Reports: Population Profile of the United States, 1999* (Washington, DC, 2001), pp. 7, 15.
19. See Richard Briffault, "Our Localism, Part I: The Structure of Local Government" (1990) 90 *Columbia Law Review* 1; Briffault, "What About the 'Ism'."
20. Bruce Ackerman, *Social Justice in the Liberal State* (New Haven, 1980).
21. See, e.g., John Braithwaite, *Restorative Justice and Responsive Regulation* (Oxford, 2001); Michael Dorf and Charles Sabel, "A Constitution of Democratic Experimentalism" (1998) 98 *Columbia Law Review* 267; Jerry Mashaw (this volume); Jody Freeman (this volume).
22. See, e.g., Peter Berger and Thomas Luckmann, *The Social Construction of Reality: A Treatise in the Sociology of Knowledge* (Garden City, NY, 1967).
23. See Jean Cohen and Andrew Arato, *Civil Society and Political Theory* (Cambridge, MA, 1992); Jurgen Habermas, *Between Facts and Norms: Contributions to a Discourse Theory of Law and Democracy* (William Rehg, trans., Cambridge, MA, 1996), pp. 359–387.
24. See Janos Kornai, *The Socialist System: The Political Economy of Communism* (Princeton, 1992).
25. See, e.g., Ian Ayres and John Braithwaite, *Responsive Regulation: Transcending the Deregulation Debate* (New York, 1992); Bronwen Morgan, *Social Citizenship in the Shadow of Competition: The Bureaucratic Politics of Regulatory Justification* (Aldershot, 2003); Neil Gunningham and Darren Sinclair, "Regulatory Pluralism: Designing Policy Mixes for Environmental Protection" (1999) 21 *Law and Policy* 49; Jody Freeman, "Collaborative Governance in the Administrative State" (1997) 34 *UCLA Law*

Review 1; Todd Rakoff, "The Choice Between Formal and Informal Modes of Administrative Regulation" (2000) 52 *Administrative Law Review* 159.

26. Weber, *Economy and Society*, pp. 8–9; Max Weber, "Objectivity in Social Science and Social Policy," in Max Weber, *The Methodology of the Social Sciences* (Edward Shils & Henry Finch, trans., New York, 1949), pp. 49, 50–85.
27. United States Sentencing Commission, *2001 Federal Sentencing Guidelines Manual* (Washington, DC, 2001), § 8A.1.2.
28. Pub. L. No. 107-204, 116 Stat. 745 (2002), codified at 15 USC §§ 7201–7266 (2002).
29. See John Braithwaite, *Restorative Justice and Responsive Regulation* (Oxford, 2002); John Braithwaite, *Regulation, Crime, Freedom* (Aldershot 2000); Brent Fisse and John Braithwaite, *Corporations, Crime and Accountability* (Cambridge, 1983).
30. See Norman Macintosh, *Management Accounting and Control Systems: An Organizational and Behavioral Approach* (Chichester, 1994), pp. 246–249.
31. But see Mashaw (this volume).
32. See Michael Dorf and Charles Sabel, "Drug Treatment Courts and Experimentalist Government" (2000) 53 *Vanderbilt Law Review* 831.
33. Jean Genet, *Our Lady of the Flowers* (Bernard Frechtman, trans., New York, 1987).
34. Ivan Petrovich Pavlov, "Lecture XVIII," in *Conditioned Reflexes: An Investigation of the Physiological Activity of the Cerebral Cortex* (G. V. Anrep, trans., New York, 1960); William Walter Sargant, *Battle for the Mind: A Physiology of Conversion and Brain-Washing* (Baltimore, 1961), pp. 51–75.
35. Robert Jay Lifton, *Thought Reform and the Psychology of Totalism: A Study of "Brainwashing" in China* (Chapel Hill, 1989); Sargant, *Battle for the Mind*, pp. 77–101.
36. See Ayres and Braithwaite, *Responsive Regulation*, pp. 20–27; Robert Kagan and John Scholz, "The Criminology of the Corporation and Regulatory Enforcement Strategies," in Keith Hawkins and John Thomas, eds., *Enforcing Regulation* (Boston, 1984), pp. 67–96.
37. See Feeley and Rubin, *Judicial Policy Making*.
38. See Michael Trebilcock and Edward Iacobucci, "Privatization and Accountability" (2003) 116 *Harvard Law Review* 1422.
39. *Ibid.*, pp. 1447–1451.
40. Richard Cyert and James March, *A Behavioral Theory of the Firm* (Englewood Cliffs, 1963); Oliver Williamson, *Markets and Hierarchies: Analysis and Antitrust Implications* (New York, 1975).
41. But see Scott (this volume).
42. See Robert Cooter and Thomas Ulen, *Law and Economics* (Boston, 2004) pp. 45–49.
43. *Ibid.*, pp. 108–116.
44. For a classic statement, see Frederick Engels, *The Condition of the Working Class in England* (David McLellan, ed., New York, 1999).

45. Neil Komesar, *Imperfect Alternatives: Choosing Institutions in Law, Economics, and Public Policy* (Chicago, 1994).
46. See, e.g., John Ely, *Democracy and Distrust* (Cambridge, 1980), pp. 131–134; Theodore Lowi, *The End of Liberalism: The Second Republic of the United States* (New York, 1979), pp. 92–126.
47. See, e.g., Steven Calabresi and Saikrishna Prakash, "The President's Power to Execute the Laws" (1994) 104 *Yale Law Journal* 541; Steven Calabresi and Kevin Rhodes, "The Structural Constitution: Unitary Executive, Plural Judiciary" (1992) 105 *Harvard Law Review* 1153.
48. See, e.g., Evan Caminker, "State Sovereignty and Subordinacy: May Congress Commandeer State Officers to Implement Federal Law?" (1995) 95 *Columbia Law Review* 1001; Vicki Jackson, "Federalism and the Uses and Limits of Law: *Printz* and Principle" (1998) 111 *Harvard Law Review* 2180, pp. 2195–2205.
49. Edward L. Rubin, "Getting Past Democracy" (2001) 149 *University of Pennsylvania Law Review* 711.
50. See Peter Drucker, *The New Society: The Anatomy of the Industrial Order* (New York, 1950), pp. 210–212; H. R. Trevor-Roper, *The Last Days of Hitler* (New York, 1947), pp. 3–10.
51. See Hannah Fenichel Pitkin, *The Concept of Representation* (Berkeley, 1967).
52. For example, some of the medieval models from which modern elections derive, such as the election of the Pope or the Holy Roman Emperor, were not conceived in representational terms. See Paula Sutter Fichtner, *The Habsburg Monarchy 1490–1848: Attributes of Empire* (New York, 2003).
53. Benjamin Page and Robert Shapiro, "Effects of Public Opinion on Policy" (1983) 77 *American Political Science Review* 175.
54. See, e.g., Richard Fenno, *Congressmen in Committees* (Boston, 1973),
55. See, e.g., David Mayhew, *Congress: The Electoral Connection* (New Haven, 1974).
56. See John Alford and David Brady, "Personal and Partisan Advantage in Elections," in Lawrence Dodd, ed., *Congress Reconsidered* (5th ed., Washington, DC, 1993), p. 149; Gary Cox and Jonathan Katz, "Why Did the Incumbency Advantage in US House Elections Grow?" (1996) 40 *American Journal of Political Science* 478.
57. See Jean Baudrillard, *In the Shadow of the Silent Majorities* (New York, 1983); Jean Baudrillard, *Simulations* (New York, 1983); Murray Edelman, *Constructing the Political Spectacle* (Chicago, 1988).
58. See Larry Bartels, "Uninformed Votes: Information Effects in Presidential Elections" (1996) 40 *American Journal of Political Science* 194.
59. See Bernard Berelson, Paul Lazarsfeld and William McPhee, *Voting: A Study of Opinion Formation in a Presidential Campaign* (Chicago, 1954); Paul F. Lazarsfeld, Bernard Berelson and Hazel Caudet, *The People's Choice: How the Voter Makes up His Mind in a Presidential Campaign* (New York, 1948).
60. See Donald R. Kinder, Mark D. Peters, Robert P. Abelson and Susan T. Fiske, "Presidential Prototypes" (1980) 2 *Political Behavior* 315;

Theresa Levitan and Warren Miller, "Ideological Interpretations of Presidential Elections" (1979) 73 *American Political Science Review* 751.

61. Benjamin Page and Robert Shapiro, *The Rational Public: Fifty Years of Trends in Americans' Policy Preferences* (Chicago, 1992).
62. Warren Miller and J. Merrill Shanks, *The New American Voter* (Cambridge, 1996), pp. 326–413; see also Derek Bok, *The Trouble with Government* (Cambridge, 2001), pp. 129–132.
63. See Jerry Mashaw, *Greed, Chaos, and Governance: Using Public Choice to Improve Public Law* (New Haven, 1997), pp. 152–156; Jerry Mashaw, "Prodelegation: Why Administrators Should Make Political Decisions" (1985) 1 *Journal of Law, Economics, and Organization* 81.
64. See James R. Bowers, *Regulating the Regulators: An Introduction to the Legislative Oversight of Administrative Rulemaking* (New York, 1990); Richard J. Lazarus, "The Neglected Question of Congressional Oversight of EPA: Quis Custodiet Ipsos Custodes (Who Shall Watch the Watchers Themselves)" (1991) 54 *Law and Contemporary Problems* 205.
65. The development of this idea is explored in Dowdle (this volume, Chapter 13).
66. See, e.g., Martha Derthick and Paul J. Quirk, *The Politics of Deregulation* (Washington, DC, 1985); Thomas McCraw, *Prophets of Regulation: Charles Francis Adams, Louis D. Brandeis, James M. Landis, Alfred E. Kahn* (Cambridge, MA, 1984), pp. 259–299.
67. See, e.g., McCraw, *Prophets of Regulation*, pp. 226–259.
68. 521 US 898 (1997).
69. 505 US 144 (1992).
70. See Caminker, "State Sovereignty and Subordinacy"; Jackson, "Federalism and the Uses and Limits of Law."
71. 521 US 898 at 920.
72. See Daniel J. Elazar, *Exploring Federalism* (University, AL, 1987).
73. *Hunter* v. *City of Pittsburgh*, 207 US 161, 178–179 (1907). See generally John Forrest Dillon, *Commentaries on the Law of Municipal Corporations* (5th ed., Boston, 1911); Gerald Frug, "The City as a Legal Concept" (1980) 93 *Harvard Law Review* 1057.
74. See Gordon Clark, *Judges and the Cities: Interpreting Local Autonomy* (Chicago, 1985), p. 70; Clayton P. Gillette, "The Exercise of Trumps by Decentralized Governments" (1997) 83 *Virginia Law Review* 1347, pp. 1363–1365.
75. Richard Briffault, "Our Localism"; Briffault, "What About the 'Ism'."
76. See James Q. Wilson, *Bureaucracy: What Government Agencies Do and Why They Do It* (New York, 1989), pp. 3–24; see especially *ibid.*, p. 14.
77. Mark Seidenfeld, "Cognitive Loafing, Social Conformity, and Judicial Review of Agency Rulemaking" (2002) 87 *Cornell Law Review* 486.
78. *Ibid.*, pp. 508–526.
79. See generally *ibid.*
80. See generally Herbert Simon, *Administrative Behavior: A Study of Decision-Making Processes in Administrative Organization* (New York, 1957).

81. See also Rubin, "Getting Past Democracy"; Edward Rubin, "Discretion and Its Discontents," (1997) 72 *Chicago-Kent Law Review* 1299.
82. Weber, *Economy and Society*, pp. 212–226.
83. See Weber, *Economy and Society*, pp. 971–987; see also Wolfgang J. Mommsen, *The Age of Bureaucracy: Perspectives on the Political Sociology of Max Weber* (Oxford, 1974).
84. Geoffrey Barraclough, *The Origins of Modern Germany* (New York, 1984); Heinrich Fichtenau, *The Carolingian Empire* (Oxford, 1978).
85. See, e.g., Trebilcock and Iacobucci, "Privatization and Accountability," p. 1449.
86. Cf. Drucker, *The New Society*, pp. 281–298.
87. See Bray Hammond, *Banks and Politics in America: From the Revolution to the Civil War* (Princeton, 1957).
88. See Frederick Jackson Turner, *The Frontier in American History* (New York, 1920).
89. See Reinhart Bendix, *Nation-Building and Citizenship: Studies of Our Changing Social Order* (Berkeley, 1977); Adam Przeworski, *Capitalism and Social Democracy* (New York, 1985); Seymour M. Lipset, "Radicalism or Reformism: The Sources of Working Class Politics" (1983) 77 *American Political Science Review* 1.
90. See generally Cornelius Kerwin, *Rulemaking: How Government Agencies Write Law and Make Policy* (Washington, DC, 1994); Jerry L. Mashaw, *Bureaucratic Justice: Managing Social Security Disability Claims* (New Haven, 1983).
91. Edward L. Rubin, "Law and Legislation in the Administrative State" (1989) 89 *Columbia Law Review* 369.
92. See Gary Lawson, "Delegation and Original Meaning" (2002) 88 *Virginia Law Review* 327; David Schoenbrod, *Power Without Responsibility: How Congress Abuses the People through Delegation* (New Haven, 1993); Lowi, *The End of Liberalism*.
93. See, e.g., *Mistretta* v. *United States*, 488 US 361 (1989); *Amalgamated Meat Cutters* v. *Connallly*, 337 F Supp 737 (DDC 1971).
94. See *Whitman* v. *American Trucking Association, Inc.*, 531 US 457 (2001).
95. See Lawrence Lessig and Cass Sunstein, "The President and the Administration" (1994) 94 *Columbia Law Review* 1; Edward Rubin, "Independence as a Governance Mechanism," in Stephen Burbank and Barry Friedman, eds., *Judicial Independence at the Crossroads: An Interdisciplinary Approach* (Thousand Oaks, 2002), p. 56.
96. 5 USC §§ 551–805 (2000).
97. *Home Box Office, Inc.* v. *FCC*, 567 F 2d 9, 57 (DC Cir.), cert. denied, 434 US 829 (1977).
98. See Elena Kagan, "Presidential Administration" (2001) 114 *Harvard Law Review* 2245.
99. See, e.g., The Personal Responsibility and Work Reconciliation Act, Pub. L. No. 104-193, 110 Stat. 205, 42 USC §§ 601–617 (2000).
100. See, e.g., Howard G. Brown, *War, Revolution, and the Bureaucratic State: Politics and Army Administration in France, 1791–1799* (Oxford, 1995);

Charles Tilly, ed., *The Formation of Nation States in Western Europe* (Princeton, 1975).

101. See, e.g., *Board of Trustees of the University of Alabama* v. *Garrett*, 531 US 356 (2001); *New York* v. *United States*, 505 US 144 (1992).
102. See, e.g., *Solid Waste Agency of Northern Cook County* v. *US Army Corps of Engineers*, 531 US 159 (2001).
103. See, e.g., *United States* v. *Morrison*, 529 US 598 (2000); *City of Bourne* v. *Flores*, 521 US 507 (1997).
104. See also Ann Althouse, "Vanguard States, Laggard States: Federalism and Constitutional Rights" (2004) 152 *University of Pennsylvania Law Review* 1745.

4 Extending public accountability through privatization: from public law to publicization

1. Jody Freeman, "The Private Role in Public Governance" (2000b) 75 *New York University Law Review* 543, pp. 637–638.
2. See Richard W. Roper, "A Shifting Landscape: Contracting for Welfare Services in New Jersey," Rockefeller Reports, No. 10, Albany, December 23, 1998, p. 7.
3. Freeman, "The Private Role in Public Governance", p. 547.
4. *Ibid.*, pp. 663–664.
5. *Ibid.*, pp. 549, 575–592 (describing four traditional accountability mechanisms that may need to be rethought).
6. See also Gerald E. Frug, "Is Secession from the City of Los Angeles a Good Idea?" (2002) 49 *UCLA Law Review* 1783.
7. See John D. Donahue, *The Privatization Decision: Public Ends, Private Means* (New York, 1989), p. 4.
8. Harvey B. Feigenbaum and Jeffrey R. Henig, "The Political Underpinnings of Privatization: A Typology" (1994) 46 *World Politics* 185, pp. 185–186.
9. Cf. Simon Domberger and Paul Jensen, "Contracting Out by the Public Sector: Theory, Evidence, Prospects" (1997) 13(4) *Oxford Review of Economic Policy* 67, p. 75.
10. See also Donahue, *The Privatization Decision*, pp. 38–56.
11. See Oliver Hart, Andrei Shleifer and Robert W. Vishny, "The Proper Scope of Government: Theory and an Application to Prisons" (1997) 112 *Quarterly Journal of Economics* 1127, p. 1143.
12. See Domberger and Jensen, "Contracting Out by the Public Sector", pp. 72–75.
13. See, e.g., Elliott D. Sclar, *You Don't Always Get What You Pay For* (Ithaca, NY, 2000), pp. 69–93; Hart, Shleifer and Vishny, "The Proper Scope of Government," p. 1129.
14. See Mark Aronson, "A Public Lawyer's Responses to Privatisation and Outsourcing," in Michael Taggart, ed., *The Province of Administrative Law* (Oxford, 1997), p. 43.
15. See, e.g., Freeman, "The Private Role in Public Governance," p. 631.

16. See, e.g., Martha Minow, "Public and Private Partnerships: Accounting for the New Religion" (2003) 116 *Harvard Law Review* 1229, p. 1261.
17. 5 USC §§ 551–559, 701–706 (2002).
18. See Harold I. Abramson, "A Fifth Branch of Government: The Private Regulators and Their Constitutionality" (1989) 16 *Hastings Constitutional Law Quarterly* 165, pp. 196–197. See also *J. W. Hampton, Jr & Co.* v. *United States*, 276 US 394, 409 (1928).
19. See, e.g., *Blum* v. *Yaretzky*, 457 U.S. 991, 1008–12 (1982).
20. See, e.g., *Brentwood Academy* v. *Tennessee Secondary School Athletic Association*, 531 US 288, 291 (2001).
21. 5 USC § 552 (2002). See also *Forsham* v. *Califano*, 587 F 2d 1128, 1136 (DC Cir. 1978).
22. See, e.g., the Government in the Sunshine Act of 1976, 5 USC § 552b (2002); see also the Federal Register Act, 44 USC §§ 1501–1511 (2002).
23. See Daniel Guttman, "Public Purpose and Private Service: The Twentieth Century Culture of Contracting Out and the Evolving Law of Diffused Sovereignty" (2000) 52 *Administrative Law Review* 859, pp. 891–901.
24. Pub. L. No. 104-193, 110 Stat. 2105 (1996), codified as amended in scattered sections of 42 USC.
25. *Ibid.*, §§ 101–116, 110 Stat. at 2110–2185.
26. See Roper, "A Shifting Landscape", p. 2; Barbara L. Bedzek, "Contractual Welfare: Non-Accountability and Diminished Democracy in Local Government Contracts for Welfare-to-Work Services" (2001) 28 *Fordham Urban Law Journal* 1559, pp. 1564–1568; see also Matthew Diller, "The Revolution in Welfare Administration: Rules, Discretion, and Entrepreneurial Government" (2000) 75 *New York University Law Review* 1121, p. 1147.
27. *Ibid.*, p. 1180.
28. *Ibid.*, p. 1181 and n. 313.
29. See Bedzek, "Contractual Welfare," p. 1560.
30. See Diller, "The Revolution in Welfare Administration," pp. 1128, 1198–1199.
31. See Jody Freeman, "The Contracting State" (2000) 28 *Florida State University Law Review* 155.
32. See Diller, "The Revolution in Welfare Administration," p. 1208.
33. See Hart, Shleifer and Vishny, "The Proper Scope of Government," p. 1152.
34. See also Richard B. Stewart, "The Reformation of American Administrative Law" (1975) 88 *Harvard Law Review* 1667, pp. 1723, 1750–1752.
35. See generally Tom R. Tyler, *Why People Obey the Law* (New Haven, 1990). See also Jody Freeman and Laura I. Langbein, "Regulatory Negotiation and the Legitimacy Benefit" (2000) 9 *NYU Environmental Law Journal* 60, p. 63.
36. Minow, "Public and Private Partnerships," pp. 1242–1243.

37. William J. Novak, *The People's Welfare: Law and Regulation in Nineteenth-Century America* (Chapel Hill, 1996), pp. 87, 105–111.
38. See *ibid.*, pp. 60–70.
39. See also Freeman, "The Private Role in Public Governance," pp. 587–588.
40. See, e.g., James W. Fossett, "Managed Care and Devolution," in Frank J. Thompson and John J. Dilulio, Jr, eds., *Medicaid and Devolution: A View from the States* (Washington, DC, 1998), pp. 131–132.
41. See, e.g., Hart, Shleifer and Vishny, "The Proper Scope of Government," pp. 1153–1154.
42. David R. Beam and Timothy J. Conlan, "Grants," in Lester M. Salamon, ed., *The Tools of Government: A Guide to the New Governance* (New York, 2002), p. 353.
43. *Ibid.*, p. 354.
44. See *Flagg Bros., Inc.* v. *Brooks*, 436 US 149, 158–159, 163 (1978).
45. See Harold J. Krent, "Fragmenting the Unitary Executive: Congressional Delegations of Administrative Authority Outside the Federal Government" (1990) 85 *Northwestern University Law Review* 62.
46. Jack M. Beermann, "Privatization and Political Accountability" (2001) 28 *Fordham Urban Law Journal* 1507, p. 1516; see also *New York* v. *United States*, 505 US 144, 207 (1992).
47. See Beermann, "Privatization and Political Accountability," p. 1518.
48. See Gillian E. Metzger, "Privatization as Delegation: Rethinking State Action in Private Delegation Terms," § V.B.2.a (Cambridge, MA, August 18, 2002) (unpublished manuscript on file with the Library of the Harvard Law School).
49. *Whitman* v. *American Trucking Associations*, 531 US 457, 472–476 (2001).
50. See "Developments in the Law – The Law of Prisons" (2002) 115 *Harvard Law Review* 1838, p. 1882.
51. See Beermann, "Privatization and Political Accountability," p. 1511.
52. See, e.g., *Euresti* v. *Stenner*, 458 F 2d 1115, 1119 (10th Cir. 1972); *Fuzie* v. *Manor Care, Inc.*, 461 F Supp 689 (ND Ohio 1977).
53. See *Heckler* v. *Chaney*, 470 US 821, 836–837 (1985); Bradford C. Mank, "The Environmental Protection Agency's Project XL and Other Regulatory Reform Initiatives: The Need for Legislative Authorization" (1998) 25 *Ecology Law Quarterly* 1.
54. See *Scanwell Labs., Inc.* v. *Shaffer*, 424 F 2d 859 (DC Cir. 1970).
55. See, e.g., *Pinsker* v. *Pacific Coast Society of Orthodontists*, 12 P 3d 253 (Cal. 1974); Michael Asimow and Marsha N. Cohen, *California Administrative Law* (St. Paul, 2002), pp. 64–66.
56. See *Cotran* v. *Rollings Hudig Hall International, Inc.*, 948 P 2d 412 (Cal. 1998). See generally Asimow and Cohen, *California Administrative Law*, pp. 64–66.
57. See *Gay Law Students Association* v. *Pacific Telephone and Telegraph Co.*, 595 P 2d 592, 598–601 (Cal. 1979).
58. See, e.g., Federal Tort Claims Act, 28 USC § 2680 (2002).

59. Beermann, "Privatization and Political Accountability," pp. 1721–1724.
60. *Ibid.*, p. 1721.
61. *Ibid.*, pp. 1721–1722.
62. *Ibid.*, p. 1723.
63. See generally Steven Rathgeb Smith and Michael Lipsky, *Nonprofits for Hire: The Welfare State in the Age of Contracting* (Cambridge, MA, 1993).
64. See, e.g., Robert E. Suggs, "Racial Discrimination in Business Transactions" (1991) 42 *Hastings Law Journal* 1257.
65. Jane Ennis Sheehan, "Mixed Finance: A Real Estate Lawyer's 'Field of Dreams'" (1998) 7 *Journal of Affordable Housing and Community Development Law* 289, pp. 289–290.
66. See Alfred C. Aman, Jr, "Administrative Law for a New Century," in Michael Taggart, ed., *The Province of Administrative Law* (Oxford, 1997), p. 95; Aronson, "A Public Lawyer's Responses to Privatisation and Outsourcing," p. 70.
67. See Paul Charles Light, *The True Size of Government* (Washington, DC, 1999), pp. 61–67.
68. See Nelson Lund, "Lawyers and the Defense of the Presidency" (1995) *Brigham Young University Law Review* 17, pp. 19–20.
69. See Mathew D. McCubbins, Roger G. Noll and Barry R. Weingast, "Administrative Procedures as Instruments of Political Control" (1987) 3 *Journal of Law and Economic Organization* 243, p. 244.
70. See Light, *The True Size of Government*, p. 76.
71. Krent, "Fragmenting the Unitary Executive," pp. 72–73.
72. *Ibid.*, pp. 108–109.
73. See "California Residents Respond to State's Energy Crisis," Knowledge Networks Press Release, February 8, 2001 (Menlo Park, CA, 2001).
74. See "Developments in the Law," p. 1869 (note 50 above).
75. See *Zelman* v. *Simmons-Harris*, 536 US 639 (2002). See also Charles Fried, "The Supreme Court, 2001 Term – Comment: Five to Four: Reflections on the School Voucher Case" (2002) 116 *Harvard Law Review* 163, p. 164, n. 9.
76. See Eleanor D. Kinney, "Tapping and Resolving Consumer Concerns About Health Care" (2000) 26 *American Journal of Law and Medicine* 335, pp. 335–336 and n. 4. See also *Rush Prudential HMO, Inc.* v. *Moran*, 122 S Ct 2151, 2171 (2002).
77. See Michael E. Levine and Jennifer L. Forrence, "Regulatory Capture, Public Interest, and the Public Agenda: Toward a Synthesis" (1990) 6 *Journal of Law and Economic Organization* (Special Issue) 167, p. 192.
78. Cf. Donald P. Green and Ian Shapiro, *Pathologies of Rational Choice Theory: A Critique of Applications in Political Science* (New Haven, 1994).
79. Administrative Dispute Resolution Act of 1996, 5 USC §§ 571–584 (2002).
80. See, e.g., *Gonzaga Universtiy* v. *Doe*, 122 S Ct 2268, 2273–2274 (2002).
81. 487 US 42 (1988).
82. *Ibid.*, p. 56.
83. 836 F Supp 698 (D. Ariz. 1993).

84. *Ibid.*, p. 699.
85. See *Brentwood Academy* v. *Tennessee Secondary School Athletic Association*, 531 US 288 (2001); *West* v. *Atkins*, 487 US 42 (1988); *Flagg Bros., Inc.* v. *Brooks*, 436 US 149 (1978).
86. Beermann, "Privatization and Political Accountability," p. 1736; see also Donahue, *The Privatization Decision*, pp. 128–129.
87. Domberger and Jensen, "Contracting Out by the Public Sector," p. 71.
88. Hart, Shleifer and Vishny, "The Proper Scope of Government," p. 1129.
89. See *ibid.*, p. 1134.
90. Domberger and Jensen, "Contracting Out by the Public Sector," p. 71.
91. Donahue, *The Privatization Decision*, p. 82.
92. See Domberger and Jensen, "Contracting Out by the Public Sector," p. 71.
93. See generally Albert O. Hirschman, *Exit, Voice, and Loyalty: Responses to Decline in Firms, Organizations, and States* (Cambridge, MA, 1970).
94. See Donahue, *The Privatization Decision*, pp. 150–151.
95. See "Developments in the Law – The Law of Prisons," p. 1878 (note 50 above).
96. Feigenbaum and Henig, "The Political Underpinnings of Privatization," p. 191.
97. See, e.g., Tony Prosser, "Public Service Law: Privatization's Unexpected Offspring" (2000) 63 *Law and Contemporary Problems* 63, p. 65.
98. See "Developments in the Law – The Law of Prisons," p. 1872 (note 50 above). See, e.g., David Shichor, *Punishment for Profit: Private Prisons/Public Concerns* (Thousand Oaks, CA, 1995), pp. 238–241.
99. See Freeman, "The Private Role in Public Governance," pp. 664–666; Minow, "Public and Private Partnerships," pp. 1266–1270.
100. See also John Hart Ely, *Democracy and Distrust: A Theory of Judicial Review* (Cambridge, MA, 1980), pp. 131–134; Theodore J. Lowi, *The End of Liberalism: The Second Republic of the United States* (2nd ed., New York, 1979), pp. 105–107.
101. See generally Dennis C. Kinlaw, *Continuous Improvement and Measurement for Total Quality: A Team-Based Approach* (San Diego, 1992).
102. See Robert W. Hamilton, "Prospects for the Nongovernmental Development of Regulatory Standards" (1983) 32 *American University Law Review* 455, pp. 460–469.
103. See, e.g., *ibid.*, pp. 463–464.
104. See Tyler, *Why People Obey the Law*, p. 64.
105. See, e.g., Robert A. Kagan and John T. Scholz, "The 'Criminology of the Corporation' and Regulatory Enforcement Strategies," in Keith Hawkins and John M. Thomas, eds., *Enforcing Regulation* (Boston, 1984), pp. 76–77.
106. See also Keith Hawkins and John M. Thomas, "The Enforcement Process in Regulatory Bureaucracies," in Keith Hawkins and John M. Thomas, eds., *Enforcing Regulation* (Boston, 1984).

5 Accountability and institutional design: some thoughts on the grammar of governance

1. See generally Richard Mulgan, *Holding Power to Account: Accountability in Modern Democracies* (New York, 2003).
2. See, e.g., *Webster's New Collegiate Dictionary* (Springfield, MA, 1959).
3. See also Mulgan, *Holding Power to Account*, pp. 22–30.
4. G. W. F. Hegel, *Philosophy of Right* (T. M. Knox trans., Oxford, 1967).
5. Claus Offe, "Political Corruption: Conceptual and Practical Issues," in Janos Kornai and Susan Rose-Ackerman, eds., *Building a Trustworthy State in Post-Socialist Transition* (New York, 2004), p. 77.
6. See also Patricia Day and Rudolf Klein, *Accountabilities: Five Public Services* (London, 1987), pp. 4–29.
7. See also Jerry L. Mashaw, "Judicial Review of Administrative Action: Reflections on Balancing Political, Managerial and Legal Accountability," paper prepared for a conference on Economic and Social Regulation, Accountability in Democracy, Sao Paulo, Brazil, March 15–16, 2004.
8. Richard Mulgan, "Contracting Out and Accountability" (1997) 56(4) *Australian Journal of Public Administration* 106, p. 115. But see John D. Donahue, "Market-Based Governance and the Architecture of Accountability," in John D. Donahue and Joseph S. Nye, Jr, eds., *Market-Based Governance: Supply Side, Demand Side, Upside and Downside* (Washington, DC, 2002), p. 1.
9. See Andrew Dunsire, *Implementation in a Bureaucracy* (New York, 1978); and Andrew Dunsire, *Control in a Bureaucracy* (New York, 1978).
10. See Charles E. Lindblom, *The Market System: What It Is, How It Works and What to Make of It* (New Haven, CT, 2001).
11. See also Michael J. Trebilcock, Ron Daniels and Malcolm Thorburn, "Government by Voucher" (2000) 80 *Boston University Law Review* 205.
12. See, e.g., G. R. Semin and A. S. R. Manstead, *The Accountability of Conduct: A Social Psychological Analysis* (London, 1983); Peter Marsh, Elizabeth Rosser and Rom Harre, *The Rules of Disorder* (London, 1978). See also Anita L. Allen, *Why Privacy Isn't Everything: Feminist Reflections on Personal Accountability* (Lanham, MD, 2003).
13. See generally Collin Scott, "Private Regulation of the Public Sector: A Neglected Facet of Contemporary Governance" (2002) 29 *Journal of Law and Society* 56.
14. Jody Freeman, "The Private Role in Public Governance" (2000) 75 *New York University Law Review* 543.
15. See, e.g., Niklas Luhmann, *Social Systems* (John Bednarz, Jr and Dirk Baecker, trans., Stanford, CA, 1995). But see Jürgen Habermas, *Between Facts and Norms: Contributions to a Discourse Theory of Law and Democracy* (Cambridge, MA, 1996).
16. Robert Cover, "The Supreme Court Term, 1982 Term – Foreword: Nomos and Narrative" (1983) 97 *Harvard Law Review* 4.
17. See, e.g., James Thompson, *Organizations in Action: Social Science Bases of Administrative Theory* (New York, 1967); Charles Perrow, "A Framework

for Comparative Organizational Analysis" (1967) 32 *American Sociological Review* 194.
18. E.g., Gunter Teubner, *Law as an Autopoietic System* (Anne Bankowska and Ruth Adler, trans., Zenon Bankowski, ed., Oxford, 1993); Collin Scott, "Analyzing Regulatory Space: Fragmented Resources and Institutional Design" (2001) *Public Law* 329.
19. See Philippe Nonet and Phillip Selznick, *Law and Society in Transition: Toward Responsive Law* (New York, 1978); Gunter Teubner, "Substantive and Reflexive Elements in Modern Law" (1983) 17 *Law and Society Review* 239.
20. See, e.g., Phillip Harder, "First Judicial Review of Reg-Neg: A Disappointment," *Administrative and Regulatory Law News*, Fall 1996, p. 1; Declan Roche, *Accountability in Restorative Justice* (Oxford, 2003).
21. See generally John D. Donahue and Joseph S. Nye, Jr, eds., *Market-Based Governance: Supply Side, Demand Side, Upside and Downside* (Washington, DC, 2002).
22. See generally James Bohman and William Rehg, *Deliberative Democracy: Essays on Reason and Politics* (Cambridge, MA, 1997). See also Jody Freeman and Laura Langbein, "Regulatory Negotiation and the Legitimacy Benefit" (2000) 9 *New York University Environmental Law Journal* 60.
23. See, e.g., Robert C. Ellickson, *Order Without Law: How Neighbors Settle Disputes* (Cambridge, MA, 1991).
24. See, e.g., William Funk, "Bargaining Toward the New Millennium: Regulatory Negotiation and a Subversion of the Public Interest" (1997) 46 *Duke Law Journal* 1351.
25. See Jonathan Boston *et al.*, *Public Management: The New Zealand Model* (Auckland, 1996), pp. 16–40 (the introductory essay). See also Lester M. Salamon, ed., *The Tools of Government: A Guide to the New Governance* (Oxford, 2002); John D. Donahue, *The Privatization Decision: Public Ends, Private Means* (New York, 1989).
26. See US Bureau of the Census, *Historical Statistics of the United States, Colonial Times to 1970* (Washington, DC, 1975); US Bureau of the Census, *2001 Statistical Abstract of the United States* (Washington, DC, 2002).
27. Paul C. Light, *The True Size of Government* (Washington, DC, 1999).
28. See, e.g., Harrington and Umat (this volume); Matthew Diller, "The Revolution in Welfare Administration: Rules, Discretion and Entrepreneurial Government" (2000) 75 *New York University Law Review* 1121; Mark Seidenfeld, "An Apology for Administrative Law in the 'Contracting State'" (2000) 28 *Florida State University Law Review* 215.
29. See Mark H. Moore, Introduction, "Symposium: Public Values in an Era of Privatization" (2003) 116 *Harvard Law Review* 1212.
30. But see John J. Dilulio, Jr, "Government by Proxy: A Faithful Overview" (2003) 116 *Harvard Law Review* 1271.
31. See generally Diller, "The Revolution in Welfare Administration."
32. Compare the Freedom of Information Act, 5 USC § 552 (2000) with the Trade Secrets Act, 18 USC § 1905 (2000).

33. See generally Jon Michaels, "Beyond Accountability: The Constitutional, Democratic, and Strategic Problems with Privatizing War" (2004) 84(2) *Washington University Law Quarterly* 1001–1127.
34. See Martha Minow, "Public and Private Partnerships: Accounting for the New Religion" (2003) 116 *Harvard Law Review* 1229, pp. 1253–1255.
35. See, e.g., Donald F. Kettl, *Government by Proxy: (Mis?)managing Federal Programs* (Washington, DC, 1988); H. Brenton Milward, Keith Provan and Barbara Else, "What Does the Hollow State Look Like?," in Barry Bozeman, ed., *Public Management: The State of the Art* (San Francisco, CA, 1993), p. 309.
36. See generally Trebilcock *et al.*, "Government by Voucher."
37. See, e.g., Deborah A. Stone, *The Disabled State* (Philadelphia, PA, 1984); Edward D. Berkowitz, *Disabled Policy: America's Programs for the Handicapped* (New York, 1987).
38. See generally Jerry L. Mashaw, *Bureaucratic Justice, Managing Social Security Disability Claims* (New Haven, CT, 1983); Jerry L. Mashaw *et al.*, *Social Security Hearings and Appeals: A Study of the Social Security Administration Hearing System* (Lexington, MA, 1978); Jerry L. Mashaw and Virginia P. Reno, eds., *Balancing Security and Opportunity: The Challenge of Disability Income Policy* (Washington, DC, 1996); Goloo S. Wunderlich, Dorothy P. Rice and Nicole L. Amado, eds., *The Dynamics of Disability: Measuring and Monitoring Disability for Social Security Programs* (Washington, DC, 2002).
39. See Social Security Administration, Office of Research, Evaluation and Statistics, *Annual Statistical Supplement to the Social Security Bulletin* (Washington, DC, 2002).
40. Martha Derthick, *Policymaking for Social Security* (Washington, DC, 1979).
41. *Mathews* v. *Eldridge*, 424 US 319 (1976).
42. *Heckler* v. *Campbell*, 461 US 458 (1983).
43. *Bowen* v. *City of New York*, 476 US 467 (1986).
44. See Mashaw, *Bureaucratic Justice*, pp. 103–168.
45. United States House of Representatives Ways and Means Committee, *Committee Staff Report on the Disability Insurance Program* (Washington, DC, 1974), pp. 111–112. See also Derthick, *Policymaking for Social Security*, p. 303.
46. See Mashaw, *Bureaucratic Justice*, pp. 188–189.
47. Compare *Books* v. *Chater*, 91 F 3d 972, 979 (7th Cir. 1996) with 20 *Code of Federal Regulations* § 404.1527(d)(2) (2004).
48. See General Accounting Office, *The Social Security Administration Should Provide More Management and Leadership in Determining Who is Eligible for Disability Benefits* (Washington, DC, 1976).
49. See generally Jerry L. Mashaw, "Disability Insurance in an Age of Retrenchment: The Politics of Implementing Rights," in Theodore R. Marmor and Jerry L. Mashaw, eds., *Social Security: Beyond the Rhetoric of Crisis* (Princeton, NJ, 1988), p. 151.

50. See Wunderlich, Rice and Amado, eds., *The Dynamics of Disability*, pp. 140–147.
51. See Mashaw and Reno, eds., *Balancing Security and Opportunity*, pp. 104–120.
52. Pub. L. No. 106-170, 113 Stat. 1860 (1999) (codified at 42 USC § 1320b-19 (2000)).
53. Gunther Teubner, "After Legal Instrumentalism? Strategic Models of Post-Regulatory Law," in Gunther Teubner, ed., *Dilemmas of Law in the Welfare State* (Berlin, 1985), p. 311.

6 Emerging labor movements and the accountability dilemma: the case of Indonesia

1. David Edelstein and Malcolm Warner, *Comparative Union Democracy: Organization and Opposition in British and American Unions* (London, 1975); Jack Fiorito, Paul Jarley and John T. Delaney, "National Union Effectiveness in Organizing: Measures and Influences" (1995) 48 *Industrial and Labor Relations Review* 613; Richard Hyman and Robert Fryer, "Trade Unions: Sociology and Political Economy," in Tom Clarke and Laurie Clements, eds., *Labour Unions Under Capitalism* (Hassocks, 1978).
2. John Hemingway, *Conflict and Democracy: Studies in Trade Union Government* (Oxford, 1978); Huw Morris and Patricia Fosh, "Measuring Trade Union Democracy: The Case of the UK Civil and Public Services Association" (2000) 38 *British Journal of Industrial Relations* 95.
3. Morris and Fosh, "Measuring Trade Union Democracy."
4. Deborah Eade, "Editorial Overview" (2004) 14 *Development in Practice* 5; Dan Gallin, "Labour Unions and NGOs: A Necessary Partnership for Social Development," United Nations Research Institute for Social Development, Civil Society and Social Movements Programme Paper No. 1 (Geneva, 2000).
5. See Courville (this volume); see also Jan Aart Scholte, "Civil Society and Democratically Accountable Global Governance" (2004) 39 *Government and Opposition* 211.
6. Gallin, "Labour Unions and NGOs"; Lance Compa, "Trade Unions, NGOs, and Corporate Codes of Conduct" (2004) 14 *Development in Practice* 210; Lance Compa, "NGO–Labor Union Tensions on the Ground" (2000) 2(4) *Human Rights Dialogue: Who Can Protect Workers' Rights? The Workplace Codes of Conduct Debates* 12.
7. Voravidh Charoenloet, Napaporn Ativanichayapong and Phan Wanabriboon, "The Impact of Trade Union Solidarity Support Organisations in Thailand 1993–2002," Chulalongkorn University Political Economy Study Center (Bangkok, 2004) (available at http://www.fes-thailand.org/Impact%20Study%20(1).pdf).
8. Souley Adji, "Globalization and Union Strategies in Niger," in A. V. Jose, ed., *Organized Labour in the 21st Century* (Geneva, 2002); Marina Prieto and Carolina Quinteros, "Never the Twain Shall Meet? Women's Organisations and Trade Unions in the *Maquila* Industry in Central America" (2004) 14 *Development in Practice* 149.

9. Michele Ford, "New Forms of Labour Activism: A Southeast Asian Perspective," in *Proceedings of the Refereed Stream of the Association of Industrial Relations Academics of Australia and New Zealand (AIRAANZ) Annual Conference*, February 3–6, 2004 (Noosa, 2004); Michele Ford, "NGO as Outside Intellectual: A History of Non-Governmental Organizations' Role in the Indonesian Labour Movement," University of Wollongong, unpublished PhD dissertation (Wollongong, 2003); Michele Ford, "Substitute Trade Union or Novel Form of Labour Movement Organization? Understanding Indonesia's Labour NGOs" (2003) 14 *Economic and Labour Relations Review* 90; Michele Ford, "Challenging the Criteria of Significance: Lessons from Contemporary Indonesian Labour History" (2001) 47 *Australian Journal of Politics and History* 100.
10. Eade, "Editorial Overview."
11. See, e.g., Charoenloet, Ativanichayapong and Wanabriboon, "The Impact of Trade Union Solidarity Support Organisations in Thailand."
12. Morris and Fosh, "Measuring Trade Union Democracy."
13. See, e.g., Alfred Stepan, *The State and Society: Peru in Comparative Perspective* (Princeton, 1978).
14. *Ibid.*; see also Michele Ford, "Testing the Limits of Corporatism: Reflections on Industrial Relations Institutions and Practices in Suharto's Indonesia" (1999) 41 *Journal of Industrial Relations* 372.
15. Michele Ford, "A Challenge for Business? Developments in Indonesian Trade Unionism after Soeharto," in M. Chatib Basri and Pierre van der Eng, eds., *Changes and Challenges in Business in Indonesia* (Singapore, 2004); Dave Spooner, "Trade Unions and NGOs: The Need for Cooperation" (2004) 14 *Development in Practice* 19.
16. Ford, "Testing the Limits of Corporatism"; Vedi R. Hadiz, *Workers and the State in New Order Indonesia* (London, 1997).
17. John Ingleson, *In Search of Justice: Workers and Unions in Colonial Java, 1908–1926* (Singapore, 1986); Jan Elliott, "Bersatoe Kita Berdiri Bertjerai Kita Djatoeh [United We Stand Divided We Fall]: Workers and Unions in Indonesia: Jakarta 1945–1965," University of New South Wales, unpublished PhD dissertation (Kensington, 1997).
18. Hadiz, *Workers and the State in New Order Indonesia.*
19. Ford, "Testing the Limits of Corporatism"; Hadiz, *Workers and the State in New Order Indonesia.*
20. Ford, "Testing the Limits of Corporatism"; Ford, "NGO as Outside Intellectual"; Hadiz, *Workers and the State in New Order Indonesia*; Douglas Kammen, "A Time to Strike: Industrial Strikes and Changing Class Relations in New Order Indonesia," Cornell University, unpublished PhD dissertation (Ithaca, 1997).
21. David Reeve, *Golkar of Indonesia: An Alternative to the Party System* (Singapore, 1985).
22. Sri Kusyuniati, "Strikes in 1990–1996: An Evaluation of the Dynamics of the Indonesian Labour Movement," Swinburne University of Technology, unpublished PhD dissertation (Melbourne, 1998).
23. Ford, "NGO as Outside Intellectual."

24. *Ibid.*
25. *Ibid.*; Hadiz, *Workers and the State in New Order Indonesia.*
26. Ford, "NGO as Outside Intellectual."
27. Michele Ford, "The Place of NGOs in the Organized Labor Movements of Indonesia and Malaysia," paper presented at the 2002 Annual Meeting of the Association for Asian Studies, Washington, DC, April 4–7, 2002; Steven McKay, "The Squeaky Wheel's Dilemma: New Forms of Labor Organizing in the Philippines," paper presented at the 2002 Annual Meeting of the Association for Asian Studies, Washington, DC, April 4–7, 2002.
28. Ford, "NGO as Outside Intellectual"; Ford, "Challenging the Criteria of Significance."
29. Ford, "NGO as Outside Intellectual."
30. See, e.g., Dan La Botz, *Made in Indonesia: Indonesian Workers Since the Fall of Suharto* (Cambridge, 2001).
31. Courville (this volume).
32. David Bourchier, "Solidarity: The New Order's First Free Trade Union," in David Bourchier, ed., *Indonesia's Emerging Proletariat: Workers and Their Struggles* (Clayton, 1994), pp. 52–63.
33. Ford, "NGO as Outside Intellectual."
34. *Ibid.*
35. *Ibid.*
36. Gerard Greenfield, "Organizing, Protest and Working Class Self-Activity: Reflections on East Asia," in Leo Panitch and Colin Leys, eds., *Socialist Register 2001: Working Classes, Global Realities* (New York, 2001), p. 241.
37. Interviews with KSBSI officials (June 2003).
38. Interviews with officials from KSPSI, KSPI and KSBSI (June/July 2003).
39. DPP-SBSI, *Laporan Pertanggungjawaban Dewan Pengurus Pusat Serikat Buruh Sejahtera Indonesia (DPP-SBSI) Periode April 2000–April 2003* (Jakarta, 2003).
40. American Center for International Labor Solidarity, "Monthly Report for May" (Jakarta, 1999); American Center for International Labor Solidarity, "Monthly Report for July" (Jakarta, 1999).
41. Interview with Dita Sari (July 13, 2003).
42. Interviews (1999, 2000, 2001).
43. Ford, "NGO as Outside Intellectual."
44. Interview with ACILS staff (July 2003).
45. Interviews with labor NGO activists (2001, 2003).
46. Interviews with NGO activists (2001, 2003).
47. Interviews (1999, 2001, 2003).
48. Interviews (1999, 2001, 2003).
49. Ford, "A Challenge for Business?"

7 Spontaneous accountability

1. Better Regulation Task Force, *Alternatives to State Regulation* (London, 2000); Julia Black, "Decentring Regulation: The Role of Regulation and Self-Regulation in a 'Post-Regulatory' World" (2001) 54 *Current Legal*

Problems 103; Neil Gunningham and Peter Grabosky, *Smart Regulation: Designing Environmental Policy* (Oxford, 1998).

2. E. Leslie Normanton, *The Accountability and Audit of Governments* (Manchester, 1966).
3. Rubin (this volume); Richard Mulgan, *Holding Power to Account: Accountability in Modern Democracies* (London, 2003).
4. Robert Behn, *Rethinking Democratic Accountability* (Washington, DC, 2001); Bruce Stone, "Administrative Accountability in the 'Westminster' Democracies: Towards a New Conceptual Framework" (1995) 8 *Governance* 505.
5. Marc Allen Eisner, *Regulatory Politics in Transition* (Baltimore, 2000); Christopher Hood, Henry Rothstein and Robert Baldwin, *The Government of Risk* (Oxford, 2001).
6. Peter Grabosky, "Beyond the Regulatory State" (1994) 27 *Australian and New Zealand Journal of Criminology* 192; Peter N. Grabosky, "Using Non-Governmental Resources to Foster Regulatory Compliance" (1995) 8 *Governance* 527; Neil Gunningham and Peter Grabosky, *Smart Regulation.*
7. Christine Parker, *The Open Corporation: Self-Regulation and Democracy* (Melbourne, 2002).
8. See Mashaw (this volume); Robert E. Goodin, "Democratic Accountability: The Distinctiveness of the Third Sector" (2003) 44 *European Archives of Sociology* 359; Claus Offe, "Civil Society and Social Order: Demarcating and Combining Market, State and Community" (2000) 41 *Revue Europeennes de Sociologie* 71; Jon Pierre and B. Guy Peters, *Governance, Politics and the State* (Basingstoke, 2000).
9. Mashaw (this volume).
10. Samuel Bowles and Herbert Gintis, "Social Capital and Community Governance" (2002) 112 *Economic Journal* 419.
11. Christopher Hood, *The Art of the State* (Oxford, 1998).
12. Julia Black, "Decentring Regulation: The Role of Regulation and Self-Regulation in a 'Post-Regulatory' World" (2001) 54 *Current Legal Problems* 103.
13. Hood, *The Art of the State.*
14. Lawrence Lessig, *Code: and Other Laws of Cyberspace* (New York, 1999).
15. Mulgan, *Holding Power to Account.*
16. See generally Freeman (this volume).
17. Christopher Hood *et al.*, *Regulation Inside Government: Waste-Watchers, Quality Police, and Sleaze-Busters* (Oxford, 1999).
18. Michael Moran, *The British Regulatory State: High Modernism and Hyper-Innovation* (Oxford, 2003).
19. Christopher Hood *et al.*, *Controlling Modern Government: Variety, Commonality and Change* (Cheltenham, 2004).
20. Albert O. Hirschman, *Exit, Voice and Loyalty: Responses to Decline in Firms, Organizations and States* (Cambridge, MA, 1970).
21. Mashaw (this volume).
22. Freeman (this volume); Hugh Collins, *Regulating Contracts* (Oxford, 1999), p. 19.

23. Richard V. Ericson, Aaron Doyle and Dean Barry, *Insurance as Governance* (Toronto, 2003).
24. Goodin, "Democratic Accountability," p. 367.
25. Adam Smith, *Wealth of Nations* (Harmondsworth, 1970) (originally published 1776).
26. Donahue, "Market-Based Governance."
27. Collins, *Regulating Contract*, p. 19.
28. Donahue, "Market-Based Governance," p. 12.
29. William Bratton *et al.*, eds., *International Regulatory Competition and Coordination* (Oxford, 1996).
30. Goodin, "Democratic Accountability," p. 392.
31. Pierre and Peters, *Governance, Politics and the State*, pp. 19–22.
32. Burkard Eberlein, "Competition and Regulation" (2003) 4 *Journal of Network Industries* 137.
33. Anne-Marie Slaughter, *A New World Order* (Princeton, 2004).
34. Geoffrey Brennan and Philip Pettit, *The Economy of Esteem* (Oxford, 2004).
35. Goodin, "Democratic Accountability," p. 367.
36. Neil Duxbury, *Random Justice: On Lotteries and Legal Decision-Making* (Oxford, 1999).
37. Hood, *The Art of the State*, pp. 157–165.
38. Lessig, *Code: And Other Laws of Cyberspace*, pp. 235–239.
39. Clifford D. Shearing and Philip C. Stenning, "From the Panopticon to Disney World: The Development of the Discipline," in Anthony N. Doob and Edward L. Greenspan, eds., *Perspectives in Criminal Law* (Toronto, 1985).
40. See especially Hood, *The Art of the State*, Chapter 3.
41. Andrew Murray and Colin Scott, "Controlling the New Media: Hybrid Responses to New Forms of Power" (2002) 65 *Modern Law Review* 491.
42. Roger Brownsword, "Code, Control, and Choice: Why East is East and West is West" (2005) 25 *Legal Studies* 1.
43. Colin Scott, "Between the Old and the New: Innovation in the Regulation of Internet Gambling," in Julia Black *et al.*, eds., *Regulatory Innovation* (Cheltenham, 2005).
44. Lee Tien, "Architectural Regulation and the Evolution of Social Norms" (2004) 9 *International Journal of Communications Law and Policy* 1, p. 6.
45. Lessig, *Code: And Other Laws of Cyberspace*, pp. 224–225; Tien, "Architectural Regulation," p. 2.
46. Brownsword, "Code, Control, and Choice."
47. *Ibid.*
48. See Freeman (this volume).
49. See Braithwaitte (this volume).
50. Julia Black, "Constitutionalising Self-Regulation" (1996) 59 *Modern Law Review* 24.
51. John Braithwaite, "Accountability and Governance Under the New Regulatory State" (1999) 58 *Australian Journal of Public Administration* 90, p. 91.

52. Goodin, "Democratic Accountability," p. 390.
53. Jody Freeman, "Private Parties, Public Functions and the New Administrative Law" (2000b) 52 *Administrative Law Review* 813; Peter Self, *Government by the Market? The Politics of Public Choice* (Basingstoke, 1993).
54. See also John Braithwaite, "On Speaking Softly and Carrying Big Sticks: Neglected Dimensions of a Republican Separation of Powers" (1997) 47 *University of Toronto Law Journal* 305.
55. Goodin, "Democratic Accountability," p. 367.
56. Scott, "Accountability in the Regulatory State."
57. John Owen Haley, *Authority Without Power: Law and the Japanese Paradox* (New York, 1991), p. 14.
58. Christopher Hood, *The Tools of Government* (London, 1984).
59. Hugh Heclo and Aaron Wildavsky, *The Private Government of Public Money* (London, 1974).
60. Mulgan, *Holding Power to Account*, pp. 131–136.
61. *Ibid.*, pp. 119–131.
62. Arthur Stinchcombe, "Contracts as Hierarchical Documents," in Arthur Stinchcombe and Carol Heimer, eds., *Organizational Theory and Project Management* (Bergen, 1985).
63. Colin Scott, "Privatization, Control and Accountability," in Joseph McCahery *et al.*, eds., *Corporate Control and Accountability* (Oxford, 1993).
64. Hugh Beale and Tony Dugdale, "Contracts Between Businessmen: Planning and the Use of Contractual Remedies" (1975) 2 *British Journal of Law and Society* 45; Stuart Macaulay, "Non-Contractual Relations in Business: A Preliminary Study" (1963) 28 *American Sociological Review* 55.
65. John D. Donahue, "Market-Based Governance and the Architecture of Accountability," in John D. Donahue and Joseph S. Nye, eds., *Market-Based Governance: Supply Side, Demand Side, Upside and Downside* (Washington, DC, 2002), p. 2.
66. Sasha Courville, "Social Accountability Audits: Challenging or Defending Democratic Governance?" (2003) 25 *Law and Policy* 269.
67. Goodin, "Democratic Accountability," pp. 373–379.
68. Colin Scott, "Private Regulation of the Public Sector: A Neglected Facet of Contemporary Governance" (2002) 29 *Journal of Law and Society* 56, p. 74.
69. Black, "Constitutionalising Self-Regulation."
70. Richard Lewis, "Insurers' Agreements Not to Enforce Strict Legal Rights: Bargaining with the Government and in the Shadow of the Law" (1985) 48 *Modern Law Review* 275.
71. Joseph Rees, "The Development of Communitarian Regulation in the Chemical Industry" (1997) 19 *Law and Policy* 477.
72. Benjamin Cashore, "Legitimacy and the Privatization of Environmental Governance: How Non-State Market-Driven (NSMD) Governance Systems Gain Rule Making Authority" (2002) 15 *Governance* 503.

73. Hood *et al.*, *Controlling Modern Government.*
74. Peter Self, *Government by the Market? The Politics of Public Choice* (Basingstoke, 1993). See especially Chapter 5.
75. Mashaw (this volume).

8 Accounting for accountability in neoliberal regulatory regimes

1. See Jerold. S. Auerbach, *Unequal Justice: Lawyers and Social Change in Modern America* (New York, 1977); Martin Shapiro, "Administrative Law Unbounded: Reflections on Government and Governance" (2001) 8 *Indiana Journal of Global Legal Studies* 369.
2. See Peter Fitzpatrick, *Modernism and the Grounds of Law* (Cambridge, 2001); John Comaroff and Simon Roberts, *Rules and Processes: The Cultural Logic of Dispute in an African Context* (Chicago, 1981).
3. See Federal Administrative Procedure Act (APA), Pub. L. No. 79-404, 60 Stat. 237 (1946) (current version 5 USC §§ 551–559, 801–808 (2000)).
4. Christine B. Harrington, "Regulatory Reform: Creating Gaps and Making Markets" (1988) 10 *Law and Policy* 293.
5. Pub. L. No. 101-648, 104 Stat. 4969 (1990) (codified as amended at 5 USC §§ 561–570 (1994)) (reauthorized by the Administrative Dispute Resolution Act of 1996, Pub. L. No. 104-320, amending Pub. L. No. 101-648).
6. Cary Coglianese, "Litigating Within Relationships: Disputes and Disturbance in the Regulatory Process" (1996) 30 *Law and Society Review* 735; Cary Coglianese, "Assessing Consensus: The Promise and Performance of Negotiated Rulemaking" (1997) 46 *Duke Law Journal* 1255; Harrington, "Regulatory Reform: Creating Gaps and Making Markets"; Christine B. Harrington, "Using 'Bundles of Input' to Negotiate an Environmental Dispute: Howard Bellman," in D. M. Kolb, ed., *When Talk Works: Profiles of Mediators* (San Francisco, 1994).
7. Sungham Im, *Bureaucratic Power, Democracy and Administrative Democracy* (Aldershot, 2001); H. T. Wilson, *Bureaucratic Representation* (Leiden, 2001).
8. Camilla Stivers, *Democracy, Bureaucracy and the Study of Administration* (Boulder, 2001); Christian Hunold, "Corporatism, Pluralism, and Democracy: Toward a Deliberative Theory of Bureaucratic Accountability" (2001) 14 *Governance* 151.
9. See Richard Stewart, "Administrative Law in the 21st Century" (2003) 78 *New York University Law Review* 437.
10. For a critical discussion, see Bob Jessop, "Narrating the Future of the National Economy and the National State," in George Steinmetz, ed., *State/Culture: State Formation after the Cultural Turn* (Ithaca, 1999); Neil Brenner, *New State Spaces: Urban Governance and the Rescaling of Statehood* (Oxford, 2004).
11. Mark Considine, "The End of the Line? Accountable Governance in the Age of Networks, Partnerships, and Joined-Up Services" (2002) 15 *Governance* 21; Donald E. Klingner, John Nalbandian and Barbara

S. Romzek, "Politics, Administration and Markets: Conflicting Expectations and Accountability" (2002) 32 *American Review of Public Administration* 117.

12. Mark Considine and Jenny Lewis, "Governance at Ground Level: The Frontline Bureaucrat in the Age of Markets and Networks" (1999) 59 *Public Administration Review* 467.
13. See Stewart, "Administrative Law in the 21st Century"; Charles F. Sabel, "Beyond Principal–Agent Governance: Experimentalist Organizations, Learning and Accountability," in E. R. Engelen and M. Sie Dhian Ho, eds., *De Staat van de Democratie Voorbij de Staat* (Amsterdam, 2004), pp. 173–195.
14. See also Mashaw (this volume).
15. James Fearon, "Electoral Accountability and the Control of Politicians: Selecting Good Types versus Sanctioning Poor Performance," in Adam Przeworski *et al.*, eds., *Democracy, Accountability, and Representation* (New York, 1999), p. 55, at p. 55; see also John Ferejohn, "Accountability and Authority: Toward a Theory of Political Accountability," in Adam Przeworski *et al.*, eds., *Democracy, Accountability, and Representation* (New York, 1999), p. 131.
16. Delmer Dunn, "Mixing Elected and Non-Elected Officials in Democratic Policy Making: Fundamentals of Accountability and Responsibility," in Adam Przeworski *et al.*, eds., *Democracy, Accountability, and Representation* (New York, 1999), p. 297, at p. 298.
17. Waldrauch defines horizontal accountability as the "capacity of governmental institutions including such 'agencies of restraint' as courts, independent electoral tribunals, anticorruption bodies, central banks, auditing agencies, and ombudsmen to check abuses by other public agencies and branches of government." Harold Waldrauch, "Institutionalizing Horizontal Accountability: A Conference Report," in Institute for Advanced Studies, Political Science Series, No. 55 (Vienna, 1998), p. 1; see also Guillermo O'Donnell, "Horizontal Accountability in New Democracies" (1998) 9 *Journal of Democracy* 112.
18. O'Donnell, "Horizontal Accountability in New Democracies."
19. Fearon, "Electoral Accountability and the Control of Politicians: Selecting Good Types versus Sanctioning Poor Performance"; John Ferejohn, "Accountability and Authority: Toward a Theory of Political Accountability."
20. See also Rubin (this volume).
21. Arthur Maass and Laurence Radway, "Gauging Administrative Responsibility" (1949) 19 *Public Administration Review* 182.
22. See, e.g., Considine, "The End of the Line"; Alfred Aman, Jr, "The Limits of Globalization and the Future of Administrative Law: From Government to Governance" (2001) 8 *Indiana Journal of Global Legal Studies* 379; Jody Freeman, "The Private Role in Public Governance" (2000) 75 *New York University Law Review* 543; Michael Dorf and Charles Sabel, "A Constitution of Democratic Experimentalism" (1998) 98 *Columbia Law Review* 267.

23. Howard Ball, *Federal Administrative Agencies* (Englewood Cliffs, NJ, 1984).
24. Dorf and Sabel, "A Constitution of Democratic Experimentalism."
25. See generally Paul Light, *The Tides of Reform: Making Government Work 1945–1995* (New Haven, 1997).
26. See generally Dorf and Sabel, "A Constitution of Democratic Experimentalism."
27. Executive Order No. 12291 (3 CFR § 127 (1982)), issued by the Reagan administration, formalized the Office of Management and Budget's review powers over regulatory actions. Executive Order No. 12866 (3 CFR 638 (1993)), issued by President Clinton, replaced Executive Order 12291, and retained the OMB review process.
28. See, e.g., Michael Dorf and Charles Sabel, "Drug Treatment Courts and Emergent Experimentalist Government" (2000) 53 *Vanderbilt Law Review* 829.
29. Wolf Heydebrand, "Process Rationality as Legal Governance: A Comparative Perspective" (2003) 18 *International Sociology* 325.
30. Joel Wolfe, *Power and Privatization* (New York, 1996), p. 26.
31. Aman, "The Limits of Globalization and the Future of Administrative Law: From Government to Governance," p. 382.
32. Coglianese, "Assessing Consensus: The Promise and Performance of Negotiated Rulemaking," p. 22; see also Charles H. Koch, Jr and Beth Martin, "FTC Rulemaking Through Negotiation" (1983) 61 *North Carolina Law Review* 275.
33. Donald R. Brand, *Corporatism and the Rule of Law: A Study of the National Recovery Administration* (Ithaca, 1988).
34. Morton Horwitz, *The Transformation of American Law 1780–1850* (Cambridge, MA, 1977); Karl Klare, "Judicial Deradicalization of the Wagner Act and the Origins of Modern Legal Consciousness: 1937–1941" (1978) 62 *Minnesota Law Review* 265.
35. See Alfred Aman, Jr, *Administrative Law in a Global Era* (Ithaca, 1992) for an analysis of the global aspects of this trend.
36. See *Wolff* v. *McDonnell*, 418 US 539 (1974); *Mathews* v. *Eldridge*, 424 US 319 (1976); and *Ingraham* v. *Wright*, 430 US 651 (1977).
37. See *Chevron* v. *Natural Resource Defense Council*, 467 US 837 (1984). For an empirical study of the jurisprudential effects of *Chevron*, see Richard Herbert Kritzer, Mark Richards and Joseph Smith, "Deciding the Supreme Court's Administrative Law Cases: Does Chevron Matter?," paper presented at the annual meeting of the American Political Science Association, Boston, MA, 2002.
38. Mark S. Hurwitz, "Ideology and Deference in US Courts of Appeals Decision Making on Administrative Law," paper presented at the 2003 Annual Meeting of the American Political Science Association, Philadelphia, August 28–31, 2003, pp. 5–9.
39. See, e.g., Doreen McBarnet, "Legal Creativity: Law, Capital and Legal Avoidance," in Maureen Cain and Christine B. Harrington, eds., *Lawyers in a Postmodern World: Translation and Transgression* (New York,

1994); Yves Dezalay, "The Forum Should Fit the Fuss: The Economics and Politics of Negotiated Justice," in Maureen Cain and Christine B. Harrington, eds., *Lawyers in a Postmodern World: Translation and Transgression* (New York, 1994), p. 155.
40. See Robert C. Lieberman, "Ideas, Institutions, and Political Order: Explaining Political Change" (2002) 96 *American Political Science Review* 697. See also Dowdle (Chapter 1, this volume).
41. Karl Polanyi, *The Great Transformation* (Boston, 1944); see also Beth Silver and Giovanni Arrighi, "Polanyi's 'Double Movement': The Belle Époques of British and US Hegemony Compared" (2003) 31 *Politics and Society* 325; Bob Jessop, "Regulationist and Autopoieticist Reflections on Polanyi's Account of Market Economies and the Market Society" (2001) 6 *New Political Economy* 213.
42. Stephen Gill, "Globalisation, Market Civilisation, and Disciplinary Neoliberalism" (1995) 24 *Millennium* 418.
43. Jamie Peck, *The Workfare State* (New York, 2001).
44. Neil Brenner and Nik Theodore, "Cities and the Geographies of 'Actually Existing Neoliberalism'" (2002) 34 *Antipode* 356.
45. Jamie Peck and Adam Tickell, "Making Global Rules: Globalisation or Neoliberalisation?," in Jamie Peck and H. Yeung, eds., *Remaking the Global Economy: Economic-Geographical Perspectives* (London, 2003).
46. See Anthony Giddens, *The Constitution of Society: Outline of the Theory of Structuration* (Berkeley, 1984) for a detailed discussion of the concept, "structuration."
47. See also Wolfe, *Power and Privatization*.
48. Administrative Conference of the US, "Recommendation No. 86-3: Agencies' Use of Alternative Means of Dispute Resolution," 1 CFR 305.86-3 (1993).
49. 5 USC Appendix §§ 1–15 (1982).
50. Lawrence Susskind, Elieen Babbitt and Peter Segal, "When ADR Becomes the Law: A Review of Federal Practice" (1993) 9 *Negotiation Journal* 59.
51. For a description and legislative history of, and technical details about, negotiated rulemaking, see David Pritzker, *Negotiated Rulemaking Sourcebook* (Washington, DC, 1995).
52. Philip J. Harter, "The Political Legitimacy and Judicial Review of Consensual Rules" (1983) 32 *American University Law Review* 471.
53. Philip J. Harter, "Negotiating Regulations: A Cure for Malaise" (1982) 71 *Georgetown Law Journal* 1.
54. Lawrence Susskind and Gerard MacMahon, "Theory and Practice of Negotiated Rulemaking" (1985) 3 *Yale Journal on Regulation* 133, p. 159.
55. But see Coglianese, "Assessing Consensus: The Promise and Performance of Negotiated Rulemaking."
56. See also Aman, "The Limits of Globalization and the Future of Administrative Law: From Government to Governance."
57. See Jurgen Habermas, *The Legitimation Crisis* (Boston, 1975).

58. Harter, "The Political Legitimacy and Judicial Review of Consensual Rules"; but see Harrington, "Regulatory Reform: Creating Gaps and Making Markets."
59. See Alfred Aman, Jr, *The Democracy Deficit* (New York, 2004).
60. Harrington, "Regulatory Reform: Creating Gaps and Making Markets."
61. See Martin Shapiro, "Administrative Law Unbounded: Reflections on Government and Governance" (2001) 8 *Indiana Journal of Global Legal Studies* 369, p. 373.
62. For discussion of this crisis of legitimacy, see Habermas, *The Legitimation Crisis*; James O'Connor, *Fiscal Crisis of the State* (New York, 1973); Eric O. Wright, *Class, Crisis and the State* (London, 1978); Hector Schamis, *Re-forming the State* (Ann Arbor, 2002).
63. These trends are also evident in several other areas within administrative law, such as (1) statutory interpretation; (2) administrative search and seizures; (3) judicial review of agency action; and (4) administrative liability. See Lief Carter and Christine B. Harrington, *Administrative Law and Politics: Cases and Comments* (3rd ed., New York, 1999).
64. See Administrative Conference of the US, "Recommendation No. 86-3."
65. See Negotiated Rulemaking Act of 1990, 5 USC § 561.
66. 5 USC § 570.
67. LEXIS identifies twenty-three cases in the Federal District Courts and the US Courts of Appeal decided during this period.
68. 65 F 3d 313 (5th Cir. 2001).
69. See, e.g., 5 USC § 563(a) ("An agency may establish a negotiated rulemaking committee . . ."); 5 USC § 563(b) ("An agency may use the services of a convener . . . ").
70. 209 F Supp 2d 102 (DDC 2002).
71. Pub. L. No. 107-110, 113 Stat. 1423 (2002) (codified at 5 USC 570).
72. 209 F Supp 2d at 108.
73. *Ibid.*, at 105.
74. *Ibid.*, at 114–115.
75. See also Cary Coglianese, "Is Consensus an Appropriate Basis for Regulatory Policy?," in Eric Orts and Kurt Deketelaere, eds., *Environmental Contracts: Comparative Approaches to Regulatory Innovation in the United States and Europe* (Boston, 2001), p. 93, n. 2; Coglianese, "Assessing Consensus: The Promise and Performance of Negotiated Rulemaking," p. 1256, n. 5.
76. 198 F 3d 944 (DC Cir. 1999).
77. 49 CFR §§ 214.301–214.355a.
78. 198 F 3d at 950.
79. *Ibid.*, at 949–950. The "definitive interpretation" threshold for notice and comment rulemaking was articulated in *Alaska Professional Hunters Association, Inc.* v. *FAA*, 177 F 3d 1030 (DC Cir. 1999).
80. 198 F 3d at 950.
81. 82 F 3d 708 (7th Cir. 1996).
82. Pub. L. No. 102-325, § 485(a), 106 Stat. 448, 619–620 (1992) (amending 20 USC § 1098(b)).

83. 82 F 3d at 714.
84. *Ibid.*
85. *Ibid.*
86. *Ibid.*, at 715.
87. *Ibid.*
88. Harrington, "Using 'Bundles of Input' to Negotiate an Environmental Dispute: Howard Bellman."
89. Gunther Teubner, *Law as an Autopoietic System* (Cambridge, MA, 1993); Heydebrand, "Process Rationality as Legal Governance: A Comparative Perspective."
90. Jody Freeman and Laura Langbein, "Regulatory Negotiation and the Legitimacy Benefit" (2000) 9 *New York University Environmental Law Journal* 60.
91. See also Stephen Breyer *et al.*, *Administrative Law and Regulatory Policy: Problems, Texts, and Cases* (5th ed., New York, 2002), p. 737.
92. Robert Choo, "Judicial Review of Negotiated Rulemaking: Should Chevron Deference Apply?" (2000) 52 *Rutgers Law Review* 1069.
93. Susan R. Ackerman, "American Administrative Law under Siege: Is Germany a Model?" (1994) 107 *Harvard Law Review* 1279.
94. Marc Galanter, "Why the 'Haves' Come out Ahead? Speculations on the Limits of Legal Change" (1974) 9 *Law and Society Review* 165.

9 The mark of responsibility (with a postscript on accountability)

1. Ronald Dworkin, *Sovereign Virtue: The Theory and Practice of Equality* (Cambridge, MA, 2000), p. 287.
2. See Aristotle, *Nicomachean Ethics* 1097^{b}24–1098^{a}17, 1103^{a}23–25, 1168^{a}5–9.
3. See also John Gardner, "Justifications and Reasons," in A. P. Simester and A. T. H. Smith, eds., *Harm and Culpability* (Oxford, 1996); John Gardner, "The Gist of Excuses" (1997) 1 *Buffalo Criminal Law Review* 575.
4. See especially *R.* v. *Thornton* [1992] 1 All ER 306; *R.* v. *Ahluwalia* [1992] 4 All ER 859; *R.* v. *Humphreys* [1995] 4 All ER 1008; *R.* v. *Thornton (No. 2)* [1996] 2 All ER 1023.
5. On the logic of pleading both defenses together, see R. D. Mackay, "Pleading Provocation and Diminished Responsibility Together" (1988) *Criminal Law Review* 411.
6. See also Donald Nicolson and Rohit Sangvi, "Battered Women and Provocation: The Implications of R. v. Ahluwalia" (1993) *Criminal Law Reporter* 728; John Gardner and Timothy Macklem, "Nine Fallacies in R. v. Smith" (2001) *Criminal Law Reporter* 623.
7. See also Anthony Kenny, *Freewill and Responsibility* (London, 1978), pp. 82–83.
8. See, e.g., Aristotle, *Nicomachean Ethics* 1139^{a}4–5; Aristotle, *Eudemian Ethics* 1219^{b}29 ff.
9. See, e.g., Aristotle, *Rhetoric* 1355^{b}1; Aristotle, *Politics* 1253^{a}10.
10. Cf. Aristotle, *Nicomachean Ethics* 1147^{b}1 ff.

11. Cf. Aristotle, *Politics* 1253a10 ff.
12. See, e.g., Richard Rorty, "Is Truth a Goal of Enquiry? Davidson vs. Wright" (1995) 45 *Philosophical Quarterly* 281, p. 283; John Rawls, *A Theory of Justice* (Cambridge, MA, 1971), pp. 580–581.
13. See Richard Rorty, "Solidarity or Objectivity?," in Richard Rorty, *Objectivity, Relativism, and Truth* (Cambridge, 1991), pp. 21–34.
14. See also John McDowell, "Towards Rehabilitating Objectivity," in Robert Brandom, ed., *Rorty and His Critics* (Oxford, 2000), pp. 109–123.
15. See also George Fletcher, "The Nature of Justification," in Stephen Shute, John Gardner and Jeremy Horder, eds., *Action and Value in Criminal Law* (Oxford, 1993), pp. 264–276.
16. See G. W. F. Hegel, *Philosophy of Right* (T. M. Knox, trans., Oxford, 1942), p. 70.
17. Immanuel Kant, *The Metaphysics of Morals* (Mary Gregor, trans. and ed., Cambridge, 1996), p. 108.
18. Immanuel Kant, *Groundwork of the Metaphysic of Morals* (H. J. Paton, trans., New York, 1964), p. 64.
19. See, e.g., Aristotle, *Nicomachean Ethics* 1140a24–28.
20. See also Jonathan Bennett, "Accountability," in Zak van Straaten, ed., *Philosophical Subjects* (Oxford, 1980), pp. 14–47.
21. See also John Finnis, Joseph Boyle and Germain Grisez, *Nuclear Deterrence, Morality and Realism* (Oxford, 1988).
22. See generally John Martin, "Changing Accountability Relations: Politics, Consumers and the Market" (Paris, 1997).
23. See also Onora O'Neill, *A Question of Trust* (Cambridge, 2002), Chapter 3. Cf. Michael Power, *The Audit Society: Rituals of Verification* (Oxford, 1997).

10 Technocratic v. convivial accountability

1. Colin Scott, "Accountability in the Regulatory State" (2000) 27 *Journal of Law and Society* 38, p. 38.
2. Anne-Marie Slaughter, "Disaggregated Sovereignty: Towards the Public Accountability of Global Government Networks" (2004) *Government and Opposition* 159; Jody Freeman, "The Private Role in Public Governance" (2000) 75 *New York University Law Review* 101; Andrew Dunsire, "Manipulating Social Tensions: Collibration as an Alternative Mode of Government Intervention," Max Planck Institute Discussion Paper No. 93/7 (1993) (available at www.mpi-fg-koeln.mpg.de/pu/mpifg_dp/dp93–7.pdf), pp. 1–13, 32–43.
3. Jody Freeman, "Private Parties, Public Function and the Real Democracy Problem in the New Administrative Law?," in David Dzyenhaus, ed., *Recrafting the Rule of Law* (Oxford, 1999), p. 331.
4. Edward L. Rubin, *Beyond Camelot: Rethinking Politics and Law for the Modern State* (Princeton, 2005).
5. Martin Shapiro and Alec Stone Sweet, *On Law, Politics and Judicialization* (Oxford, 2002), p. 211.
6. *Ibid.*, p. 212.

7. Judith L. Goldstein *et al.*, eds., *Legalization and World Politics* (Cambridge, MA, 2001), p. ix.
8. *Ibid.*, p. 35.
9. Colin Scott, "The Juridification of Relations in the UK Utility Sector," in Julia Black *et al.*, eds., *Commercial Regulation and Judicial Review* (Oxford, 1998), p. 20. See also Adrienne Heritier and Moral Soriano Leonor, "Differentiating and Linking Politics and Adjudication: the Example of European Electricity Policy" (2002) 8 *European Law Journal* 363.
10. Sara Dillon, *International Trade and Economic Law and the European Union* (Oxford, 2001); John McGinnis and Mark Movsesian, "The World Trade Constitution: Reinforcing Democracy Through Trade" (2000) 114 *Harvard Law Review* 511; Alec Stone Sweet, *Governing with Judges – Constitutional Politics in Europe* (Oxford, 2000); Stephen Weatherill, "New Strategies for Managing the EC's Internal Market" (2000) 53 *Current Legal Problems* 595.
11. James Thayer, "The Trade of Cross-Border Gambling and Betting: The WTO Dispute between Antigua and the United States" (2004) *Duke Law and Technology, Review* 13.
12. Christopher Hood *et al.*, "Regulation of Government: Has It Increased, Is It Increasing, Should It Be Diminished?" (2000) 78 *Public Administration* 283, p. 284.
13. Pablo Spiller, "Regulatory Agencies and the Courts," in Peter Newman, ed., *The New Palgrave Dictionary of Economics and the Law* (New York, 1998), vol. 3, p. 263.
14. Bronwen Morgan, *Social Citizenship and the Shadow of Competition: The Bureaucratic Politics of Regulatory Justification* (Aldershot, 2003).
15. Morgan, *Social Citizenship and the Shadow of Competition*. See also Sweet, *Governing with Judges*, p. 13; Mark V. Tushnet, "Nonjudicial Review," Georgetown Public Law Research Paper No. 298007 (2001), pp. 3–4 (available from the SSRN Electronic Paper Collection, at http://papers.ssrn.com/sol3/papers.cfm/abstract_id=298007).
16. Goldstein *et al.*, *Legalization and World Politics*, p. 35.
17. Mauro Cappelletti, *Judicial Process in Comparative Perspective* (Oxford, 1989).
18. S. P. Sathe, *Judicial Activism in India: Transgressing Borders and Enforcing Limits* (New Delhi, 2002); Sweet, *Governing with Judges*.
19. Tushnet, "Nonjudicial Review"; Jeremy Waldron, *Law and Disagreement* (Oxford, 2001).
20. Stephen Gardbaum, "The New Commonwealth Model of Constitutionalism" (2001) 49 *American Journal of Comparative Law* 707; Tushnet, "Nonjudicial Review."
21. Tushnet, "Nonjudicial Review," pp. 3–4.
22. Peter Lindseth, "Delegation is Dead – Long Live Delegation: Managing the Democratic Disconnect in the European Market Polity," in Joerges and Dehousse, eds., *Good Governance in Europe's Integrated Market* (Oxford, 2002); Miguel Poiares Maduro, "Europe and the Constitution:

What if This Is as Good as It Gets?," in Joseph Weiler and Margareta Mind, eds., *Rethinking European Constitutionalism* (Cambridge, 2000), p. 74; McGinnis and Movsesian, "The World Trade Constitution: Reinforcing Democracy Through Trade."

23. Benjamin Barber, "Interview on American Political Culture" (2004) 3(4) *Logos* (http://www.logosjournal.com/issue_3.4/barber_interview.htm).
24. John Braithwaite, *Restorative Justice and Responsive Regulation* (Oxford, 2002).
25. Michael C. Dorf and Charles F. Sabel, "A Constitution of Democratic Experimentalism" (1998) 98 *Columbia Law Review* 267.
26. Charles F. Sabel, "Theory of a Real Time Revolution," in Charles Heckscher and Paul Adler, eds., *Collaborative Community* (Oxford, 2005, forthcoming).
27. *Ibid.*, pp. 12–13.
28. Dara O'Rourke, "Outsourcing Regulation: Analyzing Nongovernmental Systems of Labor Standards and Monitoring" (2003) 31 *Policy Studies Journal* 1.
29. Morgan, *Social Citizenship and the Shadow of Competition.*
30. Dawn Oliver, "The Underlying Values of Public and Private Law," in Michael Taggart, ed., *The Province of Administrative Law* (Oxford, 1997); Tony Prosser, *Law and Regulators* (Oxford, 1997); Mark Freedland and Silvana Sciarra, *Public Services and Citizenship in European Law* (Oxford, 1998).
31. Gerald E. Frug, "The Ideology of Bureaucracy" (1984) 97 *Harvard Law Review* 1276; Benjamin Barber, *Strong Democracy: Participatory Politics for a New Age* (Berkeley, 1984); Sol Picciotto, "Liberalization and Democratization: The Forum and the Hearth in the Era of Cosmopolitan Post-Industrial Capitalism" (2000) 63 *Law and Contemporary Problems* 157.
32. Thorsten Benner, Wolfgang H. Reinicke and Jan Martin Witte, "Multisectoral Networks in Global Governance: Towards a Pluralistic System of Accountability" (2004) 39 *Government and Opposition* 191.
33. Christian Joerges and Jürgen Neyer, "From Intergovernmental Bargaining to Deliberative Political Processes: The Constitutionalization of Comitology" (1997) 3 *European Law Journal* 274.
34. *Ibid.*; see also Slaughter, "Disaggregated Sovereignty."
35. Picciotto, "Liberalization and Democratization"; Claire Cutler, "Locating 'Authority' in the Global Political Economy" (1999) 43 *International Studies Quarterly* 59.
36. Bronwen Morgan, "The Regulatory Face of the Human Right to Water" (2004) 15 *Journal of Water Law* 179; Bronwen Morgan, "Social Protest against Privatization of Water: Forging Cosmopolitan Citizenship?," in Marie-Clair Cordonier Seggier and Justice Weeramantry, eds., *Sustainable Justice: Reconciling International Economic, Environmental and Social Law* (Leiden, 2005).
37. See also Roberto Unger, *Politics: A Work in Constructive Social Theory* (Cambridge, 1987).

38. Nina Laurie, "Establishing Development Orthodoxy: Negotiating Masculinities in the Water Sector" (2005) 36 *Development and Change* 527–549.
39. John Friedmann, "Citizenship: Statist, Cosmopolitan, Insurgent," in *The Prospect of Cities* (Minneapolis, 2002), p. 77.
40. Dan Jacobson, "If England Was What England Seems," *Times Literary Supplement*, March 11, 2005, pp. 11–12.
41. Ivan Illich, *Tools for Conviviality* (New York, 1973), p. 12.
42. Charles F. Sabel, "Theory of a Real Time Revolution," in Charles Heckscher and Paul Adler, eds., *Collaborative Community* (Oxford, 2005).

11 Understanding NGO-based social and environmental regulatory systems: why we need new models of accountability

1. Sasha Courville and Clifford Shearing, *Social and Environmental Certification Systems as Expressions of Nodal Governance – Working Draft* (Canberra, 2003).
2. See Dowdle (Chapter 1, this volume).
3. Saskia Sassen, "Making the Global Economy Run the Role of National States and Private Agents" (1999) 51 *International Social Science Journal* 409.
4. See Morgan (this volume).
5. Paul Wapner, "Introductory Essay: Paradise Lost? NGOs and Global Accountability" (2002) 3 *Chicago Journal of International Law* 155.
6. Anna Vakil, "Confronting the Classification Problem: Toward a Taxonomy of NGOs" (1997) 25 *World Development* 2057.
7. Debora Spar and James Dail, "Of Measurement and Mission: Accounting for Performance in Non-Governmental Organizations" (2002) 3 *Chicago Journal of International Law* 171. See also Ford (this volume).
8. "NGOs: Sins of the Secular Missionaries," *Economist*, January 29, 2000, p. 25.
9. John Clark, *The Role of Non-Profit Organizations in Development: The Experience of the World Bank* (Washington, DC, 1999); "NGOs: Sins of the Secular Missionaries," *Economist*, January 29, 2000, p. 25.
10. Robert O. Keohane, "Commentary on the Democratic Accountability of Non-Governmental Organizations" (2002) 3 *Chicago Journal of International Law* 477.
11. Lisa Jordan and Peter Van Tuijl, "Political Responsibility in Transnational NGO Advocacy" (2000) 28 *World Development* 2051. See also Morgan (this volume).
12. Alison Maitland, "Coping with a More Influential Role: Non-Governmental Organisations: The Higher Profile of Pressure Groups is Demanding Greater Accountability," *Financial Times*, February 13, 2002, p. 13.
13. Kenneth Anderson, "The Limits of Pragmatism in American Foreign Policy: Unsolicited Advice to the Bush Administration on Relations with International Nongovernmental Organizations" (2001) 2 *Chicago Journal of International Law* 371.

14. Peter Spiro, "Accounting for NGOs" (2002) 3 *Chicago Journal of International Law* 161.
15. Wapner, "Paradise Lost?"
16. Jim Lobe, "Politics: NGOs and Corporations Criticised on Accountability" (Global Information Network, New York, 2003).
17. Anthony Adair, "Codes of Conduct Are Good for NGOs Too" (1999) 51 *IPA Review* 26.
18. Adair, "Codes of Conduct Are Good for NGOs Too"; Spiro, "Accounting for NGOs."
19. Spiro, "Accounting for NGOs."
20. Jordan and van Tuijl, "Political Responsibility in Transnational NGO Advocacy."
21. See also Ford (this volume).
22. Maitland, "Coping with a More Influential Role."
23. Spiro, "Accounting for NGOs."
24. Albert O. Hirschman, *Exit, Voice and Loyalty: Responses to Decline in Firms, Organizations and States* (Cambridge, MA, 1970).
25. Spiro, "Accounting for NGOs."
26. Dorothea Hilhorst, "Being Good at Doing Good? Quality and Accountability of Humanitarian NGOs" (2002) 26 *Disasters* 193.
27. Hilhorst, "Being Good at Doing Good?"
28. Maitland, "Coping with a More Influential Role."
29. Spiro, "Accounting for NGOs."
30. Paul Wapner, "Defending Accountability in NGOs" (2002) 3 *Chicago Journal of International Law* 197.
31. *Ibid.*
32. Pat Mallet, *ISEAL Alliance: Strengthening Voluntary Standards and Verification* (Kaslo, 2002).
33. ISEAL, *ISEAL Alliance Vision Document* (Kaslo, 2002).
34. ISEAL, *Membership Application Procedures* (Kaslo, 2003).
35. IFOAM, *IFOAM Basic Standards – Final Revision Draft* (Bonn, 2004).
36. *Ibid.*
37. FLO International, *Annual Report 03/04: Shopping for a Better World* (Bonn, 2004).
38. The IAF eventually changed its membership criteria to allow international accreditation bodies to become members.
39. See General Agreement on Tariffs and Trade, October 30, 1947, 61 Stat. A-3, 55 UNTS 187, Arts. I and II.
40. See generally Agreement on Technical Barriers to Trade, April 15, 1994, Marrakesh Agreement Establishing the World Trade Organization, Annex 1A, in *Legal Instruments – Results of the Uruguay Round*, vol. 1 (1994), 18 ILM 1079 (1979) (available at http://docsonline.wto.org).
41. *Ibid.*
42. Cora Dankers, "Environmental and Social Standards, Certification and Labelling for Cash Crops," FAO Commodities and Trade Technical Paper 2, 1729–9829, Rome, 2003, p. 85.

43. ISEAL, *Code of Good Practice for Setting Social and Environmental Standards* (Bonn, 2004), p. 6.
44. ISEAL, *ISEAL Alliance Vision Document* (Kaslo, 2002).
45. Bernward Geier, "Reflections on Standards for Organic Agriculture" (1997) *Ecology and Farming* 10; Swedish National Board of Trade, *Market Access for Organic Agriculture Products from Developing Countries: Analysis of the EC Regulation (2092/91)* (Stockholm, 2003), p. 16.
46. Diane Bowen, "International Harmonization of Organic Standards and Guarantee Systems." In *OECD Workshop on Organic Agriculture* (Washington, DC, 2002).
47. ISEAL, *ISEAL Alliance Vision Document*; ISEAL, *Code of Good Practice for Setting Social and Environmental Standards*.
48. David Dumaresq and Sasha Courville, "The Future of Organic Regulation in Australia" (unpublished manuscript, 2001); Bowen, "International Harmonization of Organic Standards and Guarantee Systems."
49. Ken Commins, *The First Ten Years of the IFOAM Accreditation Programme* (Jamestown, ND, 2002).
50. Commins, *The First Ten Years of the IFOAM Accreditation Programme*.
51. IOAS, *List of IFOAM Accredited Certification Bodies* (Jamestown, ND, 2004), p. 12.
52. Ken Commins, *Overview of Current Status of Standards and Conformity Assessment Systems – Draft* (Geneva, 2003), p. 22.
53. Michael Edwards and David Hulme, *Beyond the Magic Bullet: NGO Performance and Accountability in the Post-Cold War World* (Hartford, 1996); Danielle Beu and M. Ronald Buckley, "The Hypothesized Relationship Between Accountability and Ethical Behavior" (2001) 34 *Journal of Business Ethics* 57; Joseph E. Stiglitz, "Democratizing the International Monetary Fund and the World Bank: Governance and Accountability" (2003) 16 *Governance* 111.
54. Hilhorst, "Being Good at Doing Good?"
55. *Ibid.*
56. Active Learning Network for Accountability and Performance in Humanitarian Action, *Humanitarian Action Key Messages: Improving Performance Through Improved Learning* (London, 2002); Rachel Houghton and Kate Robertson, eds., *ALNAP Annual Review Series: Humanitarian Action: Learning from Evaluation* (London, 2001).
57. Active Learning Network for Accountability and Performance in Humanitarian Action, *Humanitarian Action Key Messages: Improving Performance Through Improved Learning* (London, 2002).
58. Lorrae Van Kerkhoff and Sasha Courville, "Mutual Dependence, Mutual Strength: The Role of Trust in Social Learning," Social Learning for Sustainability Workshop, Canberra, 2003 (unpublished working paper).
59. Mashaw (this volume), p. 000 above.
60. *Ibid.*, p. 000 above.
61. *Ibid.*, p. 000 above.
62. See also Harrington and Turem (this volume).
63. See also Dorf (this volume).

64. Stiglitz, "Democratizing the International Monetary Fund and the World Bank: Governance and Accountability."
65. Spiro, "Accounting for NGOs."
66. Keohane, "Commentary on the Democratic Accountability of Non-Governmental Organizations."

12 Problem-solving courts and the judicial accountability deficit

1. Alexander M. Bickel, *The Least Dangerous Branch: The Supreme Court at the Bar of Politics* (Ann Arbor, 1962).
2. See also Dowdle (this volume, Chapter 13).
3. See, e.g., Ronald Dworkin, *Freedom's Law: The Moral Reading of the American Constitution* (Cambridge, MA, 1996), pp. 29–31.
4. Michael C. Dorf and Charles F. Sabel, "A Constitution of Democratic Experimentalism" (1998) 98 *Columbia Law Review* 267.
5. See, e.g., Charles F. Sabel *et al.*, "Beyond Backyard Environmentalism," in Joshua Cohen and Joel Rogers, eds., *Beyond Backyard Environmentalism* (Boston, 2000), p. 3 at pp. 8–9; Dorf and Sabel, "A Constitution of Democratic Experimentalism"; Michael C. Dorf and Charles Sabel, "Drug Treatment Courts and Emergent Experimentalist Government" (2000) 53 *Vanderbilt Law Review* 831; James S. Liebman and Charles F. Sabel, "A Public Laboratory Dewey Barely Imagined: The Emerging Model of School Governance and Legal Reform" (2003) 28 *New York University Review of Law and Social Change* 183. See Charles F. Sabel and William H. Simon, "Destabilization Rights: How Public Law Litigation Succeeds" (2004) 117 *Harvard Law Review* 1016.
6. See Rubin (this volume).
7. See Dorf and Sabel, "A Constitution of Democratic Experimentalism," pp. 292–314.
8. See Francis A. Allen, *The Decline of the Rehabilitative Ideal: Penal Policy and Social Purpose* (New Haven, 1981), pp. 12–31; Morris B. Hoffman, "Therapeutic Jurisprudence, Neo-Rehabilitationism, and Judicial Collectivism: The Least Dangerous Branch Becomes Most Dangerous" (2002) 29 *Fordham Urban Law Journal* 2063, p. 2079.
9. See, e.g., C. Peter Rydell and Susan S. Everingham, *Controlling Cocaine: Supply Versus Demand Programs* (Santa Monica, 1994). Steven Belenko, *Research on Drug Courts: A Critical Review* 2001 (National Center on Addiction and Substance Abuse at Columbia University, June 2001) (available at http://www.casacolumbia.org./absolutenm/articlefiles/researchondrug.pdf).
10. See Office of Justice Programs (OJP) Drug Court Clearinghouse and Technical Assistance Project at American University, *Summary of Drug Court Activity by State and County* (May 27, 2004) (available at http://spa.american.edu/justice/publications/drgchart2k.pdf).
11. See Dorf and Sabel, "Drug Treatment Courts and Emergent Experimentalist Government," pp. 865–868.
12. I have served as an informal consultant on this project.

13. See Abram Chayes, "The Role of the Judge in Public Law Litigation" (1976) 89 *Harvard Law Review* 1281; Owen M. Fiss, "The Supreme Court 1978 Term – Foreword: The Forms of Justice" (1979) 93 *Harvard Law Review* 1.
14. See Donald L. Horowitz, *The Courts and Social Policy* (Washington, DC, 1977), pp. 17–19. But see Malcolm Feeley and Edward Rubin, *Judicial Policy Making and the Modern State* (Cambridge, 1998).
15. See Malcolm Feeley and Edward Rubin, "Judicial Policy Making and Litigation Against the Government" (2003) 5 *University of Pennsylvania Journal of Constitutional Law* 617.
16. 48 P 3d 110 (Okla. Crim. App. 2002).
17. *Ibid.*, p. 112.
18. See *ibid.*, p. 115.
19. See *ibid.* (Lumpkin J concurring specially).
20. See Ian R. MacNeil, "Relational Contract Theory: Challenges and Queries" (2000) 94 *Northwestern University Law Review* 877.
21. See Dorf and Sabel, "Drug Treatment Courts and Emergent Experimentalist Government," pp. 832–833.
22. See Jo Ann Ferdinand, Remarks, in Jo Ann Ferdinand *et al.*, "The Judicial Perspective," in "The Eleventh Annual Symposium on Contemporary Urban Challenges: Problem Solving Courts: From Adversarial Litigation to Innovative Jurisprudence" (2002) 23 *Fordham Urban Law Journal* 2011, p. 2012.
23. See, e.g., Derek A. Denckla, "Forgiveness as a Problem-Solving Tool in the Courts: A Brief Response to the Panel on Forgiveness in Criminal Law" (2000) 27 *Fordham Urban Law Journal* 1613, p. 1614.
24. See Harrington and Umut (this volume).
25. See Sabel and Simon, "Destabilization Rights."
26. See Harrington and Umut (this volume); see also Helen Hershkoff, "Positive Rights and State Constitutions: The Limits of Federal Rationality Review" (1999) 112 *Harvard Law Review* 1131, pp. 1181–1182.
27. See Ian Ayres and Robert Gertner, "Filling Gaps in Incomplete Contracts: An Economic Theory of Default Rules" (1989) 99 *Yale Law Journal* 87, pp. 91–93; Bradley C. Karkkainen, "Toward a Smarter NEPA" (2002) 102 *Columbia Law Review* 903, p. 936, n. 141.
28. See Sabel and Simon, "Destabilization Rights."
29. See also Chayes, "The Role of the Judge in Public Law Litigation," p. 1304.
30. See Feeley and Rubin, "Judicial Policy Making," p. 638.
31. See, e.g., New York State Commission on Drugs and the Courts, "Confronting the Cycle of Addiction and Recidivism: A Report to Chief Judge Judith S. Kaye" (Albany, June 2000) (available at http://www.courts.state.ny.us/reports/addictionrecidivism.shtml). See also National District Attorneys Association, "Press Release: Nation's Prosecutors Support the 'Prosecution Drug Treatment Alternative to Prison Act'" (February 13, 2001) (available at http://www.ndaa-apri.org/newsroom/pr_prosecution_drug_treatment.html).

32. See Harrington and Umut (this volume).
33. See Dowdle (this volume, Chapter 13).
34. See Eric Lane, "Due Process and Problem Solving Courts" (2003) 30 *Fordham Urban Law Journal* 955, p. 958.
35. See generally Jeffrey Abramson, *We, The Jury: The Jury System and the Ideal of Democracy* (New York, 1994).
36. See, e.g., Federal Rule of Criminal Procedure 11(c)(4).
37. Dorf and Sabel, "A Constitution of Democratic Experimentalism," pp. 409–410.
38. See Albert O. Hirschmann, *Exit, Voice and Loyalty: Responses to Decline in Firms, Organizations, and States* (Cambridge, MA, 1970).
39. See also Mashaw (this volume).
40. See Archon Fung and Eric Olin Wright, "Countervailing Power in Empowered Participatory Governance," in Archon Fung and Eric Olin Wright, eds., *Deepening Democracy* (London, 2003), p. 259.
41. See also Jean L. Cohen, *Regulating Intimacy: A New Legal Paradigm* (Princeton, 2002) p. 178.
42. See John Rawls, *Political Liberalism* (New York, 1996) p. 19.
43. See Ronald Dworkin, *Law's Empire* (Cambridge, MA, 1986) pp. 239–240.
44. See Gerald J. Postema, "'Protestant' Interpretation and Social Practices" (1986) 6 *Law and Philosophy* 283.
45. Michael C. Dorf, "The Supreme Court 1997 Term – Foreword: The Limits of Socratic Deliberation" (1998) 112 *Harvard Law Review* 4, pp. 33–43.
46. See Frank H. Easterbrook, "Ways of Criticizing the Court" (1982) 95 *Harvard Law Review* 802; Lewis A. Kornhauser and Lawrence Sager, "Unpacking the Court" (1986) 96 *Yale Law Journal* 82; Matthew L. Spitzer, "Multicriteria Choice Processes: An Application of Public Choice Theory to *Bakke*, the FCC, and the Courts" (1979) 88 *Yale Law Journal* 717.
47. See Susan Sturm, "Second Generation Employment Discrimination: A Structural Approach" (2001) 101 *Columbia Law Review* 458, pp. 492–519.
48. Cynthia L. Estlund, "Working Together: The Workplace, Civil Society, and the Law" (2000) 89 *Georgetown Law Journal* 1, p. 4.
49. 347 US 483 (1954).
50. See Herbert Wechsler, "Toward Neutral Principles of Constitutional Law" (1959) 73 *Harvard Law Review* 1, pp. 22, 34.
51. See Gerald Rosenberg, *The Hollow Hope: Can Courts Bring About Social Change?* (Chicago, 1991). See also Stephen L. Carter, "Do Courts Matter?" (1992) 90 *Michigan Law Review* 1216, p. 1221.
52. *Brown* v. *Board of Education* (Brown II)., 349 US 294, 301 (1955).
53. See generally Michael William Dowdle, "Of Parliaments, Pragmatism, and the Dynamics of Constitutional Development: The Curious Case of China" (2002) 35 *New York University Journal of International Law and Politics* 1, pp. 27–28, 152–161.

54. Cf. Liebman and Sabel, "A Public Laboratory Dewey Barely Imagined," pp. 201–283.
55. See *Faragher* v. *City of Boca Raton*, 524 US 775, 780 (1998); *Burlington Industries Inc.* v. *Ellerth*, 524 US 742, 765 (1998). See generally Dorf, "The Supreme Court 1997 Term," pp. 78–79.
56. See *Miranda* v. *Arizona*, 384 US 436, 467 (1966). See generally Michael C. Dorf and Barry Friedman, "Shared Constitutional Interpretation" (2000) *Supreme Court Review* 61; Dorf and Sabel, "A Constitution of Democratic Experimentalism," pp. 452–457.
57. Daryl J. Levinson, "Rights Essentialism and Remedial Equilibration" (1999) 99 *Columbia Law Review* 857, p. 858.
58. See *Texas* v. *Johnson*, 491 US 397 (1989).
59. See *United States* v. *O'Brien*, 391 US 367, 377 (1968).
60. See *Johnson*, 491 US 397, 430.
61. See Katharine Q. Seelye, "House Easily Passes Amendment to Ban Desecration of Flag," *New York Times*, June 29, 1995, p. A1; Helen Dewar, "Senate Falls Short on Flag Amendment," *Washington Post*, December 13, 1995, p. A1.
62. See *United States* v. *Eichman*, 496 US 310 (1990).
63. 381 US 479 (1965).
64. See *ibid.*, at 514–515 (Black J. dissenting).
65. 410 US 113 (1973).
66. See Frederick Douglass, "The Constitution of the United States: Is It Pro-Slavery or Anti-Slavery?," in Philip S. Foner, ed., *Frederick Douglass: Selected Speeches and Writings* (Chicago, 1999) (originally published 1860) p. 379.
67. Cf. Michael C. Dorf, "The Paths to Legal Equality: A Reply to Dean Sullivan" (2002) 90 *California Law Review* 791, pp. 801–807.
68. *Dred Scott* v. *Sandford*, 60 US (19 How.) 393, 455 (1856).
69. See, e.g., Dworkin, *Law's Empire*, pp. 106–107.
70. See, e.g., Larry Kramer, "The Supreme Court 2000 Term – Foreword: We the Court" (2001) 115 *Harvard Law Review* 4, p. 5; Jeremy Waldron, *Law and Disagreement* (Oxford, 1999) pp. 90–91.
71. See Dorf and Friedman, "Shared Constitutional Interpretation," pp. 67, 81–83.
72. See Mark Tushnet, *Taking the Constitution Away from the Courts* (Princeton, 1999) pp. 127, 163–165.

13 Public accountability in alien terrain: exploring for constitutional accountability in the People's Republic of China

1. See generally Clifford Geertz, *Local Knowledge: Further Essays in Interpretive Anthropology* (New York, 1983).
2. See also Dowdle (this volume, Chapter 1.
3. See, e.g., L. Neville Brown and John S. Bell, *French Administrative Law* (Oxford, 1998), pp. 3–4.
4. See, e.g., William P. Alford and Benjamin L. Liebman, "Clean Air, Clear Processes? The Struggle over Air Pollution Law in the People's Republic of China" (2001) 52 *Hastings Law Journal* 703.

5. See generally Michael W. Dowdle, "Of Parliaments, Pragmatism, and the Dynamics of Constitutional Development: The Curious Case of China" (2002) 35 *New York University Journal of International Law and Politics* 1; Michael W. Dowdle, "The Constitutional Development and Operations of the National People's Congress" (1997) 12 *Columbia Journal of Asian Legal Studies* 1.
6. See, e.g., Woodrow Wilson, *Constitutional Government in the United States* (New York, 1911), pp. 58–68, see also Robert G. Vaughn, "Ethics in Government and the Vision of Public Service" (1990) 58 *George Washington Law Review* 417; cf. Rubin (this volume).
7. See, e.g., Alexis de Tocqueville, *Democracy in America* (Garden City, NY, 1969), pp. 62–63.
8. See, e.g., Julian N. Eule, "Judicial Review of Direct Democracy" (1990) 99 *Yale Law Journal* 1503, pp. 1522–1526.
9. See Gordon Wood, *The Creation of the American Republic 1776–1787* (Chapel Hill, 1969), pp. 46–48, 53–65, 75–90; Herbert J. Storing, *What the Anti-Federalists Were For* (Chicago, 1981), p. 84, n. 12.
10. Toqueville, *Democracy in America*, pp. 71–80, 161. See also Stephen Skowronek, *Building a New American State: The Expansion of National Administrative Capacities, 1877–1920* (New York, 1982), pp. 24–31.
11. See, e.g., Wilson, *Constitutional Government*, pp. 65–68. Cf. Skowronek, *Building a New American State*, pp. 177–211.
12. Toqueville, *Democracy in America*, pp. 62–98.
13. See Alfred D. Chandler Jr, *The Visible Hand: The Managerial Revolution in American Business* (Cambridge, MA, 1977).
14. See generally Michael J. Piore and Charles F. Sabel, *The Second Industrial Divide: Possibilities for Prosperity* (New York, 1984), pp. 49–54; cf. Chandler, *The Visible Hand*, p. 8.
15. See, e.g., Rubin (this volume).
16. See, e.g., Charles F. Sabel, "Learning by Monitoring: The Institutions of Economic Development," in Neil J. Smelser and Richard Swedberg, eds., *Handbook of Economic Sociology* (Princeton, 1994).
17. See generally James C. Scott, *Seeing Like a State: How Certain Schemes to Improve the Human Condition Have Failed* (New Haven, 1998).
18. See generally Adam Przeworski *et al.*, eds., *Democracy, Accountability, and Representation* (New York, 1999).
19. See, e.g., Lon L. Fuller, *The Morality of Law* (New Haven, 1969), p. 39.
20. See Piore and Sabel, *The Second Industrial Divide*, pp. 55–65; see also Chandler, *The Visible Hand*, pp. 10–11, 212–214.
21. See generally Martin J. Sklar, *The Corporate Reconstruction of American Capitalism, 1890–1916: The Market, the Law, and Politics* (New York, 1988).
22. See Piore and Sabel, *The Second Industrial Divide*, pp. 55–65.
23. See Mark A. Covaleski, Mark W. Dirsmith and Sajay Samuel, "The Use of Accounting Information in Governmental Regulation and Public Administration: The Impact of John R. Commons and Early Institutional Economists" (1995) 22 *The Accounting Historian's Journal* 1.

24. See Paul J. Miranti, Jr, "Measurement and Organizational Effectiveness," p. 186.
25. See Chandler, *The Visible Hand*, p. 464. See also A. C. Littleton, *Accounting Evolution to 1900* (New York, 1966), p. 366.
26. See also Michael Hatfield, *A History of Accounting Thought* (Huntington, NY, 1977), p. 167.
27. See generally David Solomons, "The Historical Development of Costing," in David Solomons, ed., *Studies in Cost Analysis* (Homewood, IL, 1968).
28. See Paul J. Miranti, Jr, "Measurement and Organizational Effectiveness: The ICC and Accounting-Based Regulation, 1887–1940" (1990) 19 *Business and Economic History* 183, pp. 184–185.
29. See generally Covaleski *et al.*, "The Use of Accounting Information in Governmental Regulation and Public Administration."
30. See John Fabian Witt, "Speedy Fred Taylor and the Ironies of Enterprise Liability" (2003) 103 *Columbia Law Review* 1, pp. 30–35; Richard N. Langlois, David J. Denault and Samson M. Kimenyi, "Bursting Boilers and the Federal Power Redux: The Evolution of Safety on the Western Rivers," Economics Working Paper Archive at WUSTL: Economic History 9503002 (St. Louis, 1995); Albert Fishlow, "Productivity and Technological Change in the Railroad Sector, 1840–1910," in National Bureau of Economic Research, *Output, Employment and Productivity in the United States after 1800* (New York, 1966), vol. 30, pp. 583–646.
31. Randy S. Rabinowitz and Mark M. Hager, "Designing Health and Safety: Workplace Hazard Regulation in the United States and Canada" (2000) 33 *Cornell International Law Journal* 373, p. 375, n. 3.
32. See, e.g., Skowronek, *Building a New American State*, p. 153; Covaleski *et al.*, "The Use of Accounting Information in Governmental Regulation and Public Administration." See also Sklar, *The Corporate Reconstruction of American Capitalism.*
33. See Peter H. Argersinger, "New Perspectives on Election Fraud in the Gilded Age" (1985–1986) 100 *Political Science Quarterly* 669.
34. See, e.g., Woodrow Wilson, "The Issues of Reform," in William Bennett Munro, ed., *The Initiative Referendum and Recall* (New York, 1912); see also Theodore Roosevelt, "Nationalism and Popular Rule," in William Bennett Munro, ed., *The Initiative Referendum and Recall* (New York, 1912), p. 63.
35. See Lewis L. Gould, *The Modern American Presidency* (Lawrence, 2003), pp. 1–24. See also Wilson, *Constitutional Government*, pp. 58–59.
36. See generally Walter Dean Burnham, "The System of 1896: An Analysis," in Paul Kleppner *et al.*, eds., *The Evolution of American Electoral Systems* (Westport, CT, 1981).
37. See Skowronik, *Building a New American State*, pp. 255–259; Carol W. Gelderman, *All the Presidents' Words: The Bully Pulpit and the Creation of the Virtual Presidency* (New York, 1997), p. 2.
38. See Gould, *The Modern American Presidency*, pp. 1–34; Gelderman, *All the Presidents' Words*, pp. 1–12.

39. Cf. Samual P. Hays, *The Response to Industrialism* (Chicago, 1995), pp. 69–91.
40. See Burnham, "The System of 1896."
41. See generally Mancur Olson, *The Logic of Collective Action: Public Goods and the Theory of Groups* (Cambridge, MA, 1971).
42. See Clifton K. Yearling, *The Money Machines: The Breakdown and Reform of Governmental and Party Finance in the North, 1860–1920* (Albany, 1970), pp. 253–269. See also James A. Farley, *Behind the Ballots* (New York, 1938), p. 236; see, e.g., George M. Reynolds, *Machine Politics in New Orleans* (New York, 1936), pp. 163–166; C. R. Fish, *The Civil Service and Patronage* (Cambridge, MA, 1904).
43. See Skowronik, *Building a New American State*, p. 196.
44. Chester Lloyd Jones, "Spoils and Party" (1916) 64 *Annals* 66.
45. Yearling, *The Money Machines*, pp. 193–223.
46. Bradley A. Smith, "Campaign Finance Regulation: Faulty Assumptions and Undemocratic Consequences," in Annelise Anderson, ed., *Political Money: Deregulating American Politics – Selected Writings on Campaign Finance Reform* (Palo Alto, 2000), pp. 52–54.
47. See also Chester Lloyd Jones, "Spoils and Party" (1916) 64 *Annals* 66.
48. See generally A. James Reichley, *The Life of the Parties: A History of American Political Parties* (Lanham, MD, 2000), pp. 210–216.
49. See Richard Hofstadter, *The Age of Reform: From Bryan to F. D. R.* (New York, 1955), p. 108.
50. See, e.g., Adam Przeworski, Michael E. Alvarez, Jose Antonio Cheibub and Fernando Limongi, *Democracy and Development: Political Institutions and Well Being in the World 1950–1990* (Cambridge, 2000), pp. 92–103; Christopher Clague, Suzanne Gleason and Stephen Knack, "Determinants of Lasting Democracy in Poor Countries: Culture, Development, and Institutions" (2001) 573 *Annals of the American Academy of Political and Social Science* 16.
51. Ronald Inglehart, *Modernization and Postmodernization: Cultural, Economic, and Political Change in 43 Societies* (Princeton, 1997).
52. See Przeworski *et al.*, *Democracy and Development*, pp. 92–103.
53. Cf. Larry Diamond, "Can the Whole World Become Democratic? Democracy, Development, and International Policies," Center for the Study of Democracy Paper 03-05 (Irvine, CA, 2003).
54. Katharina Pistor and Philip A. Wellons, *The Role of Law and Legal Institutions in Asian Economic Development 1960–1995* (Hong Kong, 1998), p. 111.
55. See, e.g., Charles Sabel, "Learning by Monitoring."
56. See generally J. Mark Ramseyer and Francis McCall Rosenbluth, *Japan's Political Marketplace* (Cambridge, MA, 1993).
57. See John O. Haley, *Authority Without Power: Law and the Japanese Paradox* (New York, 1991).
58. See Tom Ginsburg, *Judicial Review in New Democracies: Constitutional Courts in Asian Cases* (New York, 2003). But see J. Mark Ramseyer and Francis McCall Rosenbluth, *Japan's Political Marketplace*.

59. See generally Pasuk Phongpaicht and Chris Baker, *Thailand's Economic Crisis* (Singapore, 2001), pp. 35–82, 97–104.
60. See generally Frederic C. Deyo, "Reform, Globalization and Crisis: Reconstructing Thai Labor" (2000) 42 *Journal of Industrial Relations* 258; see also Pasuk and Baker, *Thailand's Economic Crisis*, p. 82.
61. Pasuk and Baker, *Thailand's Economic Crisis*, pp. 80–81.
62. *Ibid.*, p. 81.
63. *Ibid.*
64. See United Nations Economic and Social Commission for Asia and the Pacific, "Social Safety Nets in Thailand: Analysis and Prospects," in *Strengthening Policies and Programmes on Social Safety Nets: Issues, Recommendations and Selected Studies* (Social Policy Paper No. 8, ST/ESCAP/2163) (New York, 2001), pp. 57–108.
65. Cf. E. P. Thompson, "Work-Discipline, and Industrial Capitalism" (1967) 38 *Past and Present* 56.
66. Cf. Bob Jessop, "Regulationist and Autopoieticist Reflections on Polanyi's Account of Market Economies and the Market Society" (2001) 6 *New Political Economy* 213, p. 213.
67. Skowronek, *Building a New American State*, pp. 24–31.
68. See generally Herbert Jacob, "Courts as Organizations," in K. Boyum and L. Mather, eds., *Empirical Theories About Courts* (New York, 1983). Cf. Mirjan Damaska, "Structures of Authority and Comparative Criminal Procedure" (1975) 84 *Yale Law Journal* 480, p. 515.
69. See Dorf, (this volume).
70. Skowronek, *Building a New American State*, pp. 24–31.
71. *Ibid.*, p. 287. See also Morton J. Horwitz, *The Transformation of American Law, 1870–1960: The Crisis of Legal Orthodoxy* (New York, 1992), p. 126.
72. Cf. Gunther Teubner, "Legal Irritants: How Unifying Law Ends Up in New Differences," in Peter A. Hall and David Soskice, eds., *Varieties of Capitalism: The Institutional Foundations of Comparative Advantage* (Oxford, 2001), pp. 417–441.
73. See generally Howard Margolis, *Patterns, Thinking, and Cognition: A Theory of Judgment* (Chicago, 1987). See also Francisco J. Varela, Evan Thompson and Eleanor Rosch, *The Embodied Mind: Cognitive Science and Human Experience* (Cambridge, MA, 1991).
74. See Albert Venn Dicey, *Introduction to the Study of the Law of the Constitution* (London, 1959), pp. 369–405.
75. See Sir William Wade and Christopher Forsyth, *Administrative Law* (9th ed., Oxford, 2004), pp. 18–19.
76. *Ibid.*, pp. 15–16. See also JUSTICE-All Souls Review Committee, *Administrative Justice: Some Necessary Reforms* (Oxford, 1988).
77. See, e.g., L. Neville Brown and John S. Bell, *French Administrative Law* (4th ed., Oxford, 1993), pp. 3–4.
78. See, e.g., *Council of Civil Service Unions* v. *Minister for the Civil Service* [1985] AC 374, 410 (opinion of Lord Diplock).
79. But see Tony Saich, "Negotiating the State: The Development of Social Organizations in China" (2000) 161 *China Quarterly* 124.

80. See generally Dowdle, "Constitutional Development," pp. 1–30; Dowdle, "Of Parliaments, Pragmatism," pp. 2–6.
81. Dowdle, "Of Parliaments, Pragmatism," pp. 70–76, 162–172.
82. See also Dowdle, "Constitutional Development," pp. 8–11.
83. See generally Alford and Liebman, "Clean Air, Clear Processes?"
84. See *ibid.*, pp. 713–716.
85. See also Dowdle, "Constitutional Development," pp. 41–45.
86. See Alford and Liebman, "Clean Air, Clear Processes?," pp. 717–718.
87. See *ibid.*, pp. 726–733.
88. See *ibid.*, pp. 733–736.
89. *Ibid.*, p. 748.
90. See, e.g., *ibid.*, p. 704.
91. *Ibid.*, p. 748.
92. *Ibid.*, p. 741.
93. *Ibid.*, p. 739.
94. *Ibid.*, pp. 747–748.
95. *Ibid.*, p. 739.
96. *Ibid.*, p. 740.
97. *Ibid.*, p. 741.
98. *Ibid.*, p. 732.
99. *Ibid.*, pp. 729–730.
100. *Ibid.*, p. 748.
101. *Ibid.*, p. 736.
102. See generally Ronald S. Burt, *Structural Holes: The Social Structure of Competition* (Cambridge, MA, 1992).
103. See also Ronald S. Burt, "The Social Capital of Opinion Leaders" (1999) 566 *Annals of the American Academy of Political and Social Science* 37.
104. See also Dowdle, "Of Parliaments, Pragmatism," pp. 162–183.
105. See also *ibid.*, pp. 184–185.
106. Alford and Liebman, "Clean Air, Clear Processes?," pp. 747–748.
107. See generally Haley, *Authority Without Power.*
108. Cf. Randall P. Peerenboom, *China's Long March Toward Rule of Law* (New York, 2002), pp. 424–431.
109. Alford and Liebman, "Clean Air, Clear Processes," p. 748.
110. See Michael C. Dorf, "The Supreme Court 1997 Term – Foreword: The Limits of Socratic Deliberation" (1998) 112 *Harvard Law Review* 4, pp. 33–43.
111. See also Dowdle, "Of Parliaments, Pragmatism," pp. 183–194.
112. Gardner (this volume).

BIBLIOGRAPHY

I. BOOKS, ARTICLES AND UNPUBLISHED STUDIES

Abramson, Harold I. 1989. "A Fifth Branch of Government: The Private Regulators and Their Constitutionality." *Hastings Constitutional Law Quarterly* 16: 165–220.

Abramson, Jeffrey. 1994. *We, The Jury: The Jury System and the Ideal of Democracy*. New York: Basic Books.

Ackerman, Bruce. 1980. *Social Justice in the Liberal State*. New Haven: Yale University Press.

Adair, Anthony. 1999. "Codes of Conduct Are Good for NGOs Too." *IPA Review* 51(1): 26–27.

Adji, Souley. 2002. "Globalization and Union Strategies in Niger." In *Organized Labour in the 21st Century* (A. V. Jose, ed.). Geneva: International Institute for Labour Studies.

Administrative Conference of the United States. 1993. "Recommendation No. 86-3: Agencies' Use of Alternative Means of Dispute Resolution." *Code of Federal Regulations* 1: 305.86-3.

AFL–CIO. 2001. *AFL–CIO Twenty-Fourth Biennial Convention 2001: Executive Council Report*. Washington, DC: AFL–CIO.

Alford, John and David Brady. 1993. "Personal and Partisan Advantage in Elections." In *Congress Reconsidered* (Lawrence Dodd and Bruce I. Oppenheimer, eds.). 5th ed., Washington, DC: CQ Press, p. 149.

Alford, William P. and Benjamin L. Liebman. 2001. "Clean Air, Clear Processes? The Struggle over Air Pollution Law in the People's Republic of China." *Hastings Law Journal* 52: 703–748.

Allen, Anita L. 2003. *Why Privacy Isn't Everything: Feminist Reflections on Personal Accountability*. Lanham: Rowman & Littlefield.

Allen, Francis A. 1981. *The Decline of the Rehabilitative Ideal: Penal Policy and Social Purpose*. New Haven: Yale University Press.

ALNAP. 2002. "Humanitarian Action Key Messages: Improving Performance through Improved Learning." London: Active Learning Network for Accountability and Performance in Humanitarian Action.

Althouse, Ann. 2004. "Vanguard States, Laggard States: Federalism and Constitutional Rights." *University of Pennsylvania Law Review* 152: 1745–1796.

Aman, Alfred C. 1992. *Administrative Law in a Global Era*. Ithaca: Cornell University Press.

1997. "Administrative Law for a New Century." In *The Province of Administrative Law* (Michael Taggart, ed.). Oxford: Hart Publishing, pp. 90–117.

2001. "The Limits of Globalization and the Future of Administrative Law: From Government to Governance." *Indiana Journal of Global Legal Studies* 8: 379–400.

2004. *The Democracy Deficit: Taming Globalization through Law Reform*. New York: NYU Press.

Amar, Akhil. 1991. "Some New World Lessons for the Old World." *University of Chicago Law Review* 58: 483.

American Center for International Labor Solidarity. 1999. "Monthly Report for July." Jakarta: American Center for International Labor Solidarity.

1999. "Monthly Report for May." Jakarta: American Center for International Labor Solidarity.

Amnesty International. 1997. "Statement by Amnesty International on the Occasion of the World Bank/IMF Annual Meetings Hong Kong" (September 23, 1997) (AI Index: IOR 30/04/97) (available at http://web.amnesty.org/library/Index/ENGIOR300041997?open&of=ENG-312/).

Anderson, Kenneth. 2001. "The Limits of Pragmatism in American Foreign Policy: Unsolicited Advice to the Bush Administration on Relations with International Nongovernmental Organizations." *Chicago Journal of International Law* 2: 371–388.

Anechiarico, Frank and James B. Jacobs. 1996. *The Pursuit of Absolute Integrity: How Corruption Control Makes Government Ineffective*. Chicago: University of Chicago Press.

Argersinger, Peter H. 1985–1986. "New Perspectives on Election Fraud in the Gilded Age." *Political Science Quarterly* 100: 669–687.

Aristotle. *Eudemian Ethics*.

Nicomachean Ethics.

Politics.

Rhetoric.

Aronson, Mark. 1997. "A Public Lawyer's Responses to Privatisation and Outsourcing." In *The Province of Administrative Law* (Michael Taggart, ed.). Oxford: Hart Publishing, pp. 40–70.

Arrow, Kenneth and Leonid Hurweiz. 1960. "Decentralization and Computation in Resource Allocation." *Essays in Economics and Econometrics: A Volume in Honor of Harold Hotelling* (Ralph Pfourts, ed.). Chapel Hill: University of North Carolina Press, pp. 34–104.

Asimow, Michael and Marsha N. Cohen. 2002. *California Administrative Law*. St. Paul: West Publishing.

Auerbach, Jerold S. 1977. *Unequal Justice: Lawyers and Social Change in Modern America*. New York: Oxford University Press.

Ayres, Ian and John Braithwaite. 1992. *Responsive Regulation: Transcending the Deregulation Debate*. New York: Oxford University Press.

Ayres, Ian and Robert Gertner. 1989. "Filling Gaps in Incomplete Contracts: An Economic Theory of Default Rules." *Yale Law Journal* 99: 87–130.

Bakhtin, M. M. 1986. *Speech Genres and Other Late Essays* (Vern W. McGee, trans., Caryl Emerson and Michael Holquist, eds.). Austin: Texas University Press.

Ball, Howard (ed.). 1984. *Federal Administrative Agencies*. Englewood Cliffs, NJ: Prentice Hall.

Barber, Benjamin. 1984. *Strong Democracy: Participatory Politics for a New Age*. Berkeley: University of California Press.

2004. "Interview on American Political Culture." *Logos*. Issue 3.4 (available at http://www.logosjournal.com/issue_3.4/barber_interview.htm) (last accessed April 19, 2005).

Barraclough, Geoffrey. 1984. *The Origins of Modern Germany*. New York: W. W. Norton.

Bartels, Larry. 1996. "Uninformed Votes: Information Effects in Presidential Elections." *American Journal of Political Science* 40: 194–230.

Baudrillard, Jean. 1983. *In the Shadow of the Silent Majorities* (Paul Foss, Paul Patton and John Johnston, trans.). New York: Semiotext(e).

1983. *Simulations* (Paul Foss, Paul Patton and Philip Beitchman, trans.). New York: Semiotext(e).

Bazemore, Gordon and Mara Schiff. 2005. *Juvenile Justice Reform and Restorative Justice*. Portland: Willan Publishing.

Beale, Hugh and Tony Dugdale. 1975. "Contracts Between Businessmen: Planning and the Use of Contractual Remedies." *British Journal of Law and Society* 2: 45–60.

Beam, David R. and Timothy J. Conlan. 2002. "Grants." In *The Tools of Government: A Guide to the New Governance* (Lester M. Salamon, ed.). New York: Oxford University Press, pp. 340–380.

Bedzek, Barbara L. 2001. "Contractual Welfare: Non-Accountability and Diminished Democracy in Local Government Contracts for Welfare-to-Work Services." *Fordham Urban Law Journal* 28: 1559–1610.

Beermann, Jack M. "Privatization and Political Accountability." *Fordham Urban Law Journal* 28: 1507–1557.

Behn, Robert. 2001. *Rethinking Democratic Accountability*. Washington, DC: Brookings Institution.

Belenko, Steven. 2001. *Research on Drug Courts: A Critical Review 2001*. New York: National Center on Addiction and Substance Abuse at Columbia University (available at http://www.casacolumbia.org/absolutenm/articlefiles/researchondrug.pdf).

Bendix, Reinhart. 1977. *Nation-Building and Citizenship: Studies of Our Changing Social Order*. Berkeley: University of California Press.

Benner, Thorsten, Wolfgang H. Reinicke and Jan Martin Witte. 2004. "Multisectoral Networks in Global Governance: Towards a Pluralistic System of Accountability." *Government and Opposition* 2004: 191–210.

Bennett, Jonathan. 1980. "Accountability." *Philosophical Subjects: Essays Presented to P. F. Strawson* (Z. Van Straaten, ed.). Oxford: Clarendon Press, pp. 14–47.

Bensch, Jennifer A. 1993. "Government in the Sunshine Act: Seventeen Years Later: Has Government Let the Sun Shine In?" *George Washington Law Review* 61: 1475–1513.

Berelson, Bernard, Paul Lazersfeld and William McPhee. 1954. *Voting: A Study of Opinion Formation in a Presidential Campaign*. Chicago: University of Chicago Press.

Berger, Peter L. and Thomas Luckman. 1966. *The Social Construction of Reality: A Treatise in the Sociology of Knowledge*. Garden City, NY: Doubleday.

Berkowitz, Edward D. 1987. *Disabled Policy: America's Programs for the Handicapped*. New York: Cambridge University Press.

Better Regulation Task Force. 2000. "Alternatives to State Regulation." London: Cabinet Office.

Beu, Danielle and M. Ronald Buckley. 2001. "The Hypothesized Relationship Between Accountability and Ethical Behavior." *Journal of Business Ethics* 34: 57–73.

Bickel, Alexander M. 1962. *The Least Dangerous Branch: The Supreme Court at the Bar of Politics*. Ann Arbor: University of Michigan Press.

Black, Julia. 1996. "Constitutionalising Self-Regulation." *Modern Law Review* 59: 24–56.

2001. "Decentring Regulation: The Role of Regulation and Self-Regulation in a 'Post-Regulatory' World." *Current Legal Problems* 54: 103–146.

Blau, Peter and Richard Scott. 1962. *Formal Organizations: A Comparative Approach*. San Francisco: Chandler Publishing Co.

Bohman, James and William Rehg. 1997. *Deliberative Democracy: Essays on Reason and Politics*. Cambridge, MA: MIT Press.

Bok, Derek. *The Trouble With Government*. Cambridge, MA: Harvard University Press.

Boston, Jonathan *et al.* 1996. *Public Management: The New Zealand Model*. Auckland: Oxford University Press.

Bourchier, David. 1994. "Solidarity: The New Order's First Free Trade Union." In *Indonesia's Emerging Proletariat: Workers and Their Struggles* (Davide Bourchier, ed.). Clayton: Centre of Southeast Asian Studies, Monash University, pp. 52–63.

Bovens, Mark. 1998. *The Quest for Responsibility*. Cambridge: Cambridge University Press.

Bowen, Diane. 2002. "International Harmonization of Organic Standards and Guarantee Systems." In *OECD Workshop on Organic Agriculture*. Washington, DC: OECD.

Bowers, James R. 1990. *Regulating the Regulators: An Introduction to the Legislative Oversight of Administrative Rulemaking*. New York: Praeger.

Bowles, Samual and Herbert Gintis. 2002. "Social Capital and Community Governance." *Economic Journal* 112: 419–436.

Braithwaite, John. 1997. "On Speaking Softly and Carrying Sticks: Neglected Dimensions of Republican Separation of Powers." *University of Toronto Law Journal* 47: 1–57.

1999. "Accountability and Governance Under the New Regulatory State." *Australian Journal of Public Administration* 58: 90–97.

2000. *Regulation, Crime, Freedom*. Aldershot: Ashgate.

2002. *Restorative Justice and Responsive Regulation*. Oxford: Oxford University Press.

Braithwaite, John and Christine Parker. 1999. "Restorative Justice is Republican Justice." In *Restoring Juvenile Justice: Repairing the Harm of Youth Crime* (Lode Walgrave and Gordon Bazemore, eds.). Monsey, NY: Criminal Justice Press, pp. 103–126.

Braithwaite, John and Declan Roche. 2000. "Responsibility and Restorative Justice." In *Restorative Community Justice: Repairing Harm and Transforming Communities* (M. Schiff and G. Bazemore, eds.). Cincinnati: Anderson, pp. 63–84.

Brand, Donald R. 1988. *Corporatism and the Rule of Law: A Study of the National Recovery Administration*. Ithaca: Cornell University Press.

Bratton, William, Joseph McCahery, Sol Picciotto and Colin Scott (eds.). 1996. *International Regulatory Competition and Coordination*. Oxford: Oxford University Press.

Brennan, Geoffrey and Philip Pettit. 2004. *The Economy of Esteem*. Oxford: Oxford University Press.

Brenner, Neil. 2004. *New State Spaces: Urban Governance and the Rescaling of Statehood*. New York: Oxford University Press.

Brenner, Neil and Nik Theodore. 2002. "Cities and the Geographies of 'Actually Existing Eoliberalism'." *Antipode* 34: 356–386.

Breyer, Stephen, Richard Stewart, Cass Sunstein and Mathew Spitzer. 2002. *Administrative Law and Regulatory Policy: Problems, Texts, and Cases*. 5th ed., New York: Aspen Publishers.

Briffault, Richard. 1990. "Our Localism, Part I: The Structure of Local Government." *Columbia Law Review* 90: 1–115.

1994. "'What About the "Ism"'? Normative and Formal Concerns in Contemporary Federalism." *Vanderbilt Law Review* 47: 1303–1353.

Brown, Howard G. 1995. *War, Revolution, and the Bureaucratic State: Politics and Army Administration in France, 1791–1799*. Oxford: Clarendon Press.

Brown, Jennifer Gerada. 1994. "The Use of Mediation to Resolve Criminal Cases: A Procedural Critique." *Emory Law Journal* 43: 1247–1309.

Brown, L. Neville and John S. Bells. 1998. *French Administrative Law*. Oxford: Oxford University Press.

Brownsword, Roger. 2005. "Code, Control, and Choice: Why East Is East and West Is West." *Legal Studies*. 25: 1–20.

Burnham, Walter Dean. 1981. "The System of 1896: An Analysis." In *The Evolution of American Electoral Systems* (Paul Kleppner *et al.*, eds.). Westport, CT: Greenwood Press, pp. 147–202.

Burt, Ronald S. 1992. *Structural Holes: The Social Structure of Competition*. Cambridge, MA: Harvard University Press.

1999. "The Social Capital of Opinion Leaders." *Annals of the American Academy of Political and Social Science* 566: 37–54.

Butler, Henry and Jonathan R. Macey. 1996. "Externalities and the Matching Principle: The Case for Reallocating Environmental Regulatory Authority." *Yale Law and Policy Review/Yale Journal on Regulation* 14: 23–66.

1996. *Using Federalism to Improve Environmental Policy*. Washington, DC: American Enterprise Institute.

Buzbee, William W. 1999. "Urban Sprawl, Federalism, and the Problem of Institutional Complexity." *Fordham Law Review* 68: 57–136.

Calabresi, Steven and Kevin Rhodes. 1992. "The Structural Constitution: Unitary Executive, Plural Judiciary." *Harvard Law Review*. 105: 1153–1216.

Calabresi, Steven and Saikrishna Prakash. 1994. "The President's Power to Execute the Laws." *Yale Law Journal* 104: 541–666.

Caminker, Evan. 1995. "State Sovereignty and Subordinacy: May Congress Commandeer State Officers to Implement Federal Law?" *Columbia Law Review* 95: 1001.

Cane, Peter. 2002. *Responsibility in Law and Morality*. Oxford: Hart Publishing.

Cappelletti, Mauro. 1989. *Judicial Process in Comparative Perspective*. Oxford: Oxford University Press.

Carter, Lief and Christine B. Harrington. 2000. *Administrative Law and Politics: Cases and Comments*. 3rd ed., New York: Longman.

Carter, Stephen L. 1992. "Do Courts Matter." *Michigan Law Review* 90: 1216–1224.

Cashore, Benjamin. 2002. "Legitimacy and the Privatization of Environmental Governance: How Non-State Market-Driven (NSMD) Governance Systems Gain Rule Making Authority." *Governance* 15: 503–529.

Chandler, Alfred D., Jr. 1977. *The Visible Hand: The Managerial Revolution in American Business*. Cambridge, MA: Belknap Press.

Charoenloet, Voravidh, Napaporn Ativanichayapong and Phan Wanabriboon. 2004. "The Impact of Trade Union Solidarity Support Organizations in Thailand 1993–2002." Bangkok: Political Economy Study Center, Chulalongkorn University (available at http://www.fes-thailand. org/Impact%20Study%20(1).pdf) (accessed March 29, 2005).

Chatfield, Michael. 1977. *A History of Accounting Thought*. Huntington, NY: R. E. Krieger Publishing Co.

Chayes, Abram. 1976. "The Role of the Judge in Public Law Litigation." *Harvard Law Review* 89: 1281–1316.

Choo, Robert. 2000. "Judicial Review of Negotiated Rulemaking: Should *Chevron* Defence Apply?" *Rutgers Law Review* 52: 1069–1120.

Christie, Nils. 1977. "Conflicts as Property." *British Journal of Criminology* 17: 1–26.

Clague, Christopher, Suzanne Gleason and Stephen Knack. 2001. "Determinants of Lasting Democracy in Poor Countries: Culture, Development, and Institutions." *Annals of the American Academy of Political and Social Science* 573: 16–41.

Clark, Gordon. 1985. *Judges and the Cities: Interpreting Local Autonomy*. Chicago: University of Chicago Press.

Clark, John. 1999. "The Role of Non-Profit Organizations in Development: The Experience of the World Bank." Washington, DC: World Bank.

Coglianese, Cary. 1996. "Litigating Within Relationships: Disputes and Disturbance in the Regulatory Process." *Law and Society Review* 30: 735–766.

1997. "Assessing Consensus: The Promise and Performance of Negotiated Rulemaking." *Duke Law Journal* 46: 1255–1349.

2001. "Is Consensus an Appropriate Basis for Regulatory Policy?" In *Environmental Contracts: Comparative Approaches to Regulatory Innovation in the United States and Europe* (Eric Orts and Kurt Deketelaere, eds.). London and Boston: Kluwer Law International, pp. 93–113.

Cohen, Jean. 1985. "Strategy or Identity: New Theoretical Paradigms and Contemporary Social Movements." *Social Research* 52: 663–716.

2002. *Regulating Intimacy: A New Legal Paradigm*. Princeton: Princeton University Press.

Cohen, Jean and Andrew Arato. 1992. *Civil Society and Political Theory*. Cambridge, MA: MIT Press.

Collins, Hugh. 1999. *Regulating Contracts*. Oxford: Oxford University Press.

Collins, Ronald and David Skover. 1996. *The Death of Discourse*. Boulder, CO: Westview Press.

Comaroff, John L. and Simon Roberts. 1981. *Rules and Processes: The Cultural Logic of Dispute in an African Context*. Chicago: University of Chicago Press.

Commins, Ken. 2002. *The First Ten Years of the IFOAM Accreditation Programme*. Jamestown: IOAS.

2003. "Overview of Current Status of Standards and Conformity Assessment Systems." Geneva: International Task Force on Harmonization (unpublished draft).

Compa, Lance. 2000. "NGO–Labor Union Tensions on the Ground." *Human Rights Dialogue: Who Can Protect Workers' Rights? The Workplace Codes of Conduct Debates* 2(4): 12. New York: Carnegie Council on Ethics and International Affairs (available at http://www.carnegiecouncil.org/viewMedia.php/prmTemplateID/8/prmID/895? PHPSESSID=8eb222d4004f884028af455856164caa/) (accessed March 29, 2005).

2004. "Trade Unions, NGOs, and Corporate Codes of Conduct." *Development in Practice* 2004: 210–215.

Considine, Mark. 2002. "The End of the Line? Accountable Governance in the Age of Networks, Partnerships, and Joined-Up Services." *Governance* 15: 21–40.

Considine, Mark and Jenny Lewis. 1999. "Governance at Ground Level: The Frontline Bureaucrat in the Age of Markets and Networks." *Public Administration Review* 59: 467–480.

Cooter, Robert and Thomas Ulen. 2004. *Law and Economics*. 4th ed., Boston: Pearson Addison Wesley.

Courville, Sasha. 2003. "Social Accountability Audits: Challenging or Defending Democratic Governance?" *Law and Policy* 25: 269–297.

Courville, Sasha and Clifford Shearing. 2003. "Social and Environmental Certification Systems as Expressions of Nodal Governance." Canberra, Australian National University (unpublished draft).

Covaleski, Mark A., Mark W. Dirsmith and Sajay Samuel. 1995. "The Use of Accounting Information in Governmental Regulation and Public Administration: The Impact of John R. Commons and Early Institutional Economists." *The Accounting Historian's Journal* 22: 1–33.

Cover, Robert. 1983. "The Supreme Court Term, 1982 Term – Foreword: Nomos and Narrative." *Harvard Law Review* 97: 4–68.

Cox, Gary and Jonathan Katz. 1996. "Why Did the Incumbency Advantage in US House Elections Grow?" *American Journal of Political Science* 40: 478–497.

Cutler, Claire. 1999. "Locating 'Authority' in the Global Political Economy." *International Studies Quarterly* 43: 59–68.

Cyert, Richard and James March. 1963. A *Behavioral Theory of the Firm*. Englewood Cliffs, NJ: Prentice-Hall.

Dahl, Robert. 1989. *Who Governs? Democracy and Power in an American City*. New Haven: Yale University Press.

Dale, Ernest. 1967. *Organization*. New York: American Management Association.

Damaska, Mirjan. 1975. "Structures of Authority and Comparative Criminal Procedure." *Yale Law Journal* 84: 480–544.

Dankers, Cora. 2003. "Environmental and Social Standards, Certification and Labelling for Cash Crops," FAO Comodities and Trade Technical Paper 2, 1729–9829, Food and Agriculture Organization, Rome.

Day, Patricia and Rudolf Klein. 1987. *Accountabilities: Five Public Services*. London: Tavistock.

deLisle, Jacques. 1999. "Lex Americana? United States Legal Assistance, American Legal Models, and Legal Change in the Post-Communist World and Beyond." *University of Pennsylvania Journal of International Economic Law* 20: 179–308.

della Porta, Donatella and Mario Diani. 1999. *Social Movements: An Introduction*. Oxford: Blackwell.

Denckla, Derek A. 2000. "Forgiveness as a Problem-Solving Tool in the Courts: A Brief Response to the Panel on Forgiveness in Criminal Law." *Fordham Urban Law Journal* 27: 1613–1619.

Derthick, Martha. 1979. *Policymaking for Social Security*. Washington, DC: Brookings Institution.

Derthick, Martha and Paul J. Quirk. 1985. *The Politics of Deregulation*. Washington, DC: Brookings Institution.

"Developments in the Law – The Law of Prisons." 2002. *Harvard Law Review* 115: 1838–1963.

Dewar, Helen. 1995. "Senate Falls Short on Flag Amendment." *The Washington Post*, December 13, 1995, p. A1.

Deyo, Frederic C. 2000. "Reform, Globalization and Crisis: Reconstructing Thai Labor." *Journal of Industrial Relations* 42: 258–274.

Dezalay, Yves. 1994. "The Forum Should Fit the Fuss: The Economics and Politics of Negotiated Justice." In *Lawyers in a Postmodern World: Translation and Transgression* (Maureen E. Cain and Christine B. Harrington, eds.). New York: NYU Press, pp. 155–182.

Diamond, Larry. 2003. "Can the Whole World Become Democratic? Democracy, Development, and International Policies." Center for the Study of Democracy Paper 03-05, Irvine, CA: University of California at Irvine (available at http://repositories.cdlib.org/cgi/viewcontent.cgi?article=1022&context=csd).

Dicey, Albert Venn. 1959. *Introduction to the Study of the Law of the Constitution* (10th ed., E. C. S. Wade, ed.). London: Macmillan.

1959. "The Development of Administrative Law in England." In *Introduction to the Study of the Law of the Constitution* (10th ed., E. C. S. Wade, ed.). London: Macmillan, pp. 493–499.

Diller, Matthew. 2000. "The Revolution in Welfare Administration: Rules, Discretion, and Entrepreneurial Government." *New York University Law Review* 75: 1121–1220.

Dillon, John Forrest. 1911. *Commentaries on the Law of Municipal Corporations* (5th ed.). Boston: Little, Brown.

Dillon, Sara. 2001. *International Trade and Economic Law and the European Union*. Oxford: Hart Publishing.

Dilulio, John J., Jr. 2003. "Government by Proxy: A Faithful Overview." *Harvard Law Review* 116: 1271–1284.

Dilulio, John, Jr. and Donald Kettl. 1995. *Fine Print: The Contract with America, Devolution and the Administrative Realities of American Federalism*, Brookings Institution Center for Public Management, CPM 95-1 (March 1, 1995). Washington, DC: Brookings Institution.

Dolinko, David. 2003. "Restorative Justice and the Justification of Punishment." *Utah Law Review* 2003: 319–342.

Domberger, Simon and Paul Jensen. 1997. "Contracting Out by the Public Sector: Theory, Evidence, Prospects." *Oxford Review of Economic Policy* 13(4): 67–78.

Donahue, John D. 1989. *The Privatization Decision: Public Ends, Private Means*. New York: Basic Books.

2002. "Market-Based Governance and the Architecture of Accountability." In *Market-Based Governance: Supply Side, Demand Side, Upside and Downside* (John D. Donahue and Joseph S. Nye, Jr., eds.). Washington, DC: Brookings Institution, pp. 1–25.

Donahue, John D. and Joseph S. Nye, Jr. (eds.). 2002. *Market-Based Governance: Supply Side, Demand Side, Upside and Downside*. Washington, DC: Brookings Institution.

Dop, Erik. 2000. "A Dialogic Epistemology: Bakhtin on Truth and Meaning." *Dialogism: An International Journal of Bakhtin Studies* 4: 7–33.

Dorf, Michael C. 1998. "The Supreme Court 1997 Term – Foreword: The Limits of Socratic Deliberation." *Harvard Law Review* 112: 4–83.

2002. "The Paths to Legal Equality: A Reply to Dean Sullivan." *California Law Review* 90: 791–812.

Dorf, Michael C. and Barry Friedman. 2000. "Shared Constitutional Interpretation." *Supreme Court Review* 2000: 61–107.

Dorf, Michael C. and Charles F. Sabel. 1998. "A Constitution of Democratic Experimentalism." *Columbia Law Review* 98: 267–473.

2000. "Drug Treatment Courts and Emergent Experimentalist Government." *Vanderbilt Law Review* 53: 831–883.

Douglass, Frederick. 1999. "The Constitution of the United States: Is It Pro-Slavery or Anti-Slavery?" In *Frederick Douglass: Selected Speeches and Writings* (Philip S. Foner, ed.). Chicago: Lawrence Hill Books, pp. 379–390.

Dowdle, Michael W. 1997. "The Constitutional Development and Operations of the National People's Congress." *Columbia Journal of Asian Legal Studies* 12: 1–125.

2002. "Of Parliaments, Pragmatism, and the Dynamics of Constitutional Development: The Curious Case of China." *New York University Journal of International Law and Politics* 35: 1–200.

DPP-SBSI. 2003. *Laporan Pertanggungjawaban Dewan Pengurus Pusat Serikat Buruh Sejahtera Indonesia (DPP SBSI) Periode April 2000–April 2003.* Jakarta: DPP-SBSI.

Drucker, Peter. 1949. *The New Society: The Anatomy of the Industrial Order.* New York: Harper.

Dumaresq, David and Sasha Courville. 2001. "The Future of Organic Regulation in Australia." Canberra: Australian National University (unpublished draft).

Dunn, Delmar D. 1999. "Situating Democratic Political Accountability." In *Democracy, Accountability, and Representation* (Adam Przeworski, Susan S. Stokes and Bernard Manin, eds.). New York: Cambridge University Press, pp. 327–345.

Dunsire, Andrew. 1978. *Control in a Bureaucracy*. New York: St. Martin's Press.

1978. *Implementation in a Bureaucracy*. Oxford: Martin Robertson.

1993. "Manipulating Social Tensions: Collibration as an Alternative Mode of Government Intervention." Max Planck Institute Discussion Paper 93/7 (available atwww.mpi-fg-koeln.mpg.de/pu/mpifg_dp/dp93-7.pdf).

Duxbury, Neil. 1999. *Random Justice: On Lotteries and Legal Decision-Making.* Oxford: Oxford University Press.

Dworkin, Ronald. 1986. *Law's Empire*. Cambridge, MA: Belknap Press.

1996. *Freedom's Law: The Moral Reading of the American Constitution.* Cambridge, MA: Harvard University Press.

2000. *Sovereign Virtue: The Theory and Practice of Equality*. Cambridge, MA: Harvard University Press.

Eade, Deborah. 2004. "Editorial Overview." *Development in Practice* 14(1 & 2): 5–12.

Easterbrook, Frank H. 1982. "Ways of Criticizing the Court." *Harvard Law Review* 95: 802–832.

Eberlein, Burkard. 2003. "Competition and Regulation." *Journal of Network Industries* 4: 137–155.

Edelman, Murray. 1988. *Constructing the Political Spectacle*. Chicago: University of Chicago Press.

Edelstein, J. David and Malcolm Warner. 1975. *Comparative Union Democracy: Organization and Opposition in British and American Unions*. London: Allen & Unwin.

Edwards, Michael and David Hulme. 1996. *Beyond the Magic Bullet: NGO Performance and Accountability in the Post-Cold War World.* Hartford: Kumarian Press.

Eisner, Marc Allen. 2000. *Regulatory Politics in Transition*. Baltimore: Johns Hopkins University Press.

Elazar, Daniel J. 1987. *Exploring Federalism*. University, AL: University of Alabama Press.

Ellickson, Robert C. 1991. *Order Without Law: How Neighbors Settle Disputes*. Cambridge, MA: Harvard University Press.

Elliott, Jan. 1997. "Bersatoe Kita Berdiri Bertjerai Kita Djatoeh [United We Stand Divided We Fall]: Workers and Unions in Indonesia: Jakarta 1945–1965." Kensington, University of New South Wales (unpublished PhD dissertation).

Ely, John Hart. 1980. *Democracy and Distrust: A Theory of Judicial Review*. Cambridge, MA: Harvard University Press.

Engels, Frederick. 1999. *The Condition of the Working Class in England* (David McLellan, ed.). New York: Oxford University Press.

Epstein, Barbara. 1991. *Political Protest and Cultural Revolution: Nonviolent Direcbt Action in the 1970s and 1980s*. Berkeley: University of California Press.

Ericson, Richard V., Aaron Doyle and Dean Barry. 2003. *Insurance as Governance*. Toronto: University of Toronto Press.

Estlund, Cynthia L. 2000. "Working Together: The Workplace, Civil Society, and the Law." *Georgetown Law Journal* 89: 1–96.

Eule, Julian N. 1990. "Judicial Review of Direct Democracy." *Yale Law Journal* 99: 1503–1586.

Farley, James A. 1938. *Behind the Ballots*. New York: Harcourt, Brace & Co.

Fearon, James. 1999. "Electoral Accountability and the Control of Politicians: Selecting Good Types versus Sanctioning Poor Performance." In *Democracy, Accountability, and Representation* (Adam Przeworski, Susan S. Stokes and Bernard Manin, eds.). New York: Cambridge University Press, pp. 55–97.

Feeley, Malcolm and Edward L. Rubin. 1998. *Judicial Policy Making and the Modern State*. Cambridge: Cambridge University Press.

2003. "Judicial Policy Making and Litigation Against the Government." *University of Pennsylvania Journal of Constitutional Law* 5: 617–653.

Feigenbaum, Harvey B. and Jeffrey R. Henig. 1994. "The Political Underpinnings of Privatization: A Typology." *World Politics* 46: 185–208.

Fenno, Richard. 1973. *Congressmen in Committees*. Boston: Little, Brown.

Ferdinand, Jo Ann *et al.* 2002. "The Judicial Perspective." In "The Eleventh Annual Symposium on Contemporary Urban Challenges: Problem Solving Courts: From Adversarial Litigation to Innovative Jurisprudence." *Fordham Urban Law Journal* 23: 2011–2040.

Ferejohn, John. 1999. "Accountability and Authority: Toward a Theory of Political Accountability." In *Democracy, Accountability, and*

Representation (Adam Przeworski, Susan S. Stokes and Bernard Manin, eds.). New York: Cambridge University Press, pp. 131–153.

Fichtenau, Heinrich. 1978. *The Carolingian Empire* (Peter Munz, trans.). Oxford: Blackwell.

Fichtner, Paula Sutter. 2003. *The Habsburg Monarchy 1490–1848: Attributes of Empire*. New York: Palgrave Macmillan.

Finnis, John, Joseph Boyle and Germain Grisez. 1988. *Nuclear Deterrence, Morality and Realism*. Oxford: Oxford University Press.

Fiorito, Jack, Paul Jarley and John T. Delaney. 1995. "National Union Effectiveness in Organizing: Measures and Influences." *Industrial and Labor Relations Review* 48: 613–635.

Fischel, William. 2001. *The Homevoter Hypothesis: How Home Values Influence Local Government Taxation, School Finance, and Land-Use Policies*. Cambridge, MA: Harvard University Press.

Fish, C. R. 1904. *The Civil Service and Patronage*. Cambridge, MA: Harvard University Press.

Fish, Stanley. 1991. "Almost Pragmatism: The Jurisprudence of Richard Posner, Richard Rorty, and Ronald Dworkin." In *Pragmatism in Law and Society* (Michael Brint and William Weaver, eds.). Boulder, CO: Westview Press, pp. 47–82.

Fishlow, Albert. 1966. "Productivity and Technological Change in the Railroad Sector, 1840–1910." In National Bureau of Economic Research, *Output, Employment and Productivity in the United States after 1800*. New York: Columbia University Press, vol. 30, pp. 583–646.

Fiss, Owen M. 1979. "The Supreme Court 1978 Term – Foreword: The Forms of Justice." *Harvard Law Review*. 93: 1–58.

Fisse, Brent. 1983. "Reconstructing Corporate Criminal Law: Deterrence, Retribution, Fault, and Sanctions." *Southern California Law Review* 56: 1141–1246.

Fisse, Brent and John Braithwaite. 1983. *Corporations, Crime and Accountability*. Cambridge: Cambridge University Press.

Fitzpatrick, Peter. 1992. *The Mythology of Modern Law*. New York: Routledge.

Fletcher, George. 1993. "The Nature of Justification." In *Action and Value in Criminal Law* (Stephen Shute, John Gardner and Jeremy Horder, eds.). Oxford: Clarendon Press, pp. 264–276.

FLO International. 2004. *Annual Report 03/04: Shopping for a Better World*. Bonn: Fairtrade Labelling Organizations International.

Foglesong, Richard. 2001. *Married to the Mouse: Walt Disney World and Orlando*. New Haven: Yale University Press.

Foley, Michael. 1990. *Laws, Men and Machines: Modern American Government and the Appeal of Newtonian Mechanics*. London: Routledge.

Ford, Michele. 1999. "Testing the Limits of Corporatism: Reflections on Industrial Relations Institutions and Practices in Suharto's Indonesia." *Journal of Industrial Relations* 41: 372–392.

2001. "Challenging the Criteria of Significance: Lessons from Contemporary Indonesian Labour History." *Australian Journal of Politics and History* 47: 100–113.

2002. "The Place of NGOs in the Organized Labor Movements of Indonesia and Malaysia." Paper presented at the 2002 Annual Meeting of the Association for Asian Studies, Washington, DC, April 4–7, 2002.

2003a. "NGO as Outside Intellectual: A History of Non-Governmental Organizations' Role in the Indonesian Labour Movement." Wollongong: University of Wollongong (unpublished PhD dissertation).

2003b. "Substitute Trade Union or Novel Form of Labour Movement Organization? Understanding Indonesia's Labour NGOs." *Economic and Labour Relations Review* 14: 90–103.

2004a. "New Forms of Labour Activism: A Southeast Asian Perspective." In *Proceedings of the Refereed Stream of the AIRAANZ Annual Conference* (February 3–6, 2004). Noosa: Association of Industrial Relations Academics of Australia and New Zealand.

2004b. "A Challenge for Business? Developments in Indonesian Trade Unionism after Soeharto." In *Changes and Challenges in Business in Indonesia* (M. Chatib Basri and Pierre van der Eng, eds.). Singapore: ISEAS, pp. 221–233.

Fossett, James W. 1998. "Managed Care and Devolution." In *Medicaid and Devolution: A View from the States* (Frank J. Thompson and John J. Dilulio, Jr. eds.). Washington, DC: Brookings Institution, pp. 106–153.

Freedland, Mark and Silvana Sciarra. 1998. *Public Services and Citizenship in European Law*. Oxford: Clarendon Press.

Freeman, Jody. 1997. "Collaborative Governance in the Administrative State." *UCLA Law Review* 34: 1–98.

1999. "Private Parties, Public Functions and the New Administrative Law." In *Recrafting the Rule of Law: The Limits of Legal Order* (David Dyzenhaus, ed.). Toronto: Hart Publishing, pp. 331–369.

2000a. "The Contracting State." *Florida State University Law Review* 28: 155–214.

2000b. "The Private Role in Public Governance." *New York University Law Review* 75: 543–675.

2000c. "Private Parties, Public Functions and the New Administrative Law." *Administrative Law Review* 52: 813–858.

Freeman, Jody and Laura I. Langbein. 2000. "Regulatory Negotiation and the Legitimacy Benefit." *NYU Environmental Law Journal* 9: 60–151.

Fried, Charles. 2002. "The Supreme Court, 2001 Term – Comment: Five to Four: Reflections on the School Voucher Case." *Harvard Law Review* 116: 163–189.

Friedmann, John. 2002. "Citizenship: Statist, Cosmopolitan, Insurgent." In *The Prospect of Cities*. Minneapolis: University of Minnesota Press, pp. 67–86.

Frug, Gerald E. 1980. "The City as a Legal Concept." *Harvard Law Review* 93: 1057– 1154.

1984. "The Ideology of Bureaucracy." *Harvard Law Review* 97: 1276–1377.

2002. "Is Secession from the City of Los Angeles a Good Idea?" *UCLA Law Review* 49: 1783–1798.

Fuller, Lon L. 1969. *The Morality of Law* (rev. ed.). New Haven: Yale University Press.

Fung, Archon and Eric Olin Wright. 2003. "Countervailing Power in Empowered Participatory Governance," in *Deepening Democracy* (Archon Fung and Eric Olin Wright, eds.). London: Verso Press, pp. 259–289.

Funk, William. 1997. "Bargaining Toward the New Millennium: Regulatory Negotiation and the Subversion of the Public Interest." *Duke Law Journal* 46: 1351–1388.

Galanter, Marc. 1974. "Why the 'Haves' Come out Ahead? Speculations on the Limits of Legal Change." *Law and Society Review* 9: 165–230.

Gallin, Dan. 2000. *Trade Unions and NGOs: A Necessary Partnership for Social Development. Civil Society and Social Movements Programme Paper Number 1*. Geneva: United Nations Research Institute for Social Development.

Gamson, William. 1990. *The Strategy of Social Protest* (2nd ed.). Belmont, CA: Wadsworth Publishing Co.

Gardbaum, Stephen. 2001. "The New Commonwealth Model of Constitutionalism." *American Journal of Comparative Law* 49: 707–760.

Gardner, John. 1996. "Justifications and Reasons." In *Harm and Culpability* (A. P. Simester and A. T. H. Smith, eds.). Oxford: Clarendon Press, pp. 103–129.

1997. "The Gist of Excuses." *Buffalo Criminal Law Review* 1: 575–598.

Gardner, John and Timothy Macklem. 2001. "Nine Fallacies in *R.v. Smith*." *Criminal Law Review* 2001: 623–635.

Gathii, James Thuo. 2000. "Retelling Good Governance Narratives on Africa's Economic and Political Predicaments: Continuities and Discontinuities in Legal Outcomes Between Markets and States." *Villanova Law Review* 45: 971–1035.

Geertz, Clifford. 1983. *Local Knowledge: Further Essays in Interpretive Anthropology*. New York: Basic Books.

Gelderman, Carol W. 1997. *All the Presidents' Words: The Bully Pulpit and the Creation of the Virtual Presidency*. New York: Walker & Co.

General Accounting Office. 1976. *The Social Security Administration Should Provide More Management and Leadership in Determining Who Is Eligible for Disability Benefits*. Washington, DC: General Accounting Office.

Genet, Jean. 1965. *The Thief's Journal* (Bernard Frechtman, trans.). New York: Grove Press.

1987. *Our Lady of the Flowers* (Bernard Frechtman, trans.). New York: Grove Press.

Giddens, Anthony. 1984. *The Constitution of Society: Outline of the Theory of Structuration*. Berkeley: University of California Press.

Gill, Stephen. 1995. "Globalisation, Market Civilisation, and Disciplinary Neoliberalism." *Millennium* 24: 418–422.

Gillette, Clayton P. 1997. "The Exercise of Trumps by Decentralized Governments." *Virginia Law Review* 83: 1347–1417.

Ginsburg, Tom. 2003. *Judicial Review in New Democracies: Constitutional Courts in Asian Cases*. New York: Cambridge University Press.

Goldstein, Judith L. *et al.* (eds.). 2001. *Legalization and World Politics*. Cambridge, MA: MIT Press.

Goodin, Robert E. 2003. "Democratic Accountability: The Distinctiveness of the Third Sector." *European Archives of Sociology* 44: 359–396.

Gore, Albert. 1993. *Creating a Government That Works Better and Costs Less: From Red Tape to Results*. Washington, DC: US Government Printing Office.

Gould, Lewis L. 2003. *The Modern American Presidency*. Lawrence: University of Kansas Press.

Grabosky, Peter. 1994. "Beyond the Regulatory State." *Australian and New Zealand Journal of Criminology* 27: 192–197.

1995. "Using Non-Governmental Resources to Foster Regulatory Compliance." *Governance* 8: 527–550.

Graebner, William. 1976. *Coal-Mining Safety in the Progressive Period: The Political Economy of Reform*. Lexington, KY: University Press of Kentucky.

Green, Donald P. and Ian Shapiro. 1994. *Pathologies of Rational Choice Theory: A Critique of Applications in Political Science*. New Haven: Yale University Press.

Greenfield, Gerard. 2000. "Organizing, Protest and Working Class Self-Activity: Reflections on East Asia." In *Socialist Register 2001: Working Classes, Global Realities* (Leo Panitch and Colin Leys, eds.). New York: Monthly Review Press, pp. 239–248.

Gunningham, Neil and Peter Grabosky. 1998. *Smart Regulation: Designing Environmental Policy*. Oxford: Oxford University Press.

Gunningham, Neil and Darren Sinclair. 1999. "Regulatory Pluralism: Designing Policy Mixes for Environmental Protection." *Law and Policy* 21: 49–76.

Guttman, Daniel. 2000. "Public Purpose and Private Service: The Twentieth Century Culture of Contracting Out and the Evolving Law of Diffused Sovereignty." *Administrative Law Review* 52: 859–926.

Habermas, Jürgen. 1975. *The Legitimation Crisis*. Boston: Beacon Press.

1996. *Between Facts and Norms: Contributions to a Discourse Theory of Law and Democracy* (William Rehg, trans.). Cambridge, MA: MIT Press.

Hadiz, Vedi R. 1997. *Workers and the State in New Order Indonesia*. London: Routledge.

Haley, John Owen. 1991. *Authority Without Power: Law and the Japanese Paradox*. New York: Oxford University Press.

Hamilton, Robert W. 1983. "Prospects for the Nongovernmental Development of Regulatory Standards." *American University Law Review* 32: 455–469.

Hammond, Bray. 1957. *Banks and Politics in America: From the Revolution to the Civil War*. Princeton: Princeton University Press.

Harder, Phillip. 1996. "First Judicial Review of Reg-Neg: A Disappointment." *Administrative and Regulatory Law News* 22: 1–12.

Hardin, Russell. 2002. *Trust and Trustworthiness*. New York: Russell Sage Foundation.

Harrington, Christine B. 1984. "The Politics of Participation and Nonparticipation in Dispute Processes." *Law and Policy* 6: 203–230.

1988. "Regulatory Reform: Creating Gaps and Making Markets." *Law and Policy* 10: 293–316.

1994. "Using 'Bundles of Input' to Negotiate an Environmental Dispute: Howard Bellman." In *When Talk Works: Profiles of Mediators* (Deborah M. Kolb, ed.). San Francisco: Jossey-Bass Publications, pp. 105–147.

Hart, Oliver, Andrei Shleifer and Robert W. Vishny. 1997. "The Proper Scope of Government: Theory and an Application to Prisons." *Quarterly Journal of Economics* 112: 1127–1161.

Harter, Philip J. 1982. "Negotiating Regulations: A Cure for Malaise." *Georgetown Law Journal* 71: 1–118.

1983. "The Political Legitimacy and Judicial Review of Consensual Rules." *American University Law Review* 32: 471–496.

2000. "Assessing the Assessors: The Actual Performance of Negotiated Rulemaking." *NYU Environmental Law Journal* 9: 32–59.

Hawkins, Keith and John M. Thomas. 1984. "The Enforcement Process in Regulatory Bureaucracies." In *Enforcing Regulation* (Keith Hawkins and John M. Thomas, eds.). Boston: Kluwer-Nijhoff, pp. 3–22.

Hays, Samual P. 1995. *The Response to Industrialism*. Chicago: University of Chicago Press.

Heclo, Hugh and Aaron Wildavsky. 1974. *The Private Government of Public Money*. London: Macmillan.

Hegel, Georg Wilhelm Friedrich. 1942. *Philosophy of Right* (T. M. Knox, trans.). Oxford: Clarendon Press.

Hemingway, John. 1978. *Conflict and Democracy: Studies in Trade Union Government*. Oxford: Clarendon Press.

Heritier, Adrienne and Moral Soriano Leonor. 2002. "Differentiating and Linking Politics and Adjudication: The Example of European Electricity Policy." *European Law Journal* 8: 363–383.

Hershkoff, Helen. 1999. "Positive Rights and State Constitutions: The Limits of Federal Rationality Review." *Harvard Law Review* 112: 1131–1196.

Heydebrand, Wolf. 1990. "Government Litigation and National Policymaking: From Roosevelt to Reagan." *Law and Society Review* 24: 477–495.

2003. "Process Rationality as Legal Governance: A Comparative Perspective." *International Sociology* 18: 325–349.

Hilhorst, Dorothea. 2002. "Being Good at Doing Good? Quality and Accountability of Humanitarian NGOs." *Disasters* 26(3): 193–212.

Hirschman, Albert O. 1970. *Exit, Voice and Loyalty: Responses to Decline in Firms, Organizations and States*. Cambridge, MA: Harvard University Press.

Hoffman, Morris B. 2002. "Therapeutic Jurisprudence, Neo-Rehabilitationism, and Judicial Collectivism: The Least Dangerous Branch Becomes Most Dangerous." *Fordham Urban Law Journal* 29: 2063–2098.

Hofstadter, Richard. 1955. *The Age of Reform: From Bryan to F. D. R.* New York: Knopf.

Hohfeld, Wesley Newcomb. 2001. *Fundamental Legal Conceptions as Applied in Judicial Reasoning* (David Campbell and Philip Thomas, eds.). Aldershot: Ashgate/Dartmouth.

Hood, Christopher. 1984. *The Tools of Government*. London: Macmillan.

1998. *The Art of the State*. Oxford: Oxford University Press.

Hood, Christopher, Oliver James, Guy Peters and Colin Scott. 2004. *Controlling Modern Government: Variety, Commonality and Change*. Cheltenham: Edward Elgar.

Hood, Christopher, Oliver James and Colin Scott. 2000. "Regulation of Government: Has It Increased, Is It Increasing, Should It Be Diminished? *Public Administration* 78: 283–304.

Hood, Christopher, Henry Rothstein and Robert Baldwin. 2001. *The Government of Risk*. Oxford: Oxford University Press.

Hood, Christopher, Colin Scott, Oliver James, George Jones and Tony Travers. 1999. *Regulation Inside Government: Waste-Watchers, Quality Police, and Sleaze-Busters*. Oxford: Oxford University Press.

Horowitz, Donald L. 1977. *The Courts and Social Policy*. Washington, DC: Brookings Institution.

Horwitz, Morton. 1977. *The Transformation of American Law 1780–1850*. Cambridge, MA: Harvard University Press.

1992. *The Transformation of American Law, 1870–1960: The Crisis of Legal Orthodoxy*. New York: Oxford University Press.

Houghton, Rachel and Kate Robertson (eds.). 2001. "Humanitarian Action: Learning from Evaluation." *ALNAP Annual Review Series 2001*. London: Overseas Development Institute.

Human Rights Watch. 1998. "World Bank Should Monitor Abuses in India" (Press Release, April 21, 1998) (available at http://hrw.org/english/docs/1998/04/21/india1083.htm).

1999. "No Kosovo Settlement Without Accountability for War Crimes" (Press Release, February 6, 1999) (available at http://hrw.org/english/docs/1999/02/06/serbia812.htm).

Hunold, Christian. 2001. "Corporatism, Pluralism, and Democracy: Toward a Deliberative Theory of Bureaucratic Accountability." *Governance* 14: 151–167.

Hunter, Dan. 2001. "Reason Is Too Large: Analogy and Precedent in Law." *Emory Law Journal* 50: 1197–1264.

Hurwitz, Mark S. 2003. "Ideology and Deference in US Courts of Appeals Decision Making on Administrative Law." Paper presented at the 2003 Annual Meeting of the American Political Science Association Annual Meeting, Philadelphia, August 28–31, 2003.

Hyman, Richard and Robert Fryer. 1978. "Trade Unions: Sociology and Political Economy." In *Labour Unions Under Capitalism* (Tom Clarke and Laurie Clements, eds.). Hassocks: Harvester Press.

IFOAM. 2002. *IFOAM Basic Standards*. Victoria: IFOAM.

2004. *IFOAM Basic Standards – Final Revision Draft*. Bonn, International Federation of Organic Agriculture Movements.

Illich, Ivan. 1971. *Celebration of Awareness: A Call for Institutional Revolution*. New York: Harper and Row.

1973. *Tools for Conviviality*. New York: Harper and Row.

Im, Sungham. 2001. *Bureaucratic Power, Democracy and Administrative Democracy*. Aldershot: Ashgate.

Inglehart, Ronald. 1997. *Modernization and Postmodernization: Cultural, Economic, and Political Change in 43 Societies*. Princeton: Princeton University Press.

Ingleson, John. 1986. *In Search of Justice: Workers and Unions in Colonial Java, 1908–1926*. Singapore: Oxford University Press.

IOAS. 2004. "List of IFOAM Accredited Certification Bodies." Jamestown, ND: IOAS.

ISEAL. 2002. *ISEAL Alliance Vision Document*. Kaslo: ISEAL Alliance.

2003. *Membership Application Procedures*. Kaslo: ISEAL Alliance.

2004. *Code of Good Practice for Setting Social and Environmental Standards*. Bonn: ISEAL Alliance.

Jackson, Vicki. 1998. "Federalism and the Uses and Limits of Law: *Printz* and Principle." *Harvard Law Review* 111: 2180–2259.

Jacob, Herbert. 1983. "Courts as Organizations." In *Empirical Theories About Courts* (K. Boyum and L. Mather, eds.). New York: Longman, Inc., pp. 191–215.

Jacobson, Dan. 2005. "If England Was What England Seems." *Times Literary Supplement*, March 11, 2005, pp. 11–12.

Janis, Irving L. 1971. "Groupthink Among Policy Makers." In *Sanctions for Evil* (N. Sanford and C. Comstock, eds.). San Francisco: Jossey-Bass Publications, pp. 71–89.

Jayasuriya, Kanishka. 2001. "Governance, Post Washington Consensus and the New Anti-Politics." In *Corruption in Asia: Rethinking the Governance Paradigm* (Tim Lindsey and Howard Dick, eds.). Annandale, NSW: Federation Press, pp. 24–36.

Jessop, Bob. 1999. "Narrating the Future of the National Economy and the National State." In *State/Culture: State Formation after the Cultural Turn* (George Steinmetz, ed.). Ithaca: Cornell University Press, pp. 378–405.

2001. "Regulationist and Autopoieticist Reflections on Polanyi's Account of Market Economies and the Market Society." *New Political Economy* 6: 213–232.

Joerges, Christian and Jürgen Neyer. 1997. "From Intergovernmental Bargaining to Deliberative Political Processes: The Constitutionalization of Comitology." *European Law Journal*. 3: 273–299.

Jones, Chester Lloyd. 1916. "Spoils and Party." *Annals* 64: 66–76.

Jordan, Lisa and Peter Van Tuijl. 2000. "Political Responsibility in Transnational NGO Advocacy." *World Development* 28: 2051–2065.

JUSTICE-All Souls Review Committee. 1988. *Administrative Justice: Some Necessary Reforms*. Oxford: Clarendon Press.

Kagan, Elena. 2001. "Presidential Administration." *Harvard Law Review* 114: 2245–2385.

Kagan, Robert A. and John T. Scholz. 1984. "The 'Criminology of the Corporation' and Regulatory Enforcement Strategies." In *Enforcing Regulation* (Keith Hawkins and John M. Thomas, eds.). Boston: Kluwer-Nijhoff, pp. 67–95.

Kammen, Douglas. 1997. "A Time to Strike: Industrial Strikes and Changing Class Relations in New Order Indonesia." Ithaca: Cornell University (unpublished PhD dissertation).

Kant, Immanual. 1964. *Groundwork of the Metaphysic of Morals* (H. J. Paton, trans.). New York: Harper and Row.

1996. *The Metaphysics of Morals* (Mary Gregor, trans. and ed.). Cambridge: Cambridge University Press.

Karkkainen, Bradley C. 2002. "Toward a Smarter NEPA." *Columbia Law Review* 102: 903–972.

Kellner, Douglas. 1990. *Television and the Crisis of Democracy*. Boulder, CO: Westview Press.

Kello, Carolyn Bingham. 2003. "Drawing the Curtain on Open Government? In Defense of the Federal Advisory Committee Act." *Brooklyn Law Review* 69: 345–393.

Kennedy, Duncan. 1980. "Toward an Historical Understanding of Legal Consciousness: The Case of Classical Legal Thought in America, 1850–1940." *Research in Law and Society* 3: 3–24.

Kenny, Anthony. 1978. *Freewill and Responsibility*. London: Routledge and Kegan Paul.

Keohane, Robert O. 2002. "Commentary on the Democratic Accountability of Non-Governmental Organizations." *Chicago Journal of International Law* 3: 477–479.

Keohane, Robert O. and Joseph S. Nye. 2001. "Democracy, Accountability and Global Governance." Politics Research Group Working Papers on International Relations. Cambridge, MA: Harvard University, Kennedy School of Government (June 27, 2001) (available at http://www.ksg.harvard.edu/prg/nye/ggajune.pdf).

Kerwin, Cornelius M. 1994. *Rulemaking: How Government Agencies Write Law and Make Policy*. Washington, DC: CQ Press.

1999. *Rulemaking: How Government Agencies Write Law and Make Policy* (2nd ed.). Washington, DC: CQ Press.

Kettl, Donald F. 1988. *Government by Proxy: (Mis?)Managing Federal Programs*. Washington, DC: CQ Press.

Keyssar, Alexander. 2000. *The Right to Vote: The Contested History of Democracy in the United States*. New York: Basic Books.

Kinder, Donald R., Mark D. Peters, Robert P. Abelson and Susan T. Fiske. 1980. "Presidential Prototypes." *Political Behavior* 2: 315–337.

King, Peter. 2000. *Crime, Justice, and Discretion in England, 1740–1820*. Oxford: Oxford University Press.

Kinlaw, Dennis C. 1992. *Continuous Improvement and Measurement for Total Quality: A Team-Based Approach*. San Diego: Pfeiffer & Co.

Kinney, Eleanor D. 2000. "Tapping and Resolving Consumer Concerns About Health Care." *American Journal of Law and Medicine* 26: 335–399.

Klandermans, Bert. 1991. "New Social Movements and Resource Mobilization: The European and American Approach Revisited." *Research on Social Movements: The State of the Art in Western Europe and the USA* (Dieter Rucht, ed.). Boulder, CO: Westview Press, pp. 17–44.

Klare, Karl. 1978. "Judicial Deradicalization of the Wagner Act and the Origins of Modern Legal Consciousness: 1937–1941." *Minnesota Law Review* 62: 265–339.

Klingner, Donald E., John Nalbandian and Barbara R. Romzek. 2002. "Politics, Administration and Markets: Conflicting Expectations and Accountability." *American Review of Public Administration* 32: 117–144.

Knowledge Networks 2001. "California Residents Respond to State's Energy Crisis" (Press Release, February 8, 2001). Menlo Park, CA: Knowledge Networks (available at http://www.knowledgenetworks.com/info/press/releases/2001/020801_CAEnergyA.html).

Koch, Charles H., Jr. and Beth Martin. 1983. "FTC Rulemaking Through Negotiation." *North Carolina Law Review* 61: 275–311.

Kochen, Manfred and Karl Deutsch. 1980. *Decentralization: Sketches Toward a Rational Theory*. Cambridge, MA: Oelgeschlager, Gunn and Hain.

Komesar, Neil. 1994. *Imperfect Alternatives: Choosing Institutions in Law, Economics, and Public Policy*. Chicago: University of Chicago Press.

Kornai, Janos. 1992. *The Socialist System: The Political Economy of Communism*. Princeton: Princeton University Press.

Kornhauser, Lewis A. and Lawrence Sager. 1986. "Unpacking the Court." *Yale Law Journal* 96: 82–117.

Kramer, Larry. 2001. "The Supreme Court 2000 Term – Foreword: We the Court." *Harvard Law Review* 115: 4–169.

Krent, Harold J. 1990. "Fragmenting the Unitary Executive: Congressional Delegations of Administrative Authority Outside the Federal Government." *Northwestern University Law Review* 85: 62–112.

Kritzer, Herbert, Mark Richards and Joseph Smith. 2002. "Deciding the Supreme Court's Administrative Law Cases: Does *Chevron* Matter?" Annual Meeting of the American Political Science Association, Boston, August 2002.

Krugman, Paul. 2005. "The Ugly American Bank." *New York Times*, March 18, 2005, p. A21.

Kusyuniati, Sri. 1998. "Strikes in 1990–1996: An Evaluation of the Dynamics of the Indonesian Labour Movement." Melbourne: Swinburne University of Technology (unpublished PhD dissertation).

La Botz, Dan. 2001. *Made in Indonesia: Indonesian Workers Since the Fall of Suharto*. Cambridge: Cambridge University Press.

Lakoff, George and Mark Johnson. 1980. *Metaphors We Live*. Chicago: University of Chicago Press.

Lane, Eric. 2003. "Due Process and Problem Solving Courts." *Fordham Urban Law Journal* 30: 955–1026.

Langbein, John H. 2003. *The Origins of the Adversary Criminal Trial*. Oxford: Oxford University Press.

Langlois, Richard N., David J. Denault and Samson M. Kimenyi. 1995. "Bursting Boilers and the Federal Power Redux: The Evolution of Safety on the Western Rivers." Economics Working Paper Archive at

WUSTL: Economic History 9503002, St. Louis, Washington University of St. Louis.

Latimer, Jeff, Craig Dowden and Danielle Muise. 2001. *The Effectiveness of Restorative Justice Practices: A Meta-Analysis*. Ottawa: Department of Justice, Canadian Government.

Laurie, Nina. 2005. "Establishing Development Orthodoxy: Negotiating Masculinities in the Water Sector." *Development and Change*. 36: 527–549.

Lawson, Gary. 2002. "Delegation and Original Meaning." *Virginia Law Review* 88: 327–404.

Lazarsfeld, Paul F., Bernard Berelson and Hazel Gaudet. 1948. *The People's Choice: How the Voter Makes Up his Mind in a Presidential Campaign*. New York: Columbia University Press.

Lazarus, Richard J. 1991. "The Neglected Question of Congressional Oversight of EPA: Quis Custodiet Ipsos Custodes (Who Shall Watch the Watchers Themselves)?" *Law and Contemporary Problems* 54: 205–239.

Lessig, Lawrence. 1999. *Code: and Other Laws of Cyberspace*. New York: Basic Books.

Lessig, Lawrence and Cass Sunstein. 1994. "The President and the Administration." *Columbia Law Review* 94: 1–120.

Levine, Michael E. and Jennifer L. Forrence. 1990. "Regulatory Capture, Public Interest, and the Public Agenda: Toward a Synthesis." *Journal of Law and Economic Organization* 6 (Special Issue): 167–196.

Levinson, Daryl J. 1999. "Rights Essentialism and Remedial Equilibration." *Columbia Law Review* 99: 857–940.

Levitan, Theresa and Warren Miller. 1973. "Ideological Interpretations of Presidential Elections." *American Political Science Review* 79: 751–771.

Lewis, Richard. 1985. "Insurers' Agreements Not To Enforce Strict Legal Rights: Bargaining With the Government and in the Shadow of the Law." *Modern Law Review* 48: 275–292.

Lieberman, Robert C. 2002. "Ideas, Institutions, and Political Order: Explaining Political Change." *American Political Science Review* 96: 697–712.

Liebman, James S. and Charles F. Sabel. 2003. "A Public Laboratory Dewey Barely Imagined: The Emerging Model of School Governance and Legal Reform." *New York University Review of Law and Social Change* 28: 183–304.

Lifton, Robert Jay. 1989. *Thought Reform and the Psychology of Totalism: A Study of "Brainwashing" in China*. Chapel Hill: University of North Carolina Press.

Light, Paul. 1997. *The Tides of Reform: Making Government Work 1945–1995*. New Haven: Yale University Press.

1999. *The True Size of Government*. Washington, DC: Brookings Institution Press.

Lindblom, Charles E. 2001. *The Market System: What It Is, How It Works and What to Make of It*. New Haven: Yale University Press.

Linde, Hans A. 1999. "Structures and Terms of Consent: Delegation, Discretion, Separation of Powers, Representation, Participation, Accountability?" *Cardozo Law Review* 20: 823.

Lindseth, Peter. 2002. "Delegation Is Dead – Long Live Delegation: Managing the Democratic Disconnect in the European Market Polity." In *Good Governance in Europe's Integrated Market* (Christian Joerges and Renaud Dehousse, eds.). Oxford: Oxford University Press, pp. 139–165.

Lipset, Seymour M. 1983. "Radicalism or Reformism: The Sources of Working Class Politics." *American Political Science Review* 77: 1–18.

Littleton, A. C. 1966. *Accounting Evolution to 1900*. New York: Russell & Russell.

Lobe, Jim. 2003. *Politics: NGOs and Corporations Criticised on Accountability*. New York: Global Information Network.

Looney, Robert. 2003. "DARPA's Policy Analysis Market for Intelligence: Outside the Box or Off the Wall?" *Strategic Insights* Vol. 2, No. 9 (September 2003). Center for Contemporary Conflict, Monterey, CA (available at http://www.ccc.nps.navy.mil/si/sept03/terrorism.asp).

LoPucki, Lynn M. 1996. "Legal Culture, Legal Strategy, and the Law in Lawyers' Heads." *Northwestern University Law Review* 90: 1498–1556.

Lowi, Theodore J. 1979. *The End of Liberalism: The Second Republic of the United States* (2nd ed.). New York: W. W. Norton.

Luhmann, Niklas. 1995. *Social Systems* (John Bednarz, Jr. and Dirk Baecker, trans.). Stanford: Stanford University Press.

Lund, Nelson. 1995. "Lawyers and the Defense of the Presidency." *Brigham Young University Law Review* 1995: 17–98.

Macaulay, Stuart. 1963. "Non-Contractual Relations in Business: A Preliminary Study." *American Sociological Review* 28: 55–83.

Macintosh, Norman. 1994. *Management Accounting and Control Systems: An Organizational and Behavioral Approach*. Chichester: Wiley.

Mackay, R. D. 1988. "Pleading Provocation and Diminished Responsibility Together." *Criminal Law Review* 1988: 411–423.

MacNeil, Ian R. 2000. "Relational Contract Theory: Challenges and Queries." *Northwestern University Law Review* 94: 877–907.

Madison, James. 1961. "The Federalist No. 52." In *The Federalist* (Jacob E. Cooke, ed.). Middletown, CT: Wesleyan University Press, pp. 353–359.

1961. "The Federalist No. 57." In *The Federalist* (Jacob E. Cooke, ed.). Middletown, CT: Wesleyan University Press, pp. 384–390.

Maduro, Miguel Poiares. 2000. "Europe and the Constitution: What If This Is As Good As It Gets?" In *Rethinking European Constitutionalism* (Joseph

Weiler and Margareta Mind, eds.). Cambridge: Cambridge University Press, pp. 74–102.

Maitland, Alison. 2002. "Coping with a More Influential Role: Non-Governmental Organisations: The Higher Profile of Pressure Groups Is Demanding Greater Accountability." *Financial Times*, February 13, 2002, p. 13.

Mallet, Pat. 2002. *ISEAL Alliance: Strengthening Voluntary Standards and Verification*. Kaslo: ISEAL Alliance.

Mank, Bradford C. 1998. "The Environmental Protection Agency's Project XL and Other Regulatory Reform Initiatives: The Need for Legislative Authorization." *Ecology Law Quarterly* 25: 1–88.

Margolis, Howard. 1987. *Patterns, Thinking, and Cognition: A Theory of Judgment*. Chicago: University of Chicago Press.

Marsh, Peter, Elizabeth Rosser and Rom Harre. 1978. *The Rules of Disorder*. London: Routledge and Kegan Paul.

Martin, John. 1997. "Changing Accountability Relations: Politics, Consumers and the Market." Paris: OECD Public Management Service (available at http://www.oecd.org/dataoecd/10/58/1902695.pdf).

Mashaw, Jerry L. 1983. *Bureaucratic Justice, Managing Social Security Disability Claims*. New Haven: Yale University Press.

1985. "Prodelegation: Why Administrators Should Make Political Decisions." *Journal of Law, Economics, and Organization* 1: 81–100.

1988. "Disability Insurance in an Age of Retrenchment: The Politics of Implementing Rights." In *Social Security: Beyond the Rhetoric of Crisis* (Theodore R. Marmor and Jerry L. Mashaw, eds.). Princeton: Princeton University Press, pp. 151–176.

1997. *Greed, Chaos, and Governance: Using Public Choice to Improve Public Law*. New Haven: Yale University Press.

2004. "Judicial Review of Administrative Action: Reflections on Balancing Political, Managerial and Legal Accountability." Paper prepared for a conference on Economic and Social Regulation, Accountability in Democracy, Sao Paulo, Brazil (March 15–16, 2004).

Mashaw, Jerry L. and Virginia P. Reno (eds.). 1996. *Balancing Security and Opportunity: The Challenge of Disability Income Policy*. Washington, DC: National Academy of Social Insurance.

Mashaw, Jerry L. *et al.* 1978. *Social Security Hearings and Appeals: Study of the Social Security Administration Hearing System*. Lexington, MA: Lexington Books.

Mayhew, David. 1974. *Congress: The Electoral Connection*. New Haven: Yale University Press.

Mazower, Mark. 1999. *Dark Continent: Europe's Twentieth Century*. New York: A. A. Knopf.

McBarnet, Doreen. 1994. "Legal Creativity: Law, Capital and Legal Avoidance." In *Lawyers in a Postmodern World: Translation and Transgression* (Maureen Cain and Christine B. Harrington, eds.). New York: NYU Press, pp. 73–84.

McConnell, Michael. 1987. "Federalism: Evaluating the Founders' Design." *University of Chicago Law Review* 54: 1484–1512.

McCraw, Thomas. 1984. *Prophets of Regulation: Charles Francis Adams, Louis D. Brandeis, James M. Landis, Alfred E. Kahn*. Cambridge, MA: Belknap Press.

McCubbins, Mathew D., Roger G. Noll and Barry R. Weingast. 1987. "Administrative Procedures as Instruments of Political Control." *Journal of Law and Economic Organization* 3: 243–277.

McDowell, John. 2000. "Towards Rehabilitating Objectivity." In *Rorty and His Critics* (Robert Brandom, ed.). Oxford: Blackwell Publishers, pp. 109–123.

McGinnis, John and Mark Movsesian. 2000. "The World Trade Constitution: Reinforcing Democracy Through Trade." *Harvard Law Review* 114: 511–605.

McKay, Steven. 2002. "The Squeaky Wheel's Dilemma: New Forms of Labor Organizing in the Philippines." Paper presented at the 2002 Annual Meeting of the Association for Asian Studies, Washington, DC, April 4–7, 2002.

Melucci, Alberto. 1989. *Nomads of the Present: Social Movements and Individual Needs in Contemporary Society* (John Keane and Paul Mier, eds.). Philadelphia: Temple University Press.

Merritt, Deborah. 1988. "The Guarantee Clause and State Autonomy: Federalism for a Third Century." *Columbia Law Review* 88: 1–78.

Metzger, Gillian E. 2002. "Privatization as Delegation: Rethinking State Action in Private Delegation Terms." Unpublished manuscript, August 18, 2002, on file with the Library of the Harvard Law School, Cambridge, MA.

Michaels, Jon. 2004. "Beyond Accountability: The Constitutional, Democratic, and Strategic Problems with Privatizing War." *Washington University Law Quarterly* 84(2): 1001–1127.

Miller, Warren E. and J. Merrill Shanks. 1996. *The New American Voter*. Cambridge, MA: Harvard University Press.

Milward, H. Brenton, Keith Provan and Barbara Else. 1993. "What Does the Hollow State Look Like?" In *Public Management: The State of the Art* (Barry Bozeman, ed.). San Francisco: Jossey-Bass, pp. 309–322.

Minow, Martha. 2003. "Public and Private Partnerships: Accounting for the New Religion." *Harvard Law Review* 116: 1229–1270.

Miranti, Paul J., Jr. 1990. "Measurement and Organizational Effectiveness: The ICC and Accounting-Based Regulation, 1887–1940." *Business and Economic History* 19: 183–192.

Mommsen, Wolfgang J. 1974. *The Age of Bureaucracy: Perspectives on the Political Sociology of Max Weber*. Oxford: Blackwell.

Moore, Mark H. 2003. "Symposium: Public Values in an Era of Privatization: Introduction." *Harvard Law Review* 116: 1212–1228.

Moran, Michael. 2003. *The British Regulatory State: High Modernism and Hyper-Innovation*. Oxford: Oxford University Press.

Morgan, Bronwen. 2003. *Social Citizenship and the Shadow of Competition: The Bureaucratic Politics of Regulatory Justification*. Aldershot: Ashgate.

2004. "The Regulatory Face of the Human Right to Water." *Journal of Water Law* 15: 179–187.

2005. "Social Protest Against Privatization of Water: Forging Cosmopolitan Citizenship?" In *Sustainable Justice: Reconciling Economic, Environmental and Social Law* (Marie-Clair Cordonier Seggier and Justice Weeramantry, eds.). Leiden: Martinus Nijhoff, pp. 339–352.

Morris, Huw and Patricia Fosh. 2000. "Measuring Trade Union Democracy: The Case of the UK Civil and Public Services Association." *British Journal of Industrial Relations* 38: 95–114.

Morris, Walter. 1968. *Decentralization in Management Systems*. Columbus, OH: Ohio State University Press.

Morrison, Brenda. 2006 *Restoring Safe School Communities: A Whole School Response to Bullying, Violence and Alienation*. Sydney: Federation Press.

Mulgan, Richard. 1997. "Contracting Out and Accountability." *Australian Journal of Public Administration* 56 (4): 106–117.

1997. "The Processes of Public Accountability." *Australian Journal of Public Administration* 56: 25–36.

2000. "'Accountability': An Ever-Expanding Concept?" *Public Administration* 78: 555–573.

2003. *Holding Power to Account: Accountability in Modern Democracies*. London: Palgrave Macmillan.

Murray, Andrew and Colin Scott. 2002. "Controlling the New Media: Hybrid Responses to New Forms of Power." *Modern Law Review* 65: 491–516.

Nagel, Thomas. 1986. *A View from Nowhere*. New York: Oxford University Press.

National District Attorneys Association. 2001. "Press Release: Nation's Prosecutors Support the 'Prosecution Drug Treatment Alternative to Prison Act'" (Press Release, February 13, 2001) (available at http://www.ndaa-apri.org/newsroom/pr_prosecution_drug_treatment.html).

New York State Commission on Drugs and the Courts. 2000. "Confronting the Cycle of Addiction and Recidivism: A Report to Chief Judge Judith

S. Kaye" (June 2000). Albany: New York State Commission on Drugs and the Courts (available at www.courts.state.ny.us/reports/addictionrecidivism.shtml).

Ngugi, Joel. 2002. "Searching for the Market Criterion: Market-Oriented Reforms in Legal and Economic Development Discourses." Cambridge, MA: Harvard Law School (unpublished SJD dissertation).

Nicolson, Donald and Rohit Sangvi. 1993. "Battered Women and Provocation: The Implications of *R.* v. *Ahluwalia*." *Criminal Law Review* 1993: 728–738.

Niebuhr, H. Richard. 1963. *The Responsible Self: An Essay in Christian Moral Philosophy*. New York: Harper & Row.

"NGOs: Sins of the Secular Missionaries." *Economist*, January 29, 2000, p. 25.

Nonet, Philippe and Phillip Selznick. 1978. *Law and Society in Transition: Toward Responsive Law*. New York: Octagon Books.

Normanton, E. Leslie. 1966. *The Accountability and Audit of Governments*. Manchester: Manchester University Press.

Novak, William J. 1996. *The People's Welfare: Law and Regulation in Nineteenth-Century America*. Chapel Hill: University of North Carolina Press.

O'Connor, James. 1973. *Fiscal Crisis of the State*. New York: St. Martin's Press.

O'Donnell, Guillermo. 1998. "Horizontal Accountability in New Democracies." *Journal of Democracy* 9: 112–126.

O'Neill, Onora. 2002. *A Question of Trust*. Cambridge: Cambridge University Press.

Offe, Claus. 1985. "New Social Movements: Challenging the Boundaries of Institutional Politics." *Social Research* 52: 117–167.

2000. "Civil Society and Social Order: Demarcating and Combining Market, State and Community." *Revue Europeennes de Sociologie* 41: 71–93.

2004. "Political Corruption: Conceptual and Practical Issues." In *Building a Trustworthy State in Post-Socialist Transition* (Janos Kornai and Susan Rose-Ackerman, eds.). New York: Palgrave Macmillan, pp. 77–99.

OJP Drug Court Clearinghouse and Technical Assistance Project. 2004. *Summary of Drug Court Activity by State and County* (May 27, 2004). Washington, DC: American University (available at http://spa.american.edu/justice/publications/drgchart2k.pdf).

Oliver, Dawn. 1997. "The Underlying Values of Public and Private Law." In *The Province of Administrative Law* (Michael Taggart, ed.). Oxford: Hart Publishing, pp. 212–245.

Olson, Mancur. 1971. *The Logic of Collective Action: Public Goods and the Theory of Groups*. Cambridge, MA: Harvard University Press.

O'Rourke, Dara. 2003. "Outsourcing Regulation: Analyzing Nongovernmental Systems of Labor Standards and Monitoring." *Policy Studies Journal* 31: 1–25.

Orr, Julian E. 1990. "Sharing Knowledge, Celebrating Identity: Community Memory in a Service Culture." In *Collective Remembering* (David Middleton and Derek Edwards, eds.). London: Sage Publications, pp. 169–189.

Osborne, David and Ted Gaebler. 1992. *Reinventing Government*. Reading, MA: Addison-Wesley Publishers.

Page, Benjamin and Robert Shapiro. 1983. "Effects of Public Opinion on Policy." *American Political Science Review* 77: 175–190.

1992. *The Rational Public: Fifty Years of Trends in Americans' Policy Preferences*. Chicago: University of Chicago Press.

Parker, Christine. 1999. *Just Lawyers*. Oxford: Oxford University Press.

2002. *The Open Corporation: Self-Regulation and Democracy*. Melbourne: Cambridge University Press.

Pasuk, Phongpaichit and Chris Baker. 2000. *Thailand's Crisis*. Singapore: Institute of Southeast Asian Studies.

Pavlov, Ivan Petrovich. 1960. *Conditioned Reflexes: An Investigation of the Physiological Activity of the Cerebral Cortex* (G. V. Anrep, trans.). New York: Dover Publications.

Peck, Jamie. 2001. *The Workfare State*. New York: Guilford Press.

Peck, Jamie and Adam Tickell. 2003. "Making Global Rules: Globalisation or Neoliberalisation?" In *Remaking the Global Economy: Economic-Geographical Perspectives* (Jamie Peck and Henry Wai-Chung Yeung, eds.). London: Sage Publications, pp. 163–181.

Peerenboom, Randall P. 2002. *China's Long March Toward Rule of Law*. New York: Cambridge University Press.

Perrow, Charles. 1967. "A Framework for Comparative Organizational Analysis." *American Sociological Review* 32: 194–208.

Peterson, Paul E. 1981. *City Limits*. Chicago: University of Chicago Press.

Picciotto, Sol. 2000. "Liberalization and Democratization: The Forum and the Hearth in the Era of Cosmopolitan Post-Industrial Capitalism." *Law and Contemporary Problems* 63: 157–178.

Pierre, Jon and B. Guy Peters. 2000. *Governance, Politics and the State*. Basingstoke: Macmillan.

Pinker, Steven. 2002. *The Blank Slate: The Modern Denial of Human Nature*. New York: Penguin Books.

Piore, Michael J. and Charles F. Sabel. 1984. *The Second Industrial Divide: Possibilities for Prosperity*. New York: Basic Books.

Pistor, Katharina and Philip A. Wellons. 1998. *The Role of Law and Legal Institutions in Asian Economic Development 1960–1995*. Hong Kong: Oxford University Press.

Pitkin, Hannah Fenichel. 1967. *The Concept of Representation*. Berkeley: University of California Press.

Polanyi, Karl. 1944. *The Great Transformation*. Boston: Beacon Press.

Polsby, Nelson. 1963. *Community Power and Political Theory*. New Haven: Yale University Press.

Postema, Gerald J. 1986. "'Protestant' Interpretation and Social Practices." *Law and Philosophy* 6: 283–319.

Poulson, Barton. 2003. "A Third Voice: A Review of Empirical Research on the Psychological Outcomes of Restorative Justice." *Utah Law Review* 2003: 167–203.

Powell, G. Bingham. 1993. "American Voter Turnout in Comparative Perspective." *Controversies in Voting Behavior* (Richard Niemi and Herbert Weisberg, eds.) (3rd ed.) Washington, DC: CQ Press, pp. 56–85.

Power, Michael. 1997. *The Audit Society: Rituals of Verification*. Oxford: Oxford University Press.

Prieto, Marina and Carolina Quinteros. 2004. "Never the Twain Shall Meet? Women's Organizations and Trade Unions in the *Maquila* Industry in Central America." *Development in Practice* 14: 149–157.

Pritzker, David. 1995. *Negotiated Rulemaking Sourcebook*. Washington, DC: Office of the Chairman, Administrative Conference of the United States.

Prosser, Tony. 1997. *Law and Regulators*. Oxford: Clarendon Press.

2000. "Public Service Law: Privatization's Unexpected Offspring." *Law and Contemporary Problems* 63: 63–80.

Przeworski, Adam. 1985. *Capitalism and Social Democracy*. New York: Cambridge University Press.

Przeworski, Adam, Michael E. Alvarez, Jose Antonio Cheibub and Fernando Limongi. 2000. *Democracy and Development: Political Institutions and Well Being in the World 1950–1990*. Cambridge: Cambridge University Press.

Przeworski, Adam, Susan S. Stokes and Bernard Manin (eds.). 1999. *Democracy, Accountability, and Representation*. New York: Cambridge University Press.

Putnam, Robert. 1996. *Bowling Alone: The Collapse and Revival of American Community*. New York: Simon & Schuster.

Rabinowitz, Randy S. and Mark M. Hager. 2000. "Designing Health and Safety: Workplace Hazard Regulation in the United States and Canada." *Cornell International Law Journal* 33: 373–434.

Rakoff, Todd. 2000. "The Choice Between Formal and Informal Modes of Administrative Regulation." *Administrative Law Review* 52: 159–174.

Ramseyer, J. Mark and Francis McCall Rosenbluth. 1993. *Japan's Political Marketplace*. Cambridge, MA: Harvard University Press.

Rawls, John. 1971. *A Theory of Justice*. Cambridge, MA: Harvard University Press.

1996. *Political Liberalism*. New York: Columbia University Press.

Rees, Joseph. 1997. "The Development of Communitarian Regulation in the Chemical Industry." *Law and Policy* 19: 477–528.

Reeve, David. 1985. *Golkar of Indonesia: An Alternative to the Party System.* Singapore: Oxford University Press.

Revesz, Richard. 1997. "Environmental Regulation, Ideology and the DC Circuit." *Virginia Law Review* 83: 1717–1772.

Reynolds, George M. 1936. *Machine Politics in New Orleans.* New York: Columbia University Press.

Roche, Declan. 2003. *Accountability in Restorative Justice.* Oxford: Oxford University Press.

Rodrik, Dani. 1999. *The New Global Economy and Developing Countries: Making Openness Work.* Washington, DC: Institute for International Economics.

Roosevelt, Theodore. 1912. "Nationalism and Popular Rule." In *The Initiative Referendum and Recall* (William Bennett Munro, ed.). New York: Appleton, pp. 52–68.

Roper, Richard W. 1998. "A Shifting Landscape: Contracting for Welfare Services in New Jersey." Rockefeller Reports, No. 10. Albany: Nelson A. Rockefeller Institute of Government, State University of New York (December 23, 1998).

Rorty, Richard. 1991. "Solidarity or Objectivity?" In Richard Rorty, *Objectivity, Relativism, and Truth.* Cambridge: Cambridge University Press, pp. 21–34.

1995. "Is Truth a Goal of Enquiry? Davidson vs. Wright." *Philosophical Quarterly* 45: 281–300.

Rose-Ackerman, Susan. 1992. *Rethinking the Progressive Agenda: The Reform of the American Regulatory State.* New York: Free Press.

1994. "American Administrative Law under Siege: Is Germany a Model?" *Harvard Law Review* 107: 1279–1302.

Rosenberg, Gerald. 1991. *The Hollow Hope: Can Courts Bring About Social Change?* Chicago: University of Chicago Press.

Rubin, Edward L. 1989. "Law and Legislation in the Administrative State." *Columbia Law Review* 89: 369–426.

1996. "The New Legal Process, the Synthesis of Discourse, and the Microanalysis of Institutions." *Harvard Law Review* 109: 1393–1438.

2001. "Getting Past Democracy." *University of Pennsylvania Law Review* 149: 711–792.

2002. "Independence as a Governance Mechanism." In *Judicial Independence at the Crossroads: An Interdisciplinary Approach* (Stephen Burbank and Barry Friedman, eds.). Thousand Oaks, CA: Sage Publications, pp. 56 –101.

2005. *Beyond Camelot: Rethinking Politics and Law for the Modern State.* Princeton: Princeton University Press.

Rubin, Edward L. and Malcolm Feeley. 1994. "Federalism: Some Notes on a National Neurosis." *UCLA Law Review* 41: 903–951.

Rydell, C. Peter and Susan S. Everingham. 1994. *Controlling Cocaine: Supply Versus Demand Programs*. Santa Monica: Rand.

Sabel, Charles F. 1994. "Learning by Monitoring: The Institutions of Economic Development." In *Handbook of Economic Sociology* (Neil J. Smelser and Richard Swedberg, eds.). Princeton: Princeton University Press, pp. 137–165.

2004. "Beyond Principal–Agent Governance: Experimentalist Organizations, Learning and Accountability." Draft discussion paper presented at theWetenschappelijke Raad voor het Regeringsbeleid Meeting. Amsterdam, May 10–14, 2004.

2005. "Theory of a Real Time Revolution." In *Collaborative Community* (Charles Heckscher and Paul Adler, eds.). Oxford: Oxford University Press (forthcoming) (available at http://www2.law.columbia.edu/sabel/papers.htm) (last accessed April 19, 2004).

Sabel, Charles F. and William H. Simon. 2004. "Destabilization Rights: How Public Law Litigation Succeeds." *Harvard Law Review* 117: 1016–1101.

Sabel, Charles F. *et al.* 2000. "Beyond Backyard Environmentalism." In *Beyond Backyard Environmentalism* (Joshua Cohen and Joel Rogers, eds.). Boston: Beacon Press, pp. 3–47.

2004. "Beyond Principal–Agent Governance: Experimentalist Organizations, Learning and Accountability." In *De Staat van de Democratie: De Democratie Voorbij De Staat* (E. R. Engelen and M. Sie Dhian Ho, eds.). Amsterdam: Amsterdam University Press, pp. 173–195.

Saich, Tony. 2000. "Negotiating the State: The Development of Social Organizations in China." *China Quarterly* 161: 124–141.

Salamon, Lester M. (ed.). 2002. *The Tools of Government: A Guide to the New Governance*. Oxford: Oxford University Press.

Sargant, William Walter. 1961. *Battle for the Mind: A Physiology of Conversion and Brain-Washing*. Baltimore: Penguin Books.

Sassen, Saskia. 1999. "Making the Global Economy Run: The Role of National States and Private Agents." *International Social Science Journal* 51: 409–415.

Sathe, S. P. 2002. *Judicial Activism in India: Transgressing Borders and Enforcing Limits*. New Delhi: Oxford University Press.

Schamis, Hector. 2002. *Re-forming the State*. Ann Arbor: University of Michigan Press.

Schedler, Andreas. 1999. "Conceptualizing Accountability." In *The Self Restraining State – Power and Accountability in New Democracies* (Andreas Schedler, Larry Diamond and Marc Plattner, eds.). Boulder: Lynne Rienner Publishers, pp. 13–28.

Schedler, Andreas, Larry Diamond and Marc Plattner, eds., *The Self Restraining State - Power and Accountability in New Democracies*. Boulder: Lynne Rienner Publishers.

Schoenbrod, David. 1993. *Power Without Responsibility: How Congress Abuses the People Through Delegation*. New Haven: Yale University Press.

Scholte, Jan Aart. 2004. "Civil Society and Democratically Accountable Global Governance." *Government and Opposition* 39: 211–233.

Sclar, Elliott D. 2000. *You Don't Always Get What You Pay For*. Ithaca, NY: Cornell University Press.

Scott, Colin. 1993. "Privatization, Control and Accountability." In *Corporate Control and Accountability: Changing Structures and the Dynamics of Regulation* (Joseph McCahery, Sol Picciotto and Colin Scott, eds.). Oxford: Oxford University Press, pp. 231–246.

1998. "The Juridification of Relations in the UK Utility Sector." In *Commercial Regulation and Judicial Review* (Julia Black *et al.*, eds.). Oxford: Hart Publishing.

2000. "Accountability in the Regulatory State." *Journal of Law and Society* 27: 38–60.

2001. "Analyzing Regulatory Space: Fragmented Resources and Institutional Design." *Public Law* 2001: 329–353.

2002. "Private Regulation of the Public Sector: A Neglected Facet of Contemporary Governance." *Journal of Law and Society* 29: 56–76.

2003. "Speaking Softly Without Big Sticks: Meta-Regulation and Public Sector Audit." *Law and Policy* 25: 203–219.

2005. "Between the Old and the New: Innovation in the Regulation of Internet Gambling." In *Regulatory Innovation* (Julia Black, Martin Lodge and Mark Thatcher, eds.). Cheltenham: Elgar.

Scott, James C. 1998. *Seeing Like a State: How Certain Schemes to Improve the Human Condition Have Failed*. New Haven: Yale University Press.

Seelye, Katharine Q. 1995. "House Easily Passes Amendment to Ban Desecration of Flag." *New York Times*, June 29, 1995, p. A1.

Seidenfeld, Mark. 2000. "An Apology for Administrative Law in the 'Contracting State'." *Florida State University Law Review* 28: 215–239.

2002. "Cognitive Loafing, Social Conformity, and Judicial Review of Agency Rulemaking." *Cornell Law Review* 87: 486–548.

Self, Peter. 1993. *Government by the Market? The Politics of Public Choice*. Basingstoke: Macmillan.

Semin, G. R. and A. S. R. Manstead. 1983. *The Accountability of Conduct: A Social Psychological Analysis*. London: Academic Press.

Shane, Peter. 1998. "Interbranch Accountability in State Government and the Constitutional Requirement of Judicial Independence." *Law and Contemporary Problems* 61: 21–54.

Shapiro, Martin. 1988. *Who Guards the Guardians? Judicial Control of Administration*. Athens, GA: University of Georgia Press.

2001. "Administrative Law Unbounded: Reflections on Government and Governance." *Indiana Journal of Global Legal Studies* 8: 369–377.

Shapiro, Martin and Alec Stone Sweet. 2002. *On Law, Politics and Judicialisation*. Oxford: Oxford University Press.

Shearing, Clifford D. and Philip C. Stenning. 1985. "From the Panopticon to Disney World: The Development of Discipline." In *Perspectives in Criminal Law* (Anthony N. Doob and Edward L. Greenspan, eds.). Toronto: Canada Law Book Inc., pp. 300–304.

Sheehan, Jane Ennis. 1998. "Mixed Finance: A Real Estate Lawyer's 'Field of Dreams'." *Journal of Affordable Housing and Community Development Law* 7: 289–303.

Shichor, David. 1995. *Punishment for Profit: Private Prisons/Public Concerns*. Thousand Oaks, CA: Sage Publications.

Silver, Beth and Giovanni Arrighi. 2003. "Polanyi's 'Double Movement': The Belle Epoques of British and US Hegemony Compared." *Politics and Society* 31: 325–355.

Simon, Herbert. 1957. *Administrative Behavior: A Study of Decision-Making Processes in Administrative Organization*. New York: Macmillan.

Sklar, Martin J. 1988. *The Corporate Reconstruction of American Capitalism, 1890–1916: The Market, the Law, and Politics*. New York: Cambridge University Press.

Skowronek, Stephen. 1982. *Building a New American State: The Expansion of National Administrative Capacities, 1877–1920*. New York: Cambridge University Press.

Slaughter, Anne-Marie. 2001. "The Accountability of Government Networks." *Indiana Journal of Global Legal Studies* 8: 347–367.

2004. "Disaggregated Sovereignty: Towards the Public Accountability of Global Government Networks." *Government and Opposition* 2004: 159–190.

2004. *A New World Order*. Princeton: Princeton University Press.

Smith, Adam. 1970. *Wealth of Nations*. Harmondsworth: Penguin.

Smith, Bradley A. 2000. "Campaign Finance Regulation: Faulty Assumptions and Undemocratic Consequences." In *Political Money: Deregulating American Politics – Selected Writings on Campaign Finance Reform* (Annelise Anderson, ed.). Palo Alto: Hoover Institution Press, pp. 36–72.

Smith, Stephen Rathgeb and Michael Lipsky. 1993. *Nonprofits for Hire: The Welfare State in the Age of Contracting*. Cambridge, MA: Harvard University Press.

Social Security Administration, Office of Research, Evaluation and Statistics. 2002. *Annual Statistical Supplement to the Social Security Bulletin*. Washington, DC: US Department of Health and Human Services, Social Security Administration.

Solomons, David. 1968. "The Historical Development of Costing." In *Studies in Cost Analysis* (David Solomons, ed.). Homewood, IL: Richard D. Irwin, pp. 3–50.

Spar, Debora and James Dail. 2002. "Of Measurement and Mission: Accounting for Performance in Non-Governmental Organizations." *Chicago Journal of International Law* 3: 171–181.

Spiller, Pablo. 1998. "Regulatory Agencies and the Courts." In *The New Palgrave Dictionary of Economics and the Law* (Peter Newman, ed.). New York: Stockton Press, vol. 3, pp. 263–266.

Spiro, Peter. 2002. "Accounting for NGOs." *Chicago Journal of International Law* 3: 161–169.

Spitzer, Matthew L. 1979. "Multicriteria Choice Processes: An Application of Public Choice Theory to Bakke, the FCC, and the Courts." *Yale Law Journal* 88: 717–780.

Spooner, Dave. 2004. "Trade Unions and NGOs: The Need for Cooperation." *Development in Practice* 14(1 & 2): 19–33.

Stepan, Alfred. 1978. *The State and Society: Peru in Comparative Perspective*. Princeton: Princeton University Press.

Stewart, Richard B. 1975. "The Reformation of American Administrative Law." *Harvard Law Review* 88: 1667–1813.

2003. "Administrative Law in the 21st Century." *New York University Law Review* 78: 437–460.

Stiglitz, Joseph E. 2002. *Globalization and Its Discontents*. New York: W. W. Norton & Co.

2003. "Democratizing the International Monetary Fund and the World Bank: Governance and Accountability." *Governance* 16: 111–139.

Stinchcombe, Arthur. 1985. "Contracts as Hierarchical Documents." In *Organizational Theory and Project Management* (Arthur Stinchcombe and Carol Heimer, eds.). Bergen: Norwegian University Press, pp. 121–171.

Stivers, Camilla. 2001. *Democracy, Bureaucracy and the Study of Administration*. Boulder: Westview.

Stone, Bruce. 1995. "Administrative Accountability in the 'Westminster' Democracies: Towards a New Conceptual Framework." *Governance* 8: 505–526.

Stone, Deborah A. 1984. *The Disabled State*. Philadelphia: Temple University Press.

Stone Sweet, Alec. 2000. *Governing with Judges: Constitutional Politics in Europe*. Oxford: Oxford University Press.

Storing, Herbert J. 1981. *What the Anti-Federalists Were For*. Chicago: University of Chicago Press.

Strang, Heather. 2002. *Repair or Revenge: Victims and Restorative Justice*. Oxford: Oxford University Press.

Strang, Heather and Lawrence Sherman. 2003. "Effects of Face-to-Face Restorative Justice on Repeat Offending and Victim Satisfaction."

Canberra: Australian National University (unpublished manuscript dated May 16, 2003).

Sturm, Susan. 2001. "Second Generation Employment Discrimination: A Structural Approach." *Columbia Law Review* 101: 458–568.

Suggs, Robert E. 1991. "Racial Discrimination in Business Transactions." *Hastings Law Journal* 42: 1257–1323.

Sunstein, Cass. 1988. "Beyond the Republican Revival." *Yale Law Journal* 97: 1539–1590.

Susskind, Lawrence, Eileen Babbitt and Peter Segal. 1993. "When ADR Becomes the Law: A Review of Federal Practice." *Negotiation Journal* 9: 59–75.

Susskind, Lawrence and Gerard MacMahon. 1985. "Theory and Practice of Negotiated Rulemaking." *Yale Journal on Regulation* 3: 133–165.

Swedish National Board of Trade. 2003. *Market Access for Organic Agriculture Products from Developing Countries: Analysis of the EC Regulation (2092/91)*. Stockholm: Kommerskollegium.

Teixeira, Ruy. 1992. *The Disappearing American Voter*. Washington, DC: Brookings Institution.

Teubner, Günther. 1983. "Substantive and Reflexive Elements in Modern Law." *Law and Society Review* 17: 239–285.

1985. "After Legal Instrumentalism? Strategic Models of Post-Regulatory Law." In *Dilemmas of Law in the Welfare State* (Gunther Teubner, ed.). Berlin: Walter de Gruyter, pp. 299–325.

1993. *Law as an Autopoietic System* (Anne Bankowska and Ruth Adler, trans., Zenon Bankowski, ed.). Oxford: Blackwell.

2001. "Legal Irritants: How Unifying Law Ends Up in New Differences." In *Varieties of Capitalism: The Institutional Foundations of Comparative Advantage* (Peter A. Hall and David Soskice, eds.). Oxford: Oxford University Press, pp. 417–441.

Thayer, James. 2004. "The Trade of Cross-Border Gambling and Betting: The WTO Dispute between Antigua and the United States." *Duke Law and Technology Review* 2004: 13 (online publication, available at http://www.law.duke.edu/journals/dltr/articles/2004dltr0013.html).

Thompson, E. P. 1967. "Time, Work-Discipline, and Industrial Capitalism." *Past and Present* 38: 56–97.

Thompson, James. 2003. *Organizations in Action: Social Science Bases of Administrative Theory*. New Brunswick: Transaction Publishers.

Tien, Lee. 2004. "Architectural Regulation and the Evolution of Social Norms." *International Journal of Communications Law and Policy* 9 (Special Issue on Cybercrime): 1–14.

Tilly, Charles (ed.) 1975. *The Formation of National States in Western Europe*. Princeton: Princeton University Press.

Tocqueville, Alexis de. 1969. *Democracy in America* (J. P. Mayer, ed., George Lawrence, trans.). Garden City, NY: Doubleday.

Trebilcock, Michael J., Ron Daniels and Malcolm Thorburn. 2000. "Government by Voucher." *Boston University Law Review* 80: 205–232.

Trebilcock, Michael and Edward Iacobucci. 2003. "Privatization and Accountability." *Harvard Law Review* 116: 1422–1454.

Trevor-Roper, H. R. 1947. *The Last Days of Hitler*. New York: The Macmillan.

Turner, Frederick Jackson. 1920. *The Frontier in American History*. New York: H. Holt and Co.

Tushnet, Mark. 1999. *Taking the Constitution Away from the Courts*. Princeton: Princeton University Press.

2001. "Nonjudicial Review." Georgetown Public Law Research Paper No. 298007 (available from http://papers.ssrn.com/sol3/papers.cfm?abstract_id=298007) (last accessed April 18, 2005).

Tyler, Tom R. 1990. *Why People Obey the Law*. New Haven: Yale University Press.

Uhr, John. 1998. *Deliberative Democracy in Australia: The Changing Face of Parliament*. Melbourne: Cambridge University Press.

Unger, Roberto M. 1987. *Politics: A Work in Constructive Social Theory*. Cambridge: Cambridge University Press.

United Nations Economic and Social Commission for Asia and the Pacific. 2001. "Social Safety Nets in Thailand: Analysis and Prospects." In *Strengthening Policies and Programmes on Social Safety Nets: Issues, Recommendations and Selected Studies* (Social Policy Paper No. 8, ST/ESCAP/2163). New York: United Nations, pp. 57–108.

United States Bureau of the Census. 1975. *Historical Statistics of the United States: Colonial Times to 1970*. Washington, DC: US Government Printing Office.

2001. *Current Population Reports: Population Profile of the United States, 1999*. Washington, DC: US Government Printing Office.

2002. *2001 Statistical Abstract of the United States*. Washington, DC: US Government Printing Office.

United States House of Representatives Ways and Means Committee. 1974. *Committee Staff Report on the Disability Insurance Program*. Washington, DC: House Ways and Means Committee.

United States Sentencing Commission. 2001. *2001 Federal Sentencing Guidelines Manual*. Washington, DC: United States Sentencing Commission.

Vakil, Anna. 1997. "Confronting the Classification Problem: Toward a Taxonomy of NGOs." *World Development* 25: 2057–2070.

Van Kerkhoff, Lorrae and Sasha Courville. 2003. "Mutual Dependence, Mutual Strength: The Role of Trust in Social Learning." Canberra: Australian National University (unpublished working paper).

Varela, Francisco J., Evan Thompson and Eleanor Rosch. 1991. *The Embodied Mind: Cognitive Science and Human Experience*. Cambridge, MA: MIT Press.

Vaughn, Robert G. 1990. "Ethics in Government and the Vision of Public Service." *George Washington Law Review* 58: 417–450.

Wade, Sir William and Christopher Forsyth. 2004. *Administrative Law*. 9th ed., Oxford: Oxford University Press.

Waldrauch, Harald. 1998 "Institutionalizing Horizontal Accountability: A Conference Report." Reihe Politikwissenschaft / Political Science Series No. 55. Vienna: Institute for Advanced Studies (available at http://www.ihs.ac.at/publications/pol/pw_55.pdf).

Waldron, Jeremy. 2001. *Law and Disagreement*. Oxford: Oxford University Press.

Wapner, Paul. 2002. "Defending Accountability in NGOs." *Chicago Journal of International Law* 3: 197–205.

2002. "Introductory Essay: Paradise Lost? NGOs and Global Accountability." *Chicago Journal of International Law* 3: 155–160.

Warner, Kate. 1994. "The Rights of the Offender in Family Conferences." In *Family Conferencing and Juvenile Justice: The Way Forward or Misplaced Optimism?* (C. Alder and J. Wundersitz, eds.). Canberra: Australian Institute of Criminology, pp. 153–166.

Weatherill, Stephen. 2000. "New Strategies for Managing the EC's Internal Market." *Current Legal Problems* 53: 595–619.

Weber, Max. 1949. "Objectivity in Social Science and Social Policy." In *The Methodology of the Social Sciences* (Edward Shils and Henry Finch, trans.). New York: Free Press.

1968. *Economy and Society* (Guenther Roth and Claus Wittich, eds.). Berkeley: University of California Press.

Webster's New Collegiate Dictionary. 1959. Springfield, MA: Merriam-Webster.

Wechsler, Herbert. 1959. "Toward Neutral Principles of Constitutional Law." *Harvard Law Review* 73: 1–35.

White, G. Edward. 1978. *Patterns of American Legal Thought*. Indianapolis: Bobbs-Merrill.

Wiebe, Robert H. 1967. *The Search for Order 1877–1920*. New York: Hill and Wang.

Wilks, Stephen. 1998. "Utility Regulation, Corporate Governance, and the Amoral Corporation." In *Changing Regulatory Institutions in Britain and North America* (G. Bruce Doern and Stephen Wilks, eds.). Toronto: University of Toronto Press, pp. 133–161.

Williams, Bernard. 1981. *Moral Luck*. Cambridge: Cambridge University Press.

Williams, Raymond. 1973. *The Country and the City*. New York: Oxford University Press.

Williamson, Oliver. 1975. *Markets and Hierarchies: Analysis and Antitrust Implications*. New York: Free Press.

Wilson, Edward O. 1998. *Consilience: The Unity of Knowledge*. New York: Alfred A. Knopf.

Wilson, H. T. 2001. *Bureaucratic Representation*. Leiden: Brill.

Wilson, James Q. 1989. *Bureaucracy: What Government Agencies Do and Why They Do It*. New York: Basic Books.

Wilson, Woodrow. 1911. *Constitutional Government in the United States*. New York: Columbia University Press.

1912. "The Issues of Reform." In *The Initiative Referendum and Recall* (William Bennett Munro, ed.). New York: Appleton, pp. 69–90.

Witt, John Fabian. 2003. "Speedy Fred Taylor and the Ironies of Enterprise Liability." *Columbia Law Review* 103: 1–49.

Wolfe, Joel. 1996. *Power and Privatization*. New York: St. Martin's Press.

Wood, Gordon. 1969. *The Creation of the American Republic 1776–1787*. Chapel Hill: University of North Carolina Press.

Wright, Eric O. 1978. *Class, Crisis and the State*. London: New Left Books.

Wunderlich, Goloo S., Dorothy P. Rice and Nicole L. Amado (eds.). 2002. *The Dynamics of Disability: Measuring and Monitoring Disability for Social Security Programs*. Washington, DC: US National Academy Press.

Yearling, Clifton K. 1970. *The Money Machines: the Breakdown and Reform of Governmental and Party Finance in the North, 1860–1920*. Albany: State University of New York Press.

Zaret, David. 2000. *Origins of Democratic Culture: Printing, Petitions, and the Public Sphere in Early-Modern England*. Princeton: Princeton University Press.

Zehr, Howard. 2003. *The Little Book of Restorative Justice*. Intercourse, PA: Good Books.

II. CASES

Alexander v. *State*, 48 P 3d 110 (Okla. Crim. App. 2002).

Amalgamated Meat Cutters and Butcher Workmen of North America, AFL–CIO v. *Connally*, 337 F Supp 737 (DDC 1971).

Association of American Railroads v. *Department of Transportation*, 198 F 3d 944 (DC Cir. 1999).

Blum v. *Yaretzky*, 457 US 991 (1982).

Board of Trustees of the University of Alabama v. *Garrett*, 531 US 356 (2001).

Books v. *Chater*, 91 F 3d 972 (7th Cir. 1996).

Bowen v. *City of New York*, 476 US 467 (1986).

Brentwood Academy v. *Tennessee Secondary School Athletic Association*, 531 US 288 (2001).

Brown v. *Board of Education*, 347 US 483 (1954).

Brown v. *Board of Education* (*Brown II*), 349 US 294 (1955).
Burlington Industries Inc. v. *Ellerth*, 524 US 742 (1998).
Center for Law and Education, et al. v. *Department of Education*, 209 F Supp 2d 102 (DDC 2002).
Chevron v. *Natural Resource Defense Council*, 467 US 837 (1984).
City of Bourne v. *Flores*, 521 US 507 (1997).
Cotran v. *Rollings Hudig Hall International, Inc.*, 948 P 2d 412 (Cal. 1998).
Council of Civil Service Unions v. *Minister for the Civil Service* [1985] AC 374.
Dred Scott v. *Sandford*, 60 US (19 How.) 393 (1856).
Euresti v. *Stenner*, 458 F 2d 1115 (10th Cir. 1972).
Faragher v. *City of Boca Raton*, 524 US 775 (1998).
Flagg Bros., Inc. v. *Brooks*, 436 US 149 (1978).
Forsham v. *Califano*, 587 F 2d 1128 (DC Cir. 1978).
Fuzie v. *Manor Care, Inc.*, 461 F Supp 689 (ND Ohio 1977).
Gay Law Students Association v. *Pacific Telephone and Telegraph Co.*, 595 P 2d 592 (Cal. 1979).
Gonzaga University v. *Doe*, 536 US 273 (2002).
Griswold v. *Connecticut*, 381 US 479 (1965).
Heckler v. *Campbell*, 461 US 458 (1983).
Heckler v. *Chaney*, 470 US 821 (1985).
Home Box Office, Inc. v. *FCC*, 567 F 2d 9 (DC Cir. 1977), cert. denied, 434 US 829 (1977).
Hunter v. *City of Pittsburgh*, 207 US 161 (1907).
Ingraham v. *Wright*, 430 US 651 (1978).
J. K. ex rel. R. K. v. *Dillenberg*, 836 F Supp 698 (D. Ariz. 1993).
J. W. Hampton, Jr. & Co. v. *United States*, 276 US 394 (1928).
Mathews v. *Eldridge*, 424 US 319 (1976).
Miranda v. *Arizona*, 384 US 436 (1966).
Mistretta v. *United States*, 488 US 361 (1989).
Natural Resources Defense Council, Inc. v. *EPA*, 859 F 2d 156 (DC Cir. 1988).
New York v. *United States*, 505 US 144 (1992).
NLRB v. *Sears, Roebuck & Co.*, 421 US 132 (1975).
Pinsker v. *Pacific Coast Society of Orthodontists*, 12 P 3d 253 (Cal. 1974).
Printz v. *United States*, 521 US 898 (1997).
R. v. *Ahluwalia* [1992] 4 All ER 859.
R. v. *Humphreys* [1995] 4 All ER 1008.
R. v. *Smith (Morgan)* [2000] 4 All ER 289.
R. v. *Thornton* [1992] 1 All ER 306.
R. v. *Thornton (No. 2)* [1996] 2 All ER 1023.
Roe v. *Wade*, 410 US 113 (1973).
Rush Prudential HMO, Inc. v. *Moran*, 536 US 355 (2002).
Scanwell Labs, Inc. v. *Shaffer*, 424 F 2d 859 (DC Cir. 1970).

Solid Waste Agency of Northern Cook County v. *US Army Corps of Engineers*, 531 US 159 (2001).
Texas Office of Public Utility Counsel v. *FCC*, 65 F 3d 313 (5th Cir. 2001).
Texas v. *Johnson*, 491 US 397 (1989).
United States v. *Eichman*, 496 US 310 (1990).
United States v. *Morrison*, 529 US 598 (2000).
United States v. *O'Brien*, 391 US 367 (1968).
USA Group Loan Service Inc. v. *Riley, Secretary of US Department of Education*, 82 F 3d 708 (7th Cir. 1996).
West v. *Atkins*, 487 US 42 (1988).
Whitman v. *American Trucking Association, Inc.*, 531 US 457 (2001).
Wolff v. *McDonnell*, 418 US 539 (1974).
Zelman v. *Simmons-Harris*, 536 US 639 (2002).

III. DOMESTIC LEGISLATION

Administrative Dispute Resolution Act of 1996, Pub. L. No. 104-320, § 12(d), 110 Stat. 3870, 3875, codified as amended at 5 USC §§ 571–584 (2002).
Administrative Procedure Act, Pub. L. 79-404, 60 Stat. 237 (1946), codified as amended at 5 USC §§ 551–559, 801–808 (2002).
Code of Federal Regulations, Chapter 20 § 404.1527(d)(2) (2004).
Executive Order 12291 of February 17, 1981, 46 Fed. Reg. 13193.
Executive Order 12866 of September 30, 1993, 58 Fed. Reg. 51735.
Federal Advisory Committee Act, Pub. L. No. 92-463, 86 Stat. 770 (1972), codified as amended at 5 USC Appendix 2 (2002).
Federal Register Act of 1935, Pub. L. No. 74-220, Chapter 417, §§ 2 and 7, 49 Stat. 500, 502 (1935), codified as amended at 44 USC §§ 1501–1511 (2002).
Federal Rules of Criminal Procedure 11(c)(4).
Federal Tort Claims Act, Chapter 753, 60 Stat. 842 (1946), codified as amended at 28 USC §§ 1346(b), 2671–2680 (2002).
Freedom of Information Act, Pub. L. No. 93-502, 1–3, 88 Stat. 1561, 1563–1564 (1974), codified as amended at 5 USC § 552 (2002).
Government in the Sunshine Act of 1976, Pub. L. No. 94-409, 90 Stat. 124 (1976), codified as amended at 5 USC § 552b (2002).
Negotiated Rulemaking Act of 1990, Pub. L. No. 101-648, 104 Stat. 4969 (1990), codified as amended at 5 USC §§ 561–570 (2002).
No Child Left Behind Act of 2001, Pub. L. No. 107-110, 115 Stat. 1425 (2001), codified as amended at 20 USC §§ 6301 et seq. (2002).
Personal Responsibility and Work Opportunity Reconciliation Act of 1996, Pub. L. No. 104-193, 110 Stat. 2105 (1996), codified as amended in scattered sections of 42 USC (2002).

Sarbanes–Oxley Act of 2002, Pub. L. No. 107-204, 116 Stat. 745 (2002), codified as amended at 15 USC §§ 7201–7266 (2002).

Ticket to Work and Work Incentive Improvement Act, Pub. L. No. 106-170, 113 Stat. 1860 (1999), codified as amended at 42 USC § 1320b-19 (2002).

Trade Secrets Act, 62 Stat. 791 (1948), codified as amended at 18 USC § 1905 (2000).

IV. INTERNATIONAL LEGISLATION AND TREATIES

Agreement on Technical Barriers to Trade, April 15, 1994, Marrakesh Agreement Establishing the World Trade Organization, Annex 1A, in *Legal Instruments – Results of the Uruguay Round*, vol. 1 (1994), 18 ILM 1079 (1979) (available at http://docsonline.wto.org).

General Agreement on Tariffs and Trade, October 30, 1947, 55 UNTS 187, Arts. I and II.

INDEX

abortion, restrictions on 320
accountability 3, 13, 52–54, 115
  crisis/problems in 1–3, 33–34, 197–202, 256
  experiences and epistemology 11–16
  fragmentation of concept 9–11, 15
  history of concept 3–6
  meanings 117–118, 175, 243
  real nature of 74–77
  stability and contiguity of notion 6–8
  taxonomy of accountability regimes 118–126
    fixing ideas 127–129
    market accountability 119, 122–124, 127, 129, 139, 153
    overlapping regimes 130
    public governance accountability 119, 120–122, 127–129, 131–132, 153, 155
    social accountability 119, 124–126, 127, 129, 139, 153
    uses of taxonomy 130–134
  see also individual topics
accounts, uniform system of 335–336
accreditation systems 96
Ackerman, Bruce 59
Active Learning Network for Accountability and Performance in Humanitarian Action (ALNAP) 291
Adams, Henry Carter 336
Advertising Standards Authority 189
affirmative action 320
agency *see* principal/agent relationships
Alford, William P. 349–356
American Bar Association (ABA) 126
American Center for International Labor Solidarity (ACILS) 161, 170, 171
Amnesty International 275
anti-administrative impulse 53, 75, 77–82
appeals, problem-solving courts and 314–319
architecture, modes of control and 174, 181–183, 189–190
argument 227
Aristotelianism, responsibility and 221, 222, 227–228, 230, 235
Asian Development Bank (ADB) 342
auditing 44, 97, 103
  modes of control and 182
  social 255
  social security disability insurance (SSDI) 142–144
Australia
  competition in 248, 250–251
  Fairtrade labeling in 282, 283
  migration advice 256–257, 258
  regulation in 41, 248, 250–251, 253, 256–257
Australian Capital Territory, restorative justice in 50
Australian Council of Trade Unions 171
Austria, restorative justice in 36

banks 79
Barber, Benjamin 254
basic responsibility 224, 229, 230, 234, 235, 236
Beermann, Jack 93, 94, 95, 96, 103
Bellman, Howard 215–216
benchmarking 200, 255
bias 154
Bickel, Alexander 301
black market 61
blurring of accountability 135–136
Bolivia, water struggles in 263–265
boundaries 296–299
Bovens, Mark 42
Braithwaite, John 254, 255
Brazil, NGOs in 273
Brownsword, Roger 182, 183
Bryan, William Jennings 337–338, 340
bullying 34
bureaucracy 4, 6, 7, 8, 9, 15, 17, 115, 198
  accountability 18, 28, 120, 121, 197, 199, 201
  anti-administrative impulse 53, 75, 77–82
  authority systems 124
  employee protection in 86
  hierarchies 75–76, 124, 197
  restorative justice and 34
Burt, Ronald 354

Canada, restorative justice in 39
capacities, privatization and 138
capture theories 138
Carter, Jimmy 71
celebration circles 46
China
  clean air legislation 349–356
  constitutional system in 27, 330, 347–349, 357
  Parliament 347–349
City Panel on Takeovers and Mergers 189
clean air legislation 349–356
Cochabamba Declaration 263–265, 266
Coglianese, Cary 203
Cold War 10
common law system 231, 232–233
communities 18, 345
  globalization and 259–261
  implicit 259, 263–265
  modes of control and 174, 177, 180–181
  spontaneous accountability in 188–189
Compa, Lance 159
comparative constitutional law 329–330
competition 66, 122
  modes of control and 174, 178–180
  neo-Madisonian 200
  privatization and 87
  regulation 248, 250–251
computer software, modes of control and 181, 182, 189
conflicts of interest, NGOs and 274, 278
consent agreement, negotiated rulemaking and 213–216
  enforcement 213–216
consequential responsibility 220, 224, 226, 229, 231, 234–235
Considine, Mark 198
consilience 16, 28–29
constitutions 27, 329–331
  China 27, 330, 347–349, 357
  constitutional law 329–330
  inductive accountability
    non-regulatory environments 344–345
    towards inductive methodology for exploring constitutional accountability 345–347
  regulatory model of constitutional accountability 331–344
    history and development 332–341
    limitations 341–344
consultation, privatization and 90
consumers
  privatization and 106–108
  product market accountability and 122
contraception 325
contracts
  contracting out *see* privatization and contracting out
  court scrutiny 93, 95
  design of 103
  discretion in 105–106
  ease of specification 105–106
  enforcement 186
  ignoring terms of 187
  negotiation 111
control *see* modes of control
convivial accountability 21, 22, 245–246, 256–261, 267–268
  incipient routinization 265–267
  reframing, participation and implicit communities 256–259
  territorial and functional communities in the shadow of globalization 259–261
corporations 115, 176, 297, 334–335
  corporate law and privatization 95–96
  information disclosure requirements 95–96, 103
  private law accountability and 33
  restorative justice in 34
corporatism 162, 249
  Indonesia 165
corruption 119
  privatization and 108
cost accounting 335
cost-benefit analysis 201, 202, 209
counter-majoritarian difficulty 301
courts 4–5
  accountability and 26, 301–304
  anti-modern nature 344–345
  drug treatment programs and 305–307, 309–314, 316, 318–319
  economic policymaking and 249
  enforcement of contracts by 186
  experimentalist 25, 305–309, 320–328
  gap filling 105–106, 302
  judicial review of human rights 251–253
  privatization and 93–96, 99–100, 101
  problem-solving 305–314
    appellate judging and 314–319
    from hard cases to big cases 320–327
  responsibility and 231, 232–233
Courville, Sasha 159, 160, 167
Cover, Robert 129
credit rating agencies 179, 184
crime
  fault and 43
  restorative justice and 34, 36, 37, 38, 43
crises
  in accountability 1–3, 33–34, 197–202, 256
  Asian financial crises 342–343
  in democracy 33–34

crises (*cont.*)
of legitimacy 208, 217, 219
in regulation 204
culture
problems of buying into professional culture 145–148
social accountability and 119, 124–126, 127, 129, 139

damages 240
decentralization 55–56, 198
delegation, government and 71, 88, 89, 93, 98, 195
democracy 7
accountability and 52, 53, 201, 337
crisis in 197–202
spoils system 339
technocratic accountability 253–256, 258
counter-majoritarian difficulty 301
crisis in 33–34
labor unions 158, 161, 162
NGOs and 273, 275, 296–299
participatory government/democracy 12, 54, 58–59
restorative justice and 34, 44, 49–51
as solution to succession problems 68–69
see also elections
deregulation 66, 71, 132, 197, 204
privatization and 103
Derthick, Martha 142
desegregation in schools 322–323
design
of accountability 13, 18–20, 28
of institutions 131–134, 153
spontaneous accountability and 189–190
deterrence 41
devolution
accountability and 53, 54–67, 78, 82
devolution to localities and the political process 54–60
devolution to private parties and the enforcement process 60–67
salience 56
Dicey, Albert Venn 5, 347
diminished responsibility 223
Diplock, Lord 347
disability
medicalization of 154
social security disability insurance 139–151, 154–155
auditing 142–144
gaining political accountability 148–149
lessons learned 151–152
opacity and entropy 149–150, 151
overview of system 140–142
problems of buying into professional culture 145–148
shifting to market accountability 150–151
systemic perspective 144–151
discretion, contracts and 105–106
disentrenching capacity 311
disinterestedness 257
distance, problems of accountability and 197
Dolinko, David 37
donor funding, NGOs and 276
Dorf, Michael C. 254
doublethink 40
drugs 305
drug abuse programs 64, 305–307, 309–314, 316, 318–319
Dublin Principles 262
Dworkin, Ronald 220, 320

Earth First 275
eBay 188
economic development agencies, accountability and 1
education 105
desegregation in schools 322–323
labor NGOs and 170
privatization and 91, 98, 99, 130, 137, 138, 320
spontaneous accountability in 189
efficiency 100, 123
privatization and 86
elections
accountability and 4, 7, 53, 67–74, 77, 121, 337
spoils system 339
desire for re-election 69, 98
as entertainment 70
incumbency advantages 70
party politics and 70
public ignorance and 70
reforms 340–341
values and interests in 69
electricity services, privatization and 109
emotional authenticity, restorative justice and 38–39
employees
privatization and 95
protection of 86
enforcement
consent agreement 213–216
contracts 186
devolution to private parties and 60–67
entertainment 57
elections as 70
entropy issue 137–138, 149–150, 151
Estlund, Cynthia 321
European Union (EU/EC) 181, 249
European Court of Justice 244
Euro-Retailer Produce Working Group 282

excuses 224, 225, 226, 228–229, 236, 239
exit and voice 276
experience 200
experimentalism 24, 200, 201, 302–303
courts 25, 305–309, 320–328

fairness 231
Fairtrade Labeling Organizations International (FLO) 281, 282–283, 286, 289–290, 294
families, accountability in 124–125
fatalism, modes of control and 182
fault, crime and 43
Fearon, James 198, 199
federalism 54, 55–56, 71–72, 72–74, 81–82
Ferejohn, John 199
feudalism 78
financial markets
accountability in 122, 187
disclosure requirements 95
Fisse, Brent 43
flag burning 324–325
Food and Agriculture Organization (FAO) 285
Ford Foundation 171
Forest Stewardship Council 189
Fosh, Patricia 159, 162
France, administrative law 347
fraud 96
freedom, responsibility and 235, 236
Freeman, Jody 244
Friedmann, John 265
Friedrich Ebert Foundation (FES) 171
Fung, Archon 317

Gallin, Dan 159
gambling 250
gap filling 105–106, 302
Gardner, John 357
General Agreement on Tariffs and Trade 284
globalization 197, 255, 272
accountability and 11
communities and 259–261
governance *see* modes of control
government and the state 16–18, 53
accountability 49, 50, 53, 67–77, 202, 297
spontaneous 186
anti-administrative impulse 53, 75, 77–82
delegation by 71, 88, 89, 93, 98, 195
deliberative 40
devolution by *see* devolution
experimentalist 24, 200, 201
courts 25, 305–309, 320–328
federalism 54, 55–56, 71–72, 72–74, 81–82
injustice and 47–48
labor unions and 162–163
Indonesia 165
market-based reforms 6, 8
modes of control and 176, 177–178
nation states 260
open government 6, 8
participatory government/democracy 12, 54, 58–59
public governance accountability 119, 120–122, 127–129, 131–132, 153, 155
regulation by *see* regulation
repressive regimes 61
restorative justice and 48, 50
succession problems 68
electoral democracy as solution to 68–69
unitary executive 71, 81
Greenfield, Gerard 169

Haley, John 356
Harrington, Christine 215
Hart, Oliver 106, 108
health care 186
privatization and 95, 99, 100
Hegel, G. W. F. 119, 234
hegemony 10
hierarchies
bureaucracies 75–76, 124, 197
hierarchical accountability 37, 39, 75–76, 77, 110, 175, 190
hierarchical modes of control 174, 175–177, 177–178
Hirschman, Albert O. 276
Hobbes, Thomas 227
honesty, rules on 187
Hood, Christopher 181, 182, 250
horizontal accountability 17, 199
human rights issues
accountability and 10, 11
technocratic accountability 251–253
judicial review 251–253
hybrid accountability regimes 184–190
communities 188–189
design hybrids 189–190
markets 186–188
public government 186

identity-oriented theory of social movements 57
ideology, privatization and 84–85, 99, 108
implementation of social programs 61–66, 78–79
incapacitation 41, 47
incumbency advantages 70
individuals, accountability and 11–12, 77
Indonesia 164
corporatism 165
labor NGOs 19, 161, 165–169
accountability 168, 170–173
funding 168, 171

Indonesia (*cont.*)
  labor unions 19, 164–165, 167, 168, 169–170
    accountability 169, 170–173
    foreign interest groups and 170
    funding 169, 171
    state and 165
inductive accountability, non-regulatory environments 344–345
industrialization 9, 333, 334–335, 339–340, 344
inequalities 67
infinite regress problem 39–40
information disclosure requirements 95–96, 103
Inglehart, Ronald 341
institutions 60–61
  design of 131–134, 153
  local institutions 52, 53, 54–60, 72, 73–74, 77
    federalism 54, 55–56, 71–72, 72–74
insurance industry 179, 184, 240
  disclosure requirements 95
insurgent citizenship 265
interdependency 25
interest groups 69, 244, 257, 338
International Accreditation Forum (IAF) 282, 283
International Federation of Organic Agriculture Movements (IFOAM) 275, 279–280, 282, 284, 285, 286, 287–289, 295, 297–299, 300
International Organic Accreditation Service (IOAS) 286
International Social and Environmental Accreditation and Labeling Alliance (ISEAL) 271, 275, 278–286
  accountability 281–286
    boundaries and democracy 296–299
    evolution v. architectural design 286–290
    as learning 290–296
    limits 299–300
  establishment and objectives 278–279
  membership 279, 281
    FLO 281, 282–283, 286, 289–290, 294
    IFOAM 275, 279–280, 282, 284, 285, 286, 287–289, 295, 297–299, 300
Internet commerce 188
investment industry, disclosure requirements 95

Jackson, Andrew 339
Jacobson, Dan 268
Japan 341, 356
  Japanese paradox 186
  Miyazawa Scheme 343
Jessop, Bob 344
judges 305
  accountability 238–239
    technocratic accountability 246–248
  economic policymaking and 249
  gap filling 105–106, 302
judicial review
  accountability and 4–5, 7–8
  human rights issues 251–253
justice, restorative *see* restorative justice
justification 221–222, 226, 228–229, 236, 239, 255

Kagan, Elena 7
Kant, Immanuel 235–236

labor NGOs 157–158
  accountability 159–161, 164
    Indonesia 168, 170–173
  funding, Indonesia 168, 171
  Indonesia 19, 165–169
    accountability 168, 170–173
    funding 168, 171
labor unions 157
  accountability 10, 158–159, 161–164
    Indonesia 169, 170–173
  funding 163
    Indonesia 169, 171
  Indonesia 19, 164–165, 167, 168, 169–170
    accountability 169, 170–173
    foreign interest groups and 170
    funding 169, 171
    state and 165
  state and 162–163
    Indonesia 165
law
  accountability of judges 238–239
    technocratic accountability 246–248
  common law system 231, 232–233
  comparative constitutional law 329–330
  constitutional law 329–330
  legal public accountability regime 120
  liberal legality 131
  negotiated rulemaking and 210–216
  private law accountability 33, 203
  public *see* public law
  rule of law 5, 40, 341, 342
  social accountability and 125
  value of legal process 231
  see also courts
learning
  accountability as 23, 24, 290–296
    implications for organizational structure 293–296
    quality and learning 290–292
    role of learning in accountability regimes 292–293
  by doing 138

legal development agencies, accountability and 1
legal-process school 5
legitimacy
  crises of 208, 217, 219
  NGOs 277
Lessig, Lawrence 181, 182
Levinson, Daryl 324
liberalism 131, 198, 244
Liebman, Benjamin L. 349–356
local institutions 52, 53, 54–60, 72, 73–74, 77
  federalism 54, 55–56, 71–72, 72–74

Madison, James 4
mail delivery services, privatization and 107
Malaysia, labor NGOs in 165
markets
  accountability and 18, 52, 67, 119, 122–124, 127, 129, 139, 153, 201, 217, 244, 345
    disability insurance and 150–151
    spontaneous accountability 186–188
  failures 67, 133, 187
  market-based reforms of government 6, 8
  modes of control and 174, 177, 178–180
Martin-Marietta Corporation 135
Mashaw, Jerry L. 190, 290, 292, 296
mediation 231
  restorative justice compared with 35
mental illness, responsibility and 223, 225
military, privatization and 98, 137
mistrust 241, 242
Miyazawa Scheme 343
modernism/modernization 334, 344
  retreat of 10
modes of control 174, 176
  architecture and 174, 181–183, 189–190
  competition/markets and 174, 177, 178–180
  hierarchical 174, 175, 176, 177–178, 190
  hybrid accountability regimes 184–190
    communities 188–189
    design hybrids 189–190
    markets 186–188
    public government 186
  networks/communities 174, 177, 180–181, 200, 244
  public governance accountability 119, 120–122, 127–129, 131–132, 153, 155
monopoly, privatization and 107
moral diversity 320
Morris, Huw 159, 162
Mulgan, Richard 123
murder
  diminished responsibility 223
  provocation defense 222–224

nation states 260
negotiation 111, 196, 203, 204
  rulemaking and 21, 22, 196, 206–209, 218
    accountability and 207
    advantages 206–207
    consent agreement 213–216
    jurisprudence 210–216
    participation 207, 208, 209, 211–212, 218
    stakeholders 208
    transparency and 209
neoliberalism 195, 272
  administrative mechanisms 202–210, 216–219
  meaning 204–205
neo-Madisonian competition 200
Netherlands Organization for International Development Cooperation (NOVIB) 171
networks
  transnational 260
  see also social networks
New Deal 195, 203
New Public Management 62, 63, 178, 186, 241
New Zealand
  Fairtrade labeling in 282, 283
  restorative justice in 36
Nirvana fallacy 139
non-governmental organizations (NGOs) 176, 180, 255, 256
  accountability 271–274
    alternatives for 275–278
    boundaries and democracy 296–299
    evolution v. architectural design 286–290
    ISEAL study 271, 275, 278–296, 299–300
    as learning 290–296
    limits 299–300
  labor movement *see* labor NGOs
non-participation 59
non-regulatory environments 344–345
non-regulatory state 79
normative issues in accountability 152–154, 155
normative reasoning 320–322
Norway, restorative justice in 36

Offe, Claus 119
Olson, Mancur 339
opacity issue 136–137, 138, 149–150, 151
open government, accountability and 6, 8
output accountability 200

Pakpahan, Muchtar 167, 169
Parker, Christine 40, 50
participation 21
  convivial accountability and 258–259

participation (*cont.*)
negotiated rulemaking 207, 208, 209, 218
right to participate 211–212
participatory government/democracy 12, 54
party politics 70, 121
Pavlov, Ivan Petrovich 64
peer reviews 200
Philippines, NGOs in 273
labor NGOs 165
Pistor, Katharina 341
Polanyi, Karl 204
police 39
accountability of 37
political process
devolution to localities and 54–60
party politics 70, 121
political accountability 121, 148–149
crisis in 197–202
privatization and 87
public governance accountability 119, 120–122, 127–129, 131–132, 153, 155
Poulson, Barton 39
power 13, 14
see also modes of control
pre-modern societies 119
principal/agent relationships 197, 199
accountability and 198–199
prisons 105
privatization and 91, 94, 98, 99, 100, 101, 107, 137
reforms 65–66
spontaneous accountability in 189
private law accountability 33, 203
private parties, devolution to 60–67
privatization and contracting out 1, 8, 186, 198, 204, 244, 255
accountability and 83–84, 87, 88, 89, 90, 93, 96–97, 99–100, 103, 109–111, 115, 134–156, 157
blurring issue 135–136
concerns associated with contracting out 134–138
entropy issue 137–138, 149–150, 151
lessons learned 151–152
opacity issue 136–137, 138, 149–150, 151
putting concerns in context 138–139
social security disability insurance (SSDI) example 139–151, 154–155
structure of accountability 134
ideological arguments 84–85, 99, 108
pragmatic arguments 85–90, 109
public law view 87–97
accountability and 109–111
conflicting factors 109
ease of specification and degree of discretion 105–106
impasse 90–91
judicial mechanisms 93–96
legislative mechanisms 91–93
motivation 97–101, 108–109
potential impact of service on the consumer 106–108
publicization not working 101–103
skepticism about 97–104
strongest cases for publicization 104–109
supplemental measures 96–97
undermining gains from privatization 103–104
problems in accountability 1–3, 33–34, 197–202
problem-solving courts 305–314
appellate judging and 314–319
from hard cases to big cases 320–327
process school 5
product markets, accountability in 122
professionalism, problems of buying into professional culture 145–148
profit motive, privatization and 101
property rights 186
provocation defense 222–224
Przeworski, Adam 341
public choice theory 98
public goods 67
public governance accountability 119, 120–122, 127–129, 131–132, 153, 155
public interest 202, 255
public law 83, 131–132, 207, 217
accountability and 203
privatization and 87–97
accountability and 109–111
conflicting factors 109
ease of specification and degree of discretion 105–106
impasse 90–91
judicial mechanisms 93–96
legislative mechanisms 91–93
motivation 97–101, 108–109
potential impact of service on the consumer 106–108
publicization not working 101–103
skepticism about 97–104
strongest cases for publicization 104–109
supplemental measures 96–97
undermining gains from privatization 103–104
public–private partnerships 83
punishment 239
Putnam, Robert 58, 59

quality 293
learning and 290–292
quality-shading hypothesis 106
specification 105–106

race
affirmative action 320
desegregation in schools 322–323
racial bias 154
randomness, modes of control and 181
rationality, responsibility and 221–224, 226, 228, 231, 235
Rawls, John 228
Reagan, Ronald 71
reasoning, normative 320–322
regulation 9, 67, 79, 81, 102, 104, 123, 131–132, 195–197
competition 248, 250–251
crisis in 204
deregulation 66, 71, 132, 197, 204
privatization and 103
neoliberalism and 202–210, 216–219
non-regulatory environments 344–345
privatization and 99
reforms, accountability and 1
regulatory model of constitutional accountability 331–344
history and development 332–341
limitations 341–344
regulatory trilemma 154
responsive 255
self-regulation 97, 126, 135, 183–184, 188–189
technocratic accountability and 249–251
rehabilitation 41
drug abuse programs 64, 305–307, 309–314, 316, 318–319
religious organizations 320
privatization and 135, 136
rent-seeking 244
reparation 229
damages 240
repressive regimes 61
reputation, NGOs 277
resource mobilization theory of social movements 57
responsibility
accountability and 44–49, 198, 237–242
active/passive 40–44
Aristotelianism and 221, 222, 227–228, 230, 235
avoidance of 220
basic 224, 229, 230, 231, 234, 235, 236
consequential 220, 224, 226, 229, 231, 234–235
diminished 223
excuses 224, 225, 226, 228–229, 236, 239
freedom and 235, 236
justification 221–222, 226, 228–229, 236, 239
legal system 223, 231, 232–233, 237, 238
rationality and 221–224, 226, 228, 231, 235
relational view 228–230, 231
restorative justice and 34–35, 36–39, 40–49
settlement of 225–226
responsive regulation 255
restorative justice 17, 34–35
accountability and 36–39
concept of 35–36
crime and 34, 36, 37, 38, 43
democracy and 34, 44, 49–51
government/state and 48, 50
responsibility and 34–35, 36–39, 40–49
rule of law and 40
stakeholders 35, 36, 38, 43, 46, 49
rights *see* human rights issues
Roche, Declan 37, 38, 40, 43, 44
Roosevelt, Theodore 338
Rorty, Richard 228, 230
Rubin, Edward 244
rule of law 5, 40, 341, 342
rulemaking 90
negotiated 21, 22, 196, 206–209, 218
accountability and 207
advantages 206–207
consent agreement 213–216
jurisprudence 210–216
participation 207, 208, 209, 211–212, 218
stakeholders 208
transparency and 209
Russia/Soviet Union
black market in 61
collapse of communist regime 10
NGOs in 273

Sabel, Charles 254–255, 268, 302–303, 306, 317
safety regulation 336
sanctions 129, 238–239
punishment 239
Sari, Ditar 167
schools, restorative justice in 34
Scott, James 334
Seidenfeld, Mark 75
self-interest 98
self-regulation 97, 126, 135, 183–184
sexual harassment 321, 324
Shapiro, Martin 247
shareholders 95, 297
Shleifer, Andrei 106, 108
Skowronek, Stephen 344
slavery 326
social auditing 255
social networks
accountability in 119, 124–126, 127, 129, 139, 153
identity-oriented theory of social movements 57

social networks (*cont.*)
loss of social solidarity 58
modes of control and 174, 177, 180–181, 200, 244
social programs, implementation of 61–66, 78–79
social security *see* welfare systems
Socratic deliberation 321
soft law techniques 132–133
software, modes of control and 181, 182, 189
South Africa, Truth and Reconciliation Commission 36
specification, ease of 105–106
spoils system 339
spontaneous accountability 174, 175–176, 183–184
in hybrid accountability regimes 184–190
communities 188–189
design hybrids 189–190
markets 186–188
public government 186
stakeholders 195, 202, 204, 218
restorative justice and 35, 36, 38, 43, 46, 49
rulemaking and 208
standardization 333
uniform system of accounts 335–336
standards of accountability 76
state *see* government and the state
Stepan, Alfred 162
stock markets, accountability in 187
Strang, Heather 38
stress 65
succession problems 68
electoral democracy as solution to 68–69
supranational organizations 115–117
suspicion 241, 242
systemic perspective, privatization/contracting out in 144–151
gaining political accountability 148–149
opacity and entropy 149–150, 151
problems of buying into professional culture 145–148
shifting to market accountability 150–151

taxation 339
taxonomy of accountability regimes 118–126
fixing ideas 127–129
market accountability 119, 122–124, 127, 129, 139, 153
overlapping regimes 130
public governance accountability 119, 120–122, 127–129, 131–132, 153, 155
social accountability 119, 124–126, 127, 129, 139, 153
uses of taxonomy 130–134
critique, dysfunction and conflict 130–131
perplexities of institutional design 131–134
Technical Barriers to Trade (TBT) Agreement 284
technocratic accountability 245, 246–256, 257, 267
democratic accountability and 253–256, 258
economic and regulatory policymaking 249–251
human rights and 251–253
judicial accountability and beyond 246–248
triadic logic 246–248
water struggles as challenge to 261–267
creation of implicit communities across distended territory 263–265
incipient routinization of convivial accountability 265–267
resisting routinization and unruly accountability 263
Teubner, Gunther 154
Thailand, social welfare in 342–343
time
responsibility and 225–226
restorative justice and 38
tit for tat strategy 65
Tocqueville, Alexis de 7, 333, 337
torture 65
trade unions *see* labor unions
transnational networks 260
transparency 207, 209
loss of 136–137, 138, 149–150
NGOs 274
rulemaking and 209
triadic logic 246–248
trust 241
Turner, Frederick Jackson 79

Unger, Roberto 263
unions *see* labor unions
United Kingdom
administrative bureaucracy in 4
judicial review in 7
provocation defense to murder in 222–224
public sector reforms in 6, 178
regulation in 248
United Nations 285
United States of America
bureaucracy in 7, 8
anti-administrative impulse 80–82
contraception use in 325
desegregation in schools 322–323
drug treatment programs 305–307, 309–314, 316
education in 91, 98, 99

elections in 4, 7
export of ideas from 9
federalism in 55, 71–72, 72–74, 81–82
flag burning 324–325
gambling in 250
health care in 95, 99, 100
judicial review in 7, 5
loss of social solidarity in 58
market reforms in 6
negotiated rulemaking in 21, 22, 206–209, 210–216
agencies mandated to convene NR 210–211
consent agreement 213–216
right to participate 211–212
New Deal 195, 203
NGOs in 273
non-regulatory state 79
open government in 6, 8
organizational sentencing guidelines 62
political participation in 56–59
presidency 71, 81
prisons in 65–66, 94, 99, 100, 101
privatization and contracting out in 134
ideological arguments 84–85, 99, 108
judicial mechanisms 93–96
legislative mechanisms 91–93
pragmatic arguments 85–90, 109
public law view 87–90, 91–97
supplemental measures 96–97
regulation in 195–197
neoliberal 202–210, 216–219
regulatory model of constitutional accountability 332–341
restorative justice in 36
slavery in 326
state officials 72, 73–74
welfare systems in 88–89, 136
social security disability insurance (SSDI) 139–151, 154–155
unruly accountability 263
utilities, privatization 109, 186

Vakil, Anna 272
values
electoral democracy and 69
restorative justice and 36
vertical accountability 199
Vishny, Robert W. 106, 108
voice and exit 276

war, restorative justice and 34
waste collection, privatization and 107
water
privatization of water services 109
transnational struggles over 261–267
creation of implicit communities across distended territory 263–265
incipient routinization of convivial accountability 265–267
resisting routinization and unruly accountability 263
wealth 33
Weber, Max 61
welfare systems
financial crises and 342–343
privatization and 88–89, 105, 136
social security disability insurance (SSDI) 139–151, 154–155
auditing 142–144
gaining political accountability 148–149
lessons learned 151–152
opacity and entropy 149–150, 151
overview of system 140–142
problems of buying into professional culture 145–148
shifting to market accountability 150–151
systemic perspective 144–151
Wellons, Philip 341
White, G. Edward 5
Wilson, Edward O. 16
Wilson, Woodrow 339
workers' compensation 336
World Bank 11, 342
Social Investment Fund (SIF) 342–343
World Commission on Dams (WCD) 266–267
World Trade Organization (WTO) 244, 248, 249